HISTORY OF THE BALKANS
From Mohammed the Conqueror to Stalin

Georges Castellan

Translated by Nicholas Bradley

EAST EUROPEAN MONOGRAPHS, BOULDER
DISTRIBUTED BY COLUMBIA UNIVERSITY PRESS, NEW YORK
1992

EAST EUROPEAN MONOGRAPHS, NO. CCCXXV

Copyright © 1992 by Georges Castellan

ISBN 0-88033-222-0
Library of Congress Catalog Card Number 91-78352

Printed in the United States of America

Contents

Introduction 1
The Balkans—Its Countries and Peoples, 1
The Region, 1
The Peoples, 4

1 The Historical Tradition: Countries and Cultures 11
The Hellenic Period: From the Grecian City
   to the Macedonian Empire, 11
Roman Rule, 14
The Birth of Byzantium and
   the Foundation of the Slavs, 16
The Byzantine Empire and the Slavic States, 18
The Decline of Byzantium and
   the Feudal Division, 1204–1453, 24
The Rise and Fall of the Slavic States:
   Bulgaria and Serbia, 27
The Balkans Against the Ottomans, 30
Notes, 32

2 The Origins of the Conquering Ottomans 33
The Origins of the Turks
   and the Seldjuk Empire, 33
The Ghazis and the Sultanate of Rum, 35
The Early Days of the Ottomans up to 1361, 41
Notes, 47

3 The Conquest of the Balkans, 1362–1451 49
The Building of Ottoman Suzerainty: Murad I,
   1361–1389, 49
The Expansionism of Sultan Bayezid
   Known as the Lightning, 1389–1402, 55
The Pause During the Interregnum
   and the Restoration of the Empire: Mehmed I, 60

The Renewal of the Balkan Conquest:
Murad II, 1421–1451, 65
Notes, 74

4   **Constantinople-Istanbul, Capital of a New
    World Empire** 75
    Mehmed II Fatih: Mohammed II, Conqueror
       of Byzantium, 75
    Mehmed II, Conqueror of the Byzantine Inheritance, 80
    Domination of the Eastern Mediterranean:
       Bayezid II and Selim I, 86
    Suleyman I: Soliman the Magnificent—Arbiter of
       Europe, 1520–1566, 90
    The Ottoman State: Power and Institutions, 99
    Notes, 107

5   **The Balkans Under Ottoman Domination** 109
    The Inhabitants: Christians and Muslims, 109
    The Provincial Government of the Great Lord, 116
    The Timar System and the Organization of the
       Countryside, 120
    The Towns, 127
    Scholastic and Popular Culture, 135
    Notes, 143

6   **The Porte's Vassal States: Wallachia, Moldavia,
    Transylvania and Ragusa up to 1566** 145
    The Principality of Wallachia, 145
    The Principality of Moldavia, 151
    Notes, 154

7   **"Fish Rot from the Head Downwards"—1566 to 1683** 155
    The Institutional Crisis, 155
    On the Empire's Borders: The Balance of Power
       in Europe, 161
    The Transformation of the Balkans, 171
    Romanian Princes and Ragusian Nobles, 177
    Notes, 182

Contents

8 The Ottoman Empire Against the European Powers, 1684–1792 185

The Christian Reconquest and the Habsburgs' Advance, 1684–1739, 185
Russia's Southward Descent: The Road to Constantinople, 1736–1792, 189
Internal Crisis and the Problem of Reform, 194
The Ottoman Balkans in the 18th Century, 201
The Vassal Principalities, 205
Conclusion, 209
Notes, 212

9 Napoleon's Conquest in the East 213

Wars and Alliances: The Games of the Great Powers, 1798–1815, 213
Resistance to Reform, 217
The Complexities of Ottoman and Balkan Culture, 221
Notes, 226

10 The Serbian and Greek Revolts 227

The Serbians at the Dawn of the 19th Century, 227
The First Serbian Uprising: Karageorge, 1804–1813, 233
The Second Uprising and the Struggle for Autonomy: Milos, 1815–1834, 242
The Greeks at the Dawn of the 19th Century, 248
The Greek Revolt, 1821–1825, 253
Greek Independence: A European Problem, 1826–1833, 257
Notes, 261

11 The Eastern Question: Crises, 1832–1859 263

The Tanzimat, 263
The First Balkan Crisis: Mehmed Ali, 1832–1841, 268
The Danubian Principalities Under Russian Protectorate, 1812–1847, 270
The Romanian Nationalist Movement and the Crimean War: United Romania, 1847–1859, 276
Notes, 283

12 **The New Christian States and the Third Eastern Crisis, 1833–1878** 285

Greece Under King Othon, 1833–1862, 285
The Autonomous Principality of Serbia: Obrenovic and
  Karageorgevic, 1834–1868, 292
Montenegro: From the Vladika to a Secular Prince,
  1830–1860, 298
The Prodomes of the Third Balkan Crisis, 1840–1868, 301
The Making of a Romanian State, 1859–1875, 305
The Bulgarian Problem, 1840–1876, 308
The Third Balkan Crisis: The 1875/76 Uprising
  and the Russo-Turkish War, 313
Notes, 320

13 **Rivalries Between the Various Christian States, 1878–1912** 323

The New Bulgarian State: Princes Alexander and
  Ferdinand, 323
Serbia: Dynastic Upheavals and Radical Domination, 328
Greece Under George I, 1863–1913, 334
Romania Under Carol I, 1878–1914, 339
Capitalist Advance and the Discovery of National
  Identity, 343
Notes, 349

14 **The Balkans "Under the Yoke," 1878–1912** 351

Bosnia-Herzegovina Under Austrian Occupation,
  1878–1903, 351
The Macedonian Imbroglio, 1850–1908, 354
The Albanian Renaissance: Rilindja, 1850–1908, 363
The Rebellion of the Young Turks and the Fourth Eastern
  Crisis, 1908–1912, 368

15 **The Balkans as a Source of Conflicts in Europe, 1912–1918** 377

Balkan Wars, 1912–1913, 377
The Creation of an Albanian State, 1912–1914, 382
The "Yugoslav" Question and the Sarajevo Assassination,
  1878–1914, 385
The Calvary of Serbia, 1914–1916, 390

The Transylvania Dream and the Romanian Disasters,
    1914–April 1918, 394
The Rape of Greece and Allied Victory in the East,
    1910–1918, 400

16 **The Triumph and Failure of the National States,
    1919–1939** 407
    The Versailles Order: Victors and Vanquished, 409
    Yugoslavia Under King Alexander, 419
    Romania Under Carol, 425
    Divided Greece, 432
    Unrest in Bulgaria, 436
    Unrest in Albania, 440
    From the Light of Democracy to the Shadow of
        Dictatorship, 445
    Notes, 448

17 **The Balkans in World War II, 1939–1945**............................ 451
    The Axis Powers Impose their Rule over the Balkans,
        1939–1941, 451
    Romania and Bulgaria Under German Occupation,
        May 1941–Spring 1944, 460
    Peoples at War: Yugoslavs, Albanians and Greeks,
        Spring 1941–Spring 1944, 467
    Arrival of the Red Army, April–December 1944, 479
    Conclusion, 488

Introduction

The Balkans: Its Countries and Peoples

Traditional history, in the same way as the contemporary press, prefers tidy theories. The Balkans . . . bridge or crossroads between Europe and Asia, mixing point or melting pot of races, powder room or battlefield of Europe. These are valid descriptions, or were so at different periods of history, yet fail to plumb the richness and variety of these countries and the peoples who live in this peninsula.

A Peninsula; characterized by seas on three sides: the Adriatic to the west, the Mediterranean to the south and the Aegean and Black Seas to the east. The fourth side, the northern border is defined geographically by the Danube, yet its history, which includes the Romanian countries, is intimately linked to that of Central Europe and the Russian steppes.

The Region

Balkan comes from the Turkish word meaning mountain and in fact when an airplane approaches Athens, Tirana or Sofia its passengers will observe a broken and rugged landscape, while the more accessible airports of Belgrade or Bucharest are on the very edge of the foothills of the Sumadjan and Carpathian ranges. Mountains are everywhere present.

Three main areas can be distinguished. The swathe of the Carpathians to the north rising to 2520m., a tertiary range moulded from the collapsed Pannonian mole, its calcium sides and valleys covered by dense forests. Extending south of the Danube, the Balkan range (known to antiquity as Haemus and to the Slavs as the Stara Planina) and the Rhodope escarpment pointing to the east.

In the centre old weathered Hercinian ranges thrust up by alpine movement; Rhodope, Rila and Pirin whose crystalline rock are covered by fresh pastures and forests giving Bulgaria the highest point in all the Peninsula—2920m. even higher than the famous monastery at Rila.

To the west and to the south are enormous dinaric folds, the Sar and Pindhos massifs and the Peloponnesian mountains. The shores of the Adriatic, an area of subsidence, are made up of sheer limestone cliffs, rising sharply and exposing their flanks to the blazing southern sun; in amongst this rock, crystaline formations, found as high as 2916m on mount Olympus, 2523m in the Montenegrin Dumitor region and 2457m in the Attican Parnassus. The Yugoslav and Greek islands are part of this dinaric system and are unbelievably white. Framing or bordering these mountain ranges, plains and plateaux which soften the contours of the peninsula. To the north and outside the Balkan area, the sub-Carpathian foothills merge with the borders of the Ukrainian steppes. South of the Danube, the Carpathian mountain range is the Iron Gate that joins the Pannonian Basin to the Black Sea, the vast alluvial plains of Wallachia and south the Bulgarian Plateau which climbs gently up to the Stara Planina. Up-river, its tributary the river Sava runs along the edge of the Hungarian plain, marked with crystaline rock formations such as the Medvenica at Zagreb, Papuk at Daruvar and the Fruska Gora of Novi Sad with its monasteries perched precariously on high. South between the three seas are coastal plains or lowlands such as the Skoder Basin, Myzeke in Albania, the Gulf of Arta, the Attican Plain, the Plain of Thessaly, the Campania of Salonika and of course Turkish Thrace which separates the Sea of Marmara from the Dardanelles and the Bosphorous. All well drained, malaria-free, fertile, heavily populated, agricultural areas. Tranverse valleys, like jagged gaps made with a bayonet, a characteristic of a limestone landscape—known as "clues" in the Alps and called "klisur" by the Slavs, link the enclosed valleys and channel water down from the smaller rivers into the larger rivers and from the large rivers into the sea: from the Soca at Trieste to the Maritsa of Thrace, these various connecting corridors were vital for the movement of peoples and goods.

To sum up then, a region of contrasts, its mountain ranges just about accessable—none exceed 3000 metres—yet nevertheless a hindrance for the traveller and imposing certain fixed routes. The main roads of the Balkans have remained the same for thousands of years: the Morava-Varda highway which joins Belgrade to Salonika, the Morava-Maritsa which goes from the Danube to Byzantium, the Via Egnatia which runs from east to west and links Durres (Durazzo) to Salonika and the pass of Fiume which was to make Trieste and Rijeka the main ports of the Austro-Hungarian

Empire. Outside these main axes, often very close, lie remote areas cut off from the Attican and Peloponnesian coastal plains or the lowlands of Ohrid and Prespa; the deep valleys of Bosnia, the Karstic Plateau in the Croatian Lika area, the highlands of the Rhodope and the Pindhos and to the north of the Danube the Transylvanian basin squashed up between the Apuseni and Carpathian mountains. Places of refuge and sanctuary, retaining strong cultural traditions: from the city state of ancient Greece to the Montenegrin and Fis Albanian tribes which still existed at the dawn of the 20th century and of course the Romanian peoples of the late Middle Ages.

In these diverse areas, climate also varies greatly depending on whether its influence is Mediterranean to the south or continental. The southern influence is strongest up to the entrance of the Dardanelles at least in coastal regions, with warm summers and mild winters—snow is rare in Athens—and there is rain in the spring and in autumn. The Greek islands of the Peloponnese and the gulf of Corinth and the Yugoslavian coastline with their olive trees, citrous fruit and cypresses are the modern tourist's paradise and give classic holiday snaps. Yet even in the southern lattitudes the broken relief troubles the blue skies: Parnassus is crowned with snow several months of the year and the Albanian Alps fully justify their name. In the north the continental influence gives extreme seasonal variations. In Bucharest for instance the temperature can vary between -30 and +40 and Belgrade can experience violent snowstorms as well as severe summer droughts. The olive trees disappear north of the Bosphorous to be replaced by oaks and conifers in the Bulgarian mountains and by firs and birches (northern European forests) in the Carpathians. Therefore two elements single out the Balkans: the existence of many microclimates, violent winds due to contiguous and contrasting isotherms eg. the winter Bora of the dinaric Karst, the Kosava of Yugoslavia, the Vardarac of Salonika, the Meltemi which in summer is so pleasant in the Aegean islands and the very dry, hot winds of the Ukraine (Sukhovi) which burn the Moldavian steppes and isolated rift areas such as Sofia, Ohrid, Sarajevo and many others.

The peninsula offers rich pastures and fertile land for wheat farming on chalky land which has largely been replaced since the 16th century by maize which is now the most widespread cereal grown in the Balkans. Vineyards thrive up to the foothills of the

Carpathians, cotton, rice and tobacco grow side by side on the small southern plains, apple and plum trees dominate the Serbian and Bulgarian Slivovitsa regions. In the highlands sheep rearing dominates in the north and cattle in the south, and often a mixture of both while in northern Moldavia it is mainly transhumant shepherding. From the earliest times the wealth of the sub-soil has been a strong pull, gold attracting Trajan and his army to the Carpathian rivers and in the Middle Ages the wealth of the Serbian and Bulgarian princes who owned the copper and silver mines was well known. Even today modern industry is drawn by Albanian ferrous-nickel and Wallachian, central Albanian, Croatian and Aegean oil.

The Peoples

These relatively favourable natural conditions have made the peninsula a magnet for people since the dawn of man. The earliest Paleolithic peoples have left traces of their stone culture in Macedonia and Romanian Oltenia. The first staging post for Asian civilisations who left the neolithic period 8,000 years B.C., the Balkans were to experience the terrific changes of agricultural settlement, the birth of the first towns and the widespread use of utensils 2,000 years later. Neolithic civilisation reached northern Greece by the end of the 7th millenium going through the peninsula on its way to the rest of Europe.

From time immemorial man has migrated, through coercion or voluntarily, and history has traced many of these incredible movements. The successive waves have intermingled in an alchemy of integration and rejection which has given birth to the present-day peoples of the Balkans. "Peoples" that the ideology of the French Revolution would classify as Nation States yet all too often break loose of this rigid frontier definition. With cultures going back two thousand years they are the human ingredient of a peninsula on which subsequent conquerors or settlers have grafted their own contributions.

The oldest Balkan peoples are probably the Greeks and the Illyrians of Albania. Speaking Indo-European languages they moved southwards, initially in the 1st millenium B.C. intermingling with the indigenous population and dominated by Crete which gave birth to the Mycean civilisation (1600–1100 B.C.) and then the civilisation of classical Athens. The 2nd wave of settlers pushing from the Danubian delta to the Adriatic where they survived for 2000 years, with several successive influxes, above all of Slavs, which gave birth to the Albanian people.

Present-day Romanians refer to their ancestors the Dacians—part of a Traco-Dacian Indo-European culture which became separated about 2000 years B.C. Romanized following the 150 year occupation, from Trajan to Aurelius (A.D. 106–271) they retained a language which was similar to French and derived from Latin, also later experiencing the influence of the Goths and above all the Slavs. Scattered around the peninsula the Vlahs have called themselves Aromanians and are also referred to by several other names, the Tsintsares of Pindhos and northern Greece, the Vlasi in eastern Serbia and Bosnia, the Morlachians of the Dalmatian coast and Istria. These are also Thracians but for five centuries they were Romanized and never had a country of their own. Their only common link is their language Aromanian, a language akin to Latin but limited to the parlance of shepherds.

The Slavs form the largest group. Originally from the plains of the Oder and Dnepr they moved south across the Carpathians and the Moravian corridor. Under Justinian they reached the Dalmatian coast and terrorized Salona (near Split) and Dyrrachium (Durres). Subjugated by the Avars who had come from Altai, in the next century they invaded the Byzantine Empire, swamping the provinces of Istria, the Peloponnese and Crete. In 629 they unsuccessfully besieged Byzantium. Place names throughout the peninsula attest to their presence for unlike their Avar masters these were not satisfied with sacking the towns of antiquity but formed agricultural communities (Zadruga), farming the land, grouped together into clans and tribes forming "Slavines" which were to remain independent of the neighbouring powers. The central Croatian and Serbian tribes, having freed themselves from the Avars with the help of Charlemagne's Franks, formed their first state in the 9th and 10th centuries , while those in the northwest who had settled in the Alpine valleys, having freed themselves of Frank rule were to fall under German domination and it was only in 1918 that the Slovenes were to have a country of their own. The eastern tribes were conquered during the second half of the 7th century by the Turanians, the forebears of the Turks also called Protobulgarians. They were sufficiently powerful to force Byzantium to recognize their state in A.D. 681. They gave their new subjects their name but acquired their languages and culture. Bulgarians, Serbs, Croats and Slovenes still form the four Slavic groups in the Balkans. The Slav tribes in Greece were subjected from the 9th century on to a religious and cultural hellenization with the result that the original characteristics of their society gradually disappeared while the Slavs of Macedonia, attacked by their neighbours on every side were to wait until the 20th century before acquiring their own specific identity. Further to these basic ethno-linguistic groups, characterized by their language and traditions, there existed in the past groups strong enough to retain their own identities but not strong enough to destroy the previous order. First of all the Turks whose Ottoman Empire dominated the whole of the peninsula. In 1356 Orkhan the son of Osman, founder of the Osman line, settled in Thrace Turcomans from Anatolia to prevent the Christian kings forcing him from the west bank of the Bosphorous. Mehmed II, conqueror of Constantinople, brought further Turcomans over to repopulate the capital and the surrounding area, and then the Imperial cities attracted soldiers, administrators and merchants. Certain strategic regions, depopulated by war or epidemics, were colonized, for instance the Dobrudja, the banks of the Danube, the Bulgarian coastline and Macedonia. Yet appearances can be misleading for up to the 19th century all Muslims were called Turks and even today in Yugoslavia and Bulgaria the distinction between religion and ethnic group still causes problems. What is certain is that "Wars of Liberation" were cruelly waged and involved deporting and massacring supposedly Turkish populations. There were also other migrations ordered or encouraged by the Sultans such as that of the Tcherkess from the Caucasus who settled in Moldavia, the Tartars of the Crimea who resettled on the Bulgarian plateau and the Gagauzians who were descended from the Christian Petcheneg converts and are found around Varna. Also of course Armenians who scattered all over the Empire from the 16th century onwards and their commercial rivals the Jews; Sefardim expelled from Spain in 1492 who found refuge under the Sultan and were later joined by the Askenazim driven out of the Tsarist Empire and finally the Gipsies, the eternal wanderers who arrived from India in the 16th century, for a long time were slaves and always remained outsiders.

In this century nationalist intolerance has produced further migrations; the Greeks from Asia Minor with 1.5 million repatriated following the treaty of Lausanne in 1923 and whose resettlement in northern Greece virtually wiped out all traces of the Slavs in this region; the Germans (Volkdeutsche) who were driven out in 1944–45 of Romanian Transylvania, the Banat and Serbian Backa; the Bulgarian Turks or Pomaci (Bulgarian Muslims) who in the 1950s (200,000 approx.) prefered to go to Turkey.

This mosaic of peoples is further blurred by their religious distribution. The matching of state and ethnic group is bound to be vague and so in the same way is that of peoples and religion. The start-point is 395AD when following almost a century of quasi-separation Emperor Theodor divided up his Roman Empire between his sons. However the east-west border of the empires ran from Sirmium (Sremski-Karlovici on the Danube) to the mouth of the river Kotor(Cattaro) giving Constantinople the whole of the peninsula but leaving Rome with the whole of Illyrian Dalmatia. In spite of clerical disobedience and liturgical quarrels this political frontier was to become the border of the eastern and Roman churches following the excommunication of the Byzantine Patriarch Michael Cerularius. No doubt this was nothing more than the logical, be it spectacular, conclusion of a conflict which had been developing for some time between the Ecclesiastical Sees of Rome and Byzantium, however henceforth in the face of Roman Church's claim to be universal the Eastern Church was formed but limited in its actions to the Byzantine Empire. The Eastern Church was to share many of the beliefs of its Latin rival apart from the order of the Holy Spirit (Filioque), belief in Purgatory and the primacy of Rome. Yet the two differed fundamentally on ecclesiastical discipline: the Patriarch shared his authority with the Holy Synod and would grant autonomy to various Churches—called autocephalic—giving them permission to celebrate the liturgy in Greek but also in their own tongues, including in Church Slavonic in the Balkan Peninsula. Monks were the only ones able to occupy an Episcopal See and priests were allowed to marry. The Middle Ages were to see the simultaneous establishment of kingdoms and autonomous churches for instance in Bulgaria and Serbia. The Ottoman conquest weakened these to the advantage of the Ecumenical Patriarch of Constantinople who was seen by the Sultan as the leader of his Christian subjects, organized into the "Rum Millet," and their head figured in Ottoman protocol as a "Lord with 3 horse's tails." The independence movements of the 19th century were naturally accompanied by a struggle against the hellenization of the Church and they tended to nationalize the Church organisations. In spite of disciplinary arguments the Orthodox Church in the Balkans still constitutes a community grouped round the Ecumenical Patriarch of Constantinople and bolstered by 1000 years of tradition it still would like to be treated as an equal to the Roman Church as was illustrated during the visit of Pope Paul VI in 1964.

The Catholics were contained, found only in the western Slav regions, even though Rome has never renounced the idea of union with its "separated Eastern brothers." Up until the Ottoman conquest there had been many attempts at union either attempted by princes such as the Bulgarian Tsar Kaloyan who in 1204 was given his crown by the Pope or else directly through the religious leaders such as the Council of Lyons (1274) or Florence (1439). The Ottoman Sultans authorized missionary activities by Franciscans in Bosnia after the 15th century, in Bulgaria from the 16th and 17th centuries where the Catholic archbishop of Sofia, P.Bogdan, was to make a lasting impression and in northern Albania in the 19th century when Italian and Austrian priest were to be auxiliaries for their governments. But whereas the Catholic ecclesiastical authorities were present in the Balkan capitals the communities were small and the only Catholic regions are Slovenia, Dalmatia round Split and Dubrovnik, Croatia and Albania in the Shkodra area. Transylvania and the Banat were also to have large Catholic populations but this was more to do with their secular dependency on the Catholic Habsburg Empire and even then it was no longer a part of the Balkans.

Although based on a religious ideal, the Ottoman Conquest was not accompanied by sytematic forced conversions. Naturally this did take place for various reasons but, apart from Bosnia which was deeply affected by the Bogomil heresy, there was no large-scale conversion to Islam. It was later, in the 17th century, that a Muslim population in Albania, Macedonia and Bulgaria grew up and for complex reasons. First of all there was the colonization of Anatolia, the Dobrudja, Macedonia and northern Bulgaria by Turks who were Muslims adding to the original body in Thrace. There was also more or less voluntary conversions of Bulgarians, the Pomacks of the Rhodope, Macedonian Slavs and Albanians in the Kosovo region that travellers were to refer to as "Turks" and who at the time of the 19th century nationalist movements would have been considered as such. Even today we talk of the problem of the Bosnian Muslims who are refered to as an ethnic group within Yugoslavia.

As well as these three major religions there are, mostly in Catholic areas (Transylvania, the Banat, Slovenia and Croatia), attesting to the great upheaval of the Reformation, Lutherans in the Slovenian Alps and Saxon Transylvania, Hungarian Protestants, Yugoslav Protestants in Vojvodina and Romanian Protestants in Transylvania. There were also Jews, decimated during the genocide of the Second World War but whose presence was widespread throughout the Balkans, alongside the Armenians who followed the autonomous Church in Antioch.

Between ethno-linguistic groups and religious denomination, a multi-secular dialectic was to develop which is at the root of the national identity. The Ottoman Millet system hid some of the variety, making the religious leaders administrators answerable for their communities whereas the followers would only escape through apostacy. On the negative side this status resulted in a total absence of theological argument of the type which had so affected the Byzantine Church; there was no equivalent to the Renaissance or the Reformation. On a positive level the Millet allowed Christians to retain their faith and worship, and its practice even in competition to the dominant religion: Islam, which was to provide a structure for national awareness to the point that the words "Greek" and "Orthodox," or "Serbian" and "Orthodox" or "Bulgarian" and "Orthodox" were to become synonymous. For the peoples of the Balkans the past has placed great importance on the religious element in the development and preservation of their cultures.

1

The Historical Tradition: Countries and Cultures

When the Ottoman Turks began the conquest of the Balkan peninsula in 1354 they encountered a people with a long and varied history and whose stratified culture was colored by the passage of time on a specific ethno-religious background.

The Hellenic Period: From the Grecian City to the Macedonian Empire

The oldest historical strata is that of the Hellenic period. A truly remarkable period in which small Attican, Argol and Peloponnesian villages organized themselves into City States, spreading through a system of colonies all over the Mediterranean and the Black Sea, and above all developing a culture which for 2000 years has remained one of the high points of reference for the whole of mankind.

It was a maritime culture; the island of Crete, melting pot of ideas coming from Asia Minor, Phoenicia and Egypt, has provided archaeologists with the oldest linear B Greek language (15th century before Christ). Cretan sea power also enabled them to control the Cyclades and the western shores of the Aegean.

The other influence was continental; two thousand years before Christ the Acheans, an indo-european people who spoke Greek, arrived in the southern Balkan Peninsula. Coming from the north they settled in Thessaly (in central Greece) and the Peloponnese, avoiding the maritime areas which they called by the pre-Hellenic word "Thalassa." But through contact with Crete, and hence the Egyptians and the Hittites, there emerged what is known as the Mycean civilisation (from the 16th–12th centuries) which was to spread all the way to Sicily. Their military expeditions, both piratical and colonial, resulted in the conquest of Crete and the

arrival of other invaders forced them to organize the campaign against Troy.

The second Greek wave, the Dorians, arrived around the 11th century B.C. Fierce warriors armed with iron swords, they came from what today constitutes Macedonia and Bulgaria, and from whence they had been driven by the Thracians and Illyrians. They were to settle in Epirus, Akarnania and all over the Peloponnese. Sparta became the centre of a militaristic culture which extended to colonies in Sicily and the Black Sea, and which was to inspire Homer's poetic muse.

Attica however was to remain independent as well as the eastern coastal regions and the islands of the Aegean where the Acheans continued to dominate. Through contact with the Anatolian east there developed what today is known as the Ionic culture, which was adopted by Athens at the height of its power. This district had few natural resources but being close to the sea it developed into a city state where power was transferred from royalty to landed aristocracy and finally to a slave based democracy. This was the golden age of the 5th century B.C. remembered for its wonderful monuments, philosophers, writers and noble statesmen, and symbolized above all by Pericles. Competing with Athens, Corinth, Thebes and Sparta became alternative centers of a multi-faceted Grecian culture, accredited with the intellectual revolution of "logic," the foundation stone of rationalism. No doubt these city states, which were primarily maritime, had only limited influence in the remote hinterland, for Greek civilization was fundamentally urban. Yet internal political rivalry, social unrest and commercial competition between the various towns was to stimulate, between the 7th and the 4th centuries B.C., a colonial period which saw the founding, outside ethnic Greek areas, of a number of satellite towns along the Balkan coast: in Illyria in the west Epidammos (Durres), Apollonia (near Fieri in Albania), and Kerkira (Corfu); to the east: Thrace, Abdera (near Xanthi), Anos (Enez), Byzantion, Apollonia (Sozopol), Messambria (Neseber), Odessos (Varna) and to the north Istros which is called Tomis on the Romanian coast. Many places from which Hellenic ideas and culture were disseminated.

The Macedonian era was altogether different; encompassing the whole of the Balkan peninsula and further afield to Egypt, the Pamir mountains and even reaching the Indus. Its origins are unclear. Even in ancient times opinion differed as to whether the people of this northern Hellenic region were Greek or Hellenized Thracians. Notwithstanding, their institutions had more in common with Dorian culture than with classical Greece: a strong royalty, a feudal style nobility and a bound peasant class. At the start of the Medicean Wars in the 7th century B.C., Macedonia was a subject kingdom under Persian rule, which regained its independence following the War of the Plates (479) but became embroiled in the rivalry between Sparta and Athens. Philip II (359–336) created an army on the basis of the phalanx. His son Alexander (336–323), known as Alexander the Great, became leader of a Pan-Hellenic movement which was to dominate Egypt and all of Asia Minor, including India. Of course this huge empire could not survive its creator's death and the generals divided it up among themselves. Macedonia under Antipater tried to retain dominion over the whole of Greece, but was dragged into a succession of wars for over a century against other Hellenic cities which resulted in some very strange alliances. Roman intervention made the Greeks settle their differences, but in 168 B.C. Macedonia was soundly defeated by Consul Paulus Emilius at Pydna.

Although short-lived the Alexandrian era did have important repercussions. For a century and a half, Hellenism was the dominant civilisation and one has only to look at a map of Greek cities founded during this period to see that they formed a dense network: from Alexandria in Egypt to Alexandria in Fergana, the coast of western Anatolia, Syria, Lebanon and Israel. Also of interest is the incredible Greco-Buddhist art of Gandhara (1st century B.C.–6th century A.D.). In the Balkan peninsula Hellenic culture was also dominant: the Macedonians adopted the Attican tongue and brought the gods of Olympus into their ancestral pantheons. From Scythia to the lakes of Ohrid, from Prespa to Pirin and the Rhodope, two-thirds of the Peninsula were Hellenic. The Illyric-Epirot border was a bilingual area and there is plenty of evidence of the influence of Greek civilisation in the Thracian kingdom of Odrisses, to the north east, with cupola'ed tombs at Kazanluk, Brezovo and Panagyurishte at the foot of the Sredna Gora, and their many treasures and paintings. Yet during this period the towns of classical mainland Greece were on the decline, only Corinth managing to keep its share of Mediterranean trade which from now on was dominated by Alexandria in Egypt, Antioch in Syria and Ephesus in Asia Minor. Meanwhile the Attican and Peloponnesian hinterland became progressively less populated in favour of the new Hellenic cities across the seas. Anyway, for the first time, Alexander had brought the whole of the Balkan Peninsula under one rule.

Roman Rule

The Greek Balkans underwent a further politico-cultural change by being incorporated into the Roman Empire. The quarrels of Alexander's successors gave the Roman Senate a pretext for intervention in the peninsula. During the 3rd and 2nd centuries B.C. the legions reached the eastern shores of the Adriatic, Epirus in the Peloponnese and Macedonia. The Roman civil war actually ended on Greek territory: Caesar defeated Pompeii at Pharsali in Thessaly (48 B.C.) and Octavius sank Antony and Cleopatra's fleet at Actium near the Gulf of Artes (31 B.C.). The Danube was reached and after Augustus, the Balkans were divided up into provinces: Crete, Archea, Epirus, Macedonia, Thrace, Moesia and Illyria. Dacia was added during Trajan's reign, this was north of the Danube and included Transylvania and Oltenia. Once more, as under Alexander, the whole of the peninsula came under one rule. This domination, apart from Dacia which was evacuated after 165 years, was to last for more than four centuries.

The influence of this era was to be long lasting. Naturally the Pax Romana brought total tranquillity in terms of politics. Existing organisations such as the Achean League or the Decebal Kingdom, were dismantled and provincial frontiers were drawn over Greek, Thracian and Illyrian land. Yet the new masters did not rely solely on their legions. As everywhere else in the Mediterranean they built a vast road network—the famous Roman roads—which were to penetrate the Balkan chaos. The Via Egnatia is the best known, but all the natural passes were fitted out with cobblestone highways along which would travel soldiers and administrators, traders hawking their wares and wandering artists producing their work as they went along. Rome set up colonies along the roads, inhabited by Roman citizens and these fortress towns and market towns are the origin of many of the large Balkan cities of today: Adrianopolis-Edirne, Serdica-Sofia, Naissus-Nis, Sigidum-Belgrade and many others. However not all the regions of the peninsula were to benefit in the same way from their incorporation into the Roman Empire. Greece, too similar with its agricultural products to southern Italy and too far from the sea routes of Egypt and the Middle East, became rather self-contained, a preserve of large landowners and sheep raisers, hardly exporting at all save marble for Italian villas. Illyria on the other hand underwent a period of rapid development. With its large vineyards and mines, what is present-day Bosnia became the gateway to the Balkans by way of the port of Dyrraciun (Durres). There began the Egnatia road, symbol of the penetration of Roman civilisation right into the very heart of the peninsula, and was to go via Heraclea (Bitola) to Thessalonika. Furthermore Illyria provided many soldiers for the Roman legions, some embracing a profession which was to lead them to the highest position, for example Aurelian, Diocletian and Constantine who are known to history as the Illyrian Emperors.

However, Romanization, completed in Gaul and Spain, was in the Balkans confronted with the hurdle of Hellenism. There is the saying: "Vanquished Greece conquered its unrefined conqueror." In reality Roman civilisation was imposed, as everywhere else, in its material expression: in the form of monuments, roads etc. Yet Greek culture was to be victorious as it was based on a written language (as opposed to the Celts or the Iberians) and had a comparatively well-known literature. The Greeks took pride in past achievements, which with each passing year were to become more and more glorious and attracted young Romans who came to Greece to study, above all at Athens university after it was restored by Marcus Aurelius in 176 B.C. Even though Latin was the administrative and army language, Greek was to retain its hold on the whole of the south and east of the peninsula. Yet the Greeks were proud to be Roman-Romaioi—a term used to denote a multisecular heritage. It is obvious that Roman cultural supremacy should have occured on the periphery of the former Hellenic area: so in Thrace, in the north east, where the process of Hellenization had begun even prior to Philip of Macedonia, Latinization was to fail, while in the north west the Illyrians, who had no written culture, adopted Latin relatively early, except in remote villages where the traditional tongue was to continue to be used. A few centuries later this was to become Albanian.

The case of Dacia is particularly interesting. Having at the end of the 1st century A.D. abandoned the plains bordering the Black Sea to conquering hordes from the Russian steppes, the Thraco-Dacians had at the end of 1st century A.D. formed a tribal confederation which, grouped within the protective ring of the Carpathians, was to come into contact with the Roman world. Their leader Decebal launched a series of attacks against the province of Moesia and defeated a counterattack by the Roman legions aimed at their capital Sarmizegetusa. Emperor Trajan resolved to conquer this stronghold north of the Danube; his campaign became known as the Dacian Wars lasting from A.D. 101–106 and are depicted on Trajan's Column in the New Forum in Rome. For 165 years the country became an Imperial Roman province and was later subdivided. Its natural resources: gold in rivers and silver, iron and salt mines together with its geostrategic position were to justify an active policy of colonisation. Imperial administrators built towns and roads and, in the same way as in Gaul, the native population adopted the Roman language and Roman customs. Attacked by the Goths in A.D. 271, Aurelian evacuated Dacia which was to be the first Roman province to be abandoned to the Barbarians. The extent of this evacuation and the subsequent survival of parts of this Romanized population is a subject for conjecture, but six hundred years later they reappear historically under the name Romanians. Whatever the case might be they are descendants of a Roman civilisation which was north of the Danube.

The Birth of Byzantium and the Foundation of the Slavs

The traditional dates A.D. 395 and A.D. 476: the division of the Roman Empire by Theodorus and the deposing of the last emperor, are more symbolic than real in terms of the eastern Roman Empire. In reality the 3rd century crisis and the rise of Diocletian in A.D. 295 put an end to the unity of the empire, which henceforth was ruled by two or more Augustus' or Caesars. But it was Constantine, born in Nis in the middle of the Balkans, who laid the foundations for this schism with three crucial decisions. First of all as sole Emperor, following the victory of Adrianopolis in 323, he was to concentrate into his own hands all the reins of power; making himself a god he surrounded himself with a servile court and replaced the magistrates of old Rome with a bureaucratic machine which was directly accountable to himself. The second measure was in 325 when he organized and presided over the first ecumenical council of Nicea which laid the foundations of dogma and canonic law of the Christian Church. Constantine had tolerated Christianity since the Edict of Milan of 313 but it was only on his deathbed that he was baptized. The third move was in 330 when he proclaimed Constantinopolis, former Greek colony of Byzantion, on the shores of the Bosphorus, the capital of the empire thus transferring the centre of the Roman world away from Italy to the Balkans. Thereafter: the official schism in 395, the sack of Rome by Alaric's Visigoths in 410 and the overthrow of Romulus Augustulus in 476, gave the eastern Roman Empire unrivalled supremacy over the west, henceforth dominated by Germanic peoples organized into barbarian kingdoms. The loosening and subsequent breakdown of political and administrative links with Rome brought about a decline in the Latin character of the civilisation in favour of Hellenism based on a capital with a population of half a million inhabitants, the great majority Greek speaking. On the other hand Christianity, which was in the ascendency, had been organized into the autocephalic Churches of Rome, Alexandria and Antioch, to which in 381 was added, following the council of Constantinople, the "New Rome" which immediately proclaimed its pre-eminence as the seat of Saint Peter. Yet the Church of Constantinople, Greek with its Patriarchate, language, and liturgy, and more importantly its Greek theology which had assimilated many of the ideas of classical philosophy. It was also the belief of the rulers of Constantinople that they were the descendants of the Emperors of Rome, and consequently the supreme rulers of the world. Up to the Ottoman conquest in 1453 they were to remain the embodiment of the Imperial Roman dream.

The Byzantine empire and civilisation had its origins in this symbiosis of Roman state structures, Hellenic culture and the Christian religion.

This was the third transformation of the Balkans, soon to be paralleled by another major event in the history of the area: the migration of the Slavs. From A.D. 527–565 during the rule of Justin I and his nephew Justinian, the Slavs started to stage brutal raids over the Danube, reaching as far down as the Adriatic, the gulf of Corinth and the Aegean Sea. Attacking towns along the way they would finally withdraw once more north of the river. During the 580s these tribes, ruled over by the Avars (Mongol nomads who had created a kingdom in the Pannonian Plains), were forced out of their own area and in ever increasing numbers settled in Byzantine territory. Avar rule came to an end in August 626 when

Heraclius (610–641) defeated the hordes besieging Byzantium. The Slavs nonetheless remained in the Balkans, their territory reaching down into the Peloponnese which was to remain for two centuries under their control. This invasion caused the population of the hinterland to flood down to the coastal island areas thus reinforcing the Greek character of the East and the Illyro-Roman of the west. The Byzantine administration however managed to survive and even regained control of the situation, adapting to the tribal organization of the villages which they referred to as "Slavenes." In the midst of this ethnic transformation Heraclius allowed the Serbs and Croats to leave their territories to the north of the Carpathians and settle in their present day territory having first of all pushed out the Avars. In principle the new arrivals recognized the sovereign right of the Empire over their land but in reality the North and West of the peninsula were henceforth outside Byzantine control. This took place as Heraclius was finishing the Hellenization of the country, replacing Latin with Greek as the administrative and martial language and adopting the Greek title of Basileus. The Balkans were becoming fundamentally Greco-Slav.

This was the fourth transformation.

The Byzantine Empire and the Slavic States

Henceforth, for 500 years, the history of the peninsula was one of rivalry between these two competing groups, expressing itself in warfare and rival churches. Yet there were also similarities for both cultures were to retain the Imperial City as a model.

Byzantium continued to affirm its political primacy even though western Europe had permanently broken away and it was being forced by the Arabs to retrench. The Arabs had since the 8th century dominated Egypt and the east. Yet even at its height in 1025, the Byzantine Empire was limited to the peninsula up to the Danube and to lake Van in Asia Minor and its European territories were progressively being whittled away by Bulgarian and Serbian invasions.

The policy of defending the border areas absorbed all the energies of Constantine V, Michael III, Nicephorus Phocas, Michael VI and many others and also caused a great drain on the imperial treasury. Yet it was internal changes that most affected the Byzantine people. The agricultural system, inherited from Rome and based on the Latifundia and the Colonat, was seriously disrupted by the migration of more farmers, especially the Slavs. As well as the soldier-peasant—he Stratiots—from the 7th century onwards there developed a free peasantry whose rights were enshrined during the reign of Justinian II (705–711) by an agrarian statute "Nomos Georgikos" which granted the peasant the right of ownership and inheritance of his property ie. cultivated land, meadows, vineyard and vegetable garden, yet together with the other inhabitants of the village, part ownership of woods, pastures and commonland. As far as the Byzantine authorities were concerned this common ownership formed an administrative and fiscal whole on which a overall tax would be imposed and collection of which was the responsibility of everybody. It must be emphasized that this was not a residual form of the Slav idea of communal property based on the Zadruga, but a compromise between the Roman concept of property—uti et abuti—and certain Slavonic communal practices. No doubt it is possible to find similar social organization prior to this but under Byzantine rule it was to be enshrined in statutory law and for a long time to come. During the Byzantine period however there was a underlining struggle between the small-holder and the secular and ecclesiastical latifundiaries who were trying to take over the land and turn the owners into slaves. The emperors alternated between support for one group and the other. The large landowners finally carried the day and serfdom was instituted. It was however only in the 14th century with the Paleologues and the Latin Empire that a truly feudal system was to emerge modeled mainly on the western system. The peasant community however had existed and been used by the fiscal authorities for too long for it to disappear completely. It remained a permanent feature of pre-Ottoman Balkan life.

It is also to the Byzantine period that the Orthodox Church owes its special role and distinctive character. On the 16 August 1054 the Christian Church split into the Eastern Church under the Patriarch of Byzantium and the Latin Church under the Pope. This schism was the logical conclusion to secular conflicts. During the 13th and 14th centuries attempts were made to resolve their differences, but to no avail and in 1452 a high-ranking Byzantine official declared to a papal delegation that he would: "prefer to see the Turkish turban in the middle of the capital than the Roman mitre." From its very beginning the Eastern Church had had very close links with the secular state. To such an extent that the Basileuses not only felt empowered to interfere in questions of ecclesiastical discipline but also in doctrinal questions. Constantine was to organize the Council of Nicea (325) to decide on Christian doctrine. The Emperors were deeply involved in the 5th century arguments over the life of Christ and during the 8th and 9th centuries in a conflict which was to shake the Empire: the artistic representation of the human form. Their interference in these crises was very different from the duality of power which existed in Europe between the Pope and Emperor, which regularly degenerated into power struggles over appointments and over many other matters. This was not the case with the Eastern Church. There was a very strong symbiotic relationship between the Orthodox Church and the state, although even this was not exempt from personal quarrels. The Patriarch was also involved in the question of succession, in questions of secular law and in the State University; further down the hierarchy, Bishops and Archbishops often considered themselves to be lord and master of a city. For example Isidor of Salonika who organized the defense of the city against the Catalans. Thus the Eastern Church usurped some of the functions which are more usually the preserve of the secular state.

In cultural terms the Empire became so Hellenized that modern Greek historians place the start of Neo-Hellenism (in other words the use of modern Greek which is very different from Attican Greek) between the 8th and 11th centuries and situate the genesis of Neo-Hellenic literature at around the 1st millennium.[1] Everything was written in Greek which was the language of both Church and State.

Wallachians—transhumant shepherds spoke Latin based dialects—and survived only in the mountain areas, although in quite large numbers.

In the Balkans Byzantine rule was confined by its proximity to Slav kingdoms. The most powerful was the Bulgarian kingdom. During the summer of 681 Emperor Constantine IV agreed to the occupation of the province of Moesia, between the Danube and the Balkan mountain range, by troops belonging to Khan Asparuk. He also agreed to pay a due to this kingdom which would exist on Imperial territory but remain an independent entity. At the Council of Constantinople a Syrian priest blamed this defeat on vice "during the war in Bulgaria." The new kingdom was called by this name which remains to this day. A warrior race originally from Tourania, they are known to historians as Protobulgarians and were related to the Huns. In the 6th century they formed a powerful kingdom round the Azov Sea with which Basileus Heraclius strove to maintain good relations. In the middle of the 7th century the Khazars were to change this. Some Bulgarians submitted to their rule and stayed in the area, but in 680 a large group, led by Asparuk, crossed the Danube in the Delta region and occupied the Moesia area whose inhabitants were Northern Sever Slavs and were organized into an alliance of seven tribes. Thus there emerged a Bulgaro-Slav state, much in the same way as the Frankish-Gallo-Roman state. The Touranians formed an aristocratic-warrior class ruling over a mainly Slav population, which over a period of two centuries managed to assimilate them. Khan Krum's fierce warriors (803–814) set out from their capital Pliska and reached the Tisza which was on the edge of Charlemagne's Empire. Yet most of their wars were against the Byzantines who continued to refuse to accept the defeat of 681 and embarked on an endless series of military campaigns marked by numerous battles.

By the 9th century the Bulgarians, from then on fully assimilated with the Slavs, had become Christians. This was during the period of competition between missionaries from the Frankish Church and the Byzantine Church for the conversion of the pagan Slavs. In Moravia Cyril and Methodius had succeeded in introducing glagolithic script and translating the Scriptures into Macedo-Slav. This became the ecclesiastical language. Boris the Bulgarian King preferred the distant Franks and so Byzantium reacted strongly. Basileus Michael sent both an army and a fleet to the Bulgarian border; Boris capitulated. In 864 he was baptized by a Byzantine priest and placed his kingdom under the jurisdiction of the Patriarch Photius. Basileus Michael became his god-father and as well as giving him his name, henceforth Boris-Michael, he gave him a small territory as a baptism present. The conversion of Bulgaria to Christianity was to complete the ethnic and political unification of the country. The Greek clergy quickly tried to organize the Bulgarian Church yet Boris wanted the Church to be autocephalic. He appealed to Rome but this tactic, following the Council of Constantinople (867), was only to result in the excommunication of Pope Nicholas I and to a volte face by Boris. He recognized the sovereign rights of the Patriarch of Byzantium while at the same time retaining autonomy for his own Church.

The archbishop of Bulgaria was henceforth to occupy a prominent place in the hierarchy of the eastern Church. The disciples of Cyril and Methodius, including Clement "of Ohrid" and his brother Naum, were driven out of Moravia and finally organized the Bulgarian Church. They gave it a Slavonic liturgy and a new script based on Greek capital letters known as cyrillic script. Even so Bulgarian Christianity was nothing more than a variant of Byzantine Christianity using Slavonic instead of Greek.

This was very clear under Boris' son. Symeon (893–927) had studied in Constantinople, spoke perfect Greek, admired Byzantine culture and tried to implant it in his own country. He even aspired to the leadership of the Empire. Received by the young Constantine VII and the Patriarch in the capital, he was crowned with the Imperial Crown and given the title of "Basileus." But the resistance of the Empress-mother prevented him from becoming co-emperor and therefore war once more broke out with Byzantium. Symeon crushed the Imperial armies and took control of all the Balkans right up to Adrianopolis, Serres and Kastoria. He gave himself the title of Basileus of the Bulgars and the Greeks. His capital Preslav became the centre of a Slav speaking Byzantine culture, notwithstanding fierce opposition from Greek-speaking partisans. Modern historians refer to his reign as the golden age of Bulgarian literature[2] yet agree that this mainly involved translating or compiling Byzantine works. What is sure is that his capitals Pliska and Preslav were centres for the dissemination of Byzantine culture in the art and literature to the Slavs and Serbs in the Balkans and even to the Russians of Kiev.

The Bulgarian Empire went into rapid decline: in 971 Basileus John Tzimisces took power in the capital, taking Czar Boris II prisoner. He annexed most of his land and abolished the Bulgarian Patriarchate which had been created in 925 by Symeon. The resurgence of a powerful state under Samuel (991–1014) shifted emphasis from what Byzantine contemporaries felt was the continuation of Symeon's Kingdom, to the Macedonian region and above all to Ohrid where the Patriarchate was restored. Emperor Basil II known as the Bulgar was to end this in the most brutal manner. In July 1014 he surprised the Bulgarian army at the Clidion pass and took many prisoners. According to tradition there were 14,000. He had them all blinded apart from the 99th in every 100 who was blinded in one eye only so as to guide the others to Prilep. Czar

Samuel was to die from sorrow on seeing this horrific procession. Bulgaria once more became an integral part of the Byzantine Empire and was divided into "themes." The Patriarchate of Ohrid was relegated to an archbishopric—admittedly autocephalic—yet the post-holder was directly appointed by the Basileus. For the first time since the arrival of the Slavs, the whole peninsula was once more part of the Byzantine Empire.

The Serbs also managed to set up an independent kingdom. Given permission by Heraclius to move to Imperial territory the Serbian tribes were to form themselves into a loose alliance of Zupans (chiefs) to resist the Byzantine administration. No doubt there had been attempts to convert them to the Orthodox rite, especially in Dalmatian cities where the Roman Church had had some success. But after iconoclast disturbances Byzantium imposed by force its control over the region and made Dalmatia into a "theme." It also sent disciples of Methodius and Cyril to convert the Slavs and so between 867 and 874 the Serbs entered into the fold of the Byzantine Church. The Serbs in the Raska region, between the Drina and the Morava rivers, had been used by the Emperor to combat the Bulgars yet Czar Symeon of Bulgaria himself succeeded in subjugating them and incorporated them into his Patriarchate. After the Czar's death a Serbian Prince called Tchaslav rebuilt the kingdom, but subservient to Byzantium. Other principalities, such as Hum (what is today Herzegovina) and Zet (future Montenegro) were caught up by the rivalry between Byzantium and Croatia. In 1077 Prince Knez of Zeta was given a royal crown by the Pope and so was to become the first Serbian monarch—King Michael (1051-1081).

The region was rocked by the piratical raids of Robert Guiscard's Normans. In 1094, Vukan, the Zupan of Raska, tried to free himself from the sovereignty of Byzantium. By 1166/7 this had been achieved and, with the support of the king of Hungary Zupan Stephen Nemanja, Vukan proclaimed his independence. Basileus Manuel defeated him but following the latter's death Vucan once again took up arms, together with his Hungarian allies, conquered swathes of Byzantine territory, uniting Raska with Zeta and making this the first real Serbian state. Its capital Ras became the seat of a bishopric subordinate to Ohrid and responsible to the Patriarchate of Bulgaria. In March 1196 old Nemanja married his son Stephen to the daughter of the Basileus, so giving the young prince the title of Sebastocrator. He then abdicated the throne and became a monk in the Monastery of Athos. It was difficult really to escape from the Byzantine fold.

At the beginning of the 13th century both the Bulgarians and the Serbs had experienced periods of political independence yet even then they remained part of Byzantium's sphere of influence. In their religious practices and their culture they remained followers in the same way that the Germanic Kingdoms, six centuries earlier, considered themselves to be the inheritors of the Roman world, even if the Empire no longer was in Rome but at Aix and on the Rhine. In the east Constantine's creation had survived even though Constantinople had become Byzantium.

The Decline of Byzantium and the Feudal Division, 1204–1453

This creation was neither destroyed by Barbarians nor Pagans but by western Christians led astray in their Crusade to deliver the tomb of Christ.

For the capture of Constantinople in the 4th Crusade (13 April 1204) was not an unexpected surprise. Previously in 1190 Emperor Frederick Barbarossa had almost seized the city. The Basileus had allied himself to Sultan Saladin, the conqueror of Jerusalem and against whom the crusade had been organized. Venice was afraid of losing its privileges within the Byzantine Empire to its rivals Genoa and Pisa but the idea of conquering Byzantium, which was daunting to both merchants and politicians, was contemplated by the military simply in terms of the traditional Latin hostility to schismatics. The result was the horrific sack of Constantinople. For three whole days, the city of Constantine the Great, which had never been conquered before and had withstood the onslaught of Persians, Arabs, Avars and Russians, was to witness rape and pillage at the hands of western soldiery. Villehardouin openly admitted that: "never before had such fabulous plunder been taken from a city" while a Byzantine writer commented that "the Saracens themselves are kind and caring in comparison to these people who carry the cross of Christ on their shoulder."

In terms of collective psychology those few days in April 1204 were to be deeply significant right up to the Ottoman conquest two and a half centuries later. On a political level a treaty was agreed by Doge Dandolo and the crusaders on how the Byzantine territory would be divided: the Latin Emperor received a quarter, Venice half and the rest went to the military leaders in the form of Imperial fiefdoms. A western feudal structure was to supplant what was left of the Roman Empire. At the summit was the Latin Emperor Baudouin I of Flanders and his five successors: the lords of the Kingdom of Thessalonika, of the Duchy of Athens and of the Principalities of Achea and of Morea. Venice, outside Baudouin's suzerainty, created a virtual colonial empire claiming Dyrrachium and Ragusa on the Adriatic coast, the ports of Koron and Modon in the Peloponnese, the Ionian islands, Crete, the largest islands of the Archipelago, the main ports of the Hellispont and the Marmara Sea, Adrianopolis at the heart of Thrace and on top of all this three eighths of Constantinople. On the one side feudal lords destined to fight each other and on the other a trading power with a virtual monopoly on trade between these new Balkan countries.

It is said that the principality of Morea was "a piece of France in Greek territory" so closely had the French feudal structures been copied out there in the far off Peloponnese. Yet the historian G. Ostrogorsky emphasizes that the Byzantine Empire had also experienced the feudalizing processes and that fundamentally there were no real difference between the Byzantine pronoia and the western fiefdom.[3] Consequently the real owners of the land, the pronoians, submitted to the new Frankish order without much resistance once they were guaranteed possession of the pronoia and the poor peasant continued to be over-burdened by the same dues, paying taxes to a Latin lord rather than to a Greek master.

This did not however prevent animosity from developing between the Byzantine population and their conquerors. Based mainly on cultural and religious antagonisms which might only become apparent as a result of everyday pressures of occupation. Many of the Empire and Orthodox Church's high-ranking officials as well as monks and educated people left the conquered regions and went to the new Byzantine states: the countries of Nicea, Trebizond and in the Balkans that of the despotate of Epirus which for a time rivalized that of Nicea. Between these three countries, together with the machinations of another—Bulgaria—there developed a complicated system of alliances and wars which lasted half a century but which resulted in the liberation of Constantinople from the Franks and the triumphal entry on the 15 August 1261 of the Emperor of Nicea, Michael VIII, known as the Paleologos, and restorer of the Byzantine Empire.

However brief the Latin interlude might have been it was to have disastrous repercussions. In spite of Michael's victories, which restored some of the Empire's former glory, the feudal division continued and in the middle of the 14th century the "Imperium" had been reduced to Thrace, the city of Thessalonika, Mistra which was an enclave in the Peloponnese and a few minor islands. The maritime republics of Italy controlled the Byzantine waters, southern Greece remained Latin with the Duchy of Athens and the Principality of Morea and although the despot of Epirus (prior to its conquest by Dusan in 1346) was Greek it remained hostile and a rival of Constantinople. The north of the Balkan peninsula meanwhile was dominated by the Bulgars and the Serbs. In Byzantine territory and in the hereditary Principalities the process of feudalization continued to develop. The pronoia became hereditary and the holders no longer answered the Emperor's call to arms, so they had to be replaced by Norman, Catalan, Kuman and even Turkish mercenaries. Yet the sack of 1204 had dispersed the accumulated wealth of centuries and the Latin Emperors sold the valuable ornaments and precious vases of the Church to cover their costs. Byzantium was not able to overcome its financial difficulties which were to remain a constant feature of the restoration. Its currency, the nomism, which had for centuries dominated the world money markets went into decline against the Venetian ducat. A mercenary army was expensive and Andronic II cut it down to a few thousand men and abandoned the idea of maintaining a fleet. Even after these measures price increases were to create popular discontent expressed in violent uprisings and political movements such as the Zealots who divided up large holdings and dominated Thessalonika from 1342–1350.

The Frankish period was linked in the collective memory to the Roman Church and was to contribute to anti-Papist feeling among the populace which later precluded any attempt at union between the Churches. Contemplated by the Emperor of Nicea, it actually was agreed upon at the council of Lyons in 1274. Yet it was to come up against almost universal opposition from the Byzantine world and died with its instigator Michael VIII. During the next century the idea foundered over one of the most important religious issues of all Byzantine history: the Hesychaste debate. This ascetic and mystical movement, similar to French "Quietism," provoked fierce debate. The Emperor became involved and the accession of John Cantacuzenos to the throne meant the victory of hesychasm. In 1351, at a meeting held at the palace, it was officially made the doctrine of the Church. Rome had declared against this interpretation of spiritual life but the movement's principal theologians in any case were fierce opponents of the reunification of the Churches. Spilling over into the realm of culture, hesychasm manifested itself in a reaction against the Latinization of the 13th century and in an affirmation of conservative Hellenism: hostility to the Roman Church and at the same time to western culture in general.

In 1355 the situation was so worrying that the Venetian ambassador to Constantinople advised the Doge to annex the Empire which otherwise would fall prey to the Turks.

This was the history of the last hundred years of Byzantium.

The Rise and Fall of the Slavic States: Bulgaria and Serbia

The two Slav countries in the north of the peninsula were affected by the decline of the Byzantine Empire after the catastrophe of 1204.

Since 1018 the Bulgarian lands, reincorporated into the Byzantine Empire, had been subject to a religious and cultural Hellenization, together with the implanting of non-Slav ethnic groups: the Kumans, a nomadic Turkish people who in 1091 were pitted against their cousins the Petchenegs by Alexis Comnen and which he then settled on the banks of the Danube; Wallachians from the great river to Macedonia and Thessaly, known as Greater Wallachia, Jews and Armenians who were particularly numerous in Thessalonika and surrounding areas. In the autumn of 1185 two brothers Peter-Theodor and Arsen, landowners from the Hemus area of Tirnovo, demanded a pronoia in return for joining the Imperial army. They were turned down and around these two disappointed men gathered Montagnards, disgruntled with higher taxes yet euphoric over the building of a church at Saint Demeter, who they made their patron saint. There has been much discussion over the ethnic origins of the leaders of this uprising and of the make-up of their troops. Bulgarian historians admit that Theodor and Arsen came from a Bulgaro-Kuman family and that the Montagnards were essentially Wallachians but Bulgars from the plains also joined which makes this insurrection the starting point for what is called the "Second Bulgar Kingdom." Following two fruitless campaigns Emperor Isaac II Angel was forced to negotiate and recognize the new state whose capital was Tirnovo and which stretched from the Stara Planina to the Danube. An autocephalic archbishopric was set up in the capital. Yet in 1200 Pope Innocent III, in anticipation of the crusade which he was preparing, entered into discussions with Kaloyan, the youngest brother of the new state's two co-founders and sent him a royal crown, while the archbishop in the name of the Roman Church was made Primate of the Kingdom. The coronation by the papal legate Cardinal Leon took place in Tirnovo on the 8th November 1204. By that time Constantinople had already been captured by the Latins seven months previously. Yesterday's friends were to become rivals; the union with Rome was forgotten and Czar Kaloyan became a staunch opponent of the Franks, the Thracian Greek aristocracy begged him to come to their aid, promising him the Imperial Crown of Constantinople. On the 4th April 1205, close to Adrianopolis, the Bulgaro-Kuman troops destroyed the cream of western knighthood and took prisoner the first Latin Emperor Baudouin I of Flanders, who was to end his days in the fortress of Tirnovo. Kaloyan however died two years later while besieging the town of Thessalonika.

The subsequent episode in the history of the Second Bulgarian Kingdom was less dazzling. Disputes over the succession weakened the young country and religious unrest developed with a resurgence of Bogomilism[4], solemnly denounced at the Council of Tirnovo in 1211. Forced forward by the arrival of the Tatars from the Russian steppes, the Kumans, hitherto allied to the Bulgars, ravaged Bulgarian territory, soon to be followed by the Tatars themselves. The kingdom broke up and the poor king of Tirnovo trying to escape from the ferocious warriors of the Khan was to wander for several weeks through the forests around Adrianopolis. For a short time from 1299–1300 Tirnovo Bulgaria became a Tartar province. A new dynasty was to emerge from Vidin called the Sismanids whose second member married his son to the daughter of Emperor Andronic III. Byzantine influence once more was dominant in the capital where the Tirnovo cultural school distinguished itself with its final "eclat." Divided up into the two kingdoms, Tirnovo and Vidin, and open to Serbian attack, Kaloyan's Bulgarian kingdom was to disappear, overpowered by the Ottomans.

The Serbs under the Nemanjids dynasty were to be a greater

threat to Byzantine power. Notwithstanding marriage ties to the daughter of the Basileus, Stephen, son of Nemanja, turned first to Hungary and then to Emperor Barbarossa who was organizing a crusade. Stephen sending his Byzantine wife back home, recognized the supremacy of the Roman Pontiff and Hungary's right of suzerainty. In 1217 he was given a royal crown by Pope Honorius, making him the first Serbian king; he was crowned King Stephen I. His brother Sava, however, turned to the patriarch of Nicea to organize the Church in the Kingdom and was in turn consecrated autocephalic metropolitan of Serbia.

In the same way as the Bulgarians, the Serbs henceforth had their own Church (1219). Its seat was at Pec and Saint Sava was later to become its greatest saint. Although independent of the ecumenical Patriarchate and celebrating the liturgy in Church Slavonic, the Serbian Church remained Byzantine in its dogma and discipline.

The weakness of the Empire after the Latin episode and the subsequent Byzantine civil wars gave King Stephen Uros the chance of taking Skopje, previously occupied by the Bulgars, which he made his capital. He also occupied Dibar and pushed on to the coast near Durazzo. His successor gained control of the strategic fortress of Prilep and won a great victory over the Byzantines and Bulgarians at Kustendil in 1330, forever destroying the Bulgar threat and paving the way for Serbian preeminence in the Balkans. This task was to fall to Stephen Dusan (1331–1355) considered the greatest Serbian king. Supported by a land-hungry Serbian nobility, Dusan conquered all of Macedonia right up to the gates of Thessalonika. Skilfully playing one power against another (Byzantium, Hungary, Venice and also the Ottomans) he consolidated a huge territory stretching from the Danube to the Gulf of Corinth. On Easter day 1346 with great pomp and ceremony he was crowned at Skopje by the Metropolitan of Pec: "Emperor of the Serbs and Greeks." The Metropolitan in turn was elevated to the rank of Patriarch in spite of the protests of the title holder in Constantinople.

Dusan's empire plainly had a Serbian leader, so to govern the newly conquered territories the Czar appointed nobles from his entourage and although the majority of the land and its population were Greek he showed respect for their customs and their privileges. The Skopje court copied Byzantium with its tyrants, Caesars and Sebastocratrators and when in 1349 the Czar published his famous—Zakonik—code it was clearly an adaptation of Byzantine law to Serbian customs. Dusan witnessing the weakness of Byzantium also aspired to conquering Constantinople. Death robbed him of his chance. Although he had had no qualms over allying himself with the Ottomans against the Basileus, his death marked the end of the last real obstacle to the advance of the Infidel. The Serbian Empire did not survive its founder and split into rival principalities that fought each other and the remains of Byzantium, under the watchful eye of the Sultan.

The Balkans Against the Ottomans

When Murad, the first Ottoman Sultan, moved his capital, from Brusa to Adrianopolis in 1365 a new chapter of the history of the Balkans was to begin. There had been many incursions over the borders for some time by religiously inspired warriors known as the Ghazi but there now began a systematic conquest of the peninsula. What were the structures which were supposed to resist this invasion?

In political terms and consequently also in military terms, the Christian population was deeply divided. The Byzantine Empire was confined to the capital and surrounding areas, to the town of Thessalonika and its surrounding areas. There was also the semi-autonomous tyranny of Mitra in the Peloponnese which belonged to the Emperor's brother and a handful of islands. The rest of the Greek lands were divided up between the Duchy of Athens which had been sold by Florentine bankers to Venetian merchants, the Principality of Achea in the western Peloponnese sold by the Angevins to Navarra, while the Republic of Venice and its rival Genoa shared the islands of the Aegean. To the north of Arta and Velos this area, which had previously been the Empires of Kaloyan and Dusan, had exploded into numerous unstable principalities. None of these countries had enough power to resist the onslaught of the Spahis and the Janissaries (the Sultan's soldiers).

In terms of religion the situation was much less complicated. Apart from the Jews and the Armenians almost all the Balkans had stayed faithful to the eastern Church and, notwithstanding the autocephalic struggle with Tirnovo and Pec, the seat of Constantinople still retained its prestige in the eyes of the population which used the Greek or Church Slavonic liturgies. Latinization, consecutive to the Frankish invasion of 1204, had been slight and disappeared almost completely following the 1261 restoration. Its impact had been greater in the Venetian and Genoese territories where the Roman clergy lived in close rivalry with the Greek clergy. The Latin interlude rekindled the conflict between the two Churches, taking it right to the congregational level. Once the Franks had fled from Constantinople, the religious intolerance and fiscal harshness of the Venetians and Genovese nurtured anti-Papist sentiment among the populations of the islands. Even so in the face of the Ottoman threat the Byzantine Emperor, John VIII, once more agreed to the union of the Churches, which was proclaimed in Florence on July 6, 1439. However, the opposition of the clergy and of the people was so great that it remained a dead-letter and merely provided a further pretext for an outbreak of fanaticism which was hostile to the west. These were the political and military stakes: would the rulers of the Christian countries of the Empire be willing to come to the defence of Constantinople threatened by the Infidel? The Pope would try to overcome both the rivalry of western monarchs, the ambiguities of the idea of another crusade and popular resentment and on his success would depend the future of the Balkans.

The myriad of peoples in the peninsula had for centuries and centuries been subject, on a cultural level, to the influence of Byzantium. Even those like the Bulgarians and Serbs who formed cohesive independent countries had lived under the shadow of the Byzantine model. After a thousand years of Eastern Imperium Romanum the Ottomans would in the Balkans encounter a Byzantine Christian people, with similar social structures of a feudal type together with traditional peasant communities; the plains experiencing change more quickly, while mountainous areas remained inward-looking and conservative. The main difference however remained that of language and dialect, for as well as Greek which was the language of the Church and above all of a cultural elite, there was Bulgarian and Serbian, both Slavonic languages which had enjoyed written forms and even their own literature. To native speakers these provided a cultural point of reference whilst the churches and basilicas built by the old rulers, with frescos and Saintly Kings were to be the history books of the illiterate masses. A diverse heritage which during the subsequent disaster would remain in popular memory as a point of reference both of unity and diversity, of a Golden Age which it might be possible to recreate once again.

Notes

1. A. Vacalopoulos: Histoire de la Grèce Moderne p.7
2. I. Dujcev: Histoire de la Bulgarie p.116.
3. Histoire de l'État Byzantin p.447. For an explanation of the *pronoia* system refer to the same book, pages 353, 392 and 415. This question has aroused strong disagreement between Byzantine specialists.
4. Refer to Charles Peuch et A. Vaillant: Le Traité contre les Bogomiles de Cosmas le Prêtre. Imp. Et. Sl. Paris 1945.

2

The Origins of the Conquering Ottomans

By the time the Turks began the conquest of the Balkans they already had a rich history, drawing on a civilisation whose origins were both ancient and prestigious.

The Origins of the Turks and the Seldjuk Empire

The Turks were a people sharing a common language, of the Uralo-Altaic group, descended from nomads who had since the 11th century B.C. roamed in an area which is present day Outer Mongolia and Chinese Turkestan. Progressively they were to divide into three main branches: the Mongols, the Tunguz-Manchus and the Turks. Chinese chronicles portray them as horsemen organized into clans and tribes, eschewing agriculture, living on livestock husbandry and the pillaging of neighbouring settled peoples. They also record the names of their successive "Empires" which seem to have been little more than federations (quite often bogus) of tribes or peoples being harnessed into martial operations by a famous leader. So there appeared a few centuries before our own era, the Hiong-Nu who carved up a huge swathe of land from the Chinese border to the Tarim Bay before splitting up into eastern and western Hiong-Nu. It was a part of the latter who invaded Europe in the 5th century; the Huns led by Attila, who were stopped by Aetius and the Gaulish Germanic kings at the Catalan Field (451). Another "Empire" was created in the 6th and 7th centuries A.D.—Tu-Ku Chinese calling themselves Kuk or Gok, hence the name Turk, who descended from the Altai region and extended their dominion from the Great Wall of China to Sogdia. This region was at the time the centre of the silk trade between the Middle East and Europe, which brought them into contact with the Persians of Sassani and the Byzantine Empire. Basileus Justin II (565–578) even made an alliance with the Turks against the Persians in his fight to control the silk trade. This was the first contact in a long line. The Kuk-Turks disappeared from history in the middle of the 8th century when the Chinese and Arab Empires, at the height of their expansion, met on the river Oxus. The Uigurs, another Turkish people from the Orkhon area to the south of lake Baikal, invaded China. Having been in touch with Manichean missionaries from Persia they adopted their religion as well as the Sogdian script which derived from ancient Syrian. Some settled on the edge of the Transox where they became established; consequently the region, which until then had been inhabited by Indo-Iranians, became Turkish from the 9th century and there developed a civilisation derived from the various neighbouring influences and also the three religions which the Vigurs practised; Buddhism, Manicheism and Nestorianism.

It was there in this new Turkistan that the Turks converted to Islam. The Iranian Transoxian dynasty, with its capital at Bukhara had been converted to Islam for more than a century. Through trade and war they made contact with their northern neighbours and in 961 Alp Tekin, a Turkish muslim slave became governor of the Iranian province of Khorrashah, and later founded in Afghanistan the country of Ghaznevid. His son Mahmoud (998–1030), renowned for his expeditions into India, adopted the title of Ghazi and the Caliph of Baghdad gave him the title of Sultan. Under his successor the Seldjuk tribe came to the forefront.

Named after Seldjuk, an eponym—a real or mythical person, the tribe was first mentioned at the end of the 10th century living on the southern shores of the Aral Sea. They settled around Bhukhara and adopted orthodox Islam in preference to their traditional Shamanist beliefs. This choice would have far-reaching consequences, for in the same way that Clovis decided on Catholicism in contrast to the other Germanic princes of Gaul who remained Arian, so Seldjuk together with the Abbas of Baghdad became the only Sunni chief while the other Muslim chiefs became Shiia—supporters of Ali and hostile to the Caliph. In 1035 the Seldjuks took control of Khorrashah and the surrounding provinces; in 1055 Tughrill Bey, the true founder of the new dynasty, answered the Abass' call for help. He entered Baghdad and proclaimed himself protector of the Caliph who in turn gave him the title of Sultan and his daughter in marriage. This was to be the start of the "Great Seldjuks" (1055–1092) who occupied Armenia, seized Aleppo and began the conquest of the Byzantine territories in Asia Minor. In 1071 the Roman Basileus Diogenes was defeated and made prisoner at the battle of Mantzikert near lake Van. Henceforth the Seldjuks were to become involved in Byzantine politics. Fortunately for the Byzantines, following the death of Malik Shah in 1092, the Empire was divided up by his heirs and formed into rival Sultanates: Khorrashah, Persia, Syria and Asia Minor, which surrounded the Caliphate of Baghdad and fought over guardianship.

The empire of the "Great Seldjuks" had been organized around the army since the Sultan was the secular arm of the Caliphate. Nomadic Turkish troops were replaced by professional soldiers recruited from among the "mameluks"—white slaves, either taken prisoner in war or captured in raids on the Caucasus area. Apart from the Sultan's personal guard, these troops were commanded by "Emirs" responsible for raising taxes in the district to pay for their soldiers' salaries. This was known as the Iqta system which also applied to administrators. But while the "Emirs" were Turkish the administrators would have been Arabic or Persian, many left over from previous administrations and only on condition that they gave up their Shiite belief in favour of the Sunni Caliphate. At the top of the hierarchy was the Grand Vizier who also controlled the treasury and justice, consequently was the embodiment of the Sultan's power especially when there was a military campaign and the Sultan usually with his army. It was the Grand Vizier who introduced mameluk slaves into government, for he had the right of life and death over them. Some were to make brilliant careers which would lead them to the heights of the Sultan's inner council. But this system periodically came into conflict with the Turks who continued to live a nomadic existence and were still numerous in the Empire and also led to religious struggles between Sunnis and Shiites, as well as never-ending disputes over rights of succession.

The Ghazis and the Sultanate of Rum

On the problem of war in its second chapter (Surah) the Koran deals only with defensive action but countenances resistance to attacks on Islam and its followers. Included in the "five pillars of the faith" which are the basic obligations of a Muslim, besides prayer, charity, fasting and pilgrimage, there is the obligation to spread the faith. This opened the way to a wider interpretation, against those who reject the word of the prophet: the unbeliever. This proselytizing tended to degenerate and consequently the question of "attacker" and "attacked" becomes academic. On the edges of the Holy land—Dar el Islam—there were insecure border areas which, similar to the Merovingian and Carolingian "marches," attracted warriors eager for adventure and booty. Their Christian counterparts, the Crusaders, were also strongly motivated for this was the rule during these centuries of religious fervour. Defensive war became offensive war: the Jihad—holy war—and its heroes the Ghazi—soldiers of the faith. They fought against the Armenians, the Byzantines and of course the Crusaders, but also against the Persians and the Afghan Shiites.

Their most hated enemy was of course the Basileus' Christian subjects living on the Anatolian Plateau. Its climate and relief reminded the Turks of their homeland and suited their seminomadic lifestyle. Following the Seldjuk's victory at Mantzikert in 1071 they advanced, pushing the terrified Byzantine population back to the north and to the south. Soldier chiefs proclaimed themselves Emirs and set up small states, which were above all forward bases for the Ghazi; for example the Emirates of Nicea and Ephesus. Their leaders conscious of the fact that holy war could not continue for ever, eventually made peaceful contact with the Christian kings. This led to their involvement in the internecine conflicts within the Byzantine Empire. Soon after the defeat at Mantzikert, Nicephoris Botaniatis, one of the pretenders to the throne of Constantinople, asked Suleyman beg Kutulmuch, the sultan's cousin and one of the most important Seldjuk leaders in Anatolia, for help. Suleyman at the head of his mercenaries occupied the main towns of the Bosphorous, in the name of the pretender, and above all Nicea where he established himself from 1078 onwards. When Nicephoris became emperor, Suleyman refused to give up the city and gave it its present day name of Iznik. The civil war over the Byzantine throne continued and Suleyman took control of most of the plateau. The new Basileus Alexis Comnenis confirmed the status quo in 1081 when he signed a treaty with Suleyman granting him possession of Nicea and the right to make it his capital—barely 60 miles from Constantinople!—yet he kept Byzantine suzerainty over the occupied territories. The

Basileus ceded the territory to the Emir for colonization by Turks however it was still deemed part of the Empire. This was the beginning of the Sultanate of Rum, the land of the ancient Greeks—Rumaioi. Following several uprisings the new lord Suleyman by lowering taxes skilfully managed to pacify the residual Christian population, the Slavs, the Wallachians and the Syrians that the Byzantines had settled there. He reorganized the administration of the towns using local administrators. He managed to affirm his independence from the Sultan of Baghdad without himself taking the title of Sultan. In 1085 he captured Antioch but the following year he died while besieging Aleppo.

His son, still an adolescent, was taken to Baghdad as a hostage and the young Sultanate disintegrated. After the death of Malik Shah in 1092 the young prince Kilidj-Arslan was allowed to return to Anatolia and although he managed to recover the Nicea region without much difficulty, the south east continued to escape his control for around Tarsis and the Gulf of Alexandria an Armenian Kingdom (lesser Armenia) had been established. The north east also remained outside his control since an Emir had firmly established himself and had founded the Danichmendid dynasty. However a far greater danger loomed ahead: the Barons' Crusade (1st Crusade). At the end of 1096 the cream of western knighthood was gathering in Constantinople; Godefroy de Bouillon duke of Lower-Lorraine, Count Raymond of Toulouse, Hugh de Vermandois brother of the king of France, Robert of Normandy brother of the king of England, Robert of Flanders, and the Norman prince Bohemon son of Robert Guiscard of Sicily and Calabria. Emperor Alexis discomfited by their arrival tried to retain control over them. A treaty was signed early in 1097 making provision for the Crusaders to swear allegiance to the Basileus and to recapture the conquered towns previously part of the Byzantine Empire. This clause came into operation the following spring; in June 1097 Nicea was retaken by the Crusaders and handed over to Alexis. Kiligj-Arslan was to make an alliance with his traditional enemy Danichmendid, but the two Seldjuk princes were defeated by the Christian army at Dorylea (Eskishehir) on the 1 July 1097. The Turkish advance was halted for two centuries.

The progress of the Crusaders continued with the capture of the cities of Heraclia, Ceasaria and Iconium which were handed back to the Emperor, yet the Turks counter-attacked and by the following autumn Anatolia was once more outside Crusader control.

Kilidj-Arslan taking advantage of the vacuum of Danichmendid power, rebuilt a vast principality leaving Byzantium with only about a third of Asia Minor, to the west. When the inhabitants of Mossul called for his support in their uprising against the Sultan of Baghdad, Kilidj-Arslan seized control of the town and during the "Khutba"[1] had his name proclaimed instead of that of the Grand Seldjuk. This meant that he had become a sultan. Soon after however (in 1107) he died and his state once again went into decline. Nevertheless it was he who overcame the second Crusade. Conrad III, the German Emperor and Louis VII, the King of France, were defeated in separate encounters with Turkish troops and returned home without glory.

In 1155 Kilidj-Arslan II came to power and strengthened the Sultanate of Rum which from then on remained firmly established around its capital Konya—previously Iconium. Initially defeated by Basileus Manuel Comenis, the sultan went to Constantinople in 1162 to pledge his allegiance. He did however manage to avoid returning the disputed towns. Then taking advantage of Byzantine difficulties in Hungary and Italy he extended his dominion in the north (Ankara and Cankiri) and in the east (Elbistan and Malatya), and then on the 17 September 1176 routed Emperor Manuel's army at Myriokiphalon. The Basileus himself compared this defeat to the Byzantine defeat at Mantzikert a century earlier.

The death of Kilidj-Arslan II in 1204 was followed by disputes over his succession. This ended with the formation of two rival empires based on Nicea in Byzantine territory and Trezibond near the Black Sea which were ruled by the grand-sons of Basileus Andronicus I. The Emperor of Constantinople Alexis, deposed by the Latins in 1204, sought asylum at the court of Konya and persuaded the Sultan to join in an attempt to restore him to his throne. This ended in failure with the Nicean troops victorious and the Seldjuk dead on the field of battle. His successor Kaikaus I expanded his territory at the expense of the Trezibond Empire. The prince was taken prisoner and surrendered the port of Sinop providing the Sultanate of Rum with an outlet onto the Black Sea. In the south he forced the Cypriot Franks, who had established a foothold on the western coast, out of Antalya and pushed the Armenians back to south of the Shilhesa pass. He died in 1219 leaving his brother Kaiqobad I a strong state. Kaiqobad was to bring it to its zenith. Wresting a fortress from the Armenian Kingdom he named it Alanya and turned it into his winter residence. Marriage enabled him to expand the Empire to Erzurum and in the south east he even managed to capture Edessa. Conquest and a policy of consolidation and developing trade links made Kaiqobad's reign the most outstanding of his dynasty's and the Sultanate of Rum the major power in the region.

However a new storm was gathering which was to shake the whole of Asia Minor and western Europe; the invasion of the Mongols. Following the unification of the tribes in 1206 by Ghengis Khan the Turkish Empires of Central Asia were subjugated and towns such as Bukhara, Samarkand and Merv destroyed. In 1241 the Mongols captured Erzurum. John Vatatz the Emperor of Nicea quickly made an alliance with the Emperor of Rum and this alliance was also joined by the Greek emperor of Trebizond. Yet too late for the Seldjuk army, reinforced by Byzantine, Armenian and Frank mercenaries, was thoroughly defeated by Batu Khan at the battle of Koss Dagh on the 26 June 1243. The Mongols occupied Sivas and Kayseri, and the Sultan was forced to pay a tribute, though he died soon after in unknown circumstances. The Sultanate of Rum went into decline and fell more and more under the control of the victors. In 1307 the Great Khan installed a permanent representative in Konya. As everywhere else in Anatolia, the Sultanate fragmented into principalities—Beyliks—under the distant supervision of the Mongols represented by a Governor general in Kayseri.

The history of the Sultanate is that of a Ghazi new-frontier area which progressively became organized into a State. Then drawn into the region's political intrigues it was forced to conclude alliances with unbelievers—giaur. With conquest the ethnic makeup also changed; to the indigenous population of Armenians and Greeks, who in generally withdrew to the west, was added the nomadic Turkish tribes from the east, who ruled the central Anatolian plateau steppes; later came the Mongols who adopted Turkish manners and ways from the 14th century onwards.

As everywhere else in the Muslim world the land belonged by law to the Sultan and was divided into four types or categories: dominion land—Khass, land given as fiefdoms in return for armed service—Timar, land belonging to religious institutions—Wakf and private land—Wulk. All were tilled by peasants whose actual status had changed very little since the Byzantine period: the Siphani replaced the pronoia and the Bey or Emir was the real owner of the land. Turkish families were brought from Turkestan and employed as temporary or daily sharecroppers, whose existence was no better than that of the Christian peasant. A real problem was the difficulty of living with nomads since they continued to live in tribes, their grazing land theoretically restricted but was often the cause of conflict with the settled population. The Sultans tried to make them settle or gave their leaders the responsibility of defending the border areas, but without much success. A further problem was that the nomads, who theoretically were Muslim had in reality retained their traditional Shamanism and remained receptive to the power of heterodox Turkish holy men called Babas. In the towns, at cross-roads, in the fortresses and in the commercial or craft centres the Turks were administrators, the Greeks soldiers or craftsmen, and the Armenians and Jews merchants or craftsmen. The latter who were quite numerous and renowned for their ability, formed religiously orientated corporations called Akhis. The administration was both monarchist and decentralized. As with the Merovingians of France, the Seldjuks saw the state of Rum as a family concern: the eldest or the most enterprising was elected, or imposed himself, as Sultan and ruled according to Sharia or Islamic law. He would be advised by a council called a Divan whose most influential member was the Vizier. The provinces were divided between the brothers and sons of the Sultan according to their status but they would have been helped by a governor called a Vali. The border regions were often entrusted to a Beg (in Arabic Bey) who would raise taxes in return for keeping an armed force proportionate to the size of the Beylik. Some might have been made hereditary and would become independent principalities.

Because of its geographical position the Sultanate of Rum was a natural crossroads for trade; caravans coming from the Balkans, Turkestan, Mesopotamia and Syria would pass through. The major meeting points were Sivas, Sinope and Kayseri. In these towns the Greeks and the Armenians were the indispensable middle-men who would make deals with envoys from Byzantium , Venice and Genoa which had trade agreements with the Sultanate. In these towns silk, carpets, copper-work, silver-work, leather-work, sesame and resin was sold to Europe.

Traditional Seldjuk culture (an Arab-Persian culture) was greatly enriched by these many contacts. Yet the pursuit of knowledge appears to have been limited, basically historical chronicles and poetic works written almost exclusively in Arabic or Persian which were official languages as well as Turkish. Artistic achievement however was very great. The mosques of Malatya, Konya, Sivas and Kayseri bear witness as well as the Medresses of Sivas, Divrik and Konya and the tombs of Erzurum and Konya. The floral and geometrical patterns sculpted in stone are truly admirable and the white, blue and black pottery marvellous. Undoubtedly inspired by Arab, Persian, Byzantine and Armenian forms they form a unique synthesis.

Culturally as well as in terms of political and social organization the Sultanate of Rum was virtually a prototype of the Ottoman Empire.

The Early Days of the Ottomans up to 1361

When the Empire was in at its height the Sultans commissioned chroniclers of the court to write narratives of the exploits of their predecessors. These scribes eagerly set to work and pieced together, basically using oral folklore, the origins of the dynasty. Modern historians are hard pushed to distinguish true from false in these stories which are to the greater glory of the Sultan's predecessors.

The official collection of epic poems traces them back to a certain Suleyman (chief of an Oghuz tribe called Kayi) who ruled the Mahan region in the 12th century, north east Persia. Driven by the Mongols he moved them to the west but drowned crossing the Euphrates. His son Ertoghrul brought the tribe to the Anatolian plateau. There he placed his warriors, some four hundred according to the chronicle, in the service of the Seldjuk to fight against the Byzantines, where they gained their reputation as Ghazi (religious warriors). In return for his services the Sultan entrusted Ertoghrul with two small border areas—Udj—at the very edge of Bithynia, across from Constantinople. Modern Turkish historians prefer the idea that the Kayi tribe came to Anatolia in the 11th century among the wave of tribes who were to settle following the Byzantine defeat at Mantzikert in 1071. This would make the idea of kinship with the Seldjuks highly improbable. Be that as it may around 1250 Ertoghrul was title-holder of an Udj around Sogut where his son Osman was born in 1258.

During this period the Mongols had defeated the Sultan of Rum's army at Kos Dagh and Anatolia was divided up into twenty or more principalities—Beyliks. Those which were a direct threat to Ertoghrul were: Karasi around Balikesir, Aydin based on Smyrna which was to built up a very strong navy and Guermiyan which was in the Kutahya area. Ertoghrul died around 1290 leaving three sons. There were no rules of succession in the tribe's traditions; in fact the youngest son rather than the oldest took power, no doubt with the support of the Ghazi who formed a veritable confraternity. He would also have had the support of his father-in-law who was a Sheik, in other words a religious leader. So Osman—in Arabic Othman—was to start a dynasty which would survive right until the 20th century.

The new Ghazi leader organized his forces into three Udj's whose Beys harassed the feudal Byzantines of Nicomides. In 1300 he took present-day Yenisehir around which he established a fledgling principality. From then on Osman acted independently: his name was proclaimed in the "Khotba" and perhaps the Seldjuk Sultan gave him the title of Bey. The Prince then took a different tack in relation to the neighbouring Byzantines. On top of Jihad he began to form trade agreements and took sides in disputes over successions. Bursa, at the foot of Mount Olympus in Bithynia, was a strong fortress but it was cut off and surrounded by Osman's drive to the Sea of Marmara and to the port of Mudanya. On the 6 April 1326 it was captured by Osman's son Orkhan who was his principal auxiliary.

Orkhan was to succeed Osman shortly after his death. There were no problems of succession. The conquered fortress was made into the new capital city. Orkhan was the real designer of an Ottoman Principality. Asserting his independence he took the title "Emir" and struck his own coinage. Yet he is known historically as Orkhan-Ghazi—the Jihad warrior who took the Turcomans from the Anatolian Plateau under his protection, those fleeing the Mongul hordes. He was also supported by the religious fraternities—the Akhis—and above all the mystical Soufis. If we add the fact that he was the Basileus' son-in-law there emerges a relatively complex personality. Jihad made him increase access to the sea. Emperor Andronicus III tried to stop him at Philkren but he was resoundingly defeated. Soon after in March 1331 Nicea fell and was changed to Iznir, followed by Nicomedia in 1337 which became Izmit. However Orkhan also kept a watchful eye on his Turkish neighbours. Under the pretext of a quarrel of succession in the Emirate of Karasi he took control of the principality extending his dominion as far as the Dardanelles. Advised by Byzantines, some of whom had converted to Islam, he turned his attention to the affairs of the Empire and approached John Cantacuzenos who was struggling with a Paleologos rival. In 1346 Cantacuzenos asked him for help and Suleyman, according to the Chronicle, son of Orkhan, went to Thrace at the head of 5,000 men to subjugate the coastal region north of Constantinople. This was the first time that the Ottomans had intervened in the Balkans. Cantacuzenos managed to fight off his rival's challenge and as a sign of gratitude he gave Orkhan his daughter Theodora in marriage. So a Byzantine princess was to become part of the Ghazi's harem. Yet their opponent had had the support of 6,000 Seldjuk troops from the Sarukhan Emirate in the Manisa region. Relations between the Basileus and his new son-in-law however were not always good. Orkhan provided him with troops to fight against Dusan's Serbs in return for the right to pillage the region of Gallipoli and Thrace. In 1352 the struggle between the Cantacuzenos and Paleologos once more flared up in Constantinople and Orkhan was again called upon to intervene. The Ottomans systematically ravaged the Adrianopolis region held by Paleologos supporters. Suleyman at the head of 10,000 men then defeated Basileus John and his Serbian allies at Dimotika. During this intervention the Ottomans occupied the fortress of Tsympea on the Gallipoli peninsula and failed to hand it back afterwards. In 1354, taking advantage of an earthquake which destroyed a section of the city's protective wall, they occupied Gallipoli itself and a third of southern Thrace from Ipsala to Tekirdag. Tradition has it that in reply to a messenger from the Basileus demanding the return of Tsympe, Suleyman showed him the result of the earthquake and told him that it was a signal from God that he wished the Turks to stay. What is certain however is that the Ottomans had gained a foothold in Europe. What happened next was a reassessment of the traditional Ghazi policy of raids and its replacement with that of systematic conquest.

By Orkhan's death around 1361 or 1362, the Ottomans were no longer a warrior dynasty engaged in a Jihad but the incarnation of a state with a culture of its very own.

This state was still quite small in terms of land but already had a foothold on either side of the Straits: the old territories of Bithynia and Hellespont in Asia cutting a swathe of lands from Pergan on the Aegean Sea to Zonguldak on the Black Sea. In Europe it only had a small bridgehead in the south of Thrace. At its head was the Emir of the house of Osman. Its first successor,

Orkhan, had been confirmed by the Akhi, but he himself, during his lifetime chose his own heir by giving him command of the army. He did this with his eldest son Suleyman and, after the death of the latter, with his youngest, Murad. For an Ottoman was still fundamentally a military leader who led his troops into battle and took his share of the spoils. His share corresponded to a fifth of the spoils; known as the Pencik or Pendjik it also applied to prisoners who would become slaves as well as objects. In this relatively egalitarian society this was the main source of the Emir's wealth, quickly supplemented by estates in the conquered territories. He had a harem and it is surprising that from Orkhan onwards this would include Christian Princesses; Theodora, Cantacuzenos's daughter, was the first of many. Murad married first a Bulgarian and then a Byzantine and Bayezid the daughter of a Serbian prince. Even so the Emir's Ottoman family retained its power; brothers, uncles and cousins taking the highest military and civic appointments. Next were the Begs, leaders of the tribes, with clan and family links which made an unruly strata, loyal when victory brought rich spoils but changeable in defeat. Loyalty to the head of the dynasty was still an embryonic concept and tribal customs and family ties were still a strong influence.

The most important factor for the Emir was to have his own army. The Turkish hordes knew only how to fight on horseback using bows and arrows and spears which were useless against Byzantine towns ringed with strong ramparts. There did exist infantry soldiers called Yaya made up of Muslim mercenaries paid for their services and formed into groups of ten to a hundred men. There were also Christian Musellem, above all from Wallachia, who preferred to do military service rather than pay the due, called Cizye or Djizie. However these various groups were costly and lacked discipline. Around 1330 Orkhan came up with the idea of drawing from the supply of Pencik (slave) prisoners. He made Kara Khalil Cenderli responsible for organizing this new force. In Turkish "new force" is "yenitcheri" from which we get Janissary. From amongst the prisoners healthy young men would be chosen and would be converted to Islam and taught Turkish. From then on they would be part of a troop of professional soldiers, the Emir's slaves over whom the Emir had the right of life and death. Under Orkhan a thousand were recruited, yet in parallel to this force there continued to exist the other military formations which progressively became auxiliaries known as Akinci or Akindji. The

Origins of the Conquering Ottomans

Turkish cavalry would have been part of this but the Emir organized a nucleus called the Spahis, in a sense the forerunners of the Timarlis. This army might seem rather disparate but was no more so than the Byzantine, Serbian or Bulgarian armies and above all had a hard core of Muslims who were inspired with the Ghazi spirit. This was an essential factor of the military success of the early Ottomans.

The administrative system remained primitive but Osman and his descendants broke with the Turkish tradition of dividing up the principality among the members of their family and perhaps influenced by the example of Byzantium made the Emirate an indivisible state centred around themselves. So under Orkhan there were Viziers to whom he delegated aspects of civil and military operations; one was even the deputy to the Emir, a role which Orkhan himself had as Vizier fulfilled for his ageing father. Initially it was his brother Alaeddin who was honoured with the title of pasha and towards the end of the reign was made "sadr-i-azam" which translates as Grand Vizier. Other Viziers were: public treasurer, justice held by the "Kadi of Bursa" and the commanders of the army. Gathered in council round the Emir they would form what was called the "Divan." In turn the territory of the Emirate was divided up into "Eyalet" or provinces and subdivided into "Flags"—Sancak/Sandjak and then into "Regiments"—Ala. This illustrates the mixed nature of those who held authority, both civil and military. Together with their posts they would have been given fiefdoms—"Timars"—and would be responsible for raising taxes, supervise farming as well as leading the troops from their district into battle. The next most important was the Cadi/Kadi who was responsible for law and order and for local administration. It is interesting to note that at least initially Byzantine practices were preserved above all in the fiscal field.

The social basis of the state had changed enormously. The settling process which had started when they moved to the Sogut region was to accelerate at the beginning of the century by the setting up of the capital first at Yenisehir and then at Bursa. In comparison to the Anatolian plateau the fertile plains of Bithynia provided greater scope for farming yet the conquerors already found implanted a Christian peasantry organized on the Byzantine model. The landowners, the pronoia and the rest, like the soldier peasants in the "stratiot" and "akritoi" border areas, had been either killed in battle or else had fled to the hinterland but a few had stayed put and having converted to Islam retained their land. For instance Evernos Beg who was one of Murad's most brilliant generals, came from a Greek family and had been very wealthy landowners in the Bursa region. The abandoned land was generally consolidated to form a fiefdom or Timar for the Beg who would have been responsible for military and administrative matters. However the opposite might have occurred with it being divided into private land or "mulk" because Ghazi chiefs needed to attract Turcomans into their service. Many of the Christian peasantry returned to their villages once the armies had left and would often have found that they worked their new master's land under better terms than had been the case under their old feudal Byzantine masters. Their presence however posed a new dilemma for the Ottomans: what was the status of an unbeliever. The Koran said that the peoples of the Bible—Christians and Jews "Zimmi"— who did not fight against Islam had the right of life and property and freedom to practice their religion. So this is what happened with the rural populations who continued to be ruled by customary laws but paid a tribute "cizye" or "djizi" in compensation for military service which was generally forbidden to non-Muslims. So from the very beginning the Ottoman Empire was multi-ethnic and multi-denominational in spite of its Ghazi vocation.

The Ghazi spirit was very important, and even the Emirs adopted the title, yet their vision of the world was obviously modified by their intervention in international affairs in eastern Europe. Their interference in the internal quarrels of Byzantium gave them a deeper understanding of the Roman world—"Rum"— which had fascinated the Arabs before them. Also the introduction of Christian princesses into the harem, not as slaves but in marriage and part of treaties with sovereign kings. According to tradition Theodora, the daughter of John Cantacuzenos, remained a Christian after she became the wife of Orkhan and protected her fellow believers. She was Murad's mother who in turn married a Bulgarian and then a Byzantine. These wives and mothers must have had a measure of influence although this is impossible to calculate. From the 14th century onwards in politics, government and also culture Byzantine influence was apparent yet grafted onto the Ottoman Seldjuk roots.

By the time the Ottomans launched their invasion of the Balkans they were by no means barbarians in the strict sense of the term. Of course their armies spread terror among the peasant population, but in the same way as other armies, no more than their Petcheneg Kouman "cousins" or the Tatars brought into the Balkans by the Basileus' and the Bulgarian princes. The ransack of Constantinople in 1204 by the Crusaders also paints an unflattering idea of the nature of soldiers during that period. In terms of actual atrocities which were to occur during the conquest they were to be no worse than other episodes in the history of Byzantium. Similar to the lynching of Andronicus Comnenos in 1185 or when the Roman Basileus Diogenesos (rescued after his defeat at Mantzikert by the very same Seldjuks who had defeated him) blinded all those prisoners with red-hot nails. What would have inspired terror in the minds of 14th century men and women was not the fact that the Ottomans were pagans, for they could conceivably have been converted, but that they were Infidels and consequently Satan's committed henchmen.

Notes

1. During Friday prayers in the Mosque the ruling sovereign's name is pronounced.
2. A Turkish people who in the 11th century lived a nomadic existence south of the Aral Sea, and from where the Seldjuks also came.
3. 237 Kilometres from Istanbul on the road to Ankara. Osman's mound can still be seen there.
4. The "akritoi" where the Byzantine equivalent of the Ghazi ie. Christians fighting the Infidel.

3

The Conquest of the Balkans, 1362–1451

The timing of the Ottoman interlude is a subject of controversy for Balkan people. They point to the fact that the conquest began with the first bridgehead in Thrace at the start of Murad I's reign, and was to continue right up to the death of Mohammed II in 1481. But this century and a quarter is considered too long by traditional Balkan history which tends to portray the conquest as a sudden occurrence. However in fact all the Christian kingdoms, large and small, were to experience two distinct phases: the first where the Ottomans retained the sovereign lord as a vassal, and the second where they seized control and make the territory a province of the Empire. The most obvious example is Byzantium itself where the Basileus was a vassal of the Sultan from 1372 to 1453 when he and his kingdom were destroyed. The Balkan people's collective memory would rather forget the first unflattering phase so as to highlight the heroes of the final battles. Transforming into a one act epic what in reality was to be, with tragic consequences for the Christian population, an imbroglio of diplomatic intrigue and betrayal .

The Building of Ottoman Suzerainty: Murad I, 1361–1389

The second son of Orkhan, Murad, had since the death of his elder brother two years previously led the army. Once in power he continued the warlike policies of his father in Europe and was the first real conqueror of the Balkans. His objective was not only the Byzantine lands but also the Slav countries of the Peninsula.

However, this did not mean that he ignored Asia Minor since from the start of his reign he spread his rule over the region of

Ankara and over Antalia on the southern coast. Up until the arrival of the Mongols at the end of the century the Ottomans effectively tried to retain a balance of power on both sides of the Straits. Having thus secured his rear Murad completed the conquest of Thrace which he had already begun as Orkhan's lieutenant. In 1362 Dimotika and Adrianopolis fell in quick succession. The Basileus did not have any forces to throw against him and retreated to his capital whose defences still seemed a match for the Ottoman troops. So Byzantium allowed the Ghazi to go past, opening up the road to Sofia, Nis and Belgrade. In 1364 Lala Shahin their leader attacked the fortress of Philippopolis from seven sides at once and seized it. Murad gave it to him and made him the first governor of the "Roman Lands"—Beylerbey of Rumeli—based at Filib. To consolidate this conquest a large proportion of the indigenous population—predominantly Greek—were deported as slaves to Asia Minor and were then replaced by Turkish colonials from Asia Minor who were settled on the Timars of the victorious Begs (chiefs). Thrace became predominantly Turkish. In 1365 the situation seemed sufficiently stable for Murad to transfer his capital from Brus to Adrianopolis which was renamed Edirne. He was henceforth well placed to observe and later stir up the rivalries between the Christian kings. Czar John Alexander Sisman waged war on the Basileus for "reasons that we are unable to explain"[1], as one Bulgarian medieval historian comments but which in reality had much to do with gaining Ottoman favour, and lost by force of arms the port of Anchialos (Pomori) on the Black Sea. John Alexander asked Murad for support but a crusade led by Amadée de Savoie preempted him and the Italian prince recaptured Gallipoli from the Ottomans also seizing from their allies, the Bulgars, the fortresses of Messembria (Nesebar) and Sozopol and handed them back to the Basileus. Aware that the increasing power of the Emir posed a threat, the Byzantine Paleologos Emperor, John V, solicited support all over Europe. He made an abortive journey to Hungary, then visited the Pope and in October 1369 rallied the support of the Roman faith. The Catholics felt this would lead to Union of the two churches, however the Basileus had not been accompanied by any high-ranking member of the Church of Constantinople, so the latter's mission was perceived as purely secular. On the way back he also stopped over in Venice. The Byzantine Empire was a major debtor of the Republic and seemed to be defaulting, so the Doge ordered his arrest (as he would have done for any dishonest debtor) and the Basileus subsequently became intimate with Venetian prisons. It was only in October 1371 that he finally returned to his capital. A month earlier the Serbian Princes had tried to move against the Ottoman threat to their borders. Before his death Czar Dusan had requested from the Pope his appointment as Captain General of a proposed crusade, but his death in 1355 thwarted any such outcome. His Empire fragmented and the despotate of Serres was formed in Macedonia with Ugljesa as its head, while his son Uros was placed under the guardianship of the Prince of Prilep, known in Serbian annals as King Dukasin, brother of the despot Ugljesa. Having assured himself of the support of the King of Hungary, Louis the Great of Anjou, and with the Pope's blessing, the two Serbian princes launched an offensive against Adrianopolis. Muslim chroniclers tell of Murad leading an ambush on the banks of the Maritsa, while their Christian counterparts put this defeat down to local Begs for instance Beg Evrenos. Whatever the truth might be, on the 26 September 1371, the Serbo-Hungarian force, their ranks swelled by Neapolitan and Wallachian contingents, was defeated at Cernomen. Dukasin and Ugljesa were among the dead but Louis of Anjou managed to escape. Known to Ottoman history as the Rout of the Serbs—Sirp Sindigi—this battle is less famous than that of Kosovo but was in fact a very important turning point in the conquest of the Balkans. The Serbian principalities once more fragmented and their chiefs were forced to acknowledge the suzerainty of the Ottomans. Vukasin's son, Marko Kraljevic, hero of folk songs, made an act of vassalage, agreeing to pay a tribute and to assemble troops when requested. The other Christian sovereigns were to follow suit. In 1372 Basileus John V submitted and the following year he joined Murad in an expedition to Asia Minor in fulfilment of his obligation as vassal. That same year the Bulgar John Sisman, Czar of Tirnovo, also swore homage and his sister Tamara, known as Desislava—"the glorious"—was given in marriage to the Ottoman. The Tirnovo synodic book states: "Lady Tamara, daughter of the Great Czar John Alexander, noble lady, wife of the distinguished Emir Amurat (Murad) given to him for the good of the people. In going there she kept her Orthodox faith, saved her people, lived a good and pious life and died in peace."[2] Popular Bulgarian folk songs keep her memory alive. Less than twenty years after the Ottomans first established themselves in the Balkans, the three ancient Empires: Byzantium, Bulgaria and Serbia were reduced to being vassal kingdoms of the Emir of Adrianopolis.

An episode in 1373 clearly illustrates the balance of power that existed at the time. While Paleologos John V was following his suzerain Murad on an expedition, his son Andronicus tried to seize power in Byzantium and reached agreement with Sauci (Saouudji), the son of Murad, who also tried to overthrow his father. Murad quickly reacted and following Byzantine practice had Sauci's eyes poked out and made the Basileus mete out the same treatment to his son Andronicus. The Muslim Prince died as a result but his accomplice lived. He was replaced as co-emperor by his brother Manuel. The Emir even had power over the heirs of Constantine.

These seemed favourable circumstances for the two Christian powers, Venice and Genoa, to resolve their conflict over the island of Tenedos[3] whose position at the approach to the Dardanelles made it an object of attention to both navies. The Genoese decided literally to dethrone the Basileus John V who had promised it to the Venetians. They helped Andronicus escape from prison and after a siege lasting a month he seized the capital and put his father and brother into prison in August 1376. To gain the support of the Emir (who had had him blinded) he handed over the town of Gallipoli, reconquered ten years earlier during the crusade of Amadeus of Savoy. In the end John V and Manuel were returned to power in July 1379, thanks to the Ottomans to whom they renewed their bonds of vassalage ie. tribute and banns. As for Gallipoli it became a formidable Ottoman fortress.

During this Paleologos family quarrel Murad turned everything to his advantage. He forced John V to recognize Andronicus, as well as Manuel, as his legal heir and to give him the coastal towns on the Sea of Mamara which were still Byzantine, while Manuel was to govern Thessalonika and the third son took the Despotate of Morea back from the Cantacuzes. The four Paleologoss had become vassals of the emir. During this period Murad married his son Bayezid to the heir of the Emir of Germian in 1381 who brought as a dowry the region of Kutaya, thus achieving Ottoman control of the west of Asia Minor. Henceforth no Turkish sovereign could rival him and he changed his title from Emir to Sultan.

Taking advantage of his new prestige he embarked on a series of military campaigns in the Balkans, where the Ottoman armies had hardly been seen for the last ten years, marking a new stage in the conquest. The principality of Serres fell in 1383 while the Beylerbey of Filipe crossed into Bulgarian territory capturing Samokov, Ihtiman and Sofia in 1382 or 1385.[4] The main resistance came from the Serbians. Following the death of Czar Uros on the field of battle at Cernomen in 1371, Lazarus the last survivor of the Nemanja dynasty seized power in Rascia, which at the time stretched from the Danube at Prizren to Uzice and Nis. However Nis was threatened following the capture of Sofia. Prince Lazarus, who is traditionally called Czar, made an alliance with Tvrtko of Bosnia who had carved for himself a vast kingdom, and received in 1377 a royal crown from the king of Hungary. In 1388 the Bosnian thoroughly defeated an Ottoman army which had crossed his border. Encouraged by this Czar John Sisman refused to pay homage to the Sultan. The response was not slow in coming. Grand Vizier Ali Pasha invaded the Bulgarian hinterland and the Czar had to flee his capital and lock himself up in the fortress of Nikopol on the Danube. Ali Pasha occupied Tirnovo and Sumen and forced the sovereign to sue for peace. John Sisman was forced to pay his tribute and also to hand over to the Ottomans the fortress of Durostorum , which was called Silvistria—Silistra, thus giving them a foothold on the Danube. Recanting at the last moment led him to further humiliations: Sisman surrounded by his family was made to kneel in front of the Sultan to ask mercy. As a result he retained his throne but was to remain a closely observed vassal. The other Bulgarian princes, of Vidin and Dobrudja quickly renewed their oath of allegiance. The prince of Dobrudja taking advantage of the flight of the Czar to Nikopol seized the fortress of Varna, once more emphasizing the lack of Christian solidarity in the face of the Ottomans.

Murad understood that this was one of the reasons for his successes but he also understood that the Serbo-Bosnian entente, which had lasted for three years, had to be smashed by force. An attack by the Emir of Karaman in Anatolia diverted his attention at this very inopportune time. Uncertain of his Turkish troops, who abhorred fighting fellow Turcomans, he led a contingent of soldiers supplied by his Bulgarian vassals against the soldiers of Konya. It is traditionally said that this campaign was the first occasion that gunfire was used by the Ottomans—muskets and cannon—and to great effect. The Sultan was victorious and with two thirds of Asia Minor under his control he quickly returned to the Balkans to conduct a campaign in the spring of 1398 against the Slav forces. Starting from Filipe he went via Sofia to Velbuzd (Kjustendil) but not to Nis where Lazarus and Tvrtko were expecting him. From there he reached the plain of Kosovo— Kosovo Polje means the field of blackbirds—next to the present-day town of Pristina. The encounter took place on the 15 June, Saint Guy Vidovdan's Day, on open ground well suited to the movement of cavalry. The story of the battle has become legendary, the numbers of soldiers involved is uncertain and troop movements have been confused with individual acts of heroism. What is clear is that Murad's army was reinforced by contingents from his Christian vassals: Prince Constantine of Velbuzd a Bulgarian, Marko Kraljevic a Serbian and enemy of Lazarus but also Muslim vassal Emirs and allies from Asia Minor. Basileus John V was missing as he no longer was able to muster sufficient troops. Against these were drawn the armies of Lazarus and King Tvrtko which were reinforced by Wallachian contingents from the Voevod Mircea and Albanians under George Balsha and Demeter Jonima. They talk of 100,000 men on one side and 60,000 on the other, inverting these figures according to whether the source is Christian or Muslim. The battle appears to have had two distinct phases. The first was clearly in favour of the Christians; so much so that Tvrtko claimed victory and on the strength of this news a Te Deum was sung at Notre-Dame in Paris in the presence of Charles VI. Serbian tradition tells of the heroic deeds of a Zetan (Montenegrin) knight Milos Obolic who managed to reach Murad's tent and stab him before being killed by the guard. Ottoman sources—which some Bulgarian historians support—have the Sultan dying in battle. After this the fate of the two armies change and two explanations are put forward: the Serbian version which speaks of betrayal by Vuk Brankovic and his 12,000 cavalrymen and the Ottoman version which credits the heir apparent with a lightning attack—Bayezid was known henceforth as Vilderim (lightning). It would appear that the Serbian cavalry who had foolishly crossed the Lab river were surprised by his counter-attack, while the centre where Lazarus fought was finally breached. The prince was taken prisoner and in front of the corpse of Murad was beheaded with his knights.

The Expansionism of Sultan Bayezid
Known as the Lightning, 1389–1402

The violent death of Murad once more brought to a head a problem which the Ottomans had not yet resolved; the question of succession of power. The deceased left two sons; Yakud the elder and Bayezid the younger. The latter was on the spot and wreathed in glory from his victory over the Serbs, whilst Yakud was in Anatolia busy recruiting soldiers for his father's army. However their respective geographical positions took on a symbolic value as the elder was favoured by the Turcomans still faithful to the Ghazi ideal, whilst Bayezid born of the Greek Princess Helena and through her grandson of Basileus John V, was the choice of the Christian population and their vassal princes. In palace terms these tendencies expressed themselves in clan and family rivalry: the Cenderli (Candarli) stood for the traditional old Seldjuk principalities while the Evrenos family represented the new allies and vassal rulers. The latter prevailed and persuaded Bayezid to get rid of his brother who was summarily assassinated; the first case of what was to become a rule of succession. The Cenderli gave in: Bayezid was the last male of the "house of Osman."

Even so the new Sultan still encountered hostility from the Turcoman principalities in Anatolia bordering his own territories. Yet he continued his policy of European conquest, motivated less by the Ghazi spirit than by his knowledge of the workings of the Christian Balkans. From this stems the breathless nature of his reign which was to witness a succession of campaigns in Asia and Europe in quick succession, justifying in his contemporaries' eyes the title Yildirim.

In Anatolia the Emirs of the south west united with the powerful Principality of Karaman and regained possession of the lands conquered by Murad. It took several campaigns for Bayezid to destroy the coalition and bring down the Karamanid who was killed. His lands came under Ottoman control. Having removed his principal opponent the Sultan pushed eastward. Kayseri and Sivas surrendered to him. He then occupied Kastamonu and Sinope on the Black Sea. On reaching the Euphrates he seized the fortress of Erzindjan near which the Seldjuks had been defeated by the Mongols in 1243. By 1400 more than half of Anatolia was in Ottoman hands. These actions against Muslim princes did how-

theory, of the secular arm of the Caliph. Consequently he mainly used his vassal Serbian and Byzantine troops, and prior to an expedition often obtained a legal authorization—Fetwa—from the Ulemas which justified his action in terms of Koranic law since these were fellow believers.

In the Balkans he continued his father's policy of intervening in the dynastic quarrels of Byzantium, settling differences between his Christian vassals and crushing them at the smallest sign of independence. In 1390 the son of the usurper Andronicus Paleologos took control of Byzantium with Bayezid's help and became Basileus John VII. Venice saw this as a prelude to the Sultan himself taking over the throne and gave the plenipotentiaries, prior to their departure, special instructions in case they found Bayezid already master of the town. In the end old emperor John V and his son Manuel were restored to power a few months later and while the father once again took control of a weak throne, his son was held hostage in the walled palace—seraglio—of Bursa. All that was left in Asia Minor of the Byzantine Empire was the fortress of Philadelphia of Lydia[5], and even this was held by Catalan mercenaries. The Sultan forced Manuel to lead the troops his father had supplied and capture this last remaining pocket of Byzantine rule. Later he was to hand it over to the Ottomans. John V who had made repairs to the capital's defensive walls while Bayezid was occupied in his Anatolian campaign was made to demolish them before he died in 1391.

Beaten at Kosovo, Serbia continued to exist in the form of a vassal state. Stephan, son of Lazarus, became the "despot" sealing his submission by sending his daughter Maria Despina to the Sultan's harem. The new Basileus Manuel II was a man of character and Bayezid had learned to appreciate him during the many months he had previously spent at the Sultan's court. Yet the Ottoman had to use force against him. During the winter of 1393–1394, he summoned all his vassals to his camp at Serres in Macedonia and ordered them to take part in the siege of Byzantium which is known as the first Ottoman seige of Constantinople. In reality this was not sustained and continued over seven years which is why certain historians speak of six sieges prior to that of Mohammed II. What is certain is that the population of the town suffered cruelly from lack of food and rising prices.

The war was not waged to its conclusion as Bayezid lacked sufficient artillery to bring down the huge walls which dated back

The Conquest of the Balkans

to the 5th century. Even so this was a radical change from the policies of the first Ottomans; from indirect dominion through Christian vassal princes to direct dominion and annexing territories into a vast Empire. No doubt this change was influenced by exterior motives. For instance Hungary ruled by the Angevin-Luxembourgers seemed not only to be a powerful obstacle for future expansion into Europe but also a strong threat to Ottoman suzerainty in the Balkans. It was to the crown of Saint Stephan that the Christian Princes would turn for help whether they were threatened or already vassal states.

Yet the Sultan was also motivated by an ideal; the son of a Greek and ruler of Byzantium, the conquering Sultan's dream was to recreate the Empire of Rum—Rome—and to sit on the throne of Constantine, lieutenant of the descendant of the Prophet the Caliph, thus combining the medieval ideal of the eastern Empire with the Turko-Arabic Mohammedan ideal of Jihad . In 1391 the Sultans' flag floated over Uskup (Skopje) and Bayezid settled thousands of Turks in the valley of Vardar making this Macedonian region into a wild-west frontier area. Pasha Yigit Bey who was to capture Scutari and northern Albania launched his assaults from this area. The Greek renegade Evrenos Bey recaptured Thessalonika and then went on to conquer Thessaly in 1393. He then attacked the Duchy of Athens which was the possession of a Florentine merchant, father-in-law of the Despot of Morea who was Theodor Paleologos, brother of Basileus Manuel: a question of inheritance had started a quarrel between the two Christian princes and the master of Athens asked the Ottomans for help. Evrenos Bey reacted by seizing Corinth and part of Byzantine Morea. The Sultan himself intervened in the northern part against John Sisman's Bulgarian kingdom which he suspected of wanting to join an anti-Ottoman coalition with the king of Hungary and the Prince of Wallachia. In 1392 monks from Rila and the Balkan mountain (Stara Planina) took refuge north of the Danube taking their most sacred manuscripts with them. The following year Yildirim struck. In July 1393 Tirnovo was besieged during the absence of Czar John who was holed up in Nikopolis on the Danube. The defence of the capital was organized by Patriarch Efthimios but after a few days, on the 17 July the town fell. According to the Koran, armed resistance was sufficient cause for all the inhabitants to be put to death, but the Patriarch managed to get agreement that only the warlords be put to the sword. The majority of the population were deported to Anatolia and the free lands were given to Turkish settlers. Bayezid went after John Sisman who died in combat the same year. The Bulgarian kingdom was to disappear for almost five centuries.

North of the river the Wallachian Prince Mircea the Old[6] had been an ally of Lazarus on the field of battle at Kosovo Polje and compounded this, in the eyes of Bayezid, by later looking to Hungary for an alliance. In 1395 he made him pay for these errors. For the first time the Sultan crossed the Danube. The encounter took place on the 17 May 1395 in the Rovinian Plain near the present day town of Craiova in Romania. At his side Bayezid had his vassal Serbian Princes: Stephan the son of Lazarus, Marko lord of Prilep, the son of King Vukasin and Constantine Dejanovic the Prince of Eastern Macedonia. King Marko a hero in Serbian folk songs, was to die there in the Ottoman ranks. There was no real victor and Mircea retained his throne, however accepting to pay the Sultan tribute and giving up Dobrudja which he had captured a short time previously.

Hungary was now directly under threat and Sigismond of Luxembourg supported by the Pope made a appeal for a crusade against the Infidel. Venice agreed to send a few ships to the Dardanelles to act as a decoy while the cream western European knighthood and above all France, gathered at Pest. This noble cause was to end in utter failure. The great Christian army, some speak of 60,000 strong, set off for Vidin where the last ruler of the last remaining Bulgarian kingdom Czar Stratsimir welcomed them with open arms. They captured Orjahovo and began to lay siege to Nicopolis which the Ottomans had taken three years previously. The seige had been laid for sixteen days when the Sultan, who had been busy besieging Byzantium, appeared once more like a lightning bolt. The encounter took place on the 25 September 1396. The Christian army under the command of Sigismond was badly coordinated. Some blamed the indiscipline of the French knights, others the arrival during the battle of 5,000 fresh troops which Despot Stephan his Serbian vassal had sent Bayezid. Whatever the cause it was a disaster. The Sultan put the ordinary prisoners to the sword whilst knights such as Jean de Nevers, who had earned the name of "fearless" during the battle, were taken to Bursa where they were held until a ransom of 200,000 ducats was paid, which took some time. The Bavarian knight Schiltberger who took part in the battle and was taken prisoner wrote in his memoirs how King Sigismond managed to escape from the battlefield, going by boat down the Danube and the Black Sea to Byzantium and from there returning via the Aegean and Adriatic Seas to his kingdom. When the fugitive's craft passed the Dardanelles the Sultan drew up on both shores the captives who sent the vanquished and humiliated king on his way with many curses.

From then on the Danube, from Vidin to the sea, was the frontier of the Ottoman Empire. Even so north of the river the Vojvode of Wallachia was made to pay tribute whether he liked it or not. The Byzantine Empire had been reduced to the capital city and even then only inside the defensive walls; its fiefdom: the surrounding lands of Mistra and a few islands. In 1397 Athens was occupied for several months and the Ottomans ravaged the whole of the Peloponnese which still belonged to the Byzantine despot, the Navarrans of Achea and Venice. These remaining Christian parts of the Balkans seemed to be on the verge of destruction. This was the opinion of the Grand Duke of Moscow Vasilij I, the son of Dimitri Donskoi the victor of the Tatars, who forbade mention of the Emperor of Byzantium in Russian churches during mass, declaring: We have a Church, we have no Emperor.

Basileus Manuel however asked the various Russian princes for soldiers and money and turned to the Pope, the Doge of Venice and the kings of France, England and Aragon. Charles VI responded favourably sending 1200 men-at-arms under the leadership of Marshall Boucicaut[7] who having fought against the Ottomans for several months persuaded Manuel to make a voyage to the West to rally the sovereigns to the fate of the Byzantine Empire. This extraordinary tour saw the descendant of Constantine requesting the aid of Venice and the Italian Republics, then to Paris, to London and once more Paris where he stayed for almost two years. Everywhere he was received with pomp but tinged with condescension. But all to no avail. All the Basileus obtained were soon forgotten promises. During his absence Manuel, on the advice of Boucicaut, had entrusted the regency to his nephew and rival John VII, however placing his children and wife in safe keeping with his brother Theodor despot of Morea. It was while in Paris that the news of the defeat and death of Sultan Bayezid reached him.

For some years the Ottomans had observed a mounting threat on the eastern border of Anatolia. In 1370 a Turkish leader from the Transox, Timur the Lame—Timur-Leng—(from which we have

Tamerlaine) proclaimed himself Mongol Khan of the region and successor to Genghis Khan who he claimed was his forbear. He laid waste to Armenia, Azerbaidjan, the Russian lands of the Golden Horde, went into India and sacked Delhi. In 1400 at the request of the Turkish Emirs whose land Murad and Bayezid had taken in Asia Minor he arrived at the borders of Ottoman territory and captured Sivas. Yet rather than continue towards the west he turned against the Mameluks of Palestine and Egypt[8]. Aleppo, Homs and Damascus were pillaged and pyramids of heads marked the victories of the conqueror. In 1402 after having totally destroyed Baghdad, Tamerlaine advanced into Anatolia at Erzerum. Bayezid went to meet him and on the 22 July 1402 joined battle in the Cubuk plain under the walls of Ankara. It would seem that Tamerlaine had more troops and that Bayezid was weakened by Turcoman unwillingness to fight their fellow Turks, as well as the indiscipline of the vassal Serbian contingents. In the end after a ferocious encounter which lasted fourteen hours Tamerlaine crushed the main body of the Ottoman army and captured Sultan Bayezid who died in captivity several months later (1403).

This marked the end of what is known as the "First Ottoman Empire" and prolonged the survival of Byzantium by half a century.

The Pause During the Interregnum and the Restoration of the Empire: Mehmed I

The defeat at Ankara sent shock-waves through the Empire without however threatening its survival. Firstly because Tamerlaine hardly outlasted his prisoner. He remained eighteen months in Anatolia restoring the Turkish principalities which had been incorporated into or destroyed by the Ottoman conquest. The controlling part of the region was the Emirate of Karaman whose leader was proclaimed "Emir of the Marches" and whose territory extended over a third of the plateau. Along with some other small kingdoms he left two Ottoman principalities in existence, one based at Bursa and the other at Amasya on the highway from Ankara to Persia. They were all his vassals and to make sure of their loyalty the conqueror burnt towns and mosques. With towns which had remained loyal to Bayezid he made pyramids of decapitated heads at the gates. But early in 1405 he returned to Samarkand and was preparing an expedition against China when he died at Otar in the Transox. His empire was divided up and his successors were to retain little more than a theoretical suzerainty over Asia Minor.

Far more serious were the internal repercussions of the death of Bayezid. Once more there was the problem of succession for the Sultan had four sons; the eldest Suleyman then Isa, Mehmed and Musa. The latter had been taken prisoner with his father and was only released by Tamerlaine after the Sultan's death in 1403. The other three had managed to flee from the battlefield and had sought refuge in various parts of Ottoman territory. Suleyman confident of the privilege that being the first born gave him went to Europe where he proclaimed himself Sultan at Edirne. Isa installed himself at Bursa where Tamerlaine recognized him as his vassal, and Mehmed did the same at Amasya. As for Musa, following his release, with the support of his erstwhile captor he set himself up at Kutahya at the expense of the Emirate of Bursa.

This state of affairs could not continue for long but prolonged the problem of a single Ottoman power which was a necessary condition for the rebuilding of the Empire. Once Tamerlaine had died the victory of one of the four heirs would depend on the balance of interests. But the problem of the succession was to reveal a deeper crisis in terms of the very structure of Ottoman society itself. Of course this state of affairs was not unique and had been in evidence during Bayezid's rise to power but these tensions had become far more serious during his reign. In addition to having a Greek mother Bayezid had a Serbian and a Greek princess in his harem and naturally they had brought a retinue which added to the Byzantinization of the court. No doubt Bayezid was aware of this and from 1390 had taken pains to make Edirne Turkish, building a mosque in the district which was named after him and to which he added a Medresa, water fountains and other Muslim buildings. The following year he made the Basileus open up a Turkish quarter in Byzantium which had a mosque and law courts with a Kadi. Manuel agreed and this became known as the Sirkeci quarter[9] However in the latter part of his reign there was a change that fundamentalists felt was a drift away from Islam. The step which aroused the greatest resistance was the expansion of the "Porte Slaves" system known as Kapi Kulari. The Seldjuks had used mameluks—white slaves—as administrators and Orkhan had recruited from among prisoners of war given to him as Pencik to build up his personal guard, the

Janissaries. It would seem that Bayezid extended the system by introducing the practice of Devsirme[10], in other words forcibly recruiting young Christians to make them Kapi Kulari. The first mention of this is found in a Christian sermon from around 1395. However instead of limiting their use to the army, Bayezid made them pages in his Palace where after been converted to Islam and educated according to Koranic principles they became administrators. The old Turkish families and the Ghazi chiefs from the border areas who had from the beginning been holders of government and military office felt this was an intolerable threat and quickly denounced these neo-Muslims for leniency in dealing with their co-religionists and sometimes even their own families. Cause or consequence of the Byzantinization of the court and its structure of power, the Sultan's policies were deemed to be less and less motivated by Ghazi ideology and more and more by the eastern Roman Imperial idyll. It was a question of a fundamental change which was to affect the basis of the Ottoman Empire itself.

Adding to this backcloth of fundamental crisis the conflict between the pretenders to the throne was complicated by alliances, broken promises and treachery among the Muslim and Christian princes of the region. Suleyman had managed to gain the support in Edirne of the Turkish nobility from the Cenderli clan and also looked to the Christian powers for their backing. He returned Thessalonika and the coastal territories to Byzantium and dispensed with the payment of tribute, signed agreements with the Serbian despot Stephan and the maritime powers of Venice, Genoa and Rhodes. In Anatolia Isa and Mehmed in contrast cast themselves in the roles of representatives of the Ghazi tradition and adopted the surname Celebi which linked them with the mystics. They recruited soldiers from neighbouring Turkish tribes and acknowledged their status of vassal to Tamerlaine who promised support against the "Infidels' friend" in Edirne. However they soon quarrelled; Isa allied himself with Suleyman against Mehmed, was beaten and disappeared from centre stage while Mehmed proclaimed himself Sultan in Bursa, the sacred city of the Ottomans. The two sultans fought each other for five whole years till Musa allied himself with Mehmed. Musa killed Suleyman in 1411 thus becoming the master of Edirne. The new sultan instigated an anti-Christian campaign removing the Kapi Kulari and laying seige to Byzantium. Basileus Manuel therefore asked Mehmed for help. Mehmed went into the Balkans, defeated

Musa's army near Filibe, pursued his brother and had him strangled at Samokov in Bulgaria in July 1413. Mehmed, known traditionally as Sultan Mohammed I, was the only one remaining and so the interregnum came to an end.

His actual reign was short lived, from 1413 to 1421, yet it was to see the restoration of the Empire. His victory came as a result of the fact that he had been able to rally the support of both the Turkish leaders and Byzantine factions. Furthermore initially he pursued a policy of reciprocity. He maintained good relations with Byzantium returning the territories taken by Musa: Thessalonika and the coastal routes near the capital. Basileus Manuel took advantage of this and visited the recovered city and then went to the Peloponnese where the last vestiges of Hellenism shone with the neoplatonic philosophy of Gemiste-Plethon in the Despotate of Mistra. His dream was of a new city based on a conscript army and a egalitarian tax system. It was however too late to embark on wide-ranging reforms and Manuel had to content himself with building up the military defences. He constructed a huge wall, known as the hexamilion and blocked the isthmus of Corinth. He installed his eldest son John in Mistra while his second son became governor of Thessalonika. The Byzantine enclaves consequently recovered a cohesion which had been lacking for some time. This made the Basileus attempt the annexation of Achea, at that time ruled by an Italian prince, who was saved only by the intervention of Venice. Localized wars between the Christian powers continued even in the face of the Ottomans. The Ottomans at this time were tied up by events in Asia where they had to fight against the Emir of Karaman and two young kingdoms which had sprung up to the east of the Anatolian Plateau: Black Sheep and White Sheep. Mehmed beat them and deported thousands of Turcoman soldiers who were settled on Bulgarian land around Filibe (Plovdiv) hence the Tatar name—Pazarcik which is now known as Pazardzik.

Internally Mehmed systematically reinforced the Turkish nature of power: Christian wives and their retinues were forced out of the palace, Turkish and Persian were used rather than Greek and the court chroniclers were made to rewrite the Seldjuk origins of the Osman Dynasty. The Kapi Kulari were supplanted in their administrative posts and their fiefdoms were returned to Muslims who consequently recovered the high posts in the reorganized army based on the feudal Spahi cavalry. In reality power passed to the Turkish nobility who were supporters of the Cenderli line and who hoped to reactivate the push into Europe, a Jihad with promise of spoil, in contrast to Bayezid's imperial policy of conquest in Asia at the expense of Muslim princes. From this stem the military operations in Albania where the mountain tribes taking advantage of the chaos of the interregnum had massacred the Turkish garrisons. Mehmed based his control of Albania on two fortresses; at Akcahisar (Kruja) and Avlonya (Valona). The beys on the north eastern border were allowed to increase their raiding expeditions into Bosnia which was to lead to the conversion to Islam of the feudal Bogomil families and the recognition by King Stephan Tvrtko II of Ottoman suzerainty.

The end of Mehmed's reign was marked by a series of revolts due in part to religion but also to other factors, underlining the ambiguous nature of the renewed Ottoman kingdom. Sultan Musa had designated a well known lawyer and Soufi as head of the Ulema—Sheik-ul-Islam—called Bedreddin, yet his teachings were held to be heretical and anti-social by conservative Muslims. Exiled by Mehmed to Iznik, he continued to sermonize and his preaching was extremely popular since he advocated a more equitable distribution of wealth. Fearing the wrath of the Sultan he fled to the principality of Wallachia where Vojvode Mihail I still continued the anti-Ottoman policies of his father Mircea the Old. From there Bedreddin pursued his activities. His followers revolted in Anatolia forcing the Sultan and his son Murad to undertake several very difficult campaigns. Bedreddin seizing his opportunity brought thousands of his followers and many of the disaffected and dissenting factions from Mehmed's regime together in the forest of Deli Orman on the edge of the Dobrudja. His patron the Wallachian prince occupied the region. At that moment a new pretender to the throne named Mustafa Celebi claimed he was Bayezid's son who had also been taken prisoner at Ankara and been lost ever since. Supported by Cuneya the Emir of Izmir and former ally of Musa, Duzme Mustafa—Mustafa the Usurper—entered Edirne and proclaimed himself sultan. Mehmed reacted swiftly. He sent the Grand Vizier against Bedreddin who was defeated and put to death, while he himself captured Edirne from which Mustafa fled to Byzantium. The sultan made Mihail of Wallachia pay for his support of the revolt by occupying the fortress of San Giorgio on the northern side of the Danube, which became known as Yergogu[11]. In 1421 however the sultan suddenly died, but his death was kept secret until the arrival in Bursa of his eldest son Murad.

This latest episode underlined the enduring weakness of the House of Osman; the problem of succession. Another weakness was highlighted by one of the few defeats of Mehmed's reign; the inadequacy of the navy. In 1416 the Sultan had wanted to teach the Venetians a lesson. The Venetians occupied most of the islands in the Aegean and allowed pirates to operate from them against the Ottomans. On the 29 May 1416 opposite Gallipoli there was an engagement which ended in defeat for the sultan's navy, as it was short in numbers and low in quality. The Venetians continued to rule the waves. Nevertheless Mehmed had achieved his goal of rebuilding a united and peaceable Ottoman Empire.

The Renewal of the Balkan Conquest: Murad II, 1421–1451

The extended nature of Murad's reign has given us a great variety of information, which sometimes results in historians making judgements widely at variance with each other: renewal of the Jihad in the spirit of the Ghazi or expansion with the aim of founding an empire in the spirit of Constantine?

The young sovereign—he was only seventeen when he was proclaimed Sultan in the holy city of Bursa—needed to secure his hold on power. In Byzantium, John the first son of Basileus Manuel, was proclaimed co-emperor with his elderly father in 1421 who from then on played a marginal role in the affairs of state. The new Basileus listened to Mustafa who had taken refuge in the town and was making some very tempting promises. A deal was struck; Mustafa took Gallipoli which he promised to return to the Byzantines, and with his ally Cuneya marched on Edirne. Once again the house of Osman found itself at a crossroads. The supporters of Mustafa included Beys from the border areas eager for a return to the policies of expansion into Europe and the promise of rich plunder, Ghazis and neo-muslims coveting territories with rich Timar land and Christian vassal princes most notably the Byzantines. On his side Murad could rely on the old Ottoman nobility, the heads of the administration and the army whose interest was to support a centralized power which could control the Ghazi of the European frontier as well as the semi-nomadic

Turks of Anatolia. Mustafa crossed to Asia to fight Murad and was defeated near Ixnik (Nicea). Returning in haste to Edirne to gather his treasure and his harem prior to seeking refuge in Wallachia, the usurper was captured and put to death. Murad remained in control yet it had been a close shave. First of all he wanted to take revenge on John VIII and besieged Byzantium in June 1422. Once more the old wall of Theodore II resisted the Ottoman charge and the revolt of one of his brothers who seized Iznik and threatened Bursa forced the Sultan to raise the siege. Byzantium once again had a thirty year reprieve.

Based at Edirne from then onwards, Murad got down to the task of strengthening his power. He heaped money and fiefdoms on the Cenderli family and appointed as Grand Vizier Halil Cenderli, the son of Ibrahim who had been Grand Vizier to Mehmed I. Halil remained with Murad for most of his reign, from 1429–1451 and lived for a short while after the Sultans death. The drive of the Muslims was clear and the Sultan, who had ample proof of how little he could trust his vassals returned to the system of Slaves of the Porte and expanding devsirme. The Neo-Muslims were the real beneficiaries of this renewal of conquest in the Balkans.

For from 1423 the Ottoman armies returned to southern Greece where Byzantium survived with the help of the Despotate of Mistra. On their way they destroyed the Hexamilion wall which had been built at great cost by Basileus Manuel and went on to lay to waste Morea. John VIII submitted and in 1424 a peace treaty between Byzantium and the Ottomans was signed which forced them once again to pay a very large tribute. The other surviving kingdom of the empire: Thessalonika, ruled over by Andronicus the Despot, the third son of Manuel, was closely besieged by Burak Bey, the son of the great warrior Evrenos. There was famine and the inhabitants no longer dared venture out of the protective walls. The despot unable to react, allowed the town council to appeal to Venice; on condition that the municipal status and the religion of the inhabitants be respected, the Serene Republic would become master of Thessalonika. A governor with the title of Duke was sent and was welcomed with great enthusiasm in September 1423. But their joy was short lived. Ottoman pressure did not let up and Venice was forced to negotiate the payment of a tribute three times as high as the one the Byzantines had paid. Internally the Venetian administrators came into conflict with the inhabitants due to their procedures. The deposed despot Andronicus was accused of plotting, was banished from the city and retired to a monastery in Morea. Several of his former aides were imprisoned. A delegation of foremost citizens went to Venice, representing the starving and miserable population, to beseech the Doge to lower the taxes but to no avail. In 1426 Ottoman forces attacked the walls built by Theodore the Great. Three years later Murad decided to put an end to this and in the spring of 1429, and at the head of his army entered on the 29 March, this city which had been a Mecca of Hellenism, victorious Thessalonika would remain Ottoman until 1912.

At the same time the Sultan had been fighting in Anatolia to wipe out the repercussions of the Usurper Mustafa's vain attempt. In five years he restored Ottoman dominion over almost all the plateau. In Byzantium Basileus Manuel died in 1425 after having become a monk with the name Matthew. His son John VIII, already co-emperor therefore became sole ruler. However this was reduced to the city and its surrounding lands as the Despotate of Morea, although ruled by his brothers, was considered independent. The three co-despots Theodor, Constantine—future and last Emperor of Byzantium—and Thomas had soon repaired the damage caused by the most recent Ottoman raid and were pursuing their fight against their neighbouring Latin principalities. Achea was conquered in 1432 and with the exception of the enclaves of Koron, Modon, Nauplia and Argos which belonged to Venice, all the Peloponnese reverted to Byzantine dominion.

In 1424 Murad signed a truce with the Christian princes of the western Balkans: the lords of northern Albania, the despot of Serbia and above all with their ally Sigismond of Hungary, as well as one agreed the same year with Byzantium. The problems which the Sultan was experiencing in Anatolia in effect forced this measure on him. Yet Despot Stephan 1389–1427, the son of Lazarus, was to take advantage and play the Ottomans against the Hungarians. A vassal to Bayezid, he had led his troops in the Ottoman army against Tamerlaine and only just managed to get away alive from the battlefield at Ankara. On his return he considered the time was right to restore Serbia to its former glory as in the reign of Dusan.

The fortress of Belgrade had been occupied by the Hungarians after the death of the Great Czar, but was left in such a state of disrepair that popular tradition believes it was in fact built by

Prince Stephan. He made it his capital, for the first time in Serbian history, on account of its remarkable strategic position. At the same time he adopted the title of Despot which linked him with Byzantium, while still remaining the Sultan's vassal. Based in the rich Morava valley the principality enjoyed a level of prosperity which can still be seen in the fortified monastery of Manasija and by a comparative renaissance of Serbo-Byzantine culture exemplified by the philosopher Constantine. The death of Stephan in 1427 gave rise to the problem of succession and in the end it was his nephew Djurdje (George) Brancovic 1427–1456 who took power. In the face of the Ottoman threat he quickly turned for protection to Sigismond and signed a treaty of vassalage with the monarch which gave him the status in the Hungarian Kingdom's hierarchy of second only to the sovereign. Yet in return he had to hand over the fortress of Belgrade and moved his capital to Semendria (Smederevo) where a still legible inscription states: Through the endeavour of the dutiful in Christ, Djurdje Brankovic, Lord of the land[12] and the banks of the Zeta, this fortress was built in 1430. This fortress, one of the most important in the Balkans, exacted very high corvees from the peasants and popular Serbian songs caricature "Helen the Greek" the Despot's Byzantine wife. Another sign of the unpopularity of this quasi Hungarian protectorate was the open fear of the draw of Catholicism and the repression of the Franciscans because of their missionary zeal. A widespread idea among the peasantry was that the Hagarians—sons of Hagar ie. the Ottomans—were only hostile to the nobles, that they should not fight against these foreigners since they did not practice serfdom. Defeatism was widespread in rural Serbia[13]. Murad made the most of this and hostilities once more began in 1428. He claimed that Serbia was his possession arguing that Bayezid his grandfather had married a daughter of despot Stephan. Brankovic was forced to give in and renew his oath of vassalage. Thus having made Serbia a starting-point for military operations, the Sultan turned his attention to Albania. Isaac Bey Evrenos overcame the nobles who had compromised themselves with the Venetians—most notably John Kastriota the father of Skanderbeg. In order to put an end to the Doge's intrigues he annexed all the property of the nobility in central Albania, established numerous Timars and turned the region into a Sandjak with a Pasha in residence at Gjirokastra numerous Timars. But these changes alienated many people and in 1434 Murad himself came with Sinan Pasha, the Beylerbey of Rumelia, to the Sandjak borders. On the Christian side the struggle was led by George Arianit whose fame had come to Sigismond's attention and who had suggested to him an anti-Ottoman alliance.

Gradually the Sultan's vassal Christian kingdoms were being transformed into provinces of an Empire which stretched from the Balkans to Asia Minor. It was apparent that the days of Byzantium's continued survival were numbered. Basileus John VIII decided on yet another appeal to the European monarchs: in exchange for financial and military help against the Ottomans, he proposed the unification of the two Churches under the leadership of the Pope. Several such attempts had been made in the past but had come to nought because of the duplicity and egoism of the various monarchs and also because of the fanaticism of the clergy and of ordinary people. So much so that on his deathbed in 1425 Emperor Manuel had warned his son against this chimera: a Union of the Greek and Latin Churches was impossible and all attempts to achieve this would only inflame relations between Byzantine and the Catholic Kingdoms. In 1431 however preparatory talks were held and the Pope agreed to hold an extraordinary council in Italy which the Basileus himself attended. John VIII left Byzantium in November 1437 leaving his brother Constantine, co-despot of Morea, as regent. He was accompanied by his other brother Demetrius, the Patriarch, several Metropolitans and many bishops and hegumens. He landed near Ferrara where the council commenced, only to be continued in Florence. Discussions were heated with the Metropolitan of Ephesus Marc Eugenikos leading the opposition. In the end Union was proclaimed in Florence on the 6 July 1439 both in Latin and in Greek by the catholic cardinal Guiliano Cesarini and the Metropolitan of Nicea John Bessarion. In spite of the solemnity of the proceedings, in the presence of the Emperor, the end result was no better than the Union of Lyons in 1274. Roused by the sermons of Marc Eugenikos the people of Byzantium indignantly rejected the idea of submission to the Pope and the city was shaken by violent demonstrations against the Basileus and the Patriarch. In other parts of the eastern Christian world there was outrage and Vasilij II the Grand Duke of Moscow who was opposed to Union, deposed the Metropolitan of the capital for taking part in the Council and for being in favour.

Henceforth Muscovy elected its own Metropolitan and in 1440 proclaimed itself autocephalic. As for Bessarion he took refuge in Rome and became a tireless advocate of an anti-Ottoman crusade.

Indeed there was a renewal—for the last time—of the crusading spirit. Sigismond of Luxembourg, king of Hungary died after a period of rule lasting half a century in 1437 and his succession was contested by the Habsburgs and the Polish Jagellons. However during this period of royal weakness, a remarkable soldier, Janos Hunyadi (1407–1456) was to take his place at centre stage. Born of a noble Transylvanian family, who were originally Romanian, he was believed to be the bastard son of King Sigismond. He had been brought up at court, had followed the sovereign on his travels abroad and had even been a Condotierre in Italy where he had learned about the uses of modern armaments. King Vladislas made him Vojvode of Transylvania and Ispan[14] of the Comitat of Temes (Banat), in other words responsible for most of the border area facing the Ottomans. Well liked at court, master of many lands, Janos Hunyadi had everything needed to become a Christian hero. In 1442 some of the Sultan's troops launched a raid and for the first time penetrated into Transylvania. Hunyadi quickly mustered an army of feudal lords and peasants together with Hussite mercenaries who brought with them the strategy of armoured wagons used in Bohemia. At the head of 15,000 men he stopped the invaders at Ialomita near present-day Sinaia and forced them back as far as the Danube. News of this victory spread throughout Europe and the dream of a crusade was resuscitated. Hunyadi convinced the king to lead it himself and so in the autumn of 1443 the Hungarian army, bolstered by western knights and reinforced with George Brankovic's Serbs, took Nis, Sofia and threatened the road to Edirne. Murad rushed back from Anatolia, halted the Christian army at the foot of the Balkan and forced it to make a painful retreat in the middle of winter. Then Skanderbeg revolted, the Emir of Karaman renewed his attacks in Anatolia and the despot of Morea occupied Athens. In Edirne the treasury was exhausted by all the demands of the various campaigns and the Sultan became much affected by the death of his favourite son. Murad went into what we would call a depression and left his Grand Vizier in charge. Through his Serbian wife Mara he managed to make contact with Brankovic who acted as an intermediary in negotiations for a truce with the crusaders, which was known as the Truce of Szeged (June 1444). Murad obtained the assurance that he could go to Anatolia to continue his campaign against Karaman and his allies, without in the meantime being attacked in Europe. Brankovic's Serbia recovered its pre-1427 (the death of Stephan) frontiers but as with Wallachia under Vlad the Impaler (Vlad Tepes), it was to continue paying a tribute to the Sultan.

Having thus, it seemed, guaranteed the security of the House of Osman, Murad II abdicated in favour of his son Mehmed in August 1444 and retired to Bursa where he led the life of a Soufi[15] in the same way that his opponent Basileus Michael ended his life in a monastic cassock. In the 15th century the religious way was universal. No doubt this abdication also had political motives: the defeat by Hunyadi had damaged the prestige of the border beys and there was mounting fear of what was seen as a Christian counter offensive.

Christianity was to find a second hero in the person of a minor lord from northern Albania; George Kastriota known to history as Skanderbeg (1405–1468). His father, a descendant of a montagnard family, had obtained presumably from the Ottomans a fiefdom in the coastal region. But the situation had been precarious at the time of the interregnum and Mehmed I having won control of the fortress of Kruja forced his feudal neighbours to send their sons as hostages. Of the four Kastriota sons it was George who was sent to Edirne, where he was given a Muslim education at the school of Palace pages where he was known as Alexander—in Turkish Skander. On receiving his Spahi qualification he returned to his region of origin in 1438, was given the title of Bey and the office of Vali (administrator) in the Kruja region. Yet in November 1443 when Hunyadi's army took Nis Skanderbeg left the Beylerbey's camp and at the head of a small force of cavalry—300 according to tradition—he took Kruja thanks to a false Firman (title deed). The next day, the 28 November 1443, he raised a flag bearing his family's arms on the citadel: a double symbol with future import since the Skanderbeg flag became the emblem of independent Albania and the 28 November remains the national feast day. At the time it was really a feudal revolt like many others which were to occur in the Ottoman Empire but which is singular because it was to go on for a long time, from 1444–1468. Furthermore it is important because of its European dimension; the kings of Hungary, Naples and Venice supported the insurgents, at least with words and Pope Nicholas V hailed Skanderbeg as an "athlete of Christ." Right up to the hero's death from sickness at Alessio (Lezha) on the 17 January 1468, he was to remain a hindrance to the successful conclusion of the Ottoman conquest.

However, while revolt was prevailing in Albania, the crusading spirit was struck a fatal blow. The Szeged agreement had allowed for a truce of 10 years binding both Christians and the Ottomans. Yet the Roman Curia, pressured by Bessarion, was certain that it could force the Ottomans back into Asia. Bound by his promise Vladislas, the young king of Hungary and Poland, hesitated to reopen hostilities but Cardinal Cesarini went to the camp at Szeged and released the sovereign from his oath. In September the army once more was on an active footing, led by Vladislav together with Cardinal Cesarini and Janos Hunyadi. However an important ally was absent: the Serbian despot George Brankovic who was quite satisfied with his gains from the previous campaign. He even alerted the Sultan to what was happening. Relying on the support of the Venetian navy the crusader army slowly made its way through Bulgaria towards the Black Sea. This enabled the Ottomans to act. Fear of entrusting the fate of the Empire to the young Sultan who was only 12 years old, made the Grand Vizier Halil Cenderli and his clan appeal to Murad. The ex-Sultan agreed to return to power. Ferried by Genoese ships he and his army crossed over to Europe and surprised the Christian army in front of the walls of the port of Varna on the 10 November 1444. The encounter was long and bloody. The Hungarian cavalry broke through the Ottoman lines but were stopped by the Janissaries who captured Vladislas and cut off his head. There followed a rout, Hunyadi just managing to escape with Cardinal Cesarini, and thousands of knights killed in the battle or in the aftermath. The idea of crusade was finally dead and buried. Vladislas' expedition was the last attempt at collective action by the Christian monarchs to stop the Ottomans. Byzantium realized that its fate was sealed. Poor Basileus John VIII sent his congratulations to the victorious Sultan together with presents.

Murad abdicated a second time in favour of Mehmed, but the Cenderli and the nobles, fearing that the young prince might be too influenced by the Kapi Kulari, fomented an uprising of the Janissaries in Edirne which was perceived as revealing Mehmed's weakness. Once more Murad returned to power, however, leaving his son with the title of Sultan and was to spend the last years of his life consolidating Ottoman power in the Balkans.

The co-despot of Morea, Constantine, wishing to extend his power into central Greece took advantage of Ottoman problems in 1443 and captured Athens and Thebes, continuing up to Pindhos. But in 1446 Murad himself intervened, striking right into the heart of Morea, wreaking havoc everywhere and taking 60,000 captives who were subsequently sold as slaves. Allowing a small vassal despotate to remain in existence, the greater part of central Greece was made into a Sandjak. Bulgaria was to suffer the same fate. Displeased with the Christian feudal lords who had sided with Mustafa at the start of his reign he was to destroy them and replace them with Spahis. Some of the Bulgarian nobility actually became Spahis. He also settled numerous Turkish tribes to cultivate the land which was to alter the ethnic balance of certain regions.

Hunyadi for his part had not given up. On his return to Buda he was made regent to the young king and he launched a fresh attack. Murad left Albania to block his path and they met in October 1448 at Kosovo; the same place where Bayezid had been victorious sixty years earlier. Once again the Ottoman armies won the day for Brancovic had again refused to join Hungary and Skanderbeg had started out as promised but arrived too late. At this juncture Basileus John died. Being childless and Theodor his younger brother dead, the crown passed to the youngest brother Constantine, Despot of Morea, known as Draganese because his mother Helen had belonged to the princely Serbian family of Dragas who came from the Prizren region. On the 6 January 1449 he was crowned Basileus Constantine XI in Morea and two months later he made his solemn entry into Byzantium. He was its last Emperor.

Perhaps sensing his coming death, Murad married his son to the daughter of the powerful Emir of Dulgadir, lord of Black Sheep and White Sheep around Amida (Diyarbakir). By this he reinforced the influence of the older Turkish families. To avoid a struggle over the succession he drew up a written will, which was unusual for the House of Osman, and designated Mehmed as his successor. On the 5 February 1451 Sultan Murad suddenly died of a stroke in Edirne, after thirty years in power.

Undoubtedly he was the greatest conqueror of the Balkans leaving his successor the task of destroying the last remnants of the Byzantine empire and above all its symbol, Constantinople. To this end he had resoundingly crushed the Crusade and left his son with a powerful army and a vigorous administration. Finally after the great fire of 1444 he had made Edirne a truly Muslim capital gathering poets and wise men to his palace.

Notes

1. I Dujcev: History of Bulgaria reference p.230 in the French version.
2. From I Dujcev's History of Bulgaria p.236 French version.
3. Now Bozcaada
4. The exact chronology of this period is subject to discussion. Refer to Ostrogorsky: Histoire de L'Etat byzantine. Previously mentioned. p.566 note 3.
5. Now Alasehir which is 150km from Izmir.
6. Mircea cel Batrin 1386–1418.
7. Jean le Meingre, called Boucicaut 1365–1421, taken prisoner at the battle of Nicopolis and freed for a ransom.
8. Originally slave mercenaries they became rulers of Egypt in 1250 where several dynasties ruled till 1517.
9. Beneath the Garden of Gulhane, which now is where the European station stands.
10. From the verb devsirmek which means to recruit.
11. Now the Romanian town of Giurgiu. The fortress was built in the XIV century by the Genoans.
12. In other words Raska and the region along the Danube called Macva.
13. Emile Haumant: La formation de la Yougoslavie. Paris 1930. p.80.
14. The title of Vojvode was given in Hungary to the governor of Transylvania while, ever since Stephan I, the Ispan was the representative of the king in the counties (comitats).
15. The Soufis wore a white wool overcoat (in arabic suf = wool)

4

Constantinople-Istanbul, Capital of a New World Empire

When Murad's son came to power in 1451, the Kingdom of the House of Osman still retained the complex characteristics of what has been called the First Ottoman Empire. On the one hand a variety of territorial groups more or less equally balanced on each side of the Straits—Rumeli and Anadoli in Turkish—and on the other containing both directly administered provinces and vassal countries; Christian Balkans and Muslim Asia Minor. Of course in Bulgaria, Greece and Albania, Murad had already transformed territories which traditionally had a vassal status into Sandjaks, but it was left to his son, offspring of a Byzantine harem, to effect the transformation from Ghazi kingdom to Empire worthy of Byzantium. To the Christian past would be added a Muslim belief, handed down to us by the historian Ibd Khaldun, which foretold that he who captured Constantinople would become the "Mahdi"—the Messianic restorer.

Mehmed II Fatih: Mohammed II, Conqueror of Byzantium

Mehmed II, known as Mohammed II, started his long reign 1451–1481 by restoring order to the palace which had been shaken by his father abdicating twice and twice returning to power. He put his brother Ahmed to death and exiled the former Sultan's wife Mara to the Despotate of Serbia from where she had originally come. Above all he took command of the Janissary corps who for the first time in Ottoman history demanded a "gift" before they would acknowledge the new Sultan. Caught unprepared Mehmed gave in but changed their commander—the Aga—and recruited a new batch of men from the Devsirme. The Janissaries became what they had been meant to be: the Sultan's personal guard and an instrument of power for his personal use. Yet Mehmed had problems with the Grand Vizier Halil, a member of the powerful Cenderli family, inherited from his father, probably due to having been removed from power twice by the Vizier, but also clearly from political motives. The high ranking families had done well out of the subtle Balkan policy practised by Murad and were opposed to a full-scale attack on Byzantium.

The young Sultan, who was only nineteen, dreamed of conquest and began to make plans for the operation. Despite protests from the Basileus and in a record three months, he had built a fortress called Rumeli Hisar on the western shore of the Bosphorus, opposite Anadolu Hisa built by Bayezid on the eastern shore and only four miles from the town. There he stationed a garrison force of 400 Janissaries and artillery pieces capable of halting any suspect vessel. Then in the autumn of 1452 he had his troops occupy the houses outside the city walls and demanded that Constantine surrender Byzantium. Winter was spent by the Ottoman building up a formidable stock of artillery. According to tradition a Hungarian or Wallachian engineer called Urban succeeded in casting huge cannons measuring 30 inches in diameter to shatter the ramparts. As for the Christians the Basileus sent out urgent appeals to the Pope and the Italian Cities of Venice and Genoa who still retained outposts in the Balkans and the Aegean. The Pope responded by sending out a legate, Cardinal Isidore the former Metropolitan of Moscow. On the 12 December 1452, in the Basilica of Santa Sophia, he proclaimed the Union of the Churches and held mass using the Roman liturgy. It was a scandal which unbridled the anti-Latin hatred of the crowds and which an advisor of the Basileus summarized with the famous saying: "Better the Turkish turban in the centre of the capital than the Roman mitre." Also the last Patriarch who had been appointed by the Basileus, George Milissanos had sought refuge in 1450 in Rome, so during the siege there was no Patriarch in Byzantium. As for the Christian monarchs they were busy with their own quarrels although the most powerful king in the Mediterranean, Alphonso V of Aragon and Naples did have dreams of a new Latin empire which would include Constantinople. Only Genoa sent troops: 700 men from its garrison of Chios, under the command of Giustiniani, whose arrival in two galleys was greeted with great enthusiasm. Then the Golden Horn was closed to traffic by a massive chain. Yet the Byzantine forces were relying on the wall defences mainly, since many of the inhabitants had fled and the city had become deserted. Many different figures have been given for the number of defenders, but there were about seven to eight thousand in all which included a thousand "Latins" from Chios and the islands, and 200 mercenaries financed by the Pope. This was scarcely enough to man Theodor II's outside wall but after all they had already withstood twenty sieges. They had light cannon which could use Greek fire. Against them Mehmed had gathered an army of 120,000, at the core of which were 10,000 Janissaries and added to this again an unknown number of irregulars, 100,000 by some counts, attracted by the prospect of spoil. Therefore a ratio of one to twenty. But the essential superiority was in the field of artillery. Mehmed had built up what can be considered the first "artillery depot" in history. Fourteen batteries of five pieces each, made up of one big bombard 5 inches thick and four smaller pieces; in all 70 cannons. And as an observer noted the "cannon was the most important factor." On top of this there was an armada of more than 300 galleys which had carried the troops over from Anatolia and which was cruising in the Marmara Sea.

The actual siege began on the 5 April 1453 when various formations of the Ottoman army took up position to the south and west of the town while the fleet blocked the Golden Horn on the other side of the chain. The huge bombards, dragged by teams of twenty oxen each were brought adjacent to the outside moat so that the massive cannon-balls could hit the walls with greatest impact. The bombardment began the following day, at a leisurely rate since it took two hours to prepare each shot and they were restricted to six or seven shots per day. However the old 5th century wall was weakened and several breaches were made. On the 18 April Mehmed launched the first assault on the Roman Gate and Lykos valley sector where there was a weak section of the fortifications but which was bravely defended by Giustiniani who repulsed each successive wave of attackers. Two days later one Greek and 24 Genoese ships managed to break the blockade and provided the town with fresh supplies. The besieged population was greatly encouraged. Two days later however Mehmed was to surprise them. At dawn the Byzantines were stunned to find seventy to eighty ships in the Golden Horn flying the Sultan's colours. A 5–6 mile wooden road, linking the Bosphorus to the soft water stream behind Galata had been built on the advice of an Italian engineer. Transformed with a coating of oil and grease into a slip-way they had dragged the galleys during the night and so in spite of its chain barrier had entered the Golden Horn. The Byzantines tried to set them alight with Greek fire but without much success and all the Christian ships inside were either captured or destroyed. Mehmed then built a pontoon bridge across the Golden Horn so that the town was also threatened from the north. During this time the western defences were being subjected to a continuous bombardment and larger and larger breaches were being opened. On the 7 and 12 May the Sultan threw further assaults to test the defences but they were repulsed with great losses. The soldiers were beginning to grumble, the siege was taking a long time and there were serious resupply problems since the surrounding countryside had been devastated. On the 23 May the Sultan sent another ultimatum to the Basileus: surrender under certain conditions or risk a final assault. Constantine rejected it with contempt. So the Sultan brought together his advisers; the Grand Vizier once more voiced his opinion that there should be a diplomatic solution and the siege lifted. However Zagan Pasha—Zaganos the Greek, a product of the Devsirme and an opponent of the Cenderli—spoke out for military action. The town, he said, was doomed since the Christian monarchs, unable to unite themselves, had not reacted and continued to do nothing. His argument won and Mehmed fixed the attack for the 29 May and to rally his troops declared that after the city was captured there would be three day during which the victorious soldiers would be allowed to pillage. All the Ottoman camp buzzed with excitement.

In the town the Basileus also had to be careful of morale and monks and priests were requisitioned every night to hold prayer services for the defenders, whose numbers were rapidly diminishing under the bombardment and assaults. The day prior to the final attack there remained only 4 to 5,000 able-bodied men. On the 28 May Constantine surrounded by all the high ranking dignitaries of the Empire attended a solemn mass in the old basilica of his famous homonym; the last in Santa Sophia before it was transformed into a mosque. Forewarned by spies, the Basileus deployed his remaining troops in the area between the already much damaged Romanos Gate and the Charisios Gate which led to the Edirne road. Amongst the contingent was Giustiniani and his Genoese from Chios. Mehmed himself gave the order to advance under cover of darkness on the night of the 28 and 29 May just before dawn. Two waves of irregulars were sent in and repulsed by the walls, but the third, made up of Anatolian infantrymen made a breach near the Edirne Gate. The Sultan threw his Janissaries into the breach and took the defenders from the rear. Giustiniani was wounded and to evacuate him his soldiers withdrew. Having gained a foothold on the ramparts the Janissaries cleared them systematically of defenders whilst the Ottoman fleet broke through the chain in the Golden Horn and gained complete control of it. The last Christian soldiers mustered round Basileus Constantine XI who died sword in hand but in circumstances which are unknown. The terrified population sought refuge in the churches as the sack of the town began. On the evening of the 29 May Mehmed Fatih—The Conqueror—asserted his victory by entering Santa Sophia on horseback. The kingdom of Byzantium died with its last Emperor and much of its cultural riches were lost in the ensuing pillage which as the Sultan had promised lasted for three days. Even so there was less destruction than when the crusaders had sacked it in 1204 since in its dying days the capital had been poorer than in Angevin times and much had already been taken to the west.

The victor could under Koranic law have razed the town which had so bravely resisted him but this was not Mehmed's intention. Master of the second Rome he believed himself to be henceforth the heir of the Emperors and wanted to make it into the capital of a new Empire.

The first task was to repopulate the city from which all its inhabitants had fled. Many, including the surviving soldiers, had taken refuge in the Genovese colony of Galata to the north of the Golden Horn. Its Podesta had declared his neutrality during the siege but the influx of refugees was to become a problem since the Sultan claimed them as his property. Zaganos, the Sultan's advisor, reached a agreement whereby the soldiers were handed over, the leaders put to death and the rest counted as slaves to become part of the booty. As for the city it became a vassal town. A breach was opened in the walls and the last two floors of the famous tower were pulled down. However the inhabitants retained their property, their freedom of religious belief and although not subject to Devsirme, were made to pay taxes and import duty.

Mehmed's entrance into Santa Sophia was the sign for the islamization of the town. The ancient Basilica and most of the churches became mosques. The population was renewed initially by allowing inhabitants of neighbouring regions to come: Turks from Thrace, Greeks from the islands and Slavs from Turkish Macedonia. Then in a more methodical way Turkish people were brought over from Asia Minor, from towns such as Aksaray and Carsamba in the emirate of Karaman. The quarters where they settled, in the houses abandoned by the Byzantines, were named after their places of origin by the newcomers. Straightaway Byzantium became a Muslim city: Istanbul, but westerners continued to call it Constantinople. Mehmed entrusted the administration of the town to a Vizier who was to maintain law and order and to make it into a capital. To this end it needed a palace worthy of Fatih. This was completed in the winter of 1457-8 and from then onwards the City of Constantine became the capital of the Ottoman Empire in preference to Edirne. By then it had a population of 50,000 inhabitants, the majority Muslim.

However not exclusively so. On the 1 June, after the end of the sack of the town, the Sultan appointed a new Patriarch: the Greek theologian and canonist George Gennadios, known as Scholarios, who had been a bitter opponent of the Union of Florence. He also decreed the status of the head of the Christian Church qualified as "Incalculable and immutable" and whom he guaranteed the same privileges that his predecessors had previously enjoyed. The Sultan's decree gave Christians the right to have icons and bibles and guaranteed freedom of worship, conducted in one of the few churches which were to remain, for instance Pammacaristos—Church of the Miraculous Virgin—which was the Patriarch's cathedral until 1586 when it became the Fethiya Mosque. Its was in this quarter called Fener—now Phanar—that gradually the Christians who had remained or those who had recently arrived began to live. The "Greeks," as the Muslims called the Patriarch's followers, lived under his authority.

Mehmed II, Conqueror of the Byzantine Inheritance

On the 1 June 1453 Mehmed settled an old score with his advisers; Halil Cenderli was made to resign his office of Grand Vizier and was replaced by Zaganos Pasha who had become, following the victory he had predicted, the Sultan's closest advisor. On the pretext that he had received money from the Basileus not to attack the town, Halil and several members of his family were imprisoned and their wealth confiscated. Of more import than replacing an individual, this amounted to a change in the balance of power; the ancient Turkish families were being supplanted by slaves, products of the Devsirme and totally dependent on the Sultan, who was visibly becoming more autocratic.

For the youthful Mehmed the capture of Constantinople was in no way an end in itself. Installed after his victory in the seat of the Basileus he aspired to its inheritance; but the Byzantine Empire of Justinian's reign had stretched from Italy to the whole of the Balkans, to Asia Minor and Egypt and also Africa to the Straits of Gibraltar. A huge undertaking which was further fuelled by the Muslim dream of the restoration of an unified Caliphate after it had been lost with the last Abbass of Baghdad and nominally survived with the Mameluks of Egypt. Based on this bicephalic ideology, which Christian Europe saw only as a continuation of the Jihad, the conquests continued and the reign of Mehmed was to become, like those of his predecessors, a succession of military campaigns, alternating between Europe and Asia.

Very close to Constantinople were the Genoese of Galata whilst their rivals the Venetians were extremely powerful on the seas. The Sultan's first endeavour was to bring them into vassalage; the new status of Galata was confirmed with a trade agreement in the Aegean islands and also in the Crimea since from now on it was possible for the Ottomans to close off the Straits if they so wished. As for the Doge he had to make amends for participating in the Varna crusade. He was forced to negotiate with Fatih but was granted his fair share of foreign trade with the new Empire in return for a small import and export duty of 2%. This was to be supervised by a representative of Constantinople called the Bailee of Venice. This privilege was given after a large tribute: in 1454 the Doge of Venice was taxed 200,000 golden ducats[1].

Abandoning the seas, at least for the time being, to the Christians, Mehmed turned to the western Balkans where the princes of Serbia and Albania still were seeking help from the king of Hungary against the Ottomans. After four military campaigns, the last avatar of the Serbian kingdom, the despotate of George Brankovic was occupied. The first two expeditions in 1454 and 1455 resulted in the capture of the southern half of Zeta and Raska, the latter giving the Sultan use of the precious gold and silver mines of Novo Brdo. The third which was meant to take Belgrade back from the Hungarians failed; Janos Hunyadi the regent came to the rescue of the defenders in the fortress whose morale had been bolstered by the courageous sermons of a Franciscan, John of Capistiano. Having gained control of the river Mehmed together with 200 galleys entered the town but was repulsed that very same evening. The Ottoman army withdrew to Sofia, the Sultan wounded. Christianity celebrated Hunyadi's victory. Hunyadi is known in folk songs as Sibinjanin Janko[2]. However the plague broke out in the Hungarian army and the victor fell victim and died in July 1456 outside the city which he had helped save. The old Despot George Brancovic, who during the siege had maintained an unsavoury neutrality, in turn died leaving behind a daughter who was promised by her mother in marriage to the king of Bosnia. But he was a Catholic and this unleashed a religious outcry: the "Latins" supported Hungary while the "Greeks" turned to the Ottomans. Things were helped along by the fact that the commander of the despotate's army Mihajlo Andzelovic, was the Grand Vizier's very own brother. A baroque situation which had come about because of Devsirme and was by no means unique. When Mehmed returned in 1459 to Smederevo on the Danube, the citadel, reputedly impregnable, opened its gates without a fight. The Serbian kingdom was to disappear for three and a half centuries, replaced by the Sandjak of Semendria, yet Belgrade was to remain Hungarian for a further sixty years.

While the Sultan was making war on the Danube, his generals were destroying the last pockets of Byzantine resistance in the Balkans. In 1456 his navy embarked on operations to wipe out piracy in the Aegean Sea which was being conducted from Christian bases. They seized the islands of Lemnos and Thasos which were Genoese possessions and from which it was possible to block passage of the Dardanelles. At the same time the two despots of Morea who were the last Basileus' brothers, continued fighting over the remains of the Duchy of Athens and strips of the Peloponnese. Mehmed killed two birds with one stone ; Ottoman galleys appeared off Athens and occupied the town, however the Acropolis which had been transformed into a fortress was to hold out for a further two years. In 1458 the Athenian enclave ended and the Church of the Virgin, built inside the Acropolis, was converted to a mosque. Two years later it was the turn of Morea. The enemy brothers conducted their affairs in such a way that the Sultan intervened. The youngest of the two, Thomas, fled to Italy and his daughter Zoe-Sofia was later to be given in marriage to Tzar Ivan II thus passing on to Russia the bicephalic eagle of the

Paleologos and their claim to the Byzantine inheritance. The other brother Demetrius, a bitter opponent of the Union of Florence, preferred to seek refuge at the Sultan's court. There still was a chunk of Byzantine territory outside the Balkans: the Empire of Trezibond. Mehmed occupied this in 1461 during a campaign waged in Anatolia. He had embarked on this campaign to end the plotting of the Genoese in Asmara together with the Emir of Sinope and the Emir of White Sheep. The last emperor of Trezibond, David Comnenos, was put to death together with his six sons. There would be no more Greek kingdoms till the 19th century.

In Albania the Ottomans continued to be confronted by Skanderbeg and feudal lords who in 1444 had formed the League of Alessio (Lezha). Yet this was a precarious alliance and was undermined by other nobles of the region, such as Dukadjin, who preferred to negotiate with the Sultan or the Arianites who had allied themselves to the Venetians. Skanderbeg had at first turned to Hungary for support but then to Alphonso of Aragon and Naples with whom he signed an alliance at Gaet in 1451. After the fall of Constantinople Skanderbeg made a journey to Naples and brought back with him 2,000 infantrymen and some Aragon cannons to bolster up the League's army. But the failure of an attack on the Ottoman fortress of Berat led to defections over to the Sultan, even from among Skanderbeg's own family. He did however manage to stop several offensives launched by the Bey Isaac Evrenos. The Pope wanted to use this resistance to start a new crusade. Venice declared war on the Sultan and Skanderbeg, accepting their offer of help, once more went on the offensive. Yet in 1464 the Pope died and with him the idea of a crusade. Virtually unaided Skanderbeg held out for four years under repeated attacks led by the best Ottoman commanders. Ballaban Pasha died in combat against him and the Sultan himself besieged Kruja the capital three times. In January 1468 however, worn out by an attack of fever Skanderbeg died in Alesso. It was to take a further decade before the Ottomans captured all the Albanian fortresses. In 1479 a treaty was signed between Mehmed and Venice which only left the latter with the ports of Durrazo (Durres) and Scutari (Shkodra), while the rest of Albania was to become Ottoman for five hundred years.

The occupation of Serbia laid neighbouring Bosnia open to attack from the frontier Beys. King Stephan Tomasevic gave his support to Skanderbeg and, rejecting Ottoman vassalage, agreed to the Hungarian occupation of his fortresses. The Sultan reacted to this and in 1461 the whole country was conquered without much difficulty, while the king was taken prisoner. Two years later he was beheaded. The Bogomils, persecuted by the Hungarians, were to welcome the Ottomans as liberators and many were converted to Islam. The ancient principality of Hum, based on Mostar in the south, had gained independence from Bosnia and in 1448 its leader Stephan Vuksich was honoured by Emperor Frederic III with the title of Duke of Saint Sava, in German Herzog, hence the name by which the region was known; Herzegovina. During the 14th century the region had a vassal status in relation to the Sultan but was finally incorporated in 1483. The part of what had formerly been Zeta known to the Venetians as Montenegro, relied on Venice to resist Ottoman pressure. The Crnojevich family, who since 1422 ruled the country, established their capital at Zabljak to the north east of Lake Scutari, but around 1480 Knez Ivan was forced to transfer his seat of power to Cetinje at the foot of Mount Lovcen where two years previously he had founded a monastery. There began a difficult period for Montenegro, deprived of the rich plains which border the lake and caught between the Ottomans and the Venetians fighting each other for supremacy. The question of vassalage was consequently simply theoretical.

North of the Danube, Hungarian claims to Wallachia and Moldavia and the Genovese presence on the southern shore of the Black Sea made Mehmed once more intervene. Wallachia had paid a tribute since 1395 and since 1456 so too had Moldavia, therefore both were felt to be Ottoman vassal territories. The Sultan controlling the Straits also wanted control of the Genoese trading posts in the Crimea: Kaffa and Sudak, and Moncastro[3] on the mouth of the Dnestr. An Ottoman squadron was sent and forced them to pay tribute one by one. In the meantime an ultimatum was sent to the Moldavian Voevod Petru Aron, who held Kilia on the northern arm of the Danube delta. The prince gave way and accepted to pay a tribute of 2,000 Venetian ducats. In return Moncastro became a dependency of Moldavia and was given the right to trade freely with all the large towns within the Empire. In 1459 in Wallachia, Vlad the new prince refused to pay his tribute and had the Sultan's envoys, who had been sent to demand it, impaled alive thus earning the nickname "The Impaler"—Tepes. War broke out; Vlad laid waste the Ottoman region of Dobrudja while Mehmed invaded

Wallachia, burnt Tirgoviste down and put another voevod on the throne. Vlad returned to his principality twelve years later but was killed after the Ottomans once more intervened. In 1476 Wallachia became a vassal principality and remained so for 330 years. The Moldavian sovereign Stephan the Great (1457–1504) also refused to pay tribute and made overtures to Hungary, Venice and Poland who in turn had been asked by the Pope to once again undertake an anti-Ottoman crusade. Mehmed sent his Grand Vizier Suleyman Pasha to put down the rebellion. On the 10 January 1470 an encounter took place which was a resounding victory for the voevod who was hailed as "Christ's Athlete" by the Pope himself. But the crusade ended there and in 1475 the Ottoman fleet took the opportunity to destroy the Genovese trading posts. The Black Sea now became a Turkish lake.

In the Mediterranean, Aegean and Adriatic Seas, Venice was still a most formidable power with a presence at the mouth of the Cattaro, in Scutari, Durazzo, and the islands of Corfu, Modon, Koron to the south of the Peloponnese, Nauplion, Argos, Negroponte (Eubea) and Crete. When he came to power Mehmed reached agreement with Venice but from Montenegro to Greece there were many flashpoints from which conflict could break out. The Doge had also listened to the Pope's appeals and joined the 1463 crusade which was to last sixteen years. The Venetian fleet seized several islands off the Peloponnese and the Aegean but its mercenaries were thoroughly defeated on land. Hostilities were limited to a few raids on the Anatolian coast coordinated with rebel emirates and attacks on the ports of Albania and Greece. In 1470 the Sultan's fleet occupied Negropont and after the pacification of Albania, Venice sued for peace. This was signed in Constantinople on the 25 June 1479. The Serenissima handed over Eubea, Scutari and Argos and agreed to pay a tribute of 100,000 golden ducats in exchange for the right to continue trading inside the Empire and to retain a Bailee in the capital.

Having managed to pacify the whole of Asia Minor, Mehmed II had also succeeded in recapturing the territory of the Byzantine Empire lost since the Comnenos. He dreamed of continuing his conquest and recreating the Empire of Justinian. He dreamed of conquering Italy which was racked by the rivalry between Venice, Naples and Milan, but also by Pontifical intrigues. At the same time he had his eye on Mameluk[4] Egypt, the seat of power of the Caliph. Yet before he could do anything about this, Mehmed had to break what he saw as the key, the island of Rhodes, held since 1309 by the Knights of Saint John of the Cross who were also known as Hospitallers of Jerusalem. But the siege during the winter of 1479-80 failed to produce any result in the face of the town's huge ramparts. At the same time however, Gadik Ahmed Pasha the commander of the fleet sailed to Otranto, reaching it on the 11 August 1480 and creating panic in Rome and in all Italy. After this the Ottomans were preparing their next campaign in the Peninsula when news arrived of the Sultan's death in his palace at Istanbul on the 3 May 1481.

For the Balkan countries Mehmed was primarily the Fatih who transformed the old vassal Christian states into Sandjaks and created a true Empire. This Empire was to have a coherent structure based on the codification of existing laws which led to three codes—Kanunname—being compiled during his reign dealing with the structure of the Ottoman state, with the welfare and duties of his subjects, land ownership and taxes.

Domination of the Eastern Mediterranean: Bayezid II and Selim I

The last years of Mehmed II reign were troubled by the rivalry of his two sons Bayezid and Djem, both candidates for the succession. The Sultan promulgated a Kanun known as the "fratricidal law": "For the good of the state, the son whom God makes Sultan is legally permitted to put his brothers to death. The majority of the Ulemas feel that this is permissible." A very harsh application of "reason of state" but which the Fatih had tried to avoid being applied prematurely by giving his two heirs governorships of provinces equidistant to Istanbul; consequently both had the same chances of reaching the capital and proclaiming themselves Sultan. As it happens the Grand Vizier tried to stifle the news of the sovereigns death till Djem had arrived at the palace but this ploy was foiled by the Janissaries who came out in favour of Bayezid. On the 21 May 1481 Bayezid became Sultan Bayezid II. Immediately he made the Janissary aga Ishak Pasha Grand Vizier and doled out a gratuity—baksheesh—to his soldiers which was to become a traditional gift of accession. He also gave them permission to put Karami Pasha and his clan to death and to take their wealth and possessions. The new reign had started under the aegis of the Kapi Kulari, the slaves of the Porte.

Djem having lost in the capital did not admit defeat but proclaimed himself Sultan at Bursa, the holy town, and suggested that he and his brother divide the Empire between them. Bayezid replied by sending out his Janissaries and the two rival armies clashed at Yenishehir near Bursa in July. Djem was beaten and fled to Egypt and into exile. This took him to Rhodes where the Knights of Saint John welcomed him, to France where he stayed for seven years and appeared at the court of Charles VIII and finally to Naples where he died in 1495; possibly poisoned on the orders of his brother against whom the Pope and Christian monarchs had intended to make use of him.

The dream of crusade stirred Innocent VIII and Bayezid worried by this was anxious to restore the Empire's precarious finances, a task badly neglected under Fatih and the enormous strain following the almost continuous wars which had taken place during this period. Bayezid was to act cautiously in relation to the neighbouring Christian kingdoms: Hungary, Poland and the Romanian principalities. The Sultan signed a five year truce with Mathias Corvinus who was fighting the Habsburgs at the time and launched a sea and land operation against Stephan of Moldavia which ended in the summer of 1484 with the capture of the two ports: Kilia on the Danube and Akkerman on the Dnestr and so denying Moldavia, as well as Hungary and Poland, access to Black Sea trade. In spite of further efforts by Stephan, Moldavia in 1503 was forced, in the same way as Wallachia, to sign new terms reaffirming its vassal status in relation to the Sultan.

After the death of Mathias Corvinus in 1490, the Hungarian throne went to Ladislas II Jagellon, brother of the Polish king, who was won over to the idea of a crusade against the Ottomans. Bayezid hoping to deter him tried to seize the Hungarian forward post of Belgrade but failed and had to make do with forays into Transylvania and Croatia. Also the Khan of the Crimean Tatars—a vassal since 1475—emboldened by the protection of the Sultan, launched several raids on south eastern Poland, pillaging the countryside and taking slaves, reaching right to the very walls of Lemberg (Lwow) and Cracow. The king of Poland wanted to respond by making Moldavia into a vassal kingdom, but Voevod Stephan appealed to Bayezid and the Moldavian army reinforced by Wallachian and Ottoman contingents defeated he Polish army at the forest of Cosmin[5] in October 1497. The peace of Hirlau in 1499, between the Sultan, his Moldavian vassal and Poland established a "permanent peace." Renewed in 1533, it was to place relations between the Sublime Porte and the Polish Rzeczpospolita on an even keel until the 17th century.

During this reign the most serious conflict was the war against Venice lasting for more than ten years. In 1482 the Doge obtained agreement from the young Bayezid excusing him from paying the tribute prescribed by the 1479 Treaty of Constantinople. Yet there was great rivalry in the Adriatic and in 1491 the "Bailee" of Venice was expelled from Istanbul. Further incidents occurred. A fleet was built and was placed under the command of Kemal Reis, a "barbary pirate" who had operated off the French and Spanish coast. In 1499 war broke out, the Venetians were all expelled from Constantinople and their base at Lapanto was stormed. Then Modon, Navarino and Coron fell to the Ottomans and their fleet arrived off Venice. To succour his Serenity, Pope Alexander Borgia VI tried to organize a crusade. A naval expedition landed at Lesbos which troubled the Porte's advisers. A peace treaty was signed at Constantinople in December 1502 thanks to Polish mediation, whereby Venice retained its last ports in Morea and Albania. But from this time on the Ottomans were clearly the greatest maritime power in the eastern Mediterranean and also an important factor in the western Mediterranean basin. In 1482 the Andalusian Muslims turned to the Ottomans for help, and following the fall of Granada in 1492 the Barbary coast states also sought their protection against a Christian conquest.

In the face of hostile forces Bayezid consolidated the Empire which he had inherited from his father. He did the same internally by reorganizing the funding of military operations. Initially by increasing the number of horsemen which the Timar holders had to supply and then by imposing a special tax called Avariz, levied on all non-combatants as a contingency fund. These reforms had very positive results and the income of the Treasury was to double during his reign. On a personal level, as he grew older he was to become caught up in religion and mysticism, and increasingly left executive decisions to his Grand Vizier.

Once again the problem of succession arose. In 1511 Bayezid had five adult sons and therefore possible heirs. Two died and a third, very pious and educated was the favourite of the Ulemas, yet he showed little aptitude in military matters. This left the eldest, Ahmed, designated by his father to succeed him, and Selim who was a firebrand and much admired by the Janissaries. First of all the aspirants vied against each other for control of the provinces nearest to the capital. Then Selim led the Janissaries on several very rewarding incursions into Georgia and Persia. In April 1512 the Palace Janissaries forced Bayezid to abdicate in favour of Selim, whom they felt was the only one capable of defending the Empire against the threat of the Shiite Persians. Bayezid wished to withdraw to his birthplace Demotica, to end his days in meditation, but died from illness on the way, perhaps poisoned by Selim.

Selim I, unlike his father, straight away showed himself to be a warrior. The direction of the thrust of his short reign (1512–1520) was other than the Balkans and he is remembered as the conqueror of Syria and Egypt and ruler of Arabia. His accession was followed by the, by now usual, distribution of valuable "gifts" to the Janissaries who had put him on the throne. He then put his two brothers and their four children to death, thus earning himself the nickname of Yavus—the Terrible. Aware of the Persian threat he renewed agreements made by Bayezid with Venice and Hungary, and gave the Khan of the Crimean Tatars free rein to pillage Polish and Russian land. He was then able to concentrate on the Sefevids from Persia who since their rise in 1487, with Ismael I, had made Shiism the state religion and given it a militant form. Under its influence a worrying revolt had occurred in Ottoman Anatolia which had been suppressed by Bayezid's Grand Vizier with great difficulty. After a hard campaign Selim crushed Shah Ismael's army at Caldiran[6] and entered the capital Tabriz in 1514. The next year he subjugated all Kurdistan. Then in 1516 he turned on the Mameluks of Egypt and Syria. Aleppo, Homs and Damascus fell into Ottoman hands, soon followed by Ramallah, Ghaza, Nauplia and Jerusalem. The decisive encounter took place in January 1517 at the foot of Mount Mokattam on the Sinai-Nile road. The Mameluk Sultan was taken prisoner and was soon afterwards killed. In Cairo Selim I received the homage of the Mameluk emirs and the Sheik of Mecca who promised to read his name out during prayer—Khotba—thus recognizing him as defender of Islam's Holy cities—Mecca and Medina. Having returned to Istanbul, he was preparing an expedition against the Knights of Rhodes when he suddenly died on the 25 September 1520. In between his military campaigns he also found the time to expand his capital Istanbul and to transfer the remaining ministries from Edirne. Above all he built a new naval dockyard in the Kasimpasha district, the fore-bear of the present Arsenal, from which a new fleet emerged which was to assure Ottoman supremacy in the Mediterranean.

Suleyman I: Soliman the Magnificent—Arbiter of Europe, 1520–1566

The new sultan's accession to power took place without any difficulty. Selim had put three of his four sons to death for staging a revolt against him and had designated Suleyman his successor. He was twenty-four when he came to the throne and despite bad health stayed on the throne for forty-six years which earned him the nickname "Magnificent" in western Europe, whereas he is referred to as "Kanuni"—the law giver—by the Ottomans and held to be one of the greatest of rulers.

Following the now firmly established custom he distributed "baksheesh" on his accession and took immediate steps to win over those who had suffered from his father's policies. He allowed the last Abbass, Caliph al-Motawakil, who had been taken prisoner by Selim and locked up in the castle of the "Seven Towers," to return to Cairo. He also strove to curb corruption in the administration and in the courts hence the title "Kanuni." Yet he was soon involved in problems of international relations since the Ottoman Empire had become a key figure, not only in Asia but also in Europe. He himself led thirteen campaigns which follow a rhythm dictated by the military organization of the Empire; the Spahi needed to return home to raise the tithe and get supplies for winter. The army, with the Sultan at its head, would leave Istanbul in the spring and would return in the Mediterranean rainy season. The problem was how to make sure that in the same year they would not have to intervene in several conflicts in areas far apart from each other. This was the reason for Suleyman's preemptive wars which generally secured their objective, bearing in mind the difficulty and time it would take to reach other fronts. There was a maximum distance from the capital from which they could operate, so a campaign for example further than the Buda river would have been difficult.

The frontier along the Danube was the first to require his attention. For more than a hundred years the kingdom of Hungary had been the centre of all crusades against the Ottomans and the fortress of Buda was proudly known as the "Shield of Christianity." Yet since the death of Mathias Corvinus in 1490 the kingdom had experienced a serious social and political decline. The struggle for the succession resulted in a feudal "reaction" which ended with weak Ladislas Jagellon taking the throne while the barons controlled government. Furthermore there was an economic crisis partly due to price rises prompted by an influx of precious metals from South America which ended in what is known as the Dozsa revolt. This was closely associated with the anti-Ottoman crusade. Archbishop Esztergom hoping to distract the peasants' anger proclaimed a crusade which brought them streaming in the spring of 1514 into a field near Pest. There they were organized by a Captain from the border area Szekely Gyorgy who is known as "Dozsa." The barons fearful of this armed gathering cancelled the crusade. Outraged by this attitude and roused by the egalitarian sermons of the Franciscan monks, the would-be crusaders revolted. Led by Dozha they were to launch attacks on castles and massacre the nobility, but were crushed by the barons' armies near Temesvar. The ensuing repression was horrific. Dozsa, crowned with a red-hot iron crown, was burnt alive and thousands of peasants were hung (October 1514). Terrorized and henceforth subject to "bondage to the glebe in perpetuity" by order of the Diet, the Hungarian peasant masses, in the same way as their Serbian counterparts in the previous century, were open to the idea that the descendants of Hagar might be better than their lords and masters. A year later the king died and was replaced by his son Louis II Jagellon, a boy of ten. But the year before the young king had been allied to the Habsburgs by marriage; he was to marry Mary, sister of Archduke Ferdinand and of Charles the king of Spain. In 1519 Charles V was made Emperor, so Hungary had the support of this powerful empire "on which the sun never sets." In 1521 Suleyman preempted any form of action by absorbing the last remaining Christian enclaves to the south of the Sava such as Sabac, laid siege to Belgrade and took the Hungarian fortress on the 29 August. Some of the Serbian population were deported to Constantinople where they were to form the Beograd-Mahala quarter near the Gate bearing the same name. From now on the Sultan possessed the key to central Europe.

The next year he took another Christian stronghold, Rhodes. The Knights of Saint John since 1309 had made it into a formidable bastion out of which its fleet set sail to attack infidel ships all over the eastern Mediterranean. Already on two occasions, in 1444 and 1480 the mameluk Sultan of Egypt and Mehmed II had tried to destroy what they considered to be nothing more than a pirate base but without success. Backed by the fleet his father had built, Suleyman returned in June 1552 at the head, according to Christian lore, of an armada of 100,000 men. In fact the Grand Vizier led a fleet of 300 galleys transporting some 9,000 men, while the Sultan at the head of a large army made the journey by land to Marmaris from which he crossed over to the island. The Grand Master, the Frenchman Villiers de l'Ile-Adam, had appealed unsuccessfully to the western Christian kings and had only managed to muster 4,500 men on top of his 650 knights. The siege began on the 1 August and was to last until December 1522, punctuated by violent encounters, acts of bravery and of betrayal such as that of Amaral the Grand Prior of Castilla. Suleyman proposed an honourable surrender: the Knights could withdraw with their belongings, the churches would be respected and the right of the Greek Orthodox population to Christian worship guaranteed. They would also be exempted from paying taxes for five years. The agreement was signed on the 22 December. Hammer, the expert on the Ottoman Empire, relates how on the 1 January 1523 the Grand Master took his leave of the victor, kissing his hand and presenting him with four gold vases. Then he left by boat with the 200 surviving knights and some 4,000 Christians to find refuge in the Pontifical states until Charles V established the Hospitaller order in Malta in 1530. Rhodes and the surrounding islands were made into a Sandjak from which all Latins were expelled whilst the Greek Orthodox and Jewish inhabitants stayed put.

Since 1515 the Christian kingdoms had been split by the rivalry of the kings of France and the Habsburgs. The election of Charles of Habsburg, king of Spain, to the office of Emperor of the Holy Roman Empire in 1519 was a clear illustration of this and at the same time was to make him the nominal head of Christendom. Also in October 1517 in Wittenberg Luther nailed the famous 95 theses which signalled the start of the Reformation: the second renting of Christ's gown after the schism of the eastern church in 1054. This combination of religious unrest and political dynastic rivalry would mean the end of the idea of crusade in the 14th century Europe. The fall of Belgrade followed by that of Rhodes produced no reaction from the Christian side—Venice even went as far as to congratulate Suleyman for his victory over the Hospitallers, who in fact had been fierce rivals with Venice. The Pope was part of the League of Cognac which had France, Venice and Milan in an alliance against Charles V. At the same time Luther declared that to fight against the Turks was to avoid God's judgement on mankind for its sins. As for Hungary which was on the front line, it was being torn apart by the struggle between the Bathory and Zapolyai families and by an armed uprising of workers from the copper mines at Neusohl in Slovakia; this was brutally suppressed in the spring of 1526.

Suleyman felt that the time was right and in April 1526 he left Istanbul at the head of an army of 80,000 men, passing through his most recent conquest Belgrade, captured the fortress of Peterwardein[7] and continued along the right bank of the Danube to Buda. King Louis II had great trouble mustering troops from his barons and the comitats because many of the smaller feudal lords had preferred to answer the call of John Zapolyai, leader of the faction opposed to the Habsburgs. Zapolyai had gathered his own army in the north east of the country. He denounced foreign and Catholic influence which was being forced on the king to the detriment of the Hungarian nobility's "rights," especially religious freedom. In the end the royal army, under the command of a seasoned and famous soldier Archbishop Kalocsa, confronted the invader without the support of John Zapolyai's troops. The encounter between 28,000 Hungarian and 45,000 Ottoman men took place in the flooded plain of the Danube, near the village of Mohacs on the 29 August 1526. The Christians were caught unawares by a quick manoeuvre of Suleyman protected by an elevated ridge and, after regrouping, the Hungarians launched a frontal attack which was repulsed by cannon and musket shots from the Janissaries. The withdrawal became a full-scale rout and Louis II drowned when his horse dragged him into a stream. He was just twenty years old. With him perished a large proportion of his barons and clergy as well as at least half of his army since the Ottomans as usual did not take any prisoners. Mohacs became for the Hungarians what Kosovo Polje had been for the Serbs one and a half centuries before.

The road to Buda was open. Ten days later Suleyman entered unopposed and set fire to the ancient fortress which had called itself the "Shield of Christianity." Suleyman only remained there two weeks before going back to Istanbul. There has been much conjecture over why he did this, for why did he not then press on to Vienna which was within easy reach? No doubt there were primarily tactical reasons. Three hundred miles away from

Belgrade which was its last logistical base, the Ottoman army was clearly in a dangerous position. Furthermore there remained, in the north east of the country, Zapolyai's army, estimated at 40,000 men. Also Setevid propaganda was bearing fruit in Anatolia for in August 1526 revolts had broken out in Cilicia and in the north. The Sultan had to keep an eye on the eastern border. Above all Suleyman did not want to annex Hungary just at that moment into the Empire. He intended to make Hungary a vassal state in the same way as Wallachia and Moldavia, to act as a buffer zone between the Empire of the Faithful—Dar el Islam—(of which Suleyman was undisputed leader) and the Christian Empire—Holy Roman Empire—over which Charles V, head of the house of Habsburg, was endeavouring to gain control. Suleyman therefore headed back to his capital.

The Sultan left behind him a chaotic situation. The Hungaro-Bohemian branch of the Jagellons had ended with the death of Louis II. Since 1515 it had been agreed that if this line were to die out then the crown of Bohemia and Hungary would pass to the Habsburg family. Yet the Hungarian nobility rejected this "German King" and pushed for John Zapolyai. He was therefore elected king by his supporters who had gathered in an unlawful but well attended Diet on the 11 November 1527 at Stuhlweissenburg[8] The Habsburgs took their time to react. The leader of the court faction, Istvan Bathory of the Palatinate and the king's widow, Mary of Habsburg, called a sparsely attended but legal Diet at Pressburg, which appointed Ferdinand I of Habsburg, brother-in-law of the deceased king and brother of Charles V. So Hungary had two kings, but Ferdinand had in fact taken advantage of the delay and occupied most of the north of the country, so Zapolyai was forced to seek asylum at the Polish court. There he made contact with an envoy of Francis I, king of France, who advised him to appeal to the Sultan. The latter was embroiled with further unrest in Anatolia, yet in February 1529 an agreement was reached whereby Zapolyai was promised the throne of Saint Stephan as an Ottoman vassal, similar to the voevods of Moldavia and Wallachia. In May, Suleyman himself at the head of the army took the same route as in 1526 and was met by Zapolyai who brought with him a large contingent of cavalry and pledged his allegiance to the Sultan on the very field of battle. Suleyman easily recaptured Buda and continued to march towards Vienna with the intention of bringing down the Habsburgs. This was the first siege of Vienna. Ferdinand had appealed to his brother the Emperor for help, but due to the conflict with Francis I and the German Protestant Princes, he had only been able to respond with a small number of reinforcements: several thousand men from the formidable Spanish infantry together with a small contingent of troops of the Holy Roman Empire (since this time Luther had come out in favour of armed struggle against the Infidel). Twenty thousand men in all defended the town, under the command of General N von Salm. The siege began later than expected, on the 18 September 1529, and was immediately hampered by diluvian rains which soaked the earth and denied the Sultan use of his huge bombards. The lighter cannon proved useless against the city walls so they concentrated on tunnelling to undermine them and on infantry attacks. When the countryside around Vienna was totally exhausted the Ottoman troops launched raids reaching as far as Ratisbonn in Bavaria and Brno in Bohemia, and causing panic all over the Christian world. But these efforts did not bring victory and faced with mounting discontent amongst his troops, Suleyman made the decision to withdraw on the 14 October. Vienna remained intact.

This failure clearly showed that the Ottoman army had reached the furthest limits of its offensive power in the West and had found itself pitted against halberdier infantry equal to the Janissaries. As for Ferdinand he was unable to reconquer Hungary which was clearly illustrated by his failure to recapture Buda in 1530. The Sultan however, intent on wiping out the humiliation of his failure to occupy Vienna, embarked in 1532 on what historians have called the third Hungarian expedition. The "Magnificent" dreamed not only of destroying the house of Habsburg but also the Holy Roman Empire and establishing himself as the supreme ruler of the world. He gathered a huge army—believed to be about 300,000—but instead of marching on Vienna he tried to join battle with the Habsburg army but the latter continually refused to do so. The countryside was devastated but the fortresses continued to hold out and above all the fortress of Guns[9]. As the season was nearing its end the Sultan left his troops pillaging Styrian and Croatian territory and returned to Istanbul. Preoccupied by the situation in Persia the Sultan tried to broker terms on the Danube.

Agreement between Suleyman and Ferdinand was reached on the 22 June 1533 with Poland acting as mediator. For the first time ever, a Habsburg had negotiated with the Infidel. Ferdinand recognized the Sultan as a "father and suzerain" to whom he pledged his allegiance and tribute for that part of Hungary which he had retained following the battle of Mohacs. He also renounced his claim over the totality of Saint Stephan's kingdom and left the title of king to J. Zapolyai. It is worth mentioning that this agreement was never ratified by Emperor Charles V who continued to be at war with the Ottomans. However Hungary no longer existed as a regional power. The western third, arching up from the Adriatic coast to upper Tisza remained under Ferdinand and was called Royal Hungary and the rest was given to Zapolyai who was the sultan's vassal although it was to be continually overrun by Ottoman raiding parties and Habsburg mercenaries. This situation was to continue up until the death of the vassal king in 1540. Two years prior an agreement was reached between the two Christian rivals whereby the Habsburgs would recover the Crown of Saint Stephan after the death of the present holder John and the Zapolyai family would retain the Duchy of Transylvania. But their supporters refused to countenance this and proclaimed John Sigismond's son king. He then moved to the fortress of Buda. Ferdinand of Habsburg immediately besieged it and in 1541 Suleyman, at the behest of his vassal, returned with an army and lifted the siege. This time the Sultan wanted to leave his northern frontier with a solid organization. He retained Buda which became the residence of a Pasha and was called the "Shield of Islam," made an Elayet of the central plain and sub-divided this up into Sandjaks as everywhere else in the Empire. John Sigismond's son only retained the territories to the east of the Tisza—Transylvania and its border areas—and the title of king but was to pay a heavy tribute for the "protection" the Sultan provided. As for Ferdinand, who since 1531 had become King of Rome—in other words the Emperor's[10] successor, he also had to pay a large tribute for "Royal Hungary." So Hungary was divided into three parts and the heart of Europe for 150 years became a part of the Ottoman Empire. Buda was added to the roll of infidel towns together with Baghdad, Jerusalem and Cairo.

In Hungary the border between Dar el Islam and Christian lands was defined by a system of double fortifications with, on the Habsburg side a string of fortified villages linked by earth works, defended by mercenaries and military settlers. Later, strong fortresses were built around lake Balaton and a large zone under the direct authority of Vienna became known as the "military border"—Militargrenze[11] On the Ottoman side the frontier was divided up into Sandjaks under the military and administrative control of a Beg; troops were supplied by the holders of Timars but, in contrast to the regions of the mothercountry, the majority of Spahis lived in the cities of Buda, Temesvar and Gran[12] and entrusted the administration of their lands to mercenaries or former Janissaries. In the remainder of the Hungarian plain the nobles' lands were allotted to the Spahis in the form of Timars but the Berats which created them generally retained the old peasant dues—yet without the statutory labour—, allowed a fair amount of administrative autonomy in the villages and total religious freedom. The royal towns were to retain their autonomy but were forced to pay a tribute to the Sultan.

Suleyman did not have the time completely to reorganize his newly conquered lands since the war with Charles V was continuing and the western Mediterranean had become the area of theatre of action with confrontation between the Barbary and Habsburg fleets. Since 1502 Muslim pirates occupied La Goulette (the port of Tunis) and in 1616 Khaireddin, known to Christians as Barbarossa, captured Algiers and pledged vassalage to the Sultan. In 1533 Suleyman created the Beylerbeylik of Algiers and entrusted it to Khaireddin together with the title of Kapudan i Derya—Grand Admiral. He became the Muslim champion against the Genovese Admiral, Andrea Doria, in the service of Charles V and the Holy League. It was in this context that in February 1536 a trade agreement—later known as the "Capitulation"—was signed between the Sultan and Francis I. In fact it was a similar arrangement to those agreed with Venice and Genoa and which allowed the French king's subjects free trade with the Ottoman Empire, under the supervision of a "Consul" residing in Istanbul. This agreement allowed Francis I, in 1543, to ask Barbarossa for help in besieging Nice, which then belonged to Savoy, an ally of Charles V. The emphasis changed from commercial to political and there was an outcry from Catholic Europe. As a result of Khaireddin's victories—especially that of Prevesa[13] in September 1538—the Aegean and Ionian Seas had become Ottoman waters and it is significant that about the same period another of the Sultan's fleets drove the Portuguese from the Red Sea, occupied Eden and pushed on as far as India.

War soon started up again on the Danube. Under Habsburg pressure, Petru Rares, the son of Stephan the Great and the prince of Moldavia, refused to pay his tribute and so in 1538 Suleyman directed his eighth campaign against him. He pillaged the main towns of Moldavia and occupied Iassy where he later transferred the capital. The Voevod was removed from his throne and southern Bessarabia was annexed to the Empire. The Sultan organized this area into a Raia, in other words a military zone, from Tighina to Bugeac, cutting Moldavia off from the Black Sea. In 1542 he did the same to Wallachia, annexing the region round Braila, which denied the principality access to the mouth of the Danube. From now on the whole of the Black Sea coastline, from the Bosphorus to the mouth of the Danube, was part of the Sultan's Empire. In 1542 Ferdinand, reconciled with the German Protestant princes, tried to launch a further crusade. Forewarned by Francis I, Suleyman was able to send reinforcements to Buda and counterattacked. This was his fifth Hungarian campaign in 1544 and led to the annexation of Gran and Stuhlweissenburg (Fehervar) and after three years of border skirmishes finally to peace in February 1547: Ferdinand retained his Hungarian possessions in return for a payment of 30,000 golden ducats; the two signatories pledged themselves to end further raids by either side and Habsburg traders were given trading privileges within the Ottoman Empire. Francis I died just after this agreement and peace in the Danube area would ensue for the next five years.

Suleyman concentrated during this lull on a massive campaign against the Persians which took him as far as Tabriz whilst his Grand Vizier advanced into Georgia. But a further military expedition in 1555 would be needed before there was peace on the eastern border of the Empire.

By then war had broken out once more with Ferdinand over Transylvania, occupied by the Habsburg army in 1551. Suleyman gave control of operations to the Beylerbey of Rumelia, Mehmed Sokoli—a Slav from Bosnia who's real name was Sokolovich. After two campaigns in 1551 and 1552 he had captured Temesvar which became the seat of a Vilayet, and had besieged Erlau[14] which was heroically defended by Dobo Istvan. On the Sultan's orders the Transylvanian diet reinstated Zapolyai and Ferdinand renounced his claim to the region yet had to continue to pay his tribute. After ten years of sporadic hostilities a new peace treaty was signed in 1562. Two years later however, Ferdinand I died and his successor,

Emperor Maximillian of Habsburg, rejected the two clauses of the agreement. Suleyman, now an old man of 70, embarked on another campaign, his thirteenth, which was to be his last. The Ottoman army went from Belgrade up the Sava river and besieged the border stronghold, Szeged[15]. Defended by a Croat nobleman called Zrinyi Miklos it was reduced to dust by Ottoman artillery and captured on the 8 September after a last ditch stand by the garrison who fought to the last. But two days before, during the night of the 5 and 6 September 1566, Soliman the Magnificent died following a short illness. Thus, the Sultan who had made the Ottoman Empire the greatest power in Europe and arbiter of the rivalry between the Habsburgs and France, was to die on Christian soil. In Asia against the Persians he had become master of Mesopotamia and the Persian Gulf, of Armenia and some of Georgia. Finally in Africa he had extended his suzerainty from the frontiers of Egypt to the Straits of Gibraltar in the form of regencies in Tunis and Algiers. Indeed he had accomplished his dream of an Empire spanning the globe.

The Ottoman State: Power and Institutions

In the three and a half centuries that separate the start of the reign of Osman and the death of Soliman the Magnificent, the Ottoman state had obviously undergone some fundamental changes: from Ghazi Emirate on the periphery of the Muslim world, to undisputed superpower. An Empire had arisen out of a Seldjuk frontier Beylik. Mahomet II had felt he was the successor of Byzantium and Suleyman denied Charles V his imperial title because, according to him, there could only be one Emperor in the world. These Romano-Christian pretensions, product of Phanariotic thought in Istanbul, did not alter the fundamental concept of Osman. The state which he had created was destined to the defence and expansion of Islam—Dar el Islam. Therefore it was based on religious law—Sharia—and the strict enforcement of it was its very purpose. Only believers—Moslem—were allowed to become full members of society, whereas non Muslims who lived within the Empire were protegees—Zimmi[16]—whose status was markedly inferior. By law the Zimmi only existed by the grace of the conqueror who could put them to death if he so wished. This idea is borne out by the payment of a bounty—Djizya—a tax which buys back lives. Naturally they could not aspire to political or administrative office within a society whose laws they did not follow. Conversion to Islam was the sole way of overcoming this problem. This Islamic way of seeing the society had been taken, in the case of the Ottomans, from older traditions, inherited both from the Persian Sassanides and the Turco-Mongols of Central Asia who considered the Prince the shepherd of his troop—Reaya; a shepherd, guide and defender whose first task was to render justice, but also owner of the herd over which he would had absolute authority. From this stems a second fundamental division, not of a religious but a social kind: on the one hand the leader and on the other the Reaya, who pay for his protection with taxes. Since the governing powers were a product of the Jihad, Ottoman society was organized into two strata: the military class and the herd, separated by a barrier which only the Sultan's favour might overcome. By its very structures the Ottoman system threw up a double antagonism, as clearly defined by Tursun Bey, the chronicler of the 14th century: "Government based only on reason is called the Sultan's Law, whilst government, based on principles of happiness in this world and the next, is called holy law or Seriat. The Prophet preached the Seriat but only the authority of the sovereign can apply its principles. Without a ruler Man can not live in harmony and risks dying out. God gave authority to one sole person, who needs absolute obedience to maintain a just order."[17]

The Sultan therefore was not so much the highest point of a socio-political pyramid than the very heart of the system, alone able to give it a dynamic cohesion. It has been quite rightly pointed out that a change of dynasty in France or England did not result in a collapse of the kingdom, yet without the line of Osman there would not have been an Ottoman Empire[18] for six centuries this family was to provide thirty-six rulers. Yet the history of its most successful period, up to the death of Suleyman, shows how unable it was to sort out its most serious problem, the question of succession to the throne, which was very different from the process of succession of, for instance, the kings of France. Apart from two occasions, every time there was a change of sovereign it took place amid death and civil war. Islamic tradition merely made provision for the sovereign to be an adult male, of sound mind yet his accession to the throne was in the hands of God. Suleyman held it against his son Bayezid, who had plotted to usurp the throne, for not trusting in divine providence and told him before he put him to death: "If God had decided to give you the kingdom after me then no man alive could have got in the way." Yet it is clear that since 1421 the Janissaries in the capital city had become the decisive factor to accede to the throne, while the practice of fratricide, which Mehmed II legalized, got rid of the remaining competition. From the 16th century till the end of the 17th century, sixty princes of the Osman line were killed in this way on the orders of their relatives who had risen to power.

Having become the sole candidate the postulant would command that his name to included in the sermon—Hutba—during Friday prayers in all the mosques. Seated on the throne in front of the "Door of Happiness"[19] he would accept the tribute from the dignitaries and Ulemas who, kneeling in front of him would pledge their oath of allegiance—Biat—to him. The Sultan was then considered to be legally enthroned. In this way they asserted the dual nature of his role as the religious leader of Islam and the sovereign of the Empire. There has been much discussion over the title of "Supreme Caliph" which Suleyman and his successors adopted and Selim who had captured Motawakhil (the last Abbass holder of the title) and kept him prisoner in Egypt, is considered the first Ottoman Sultan to have invested himself with the Caliphate. It would seem however that, first of all Motawakhil did not actually leave the prerogative to his jailer and after the death of the latter, he returned to Cairo and continued to use his title. Also according to Sunni tradition the Caliph needed to be related to the Prophet which was not the Ottoman case and nor did the hagiographers-chroniclers try to establish this. In reality the Caliphate had disappeared in the 8th century and the avatar of Mameluk Egypt merely had nominal prestige. The Ottomans, as the greatest Muslim sovereigns added this to their list of titles without it giving him any additional power. The offices of "Protector of Mecca and Medina, and guardian of the pilgrim routes," to which they were entitled following the conquests of 1517 were in reality much more important. Whatever the case the Ottoman Sultan was recognized by the Sunni princes as the "Protector of Islam," in other words its supreme leader. Consequently he had to follow and promote Islamic law—Sharia or Koranic law—even though it limited his own power. The Ulemas and especially their leader the Sheik ul Islam were meant to make sure that the actions and conduct of the Sultan complied with the law. This was indeed the case when Bayezid asked the Ulemas for a justifying Fetwa to fight the Turcoman Emirs, and more dramatically in the 17th century when Ibrahim I was deposed and condemned to death by the Sheik ul Islam for not respecting the law. On the other hand the Sultan had unlimited power to organize everything that was not covered by Sharia law, which he did by issuing "Kanuns" to be applied everywhere in the empire or else limited to certain regions and known as "Ferman" or "Firmans." Suleyman was held in high esteem by his subjects for bringing these together into legal codes—Kanunname.

On the executive side the Sultan's power was even more absolute as it relied on a system which was quite unique: the Kapi Kulari called the "Slaves of the Porte." As has been mentioned above it developed from the Pencik (the right of the Sultan to keep a fifth of the prisoners of war as slaves) then was extended by Murad who instituted Devsirme whereby male children of Christian peasants aged 8 to 20 years old were made into slaves, originally used for the Janissary corps, then for palace duties and finally even in government. Also there was the purchase of slaves by the Sultan in specialized markets in Istanbul and Izmir. The internal history of the 15th century empire was dominated by the bloody struggles between the traditional old Turcoman families, in power since the inception of the regime and neo-Muslims over whom the Sultan had absolute power and precisely because of this he could delegate some of his power to them. The victory of the Kapi Kulari was a triumph of absolutism, in the same way as the triumph of the middle classes was a result of Louis XIV's absolutism. The Devsirme system lasted for almost three centuries, the last levy taking place in 1637. It provided the Empire with two to three thousand slaves per year, which was a very small number in comparison to the amount of slaves captured in raids by land and at sea and sold in the marketplace. Emphasized by the Romantics in the 19th century, this should not obscure the reality of the situation. On the one hand this occurred in a society where slavery was part of everyday life and secondly it above all gave its victims a chance of survival, at a time where people were very much like Tom Thumb's parents, together with the possibility of a career which could lead to riches and the highest honours. Yet for uneducated peasants, in this period of religious fervour, there would also have been the horror of apostasy and the fear of everlasting damnation. Whatever the case the young Kapi Kulari, taken mostly from the Balkans, were sent to Anatolia to the Begs' estates where they were Islamicized, learning Turkish, the Koran and Ottoman customs. Afterwards depending on their abilities, good Muslims, they would become soldiers either in Anatolia or else in Istanbul. Out of those who left Anatolia, the most gifted or most handsome would go as servants to the emperor's palaces and above all the Seraglio in Istanbul. They were pages—Icoglani—who with the backing of the Sultan or a vizier, or even a sultana could rise to the highest offices of state. It has been calculated that between 1453 and 1623, of the forty-seven Grand Viziers, thirty-seven were of Christian origin and almost all products of Devsirme[20]. This indeed was a well known paradox, that an Empire based on one religion should be led by slaves who at birth were not Muslim. This resulted in the following: the Ottoman system did not produce a noble class since public office was the sole domain of the Sultan's will and not a birthright. Devsirme resulted in the creation of a social strata which was divorced from its ethnic origins (with a few exceptions) and bound solely to the sovereign. These were the real Ottomans, in the same way as in the future the Habsburg administrators were considered the only true Austrians.

The whole system from top to bottom was directed to the sons of Osman who lived in their palace in Istanbul—Yeni Sarayi—and proximity to them determined the importance of a person. The palace was divided into two parts: the interior—Enderum—where the sultan enjoyed a private life with his harem, and the outside—Birun—to which it was joined by the "Gate of Happiness" and which was the centre of public affairs. In front of this Gate stood the Sultan's throne on which he would receive the high ranking officials of the Empire and foreign ambassadors. It was adjacent to this, in a domed room, that the Council met, hence the expression "Sublime Porte," by which foreigners used to refer to the government.

The Divan—i Humayun—denoted the council of heads of the main departments of state with the Sultan: the Grand Vizier for political affairs, the military and general administrators, the Nishanji—the council secretary—responsible for the Chancellery, the Kadishker from Anatolia and Rumeli who were the highest ranking people in the judiciary, the Defterdar who was in charge of the treasury and the Kapudan Pasha who was the Lord Admiral of the fleet. Mehmed II chaired this daily meeting; Suleyman made do with four meetings per week and often allowed the Grand Vizier to preside over it thus making him the highest-ranking official of the administration. As from the 17th century the Sultans no longer attended the Divan but western travellers would recount that since 1475, when Mehmed was an old man and stopped attending the meeting, the sovereign would stay behind a hidden window and listen to the deliberations of his advisers without being seen. As well as the general affairs of the Empire, the Divan would receive petitions from his subjects and was to become a sort of supreme court. This was the assize of last resort for the Reaya—Christian and Muslim alike—when in conflict with the local Kadi. The Sultan gladly intervened in this type of situation since it was felt that meting out justice was his most important duty. The annals of the history of the Empire are full of more or less edifying examples of the sovereign listening to the complaints of his subjects, against the wishes of his advisers. (Saint Louis' oak tree existed in different climes and in a different form.) They also discussed foreign policy, of war and peace; the appointment of governors in the provinces, of army commanders and local judges. All the measures taken by the council had to be approved by the Sultan before they could be promulgated in the form of a Kanun, or a Berat for an individual certificate, onto which the Nishanji affixed the Tugra which was the Prince's seal which he would then approve. These six high ranking officials were answerable only to the Sultan but could only use their judicial powers over civil matters. The most powerful slaves (for they were still slaves) made their way into the seraglio passing by what today is still known as the "Fountain of the Hangman," and the "Stone of Forewarning" which served as a block to chop off the heads of high-ranking officials who had lost the sovereign's favour: quite a number of favourites, Viziers and Grand Viziers left there heads there having learned of their misfortune on entering the palace by the Urtakapi—the Middle Gate.

The Grand Vizier—Vezir i Azam or Sadrazam—held the sovereign's seal which invested him with similar powers to his master. Under Suleyman he was given a yearly salary of 1,800,000 akshe[21] as well as "appointment dues" and various forms of Baksheesh, and as of 1570 an income from the island of Cyprus. He was a very rich man who had a palace, with a household similar to that of his master and was very conscious of his prerogatives. Several French ambassadors had their meeting complicated by the questions of precedence. Yet if he fell from favour he lost all his wealth which would go to the Imperial coffers, as well as his life. The Defterdar was in charge of accounts; under Selim there were three: one for Rumelia, Anatolia and Syria, yet the first had overall authority and title of Chief Treasurer—Bash Defterdar. He would have charge of all state finances and received petitions dealing with this. However he was not privy to the Sultan's treasure which was meant to cover the expenses of the Seraglio. All these high-ranking officials had under them a vast bureaucracy: the Grand Vizier had a dozen Viziers under him, called "Viziers of the Cupola" since they could be called on to attend the Divan depending on what matters they were dealing with at the time. The Nishanji had under him dozens of scribes and editors. The Bash Defterdar had 2–300 accountants under him. They were all in principle "Slaves of the Porte" but in reality they were made up of factions, often linked by family ties, and certain posts became virtually hereditary.

The Grand Vizier was also the head of the army and several had got to their high position because of their military abilities. If above all the Sultan was leader of the Jihad, as had been the case until Suleyman, from the 17th century onwards the sovereign no longer led his troops into battle. The Ottoman army consisted of two parts: the Kapi Kulari contingents and the provincial contingents[22]. A standing army was made up of the former and was paid for by the Treasury. As their name suggests they were all slaves and had come mainly from the Devsirme. The main body of men were the Janissaries who were professional footsoldiers who had to remain celibate, lived in barracks and were subjected to continuous training. Their size had increased greatly since Okhran first formed them in 1330 and under Suleyman their numbers varied from between 40,000 and 60,000. Pious Muslims, influenced by the mystic Bektasi sect, they formed the backbone of the Sultan's army and were the architects of such great victories as Mohacs. In Istanbul they guarded the palace and policed the town, and their commander the "Aga" was one of the most powerful state official. There was also an artillery corps of about 2,000 specialists, which had been formed by Murad II, and dealt with the casting, transport and firing of their pieces. They were based in the capital and in the Empire's strongholds. It is clear that artillery, as well as the Janissaries was at the base of Ottoman military superiority, yet this advantage would progressively disappear. The engineer and sapper corps were in support. The cavalry was made up of Spahi from the provinces as well as Spahi Kapikulu—the Porte's Spahi. They were also from the Devsirme and were chosen for their physical attributes. Like the Janissaries they were given a salary but slightly higher since in Istanbul they were the Sultan's guard of Honour. They were also present in most large towns and during Suleyman's reign totalled about 6,000 men and for a long time were to retain traditional weapons such as bows and arrows, scimitars, lances and axes. It is worth mentioning that the irregulars—Akinji—, who played such an important part in the conquest, in fact were to disappear after Suleyman, and had never been recruited in the capital itself.

Through the Divan and the high-ranking officials who sat on it, the Sultan was able to control government, justice, finances, the army and the navy. Yet one area was partially outside his control, notwithstanding his title of "Supreme Caliph," and that was religion. In contrast to the Byzantine Empire, the Ottoman Empire did not have a clergy distinct from the rest of its subjects. Instead there were Ulemas[23], their very title defining their nature, who were graduates of the Koranic schools. Unlike the Kapi Kulari these were Muslims by birth, free Turks or Arabs, who formed a judicial-religious hierarchy dealing with the application and enforcement of Sharia law. At the top of this hierarchy was the Sheikh ul Islam[24] who was the highest authority of Koranic law. Appointed by the Sultan, he was not a member of government but his influence on government was considerable. In many disagreements with the Grand Vizier a Fetwa—a written judgement—from the Sheikh ul Islam was all that was needed for the Sultan to ignore his prime adviser. He alone could legally topple the Sultan by accusing him of disrespect to Sharia law. He would adjudicate on appeal decisions made by the Kadiaster and through this he controlled the Kadis of the provinces. He was the ultimate authority of the Mufti who interprets the law and the teachers of Medresses—muderri—who taught the novices. In the face of the Sultan's absolutism the Sheikh ul Islam, who is sometimes compared to the president of the Supreme court of America, defined the principles of Koranic law.

It was the synthesis of these two powers that was to characterize the Ottoman empire at its height.

Notes

1. The Venetian golden ducat weighed 3.56 grams, which gives a tribute of 712 kg of gold.
2. Sibinj = Sibiu a town in Transylvania. His family were Romanian from Huneodara 60 miles from Sibiu hence the Serbian name: John of Sibiu.
3. Sudak and Teodosia in present day Crimea; Moncastro became Akkerman under the Ottomans , then Cetatea Alba under the Romanians and since 1941 Belgorod-Dnestrovski in the S.F.R. of Moldavia.
4. Masters of Egypt since 1250.
5. Near Chernovtzy (Cernauti)
6. 50 miles from Ercis on the northern shore of Lake Van.
7. Now Petrovaradin on the right bank of the Danube opposite Novi Sad.
8. Now Szekes: Fehervar on the outermost northern side of Lake Balaton.
9. Koszeg which is 60 miles south east of Vienna
10. Which he was to become in 1556 after the abdication of his brother Charles V.
11. The last sector facing Bosnia was dismantled in 1878–81.
12. Now Esztergom.
13. On the Greek coast to the south of Corfu.
14. Eger in Hungary.
15. Szigetvar in Hungary to the west of Pecs.
16. Also written as dhimmi.
17. Quote from Inalcik: The Ottoman Empire see above. p. 88.
18. In a way similar to the Japanese structure.
19. Now between the second and third courtyard of the Palace.
20. Stavrianos: The Balkans since 1453 op. cit. p.85: gives the following analysis: 17 Albanians, 11 southern Slavs, 6 Greeks, 1 Caucasian, 1 Armenian, 1 Georgian and 1 Italian. The last four were from a slave market.
21. The aksh was a Turkish coin which initially weighed 3.2 grammes and was 90% silver. A Venetian ducat was worth 120 aksh.
22. They will be looked at more closely in Chapter 5.
23. Ulem, which in Arabic is olem, means "wise man."
24. Often written as Sheik el Islam.

5

The Balkans Under Ottoman Domination

So far this account of the Ottoman conquest of the Balkans has sketched a picture of periods of violent expansion followed by periods of further but less brutal expansion, in contrast to the days of Ghengis Khan or Tamerlaine when whole peoples were wiped out. Of course Christian states were dismantled, the nobility decimated in battle, the population terrorized and the land sacked, yet the Balkans did remain Balkan and the Ottoman Empire acquired Christian peoples who for a thousand years had been influenced by Byzantium. However, the conquerors brought with them a different administrative, social and cultural system which was a product of its Turcoman and Irano-Arabic heritage. The dialectical relations between these two models was to continue for almost five centuries and was to give the Peninsula its unique characteristic which is Balkan.

The Inhabitants: Christians and Muslims

The continued survival of ethno-linguistic groups such as Greeks, Albanians, Romanians, Bulgarians and Serbians in the period prior to the Ottoman conquest has already been emphasized and this remained true even after Turkish rule. It has also been noted that there would be further migrations during the centuries of Ottoman rule; of Turcomans, Circassians, Tatars, Armenians, Gipsies and Jews therefore it would be far too simplistic to portray, as was the tendency of nationalist historians of the 19th century, ethnic stability to justify inviolate modern frontiers. The Ottoman conquest weakened these groups. Colonizing and wholesale relocation of inhabitants was part of the Sultans' policy and commerce on the edges of an Empire which spanned three continents would naturally lead to the movement of people.

The best known example is Constantinople. After the capture of the town the surviving Greek population was forced into slavery and deported. Mehmed II replaced them with Turks from Anatolia but also with Greek and Slav Christians from the Balkan regions already under Ottoman control. Later came Greeks from the islands, Armenians from Asia Minor and Jews from Salonika. This was a voluntary process since the Fatih wanted to make Constantinople the capital of his empire and supplant Cairo, which belonged to the Mameluks, as the main centre of the Muslim world. When Fatih died, Istanbul had approximately 200,000 inhabitants. His successors were to continue this policy. Bayezid II settled Wallachians in the neighbourhood of the Silivri Gate, Selim I brought craftsmen from the Caucasus who were renowned for their pottery, Soliman the Magnificent settled Serbs from Belgrade, in addition to the mainly voluntary influx of peasants escaping land duties and craftsmen, seafarers and adventurers drawn to the capital by the opportunities of work for the seraglio, the variety of opportunity and the welfare charitable institutions. Which is why by Suleyman's reign the population had increased to 400,000 inhabitants. A similar pattern of change can be seen in most of the Balkan towns: Thessalonika was repopulated by Turks, Greeks and above all Jews; the Aszkenazi Jews from Bavaria who in 1470 fled from the German principalities were joined at the end of the century by the Sephardic Jews expelled from Spain, Sicily, southern Italy, Portugal and Provence. The peasants in great numbers had fled from the sultan's armies into the hinterland as they would have from any army, even a friendly army such as the Catalans of Roger de Flor—an ally of the Basileus who for two whole years had ravaged Thrace. It was the same picture everywhere: the villagers, their popes at the front leading with reliquaries and icons, would withdraw to the forests and mountains and return to what was left of the village once the armies had left. In Wallachia they even had special carts in which the peasants would keep the necessary food and tools to survive, with a double shaft at the front and the back so that they could harness up without moving the vehicle in case it was too difficult to turn around. The Carpathian forests were the great protector of the Romanian peasants. Folk songs up until modern times are full of the feats of the "Hajduks" of the Stara Planina, Rhodope and Sumadja and the "Klephtes" of Olympus, Epirus and Achea. The mountain as a safe haven has an essential place in Mediterranean history although these desperate flights did result in many deaths. Exposure, exhaustion and malnutrition took a heavy toll on children, old people and pregnant women. It is not surprising then that whole regions were depopulated by repeated military action. Modern Greek historians have calculated that by the end of the 15th century 40% of the villages of the Peloponnese had been abandoned, yet the Turkish invasion had merely been the closing chapter of half a century of fratricidal conflict between the despots of Morea, the princes of Achea and Venetian mercenaries. Once peace had been restored the Ottomans implemented policies to repopulate the areas, for example settling Yuruk and Koniar[1] Turks in the Macedonian plains to farm the land or like eastern Thrace where for military and strategic reasons Turcomans were settled in and around Edirne, the new capital; in certain border areas such as the Dobrudja and on the Bulgarian coast where the Sultan needed to be sure of the firm support of the population, hence Muslims. Initiated from the very start of the conquest these movements of people would continue right until the 19th century. If we add the transhumance of nomadic Wallachian and Tsintsar breeders, plagues and epidemics, malaria infested areas and their depopulation, earthquakes and the resulting exodus, there emerges an idea of dynamic movement rather than settled inward-looking ethnic groups; a perpetually moving kaleidoscope of very many parts oscillating about relatively stationary centres: Romanians to the north of the Danube and Bulgarians, Serbs, Albanians and Greeks to the south.

This praetor-national ethnic idea was not shared by the Ottomans who as followers of the prophet saw their subjects as either Muslim—believers—or Zimmi—protected people, ie. non-Muslims who lived in the Empire but respected its laws. Yet these were based on the Sharia which was alien to non-believers. Therefore there developed the Millet system[2], mistakenly held up as an example of the tolerant nature of Ottoman rule. In fact similar systems of self-administration based on the religious laws of the members existed in the middle ages in Europe. It is not necessary to go back as far as the barbarians with Roman law or Vizigoth or Burgundian codes to find similar theoretical tolerance, coming from a similar theological vision of the world; an example is the law governing Jews, based on Kahal, which was passed by

Casimir the Great of Poland. The Sultans had come across examples of this in the great middle eastern empires and above all in Persia, however, the proportion of zimmi was so high, especially in the European parts of the Empire, that the Millet system had to be adjusted and extended and was to become one of the fundamental factors for Ottoman rule in the Balkans. Therefore it is a misnomer to translate the word "millet" with "nation" or "nationality" as certain historians continue to do, since "millet" was a religious entity recognized by the Ottoman authorities and responsible through its own hierarchical leaders for the self-administration of theological or moral matters but otherwise subject to the laws of the Empire. A difficult distinction in pre-secular societies where Sharia and Cannon law considered it had a right to adjudicate in individual and collective problems. Applying the law to concrete situations was the only way of distinguishing its limits and even this resulted in many conflicts which were generally settled in the interests of the stronger party ie. the Ottoman authorities. In reality the Millet had power over all that was primarily religious: religion, family, education and charity. To settle the various problems the Millet set up and paid for the necessary structures: ecclesiastical courts, schools, hospitals and hospices.

Following the conquest of Byzantium and the appointment of a Patriarch by Mehmed II, there emerged what the Ottomans later called the "Rum Millet" (meaning Greek Millet but not used in the ethnic sense of the word but as in Greek Church) in other words the Eastern Christian Church under the responsibility of the Patriarch of Constantinople. He in fact was to extend his jurisdiction to the whole of the Balkans. To the medieval mind the authority of a patriarch was linked to the existence of a dominant power and so it was understandable that it should wane with the decline of the Christian state; so the Patriarch of Tirnovo from 1402 became a Metropolitan and that of Ipek (Pecs) became subservient in 1459 to the see of Ohrid. The Rum Millet encompassed all the eastern Christian populations: Greeks, Bulgarians, Serbs, Albanians and Wallachians. Its leader, known as the Millet Basi, was the ecumenical Patriarch. As mentioned above, on the 1 June 1453, he was installed in the conquered city. Gennadios' successors were elected canonically by the Holy Synod but the candidate had to be approved by the Sultan. The Patriarch would then take his place in the Ottoman hierarchy with the title of Pasha with three "Tugs"[3]. His authority extended over various secular matters, such as raising taxes which had been usual practice during the last centuries of Byzantine rule. In the 14th century the archbishop of Thessalonika, Isidor Glabas, was considered to be the real master of the city by the inhabitants, and following the fall of Constantinople the bishops would often take the place of the civil powers, issuing passports and certificates of health to travellers and seamen. Seemingly without problem the Balkan Christians formed the Rum Millet and used it to protect themselves from what they feared could be, and in fact was, the arbitrary nature of Ottoman rule. The Kadi's tribunal, which was mandatory in conflicts between Muslims and Zimmis, also had jurisdiction over cases between Christians, however the latter did not necessarily feel that they were impartial and preferred to take their litigation to the ecclesiastical court of the archbishop or the Patriarch in whom were vested the last rights of appeal.

The structure of the Rum Millet was based on the Church. At the top was the Patriarch who lived in the Fener quarter (known as phanar in Greek) with other high-ranking clergy of the major church institutions. Otherwise there was the autocephalic Metropolitan of Ohrid who though Greek had since 1037 rivalled the Patriarchates of the former Slav kingdoms and whose authority extended over Bulgarian areas, Ipek (Pecs), previously a Greek Metropolitan but which in 1557 had been replaced by a Serbian Patriarch, brother of the Grand Vizier Mehmed Sokollu, and who had jurisdiction over Serbian, Bosnian and Hungarian territory. Under them were archbishops and bishops, particularly numerous in Greek areas, who formed the framework of the Millet. It is clear that the role of the Church was very important in keeping alive and developing the Christian identity of the Balkan population.

As well as the Rum Millet there soon developed an Armenian Millet. Already living in Byzantium since the late middle ages, Armenians were encouraged by Mehmed II to come to his new capital and settled in the Samatya and Solu Monastiri quarters[4]. They were craftsmen and traders from Sivas, Tokat and Kayseri, later joined by new arrivals from Bursa, Ankara and other Anatolian cities. The Armenian Church, since 491 faithful to the monophysite doctrine, was considered heretical by the ecumenical patriarch and had its own distinct structures. At its head was the

"Catholicos" who in 1453 still lived in the Caucasus but outside the Empire. Mehmed II called on the archbishop of Bursa, gave him the rank of Armenian Patriarch and set him up among his fellow countrymen in the Solu Monastiri. In 1461 he issued a Berat which appointed him Basi Millet and conferred the same powers as the Greek Patriarch, extending his authority to the Coptic Gipsies, the Syrian and Egyptian monophysites and even over the Bosnian Bogomils.

Soon after the fall of Byzantium a Jewish Millet was organized— Yahudi Millet—although it was not until 1839 that a legal Berat was issued. In 1453 Mehmed II himself appointed Moses Kapsali as Grand Rabbi whereas his successors had been chosen by the community. Although the followers of Moses came from many parts, as far as the Ottoman authorities were concerned they formed a single community whose Basi Millet was the Grand Rabbi of the capital. Yet in reality they were divided into Ashkenazi and Sephardi according to their place of origin and also their spoken tongue—Yiddish and Judeo-Spanish—but there was also a further group—Byzantine Jews who had always experienced a somewhat precarious legal status. They used Greek and Hebrew in their liturgy and were made up of Romaniotes, followers of the Talmud and strict orthodox Jews, and the Karaites who were more progressive. At the start of the 16th century the Romaniotes and Sephardis fought for control of the Grand Rabbinate and the latter due to their superior numbers finally won. In reality however, in the provincial towns as well as the capital each community had their own separate Rabbis and ruling councils known as the Hashgaha which dealt with internal problems and relations with the Ottoman authorities. The Jews specialized in trade, especially the silver trade but also medicine, metal-work and weaving. The first printing press in Constantinople was set up in 1494 by some Spanish Jews.

These were the three Millets which the Ottoman authorities recognized. The Catholics from Galata who were in the capital were ruled by a separate statute, yet those in the provinces were felt to be the responsibility of the Rum Millet. The problem came to a head in the 17th century in a Bulgarian area, Ciprovici[5], which German miners had made into a centre of Catholic belief. Austria became involved, the Pope making it into an archbishopric which became famous with Peter Bogdan and Peter Parcevic, and Vienna securing a Berat for its protégés which would allow them to build their own churches and practice their faith. However it would be wrong to speak of a Catholic Millet for this did not exist.

There were two types of Muslims: the conquerors and colonials—Turcomans often called Turks, Circassians and Tatars—and all the peoples of the Balkans who had converted—Greeks, Bulgars, Serbs, Albanians and Wallachians. Being part of the Sultan's "Reaya" they were under Sharia law, complemented by Kanuns, and would have been the direct responsibility of the various organs of Ottoman power. Their proportion in terms of the whole of the population would have varied a lot over the centuries but there is a lack of written documents which prevents a clear picture from emerging. Using the incomplete Census of 1520/1530 historians have put forward the following figures for the Ottoman Balkans: 19% Muslims, 80% Christians and less than 1% Jews, as well as the major trends whereby Muslims were most numerous in towns and only predominated in the districts (Kaza) of Viz and Gallipoli in Thrace (present-day Turkey), Silistra and Sumen in Bulgaria, as well as a nucleus in Bosnia, Macedonia and Thessaly. It is worth mentioning that right up to the end of the 16th century a fifth of these followers of Mohammed were still nomadic or semi-nomadic, descendants of the initial conquering Turcomans. As mentioned above, for over two centuries a number of the old families who had come over from Anatolia were to compete with the Kapi Kulari for the levers of power but were ultimately to lose due to insufficient numbers.

In terms of status it is necessary to distinguish Muslims who were the "Porte's Slaves" and free men. The former, at the very heart of the Ottoman system, would have either come from Devsirme or the slave markets. The remainder, estimated at about 70% of the faithful, would have been free subjects converted to Islam. There has been much discussion of the coercive nature of these conversions but to have a fuller understanding one must be careful not to make the mistake of anachronism. In the 16th and 17th centuries individual freedom did not have the same value as at present. The subjects of the German kingdoms were forced to become Catholic or Protestant at the wish of their prince, in the same way as the peasants of Bosnia were forced to follow Islam once their lords became Begs. In a society where only the mighty were truly free it is not surprising that whole villages would be forced to convert to the same religion as their leader. Above all conversion brought benefits in the form of exemption from Djizya—tax, equality in law, personal security, full legal guarantees on property, enfranchisement for descendants of Byzantine slaves and the possibility of admittance to the Ulema corps (civil service) and certain craft guilds. Also the practice of the Christian religion was very basic and together with the ignorance of the clergy would not have been a great obstacle to apostasy, which in any case was not a very strong commitment. Simple Byzantine Christianity had included many ancient pagan rites, and Islam reduced to its ritual obligations was not averse to similar syncretism. In the village it was not uncommon for families whose head was officially Muslim to allow the other members to worship icons and celebrate Christian feast-days. As mentioned previously the example was given by the imperial harem itself. Contrary to romantic tradition the barrier of faith was often crossed but more often by groups of people than individuals, such was the strength of group solidarity during this period.

The Provincial Government of the Great Lord

From the Danube to the Island of Cithiria—Kythira—the whole of the Balkan peninsula had become part of the Empire and from 1541 to 1699 was added the Hungarian plain up to Fulek and Erlau (Eger).

The basic territorial unit was the Sandjak (Sancak[6]) which is generally translated as province. During the conquest they had been simply tracts of land large enough to support a set number of Spahis which the Sultan would have entrusted to a Bey. He would have handed him a "Sancak," in other words a flag, which in battle was that of his cavalry unit. But these Sandjak Beys proved troublesome and from 1362 onwards they were supplanted by a Beylerbey—a Grand Bey—whose power-base gradually expanded over all occupied Europe. From this came the Beylerbeylik of Rumelia whose capital was first at Filib and then Edirne. Later the whole of the Empire was divided up into Beylerbeyliks and by the end of the 16th century their number had reached thirty-two. Five were in European territory and were known as the Beylerberliks of: Rumelia, Bosnia with its capital at Saraybosna (Sarajevo), The Aegean Archipelago (capital Gallipoli), Budin in Hungary (capital

Buda) and Tamisvar (capital Temesvar). It was these large provinces that from 1590 were designated as "Eyalet"; the head had the honorific title of Pasha hence the name Pashalik which for example was used in the 18th century in reference to the frontier province of Belgrade. Downwards the Sandjak would have been further divided into Subasilik, its leader the Subasi would command a smaller military unit. The number of Sandjaks and the areas were they existed was to change a lot, but at the end of the 16th century there were about thirty in the Balkans. The Sandjak retained its original military characteristics until the 19th century, with the Sandjak Bey as leader of the Spahis and other troops which were raised in his district. Next to him was the Kadi, the head of justice, who came from the Ulema class, only second to the Sultan in terms of power. Entrusted with the task of enforcing Sharia law and Kanuns, the Kadi was independent of the Bey and could turn to the sovereign himself for support. The Bey was unable to pass judgement or impose a fine without the assent of the Kadi, who in turn had to seek the support of the Bey to impose his decision. For legal purposes the Sandjak was sub-divided into Kazas and Nahis with their own Kadis. This duality of administrative power was felt by Ottomans to be necessary. The third most important official was the Defterdar—the treasurer—who was linked to the Grand Superintendent of Istanbul. The Sandjak Bey would bring them together in a "divan"—council—on the model of those held by the Sultan.

The three traditional areas of interest for the authorities—army/law and order, justice and finance were also of interest to the Reaya depending on whether Muslim or Zimmi. Only the former had the right to carry arms. The Spahi, owner of a Timar, was obliged to equip a certain amount of men—auxiliary Cebelu—keep horses and supply weapons and equipment for the campaign. At the behest of the Beylerbey the Sandjak Beys might call them up and would confiscate the Timars of those unable to answer the call or unable to supply the right number of Cebelus for the size of their fiefdom. Usually it was fixed so that one in ten Spahis would remain in the Sandjak to keep the peace and to raise taxes in the absence of the others. As well as the Spahis, in the provinces there were garrisons of three to five hundred Janissaries in fortresses and in most towns. Obliged to remain celibate at least till the middle of the 16th century, they had their own chiefs and were not under the authority of the Sandjak Bey. Their primary role was to stop conflicts between Muslims and Zimmis breaking out, to escort ambassadors and important travellers, to protect the trade routes and caravans and the shipment of money to the treasury. In the mountain or border areas there would have also been auxiliary forces made up of Christians, even though Sharia law forbade this; there were Wallachians in Serbia and Macedonia up until the start of the 17th century and the Debenci who guarded roads or bridges would sometimes have been Zimmi. The only military obligation that the Christian population had apart from this was Devsirme, which was raised every three to five years and affected, not craftsmen or traders from the cities, but peasants, and the Djizya—tithe—which was felt to be a compensation for not doing military service and was paid for every male over the age of twelve but not for women, children, invalids or monks.

The Sultan's law applied to everybody and was represented even in the smallest of provincial towns by a hierarchy of Kadis, even though it has been shown that Christians often avoided them, taking their business to their own Millet courts. Although paid for by the Porte, the Kadis also took a percentage of the fines that they imposed, as well as presents—Baksheesh—which it was customary to offer. This justice was expensive but was felt to give protection or at least to counterbalance arbitrary rule of the Sandjak Bey or his agents. Above all as judge, the Kadi would enforce retribution, the most frequent being drubbing, but would also be involved in supervision of the craft guilds or policing the town markets.

Ottoman finances retained its particular form which was a result of its origins. Soon after the conquest the new authorities set up an administration based both on the Timar system and the levying of taxes on the Reaya. To this end they sent commissioners to the occupied territories who set up a register of the resources of towns, villages and families. The property and income of each person was written down and served as a basis for taxation, calculated per household in towns and per village in the countryside. From this sum total the Treasury first deducted the State duties (to pay for the high ranking state officials: Grand Viziers, Beylerbeys etc.) and the rest was divided amongst the Timars within the territory. This overlapping of Imperial and Timar finances was clearly shown in the collection of taxes, which in the countryside was generally the responsibility of the Spahis; the confusion was such that as far as those who paid were concerned the distinction between the two was not always clearly understood. Muslims and Zimmis living in the villages owed the Imperial Treasury fist of all Tithe—Asar—which would have varied greatly according to the region; added to this there was a fee which allowed farmers to farm a Cift, the basic unit which a pair of oxen might till, about 7 to 17 hectares. The Muslims called this Cift Resmi and the Christians Ispence. The latter also had to pay Djizya which must have been very high since, in 1527, it is calculated it brought in 750,000 golden ducats, in other words 42% of the Treasury's income from the European part of the Empire.[7] In the cities there was also Djizya but the land tax was replaced by Mulaka which was deducted from all revenue from crafts and on commerce for example market taxes such as roasting imported coffee beans or on fish and salt. The household tax—Avaris—was theoretically a one off tax, which was meant to equip the troops should the need arise, however this soon became a regular duty. In the same way as in the countryside the overheads would differ greatly yet urban areas are said to have contributed only 25% of the Treasury's budget.

Even under Suleyman, at the Empire's zenith, the picture of provincial administration was less uniform. In spite of its centralized nature the Ottoman system also had different regional privileges as a consequence of the way they had become incorporated into the Empire. Thus the islands of the Aegean such as Rhodes and Chios retained their self-regulating bodies, benefitting from fiscal privileges in return for the provision of ships and crews for the Sultan's fleet. Certain villages on the great highways between Istanbul and Belgrade, Istanbul-Sofia were exempted from taxes as they were supposed to maintain the roads and bridges, and supply horses for the official mail. Others paid for auxiliary soldiers to safeguard the security of mountain or border regions. A curious example is the Timok region which was the Sultan's exclusive possession, his personal "Has" which the Serbians continued to administer and in which they were even allowed to bear arms. Finally we must not forget that, as in all states at the time, the actual form that government took depended on the means that were available—effective along the lines of communications and in the valleys the Sultan's authority would have been much more theoretical in mountainous regions. Northern Albania, Montenegro, the Epirus regions or the Peloponnese in fact retained some independence based on their own tribal structures and were only limited to paying a tribute which often was "forgotten."

The Timar System and the Organization of the Countryside

Modern Turkish historians are quick to emphasize the novelty of the Timar system and there has been much discussion of the existence and characteristics of Ottoman feudalism. To explain this it is necessary to go back to its origins.

The problem that the first members of the House of Osman were confronted with was the need to maintain an army as large as possible. Yet in the Middle East, as in medieval Europe, the kings and princes had a major problem: an insufficient money supply to pay the soldiers through income tax of the population. A solution was to give the warrior leaders land to provide for the upkeep of his household and also of his comrades-in-arms and subordinates. The Merovingian nobility were recompensed in this way and the Byzantines had the Pronoia system which was based on the same principle. H. Inalcik himself underlines the similarity between the Pronoia and the Timar[8]. In the Middle East this institution was used by the Persians and the Seldjuks adopted it. The Ottomans clearly inherited it from them and defined its legal basis.

At its very heart was land settlement. In accordance with Sharia law, land conquered from the Infidel was felt to be part of the spoils of Jihad. The Sultan would receive the fifth due to him under the Pencik rule and divide up the rest among the various commanders of the army. In fact since the whole world belonged to God his Caliph could share it out as he pleased. Naturally the generals had to be rewarded, but most of them were Kapi Kulari and had paid positions. The Sultan also had to make gifts to religious bodies. Consequently there were three forms of land ownership: Miri land, belonging to the state and which made up 87% of the land in 1528 and almost all the agricultural land, Vakif land which belonged to the mosques and holy institutions and Mulk land which was private property in the Roman sense of the word and of which there was a great deal in Asia Minor but very little in the Balkans. Miri land was the capital which the Sultan would draw upon to form Timars. These were not defined by their size but by their revenue. A Has had an income of more than 100,000 akces.[9], a Zeamet an income of 20–10,000 akces and the Timar, strictly speaking, an income of less than 20,000 akces. The Has was under the control of the Sultan or a high ranking official—a Beylerbey, Vizier or Sandjak Bey, the Zeamet of a Subasi or something similar and the Timars were for Spahis. While the Has or Zeamet might have contained towns, the Timar was essentially rural and it is over them that the question of Ottoman feudalism has arisen.

The financial aspects have already been mentioned: Timars provided the income of a Sandjak after deductions, for the Sultan, for high ranking official and of course the Sandjak Bey. The income would then be divided among the Spahis settled in the area. A register defined the amount and the geographical distribution. This allocation might have resulted in a single village being divided up between two Spahis. Once established the Timar became the essential unit of the Sandjak's administration. It resulted in a definition of domains and of the status of the peasants who lived in them. It was indivisible and invariable until the following cadastral survey which took place in principle every twenty to twenty-five years. If there was disagreement then the Kadi would be called on to decide.

The number of Timars varied greatly. This is known from the registers of the Spahis troop strengths—Yoklamas—which resulted in the reassessment of the traditional value of up to 200,000 Timars in the Empire. It is thought that in 1475 there were 22,000 holders of Timars—Timarli—in Rumelia and 17,000 in Anatolia. Yet it is known that Mehmed II wanted to increase the number of Spahis to provide for his wars and that in 1470 a Kanun decreed the transfer of Vakifs, which had not yet been given by the Sultan, to the Miri which led to 22,000 farms and villages being made into Timars. His successor Bayezid II revoked this measure in the face of complaints from Anatolian Turcoman families who in turn demanded the land in the form of private property—Mulk. Selim I and Suleyman I went back to the Fatih's methods and so the number of Timars varied according to the power of the Sultan, and up to the 17th century the huge preponderance of Miri land is an indicator of the Sultan's power whereas later, the increase in Mulk land indicates his decline. In 1605/1606 the Elayet of Rumelia, diminished by the secession of Bosnia and the Semendra (Smederevo) region, had 6,100 Timars with 60% having a nominal income of around 3,000 akces, 8% around 6,000, a dozen with less than 1,000 and about 50 with 50,000. It should be mentioned that the European average of 3,000 akces was higher than the Anatolian Timars which yielded only 2,000. These figures are low and corresponded more or less to the Kilic (Sword), the minimum income needed to equip a warrior. It represented also the sum of tax deductions on a dozen families, on average between 10 and 20 akces. Since the Spahi was supposed to go to war with armed auxiliaries—Celebu—he was often forced to seek further funds and might have been allowed to tax several villages which is what was meant by composite Timars.

The acquisition of a Timar was reserved to a member of the military class and consequently those in the Reaya—both Muslims and Christians—were excluded. However during the occupation many feudal lords in Bosnia and Serbia offered the Sultan their services, retaining their fiefdoms which were transformed into Timars. Nevertheless either they themselves or their children converted to Islam. The statistical findings for the year 1431, in the frontier region of Albania, shows that 16% of the Spahis were formerly Christian lords, 30% Anatolian Turks and 50% Kapi Kularis. Later the recruiting of Timarlis was done by the Beylerbeys. When a military inspection showed that a Timar no longer had a chief, perhaps because of death or being no longer able to bear arms, the Sandjak Bey would put forward a candidate to whom the Beylerbey would give a certificate—Tezkere. If it involved a Timar of less than 5,000 akces then this was enough, but if it was larger it was necessary to get a degree/certificate from the Sultan. The sovereign's appointment made the holder a lifelong Timarli as against a duty Spahi. In principle the Timar was not hereditary, but the son was quite likely to succeed the father on condition that he could fulfil the same military obligations and obtain a new Berat from the Sultan.

The military side of the Timar, while essential in the eyes of the Ottoman authorities, was not always perceived as such by the people it governed. For obvious reasons of simplicity the Timarli was in charge of the collection of taxes—of all the taxes—everywhere within the Timar. His own revenue was what was left over from the sum total. The Sandjak Defterdar would then oversee its distribution. Naturally this was open to abuse and the Kadis' courts were forever receiving complaints in respect of, for example, the collection of tithe which was meant to be in kind but which the Spahi often demanded in cash, or else of so-called one-off taxes being raised regularly. On top of this the Spahi was the sole armed soldier of the area and therefore had the task of policing it. He would keep the peace with his Celebu in the villages and had authority to arrest people and send them to Kadi's court. He was expected to collect fines imposed by the latter and had the right to keep half for himself while the other half would go to the Sandjak Bey. The Timarli was the lord of the countryside, the peasants always referred to him by his title of Spahi, and he could often demand a certain number of services, such as the transport of tithe produce to his barn, or even to market if this was less than one day's journey away. The Spahi had so many duties that he was virtually the master of the village.

But can he be held as the master of the land in the same way as the Romanian Boyar for example? Legally no, since he only benefitted from a part of its revenue, but for there to be an income the land needed to be cultivated and the Ottoman Empire had to face the same problem that all medieval societies at the time had to confront, namely that man was the sole source of power for tilling the land. In the same way as the former Byzantine feudal lord, the Timar relied on regular farming of the land and, in other words, the stability of the workforce. The peasants enjoyed the use of the land as long as they could meet their financial obligations and could hand down the land, without hindrance, but with the same obligations, to their heirs. However they were not allowed to sell the land since it still belonged to the State. Neither could they leave it. On this point the Ottoman authorities had only to use previous legislation to punish those who absconded. The Sultan's regime was relatively lenient on this subject; no branding or mutilation such as that happening in Christian countries, but the Spahi had fifteen years to find the fugitive, on whom the Kadi and not the Spahi would then impose a fine. If a peasant went to settle on fallow land and started to farm it then the Spahi was not allowed to force him but could impose a Cift Resmi tax on him. Finally if the peasant managed to settle in a town he would owe the Spahi compensation which was called the tax on breakers of the Cift— Cift bonaz akcesi.

At a time when land was still of the highest value the Timarli retained a certain amount of land for his own uses. This was called the Has Cift or Ciftlik which he farmed for his own needs and that of his family. The size varied depending on the quality of the soil but as has already been mentioned amounted to an area of 7–17 hectares. After the death of the Spahi this was left to the eldest son as a sort of basic minimum so that he could retain his military status and the potential of gaining further land or a new Timar through military exploits.

This was the legal framework, laid down in the Sandjak Kanuname which outlined the exact rights of the Spahis and the Timar peasants. Yet the cases which the Kadi heard shows that these customs were not unchallenged. Mostly it was a question of the continuation of statute work, which had been usual in the Byzantine, Serbian and Bulgarian kingdoms, but which was exacerbated by the fact that often the Spahi was the former Serbian or Albanian lord. Consequently the Timarli would impose days of work on their own farms although usually not very many. In this way the transformation of the Timarli into "lord of the land" did occur. It is also plain that the Timar's origins and legal framework differentiate the system from western feudalism, yet because of the similarities in farming methods and ideas the parallels between the two institutions also became stronger which would become more pronounced, as we shall see, with the decline of central government.

In the Balkan countryside in the 16th and start of the 17th centuries the great majority of the Reaya was made up of peasants on Timars. There were also small land owners, landless peasants and farm managers. There were only a few landowning peasants, the Mulk land making up only 5–6% of Balkan lands. Most of them were Muslims who came from Anatolia and had been brought over with the idea of colonizing the land. They were obliged to pay tithe and Cift Resmi and the various taxes on sheep, pastures and other things. The Christians formed a small minority, remnants of the former Byzantine order. Yet as mentioned above, throughout the history of the Eastern Empire there had been a fierce struggle between the large and small landowners and under the Paleologos the owners of large estates had gained ascendency. The Ottoman invasion broke them up and some of their peasants, and also some of those from the monasteries, managed to have their land classified as Mulk. Sharia law indeed allowed Zimmi the option of accepting to submit to the conquerors in return for a stipulation that their land would not be split up by the victors and would remain the property of the old masters in exchange for payment of a due—Kharadj or Harac—intended to pay for the army and the

Muslim community. Added to which there were the labour dues—Cift—which was called Ispence by the Christians and the other peasant taxes. The Kharadj which was paid solely by non-Muslims became amalgamated with the Cift in the 18th century as a due, whereas originally it had been a tax notionally intended to buy back the land. There were landless peasants who were either descendants of Byzantine agricultural labourers, cift-breakers who had not been caught, children from overpopulated timars and former nomads from Anatolia who had been displaced. As far as the Ottoman authorities were concerned they were part of the same fiscal class. They might find employment as temporary workers on the Timarlis' own lands but the majority would work on the Sultan's Has or for a large landowners in the Sandjak. In the latter case they were often settled on land without tenure, similar to the medieval common land and for which they paid tithe to the holder of the Has. In contrast to these landless but free peasants, the tenant farmers were slaves, either former prisoners-of-war or else bought in the marketplace for use on the land of a high-ranking official or of a Vakif. The Sultan employed them on land destined for rice production; Mehmed II settled some near Istanbul to provide for the Seraglio. They were not allowed to marry outside their class and gave the state half their harvests. Their fate was similar to that of the medieval serf yet by the end of the 16th century many had become Timar peasants.

So the status of the Christian peasantry in everyday terms under the Ottoman had changed very little from Byzantine or Slav times, especially as the new rulers had retained the traditional order within the village. This had been laid down by Byzantium in the ancient "Agricultural Law"—called Nomos Georgikos—which went back to the 7th century. This made the village as a whole responsible for the collection of taxes but also self-governing together with a council of principal farmers and a village chief whom they elected. It was on this basis that over the centuries very different rural villages had developed depending on their geographical location yet at the same time retaining similar features. Houses and gardens were marked off by small walls or hedges which closed off what was considered to be the family property, passed on according to the laws of the group. Further away, cultivated land which was generally open but which was also considered to be private property whatever the legal status.

Further out, or else mixed up in the fields were woods and pastures, often whole mountains which were used by the whole community according to traditional rules.

Apart from colonized areas where the newcomers sometimes brought with them different organizational methods, the Ottoman conquerors generally left the peasant communities alone. The title of the village chief might be different: Archon in Greek areas, Knez in Serbian and Corbadji in Bulgarian. They were chosen by the council made up of heads of families who were often known as elders and generally came from a lineage with a reputation of wealth or wisdom. It was these councils that regulated the life of the community and tried to settle conflicts in accordance with customary law. These were in general unwritten but carefully handed down from the past. Very different from each ethno-linguistic group, and even within these groups with geographical location or custom, their elaboration was the result of successive influences, with the Byzantine inheritance the most conspicuous. The survival of these structures limited contact between the Ottoman authorities and the Reaya, and consequently reduced the opportunities for conflict. When a Spahi lived in the village he might have to intervene but only in matters of taxation or law and order. In other matters the Archon or Knez was the usual conduit. However most rural communities would not have had a resident Spahi, usually he was only present when raising taxes which was in the autumn. It was on these occasions that the most common misuse of power would be brought to the Kadi's attention, namely the price which the community would have to pay to keep and feed the Spahi and his entourage over several days and often far more than that stipulated by the Kanun. Usually the Ottoman courts would only be used for matters which concerned the whole community while an individual case would have been the result of the plaintiff being in conflict with the community. For village solidarity which is most apparent in relations with the outside world and above all the Ottoman authorities, in reality hid deep tensions. Keeping these structures meant that the village chiefs and their families would have privileges, as the conduit for the Sandjakbeys, Kadis, Defterdars and other representatives of the Empire. It also had its risks and the Archon, Knez or Corbadji sometimes paid the penalty with a beating or imprisonment, more frequently than his compatriots. Yet more easily than the other peasants, he was able to obtain favours from the administration whose prime weakness was corruption. These differences, slight at the beginning of the occupation, became greater during peacetime and resulted in a social hierarchy based on wealth which was to lead to resentment. Their 18th and 19th century descendants have often been accused by nationalist historians of exploiting their fellow countrymen and collaborating with the establishment in stifling popular liberation movements.

The Towns

The antiquity of Balkan towns is well known and their economic and strategic importance, on the Roman highways, was to continue during the Byzantine period. Urban growth prior to the Ottoman conquest has been mentioned and although the decline of the capital can be precisely measured and understood, data concerning other towns is much more scarce. The new administration which was set up was based on the towns since each Sandjak was organized around an agglomeration which would have contained the representatives of government. Although it is known that 25% of the state's income came from the cities, it is much more difficult to gauge exactly what proportion of the population lived in the Balkan towns. What is certain is that this proportion as a whole increased from the 15th through to the 19th century however sporadically. Cities were the prime objective of the warring armies, and those near the frontiers experienced huge variations in the number of inhabitants because of sieges and military operations. This was the case of Buda, Belgrade, Sofia, Silistra and many others. Belgrade for example was a large town in the 16th century with over 80 mosques and six Caravanserais (hotels for caravans). Yet in 1717 when the Austrians occupied it there were only 2,000 inhabitants which by the time they left 20 years later had increased to 5,000. Also there was the scourge of plague epidemics, regional troubles such as the 1598 Tirnovo revolt which was supported by the Wallachian voevod, Michael the Brave or the greed of a particularly avaricious pasha. These various factors mean that the question can only be described adequately in the context of a specialized monograph.[10]

The Ottomans referred to the towns with the term "Sehir," which comes from the Persian. They also distinguished between, "Kasba"—a crafts and commercial town—and "Palanka" which might have been a town or a village but was fortified, and "Varos" which had been the Byzantine suburb and referred to the Christian part of town. The confessional element was fundamental in urban topography. The Reaya was divided up like everywhere else into Muslim and Zimmi, the latter subject to the Djizya. It was precisely for this fiscal reason that every 10 or 20 years a census was conducted, which gives modern historians their first insight into these city dwellers. The basic unit was the Hane, the household which can be compared with the hearth in western medieval society and which was given an average value of five people. There emerges a relatively accurate picture of the size of agglomerations and their Christian or Muslim composition. Apart from Istanbul which needs to be studied separately, at the end of the 15th and the beginning of the 16th century, there were two towns in the Balkans with more than 20,000 inhabitants: Edirne and Thessalonika, followed by Athens with 10,000, Vidin and Nikopol under 10,000 (trading cities such as Lubeck, Hamburg and Nuremberg had just under 20,000). Most of the Balkan Sehirs had about 2,000 and 4,000 inhabitants, however it is worth noting a relatively large increase during the 16th century. The most striking example is Sarajevo which had been a small medieval town known as Vrhbosna. Under Ottoman occupation from 1462 onwards, a seraglio was built for the Beylerbey in 1462, hence the name Bosna-Serai. Twenty years later there were 1,000 inhabitants but by the second half of the 16th century there were over 21,000.

From religious records it is clear that there was a increase in Muslims. While Christians had been largely in a majority during the 15th century, 75% as against 25% Muslim, a century later the latter had risen to over 50%. Yet with noteworthy variations; in 1425/30 Tirnovo was 25% Muslim and 75% Christian while at the fortress of Nikopol on the Danube the two groups were almost equally balanced. A century later the port of Varna was still almost 94% Christian while Sofia had already become predominantly Muslim, and Plovdiv even more so. The urban agglomerations were divided up into quarters—Mahalle—in which the inhabitants would live on a confessional basis. In 1529 in Edirne there were 16,400 Muslims with 2,4000 Christians in 19 Mahalles and 1,000 Jews in a further eight Mahalles. The census officer wishing to emphasize how extraordinary this was noted that there was an enclave of 16 Christian households within the Muslim district. Furthermore in some towns there would have been a Gipsy quarter which was strictly separate.

As with all the Empire's territories the towns belonged in principle to the sultan and there were three forms of ownership: Miri, Vakif and Mulk. The income from these might have been transferred to members of the military class in the form of a Has, Zeamet or Timar in the same way as in the countryside. Since they usually gave a much higher income the towns were generally considered Has' or Zeamets which was under the sovereign himself and people of the highest rank. In this way by the start of the 16th century all the towns in the Balkan peninsula became part of the Ottoman system. Out of 177 agglomerations, 45 were part of the Sultan's Has, 88 of the Grand Vizier's, the Beylerbey's and the Sandjak Bey's, 26 were Zeamets belonging to Subasis and other officials, 9 were Timars and 9 Vakifs. So the Sultan retained approximately a quarter of the towns for himself and these were the largest; Edirne, Thessalonika, Sofia, Plovdiv, Skopje, the largest ports and all the mining towns. It should be remembered however, that in certain cases he shared the revenue with the Beylerbey or a Sandjak Bey. It was not a question of territorial fiefdoms as their status could change. Athens for example was at the start of the 16th century a timar under a Kadi, in 1526 it became a Has of the Grand Vizier and twenty years later part of the Sultan's Has. The collection of revenue and allocation of resources was the responsibility of the Defterdar. It has been calculated that about half of the town revenue went to the treasury to cover the expenditure of the palace and central government, the remainder going to high officials and those with privileges. These sums of money came from "Mukataas," which were the various taxes on crops and port duties. There was also the Djizya on the Zimmi and a few other minor taxes. On average the levy per household—Hane—was around 100 to 200 akces in medium sized towns and 300 to 400 for Edirne and Thessalonika. Compared with taxation in the countryside the city dweller seems to have paid on average twice as much tax as the peasant.

The government of the towns was the responsibility of the provincial authorities; Beylerbeys, Sandjak Beys and Subasi, who had police powers in contrast to the Kadis who were masters of the courts. But the everyday life of the Mahalle was controlled by a "Muhtar" in conjunction with those responsible for the various Millets in the town and as in the countryside the Zimmi tried to keep dealings with the Ottoman authorities to the strictest minimum. Their quarters, sometimes closed off by gates, were organized around the Church or Synagogue, with a market, baths and taverns thus forming a cultural area outside which women for instance would rarely venture.

The town dweller's professions were varied and were translated into a social hierarchy: at the bottom were the craftsmen and store holders, above them traders from the town and regional markets and at the top the merchant—Tuccar or Bazirgan—who had contacts all over the Empire. All these bodies were organized into corporations—"Esnafs." There has been much discussion over the origins of these associations and their nature , Turkish historians point out the differences between the Esnaf and the medieval Christian guilds, the Greeks however insist on the similarity with those of Byzantium. There had been Collegias which had been closely controlled by the authorities and the Seldjuks had in turn had organized corporations. What is certain however is that the word Esnafs appear in Ottoman manuscripts relatively late, at the start of the 16th century in Istanbul and much later in other towns. The structures were similar: master craftsmen—Usta—, craftsmen—Kalfa—and apprentices—Cirak. The apprentice would usually live with the master and would work for nothing. At the end of two or three years he would become a craftsman. To become a master craftsman would depend on the rules of the Esnaf. There had to be a vote by a council of master craftsmen and it often required the making of a masterpiece. The newly elevated then had to obtain a "Gedik" from the Kadi which was a permit to open a workshop or a store which he could hand down to his descendants. There was the tendency therefore, more so than in Europe, for the Usta class to become closed in on itself. The assembly of master craftsmen, also known as the Council of Elders, settled internal problems and elected the head of the corporation— Kethuda—who made representations on their behalf to the authorities and whose appointment would also have been confirmed by the Kadi. There were many Esnafs, a census of Istanbul showed 1,100. Many bridged the religious divide bringing Muslims and Christians together and others kept them apart such as the slaughter and sale of pork which was forbidden by Islam. The mixed character of the Esnaf had not been very easy to achieve since they had retained certain religious traditions from their Seldjuk past. The head of the corporation was usually the Sheik—Cheykh— aided by a Duaci, yet gradually the corporations became more secular and from the 16th century the Kethuda became the real power. The Christian Esnafs also involved popes in their affairs and religious ceremonies. This progressive secularization can however be seen as a reason for the late development of the Esnafs in the Balkans. Henceforth corporations were to assume the double function of defending the interests of the profession (in the face of a government which strictly controlled the economy, especially prices) but also a social and cultural organization with rules of mutual aid, tradition and celebration.

Traders, especially store keepers, had the same type of organization, while merchants and wholesalers did not yet were very closely controlled by the authorities. The provision of food to the towns, the imports of raw materials to supply the craftsmen and the stability of prices were the major preoccupation of the civil administration. This all culminated in the town market place— Bedestan—which westerners preferred to call the Bazaar. As well as traders who had stores, there were many pedlars—Seyyars— water carriers, tumblers and also shadowgraph puppeteers[11] which made for a colourful and noisy street-life in a Balkan town.

Western travellers have left interesting, if not always accurate, accounts of these scenes. What immediately struck them was that the towns, apart from a few exceptions such as Istanbul and Thessalonika, were not enclosed by fortified walls which was the case of European cities of the same period. Also it was very rare for them to be dominated by something like a palace which might correspond to the castles of western nobles. Apart from the mosques, one or two caravanserais—Han—, a covered marketplace and baths—Hamman—generally they were described as agglomerations without any discernable order made up of small fragile houses of cob and wood, producing much dust and very mean to the eyes of the envoys of the Kings of France or of German princes. In fact each town had its very own character.

Smederevo which was dominated by its 15th century fortress remained up until the capture of Belgrade in 1521 and the annexation of the Benat region, the main Ottoman base for forward operations against the west. It had a large garrison and the army maintained numerous workshops and warehouses. The fortress was later abandoned and for the whole of the 16th century the town became a very important commercial centre. The number of Mahalles increased from seven to fourteen and the number of households rose to over 300; in other words 1,500 inhabitants three quarters of which were Christian and the rest Muslim. Its port could be compared with Belgrade and documents mention 367 shops and workshops. There were also about thirty traders from Dubrovnik. By the end of the century its decline was clear; Smederovo only had eleven quarters and 200 households—consequently only 1,000 inhabitants.

Sofia is described by a German traveller, at the start of the 17th century, as a populous commercial town as large as Worms in Germany. It had about 8,000 inhabitants of which 88% were Muslim while the Sandjak ie. the countryside was 95 % Christian. In contrast to most other conglomerations whose different ethnic population had increased, this island of Islam had lost a section of its Christian families. Part of one of the Sultan's Has' it gave him 110 akces[12] per family which was a higher charge than for the inhabitants of Edirne where it was 72 akces. The town was renowned for it leather products, armaments and animal skins.

Thessalonika—called Selanik by the Ottomans—with 25,000 inhabitants, was the second largest city, per capita, in the Balkans. It was distinctive with a large Jewish colony, Sephardis attracted by the port. In 1518 the number of Jewish households was put at 3,143 as against 1,374 Muslim and 1,087 Christian households. During the following century this number went down as they dispersed to towns further inland, while the number of Christians was to increase. The Muslims lived in the higher parts of the town, around the Acropolis. Foremost among these was the family of the renegade, Evrenos Pasha, who was very wealthy. A tiny Greek enclave had remained around the monastery of Vlatades, but both Christians and Jews shared the lower Mahalles near the port. This was the great attraction of the town and much of it due to the Jews who had built up networks with their fellows in Venice, Amsterdam and Hamburg. Their speciality was the import of wool and the manufacture of clothing. They represented a thriving cultural community with synagogues, schools, rabbinical seminaries and libraries, epitomized by scholars such as Benjamin Halevy, Eskenazi or Moses Almohino. The Christians had retained the use of a dozen churches, but by the 17th century this had risen to 30, as against 36 synagogues and 48 mosques. As well as the usual monuments in Ottoman cities, a dozen or so Hammans, sixteen Hans and a Madresses or two, Thessalonika was noteworthy for the palaces—seraglios—of its officials and notables. Its markets were noteworthy for travellers, especially the Egyptian market—Misir Carsi—which had 500 stores selling all the products of the East.

But the greatest city of all was Istanbul, the capital of the Empire, and for this very reason the most distinct and different from the rest of the Balkans. Two aspects however attach it to the region: its population and it economic position[13]. At the start of Suleyman's reign there is documentary proof that there were 46,635 Muslim households, 25,252 Christian and 8,570 Jewish; in all about 80,000 households and some 400,000 inhabitants, which in fact made it the largest conurbation in Europe and much larger than Paris which had a population of barely more than 250,000. This was a town with a population 58% Muslim and 42% Christian and Jewish. It is clear that ethno-linguistic groups must not be equated with religion and among the followers of the Prophet there were Turks, Arabs, Iranians and also Balkan peoples, from every group that lived in the peninsula and the islands, converts to Islam at different times and for different reasons, and it is impossible to calculate exactly how many. Balkan people however were in the majority amongst the Christians together with the Armenians and the westerners known as Galatan Franks. The largest group were the Greeks yet they had not been, as mentioned above, the original Byzantine population; the survivors of the siege were deported to Edirne, Bursa, Gallipoli, Filibe (Plovdiv) and replaced by Turks from Anatolia, Greeks from the Peloponnese and the islands, and also from Asia Minor as well as Armenians. A register made in 1450 shows 1,457 Greek families who came from the archipelagos; in particular Mytilin and the Black Sea trading posts—Kaffa in the Crimea and Trezibond. In the 16th and 17th centuries the capital showed a huge increase for by 1690 there was a total population of 6–700,000 inhabitants. On top of a natural increase this surplus was due to an influx from all over the Empire, but especially from the Balkans; craftsmen from other towns and peasants escaping from their miserable lot. Istanbul remained quite clearly the largest Greek city. Established on the shore of the Golden Horn the Greeks had made the Phanar a residential quarter with beautiful stone houses where wealthy merchants and traders lived, doctors and collaborators with the Ottoman administration such as interpreters—Drogman—the greatest in 1669, Grand Drogman Panayotis Nikusis and then Alexander Mavrocordatos. Thanks to a network of commissioners in the eastern Mediterranean and Black Sea ports, they controlled the bulk of maritime trade, while others performed more menial jobs associated with the sea—sailors and gunners—or owned taverns or drinking booths. Having about thirty churches within the city, with about ten in the Phanar district, they formed the largest part of the Rum Millet beneath the Patriarch and a numerous clergy. It was around this sound organization that the other Balkan peoples gravitated, mostly specializing in the craft trades, the Bulgars gardeners and tanners and the Serbs and Moldo-Wallachian cheese, fruit and vegetable sellers. The Albanians however were in the main Muslims and lived in the same Mahalles as the Turks but were pavers, well-diggers and pedlars. They often benefitted from the protection of their compatriots, who had made careers in the army or else had reached high positions in the palace.

To this human fabric which linked the capital to the Balkan peninsula, must be added the tight network of commercial contacts. An enormous city, Istanbul was also a huge consumer centre: from all over the Empire there came foodstuffs and raw materials for local industry; yet all was for consumption and there were hardly any exports. This phenomenon was due to the presence of the seraglio; employing some 15,000 people in 1690 in the Sultan's own service, to which on must add the "houses" of the Grand Vizier and other high officials: a population for whom luxury was the mandatory expression of power and whose level of consumption was very much higher than their average contemporaries. In 1674 the demand for meat in Istanbul was 200,000 oxen, four million sheep and three million lambs. The seraglio and the Janissaries alone consumed one tenth of this amount. It was therefore necessary, and this was one of the most pressing preoccupations of the authorities, regularly to supply and assuage this consuming appetite. So a system of priority selling was set up in the provinces and the vassal countries at prices fixed by the central authorities. For wheat the following areas were set aside: Thrace, the asiatic side of the Sea of Marmara, the coastal plains of the Aegean, the Danubian principalities and the Black Sea coast. Sheep and lamb came principally from the Balkans and Anatolia. At the end of the 16th century the Bulgarian provinces were supposed to supply 440,000 sheep every year. This trade conducted by wealthy merchants—Jeleb or celeb—was directed at the palace which would take a thirtieth of the total. Fowl came from Thrace, cheese from various Balkan mountain areas and honey from Moldavia and Wallachia. The sultan had control of the produce of certain villages for fruit and vegetables, for example with a steward in situ who would buy the products at a set price. For textiles Thessalonika was an important centre where cloth and uniforms were made for the Janissaries. So the capital of the Empire had a strong influence on the economy of the Balkans.

Scholastic and Popular Culture

On a group and individual level this multi-secular alchemy between the Balkan peoples and the Ottoman system expressed itself through cultures which were in evidence even to the least observant traveller. The towns they called Turkish and the countryside Greek, Bulgarian, Serbian or something else. Yet as we have already seen with city dwellers it was clear that there was a religious divide which separated Christians from Muslims. Hence two distinct cultures with differing facets.

First of all there was the Islamic culture which can be called Ottoman, as it was identified with those in power. Based on religious laws—Sharia—and the tradition—Hadith—of Sunni Islam, it was based on an official hierarchy of "doctors" of law: the Ulemas with their Sheik ul Islam and Muftis who interpreted the law, the Kadis who applied it in practice and the Muderri who taught it in the schools. The Sultan also held the title of Caliph, in other words the Prophet's successor. Of course every medieval country had its own theocratic basis, mixing religious and secular matters, so for instance the Basileus of Byzantium interfered in theological questions. However with Islam the Sultan did not have a structured church ranged against him with a clergy forming a separate social group, but an simple category of learned and cultured men who were theoretically independent. These Ulemas were inspired by the Koran, taught in schools called Medress. This institution was already there at the time of the first Seldjuks and it was Orkhan who in 1331 transformed the Church of Nicea (Iznik) into the first Ottoman Medress. But Mehmed II complained that his Ulemas had to go and study in Egypt or Persia because of the absence of quality schools within the Empire. After the occupation of Byzantium he transformed eight churches into Medresses which were clustered around his mosque, the Fatih Mehmed Camil, and became known as the Semaniye, the highest place of scholarship. Next there were those of Edirne and Bursa which were imperial foundations and others which had been created by important officials such as in Filibe (Plovdiv) or Uskup (Skopje) and then those in smaller towns. In the 16th century they were classified into eight levels; depending on which level was reached a student could aspire to the office of Kadi or Muderri. They would learn first to read the commentaries and interpretations of the Koran and Hadith according to the Hanefit[14] which had been adopted by the Turks. It was the highest science—Ilm—which was taught, and above all through Arabic authorities since the Turks were never very strong on theology. Then came Sharia and its jurisprudence. On these foundations the other disciplines then could be built: logic (Mantik) or the art of reasoning, writing skills—calligraphy, grammar, rhetoric, poetry, the sciences—mathematics, astronomy, music and medicine. It should be remembered that in the traditional Islamic way these were based on repetition and memorizing. These studies were assessed by examinations which gave the aspirant the right to teach in a lower Medress or else take office in the administration. In practice it was necessary to come from one of the Semaniye schools, undertake a long period of training and above all come from a family of Ulemas. In this way there was created and perpetuated, what R. Mantran has called an "administrative bourgeoisie."

It was they together with the ruling military class who upheld scholastic Islamic culture, based on the book and expressed in writing. Its followers developed an essentially urban culture and this gave towns the Turkish character which foreigners refers to. All the urban centres would have had several mosques whose minarets are described as forming veritable forests. There were 485 mosques in Istanbul and 4,500 district shrines, furthermore 157 convents. Each Sultan was duty bound to build his own mosque and even today Istanbul is proud of the mosques of Fatih (1452–1470), Bayezid II (1505), of Selim I (1522), Soliman (Suleymaniye) (1550–1557) and others and especially the famous Blue Mosque (Sultan Ahmet Camil) (1609–1616). The greatest architect of the Empire, Sinan (1486–1578), a Turk from Kayseri made his name there and this was a privileged arena for all the decorative arts (pottery and calligraphy). Around the mosques would be the Medress' and also Hammams where the literate would freely gather, heard readings and had discussions. Clearly a very limited audience for whom the poets and chroniclers would have written in a scholarly Turkish tongue full of Arab and Persian and imitating Eastern stereotyped models.

But unable to read or write most of the followers of Islam

would not have reached these heights. Again in the towns and on a basis of a simplified Islam, there developed a series of customs and traditions which also should be called "Ottoman" but "popular Ottoman." In the Mahalle it revolved primarily on the Mosque since religious practice was widespread and was expressed by Friday prayers and Rammadan, but also with the Esnaf where feast days and celebrations punctuated the lives of their members and all the district. It was essentially in this area that the influence of religious orders as well as of the numerous monasteries in Istanbul was felt.

Sufism, the mystic tendency of Islam is almost as old as Islam itself and the Seldjuk authorities had to deal with this trend as well as Ghazi and Dervishes, itinerant holy men. The first Ottomans had to come to an arrangement with what the Turcomans called Babas. In 1261 Baba Sari Saltuk at the head of about forty nomadic families from Anatolia took refuge in Dobrudja where he fought on behalf of the Mongol emir Nogai. This episode inspired heroic acts and a book called the Saltuk—Saltukname—was written which was appreciated by the Ottomans, whilst the Dobrudja was to remain for a long time a centre of the troublesome and heretical Simavni dervishes. In the 13th century these gyrating preachers organized themselves into a brotherhood—Tarika—which spread all over the Empire. It contained real clerics, in the western sense of the word, who had pledged a vow, undertaken a more or less lengthy initiation ceremonies and lived in convents—Tekke—bound by a strict discipline. Far more numerous were the ordinary followers who did not take an oath but remained in the real world, who had to say certain prayers and fulfil religious practice in the Tekke of the confraternity. It was during these sessions—Zikr—that they would reach a state, through chants, music and dances, of mystical exaltation which would lead to ecstasy or hysteria. Founded in the 13th century by Mevlana of Konya[15] it managed to keep in the sultan's favour. They recruited primarily among the urban bourgeoisie and were considered conservative. The Bektasi on the other hand were very troublesome. The founding father, Haci Bektash, had lived in Anatolia in the second half of the 13th century and folk tales traditionally have him as an adviser to Osman. What is certain is that his teachings borrowed from previous pre-Islamic Turcoman religions, from Shiism and Christianity. This syncretism made it very accessible to those people who were from the Turkish Yuruks and newly converted Christians, hence its extraordinary success within the corps of Janissaries and through them the regions from which they originally came. Unlike the Mevlevi they recruited among ordinary people in the large towns but also in the countryside. They were therefore to be found amongst the Turks of the Bulgarian riviera, in Dobrudja, in Rhodopes, in Macedonia, in Thessaly and Albanian areas.

The Muslim peasantry, as mentioned above, had come from various different places; Turks who had settled as colonials or other Christian populations who had converted to the religion of the conquerors at the same time as their masters. The former were from the monadic Turcomans—Yuruk—that the Ottoman authorities had tried to settle, but who for two centuries retained the traditional clan structure and were organized on a tribal basis. Their form of Islam incorporated elements of traditional shamanism. As for the Bosnian Muslim Slavs, or the Bulgarian Pomaci, or the Albanians of Myzeqe, theirs was a mixture of Christian traditions and the teachings of the Prophet. The Albanians had two expressions to describe those Mohammedans who had their children baptised and celebrated the Christian feast days: Domne—the hesitant and Laramane—multi-coloured. They all retained their own language and outside the towns the vast majority did not understand their masters' language. However as Muslims they were totally integrated at their own level of the Reaya within an Ottoman state. The Bey or the Spahi would deal with them directly, the Kadi was their judge and the Sultan their Grand Lord, both as a political leader and as a religious leader. Different in their origins, their way of life and their social organization, these Muslim peasants were to form many substrata in Ottoman society sprinkled here and there all over the Balkans.

The Christians, confined to the Rum Millet were considered by the Ottomans as a cohesive whole but geographical and historical factors divided them culturally. However with its doctrine founded on the holy texts and with its clergy, at least in part having received an intellectual training, the Christian Church developed in its organization a scholastic culture. Until the 18th century reading and teaching were the virtual monopoly of the clergy. Of the written languages of the medieval Christian countries—Byzantium, the Empire of Kaloyan, the Empire of Dusan—only those used in the liturgy remained ie. Greek and the Bulgar Church Slavonic together with a Latin tradition from the Catholic

Church in northern Albania which had been consolidated by Charles d'Anjou in the 13th century.

The Greek side of this ecclesiastic culture was by far the most powerful: based on the Ecumenical Patriarch, on the Metropolitan of Ohrid and the big monasteries of Athos and Meteora. In 1454 Gennadios set up a school which was known later as the Academy of the Patriarch and which corresponded in fact to a secondary school; teaching was entirely in Greek and aimed at future members of the clergy. As a result, a few other towns, as well as Istanbul, provided primary schooling where popes and sometimes lay members taught the basic elements of religious faith, of reading, grammar and arithmetic, to the sons of merchants and craftsmen. In 1593 Patriarch Jeremy II issued a decree forcing the metropolitans to organize schools in the areas under their jurisdiction. Its application was slow and depended on the area but due to this, and also the support of Greek merchants, from the 17th century onwards schools were opened in Hellenic areas, on the islands as well as on the continent. Some of these teachers are quite important as far as neo-Hellenism is concerned. For instance Theophil Corydallis (1570–1646), a disciple of Aristotle and supporter of the autonomy of Philosophy in relation to theology, or his disciple Eugene Etoli, who died in 1682 and who is above all known for his epistles. These authors used ecclesiastical Greek, reputed "pure"—Katharevusa—but in reality very corrupted in comparison to the authors of classical antiquity; it was hardly understood by the ordinary people who used Demotic Greek. This is at the root of the bilingual nature of Hellenic culture still present today. The Greek Church also was the source of a form of post Byzantine art which prospered from the 16th century onwards. It was first seen in the restoration work on churches in Epirus and this in spite of pernickety Ottoman regulations, then in Athens and in the Peloponnese. The frescos of this period can still be seen in very ordinary village churches. This painting reached its zenith on the island of Crete, occupied at the time by Venice, and the "Cretan School" which is illustrated by such names as Theophanos and the renegade Theotokopulos called El Greco (1541–1614). At the level of the Patriarchate an interesting but insubstantial contact was made with the Lutheran Reformation. In fact the initiative came from a Hellenic Professor at the University of Tubingen at the time of Patriarch Josaphat II (1551–1561). This dialogue went on under his successor Jeremy II Tranos when the ambassador of the Holy Roman Empire took up his post in Constantinople in 1573. He had brought with him as Chaplain Stephan Gerlach, a theologian from Tubingen, who brought with him for the Patriarch a Greek translation of the Augsburg Declaration. There took place a theological discussion which centred on purgatory and filioque over which there was a meeting of minds but which was disturbed by the Lutheran dogma of justification through faith alone. The exchange of letters was to end but was not forgotten by the Phanar See. On the other hand opposition to Rome was aggravated by the Catholic Counter Reformation and missionary activity which this had encouraged. Pope Gregory XIII (1572–1585) founded in Rome, the College of Saint Athanas, where lessons were in Greek and intended for young men who wanted to be priests or teachers in the Balkans. This was clearly in competition to the church of Constantinople which lacked educated officials. The Dominicans and Franciscans were especially active and infiltrated the mainland from the ports and islands which were still occupied by Venice and Genoa. They were under a Patriarch Vicar who lived in Galata and represented the Roman archbishop of the capital residing in Rome. Their actions were reinforced by the Jesuits who established themselves in Pera in 1583 and later in Chios. They even had contact with Athos from where several monks went to Naupli to receive training. The Capuchins were everywhere in the Balkans and extremely active. In the 17th century they were established with their schools and churches in Chios, Smyrna, Naxos, Andros, Naupli, Athens and Milos. Their popularity was due in part to the fact that they preached in ordinary Greek—Demotic, which was also used by the Jesuits. These missionary activities gave rise to a lot of criticism by Greek nationalist historians in the 19th and 20th centuries, yet although more often than not these Italian, Croat, Ragusian and other monks were much inclined to quarrelling with the eastern Church, consciously or unconsciously they brought western ideas, which together with contacts made by the merchants was to maintain the link between the Greek world and western Europe.

Ecclesiastical culture based on Church Slavonic presents the obvious paradox of a language which was very similar to Bulgarian, and from 1557, having a Patriarchate with its seat at Pecs in a Serbian area. In fact, if at a popular level there was little possibility of confusion between the ethno-linguistic Bulgarian and the Serbian groups, those who were literate did use liturgical vocabulary but corrupting and adapting it to their own uses and resulting in what linguists have called a Serbian and Bulgarian[16] Slavonic. During the 16th and 17th centuries there arose what is termed a Balkan Paleo-Slav culture and therefore one has to be careful in using modern national terms to describe these authors. A student of Eftimij, the last Patriarch of Tirnovo, Grigorij Camblak is often classified as a great Bulgarian author; in fact even though he was born at Tirnovo he was educated in Mount Athos, became an Igumen at the Serbian convent of Decani, was a priest in the Moldo-Wallachian church of Suceava before being sent for by his uncle the Metropolitan of Moscow, who had him elected to the seat of Kiev where he died in 1418. His works are claimed by Bulgarian, Serbian and Russian literature. In the next generation, Constantine of Kostenec, known as the Philosopher, is also a good example of this culture based on Slavonic. Born in a Bulgarian area, he lived in Serbia and is famous for his biography of the Serbian King Despot Stephan who died at Kosovo Polje. Up until the 18th century, on both the Serbian and Bulgarian sides, there are three or four well known writers whose achievement however is limited to translations of religious works, biographies and a few chronicles. Nevertheless they perpetuated a Slav current which was followed by the first craftsmen of the Renaissance: the monks Paisij from Rila and Dositel from Hopovo; for the monasteries were the seats of this culture. In the Serbian lands it was Gracanica, Zica and Decani who under the Ottomans retained their land and villages as before and in the Bulgarian areas Rial, Backovo and Varovidec[17]. At various times these monastic communities flourished and the number of monks at Backovo was to reach three hundred at the start of the 17th century. Varovidec was the seat of a renowned school of copyists. Yet as well as these indigenous elements, there were also outside influences. For the Serbs this was mainly from scholars of the Republic of Ragusa which will be looked at later[18] and Catholic Croat and Italian missionaries who went into Bosnia and neighbouring areas. From 1463 the Franciscans obtained a Berat from Mehmed II which allowed them to practice their ministries, and they were quite numerous as is borne out by the fact that by 1629 they had 17 monasteries, even though they were usually quite small. Then there was a decline and in 1758 the order only retained three. Venice was one of the rear bases from which were imported the Cyrillic type, used by Macarios from the monastery of Ohrid, near Cetinje, to print the first Bible in Slavonic around 1493. Educated in the Doge's city this monk was recruited by the Voevod of Wallachia, Radu cel Mare, and installed in 1508 at Tirgoviste which consequently became a centre for Slavic books for the Balkan Christians. The Bulgarian areas also benefitted from this outside influence but the most obvious acquisition was with the appointment of Catholic bishops at Ciprovci: Peter Bogdan, Philip Stanislavov and above all Peter Parcevic (1612–1674). Born in the city of Ciprovec where many Saxon miners were to be found, he studied in Rome and was appointed in 1654 Archbishop of Marcianopolis[19] and apostolic vicar of Moldavia. For since 1615, Vienna had obtained a Berat from the Porte allowing Catholics to build churches and to practice their religion freely. As the Bulgarian nuncio to the court of Vienna, Peter Parcevic was responsible for supervising its application. Consequently he became involved in wider European politics and was sent on a mission to the Cossack Hetman Bogdan Chmielnicki. It was in this context that the Bulgarian lands to the north and north west were disturbed by the War of the Holy League 1684–1699 and that contact was made with Peter the Great's Russia; so opening a further path for outside influences on the Christians of the Balkans.

These communities, Islamic as well as Christian, cohabited in the cities and gave them the "oriental" character which western travellers had noticed. More fundamentally this produced a popular oral culture in the Balkans which mixed both traditions and customs, above all on matters which did not involve religious faith. So until the 19th century Serbian women in Belgrade would go out with veils whilst their husbands wore turbans and smoked hookahs. To such an extent that in 1829 Vuk Karadzic was to write: "Only the peasants are Serbs. The few Serbs who live in the cities are called Varosani (Town dwellers) and dress in Turkish garb and follow Turkish customs." However in the countryside, having kept contact with the Ottoman authorities to a minimum, there remained and developed cultures of an ethnic group and an oral tradition of passing on knowledge and social norms. There lies the difference between Greek or Bulgarian patriarchal family, Serbian Zadruga, Albanian Fis and Montenegrin or Wallachian tribe, resulting in ways of life and value systems expressed by unwritten lore, traditional festivals and indigenous art. In other words folklore and ethic tradition.

Notes

1. The Yuruks were nomads from Anatolia. The Koniars had retained the name of their home region; Konya.
2. It is worth noting that the term "millet" appears in Ottoman texts only late on, not before the end of the 18th century.
3. Tug: horse's tail which would be carried in front of a high-ranking Ottoman official. The number showed their position in the hierarchy.
4. Solu Monastiri is to the south west of town where the Armenian Church of Saint Mary Perivlepte still remains standing.
5. On the Bulgaro-Yugoslav border on a level with Mihajlovgrad.
6. In some Ottoman documents the arab term "Liva" is used.
7. Cf. P.F. Sugar: Southeastern Europe under Ottoman Rule p.94/95.
8. The Ottoman Empire. The classical age. op. cit. p.107.
9. Silver coin—basic monetary unit of the Empire which is also translated as Aspries.
10. The fundamental study in French is: Todorov (Nicolaj): La ville balkanique aux XV—XIX siecles. Bucarest 1980. p.495.
11. The extremely popular Turkish Kara Ghuz.
12. An Okwa of bread (1.2gr) was worth 2 to 3 Akces.
13. The definitive study is that of Mantran (R): Istanbul dans la 2eme moite du XVII siecle. Paris 1962. Also consult the delightful "Vie quotidienne a Constantinople au temps de Soliman le Magnifique et de ses successeurs (XVI—XVII siecles)" Hachette 1965.
14. There existed four orthodox rites of which the Hanefit originated with Abou Hanifa who died in Baghdad in 767.
15. His Tekke with its mausoleum is still today a place of frequent pilgrimage.
16. Also called the "Bulgarian medium."
17. Next to the Bulgarian town of Etropoli.
18. See Ch.6.
19. An ancient town, 13 miles from Varna, founded by Trajan and destroyed in the 7th century.

6

The Porte's Vassal States: Wallachia, Moldavia, Transylvania and Ragusa up to 1566

Historical atlases differ over the limits of the Ottoman Empire on the death of Suleyman in 1566. Should this include the territories north of the Danube: Wallachia, Moldavia, Transylvania and the port of Ragusa on the Adriatic? The de jure and de facto differences between regions, has already been mentioned even though they might have been considered integral parts of the Empire since they were under the Sultan's administration, yet at the same time they might have enjoyed different privileges. For the above mentioned territories retained their traditional structures and in return had to fulfil certain obligations, above all payment of a tribute. In feudal Europe this obligation was a sign of vassalage hence the generally accepted term of "the Porte's Vassal States," even if in a sense, we have to include some of the possessions of Ferdinand of Habsburg, who in 1533 agreed to pay a tribute for Royal Hungary in return for peace. However, as well as these political and financial criteria, one has to add the religious one of belonging to Dar-el-Islam which would have been manifest by the existence of mosques. They exist or existed all over the Empire apart from Wallachia, Moldavia, Transylvania and Ragusa which were to remain infidel territories.

The Principality of Wallachia

Since the loss of the Roman province of Dacia, in 272 AD, the plain of the Danube to the north had witnessed the passage of a succession of peoples: Germanic tribes and nomads from the steppes. It was part of the First Bulgar Kingdom (681–end of the 10th century) then of the Petcheneg Turcoman Empire which had been used by Byzantium for two centuries against their enemies but who had fallen out with their masters and been crushed by Basileus John II in 1122. Then came their cousins the Kumans, semi-nomadic animal farmers who had settled there and been converted to Christianity, hence the creation of a Kuman Archbishopric in 1227. They ruled over indigenous Slav and Romanian peoples who were in conflict with Byzantium which was to result in the creation of the Second Bulgarian Kingdom in 1186. In 1240 the Kuman Empire was overcome by Mongol attacks. The following year two Mongol armies crossed the Carpathian mountains whilst a third laid waste to the plain of the Danube before linking up with the other two and crushing Bela IV, king of Hungary, at Mohi on the river Tisza in April 1241. The precipitous departure of the invader in 1242 allowed the Hungarian sovereign, who had escaped death, to rebuild his kingdom. It was in this context that Wallachia was created.

Under Byzantium and during the reign of Saint Stephan, small political movements had brought together semi-autonomous village communities which had continued to survive under their Kuman masters. Once free the local chiefs had wanted to strengthen their position, yet had come into conflict with Bela IV who wanted to make this area a barricade against further invasions. He tried in vain to establish the Knights of Saint John of Jerusalem and set up a feudal structure similar to that of Hungary ie. responsible to the crown. Yet after 1270 there is evidence of increasing resistance to the Magyar King. Voevod Basarab (1310–1352), who had made a name for himself against the Tatars of the Golden Horde, gave himself the title of Grand Voevod and formed a state whose capital was Cimpulung and later Arges. This state was called Wallachia and gained its independence following his victory over Charles I of Anjou, the new king of Hungary.

Inhabited mainly by Romanian Wallachians the principality retained a feudal structure but was to remain faithful to the Byzantine Church whose form of Christianity had been adopted by the population during the First Bulgarian Kingdom. In 1359 the Patriarch of Constantinople created the Metropolitan See of Arges, granting the Church of "Ungrowallachia" its autocephalic status. Politically the voevod attempted to consolidate his grasp on power, refusing the boyars the right of election. His son and heir was brought into government during his lifetime. The Hungarian suzerain reacted and there followed a ten year war between Vlaicu Voda (1364–1377) and Louis I whose outcome was inconclusive, and the Angevin had to make do with a purely nominal oath of allegiance from the Wallachian Prince.

This period of real independence was short lived, for the small principality had to confront a particularly fearsome new neighbour: the Ottomans. The capitulation of the Bulgarians of Tirnovo in 1393 brought the armies of Sultan Bayezid right up to the banks of the Danube. Previously the Wallachian Voevod, Mircea cel Batrin (1386–1418), had been aware of this threat and in 1389 had taken a contingent of soldiers to help Serbia, and fought with Prince Lazarus on the field of Kosovo. The following year he expelled an Ottoman army from the Dobrudja. In 1394 the Thunderbolt—Yildirim—was to avenge this; crossing the Danube at Orsova the Ottomans invaded the principality and forced the Wallachian army back at Rovine, near Craiova, on the 10 October. The Voevod had to seek refuge in Hungarian Transylvania, on the other side of the mountains, and his rival and successor Vlad I (1395–1397) agreed to pay the Sultan a tribute—Harac. But at Kronstadt (Brasov), Mircea pledged his allegiance to Sigismond of Luxembourg, his Hungarian sovereign, and with his help tried to reconquer his throne. Yet the powerful crusader army which at Sigismond's behest had been assembled was crushed by Bayezid on the 25 September 1396 at Nicopolis[1]. Mircea, who had been on the Christian side, just managed to escape and the Ottomans occupied the Bulgarian principality of Vidin which they then annexed. Henceforth the Sultan's Empire touched Wallachia all the way along the Danube. Mircea was restored to his throne and there was a breathing space following the Ottoman defeat of Ankara (1402) and during the struggle for Bayezid's succession. He made the most of this, and together with Sigismond and the Polish king Ladislas Jagellon, he recaptured the fortress of Silistra and part of the Dobrudja. But in 1413, after Mehmed I reunited the Ottoman Empire and once more became a threat, Mircea agreed to pay a tribute of 3,000 golden ducats a year. Even so, in 1418 (the same year as the death of Mircea) the Sultan flexed his muscles: the Dobrudja region was completely retaken and remained an Ottoman province until 1878, two bridgeheads were established on the right bank of the Danube around Turnu and Giurgiu, the whole of the plain was laid to waste and Mircea's son Mihail was killed near Arges. With the support of some of the boyars Mehmed placed Dan II, formerly a hostage at Edirne, on the Wallachian throne. From 1419 onwards the fate of Wallachia was tied to the Ottoman Empire.

Yet for more than half a century the voevods were to continue to try and recover their independence. In 1421 Dan II revolted and for the next ten years, supported by the king of Hungary, he was to alternate in power with Radu II, who was the Porte's candidate. His successor, Vlad Dracul, however was made to pay tribute and accompanied Murad II on his campaign in 1438 in Transylvania. From 1441 onwards the voevods became caught up in the anti-Ottoman struggle of Janos Hunyadi and there were Wallachian contingents at the battles of Varna (1444) and Kosovo Polje (1448). The death of the Transylvanian hero, outside the city of Belgrade (August 1456), coincides with the accession of Vlad the Impaler— Vlad Tepes (1456–1462)[2] (who seized power by killing his predecessor) to the Wallachian throne. In 1459 the new voevod refused to pay Harac (which in the meantime had risen to 10,000 ducats) to the Porte. The Sultan sent an armed detachment which issued an ultimatum. Vlad seized the two commanders and had them impaled alive at the gates of his capital thus acquiring his fearsome surname. War once more broke out in 1461. Vlad laid waste to the Ottoman Dobrudja and Mehmed invaded Wallachia. The voevod implemented a scorched earth policy. He set light to his capital Tirgoviste[3] and withdrew into the mountains. Unable to dislodge him from there the Sultan appointed a new voevod who was supported by an Ottoman garrison and some of the boyars. Vlad, who had taken refuge in Transylvania, quarrelled with the king of Hungary who imprisoned him for twelve years. He returned to Wallachia in 1476 and was reinstated as voevod by Stephan the Great of Moldavia. The Porte reacted and put forward his own aspirant who had Vlad Tepes put to death.

After this Wallachia became a more or less faithful vassal of the Sultan. The weak successors of Vlad Tepes helped the Ottomans fight against Stephan the Great. Yet in 1521, following the capture of Belgrade, Voevod Radu of Afumati made an alliance with his neighbour Janos Zapolyai, the Voevod of Transylvania, to fight Soliman the Magnificent. This resulted in his being four times deposed by rivals protected by the Porte. Hungarian support vanished after the Mohacs disaster (August 1526). Following the struggle of succession for the Crown of Saint Stephan, Janos Zapolyai turned to the Sultan and became his candidate against the Habsburgs.

Deprived of all outside help, the Voevod of Wallachia found himself an object of intrigues and even open revolt, involving several boyars whose support was essential. Due to the lack of clear guidelines on the rules of succession, the prince—Domn in Romanian—before he died tried to make his son his successor, in the Byzantine tradition. However the great boyars had the right to choose a candidate put forward by a neighbouring country or by force of arms and from the beginning of the 16th century the Porte had reserved the right to reject the thus designated voevod and had not hesitated to bribe the boyars to support their own candidates. Over twenty years, between 1509 and 1529, there were fifteen different people on the throne of Wallachia. As well as a tribute, it was customary to pay homage at the sultan's court. Vassalage had become a formal institution.

Basically the settlement which the Porte had imposed on the Wallachian voevods at the end of the 15th and beginning of 16th centuries, stipulated that a tribute be paid which, in terms of Sharia law, signified vassalage. A sum in gold coins, usually Venetian ducats[4], was set each year to be taken to Istanbul. Wallachia's tribute was almost constantly going up depending on incidence of wars and the needs of the Sultan's treasury. This was slightly mitigated by the devaluation of the coin:

Wallachia's Tribute in Golden Ducats[5]

1417	3,000
1459	10,000
1503	8,000
1541	12,000
1542	24,000
1567	55,000
1593	12,000

On top of this there was a gift—Peshchesh—given to the Sultan by the prince on accession. A Firman was issued when the Porte confirmed the appointment and the candidate would have been wise to be generous. Soliman the Magnificent made sure this was clearly understood. There was also Baksheesh for the Grand Vizier and other notables, renewed at each change of prince, which was in fact one of the reasons for the frequent changes. It has been calculated that during the short period 1581 to 1590, the sum total of gifts and Baksheesh was more than the tribute itself. On top of this the economy was subject to a variety of controls. Wallachia was obliged to provide the Sultan with a certain number of ex gratia deliveries of grain, honey and furs. The voevod was responsible for this yet left it to the boyars who took advantage of this power over the peasants. As everywhere else in the Empire the principality was subject to a system of compulsory purchase of goods, at prices fixed by the Porte, to feed its vast capital Istanbul. The purveyors—Djelep—local merchants or notables infamous for their harshness had to guarantee the deliveries. Wallachia supplied Istanbul with cattle, grain and fish from the Danube.

Having fulfilled his dues, the voevod was in theory his own master, and had power over all internal questions. He ruled the country with the help of a council—Divan—which was made up of eight to ten boyars. He would pass sovereign judgement, based on customary law which was complemented by Byzantine law. His army, with less than 10,000 men, made up of the prince's soldiers and his nobles, was above all intended for domestic use against rebellious boyars, and was called the "little army." When the need arose he could enlist support of peasant serfs who made up what was called the "Grand Army" and which had 40,000 men but was not very effective. The Sultan often used these soldiers for his own use and as mentioned above, Wallachian soldiers were present at most of the big battles of the Ottoman army during the 15th and 16th centuries.

The independence of the Principality was above all demonstrated by the fact that Sharia law was not applicable, and that Wallachia, unlike central Hungary, did not have Spahis or Kadis, nor mosques and neither were Muslims allowed to settle. Clearly it was not part of Dar-el-Islam. With one exception however for, in 1542, Suleyman fighting the Habsburgs, had transformed the port and region of Braila into "Raia" or in other words territory under military control and so cut the Principality off from the Black Sea. This was simply an annexation of Wallachian territory and Ottoman troops and mosques were to remain.

Contiguous to the Sultan's Empire, the Principality of Wallachia was to remain a vassal state up to the 19th century.

The Principality of Moldavia

The eastern Carpathian foothills, between the Dnestr and the arching mountain range, experienced a similar development. The indigenous population had been even more exposed to invasion by tribes from the Steppes than their fellows in the Danubian plain. They were to experience the rule of the Goths, Bulgarians, Avars, Petchenegs and the Kumans. In the 12th century the first political grouping around the Birlad area was formed and one of its leaders, perhaps a Wallachian, joined in the conflict between the Russian princes of Kiev and Halitch. What is certain is that the whole region was laid waste by the Mongols and that Kuman rule came to an end only to be replaced by that of the Tatars of the Golden Horde. There is a voevod called Olaha who took "gifts" to the Khan of the Horde yet this vassal status appears to have ended with the death of Khan Nagoi in 1299. There was then a period of rivalry for control of the region between the Polish and Hungarian sovereigns who both wanted to make it into a buffer zone against the Tatars. In 1325 a Moldavian contingent is reported to have taken part in Ladislas I of Poland's campaign against the Margrave of Brandenburg and merchants linking Lemberg and Cracow to the ports of the Crimean and Moncastro[6] helped develop towns such as Baia, Siret and Suceava which are first mentioned in archive documents around 1330/1350. Yet this trade route, known to seafarers of the 14th century as the Via Wallachiensis, was also of interest to the Magyars who were keen on directing some of the flow to Transylvania. In 1352–53 the king of Hungary, Louis I of Anjou, organized an expedition against the Tatars. The Voevod of Maramaros, a certain Dragos, took part and following victory, the Angevin gave him the "Moldavian Borders." The population of the border area, disaffected with Magyar rule and above all Catholic propaganda by Dragos' nephew, appealed to Bogdan his successor in Maramaros, who was in conflict with Louis I. Bogdan was made voevod in 1359 by the nobles and was the first prince of Moldavia. Despite Hungarian efforts he remained in power until his death in 1365. But Moldavia was limited to the northern region around Suceava while the south remained under the control of the Golden Horde. It was to be the task of his successor Petru to reunite the parts which had made up the old border area into the Principality of Moldavia. Petru I, as he is known in the list of Romanian princes, laid the basis for a state, fortified the capital Suceava and struck the first silver coinage. Yet the Tatar threat was to remain acute especially in 1386 when the son of the Grand Duke of Moscow, Dimitri Donskoi, escaped from the Khan's court where he was being held hostage and took refuge in Moldavia. Jagellonian Poland was at the time the main opponent of the Tatars, so Petru I went to Lemberg in 1387 to pledge vassalage to Ladislas II. While Wallachia turned for support to Byzantium and Buda, Moldavia came under the sphere of influence of Poland much in the same way as the former Kiev territories of Halitch, Podolia and Volhinia. The feudal model consequently was that of Cracow with boyars—the Slav term Boi which means fight—both masters of the land and warlords having dominion over peasant serfs who had succeeded in keeping their traditional freedom for much longer than their Polish counterpart. The towns provided a counterbalance to the power of the boyars, with elected representatives and town mayors (called Soltuzi in Romanian which comes from the Polish Soltys).

In the same way as their Wallachian cousins, the Moldavians had stayed true to the Eastern Church. In 1388 the Halitch Metropolitan ordained as bishop of the Genoese colony of Moncastro, a monk called Iosif, yet the ordination was not accepted by the Patriarch of Byzantium. A lengthy quarrel ensued but in 1401, at the request of the Grand Voevod Alexander the Good (1400–1432), a canonical inquiry concluded that the consecration had been valid and bishop Iosif was recognized as Metropolitan of Moldavia with his seat at Suceava. The new Principality henceforth enjoyed ecclesiastic autocephalism which it was felt demonstrated its sovereignty. In fact Alexander was a faithful vassal of the Polish sovereign and for example Moldavian contingents were to participate in the battle of Grunwald[7] in 1410 against the Teutonic Order. Polish historians maintain that Polish suzerainty over Moldavia continued up until 1499, but on the death of Alexander, the boyar struggle for succession pitted supporters of Poland against those of Hungary. It was at this moment that the Ottomans turned their attention to this small distant principality.

The first encounter took place in 1420, when a band of irregulars—Akinji—coming from Wallachia, crossed into Moldavia. Pillaging as they went along they reached the port of Moncastro before withdrawing once again south of the Danube. In retaliation

Alexander occupied the fortress of Kilia on the northern branch of the Danube delta. Control of the mouth of the great river was also of interest to the Crimean Tatars, and in 1428 the Khan proposed an alliance with the Ottomans who were down river. Mehmed II revived the idea and following the fall of Constantinople, sent a fleet to capture the Genoese ports of the region. This was the first coordinated action with the Tatars. Moldavia was caught in a pincer movement and the Sultan issued an ultimatum for Voevod Petru Aron to surrender. In the spring of 1456 the Prince called a Grand Assembly at Vaslui under Metropolitan Teoctist together with the boyars. After lengthy consultations they understood that they were on their own and could do nothing else save accept defeat. By the Firman of 9 June 1456, Mehmed ended the state of war with the principality in return for an annual tribute of 2,000 golden ducats. The merchants of Moncastro who were to remain the voevod's subjects were allowed to trade with Istanbul, Edirne and Bursa. Officially, from 1456 onwards, Moldavia became a vassal of the Ottoman Empire.

In fact a famous voevod did try for half a century to limit the influence of his fearsome neighbour. Stephan the Great (Stefan cel Mare 1457–1504) enjoyed a long reign during which he increased the power of the prince and stimulated economic prosperity. Moldavia became an ally to be reckoned with by Poland and Hungary, when dealing with the Sultan. Petru Aron had ascended the throne by assassinating Stephan's brother. Stephan in turn overthrew the assassin and forced him to seek refuge at the court of his suzerain, the king of Poland, Casimir IV Jagellon. The latter however was occupied in the struggle with the Teutons and Stephan took advantage of this to mark his independence. In April 1457, during his coronation as voevod, on top of the traditional acclamation of the boyars the Metropolitan anointed him, imitating the coronation of the Polish kings. Ten years later when the Hungarian sovereign Mathias Corvinus wanted to impose his suzerainty, Stephan faced up to him and beat the Magyar army at Baia.

Moldavia remained independent but isolated in the face of a mounting Ottoman threat, for ever since his accession Stephan had refused to pay tribute. So he willingly answered the call of Pope Sixtus IV to join Poland, Hungary and Venice in an anti-Ottoman crusade. Mehmed sent a large army against the rebel—chroniclers speak of 100,000 men—while Stephan with his vassals and free peasants was reinforced by his allies: Polish, Hungarian and Szekler contingents. In January 1475 the Moldavian prince won a great victory at Vaslui but was unable to persuade his allies to prolong their action. An Ottoman fleet seized the Genoese settlements of Kaffa, Cherson and Sudak and the Sultan imposed his suzerainty on the Crimean Tatars, who had been decimated by Stephan some years previously in the oak groves of Lepnic on the Dnestr. From then on the Khan was to become a vassal of the Porte and was a permanent threat to Moldavia. The vodjvod took the consequences in July 1475 and pledged allegiance to Mathias Corvinus who in turn promised to support him against the Ottomans. Resolved to settle the matter once and for all, Mehmed II summoned his vassals, the Voevod of Wallachia and the Khan of Crimea, and leading personally the army they joined battle at a place near Neamt in July 1476 and Stephan was forced to beat a retreat. Yet the Sultan failed to capture Suceava. Three years later, in October 1480, isolated after Venice had made peace with Istanbul, Stephan was forced in turn to negotiate and agreed to pay a tribute of 6,000 golden ducats. The truce was short lived for the Voevod proved recalcitrant and Bayezid II coveted the Moldavian fortress on the Danube delta. In June 1484 the Ottomans took Kilia and Moncastro. Stephan appealed to the king of Poland, Casimir IV Jagellon, and with his boyars went to Kolomyja in Red Ruthenia to pay him homage. But Jagellon, in turn threatened by the Grand Duchy of Moscow, signed a peace agreement with the Porte recognizing his possession of Kilia and of Moncastro, the latter becoming Akkerman. Once more Stephan gave in and recognized the Sultan's suzerainty, promising payment of a tribute of 5,000 ducats.

Notes

1. Now in Bulgaria, Nikopol is on the Danube.
2. Son of Vlad Dracul he is known in historical mythology by the name of Dracula.
3. Capital of Wallachia after it took over from Arges (now Curtea of Arges) in 1385.
4. Remember that the Venetian gold ducat weighed 3.56g.
5. From P. F. Sugar: Southeastern Europe above. p.122.
6. Cetatea Alba now Belgograd which was a Genoese colony since 1315.
7. German historians call it Tannenberg.

7

"Fish Rot from the Head Downwards"—1566 to 1683

This traditional Turkish proverb was aimed at what was felt to be the cause of crisis in Ottoman society. Traditionally the death of Soliman the Magnificent in 1566 is taken by historians to be the beginning of the "Decline of the Empire." In fact everybody agrees that there was a crisis of power in the second half of his great reign, after the Sultan strangled his Grand Vizier Ibrahim in 1536, and there is also agreement on the decline being uneven with sporadic upsurges. In foreign affairs the conquests of Cyprus in 1570, Crete in 1669 and the thrust into the Ukraine in 1672, together with the vigorous recovery under the Koprulu Grand Viziers in the second half of the 17th century, break the line of this descending curve. Finally this decline must be seen in relation to a period which is marked by the political and economic growth of two neighbouring countries: Austria and Russia, and which was to result in a change of the balance of power in the region. In this complex process the siege of Vienna was to mark a turning-point. Up until then the Ottoman Empire had been amongst the mightiest powers in Europe.

The Institutional Crisis

Since Orkhan the system had operated as a military and religious organization led by a Sultan whose skill as a military and political leader had been an important factor of their success. Apart from the period of interregnum, from 1402 to 1413, when several brothers had fought over the throne, the "House of Osman" had kept power for two and a half centuries with nine of its members, an average reign of almost 27 years. The period following the death of Suleyman to the siege of Vienna spans only 117 years during which time there were ten sultans, which gives an average reign of less than 12 years. In the second period there was a lack of continuity and continuity had characterized the reigns of their great predecessors in the 15th and 16th centuries. Also out of the first nine sovereigns (leaving aside the period between 1402 and 1413 when there was civil war) and even though two sultans abdicated, the Sultan himself remained inviolate, while of the ten successors, five were deposed and two assassinated: Osman II in 1622 by the Janissaries of Istanbul and Ibrahim strangled in his palace[1] in 1648.

The first reason for a possible crisis at the top was the traditional problem of succession to the throne. As previously mentioned Mehmed II had tried to resolve this problem in the most brutal of fashions by actually eliminating potential rivals. The "fratricidal law" was to continue to apply up until the beginning of the 17th century, reaching a horrific record in 1595 when Mehmed III had 19 brothers and about 20 sisters put to death at his accession, all strangled by deaf and dumb servants that very same day. Ahmed I ended this practice in 1603 when, not having any children of his own old enough to rule, he adopted the Arab tradition whereby the oldest male relative succeeded to the throne: in this case his brother, the future Mustafa I. Following this the Ottoman princes—brothers and uncles of the sovereign—were kept inside the palace in Kafes for all their life—the "golden cage" that travellers wrote about—where they lived with wives and eunuchs, lacking any military or political training and with the possibility of change, without any transition, from this life of luxury and idleness to that of responsibility and power. There was the case of Ibrahim who was known as Deli Ibrahim—the mad—whose craving for furs ruined the imperial treasury. He was deposed in favour of his son and was once again shut up in his apartments which was so traumatic for him that he became raving mad and a Fetwa from the Sheik ul Islam allowed him to be strangled.

This new method only resulted in increasing the likelihood of intrigue inside the harem. From the latter half of Suleyman I's reign it is possible to speak of a "Sultanate of women," product of the rivalry between the Sultan's mother—Valide Sultan—and his wife Hurrem of which Grand Vizier Ibrahim was in 1536 to fall foul. Later certain Sultanas were the real power behind government, for instance Safiyen who was undoubtedly of Venetian origin[2], Mehmed III's mother who let her have power. Sultana

Kosem, the wife of Ahmed I (1603–1617) dominated her brother-in-law Mustafa I. His children Murad IV (1623–1640) and Ibrahim (1640–1648) had ascended the throne but were strangled on the orders of Kosem's rival, Sultana Turkhan, a Russian slave who became the wife of Mehmed IV. About these women would grow grasping cliques, sometimes with the support of the Grand Vizier or the Sultan's teacher, sometimes the head of the eunuchs or the Aga of the palace guard. Intrigue, betrayal and assassination became the framework of Palace life in the 17th century, the Grand Vizier often being the first casualty. Osman II, fearful of the Janissaries, had Dilaver Pasha executed in 1622. Murad IV let his soldiers hang Hafiz Ahmed Pasha from the palace doors in 1631 and in 1632 he himself had Recep Pasha strangled and his body thrown onto the public highway. Ibrahim ordered the execution of Kemankes Kara Mustafa Pasha in 1644. There are many other examples and indeed it was rare for a Grand Vizier, in the first half of the 17th century to die in his bed.

These tragedies soon spilled outside the walls of the Seraglio as Janissaries and Spahis from the Istanbul garrison became the tools of the main protagonists, to the extent that the period of 1648 to 1651 is known as the "Sultanate of the Agas," when the capital's military leaders ruled. Sometimes troops from further afield would intervene. In 1631 to pacify the rebellious soldiers of Anatolia, they were permitted to come to Istanbul to voice their grievances. The city was invaded by undisciplined gangs of soldiers who straight away demanded that the Grand Vizier and Sheik el Islam be put to death, which was done only to be followed by a reign of terror with robbery, extortion, debauchery and drunkenness in public during the holy period of Ramadan. Murad IV only regained control after seven months of disorder and had to force the various commanders of the garrison to take a written oath of loyalty to him.

The decline of the military institutions—Seyfiye—had its roots in the fact that the art of war was changing. In the 16th century the Sultan's opponents in Europe, and above all the Habsburgs, were forming armies that closely coordinated infantry, cavalry and artillery. Usually made up of mercenaries, these were very different from the feudal formations which had been based on the noble cavalry. In order to face up to this the Ottoman army had to undergo a fundamental reform. As mentioned above the growth of the Empire had made it difficult to conduct campaigns on a seasonal basis and the failure at Vienna in 1683 was a graphic illustration of this problem. Furthermore the defence of thousands of miles of borders in Europe, placed new strains on meagre resources. Across Hungary and the western Ukrainian steppes, there sprang up a fortified line comprised of strongholds held by infantry and artillery. So the Spahi cavalry was no longer needed, at the very time when its obedience was to be put into question and the sovereign no longer inspired his troops. The second pillar of Ottoman military might, the Janissaries, underwent a similar decline. This slave army of which the Sultan was in theory the father figure, had begun to emancipate itself in the first half of the 16th century when they were first allowed to marry and set up families. This immediately raised the question of pay. It has been calculated that between their creation in the 1330s and 1600 their pay had quadrupled whilst the cost of living had risen tenfold. To provide for their own families the Janissaries would become more involved in craft and commercial activities than in their military duties. The majority of Esnaf armourers or butchers were Janissaries. In 1574 they were allowed to enrol their sons in the corps to provided new recruits. In the towns of the Empire, by the 17th century , the Janissaries had become a form of militia who were rather loath to answer their sovereign's call to arms. In the capital they demanded the "gift" of accession from each new Sultan, they were the essential ingredient for palace intrigues and benefitted from numerous other monetary hand-outs from Grand Viziers, various Sultanas and their supporters. Pampered and feared by the Palace, the Janissaries remained a force to be reckoned with but more for internal struggles than for border combat.

Furthermore the traditional method of recruitment, Devsirme, had fallen into abeyance, its disappearance not as a result of a greater respect for Christians but that the levy was felt to be expensive and unproductive, whereas the slave markets were well stocked because of Crimean Tatar raids on the Polish border areas. Anyhow the Janissary corps was already large enough (in theory 60,000 in the 17th century) and reluctant to see an increase in numbers which would increase the competition with their children for the privilege of joining-up. Therefore the Devsirme levies became less and less frequent and finally were to disappear, the last being during Murad IV's reign in 1637.

In fact these were indications of the need for deep-rooted reforms involving not only the army but also government and all the Kapi Kulari—the servants of the Porte—in short the whole Kul system. Since its creation in the 14th century there had developed an often violent antagonism between the old Turcoman, or at least Islamic families, and the neo-Muslims who were brought to high office by the Sultan's favour. Two centuries later they had become assimilated and the Palace struggles—often to the death—had created new allegiances: those who were ambitious sought the support of a Sultana, Grand Vizier or Chief Eunuch. The old rift between the "Turks" and "Devsirme" had been replaced by that of "parties" such as that of Sultana Mahfiruz who was opposed to Sultana Kosem, or other temporary and diverse coalitions. The old "Slaves of the Porte" had become nothing more than Muslims in the Sultan's service and only rarely slaves from the Empire's markets, such as black eunuchs. It would seem that Mehmed Koprulu, the founder of the Grand Vizier dynasty which reached its zenith in 1656, was one of the last levies of Devsirme.

The name Koprulu, together with Murad IV, brings up the question of the two periods of reform that the Empire experienced in the 17th century. Murad IV (1623—1640) brought to the throne at the age of 14 by his crafty and fearsome mother Kosem, wife of Sultan Ahmed I, found anarchy reigning in most of the provinces. It took him nine years to sort things out. Indeed there was discontent in the army when it failed to take Baghdad in 1631 and as a result it seized control of Istanbul and committed such acts of violence that the population turned to the Sultan. With the support of his adviser Koci Bey he attempted to reform the system by revamping traditional institutions. He purged the capital of rebel soldiers and allowed thousands to be massacred by the ordinary people whom they had previously terrorized. In the provinces he confiscated fiefdoms abandoned by their Spahis and gave them to the Janissaries, restoring the Timar system and the raising of taxes. Following a huge fire which burnt down a quarter of Istanbul he concluded that this was divine punishment and enforced a climate of moral puritanism: the consumption of coffee and tobacco were forbidden and the places were these were taken were closed down; traditional rules of dress and comportment were once more implemented and the Sultan himself would wander at night in disguise to check that his orders were being obeyed and have those who disobeyed immediately executed and their bodies left as an example to others. In 1636 he had Nefi, the greatest poet of his day, strangled for writing satirical works. This reaction ended with the development of a vast spy network all over the Empire.

Mehmed Koprulu who was Grand Vizier from 1656 to 1661, and his son Ahmed who followed him from 1661–67, mark the second variation of the Ottoman downward curve during the 17th century. Born around 1575 in the village of Rudnik in Albanian territory, of a Christian father, he was taken by Devsirme and entered Palace service, first in the kitchens and then in the Imperial Treasury. Rewarded with a Timar in the central Anatolian village of Kopru, he married the daughter of the Sandjak Bey and took the name of his fiefdom: Koprulu. He then embarked on an administrative career in the wake of successive Grand Viziers as well as taking part in the siege of Baghdad as a Spahi. Appointed governor of Damascus he became involved with Sultana Kosem until disastrously for him she lost all her influence. He was back in Kopru when Sultan Mehmed IV made him Grand Vizier in September 1656. The situation was critical: the Venetian fleet was blockading the Dardanelles, there were food shortages in the capital and prices were rising fast. The terrified population feared a Christian raid on the city. More than seventy years old, Mehmed came to the office of Grand Vizier with a lot of experience in government and also in Palace intrigue. He obtained full powers, above all for the appointment of high ranking officials and a promise from the Sultan that he would ignore rumours and gossip concerning his highest servant. There followed five years of strict rule over the Empire. In the Palace all those who had supported the Sultana against him were put to death and he instigated a vigorous campaign against corruption. It is reported that in 5 years he had 13,000 members of government or Ulemas executed for being guilty of embezzlement. At the same time he practised tight control of expenditure and recovered a large proportion of unoccupied or illegally held fiefdoms, the proceeds going to the Treasury, which led once again to a balanced budget. Too old to lead military operations himself, he entrusted them to his son Ahmed who turned out to be a good military commander.

Ahmed in turn was called upon by his father to succeed and continue his task. Better educated and more versatile, he brought back order to government and the army. In response to the demands of the provincial Janissaries he instituted a system of recruitment of Anatolian peasants, known as "volunteers"—gonullu—yet the reform was not completely successful, due to financial problems and the numerous wars which characterized this period. Nevertheless, under Ahmed Koprulu, the Grand Vizierate recovered the power that its 14th century predecessors had known.

Murad IV and the Koprulus were what would be called conservative reformers, for they were convinced that the fight against corruption would restore the grandeur of the Ottoman system, the best possible system in the world. However in 1632 corruption and the conduct of soldiers during Ramadan led some Ulemas to denounce the more serious crisis in religious faith itself. One of them, Kadizad Mehmed Efendi, who died in 1635, was at the root of a movement which could be called "fundamentalist" and which was named after him "Kadizadler." They advocated strict practice of the principles of the Koran and traditional faith, and renewed their attacks on supporters of Sufism, such as Sivosi Efendi who died in 1640. These quasi-scholastic disputes split the literate classes in Istanbul and Murad IV aligned himself with the supporters of Kadizad who made him implement his moral strictures. This influence was especially strong at the beginning of Mehmed IV's reign. At their behest he dissolved the mystic orders and closed their Tekkes which was not much appreciated by the inhabitants of the capital. The Kadizadlers projected an image of intolerance and narrow-mindedness which was in sharp contrast to the moral laxness of the Palace itself and underlined one of the contradictions of the Ottoman 17th century.

On the Empire's Borders: The Balance of Power in Europe

The same ambiguity is to be found in foreign affairs. In the east the Sefevid Persians remained the main opponent until the 18th century. United under Shiite Islam the Shah's empire was to reach a zenith under Abbass I (1587–1629) who transferred his capital from Tabriz (which had been captured by the Ottomans in 1534) to Ispahan and with English help reorganized his army. The Sultan's army which had occupied Azerbaijan, the whole of the Caucasus region and even Luristan was forced to withdraw, and in 1642 Abbass captured Baghdad and massacred all the Sunni Muslims. Murad IV took his revenge in 1638 and recaptured the former Abbassid capital, signing a treaty with Persia at Kasri Sirm in May 1639 which put an end to their rivalry after more than a century and setting borders which were to last until 1918. Mesopotamia, including Baghdad was to remain Ottoman while the Caucasus region, together with Erevan, Azerbaijan and Tabriz was to be returned to Persia. Access to the Persian Gulf was henceforth assured and one of the great "Spice Roads" was in the Sultan's control.

These operations in far off places explain the Porte's efforts to keep the eastern Mediterranean a "Turkish lake." Ottoman naval supremacy, inherited from Suleyman was to be maintained under Selim II (1566–1574) who was known as the "Drunk." His fleet captured Naxos, Venetian for three centuries, and wrested the island of Chios in 1566 away from the Genoese and renamed it Sakiz. They then concentrated on Cyprus. The old Lusignan kingdom, bought by Venice in 1489, was a base for Christian corsairs who in reality were engaged in out and out piracy, robbing not only Infidels but the Christian inhabitants of the islands, the Greek coast and Asia Minor[3]. In 1570 Selim asked the Doge to cede the island, whose wine he apparently greatly enjoyed. Having received a refusal, the Sultan gave Piyale Pasha responsibility for the expedition. A landing at Limassol met with little resistance, as the money grabbing, intolerant Venetians were not liked by the Greek population. The siege of Nicosia lasted two months and the town fell in September 1570. The following year Famagusta, bravely defended by Marco Antonio Bragadino, on the 1 August was forced to surrender and was granted honourable terms. However an argument broke out between the victor and Bragadino, his hostage, and he was flayed alive while all the Latins were put to death. The Greeks retained their freedom of worship and ownership but to farm the huge estates many peasants from Anatolia were brought over and are the ancestors of the present day Turkish Cypriot community. The island became part of the Grand Vizier's and the Sultan's mother's Has.

In 1568 the Serenissim of Venice turned to Pope Pius V to mobilize Christian forces: only Philip II of Spain and Genoa replied to his call to arms. A Holy League was formed in May 1571 but too late to save Cyprus. In September a fleet assembled at Messina commanded by Don Juan of Austria (the bastard son of Charles V) comprising 210 galleys of which half were Venetian. When news of the fall of Famagusta arrived in October the armada lay at anchor off the Ionian Isles. While several commanders wanted to go home, Don Juan decided to attack the Ottoman fleet which had been spotted in the Gulf of Patras. The encounter took place on the 7 October 1671, at the entry to the gulf, south of the Island of Oxia[4]. Even though numerically superior, the 270 Turkish galleys were overpowered by the Christian attackers who had more soldiers. Fifty ships were sunk and a hundred captured, which resulted in the freeing of 15,000 Christian prisoners. Only forty ships managed to get away under the command of a former Corsair, Vluk Pasha, who brought these remnants back to Istanbul. On the Christian side about a dozen ships were lost and some 8,000 men killed. Among the wounded was Cervantes who lost his arm. Celebrated by the whole of Christianity, Lepanto was the first victory over the Ottomans since the 15th century. Even so it was not decisive. While the crusaders failed to agree on further objectives for their victorious fleet, Grand Vizier Sokolu assembled the resources to rebuild Ottoman naval forces and during the winter of 1571–2, 160 galleys were built. In May 1572 Pius V died and the following year Venice signed a peace treaty with the Porte. Under the treaty of 7 March 1573, Venice renounced forever all claims on Cyprus and agreed to pay an indemnity of 300,000 golden ducats, which Istanbul saw as its tribute for retaining its trading privileges within the Sultan's Empire. The following year 1574 Ottoman galleys came and laid waste to the Sicilian and southern Italian coastline, then in 1574 wrested Tunis back from the Spaniards, which was to remain for three centuries within the Porte's orbit.

During the first half of the 17th century the western Mediterranean basin was to be the scene of Spanish, English and French rivalry, punctuated by "corses" by Barbary pirates, over whom in theory the Porte had suzerainty but in reality could not control. The eastern part however remained a "Turkish Lake," troubled in turn by Christian corsairs: mainly the galleys of the Knights of Malta but also others under the flags of the Order of Saint Stephan and Tuscan, Sicilian or Savoyard galleons. They would operate off the Peloponnese coast, in the Greek archipelagos, along the Anatolian coastline between Izmir and Adana and opposite Mount Carmel and the delta of the Nile outside Alexandria. Twice a year a seaborne caravan left Istanbul loaded with timber from the Black Sea and large amounts of currency in coins to buy merchandise from Egypt: rice, flax, sugar, and those that passed in transit through the Red Sea with coffee and spices. This caravan was the most coveted prize but, as a French contemporary who sailed the area explains: "The Christian corsairs, rather than go back empty-handed would land and kidnap those they found, so making a few "dinars" (cents) by ransoming the rich and selling the rest[5]." An Englishman called Roberts adds the detail that: "Straight away in Tripoli, Jaffa, Saint John of Acre or Beirut they would negotiate a ransom for their captives, flying a white flag." This puts into proportion, at least as far as the 17th century is concerned, the infamous buccaneers and Barbary slave trader. After the fall of Cyprus, Crete was the last territory in the eastern Mediterranean where Christian corsairs could find refuge. Since 1210 it was one of the most prized possessions of Venice. Many people had gone to colonize it and Candia [6] was made into a stronghold surrounded by formidable fortifications. Mahomet II the Conqueror is said to have wanted to capture it in 1475, but it was only in 1645 that this Ottoman dream was to come true. Weak Sultan Ibrahim, short of money and egged on by his mother Kosem, at the same time wanted to destroy this den of piracy and get his hands on some of the islands huge wealth. The ostensible pretext was the capture of some very high ranking dignitaries, on their way to pilgrimage at Mecca, by a Maltese corsair who held them prisoner on the Island of Karpathos which was a Cretan dependency. A fleet of 4,000 ships, according to the chroniclers, landed at Can in June 1645 and occupied it without much difficulty, the Greek inhabitants once more demonstrating their dislike of Venetian domination. The next year a further expedition ended with the Ottomans taking Retimo[7] and two years later laying siege to the capital. The siege of Candia was to last for twenty years, from 1648 to 1669. The Serenissim of Venice appealed to the Christian world for help. Pope Clement IX authorized him to sell some convents to obtain money and Louis XIV sent 6,000 soldiers who turned out to be useless. Venice did not give in. Not only did she still retain control of most of the island, but since 1648 she had been blockading the Dardanelles causing panic in Istanbul and leading to the fall of Ibrahim. In 1657 the Venetian grip was relaxed which allowed the Ottomans once more to circulate freely in the Aegean. The energetic Grand Vizier, Ahmed Koprulu, decided in 1669 to resolve the matter and personally took command of the siege. He threw his men at the last fortifications and at the end of August the French withdrew, leaving amongst the dead the Duke of Beaumont[8]. They were followed by various other Christian contingents who had quarrelled with the governor, Morusini, so the latter had no other option than to negotiate. The surrender was signed on the 6 September 1669: the garrison was allowed to withdraw with all its weapons, the island became the property of the Sultan, but the Serenissim of Venice retained his possessions in Dalmatia and the Ionian islands and recovered his trade privileges within the Empire. For more than two hundred years from 1669 to 1898 Crete was to be an Elayet and part of the Dar el Islam.

The struggle with Venice led the Sultan to intervene in Montenegro. Retrenched in Cetinje, the new capital, since the end of the 15th century, Knez Ivan the Black's line—Crnojevic—was to end in 1516. The monastery, around which the small principality town had grown, was held in great veneration by the population, and the bishop—Vladika—who was elected by the monks, had great prestige. This brought him into conflict with the Knez. Traditionally it is reported that the last Crnojevic handed over power to the Vladika before withdrawing to Venice. It would however appear that the bishop took advantage of the absence of the Knez, who at the time was with the Doge, to seize power for himself. Thus was born a peculiar theocratic state which was to last from 1516 to 1851. The head of state was the bishop of Cetinje who was always a Slav, elected by the local assembly, half ecclesiastical and half secular; the bishop would have been consecrated by the Patriarch of Pecs. This system guaranteed the Christian inhabitants implacable opposition to the Ottomans, since the Vladika would never compromise with the Infidel. Furthermore the sacred character of his office made it easier for him to impose his will on the leaders of the tribes. All through the 17th century the Porte tried to destroy this natural ally of Venice. Several times the Ottoman armies launched assaults on this mountainous areas in which, as an envoy of the Doge remarked: "small forces could be beaten but large forces were unable to feed themselves." Twice, in 1623 and 1687, Cetinje was reached and the Montenegrins were forced to pay a tribute, forgotten once the invaders departed. There were in fact two Montenegros: Independent Montenegro which consisted the mountains round Cetinje and subjugated Montenegro in the Moraca plain and the shores of Lake Scutari, inhabited by Muslim Slavs and a steadily growing Albanian population.

In the same way as the eastern Mediterranean was a "Turkish Lake" so too the Black Sea in the north. Since 1542, the whole of the coastline, from the Bosphorous to the mouth of the Dnepr, was part of the Empire; to the north of the Danube, the Kilia-Akkerman area to Jedisan, between the Dnestr and Dnepr, formed a block, up to Kanat in the Crimea which Mehmed had subjugated in 1475, which in fact extended over the whole of the Kuban and lower Don regions. On this northern frontier of Dar el Islam, the danger was from Poland and then from Russia. To protect himself from Tatar raids, the Rzeczpospolita had wanted to transform the principality of Moldavia into a buffer zone but Bayezid had intervened in support of Voevod Stephan and forced Poland in 1499 to make "peace in perpetuity," which was renewed in 1533. In 1572 the Jagallon dynasty came to an end and the great powers vied with each other to place on the Cracow throne their own candidate. Against Austria and the Tsar of Russia, the Porte supported the candidacy of Henry de Valois, and following his return to France, that of Stephan Bathory the Prince of Transylvania and as such the Sultan's vassal since 1566. During his reign (1576–1586) he pursued policies which were in line with Ottoman interests against the Habsburgs and received support from the Crimean Tatars in the war against Tsar Ivan IV. But these turbulent vassals were themselves struggling against Zaporogian Cossacks, the inhabitants of the "wild steppes" which formed a no man's land between the Polish provinces of Podolia and Volhinia. At the end of the 16th century the Cossacks launched their own raids on the Tatar and not only in the direction of the Crimea but also on the ports of the Empire. In 1619, Cossacks were to reach Varna. The Porte reinforced his frontier. Strong fortifications were built at Ozu[9] and the governor, Skander Pasha destroyed a Polish army at Tutova on the river Pruth in September 1620. Peace was restored the following year and Poland confirmed the Sultan's possession of the fortress of Hotin[10] on the upper branch of the Dnestr.

For the next fifty years the situation remained unchanged only troubled by Tatar and Cossack raids, until the balance of power in the region was altered by the intervention of a newcomer: the Tsar of Russia. The Porte reacted tardily to the rise of this great power, which was in fact to become its main opponent. It was only after Ivan the Terrible destroyed the Grand Khanates of Kazan and Astrakhan in 1552 and 1556 respectively and reached the Caspian Sea that Grand Vizier Mehmed Sokolu understood the real danger. In 1570 he organized a naval expedition from Kefe—Kaffa—to the mouth of the Don from which he hoped to reach Astrakhan and make it into a buffer zone against both the Russians and the Persians. It was also hoped to make this area into the point of departure for caravans to Central Asia. The attempt failed because the Khan of Crimea defected and in 1584 an Ottoman army was forced to intervene in this vassal state to impose a more obedient leader. Fifty years later Tsar Michael Romanov, at war with the Poles, appealed to the Ottomans for help. In 1633 they attempted to capture the fortress of Kamieniec in Podolia but King Vladislas IV of Poland saw the writing on the wall and came to the negotiating table: the borders were agreed and the Sultan recognized Polish sovereignty over the Zaporogian Cossacks. (This was to be challenged by the Cossacks themselves when Bogdan Chmielnicki led an uprising 1648–51.) Russia gained a common border with the Ottoman Empire after the Truce of Andrusovo in 1667, which was signed by the Rzeczpospolita and the Tsar and gave the latter, as well as Smolensk and Kiev, the Cossack territories on the northern banks of the Dnepr. The Zaporogian leaders then played the Russians off against the Poles. Hetman Doroszenko, at war with the Poles, declared himself the Sultan's vassal and appealed for help from neighbouring Tatars. After forty years of peace, war broke out between the Porte and Poland and notwithstanding the military skill of the future king, John Sobieski, the Ottoman army pushed to Lemberg (Lwow) and imposed on the Rzeczpospolita the Peace of Butchatch in 1652, which gave Dar el Islam the Podolia and the region south of Kiev. They were also forced to pay a tribute to the Infidel as a sign of vassalage. Never before had the Sultan's banners floated so far north: the Black Sea remained a "Turkish Lake." However a new regional power had come forward: Russia. This was clear soon after the peace treaty when the new Grand Vizier, Kara Mustafa Koprulu, tried to intervene in Cossack affairs and impose a hetman more obedient to the Porte. Tsar Theodore III did not hesitate in using force; this was the first Russo-Turkish war. It was limited to four campaigns between the Bug and the Dnepr and illustrated the problems that the Sultan's army had in operating so far from base. A peace treaty was signed at Bachtschi-Sarai in the Crimea[11] in 1681 and made the lower Dnepr the northern border of Dar el Islam. It was from this starting point that the Russian advance was to begin, to the detriment of the Sultan's Empire.

However it was in central Europe that a new balance of power was emerging which would sound a final halt to further Ottoman expansion. Soliman the Magnificent died in 1566 during a campaign against Emperor Maximilian (1564–1576). Maximilian had refused to pay the tribute which Ferdinand I had previously paid. He also wished to take Transylvania from the Zapolyais who were the Porte's vassal. Yet the Habsburgs lacked the means to carry out this policy and a fragile peace was signed which confirmed the borders of Royal Hungary and the Elayet of Buda, with similar terms to the 1541 treaty. In fact this peace was to be continually jeopardized by Akinji raids against Hungarian towns and villages. These irregular Ottoman soldiers were often from Bosnia, brought there by their newly converted beys and were the main beneficiaries of the Timars which Suleyman had created in the Elayet of Buda. Christian Uzkoks irregulars would in turn retaliate from their side of the frontier. In 1591 the situation degenerated and Emperor Rudolphe sent his army in and defeated the Ottomans at Sisak on the river Sava. This was the start of a war that the Hungarians call the "15 Years War." It was to last in fact thirteen years and was mainly limited to the borders but twice the fortress of Buda was besieged by the Austrians (1602–1603). The main area of battle however was Transylvania. The Pope resurrected the idea of a Holy League and Sigismond Bathory, prince of Transylvania, together with Voevod Michael the Brave (unhappy at the increase in tribute) were to join. All "Turks" found in the two principalities were massacred. Mehmed III ordered his best general, Sinan Pasha to avenge this insult and Bucharest was occupied, its churches and boyar palaces reduced to ruins. Michael nevertheless managed to stop the Ottoman advance and with the reinforcement of Moldavian forces and an Imperial army he pushed Sinan Pasha back south of the Danube. A further campaign in 1598 allowed the Moldavian army to advance right up to the Balkan mountain range. At this moment a quarrel over the succession of the Transylvanian throne gave the Wallachian voevod the chance to become prince of Transylvania and soon after to enforce his will at Suceava. In 1600 Michael the Brave—Mihai Viteazul—could call himself "Prince of Wallachia, Transylvania and Moldavia" so forming a dynastic aggregate to rival that of the Habsburgs or the Bathorys[12] but which, a few months later, came to nought. Having fallen out with General Basta, the commander of the Imperial army operating in Transylvania, Michael was assassinated by his henchmen. In 1604 the Porte actively encouraged the revolt of Istvan Bocksai against the Habsburgs, promising him the principality of Transylvania, and supported by Hungarian peasants who called themselves Hajduks, Bocksai managed to foment unrest all over Royal Hungary. However he was forced to settle his differences in Vienna in 1606. In November the following year the Habsburgs and the Sultan in turn signed the Peace of Zsitvatorok[13] which left the Ottomans with the fortresses of Kanisza and Eger. This was more than just an adjustment of the borders for it showed a substantial change in relations between the two sovereigns. Since their first encounter with the Habsburgs under Soliman the Magnificent, conscious of their role as "Protector of Islam" and heirs to Byzantium, they had always the presumed supremacy over the Holy Roman Emperor and so payment of tribute was in a sense the vindication of this idea. Yet this treaty dispensed with this pretention and was an act passed by two equal sovereigns. It was an important concession but was compensated by the restoration of Ottoman suzerainty over Transylvania following the death of Bocksai in December 1606. The new prince, Gabriel Bethlen (1613–1629), was an obedient vassal and held the neighbouring Moldavian and Wallachian voevods in subjection. Whether they liked it or not the three principalities were coming back into the Ottoman fold.

The "Thirty Years War" (1618–1648) was to fully occupy the Habsburgs and marked a time of peace with the Porte. However once the European war had ended, Vienna again started manoeuvring in Transylvania where the prince, George Rakoczi, had hopes of taking advantage of Ottoman difficulties and making Transylvania into a great European kingdom. Mehmed Koprulu understood the danger and launched the faithful Crimean Tatars against Rakoczi. Then he himself led a very large army and in 1658 Rakoczi was beaten and forced to flee. Ottoman garrisons were established in the Partium to keep an eye on the principality which once more became a vassal. His son Ahmed went to the root of the problem in 1663 and declared war on Vienna. An encounter took place with the Imperial army commanded by Montecuccoli in August 1663, near the village of Saint Gotthart on the river Raab, but was inconclusive. At the Peace of Vasvar (Eisenburg) Leopold I, agreed to evacuate the parts of Transylvania occupied during the conflict and recognized the Porte's protegee, Prince Michael Apafy. The Christian world, which had hailed the action at Saint

Gotthart as a great victory for the Emperor, were horrified and accused Leopold of pusillanimity, but the court of Vienna had in fact understood the extent of the recovery of power which had been effected by Koprulu.

The third of the Kara family, Mustafa—Mehmed's nephew—had grand designs; dreams of capturing Vienna and bringing together the Rhine and Danube territories into a vassal kingdom similar to Transylvania. In Royal Hungary the Habsburgs were struggling to suppress the uprising of the Kurutz[14] peasants who were revolting over the increase of feudal dues and were organized by Protestant nobles hostile to the dynasty. Encouraged by France, who was pursuing its own secular struggle with the House of Austria, a few Kurutz leaders such as Count Imre Thokoly, a large landowner in Upper Hungary, turned to the Porte for support and promised to recognize the Sultan's suzerainty over an independent Hungary. In 1682 Imre Thokoly was declared "King of Hungary" by Istanbul. Emperor Leopold hesitated to start up hostilities. When the French ambassador promised the Grand Vizier that Louis XIV would not send troops to help Vienna, Kara Mustafa felt that the circumstances were right for him to achieve what Soliman the Magnificent had failed to do, namely occupy the Habsburg capital. Leopold in turn could rely on the help of the king of Poland, John Sobieski, who had previously fought the Ottomans in Podolia. Conscious of the aggressive dynamism of the Koprulus, Sobieski listened to the advice of Pope Innocent XI, who had previously been a soldier, and signed an alliance with the Emperor in April 1683. A month later Kara Mustafa's army, some 200,000 men, marched out of Edirne in the direction of Belgrade, Esseg (Osijek) and Raab (Gyor). On the 15 July the siege of Vienna began. The Emperor and court had fled leaving its defence to 11,000 soldiers and a city militia under the command of Count Stahremberg. The Imperial army under the command of Charles of Lorraine withdrew to the north bank of the Danube and was joined by contingents of the Catholic southern German princes. The king of Poland hurried from Cracow and joined the Imperial forces at Nikolsburg (Mikulov) where he was given the commander-in-chief's baton. He ordered a crossing of the river on three pontoon bridges and amassed the 75,000 Christian army behind the cover of the Wienerwald hills. Kara Mustafa, who had pitched his camp to the west of the city walls understood the danger some time later and deployed 85,000 men from the village of Nussdorf to the Danube.

That night however, John Sobieski occupied the two natural vantage points of Kahlenberg and Leopoldsberg and had artillery pieces dragged up onto them. At dawn on the 12 September the Christian army attacked. The advance across the hills, covered by vineyards, was slow but at 4pm the Polish heavy cavalry emerged from the heights and swept down on the Janissaries and Ottoman artillery, cutting everything down in their path. The Grand Vizier's huge camp was reached amid indescribable scenes of panic. Kara Mustafa managed to escape on horseback whilst a handful of Janissaries held out all night in front of the city walls. The following day, without waiting for Leopold (who would later remember this), John Sobieski entered the capital amid jubilation.

The liberation of Vienna marked the final arrest of the expansion of Dar el Islam in Europe. Kara Mustafa paid for his failure with his life: in Belgrade he was given the gilded silk lancet which signified the death sentence. As for the European kings they listened more attentively to the exhortations of Innocent XI[15] and the Holy League became the instrument for the reconquest of Christian lands.

The Transformation of the Balkans

The crisis of the Ottoman system and the wars in the far reaches of the peninsula were to have a profound affect on the way of life of the Balkan inhabitants.

The long struggle against the Habsburgs took many Spahis to the frontier regions, opened the way for uprisings in the Bulgarian, Serbian and Greek regions. Yugoslav historians have drawn up an exhaustive list: 1564-5 in and around Prilep, 1575 at Ohrid and in 1590 at Kustendil. During the 15 Years War the invasion of Michael the Brave south of the Danube towards Razgrad, provoked a revolt among the population of the region; he signed up volunteers and a detachment of cavalry was created under the command of Baba Novak, a Bulgarian from Vidin. In 1598 a further campaign by the Wallachian prince produced an extensive uprising around Tirnovo and someone called Sisman, pretender to the line of the last sovereign, had himself proclaimed Tsar in the old liberated capital. The Habsburgs were too far away to be able to help and the insurrection—called the "First Tirnovo Insurrection" by historians—ended in a blood-bath. Many Bulgarians—60,000 according to tradition—found refuge in Wallachia. After the fall of the Principality of Smederevo many Serbs crossed the river into what is now Voevodina. In 1483, Mathias Corvinus in a letter to the Pope mentioned 200,000 Serbian subjects yet however many there were, they were to stay put following Soliman's conquest and were to form a sizeable part of the population of Ottoman Hungary, and in fact it was the Magyars who seem to have been in a minority perhaps as a result of emigration or suppression. It is known that most of the Timars in the Elayet of Budim were Bosnian Beys, hence Slavs, who reconstructed the ethno-social stratification of their region of origin. These functioned without serious problem as long as the Sultan's army was victorious, but at the first setback they were shaken by numerous uprisings. Also north of the border, the Kurutz movement resulted in the forming of roving peasant gangs—both Slav and Hungarian—who called themselves Hajduk—Brigands. Basically hostile to the Ottomans, they allowed themselves to be enlisted by Bocskai who gave them land in the Debrecen area of the frontier which for the whole of the 17th century remained unsettled. Yet it was in southern Serbia, especially Sudmadja and the mountainous regions towards Montenegro and Bosnia that the ideal territory for the Hajduks was to be found, glorified in folk songs known as "Pesmes." These outlaws, either volunteers or outcasts from the villages, would form gangs of 100 or even three hundred men led by former soldiers who would, as the Pesmes tell, "plough the roads of the Great Lord." They would above all attack Turks yet not the well armed soldiers: administrators, Kadis, travelling treasurers and sometimes the Spahis' Palanke[16]. Nor would they spare Christian merchants, or monks collecting money, nor even the Knez of a village. No doubt they "forced" the peasants to feed them and give them shelter, but as Stanoje Glavas, a Hajduk and companion of Karageorge, was to say in 1804: "The people and ourselves we are one." It was the proliferation of Hajduks in the 17th century, mostly deserters, that was to create in the countryside a climate of banditry which western travellers were to describe. The Hajduks were also involved in revolts in the Serbian territories, for instance the 1594–5 uprising. Albanian historians have researched the attempts at organized insurrection. In 1595 there was one under Mark Gjin with the encouragement of the Pope and another in 1601 which consisted of a huge assembly of Mati men (apparently 2,600 delegates) who decided not to pay the tribute and which was to last for fifteen years. Because of their seafaring traditions the

Greeks were directly involved in the naval wars between the Ottomans and the Christian powers. They were to be found at Lepanto on both sides, and the islands produced numerous corsairs who would not have thought twice about becoming turncoats. The mountainous areas had always been safe havens even before the conquest, and amongst these mountain people there developed the Greek version of the Hajduk: the Klephtes. To uphold law and order in these remote areas, Sultan Murad II created the Armatoliki, whose area was entrusted to a tribal chief, often also the Klephte chief. Thus they were set up around the Agrapha Massif, Olympus and all over continental Greece (excluding the Peloponnese), but the Armatols, although theoretically in Ottoman service, proved to be disobedient auxiliaries, ready to revolt against the Ottomans if their pay were delayed, or else if Venetian ducats proved more appealing. Armatols and Klephtes were the same as far as travellers were concerned and were to contributed to the growing sense of insecurity at the end of the 16th century, leading to the Klephtopolemos—the wars of the Klephtes—which were to last until Edmond About's Andartes—"King of the Mountains"—during the Second World War. Nationalist historians have tried to portray them as more or less national resistance movements, yet they were no more than a symptom of the growing inability of the Ottoman authorities to keep control or exploit the Reaya in the traditional way. Revolt was not exclusive to the Christian populations for Anatolia experienced numerous ones, which at times threatened the Sultan's very power. Muslim areas of the Balkans also experienced huge exoduses—Buyuk Kacgun—as a result of epidemics, famines or a particularly greedy Spahi. Peasants or out of work soldiers would form mercenary gangs and fight for the highest bidder. In the large towns, above all in Istanbul, the Medresse students—Sofa—were often at the root of disturbances using the capital's beggars and bums.

In the countryside one of the most important reasons for these uprisings was the way in which the Timar system had fallen into decadence and the process of replacing it with the Ciftlik system (Hypostatika in Greek regions and Beylik in Bosnian areas).There had always been Ciftliks, areas of land which were Mulk ie. free, and which belonged to the owner inalienably, for sale or passed on as inheritance. Only Muslims could own land and had to pay their "dues" to the Sultan. Quite common in Anatolia where it was at the base of the Turcoman Begs' power, it was rare in the Balkans since conquest had transformed all the land into Miri, hence property of the state, to be farmed out into Timars or Zeamets. Bosnia was an exception since many the feudal lords had converted to Islam, keeping their land and becoming Beys. This was one of the situations which the Koran deemed as mass conversion. In fact it was the result of ambiguity marking the initial period of conquest. As elsewhere in Europe, the feudal lords of Bosnia did not own their fiefs and submitting to the Sultan would have made them Timarli, yet since they were protectors of the frontier regions the Porte did not enforce the rules of inheritance. By the end of the 16th century in Bosnia and Herzegovina they had become Begs, using the land as if it were Mulk and their peasants as tenant Serfs—Kmet. The "owner" of the land would require the Kmet, in return for the price of the tenancy, to give a proportion of the harvest which might have varied from a third to a half (two to five times more than the dues of a Spahi). They would be strictly bound to the land, not by law but by necessity, for in these areas peasant farming—Cift—could not support a peasant family. They would have to take on part of the Begs land which put them in debt and bound them, virtually in perpetuity, to their creditor. In reality the fate of the Bosnian peasant, be he Muslim or Christian, would not have seemed very appealing to the Timariots of the classical age.

The passage from one condition to another was a consequence of military or economic change, for the extended war with Austria had decimated the Timarli in bordering Elayets, while the number of deserters ie. the Spahis who ignored the Sultan's call to arms, steadily rose. There were even cases of feudal lords revolting, such as the Firaris (deserters) who started in Hungary in 1596 and spread all the way to Asia Minor and were only finally quelled in 1604. The decline in the quality of soldiers came at a time when war often involved siege-war and placed more emphasis on the Janissary infantry than on the Timarli cavalry. The Yoklamas clearly show that by the beginning of the 17th century, the Timar troops were no longer the mainstay of the Ottoman army[17]. The authorities tried to react by publishing edicts confiscating property but were unable to enforce them. The Timarli would bribe the Sandjak Bey and other state employees or else at the head of Hajduk troops would resist by force of arms. In general however, they continued to benefit from their rights over the land without in return having to fulfil their military obligations. Furthermore land values at the time were at a premium. Inflation which characterized the 16th century in Europe, was also felt in the Ottoman Empire notwithstanding its closed economy. The price of agricultural products was to double and so land became a lucrative investment and a source of high profits. Provincial administrators would lay their hands on abandoned Timars while those that had stayed put became more involved in questions of farming revenue. Therefore there emerged in the countryside a section of large landowners whose estates were geared to commercial production of wheat, maize, rice and cotton. Of course this phenomenon was most evident in the fertile plains; in Thessaly, Macedonia, Thrace, "Old" Serbia (Kosovo-Metohja), coastal Albania and the Bulgarian plateau. These "new masters" forced fugitive peasants or else villages without a Spahi into their service , transforming them into tenant serfs and obliged them to give at least a third of their harvest, also corvee work, which had not existed in before in the Ottoman system. The peasant condition as a result was clearly worse at a time when that of his western counterpart was improving and as a consequence there was largescale emigration to Christian states: Austria, Royal Hungary and Transylvania (which was the opposite of what had frequently happened during the conquest). Above all there was an influx of people into Istanbul and the towns, to such an extent that travellers in the 17th century remark on the number of deserted villages which they saw in the countryside.

For a society where all was enshrined in law this development was clearly illegal, for only a firman from the Sultan could change the status of the territory and transform Miri land into Mulk. Clearly the sovereign could not accept this flouting of his authority. The Treasury tried to confiscate the Timars of dead or absent Spahis, and right through the 17th century decrees were issued forbidding corvee work. Murad IV (1623–1640) targeted disobedient Spahis, killing many of them and giving their fiefdoms to Janissaries. For a short while the Timar system was restored all over the Empire however, in the end, corruption of local administrators resulted in Ciftlik once more becoming during the 17th century, a characteristic of the Ottoman Balkans.

Another fundamental change was the spread of Islam. Historical documents show that the policy of colonizing by the central government, of transplanting Muslim populations, had largely ended by the latter half of the 16th century. A study of the Yuruks in Rumelia shows this to be the case and the mass settling of landless Anatolian peasants on the island of Cyprus just after the conquest in 1576 would seem to have been the last of this type of operation. The increase in the number of believers in the Balkans is due to other reasons. The natural demographic balance does not seem to have been particularly favourable to Muslims bearing in mind that as everywhere else, the mortality rate in towns was in general higher than in the countryside. As mentioned before, apart from the areas which were colonized, the greatest concentrations of Muslims was in the towns where they were administrators, soldiers, merchants and craftsmen. These centres were to develop significantly during the 17th century as the Djizya registers show. The stories of chroniclers give an initial clue: the climate of insecurity which reigned in certain regions, where the Spahi was often the first target, forced many of them to settle in the towns with their families and servants. They would live next to peasants who had escaped the burden of Ciftlik. This proximity would lead the Christians to note the inequalities of their everyday experience: taxes, Esnaf rules and even the prohibition of green in clothing. To escape from this condition there was a simple remedy, however worrying, of conversion to Islam. From tax registers it is clear that from the end of the 15th century, however erratically, "voluntary[18]" conversions took place and increased in the 17th century due to the socio-economic developments described above.

In the countryside whole villages would jump over the religious barrier together. This was already referred to for Bosnia-Herzegovina at the time of the conquest; the feudal Bogomils placed themselves spontaneously at the service of the Sultan and so retained their land, which was then transformed into Timars and they became Christian Spahis. Albanian historians recently drew attention to the same phenomenon in their own country[19]; in 1431 Christian Spahis had 28% of the Timars in the Korca, Permet and Konice areas and 15% in the Kosovo plateau. These Begs might have converted to Islam to insure that their children inherited their fiefdoms, which was possible under Ottoman law only in the case of a Muslim. As elsewhere in Europe when the lord recanted so did his peasants. In the middle of the 16th century in certain areas of Bosnia, 40% of the population were Muslim. The

Greek lands were no exception to this process. After the capture of Thessalonika in 1430 most of the inhabitants renounced their faith "in despair." A Vacalopoulos emphasizes the steady flow of individual and family conversions which sometimes even involved members of the clergy, monks or prelates. "In some regions the disappearance of the Christian population might have been total 100%[20]" According to him many of these conversions were to avoid Devsirme, however as was previously mentioned this "blood tax" was lightly enforced and disappeared in the 1630s at the very moment that the appeal of Islam seems to have reached a peak. In Crete, conquered in 1669, more than half the inhabitants became Muslim in less than a century. In Albania tax increases seem to have had some bearing on the matter because the Djizya went in the 16th century from 45 Aspres to 305 a year and at the start of the 17th from 780 to 1641 for certain categories of people. It was to become more and more difficult to pay and conversion would have been the only way to avoid it. Bulgarian historians still have not looked closely at the cause or circumstances surrounding the conversion to Islam of the Rhodope Bulgarians, known as Pomaks—Pomaci—whose descendants still exist. In the end what is clear is that during the 17th century there was a steady increase in the number of Muslims but that the reasons for this were varied from region to region. There was no coherent policy but rather was it a product of heightened tension between believer and non-believer during the slow process of decline of central authority. For the Balkan Christians the Ottoman system was oppressive when it worked but unbearable when it went wrong.

Romanian Princes and Ragusian Nobles

Due to their geographical position, Moldavia and Wallachia became involved in the struggle between the European powers and the Ottoman Empire. Vassal principalities since the mid-17th century, they were forced, whether they liked it or not to develop in the shadow of the Sultan. On the political front the century closed with the great figure of Michael the Brave—Mihai Viteazul (1593–1601) who fleetingly unified the two principalities of Moldavia and Transylvania, not with a view to nationhood but rather as a Renaissance prince interested in collecting titles. In the same spirit he reorganized the army, replacing the feudal Boyar contingents with Polish and Serbian mercenaries and Dorobanti who were recruited from among the free peasants in return for tax exemptions. He also tried to create a strong central government and reinforced the prince's authority vis-a-vis the nobility. He changed the structure of the council (Divan), increased the areas of central intervention and created provincial governors (Bans). Yet at the same time he followed the example of the Polish and Hungarian sovereigns and abandoned the peasants to their lords by ending freedom of movement. Michael the Brave's measures were at the root of the attachment in perpetuity to the Glebe which from then on was to characterize the status of Romanian peasants. Hence the 17th century is considered to be the century of Boyar dominion. Masters of the land their produce increasingly was exported to Istanbul. There was a similar rise in the use of peasants for corvee work—Claca. This brought huge returns enabling them to buy public office, including even that of Voevod which continued in theory to be appointed according to customary rules. The Voevod was elected by the "National Assembly" made up mainly of Boyars and high-ranking clergymen, but he needed to be confirmed in office by the Sultan who bestowed the symbols of power upon him. This is where gifts of money could weigh heavily in the balance. Rich noble families could build up a network of client families which would achieve power in their turn; the Movila, Sricci and Ureche families were the real rulers of the principalities and would vie against each other for power. Hence the frequent changes of prince: between 1601 and 1688 twenty-five princes were to rule in Wallachia for an average of three years five months, and in Moldavia forty-two princes with an average of less than two years. Nor was the Porte afraid of direct meddling. Voevods were appointed who had no legal right, for example Graziani a Dalmatian who was appointed in Moldavia (1619), and strangely enough was to ally himself with Poland, or Radu Mihnea in Wallachia (1611) appointed instead of Radu Serban who was busy fighting in Transylvania. In the second half of the 17th century, clan rivalry often degenerated into actual feuds such as civil war in Wallachia between 1663 and 1678 or trouble in Moldavia in 1691 in which the high dignitary and historian Miron Costin died.

To free themselves of the grip of these clans some of the princes brought Greeks into their service, bringing about the Phanariot phenomenon which was a characteristic of the principalities. The name is derived from the Phanar quarter of Istanbul and some of them had taken service with the Porte Following this example Radu Mihea (1611–1616) Voevod of Wallachia appointed some of them to the great anger of local Boyars. During the century there were the Cantacuzenos, Catargis, Rossetis and the Ghicas (of Albanian origin) who more or less became Romanian, found their place among the Boyars and were later to have important roles in the affairs of the principalities. Yet this provoked some resistance and in 1630 the Wallachian boyars forced the Voevod to expel some Greek officials and merchants, and annul the contributions which were made to the Patriarch of Constantinople and monasteries such as Athos. Relations with the Porte remained officially those set out in the treaty establishing the principality as a vassal state. Wallachia's tribute, which had to be taken every year to Istanbul, was to remain relatively steady from 1632 to 1715 at 130,000 golden ducats while Moldavia had to pay 38,000 golden ducats in 1620, 42,000 in 1710, and 65,000 in 1593. There was also the need to make Pesches and Baksheesh through the intermediary of the Phanariots as well as compulsory delivery of honey, grain and other products for to the palace. Also the mandatory purchase of foodstuffs for the supply of Istanbul was to increase every year.

The mediocrity of public life in the principality was sharply contrasted by a rich cultural awakening in the 17th century. However this only concerned the upper strata of society, those who had access to written works, a small privileged minority of Boyars and members of the clergy. Peasant culture continued to be handed down from generation to generation. It was based on local customs—obiceul pamintului—, regulating social and personal relations with passage rites of birth, marriage and death, seasonal rites and religious and pagan feasts. These were the overt expressions of a culture which shared its vision of the world and many characteristics with that of its neighbours but in synthesis was particular to the Romanian peasant of the different regions—Tari. Unfortunately the recurrent invasions, almost yearly, left few traces of the product of this culture prior to the 16th century: wooden churches, village houses and pottery. High culture in the 16th century remained largely traditional. Chronicles were written in Old Slavonic imitating the Byzantine chroniclers. In Moldavia there was a veritable blooming of historical chronicles. The Chronicles of Macarie, bishop of Roman, of his disciple Eftimie and their follower Azarie recount the history of the principality during the years 1504 and 1574. In Wallachia Michael the Brave had Theodorus Rudeanu write his story in the hope of publicizing his exploits in Europe. This was written in Latin and the work was published in Gorlitz in 1599. As well as these historical works, also written in Old Slavonic, there were many religious works some undoubtedly influenced by Bogomil Manicheism. The great innovation of the 16th century was the development of the printing press. As mentioned previously this was brought from Venice through Montenegro. The Wallachian Voevod Radu cel Mare (Radu the Great) brought to his capital Tirgoviste a Serbian monk called Macarie who had learned the trade in Venice and had set up the first press in the Balkans in his monastery at Obod. In 1508 a missal was produced and in 1512 the Holy Gospels thus preempting in Romania by three centuries the printing of cyrillic. The Reformation on the other hand had little effect except in Moldavia. In 1561 the Voevod Despot Voda, who was of Greek or Wallachian origin[21] granted the right of freedom of religious worship to all Protestants exiled from their own countries, among them some French Calvinists. The same year he opened a college at Cotnari, a Scola Latina similar to those springing up over Europe at that time. He appointed as its head Ioan Sommer (1542–1574), a German humanist living in Transylvania who was an opponent of the doctrine of the Holy Trinity and was to produce a biography of the prince. Later this was reformed on the line of the Jesuit Colleges, was transferred to Jassy and was reserved for the sons of the Boyars. The social climate of aristocratic patronage encouraged the parallel development of printing and education during the 17th century. In Wallachia in 1640 was printed the first book in Romanian, the Govora Code which was translated from Old Slavonic. Moldavia was greatly influenced by Kiev whose Metropolitan was from 1632 Peter Movila, a noble of Moldavia. Founder of a college which was the origin of the famous Academy, he was one of the most respected Orthodox theologians and convened an assembly of bishops at Jassy to reply to the "Catechism" of Calvin. Old Slavonic was used in these works but it was during this period that the first book in Romanian was printed. In 1688 a group of scholars finished a translation of the Bible at the Voevod's behest which was called the "Bible of Serban Cantacuzino" and enabled Romanian to vie with Old Slavonic in religious life. Further studies of import: in 1647 a Boyar V. Nasturel found a link between Latin and Romanian which was clearly helped by the renewed interest of Europe in the Ancient world whereas Grigore Ureche in his "Chronicles of Moldavia" was to claim that the Boyars were descended from the Roman legionnaires.

The art of the period has left posterity with a marvellous heritage especially in the realm of architecture. In Wallachia Voevod Neagoe Basarab had a huge monastery "Arges" built around 1512 in which many of the sculpture and paintings were inspired by Georgian and Armenian church art. In Bucharest there was the court chapel Curtea Veche (1554) which was mostly in brick. In Moldavia Stephan the Great's son Petru Rares (1527–1546) continued his father's building works and had outside wall decorated with huge frescoes and which still today are the pride of for example Saint George of Hirlau (1530), Saint George of Voronet (1547), the church at Arbore (1541), the monastery of Humor (1530), of Moldavita (1537), of Sucevita (1582) and many others. In the 17th century Moldavian art copied its southern neighbour with Armeno-Georgian decorative art which reached its zenith in the church of Three Hierarchs at Jassy (1639) and those in the monastery of Golia (1650) also at Jassy. There are also Ottoman influences, for example in the architecture and decoration of the church of Saint Sabbas of Jassy, but which is mixed with baroque influences from Central Europe; a symbolic mixing of cultures on the furthest border of the Ottoman Balkans.

The Republic of Ragusa was the Empire's window onto the Italian world. The Porte's vassal since 1458, it was to be placed in a very difficult position every time war broke out between Venice and the Porte. Up until the 18th century, there were in fact six wars[22]. Twice, in 1485 and in 1603, the Doge's fleet blockaded the city but the walls were to hold and the Venetians to withdraw. In return for paying the Sultan a tribute the Republic was allowed to continue its lucrative commercial ventures and this was checked not by anything man-made but on the 7 April 1667 by a natural disaster; a terrible earthquake which hit the Dalmatian coastline causing extensive damage and destroying most of the houses inside the ramparts with the loss of about 5,000 lives. Recovery was slow and made more difficult by the fact that Mediterranean trade was going through a sharp decline. Venice took advantage of this to enlarge its hold on the coast and the Peace of Karlowitz in 1699 set out a new frontier (called the Grimani line after the Venetian negotiator) which hemmed in Ragusa and placed Venice solidly on the Cattaro (Kotor) river.

Despite these reverses the Republic retained its patrician character which expressed itself in a Latino-Italian culture drawn from the universities of Italy. The first Slav writers of the latter part of the 16th century were poets who found their inspiration in Petrach: Siska Mencetic, George Drzic and a dramatist whose plays are still performed today, called Marin Drzic. The 17th century witnessed a veritable golden age in Slav literature with Ivan Gundulic's (1589-1638) epic poem Osman[23]. A patrician, member of the Senate and diplomat, his work, together with the epic of Kosovo and Guirland of the Mountains of Njegos, represents the best trilogy of Yugoslav epic poetry. One of his cousins Junius Palmotic, also of patrician family and a former Jesuit pupil, was a prolific writer and went to Bosnia to develop his art, whereas his cousin Jacob Palmotic, ambassador to Istanbul and Rome following the 1667 disaster, showed himself to be a skilful propagandist for his homeland in the poem "Dubrovnik Restored." In the face of such a flourishing of the arts the republic was soon known as the "Athens of the southern Slavs." In fact its immediate influence on the Balkan peoples of the Empire was negligible, the literature of Ragusa which was rediscovered by Serb and Croat intellectuals in the XIXth century was an important element in the nationalist reawakening of that century.

Notes

1. Certain historians have put forward the idea of a physical degeneracy of the "House of Osman" which goes against the highly mixed nature of the possible mothers in the imperial harem.
2. Is considered to come from the noble Venetian family of Baffo; captured by a pirate she was sold to Murad III's harem.
3. Ref. Fontenay (Michel): L'Empire Ottoman et le risque corsaire au XVII siècle—in Revue Moderne et Contemporaine. t. XXXII avril. juin 1985 pp.185-208.
4. West of Missolonghi opposite the mouth of Acheloos. Lepanto—now Nafpaktos—is the name of the port from which the Ottoman admiral departed to give battle.
5. Savary de Brives (J): Relations des voyages de Monsieur de Brives tant en Grece, en Terre Sainte et Egypte q'aux royaumes de Tunis et Alger. Paris 1688 according to Fontenay (M) op. cit. p.191.
6. Now Heraklon.
7. Now Rettimnon.

8. Francois de Vendome, duke of Beaufort (1616–1669): the popular "King of the Halles" in the Fronde revolt in France.

9. Otchakov, on the coastline 40 miles to the east of Odessa.

10. Now Khotin in the Republic of Moldavia.

11. Also known as the Peace of Radzin.

12. Romanian nationalist historians of the 19th century made this the precursor of Romanian unity. Nicolae Ceausescu was also to take this up.

13. A the place where the Zsitva enters the Danube near Komaron.

14. From the Latin: Crusiatus—crusader.

15. Pope Pius XII canonized him in 1956.

16. Fenced off enclosure in which tithe production was stored, sometimes together with the Spahi's residence.

17. V.P. Mutafcieva and St. Dimitrov. above p.17.

18. This expression is from N. Todorov in La ville balkanique. above. p.60/61.

19. Pulaha (Selami): Pronosia feudale ne tokat Shgiptare (sh.XV-XVI Tirana 1988 518p. (Feudal property and Albanian customs)

20. Vacalopoulos (Apostolos): Histoire de la Grece moderne. Horvath ed. Paris. 1975. 325 p.

21. Known as Iacob Heraclid.

22. Periods of war: 1468–1479, 1499–1502, 1538–1540, 1571–1573, 1644–1669 and 1688–1699.

23. Dealing with Osman II (1618–1622) and his campaign in 1621 against Poland.

8

The Ottoman Empire Against the European Powers, 1684–1792

The Ottoman failure to capture Vienna was the start of a territorial decline that was to continue until the Treaty of Jassy. This decline was mainly due to two other powers: Austria and Russia, the latter openly aiming at the destruction of the Ottoman Empire itself. The Porte was aware of this and all through the 18th century there was talk of reforming the army of the House of Osman and restoring the lustre of a conquering power. Yet all to no avail for the upper classes were loath to jeopardize their privileges and the few who could foresee the consequences found themselves prisoners to the traditional view of the world. The great transformation of pre-industrial capitalism, which was changing the balance of power in Europe, failed to permeate the political and psychological frontiers of a theocratic state which by its very structure rejected the ideas of Aufkärung and the French Revolution. In the Europe of the Enlightenment the Ottoman Balkans was to become a region culturally backward and economically semi-colonial.

The Christian Reconquest and the Habsburgs' Advance, 1684–1739

The raising of the siege of Vienna and the energy of Pope Innocent XI led to a resurrection of the Holy League: Venice, Malta, Tuscany and even Russia joined forces with the Habsburgs and the Poles. The Sultan's army, shaken by defeat, had to confront Habsburg armies in Hungary, Bosnia and Serbia, John III Sobieski's Poles in the Ukraine, Venice in Dalmatia and Morea and Peter the Great in the Crimea.

The main combat zone, however, was Central Europe. Kara

Mustafa's defeat turned into a rout after the defeat at Gran (Esztergom) on the 1 November 1683 and left Hungary open to Sobieski's forces. By 1684 northern Hungary and Pecs were in Habsburg hands, while Buda (the shield of Islam) was captured by the Duke of Lorraine in June 1686. The whole plain was occupied following the symbolic victory at Mohacs in 1687, and on the 8 September the Imperial army took Belgrade. The Porte tried to sue for peace. Habsburg armies penetrated into Bosnia and advanced up the Morava valley to Nis while a huge Serb uprising opened the way for the Habsburgs to occupy Vidin, Skopje and Prizren from July to November 1689. The Balkans appeared to be on the point of changing masters. At the same time Imperial forces penetrated into Wallachia and negotiated with the Boyars the transfer of suzerainty from the Sultan to the Habsburg Emperor. An episode places the crusading character of this reconquest into perspective. In 1673 George Brankovic, envoy of the prince of Transylvania to Istanbul, claiming to be a descendant of the Serbian despots of the 15th century, suggested to the Emperor's envoy that he organize an uprising of the Balkan Christians who would rally around his famous name. He brought this idea up again in 1683 during a revolt led by Thokoly Imre, envisaging the creation of a Serbian Kingdom, under his sceptre, which would include Slavonia, Sirmia, the Banat north of the Danube and the Sudmadja and Kosovo to the south of the river. This kingdom would be the everlasting ally of the Emperor and would serve as a buffer against the Ottomans and a means of pressure on the Hungarians. Vienna was interested, Brankovic became a count of the Holy Empire and his lineage was confirmed by authenticated title documents. Yet when the progress of the Austrian army showed that his prestige was not enough to provoke an uprising in the Reaya he was for "Raison d'Etat" arrested, and imprisoned at Cheb (Eger) till his death in 1711. The real reason was that a more prestigious leader, the Patriarch of Pecs, Arseni III Crnojevic, had been found. Austrian agents throughout the region spread a proclamation by the Emperor—largely inspired by Brankovic—promising "Serbs, Albanians, Mesians, Bulgarians, Illyrians, Macedonians and Rascians" all the political and religious freedom that they had enjoyed in the past "under the suzerainty of the kings of Hungary." Popes at the head of the villagers massacred the Spahis and the Muslims in neighbouring towns, but energized by the new Vizier of the Koprulu family, Grand Vizier Fazil Mustafa, the Porte was to counter-attack in the summer of 1690. Nis was recaptured and Belgrade fell on the 14 October. For fear of reprisal thousands of Christian families followed the Imperial forces in their retreat, first to Belgrade, and when the town was abandoned north of the Danube into what was to become "Serbian Hungary." The Ottomans made a defensive line on the river. The following year the death of Fazil Mustafa in battle blocked the situation and the Danube became the frontier between the two Empires.

To the north, John Sobieski's attempts to recapture the Podolian region and conquer Moldavia floundered: the Tatar raids and the resistance of some fortresses such as Kamieniec drained the Rzeczpospolita's troops and forced him to abandon Kiev forever to Russia (1686). On the Mediterranean front however Venice encountered success in Morea where the population revolted, and in Greece where they captured Athens in 1687, seriously damaging the Parthenon which the Ottoman forces had used as a gunpowder magazine. But their advance into Bosnia as well as a landing in Crete were to end in failure, while in 1694 they only managed to hold the island of Chios for a few months.

The new Sultan, Mustafa II (1695–1703), once more went on the offensive against the Habsburgs launching three successive campaigns, which earned him the title of Ghazi for his defense of Temesvar, the last Elayet north of the Danube. The response was immediate and devastating: Prince Eugene of Savoy was victorious at the battle of Zenta[1] in September 1697. The Ottomans had little alternative but to sue for peace. Emperor Leopold also wanted peace because the question of the Spanish succession was not settled and presaged hostilities with Louis XIV. Only Peter the Great who had entered the fray late, wanted to continue operations round Azov and Taganrog which were captured in 1696. He wanted to make the small fortress of Azov into a Russian naval base on the Black Sea and this was the underlying reason for his secret journey to Europe in 1697–1698. Even then, on his return, he was made to follow the allied line. Negotiations took place on the northern shore of the Danube at Karlowitz[2] starting in December 1698. They were to last 70 days and an agreement was signed on the 26 January 1699. It was based on the territorial positions of the different armies: the frontier between the two Empires henceforth was to follow the river Tisza down to where it joined the Danube, the river Sava up to the Una and the river Una to its source. The Temesvar region was to remain an Ottoman possession as Beylerbeylik of Tamishvar, while the Porte recognized Habsburg dominion of Transylvania. The Sultan was also forced to make two important concessions: guarantee freedom of worship for his Catholic subjects, which could lead to Vienna intervening in their support, and for Austrian merchants to trade freely within the Ottoman provinces. The other members of the Holy League were not forgotten. Poland recovered Podolia up to the Dnepr, thus rendering the treaty of Buczacz null and void and in the Mediterranean, Venice retained Morea, Corinth, Corfu, Zanta and Cephalonia, increased its territory in Dalmatia around Zara and had its commercial privileges within the Sultan's empire confirmed. With Peter the Great negotiations were only concluded in Istanbul in July 1700. Russia was to keep Azov and the conquered territory along the Dnestr, suzerainty over the Zaporogian Cossacks was reaffirmed while the Porte promised to restrain his loyal Tatars from making any more raids (Razzias). In spite of the efforts of his negotiators the list of lost territories was very long. The Treaty of Karlowitz was the first of a series of treaties which progressively reduced Dar el Islam in Europe.

Peace on the Danube was to last for 16 years, until an anti-Venetian group within the Palace pushed for the reconquest of Morea. The situation was propitious because Venetian taxation and the actions of the Roman Catholic clergy had alienated the Greek population. A dual expedition by land and sea resulted in the recovery of the province. But then Vienna, the Doge's ally intervened. Once again Prince Eugene defeated the Ottomans at Peterwardein (Petrovaradin) in August 1715 and after two campaigns captured Temesvar and Belgrade. The Ottomans sued for peace at Passarowitz (Pozarevac) in July 1718. The Austrians retained the conquered territories: the region of Temesvar, Belgrade, Sudmadja up to the outskirts of Nis and Wallachia up to the river Olt. They also retained their commercial privileges and obtained the right to set up consuls in the Sultan's empire. Venice was forced to abandon Morea but kept the Ionian islands and their positions in Dalmatia. The European courts began to speak of Austrian domination of the Balkans. In fact it was only to be a twenty year truce. Vienna was to take up arms again in 1737 mainly because of the grand designs of Tsarina Anna of Russia.

Hostilities began and an offensive in the direction of Nis was successful due to the support of Serbian peasants; Montenegro helped the Imperial army conquer large tracts of Bosnian territory. Yet Prince Eugene was no longer there and after the Ottomans counter-attacked they recovered Belgrade where peace was signed on the 18 September 1739. The Habsburgs gave up Oltenia and all the territory south of the Danube and the Sava. Once again, for a century, the borders of Dar el Islam were defined by these two rivers.

Russia's Southward Descent:
The Road to Constantinople, 1736–1792

Peter the Great's objective of "gaining an opening onto the sea" is well known. He was to pursue it in 1696, in the Black Sea region, when he captured Azov which he then turned into a naval base. Rivalry with Charles XII of Sweden led to extended hostilities which ended with a Russian victory on the 6 July 1709 at Poltava, in the Ukraine where the Swede unwisely engaged battle. The vanquished sovereign took refuge in Ottoman territory and in Istanbul became the centre of anti-Russian intrigues and also received financial support from Louis XIV. Warmongers, voicing the fears of the Crimean Tatars who felt threatened by the Azov base, were to hold sway in 1710. Peter the Great on the other hand, received assurances of support from the princes of Moldavia and Wallachia and persuaded by his agents that an appeal to all the Balkan Christians would result in a general uprising, he launched the 1711 campaign which was to end in disaster. When his army entered Moldavia the Romanian population fled into the mountains and showed little warmth towards the invader. No doubt when Peter reached the Danube he said to himself that he was the first Russian since prince Sviatoslav of Kiev in the 10th century, to quench the thirst of Russian horses with the waters of the great river, but this was about all he achieved. The Ottoman counter-attacked and made the Tsar withdraw to the river Pruth where he was surrounded and forced to negotiate. The Treaty of Stanilesti in July 1711 was an admission of his weakness: he was to return Azov and Taganrog to the Ottomans, promise to destroy the forts on the lower Dnepr and withdraw diplomatic representatives from Istanbul. Russia was back to square one. In the Balkans however, this first descent southwards was to have a dual outcome. In neighbouring Moldavia, Voevod Dimitri Cantemir had spoken out in favour of an alliance with the Tsar, joining him in retreat and was replaced on the throne of Jassy by a Greek named Nicholas Mavrocordatos: this was the beginning of the "Phanariot period" in the principalities. In distant Montenegro the Vladika, Danilo I Petrovic rallied to the call of Russian agents and proclaimed the Tsar the "champion of Montenegrin freedom." The Ottomans reacted in 1713 by laying siege and occupying Cetinje for several months. But the Vladika went in 1715 to the court of Peter the Great who agreed to guarantee the independence of the principality and granted him a generous subsidy. Subsequently all Danilo's successors were to make this visit to the Tsar and as a consequence it was felt that Montenegro was a Russian protectorate in the Balkans.

It was only with Tsarina Anna that her uncle's designs on the Black Sea were once again considered. She began with a secret alliance with Vienna whereby Russia was to acquire the Azov and Crimea regions while the Habsburgs would reinforce their control over the Balkans by annexing Bosnia and Herzegovina. Denouncing the continued raids (Razzias) of the Tatars (which in any case the Porte could not control) Saint Petersburg declared war in the spring of 1736. The Russian army, under the command of Marshall Munich, invaded the Crimea and took Azov. The Austrians in turn captured Nis and advanced into Bosnia. Yet in the following campaign the Ottomans counter-attacked and managed to repulse all these forces from their territories. The Imperial forces advanced on Bucharest and Banja-Luka and the following year Belgrade and Semendria (Smederevo) were captured. Without consulting its ally, Vienna sued for peace. The Peace of Belgrade was concluded in September 1739. The Danubian conflict was hindered by the simultaneous conflict with the Afshars in Persia and the Porte was to leave the Danubian principalities open to attack. Munich tried to spark off a general Christian uprising in the Balkans but failed and in 1739 captured the Ottoman fortresses of Hotin and Bender on the Dnestr, seized Jassy and was about to penetrate into Wallachia when he heard the news of the Treaty of Belgrade. He therefore accepted the good offices of the French ambassador de Villeneuve and signed at Nis in October 1739 a document which the Porte considered as a supplement to that of Belgrade. Russia evacuated Moldavia and the Crimea, returned Azov and withdrew its ships from the Black Sea. Thanks to French support the Sultan had stopped the Russian advance south, yet the war had demonstrated that Saint Petersburg had a modern army and that the reforms of Peter the Great were beginning to bear fruit.

Thirty years later Catherine the Great was to show this to great effect.

The European balance of power had been altered by the War of Spanish Succession and the Seven Years War, while in Istanbul, weak Sultans nervously observed the actions of Nadir Shah, the ruler of Persia. Ever since the peace of Nis, Russian agents had been infiltrated throughout the Balkans, and in 1767 had actively encouraged another uprising in Montenegro. An adventurer, Stephan Mali—Stephan the Small—(claiming to be Tsar Peter III who had been killed by his wife Catherine II), seized power from 1767-1774. In 1768 an incident occurred on the Polish-Ottoman frontier when the Russian army, in hot pursuit of the forces of the Confederacy of Bar, crossed into Ottoman territory. Egged on by the Tatar Khan (the Tatars were eager to fight the Cossacks who they felt were in the pay of St.Petersburg) and also by the French, the Porte demanded that the Russians evacuate Poland. Saint Petersburg refused and war was declared in October 1768. In fact neither army was on a war footing and operations only started in 1770. Prince Gallitzin occupied Jassy and Bucharest, destroyed an Ottoman army at Kardam to the south of Dobrudja and occupied the Principalities. At the same time Tsarina Catherine set into motion a daring operation, sending the Russian Baltic fleet into the Mediterranean. Under the command of count Alexis Orlov,(who together with his brother shared the favours of the Tsarina) they were helped by the English who allowed them put into port at Portsmouth. Its first target was the Mani coast in the Peloponnese where Russian agents sparked off an anti-Ottoman uprising. The fleet unloaded arms while the Muslim population of the region were massacred and the port of Navarin was captured. The Russian officers tried to organize the Maniotes but were unable to. Their excessive behaviour brought them repeatedly into conflict with their foreign allies and after a final setback at Tripolitsa (Tripolis), the disheartened Russians abandoned them to Ottoman reprisals. This unfortunate episode was to be remembered by the Greeks for a long time. Catherine's fleet sailed to the Aegean Sea and came across the Sultan's fleet at anchor at Tchesm (Cesm) off the coast near Chios. The encounter (October 1770) resulted in most of the Ottoman ships being destroyed by fire and opened up the whole of the eastern Mediterranean to attack from the Russians, who however failed to take advantage of this. Orlov, at odds with his English advisors, made do with a few unsuccessful strikes against Rhodes and the surrounding islands. On the Black Sea however, the 1771 campaign resulted in the total occupation of the Crimea which was made into a Tatar autonomous state under Russian suzerainty and a Khan who was one of Catherine's protegees. Distracted with the first division of Poland (1772) and the Pugachev uprising in the Ukraine (1773–1775) operations only restarted in 1774 under a new commander-in-chief, Alexander Suvorov. The 1774 campaign once again reached southern Dobrudja and peace negotiations took place in the Russian camp at Kutcuk-Kainardji[3]. An agreement was signed on the 21 July 1774 whereby the Crimea in principle recovered its independence and Saint Petersburg was allowed to stay in the Zaporog between the Dnepr and the Bug and also the ports of Azov and Kinburn[4] which controlled the estuaries of the Don and the Dnepr. The Russians now were to be reckoned with on the Black Sea. In return they were to withdraw from the Danubian principalities and those points in the Aegean Sea that Orlov had captured. However Catherine II, even though it was not part of the terms of the treaty, was permitted to build an Orthodox church in Istanbul and this was seen as a symbol of Russian protection for the Christian communities living within the Ottoman Empire. Furthermore preferential trade agreements were made and Russian consuls were appointed to monitor this. Lastly a war indemnity was imposed which the already overburdened Palace treasury had great difficulty in paying. This treaty was to dominate Russo-Ottoman relations for more than half a century and gave Saint Petersburg the necessary pretext increasingly to intervene in the Porte's internal affairs.

Yet Catherine was not completely satisfied. Wanting control of the whole of the north coast of the Black Sea she encouraged the internecine conflict within the Crimean Khanate, pitting a Russian protege against Istanbul's. In 1778 an uprising provided the necessary pretext for intervention and the occupation of the whole area. The way to Constantinople appeared open. Catherine then resurrected Marshall Munich's strategy: the famous "Greek Plan." It amounted to pushing the Ottoman's out of Europe and making the liberated territories into a Greek Empire with Constantinople as its capital. Istanbul would be once more Christian and its sovereign would be the Tsarina's second grandson, who had opportunely been christened Constantine. This eastern dream of a German princess, cloaked in terms of Christian solidarity and crusade, led to a very strange diplomatic pact. In 1775 Austria had exacted a price from the Sultan for its neutrality during the Russo-Ottoman war: the northern part of vassal Moldavia which had become "crown land"—Kronland of Bukovina. Austria was still very interested in the Balkans. In 1782 Catherine started secret negotiations with Joseph II and explained her grand design. Russia would first annex the Khanate of Crimea which was already occupied and the Crimean peninsula, Tauridia and the Kuban. Moldavia and Wallachia would be amalgamated into an independent state which would act as a buffer between Austria and Russia and would have its old name Dacia with the first prince, Potemkin the Tsarina's favourite. Constantinople would be united with Thrace, Macedonia, the Bulgarian territories and northern Greece and would form a new Byzantine Empire to be given to young Constantine. To balance this massive Russian move south Habsburg Austria would get most of the western Balkans: Oltania, Serbia, Epirus, Bosnia-Herzegovina and the Venetian possessions in Dalmatia. The Doge was to be compensated by the transfer of Morea, Crete and Cyprus to his rule.

With this in mind Potemkin began by colonizing the steppes of southern Ukraine and built the ports of Kherson and Sebastopol. In 1783 the Empress decreed the annexation of the Crimean Khanate which was accepted by the Porte the following year. Four years later Potemkin organized for his sovereign, accompanied by Emperor Joseph II and King Stanislav Poniatowski of Poland, a tour of the Crimea which ended in Sebastopol where a triumphal arch had been built marking the start of the road to Constantinople. Humiliated by these gestures and disturbed by the activities of "Russian agents" in the Balkans, who were in fact mostly Greeks, the Porte decided to renew hostilities. In fact Saint Petersburg was not prepared for this and Austria delayed for a year before joining Catherine. Both England and Prussia were also very much opposed to any further Russian expansion. Operations began in 1788 when Imperial armies penetrated into Bosnia and Serbia where they once more occupied Belgrade and Nis (October

1789), while Suvorov on the frontier tested Ottoman defences and the Prince of Saxa occupied Bucharest. The French revolution however, was soon to monopolize the attention of all of Europe's sovereigns and Emperor Leopold as soon as he came to the throne strove to make peace with the Porte. This he signed at Sistova[5] in August 1791 on the basis of the territorial status quo ante, however receiving a promise from the Sultan that his Christian subjects should have the protection of Austria. Abandoned by her ally, Catherine was preoccupied by developments in Poland and also the war with Sweden. Greek sailors in Russian service, in isolated incidents continued to make life difficult for Ottoman shipping and the beys of Epirus were won over by the Tsarina's money, but following the military victory at Macin on the Danube delta, she decided to make peace. The treaty was signed at Jassy in January 1792[6]. This was once more based on the terms of Kutcuk-Kainardji and the 1784 agreement, but the former Crimean Khanate up to the river Kuban in the west was to become a part of Russia under the name of Tauridia, while in the Caucasus Georgia recognized Catherine's suzerainty. In return Catherine agreed to evacuate the Danubian principalities and the forts on the Danube delta. The Dnestr therefore became the common border between the Russian Empire and Dar el Islam. To the north of this frontier the port of Odessa was to become the symbol of a further stage of the road to Constantinople.

Internal Crisis and the Problem of Reform

The Porte had suffered great losses in these various wars and the succession of treaties highlight the territorial retreat of the House of Osman. On the internal front the consequences were also dire.

War, which during the initial conquest had sustained the Treasury, was during the 18th century the prime reason for its ruin. The failure to capture Vienna and the loss of revenue from the Hungarian Has and Timars, as well as the actual cost of the campaign itself, posed an immediate problem for the treasury. The salaries of the administrators and soldiers were delayed for up to two years which became even more serious when they refused to obey orders so long as they were not paid. The Grand Defterdar tried to levy a special "campaign tax" which in theory was meant to be a one-off payment, but the revenue proved almost non existent. A century later the situation had not improved much and when, following the treaty of Kutcuk-Kainardji, the Porte was made to pay war reparations of 65,000 Venetian gold ducats, which was not very high[7], because of the disastrous shape of finances the negotiators argued forcefully for it to be spread over three years.

Yet this was not only a question of insufficient care in budgeting or of administrative chaos or even fraud but also due to a general international crisis. The phenomenon was long standing and had its roots in the 16th century following the advent of western centralized mercantile economies. The influx of South American gold resulted of course in inflation but also acted as a stimulus to manufacturing and trade. The Ottoman economy however was too closed, too regulated by fiscal and corporate rules, to be able to keep up with such changes. It experienced inflation and it has been established that during the two centuries that followed the death of Suleyman prices quadrupled. But in terms of production there was little increase and the Empire became increasingly a supplier of raw materials: wheat, wool, copper and precious metals to manufacturing European countries. In turn finished products which local corporations were unable to supply were off-loaded onto a demographically and financially expanding market. There was a permanent deficit in the balance of trade which resulted in the use of weak currencies, as against Venetian ducats or German thalers, and forced the Porte repeatedly to devalue the currency by either reducing its weight or introducing new coins. Although Ottoman dependency on Europe had already been perceptible at the end of Suleyman's reign, it was to become a major characteristic of the 18th century. The previous century had seen the development of Anglo-Dutch trade in the Mediterranean, this would be matched by the French as a result of Colbert's policies. His trade policy was to outlast him and French trade with the Levant was to reach a zenith around 1780 bringing great wealth to towns such as Marseille. At least half of this trade was in textiles. Silk came from Smyrna, cotton from Saida and leather and wool from Istanbul. Leather goods were also exported from Alexandria, wax, ash, oak gall, medicines and many types of perfumes. Europe sold fabrics, spun cotton, paper, tools and even sugar and coffee from the West Indies. The technical and scientific discoveries of the Enlightenment widened the gulf between European manufacturers and Ottoman corporations further encouraging the adoption of European products. As well as military victories the Great powers were able to add a growing economic supremacy. A significant symptom of this is that at the peace of Passarowitz in 1718, Vienna demanded trade right throughout the Empire and after the Treaty of Stanilesti in 1711, Peter the Great still was to retain free trade within the Porte's territories, even though Russia had in fact been beaten.

A few Grand Viziers were aware of the consequences, although perhaps not the causes, of this situation but generally took it to be a fiscal problem since this was the most obvious symptom. Hence Hussein Koprulu, nephew of Mehmed and in power from 1697 to 1702, tried through tax reductions to draw the peasantry back to the land and the shop-keepers back to their workshops, abandoned during the war with Austria due to excessive taxation. Damit Ibrahim Pasha who was Grand Vizier from 1718 to 1730 had to implement a policy of fiscal austerity as a result of the lavish expenditure of his master and intended on devaluing the currency but encountered opposition from the corporations. Halil Hamid (1782–1788) while retaining normal price control, stimulated a craft renaissance which had been in the doldrums due to European competition. To encourage fabric production he reintroduced the traditional rules of dressing according to the type of Millet from which one came or one's rank. Yet much more was needed to bring the Empire out of its permanent economic crisis which S. Shaw characterized after the peace of Belgrade in 1739: "The Empire was confronted by the eternal problems of inflation, plague, shortage of foodstuffs, overpopulation of the towns, rural depopulation, banditry in the countryside and indiscipline of the nobility."

Politically the crisis continued at the very top. Of the eight sultans who followed each other on the throne of Osman from the siege of Vienna to the accession of Selim I in 1789, none have gone down to posterity for their qualities of statesmanship. Mehmed IV (1648–1687) did not change his lifestyle following the defeat in 1683, but continued to spend most of his time hunting and womanizing. The soldiers upon their return from the Danube regions clamoured for his removal and a Fetwa from the Sheik ul Islam declared him unfit to fulfil his duties. He was placed in isolation with his son in an apartment in the depths of the palace. His successor Suleyman II (1687–1691) spent forty-five years of his life shut up inside the palace for fear of being assassinated. He left the task of governing to those who had placed him there and died of an attack of dropsy. Ahmed II (1691–1695) with no education or experience did not leave the harem and abdicated power to his chief eunuch and to the palace factions. Mustafa II (1695–1703) had had more of an education for he had been allowed to move freely within the palace and partake of the pleasures of riding with his brother, but was controlled by his teacher whom he made the Sheik ul Islam as soon as he came to power. In 1703 there took place what is called the "Edirne Occurrences." The Sultan would frequently visit his palace in Edirne and merchants in Istanbul were very worried lest he transfer government over there which would have affected business. In July 1703 during one of the Sultan's absences, some of the Janissaries in the capital refused to go off to war until they had received their back-pay, which amounted to three years. There was a riot, city officials were lynched and Istanbul was in the hands of the rebels. In the meantime Mustafa and the Sheik ul Islam continued to hunt in Edirne. They reacted too late and the Sultan was forced to abdicate in his brother's favour. Mustafa spent the rest of his life locked away in a distant wing of the palace. Ahmed II (1703–1730) also had a proper education and enjoyed poetry, art and calligraphy. On his accession he was forced to give a much larger "gift" than ever before to the soldiers who had nominated him, yet when other units demanded similar amounts he was unable to give them satisfaction. Gathered at Silivri on the Sea of Marmara his troops debated whether to overthrow the house of Osman and to replace it with the Crimean Khans. In the meanwhile they devastated Thrace. Perhaps this experience stifled any wish that Ahmed might have had for reform, and he is remembered in Ottoman history as the sovereign of the "Tulip Period"—Lale Devri—because this flower became exceedingly fashionable in palace circles. Huge amounts of money were spent on getting the Sultan rare bulbs. This ridiculous expenditure compounded the population's misery. In September 1730, an Albanian Janissary called Patrona Halil incited his fellow soldiers, who were supposed to be going on active service to Persia, to revolt and they were soon joined by the population at large. The rebels demanded that Grand Vizier Ibrahim, who had been in power for twelve years, be put to death. Ahmed had him strangled but still was not able to keep his throne. The Sheik ul

Islam made him abdicate in favour of his son Mustafa who became Mahmud I (1730–1754). Patrona and his men meanwhile were sweeping the streets of the capital, killing the rich and burning down their palaces. The city was to experience a reign of unparalleled terror. After a year the Sultan lured Patrona and his henchmen to the palace and had them strangled. His successors Osman III (1754–1757) and Mustafa III (1757–1774) had the good fortune and sense to provide the Empire with one of the lengthiest periods of peace in its history and let their Grand Viziers govern for them. The last on the list, Abdul Hamid (1773–1789) was on the other hand a real reformer. Fifty years old when he came to power he managed to balance the factions within the palace and replace their leaders when necessary to keep hold on power. The serious defeats inflicted by the Russians, forced him to reform the army and more generally to enlist the services of foreign technicians auguring the changes of the 19th century.

The need for reform cut across the whole period. In fact it was already evident in the 17th century when the idea of what was to be called "Traditional Reform" first appeared. Set out in the "Letters of Advice" and meant to be read by the Sultans and the Viziers, they went back all the way to the reign of Soliman the Magnificent. The best known was that of Mustafa Koci, an Albanian, a friend of Murad IV to whom he sent it in 1631. In it he analyses the causes of the decline of the Empire: the state of corruption in the Palace, the passing on of numerous Timars to women and children which weakened the army, parasites in government and in the ranks of the Ulemas and embezzlement of state funds by individuals.The problem was therefore how to reform these different areas and restore efficiency and power to the system. In a slightly modified form this analysis was taken up by Katip Celebi in his "Code of practice for reform" which he wrote in 1656. The areas which he outlined as needing reform were: the army, the treasury and fiscal policy. This was what some of the more dynamic Grand Viziers of the next century were to try and do. Hence following the defeat in Hungary, Mustafa Koprulu struck off the roll about 30,000 Janissaries who had proved unable or unwilling to fulfil their military obligations and called up eastern Turcoman tribesmen to replace them. His cousin Hussein, Grand Vizier from 1698 to 1702 completed this reform: Janissaries who had become craftsmen or traders were thrown out, the corps was reduced to 34,000 men rather than the theoretical 70,000 who had been counted on the eve of Karlowitz, and regular training was given to the Eastern Anatolian Turkish peasants. At the same time the Spahi corps was remoulded. On the economic front, confronted by virtually permanent shortages of foodstuffs, Fazil Mustafa felt there were dangers in taxing foodstuffs and Hussein tried to lower the taxes on some commodities such as oil, soap, coffee and tobacco. Up until the reign of Selim the Palace was to issue numerous kanuns outlining military obligations, kanuns to restore the Timar system and kanuns to spread taxes more equitably.

The shock which was felt following defeat and the Peace of Karlowitz had one positive result: several high-ranking officials realized that the victory of the European powers was due to their technical superiority and that, without necessarily abandoning their own system, the Ottoman Empire would gain by using these same techniques. The reforms of the 18th century often combined traditional characteristics with this idea of modernization. The origins of this are to be found during Ahmed III's Tulip reign (1703–1730), for notwithstanding certain excessive traits, this marks the beginning of an exchange of ideas with the western civilisation. Grand Vizier Damit Ibrahim, who had negotiated at Karlowitz, realized that to be able to conduct a successful Ottoman foreign policy it was essential to have a better understanding of the European powers. Hence the idea of sending to every large capital an ambassador, not only to sign and negotiate treaties and alliances but also to inform the Porte of the political and military situation in the various countries. Mehmed Efendi was sent to Paris (1720–1721) and others went to Vienna, Moscow and Warsaw. The most spectacular result of this was the construction, in the valley of Kagithane Suyu at the far end of the Golden Horn, of a palace based on a model of Fontainebleau which the Ottoman envoy had brought back with him[8]. A folly, the new building was an imitation of the lifestyle of a French king and was adopted by the notables of the Sultan's entourage. Istanbul wished to copy Paris which could have led to a cultural revolution, for as well as fashion there came western artists with commissions to decorate the palace walls and despite the religious prescriptions to paint the portraits of rich Ottomans. Along with the palaces, fountains, gardens and aqueducts there was set up the first printing press in the Ottoman capital, in fact a simple press in the unassuming house of a certain Ibrahim Muterferrika, a Transylvanian convert to Islam. The powerful scribes' corporation, fearful of potential competition, tried to stop him and the Grand Vizier settled for a compromise: printing would be limited to secular works while religious literature would continue to be written by hand. Until his death in 1745, Ibrahim printed maps of the Sea of Marmara and the Black Sea, a dictionary and about fifteen works, above all the printer's own work since he was interested in the geography of the empire and even published a work on America. The bloody revolt led by Patrona put an end to the Tulip period, yet even though many palaces were burnt down, the ideas which had been thrown up into the air did not all go up in smoke. Especially the need to copy the west in military matters to arrest the retreat of the Sultan's flag. In order to reform the army the new sovereign, Mahmud, decided to use an European adviser, the first of many, count Claude-Alexander of Bonneval (1675–1757); an officer who had fallen into disgrace with Louis XIV, joined Prince Eugene with whom he quarrelled and finally offered his services to the Ottomans. He converted to Islam and was discovered by the Grand Vizier who made him Ahmed Pasha Humbaraci after his reorganization of the Bombardiers (Humbaraci). He was helped by three other French officers, also renegades, and used Irish and Scottish mercenaries and Bosnian peasants. They were dressed in Hungarian style uniforms and trained according to French and Austrian methods. Ahmed Pasha also put forward an overall plan for the reorganization of the army on the lines of the French system but encountered the opposition of the Janissaries. His own corps, by coincidence was disbanded during the same period as the Muterferrika press was destroyed during the reign of Mustafa III. Thirty years later the reorganization of the army was again taken up by Francois of Toth (1730–1793), a Hungarian who entered the service of France and was sent to Istanbul with Ambassador Vergennes. The Sultan rented his services and entrusted him with the reorganization of the artillery. In 1774 de Toth set up a new corps with rapid fire cannons and above all established a school of mathematics to teach the officers. After his return to France his achievement was maintained and continued from 1780 to 1785 by Grand Vizier Halil Hamid who made great call on the services of French engineers and even specialized workers in artillery and marine technology and fortifications.

The Ottoman Empire was opening up, however timidly, to the outside world through the military.

The Ottoman Balkans in the 18th Century

For the first time since the original conquest the Balkan peoples had become directly involved in wars: from the west the Austrian armies had penetrated right into the heart of Kosovo, in the East the Tsar's troops had pushed into Bulgarian territories whilst Orlov's contingents cut across the Peloponnese. Following the best tradition troop movements were followed by that of the population, in this case sometimes so numerous that in some areas they were to change the very ethnic balance. So in 1690 there took place the Velika Seoba—the great migration—in which 37,000 Christian families moved to southern Hungary even though this had only recently been reconquered. Under the authority of the Patriarch of Pecs, whose see was in the Monastery of Krusedol in Fruska Gora, they were to form under Emperor Leopold's favourable gaze, a "Communitas Rasciana" with its administrative and cultural centre at Karlowitz, the real Serbian capital of the 18th century. A similar phenomenon, but of lesser proportions, took place in 1737 when the Patriarch once more had to leave Pecs following the subsequent retreat of the Imperial forces. There has been much argument over the consequences of these exoduses for the Balkans and especially Kosovo. It should first be noted that the Christians fleeing the Ottomans were not all Serbians; among them were Albanians and above all from the region round Scutari (Shkodra). The abandoned villages of the Metohja plain were repopulated by montagnards from surrounding areas who in these new surroundings were to become converts to Islam. There were also peasants on the run, thousands of them in the Balkans, from all over the place, drawn by the promise of fertile lands. In 1840 Ami Boue, a shrewd observer was to write: "The Albanians (of Metohija) are a bastard race, mixed with much Serbian blood and their many tribes and children are all descendants of mixed marriages between Serbs and Albanians."[9] The 18th century marks the Islamization of the region but it was only during the next century that signs of a national uprising were to appear. In the opposite direction, the victories of the Duke of Lorraine and Prince Eugene sent a wave back south of thousands of Spahis and their Celebu. Many we know were of Bosnian origin and had settled on Timars in areas far from Bosnia, reinforcing the Islamic composition of the population of such areas as Serbia and Macedonia. During the Ottoman counter-offensive of 1737 against the Imperial forces, the old Hungarian Timarlis were renowned for their courage and mettle, avenging their families massacred during the Christian conquest. At the other end of the Empire, in the Tatar areas, the Russian advance resulted in similar migrations, but these Muslims emigrated mainly towards Anatolia, although some actually reached Istanbul. The Porte also made use of some of these peoples to colonize strategic areas: Circassians from the Kuban were settled in southern Moldavia and the Danube delta and Tatars on the Bulgarian plateau between the Danube and the Stara Planina.

The innovative Grand Viziers also tried to halt the exodus from the villages to the towns by, for example closing down the Hans (inns) so that the peasant would not be able to find a bed or food on his journey. Kanuns fell into abeyance and although there was quite a lot of Christian resistance, Muslims ultimately had power. The decline of the town of Voskopolis (Voskopola) was due to this feeling of general insecurity. First mentioned in the 15th century, it had grown to 20,000 inhabitants at the start of the 18th century. A centre of crafts and thriving trade it could boast an "academy," a printing press and patronage of the art. Making the most of the fact that war with Russia tied down the Sultan's armies in the border areas, the leaders of the Fis and Ayans of the region had tried to capture the town. Three times, in 1769, 1772 and 1789 it was pillaged and burnt down. The Albanian, Greek, Slav and Wallachian inhabitants dispersed all over the Balkans going as far as Hungary and southern Poland. When consul François Charles Pouqueville visited the place fifteen years later he only came across "two hundred huts" inhabited by poor shepherds, and reached the conclusion that: "after ten years of devastation, plunder and war, Voskopolis had been wiped from the map of Albania."

In the end all this population migration had one major effect, the progressive Islamization of the Balkans. Modern historians prefer to emphasize this point to explain the relative decline of the Christian populations in the 18th century rather than a generalized demographic crisis within the Ottoman Empire[10].

The changes in the organization of the countryside, initiated during the previous century, were to become widespread. To contend with war expenditure the Treasury converted some of its assets, Mukata—revenue—tax on farmer generals or fiefdoms which it replaced with Malikane—concessions on property which was granted for life and passed on as inheritance. So farmer generals became feudal lords, whereas Has and Timars were transformed into Ciftlik land. Taken after the terrible reversals, these measures resulted in huge ready income but ultimately were a drain on Treasury resources. The reforming Grand Viziers tried to recover control over Mukata land. Raghib Pasha set up in 1750 a special corps of civil servants to check deeds of ownership. Halil Hamid used the same inspectors in 1780 to check up on absentee Spahis and was quick to seize the fiefdoms of those who were absent. However this development was to become more widespread. The decline of central authority was exemplified by the growth and consolidation of another group: the Ayans. These notables had originally been the servants of city or provincial governors, but unlike their masters would have come from the same area and in principle would have been elected by the inhabitants to be their representatives in the administration. In fact they were mainly large landowners who with Baksheesh had bought this lucrative and prestigious office from the governor. These were the officials who had most benefitted from the Treasury's financial problems, buying Malikanes and generally increasing their power, to such an extent that this was one of the most pressing of issues for central government in 1774 when Abdul Hamid came to the throne.

The final stage of this evolution was the creation of "Grand Pashaliks"; virtual feudal states formed in the heart of the Empire and whose head was appointed as Pasha.

They had always in fact existed in Anatolia where there remained powerful families, such as the Kara Osman Oglus who had domain over vast tracts of the south-west, the Capan Oglus who controlled most of the central plateau or the Sanikli Oglus in the north-east. Mameluk Egypt, Syria and Palestine had had similar forms of government, whereas in the Balkans this phenomenon had developed much later on and was to be a characteristic of the 18th century. During this period Edirne was controlled by the Dagdeviren Oglus, while the banks of the Danube from Ruscuk (Ruse) to Sistova was dominated by the Tirsanikli Oglus. But the most famous examples, even outside the Empire were the Busatis of Skutari, the Alis of Janina and the Pasvan Oglus of Vidin. During a period of strife and vendetta between the region's lords, the Busati family had come to power in Skutari. In 1757 Mehmet, its head known as the Old, having seized control of the city, obtained a Firman of Mutasarrif—Governor—from the Sultan. Rapidly his power extended over the whole of the Sandjaks and he therefore took the title of Pasha. Later from weak Mustafa III he managed to obtain control over the neighbouring Sandjaks of Ohrid and Dukadjin together with the title Vizier and his son was to become governor of the Elbasan Sandjak, thus placing the whole of northern Albania under Busati control. After Mehmet's death the Porte tried to appoint a more obedient governor but came against the armed resistance of Mustafa, the eldest son whom they were forced to have poisoned. The second son Kara Mahmud came into open conflict with Istanbul and had links with Vienna, Saint Petersburg and France. In 1795 he received a French Consul in Scutari together with seven military advisers sent by Bonaparte who was in Slovenia at the time. He was to die with four of the seven in an ambush by Montenegrins in September 1796. The Pashalik's autonomy disappeared with his death and his brother Ibrahim was to govern until his death in 1810 as the Sultan's loyal Mutasarrif.

Another Albanian, Ali (1744–1822) was the son of a humble Ayan from Tepelen. Left an orphan, he took up arms in a gang of Armatoles and became their leader. For twenty years they were to plunder southern Albania and Thessaly. His fame came to the Sultan's attention and in 1785 at forty-one years of age, he was given the title of Pasha and the post of Mutasarrif of the Trikalia (Trikala) Sandjak. Three years later he was master of Janina (Ioannina) which had 25,000 inhabitants and was the trading centre of Epirus. Fabulous gifts persuaded the Sultan to agree to his taking power and his son was to succeed him in Trikalia. Taking advantage of the war against Catherine II, he actually launched several military operations to occupy the Tosk region and above all Acta which gave him access to the Ionian Sea. Bonaparte's expedition to Egypt presented him with the opportunity of making a complicated deal: requesting French and then Russian support in quick succession he still managed to retain the Sultan's. He encountered strong resistance from the Suliotes of Himara whom he had massacred, so breaking a promise[11] he had made. In 1806 he turned to Napoleon to capture the seven Ionian islands and a body of correspondence was sent in which Ali calls the French Emperor, "Hero of centuries, Great Napoleon." However the Franco-Russian alliance of Tilsit marked an end of his hopes. Disappointed he took revenge on the French Consul at Janina, Francois Charles de Pouqueville, whom he kept a virtual prisoner. Ali continued to play his hand skilfully which allowed him progressively to capture the Ottoman fortresses of Berat, Vlora and Djirokastra. At its height in 1811, the Pashalik was made up of all of southern Albania, Thessaly and Epirus. In theory Ali remained the Sultan's vassal but he got rid of the Timars, Zeamets and Has and transformed them into Ciftliks. So successful was he that by the end of his life, the Pasha who had inherited only two small estates in the Tepelen region, had become proprietor of 934 working villages in the form of Ciftliks spread right through his Pashalik.

Osman Pasvan Oglu (1758-1807), an Albanian, son of an Ayan who had been executed on the Sultan's order, settled in the Vidin area as the leader of a band of Derbenders. These were armed auxiliaries who were supposed to be used to guard bridges, high ground and places of transit but who since the 17th century had progressively become organized gangs operating independently and were even involved in military rebellions in Istanbul. Occupying the Danube fortress of Vidin from 1794 onwards, Osman made it into a centre of resistance against Sultan Selim under the pretext of opposition to his reforms. Recognized as Pasha of Vidin in 1799 after defeating an Ottoman army, he was in fact to remain independent and became involved in the intrigues and fighting of the Serbian Karageorge uprising.

The "Great Pashaliks" of the Balkans were regions where the Sultan's power was almost non-existent.

The Vassal Principalities

Paradoxically it was during this same period that Istanbul was to increase its hold on Moldavia and Wallachia, by putting into place what Romanian historians have called the "Phanariot Period" from 1711-1821. The beginnings of this phenomenon have already been mentioned and the reason for its development was clearly due to the mounting threat from abroad.

When Dimitri Cantemir, Voevod of Moldavia and ally of Peter the Great, fled to Russia, the Porte decided to replace him with a man they could trust, a Greek from the Phanar district of Istanbul, Nicholas Mavrocordatos son of the High Dragoman[12]. In December 1715 the Prince of Wallachia, Stephan Cantacuzino, was executed on suspicion of being in league with Vienna and the Porte placed Nicholas Mavrocordatos on the throne of Bucharest where he remained for one year and a further period from 1719 to 1730.

This clearly shows that the Sultan considered the rulers of the Principalities as no more than provincial governors whom he could appoint, displace and remove whenever he wished. The name Voevod, which had the notion of military leader, was replaced by Hospodar which signifies "Lord[13]." The political system had features which were rather original: the princes were largely chosen from among members of Greek families living in Istanbul and were appointed by the Porte without consultation nor election by the "National Assembly"—in other words the Boyars of the Principality. Between 1711 and 1821 some eighty rulers were chosen from twelve families, of these only two were Romanian and one Albanian , the remainder were of Greek origin and had lived in the Empire's capital for quite some time. The average length of a reign in Moldavia was less than three years and in Wallachia two and a half. The princes moved frequently from one principality to the other; between 1730 and 1769 Constantine Mavrocordatos, Nicholas' son, was to have ten different reigns: six in Wallachia and four in Moldavia. The appointment by the Porte consisted of the purchase of a Firman of appointment with Mucarer as well as gifts—Pesches—for the Grand Vizier and other dignitaries. The Hospodar's enthronement was accompanied by the payment of the tribute which for Moldavia was to vary between 65,000 and 260,000 thalers and from 260,000 to 300,000 for Wallachia. From 1750 there was also a yearly tax to the Sultan and of course the mandatory supply of foodstuffs which tended to rise with the loss of certain provinces, for example the Crimean wheat was replaced by Wallachian wheat. In 1783 there were four grain levies at a price far below the Istanbul market value. It is reckoned that in 1772 Wallachia paid about 650,000 thalers to Istanbul. This was a huge sum of money and explains why taxes were high and also the acquisitiveness of the princes who would have been anxious to reimburse themselves and make a healthy profit as well. Hence the reputation for fraud and corruption which clings to the names of many of the Phanariots.

Among the Hospodar's entourage there emerged a court nobility which lived and dressed according to the fashions of the palace of Istanbul, while at the same time military duty virtually ended, due to the fact that the army had been reduced to a few units used for nothing more exciting than internal security and border duties. This was a sign that the principalities were not allowed independent foreign policies. The Hospodar was responsible with his life and that of his family for submission to the Porte's interests.

More profound changes were also taking place: the population is calculated at about 1,520,000 in Wallachia in 1791 and 980,000 in Moldavia in 1774. Of this 95% lived in the countryside where a distinction should be made between the free peasant (about a third) and the majority who were serfs. The latter worked the land and lived in villages belonging to either the Hospodar, Boyars, the Metropolitan or else monasteries. There tenancies were hereditary and they were not allowed to leave the land. As everywhere else in the Balkans peasants fleeing the land was one of the biggest problems of the Phanariot 18th century. However, unlike the regions to the south of the Danube, large estates were common. In 1780 the Boyar Constantin Brancoveanu owned 82 villages, 32 vineyards and five mountains used for pasture. Contrary to what some historians had believed these large landowners did not farm huge estates like their Polish or Russian counterparts, as most of their land was made up of peasant tenancies while the "Reserve" was small. This explains why there were few corvee work days—less than ten a year—which were often paid for in lieu. The Boyar's income came principally from a levy on produce meant for market and to a greater extent from monopolies such as mills, taverns etc, and above all from the manufacture and sale of alcohol which could only done on their domains. Towns remained small. At the start of the 18th century only the capitals were noteworthy: Bucharest had 30–40,000 inhabitants and Jassy 20,000. Although mostly Romanian they were still very cosmopolitan with Greeks, Armenians, Jews and sometimes even Ragusians. They were to become more Balkanized during the 18th century with Hans, markets and Cardaks but there were never any mosques nor palaces built.

For a long time they were summarily dismissed by Romanian historians yet the Phanariot Princes were not all bad. Some tried to reform the tax system, with the aim however of increasing its efficiency. In 1746, before the "Enlightened" Joseph II[14], Hospodar Constantin Mavrocordatos abolished serfdom in Wallachia and in Moldavia in 1749. Published in the "Mercure" in France the "Constitution" which the prince granted his subjects, was to make him famous in Europe yet encountered resistance from his own powerful landowners. They were to impose corvee work two to three times higher than before, from their former serfs. The serfs became corvee peasants, but under the authority of the Prince rather than the Boyars. This was a first step on the road to emancipation.

As previously mentioned Moldavia and Wallachia became caught up in the wars between the Porte and the neighbouring powers, Austria and Russia. Oltenia was governed by Vienna from 1718 to 1738 with Austrian methods which although harsh on the inhabitants were to influence the reforming Hospodars and above all Constantin Mavrocordatos. The first war with Catherine II brought the Russian armies right up to Bucharest and the Boyars took advantage of this by calling for their independence. The peace of Kutcuk-Kajnardji (1774) recognized the right of both princes to have an ambassador in Istanbul "enjoying the privileges of international law." Notwithstanding this and ignoring the protests of Hospodar Grigore III Ghica, the Porte gave Vienna the northern part of Moldavia, which became Bukovina, in return for the diplomatic support that Austria gave in settling problems with Russia. The Sultan had disposed of a part of the principality as if it were a part of his Empire. Two other clauses in the treaty were to have important repercussions for the two states: firstly the independence of the Crimean Tatars which meant that an old and dangerous forward post and threat to Moldavia had disappeared, and secondly the right of Russian merchant ships to use the Straits so signalling the end of the Black Sea as a "Turkish lake." The result was a series of acts from the Ottoman Chancellery which limited the practise of forced purchases in peacetime and Russian consuls were sent to Bucharest and Jassy in 1782, soon followed by Austria, France, Prussia and England, signalling the end of Istanbul's political monopoly. Both in Moldavia and Wallachia the dominion of Istanbul was henceforth counterbalanced by the growing influence of Russia.

The principality of Transylvania, independent of the Crown of Hungary since 1541, had had to accept a Firman in 1566 which established its vassal status in relation to the Sultan, whereas under the treaty of Spire in 1570 the Habsburgs recognized its independence while retaining their own right to the Zapolyai succession. For a century the princes implemented policies vis-a-vis Istanbul and Vienna which tried to mix dynastic interests, for example Stephan Bathory was also king of Poland and the Rakoczi's had dreams of creating a Protestant Empire against the

Habsburgs. Each time the candidate to the throne seemed favourable to the Habsburgs then Istanbul would intervene. So in 1613 Gabriel Bethlen, whose reign was later seen as a Golden Age in Transylvania, was imposed on the Diet by an Ottoman army, yet in the face of Austrian opposition the prince had to make a deal with Vienna. During the Thirty Years War, George I Rakoczi had been an ally of Sweden and France which meant that Transylvania took part in the peace negotiations at Westphalia in 1648 as a sovereign state. However this international prestige was not to last for very long. In 1658 under the energetic leadership of Grand Vizier Ahmed Koprulu the Ottomans returned to a more offensive policy which led them to the gates of Vienna. Transylvania was invaded and ravaged by the Sultan's armies who annexed the mountainous region of Banat, to the Beylerbeylik of Temesvar (Timisoara). Istanbul then imposed its own candidates until after the siege of Vienna when the victorious Habsburgs forced Prince Apafi at the treaty of Blasendorf, to accept their "protection" in return for 100,000 ducats and the occupation of its fortresses by Imperial troops. Henceforth Transylvania was under Austrian domination, thus escaping from the Ottoman Empire and so also from the Balkans.

Conclusion

The Ottoman Yoke

The title of Ivan Vazov's famous novel "Pod Igoto"[15] is well known and the term "Ottoman Yoke" has subsequently been used by many Balkan historians. What did it consist of at the dawn of the 19th century, at the very moment when the peoples of the Balkans were one after another, Serbia, Greece, Bulgaria and Albania, to escape from its grip?

We first need to dispel a erroneous idea, often held by nationalist writers of the 19th and 20th centuries: Ottoman occupation. A presence which lasted for five centuries and which imposed a new political, administrative and social order cannot be reduced to a temporary military situation of different peoples in conflict with each other. We must speak of Ottoman "domination" and of every aspect of life. From the beginning the Islamic theocracy permitted cohabitation, Muslims and Zimmi, as long as the Zimmi paid

Harac. The Ottoman solution was the Millet which was based on a fundamental inequality making Christians second class subjects in the same way as Jews in Medieval Europe. This Diminutio Capitis was felt and suffered no doubt by the leaders of the Christian communities. Not the nobility who were either wiped out during the invasion or else converted to Islam but the clergy, town merchants and heads of villages. As for the peasant masses—the great majority of the population—their serf status already made them a "herd" so the Ottoman notion of Reaya fitted quite well. The state, be it feudal Christian or Islamic, was felt to be an instrument of oppression and above all financial oppression. More important to them was the system of farming the land, what proportion of their labour was their own and on this question the Timar system was in theory much better than serf tenure. This was recognized to be the case in the 15th century. The Serbian peasantry was docile showing that in their opinion the Hagarians were no worse than the Brankovics and other feudal lords, borne out by the flight of Hungarian and Romanian serfs to the Sultan's Empire. There did however remain the religious antagonism, particularly important during these centuries of deep faith, which was reflected in the opposition of two "cultures" in the broadest sense of the word, or as Ralph Linton, the social psychologist defines it; the configuration of acquired and resultant behaviour, which in its basic elements are shared and transmitted by members of a particular society. Hence there existed between the followers of Islam and the Eastern Christian Church a wall of incomprehension and possibility of a whole series of large and small conflicts erupting in everyday life. In fact for as long as the Ottoman system worked, the "yoke" which was imposed on the Christians can be reduced to a cultural antagonism which was implacable, since it was based, on both sides, on a theocratic view of the world.

We have seen however that the system underwent rapid changes which were to get worse during the 17th and 18th centuries with rising and unequal taxes, corrupt government, land acquisitiveness and the transformation of Timars into Ciftliks, as well as the decline of the military—in a word the "decadence" of a state "rotting from the head downwards." The Christians were to experience this more than the Muslims since they were unable to appeal to the Sultan or to what remained of central power. Furthermore the ruinous wars, the to and fro of devastating armies, whatever their colour, the slow but continuing decline of the Empire's economic performance in relation to the rest of the world, help to understand the dismal accounts of the Balkans that European travellers in the 18th century were wont to give.

Muslims were not exempt and Istanbul had its poor. Every so often a Grand Vizier or a writer would advocate reform yet they always encountered two obstacles. On the one hand the people of privilege who refused to learn from experience and clung on to the "old methods"; everything was better in the past and must be recreated, and in the absence of any cultural revolution similar to the Renaissance, "Reformers" could only envisage a reform of the excesses and a restoration of the institutions which were a product of the traditional theocratic concept: theirs was a world where the sun orbited the world and Allah's paradise retained its profane and voluptuous attractions.

The Christians suffered the most and the stories of the period are full of complaints against prevaricating Kadis, oppressive Timarlis, highway robbing Janissaries and the climate of insecurity which was a characteristic feature of the countryside. The Serbian and Oltenian peasants experienced an alternative regime, that of Austria between 1718 and 1738, and although it was hardly caring it did give a picture of an ordered Christian country where laws were enforced and the Emperor claimed the same God as themselves. Contrary to the 15th century, the comparison was now in Austria's favour and it was to her, as well as to an almost mythical Russia, that some Christian worthies, monks, popes and merchants who in their journeys had visited Vienna, Saint Petersburg and Marseille, were to turn. They came into contact with lay Christian cultures developing the rationalism of the "Enlightenment." The Ottoman "Yoke" and even their own culture was to be reappraised in this light. The cultural antagonism between Islam and Christianity had not died down but had become complicated by new tensions which were to pit traditional and modern thought against one another.

Yet it would be giving a false impression of the Ottoman Balkans in the 18th century to portray, as the romantic writers were to do, the Manichean view of two opposing camps, with on the one hand the guardians of the occult and on the other the sons of the enlightenment. The Ottomanization of society, in other words the adoption of a way of life, without even needing to go as far as conversion, was to a large extent a necessity. Numerous Bulgarian Tchorbadjis, Serbian Knezes, Greek Arshonts and above all the Phanariots remained Christian, retained their native tongues yet lived in a Turkish manner as a result of their dealings with the Ottoman administration. Travellers frequently emphasized the Turkish nature of the cities, even those where the Christians were predominant. The wearing of the Tchartchaf was common in Thessalonika, Belgrade and Sofia and there were many churches which were divided up by wooden barriers, separating men from women, as can be seen in Bansko in Bulgaria and as was the case in Troyan and Koprivchitsa although no Muslims lived there[16]. More importantly this Islamo-Christian symbiosis reached to the very depths of the religious experience. The Pomaks and the Domnes in Albania mixed Christian and Muslim practices without any apparent difficulty. Bernard Lory calls this "contamination," for instance the wish to go on Hadjilak, pilgrimage to the Holy Places (Mecca for some and Palestine for the others) but which allowed the faithful the same name—Hadj—and the same prestige. Perhaps slightly more curious was the sharing of certain sites, such as near Varna the Teke of Ak Azala Baba which the Orthodox Church prescribed to Saint Athanas and whose feast days were celebrated on successive day, on the 1 and 2 May, first by the Muslims and then the Christians.

Four to five centuries of "shared" life had produced many shades of meaning for the term "Ottoman Yoke."

Notes

1. Now Senta on the river Tizsa in Yugoslavian Voevodina.
2. Sremski Karlovci near Novi Sad.
3. The village of the "Little Spring" near Silistra in present day Bulgaria.
4. Now Poksovsk.
5. Svistov in Bulgaria, on the Danube.
6. The 29 December 1791 according to the Orthodox calender.
7. Wallachia's tribute was then at 130,000 gold ducats.
8. Now in ruins.
9. Ami Boue: Turquie d'Europe. Paris 1840. t. II p.15.
10. cf. Maria A. Todorova: Was there a demographic crisis in the Ottoman Empire in the XVII century. Etudes Balkaniques. N-2. 1988 pp. 55/63.
11. After four years of seige in the mountains the Suliotes agreed to put down their arms on condition that they would be allowed to go to Corfu which was in Russian hands. Ali promised but attacked the refugee

caravan. The famous episode where the Suliotes women threw themselves over the precipices with their children to save them from Ali's soldiers, immortalized in Ary Scheffer's painting in the Louvre, took place in the Zalong pass.

12. The office of "Grand Translator" had been created in 1669. The first holder was a Greek from Chios. In 1673 he was succeeded by a young Greek from Phanar district of Istanbul Alexander Mavrocordatos who held the post until his death in 1706. Alexander had married a rich Greek merchant's daughter who supplied the palace with livestock.

13. In modern Romanian Gospodar means administrator.

14. The Order of the abolition of serfdom from 1781–1785.

15. "Under the Yoke" published in 1889.

16. Lory(B.): Le sort de l'heritage ottoman en Bulgarie: l'example des villes 1878–1900. Istanbul. ed. Isis. 1985. 235 p. Cf. pp. 167/8 and 176/7.

9
Napoleon's Conquest in the East

Instead of the Turkish caricature which Moliere had portrayed and which had been commonly held to be true during the reign of Louis XIV, the 18th century view was to become more sophisticated as a result of a growing interest in exploration, dreams of uncorrupted peoples and of the actual experiences of merchants from Marseilles, Amsterdam and London. Bonaparte, dividing the world with the Russian Tsar, was also to add to this experience with his brief conquest of Egypt and for the next century there developed a romantic fascination, from Chateaubriand to Pierre Loti, for what was known as the "Orient."

Wars and Alliances: The Games of the Great Powers, 1798–1815

Leopold of Austria and then Catherine II of Russia were to sign the treaties of Sistova (1791) and Jassy (1792) so as to be able to confront the revolutionary armies of France which gave the Ottoman Empire a respite of six years of uninterrupted peace. The ideas of the French Revolution did not have much influence on the Porte for they were very alien to it, yet Selim III was apparently troubled by the death of Louis XVI for he considered him a friend. Above all he was anxious at the alterations to the balance of power of Europe. The conflict between France, Austria, Russia and England was welcome, at least until October 1797 following the Treaty of Campo Formio and the dismantling of the Republic of Venice which Bonaparte gave to Vienna, since this left the presence of French troops in the Ionian Islands and at ports of Preveza and Parga in Epirus. Istanbul was very worried by this direct contact with the most powerful nation in Europe and following the death of Catherine the Great, and the succession of her son Paul I, a rapprochement took place which was to become an alliance in 1798/99. Bonaparte embarked on his Egyptian expedition. Since Selim I's conquest in 1517 this had been part of the Beylerbeylik of Misir and an integral part of the Empire (even though recurrent Mameluk revolts meant that anarchy reigned). As a result of this direct attack on Dar el Islam the Porte had to conclude a realignment of alliances to be able to repulse it by force. French citizens were imprisoned and their property seized. This was the end of a status quo which had been in place for centuries. The Russian fleet was allowed to pass through the Straits and joined the Ottoman fleet for joint operations in the Adriatic. French troops were thrown out of the Ionian Islands with the slightly dubious assistance of Ali Pasha of Jannina who coveted them himself, while at the Russo-Ottoman conference in March 1800 the Islands were confirmed as being under Ottoman suzerainty but with Russian garrisons. In Syria the Sultan's army fought the French at Jaffa, Mount Tabor and at Acra with the help of English forces. Following the disaster of Aboukir in August 1798 General Kleber reached agreement with the Grand Vizier to withdraw, but London and Saint Petersburg overruled this. In the end the French surrendered to a combined English and Ottoman force in August 1801. In Istanbul those in favour of peace gained the upper hand and in June 1802, Selim agreed to sign the Treaty of Amiens which confirmed the surrender, returned French interests and reestablished normal relations. Egypt returned to Ottoman sovereignty while the Seven Islands[1] became an independent republic. In fact it was under Russian protection and a Corfu noble, Capo d'Istria, was chosen as the head of government. Thus the Ionian Isles broke away from the Ottoman Empire.

The alliance which was formalized in the Treaty of Constantinople in January 1799 gave the Tsar the opportunity to further his interests in the Danubian Principalities. In 1802 the Porte agreed not to replace the Hospodars without the prior agreement of Saint Petersburg, which amounted to recognition that the two vassal states had become Russo-Ottoman condominions. The breach of the Peace of Amiens and the forming of a Third Coalition greatly served the Porte's interests: the appeal for help by the Karageorge Serbs, who had been in revolt since the beginning of 1804, went unanswered since Austria and Russia were intent on operations in central Europe and England was keen on maintaining the Ottoman alliance and did not want to anger the

Porte. The balance of power was changed by the Peace of Pressburg in December 1805 whereby Austria ceded Venice, Istria and Dalmatia to Napoleon who thus gained control of the Adriatic. During the summer of 1805 Bonaparte sent General Sebastiani, who in 1802 had managed to gain the Sultan's confidence, to Istanbul to convince Selim of abolishing the treaties of 1799 and 1802 which they considered were too favourable to Saint Petersburg. Selim listened to him and dismissed the Hospodars Constantin Ipsilanti of Wallachia and Alexander Moruzi of Moldavia who he felt were too obedient to the Tsar, reaffirmed his suzerainty over the Ionian Islands and closed the Straits to foreign warships. Alexander I responded by sending an army into the Principalities and in November 1806 the Sultan declared war on Russia. The Ottoman Empire was once again in alliance with France.

The Allied reaction was swift. England sent a fleet which forced the Straits of the Dardanelles and was riding off the coast near Istanbul by January 1807. The city's defences were in a bad state and General Sebastiani helped by French technicians hurriedly tried to strengthen them. The English command however delayed the attack as he was paralysed by the absence of firm orders. Two months later the British fleet again passed through the Straits, while another English fleet with an expeditionary force succeeded in capturing Alexandria yet failed to make any substantial headway into the interior of Egypt. Russia on the other hand started giving support to the Karageorge revolt. An agreement was reached in July 1807 whereby a governor and ruling body would be sent together with armaments and supplies, and Russian troops would occupy the Serbian fortresses. The Porte appealed to the powerful semi-independent Pasha Ali of Janina and Pasha Osman Pasvanoglu of Vidin promising them extra territory. Ali attacked the Russians in the Ionian Islands and Pasvanoglu threatened the Serbs. Napoleon answered the Sultan's request for assistance by sending military advisers and 500 gunners from the Dalmatian garrison. The regular Ottoman army counter-attacked in Wallachia and laid siege to Bucharest where the Russians had withdrawn.

Two things were to change the course of the war: in Istanbul on the 29 May 1807 Selim was overthrown by the Janissaries in favour of his cousin Mustafa IV and in July 1807 at Tilsit Napoleon entered into an alliance with Russia. The overwhelming Ottoman offensive ended operations north of the Danube, whereas the

Franco-Russian alliance resulted in a new situation in the Balkans. The two emperors envisaged the division of the Ottoman Empire but the negotiations in Saint Petersburg, led by Caulaincourt, floundered on the problem of control of the Straits and who would receive Istanbul. Napoleon's reply to Alexander's question is well known: "Constantinople? Never. Constantinople is the centre of a world Empire." In the meantime France in August 1807 recaptured the Seven Islands as well as their dependent territories to the great anger of Ali who had his eye on the port of Parga. Once again isolated the Porte resigned itself to peace: France acted as go-between to Istanbul and Saint Petersburg, and an agreement was signed at Slobozia[2] in March 1808 which allowed for the evacuation of Russian troops from the Principalities and passage through the Straits of the Tsar's fleet which again gained access to the Mediterranean. In fact Alexander did not ratify this treaty, sporadic fighting continued and at a meeting at Erfurt in September 1808, Napoleon planning his strategy in Spain, promised Alexander Moldavia and Wallachia. England however, anxious to divide Istanbul from France in January 1809 signed with the Porte, the Dardanelles Convention which set out the principle of closing the Straits to naval forces in time of peace.

War once again broke out in Europe in 1808 (5th Coalition). Such was the situation in Istanbul that General Sebastiani foresaw that the Tsar's armies would reach the city in a few days, however such was Alexander's mistrust of his French ally that he kept the best of his divisions in central Europe. Napoleon crushed the Habsburg forces, occupied Vienna and was victorious at Wagram, then he laid down his terms for peace in October 1809. Austria gave up its last Dalmatian possessions as well as Istria, Trieste, Carniola, Carinthia and a part of the kingdom of Croatia. These territories were to form the "Illyrian Provinces," annexed to the French Empire thus breaking the English blockade of the Mediterranean sea-routes with a land route. Ragusa was also to be incorporated into it. The Republic had since the Treaty of Presburg in December 1805 been divided between the French in Dalmatia and the Russians who controlled the mouth of the Cattaro, which in reality was Austrian territory. Napoleon had the city occupied in 1806 but only in January 1808 did he confirm its status with a decree which declared that the "Republic of Ragusa no longer exists." The following year its territories were joined to the Illyrian

Provinces. Thus one of the Porte's most faithful vassals had been destroyed.

This was a difficult period for Istanbul. It was ruled by the weak Mustafa IV who was under the threat of supporters of Selim and was overthrown in July 1808, to be replaced by Mahmud II who was keen on reform of the Empire but needed peace to do this. Alexander in turn was becoming anxious about the direction of his ally Napoleon's policies. The English ambassador to Constantinople, Canning, served as an intermediary for reaching a settlement. Peace was signed in May 1812 in Bucharest. Saint Petersburg agreed once more to evacuate the Principalities but continued to occupy the region between the Dnestr and Pruth (what had been the Ottoman Reaya of Bugak) while Moldavia was once more reduced in size giving approximately a third of its territory which was to form the new Russian province of Bessarabia. The Tsar had not wanted to abandon his protégés the Serbs of Karageorge and the Porte agreed on an amnesty and autonomy, in return for the reoccupation of the fortresses.

The Balkans were not directly involved in the drama of the subsequent period and the Congress of Vienna only mentions them in passing. Mahmud tried in vain to obtain from Saint Petersburg the return of Bessarabia but to no avail. The Treaties of 1815 did not change the Balkan frontiers and the confluence of the Danube and the Sava with the Una marked the edge of the Sultan's Empire. North of the river Wallachia remained unchanged, Moldavia already reduced in size in 1775 with the loss of Bukovina to Austria had had Russian Bessarabia sliced out of it, and on the Adriatic Austria recovered the whole of the coast right up to the river Cattaro which was known as the kingdom of Dalmatia. Finally the Ionian Islands once more became a Republic this time under the protection of the English.

Most of the Balkans still remained under the "Ottoman Yoke."

Resistance to Reform

Sultan Selim (1789–1807) had been interested in the reforms of his father Mustafa III and in particular in the artillery of Baron von Toth. Hidden away in the Palace during the reign of his uncle Abdul Hamid II, he kept abreast of developments in the outside world through his servants and above all his doctor, a Venetian in the pay of the French and Austrian embassies. During this period he maintained a more or less unbroken correspondence with Louis XVI. Yet did this make him an enlightened sovereign and would he have had sympathy with the Revolution? Some of the French officers who were sent to Istanbul by the Directorate or by Napoleon were quick to jump to this conclusion but mainly to please their superiors. What is known of the Sultan's character does not bear this out, for he was horrified by the news of Louis XVI's execution and he refused to receive officially the emissaries of the Convention. It was only in 1796 that he recognized the Directorate's envoy, Aubert-Dubayet, as the French ambassador. The principles of 1789 were too alien to his upbringing and Ottoman tradition for Selim to understand them; as for revolutionary authority or the ability to replace a society with another form, he would never have believed it. He was however impressed by the victories of the armies of the Great Nation, which showed their military superiority and so, like his father before him, he called on French officers for assistance. He saw reform of the army as the first priority. Selim was another traditional reformer but at least he chose as his agents certain partisans of a greater openess to the west, such as his favourite Ratib Efendi (Mahmud Raif Efendi) who was a great admirer of Pitt and the English political system.

In 1791 the Sultan asked the Grand Vizier to commission Ulemas and lay notables to draw up proposals—Layiha—for the desired reforms: 17 of these still exist, dealing mostly with the Janissaries and the Spahis together with all the financial implications of this reorganization. A series of Hatti Sheriffs gave substance to these ideas forming the "New system," as the new army corps was known. The new regulations imposed a review and clarification of the rules of allocating and inheriting Timars which were to be the sole domain of Spahis. The audit of the roll of Janissaries would reduce them to 30,000 men subject to regular training. More innovative was the creation of administrative officers who would be different from troop officers and the rules of promotion were changed to try and lessen the use of Baksheesh. Yet these reforms came up against the opposition of those it affected and the Spahis and Janissaries remained largely ineffective. The artillery and similar specialized corps: mortars, mines and services, benefitted from European advisers and Ottoman officers who had experienced Toth's academy. These corps were by far the best in the traditional army. Selim wanted more to make the army fit for modern warfare and formed an entirely new corps which was called the Nizam i Cedid. Organized, dressed and trained in an European way by French, English and German advisers, this was largely made up of young Anatolian peasants recruited by the provincial governors and Ayans. Quartered in September 1794 in the Levend Ciftlik within the capital it grew from 1,000 men to 10,000 in 1801. The following year a system of conscription was set up in Anatolia whereby by the end of 1806 the Nizam i Cadid had 22,600 men and 1570 officers. Half were in Istanbul and the remainder in Anatolia. The reform also aimed at armament manufacture: foundries and rifle making workshops were set up and French and English specialists were brought in. The School of Naval Engineers was expanded in 1795 and included the land army engineers ie. artillerymen, fortifications and mines. These schools were to produce the officers of the Nizam i Cedid. The navy set up a health service and European medical science was quickly adopted. Financial and administrative questions were also raised but almost exclusively in terms of supplying the army's needs, without grasping the fact that failing a general budget reform these limited reforms would be of no use. The scribe office was reorganized and became a department within the Grand Vizierate and led to less nepotism and corruption.

Selim's reforming zeal became bogged down due to internal conservative pressures but also because of foreign war. The Egyptian expedition was a harsh blow to his personal prestige since up to then he had relied almost exclusively on the French. Also the Grand Pashas of the Balkans were becoming involved in international affairs: Ali of Janina in turn conspired with Paris and then London. Pasvanoglu dreamed of an alliance with Napoleon whereas Karageorge and his Serbians were asking Saint Petersburg for support. The situation appeared to be so serious that in 1802 Bonaparte asked the Russian ambassador whether it was true that there was a Tatar prince in his country who was a descendant of Genghis Khan and whose family would be ready to supplant the house of Osman. This was in fact Pasvanoglu's idea of supporting his friend Mehmed Giray the former Khan of the Crimea.

The constitution of the Nizam i Cedid was the last straw. Although this system relied on provincial notables—Ayans and Pashas—all apart from that of Anatolia (Mehmed Ali of Egypt, Ali of Jannina and others) felt that this would be a threat to their power. Early in 1805 Selim wanted to create a new corps at Edirne with conscription throughout the Balkans. The Ayan of Rutshuk, Tersenikli Oglu, headed the opposition and formed alliances with all the large feudal lords. They refused to respond to a summons by the Beylerbey of Sofia. The Porte sent an army under the command of Radi Pasha, the head of the Nizam i Cedid but the Edirne Janissaries rose up in revolt. There was panic in Istanbul and Selim was forced to give in: the Grand Vizier and the reformers were dismissed. In May 1807 a further Janissary uprising broke out but this time in the capital. The Sultan tried to save his throne by disbanding the Nazim i Cedid and handing over its commanders to the insurgents. Selim was forced to retire to the Cafes of the Palace while on the 29 May 1807 his cousin, the conservative candidate, Mustafa IV acceded to the throne.

The new Sultan allowed those who had brought him to power a free hand: the new style army was disbanded, its officers hunted down throughout the Empire and executed, associated academies and institutions were closed down under the pretext that they infringed on traditions. This brutal reaction was short lived. The Janissary commanders became divisive and started fighting each other. Mustafa Bayraktar[3], Terseniki Oglu's successor turned coat and transformed Rutshuk into a stronghold with 25,000 men mostly irregulars—Kirdzhali—led by himself the Ayan and officers such as Baba Aga a Polish renegade and one of Bayraktar's favourites. All those disaffected with the new Sultan gathered there, especially those still faithful to Selim. A "circle of friends" was formed on the Rutshuk committee, whose purpose was to restore the deposed prince. They hatched a plot in the palace, which was divided by rivalry between the Grand Vizier and the Sheik ul Islam, whereby Bayraktar would bring his army to Istanbul under the pretext of restoring order. In July 1808 the Ayan of Rutshuk entered the capital and set about hunting down the enemies of Selim and the Janissaries. Yet when he showed no sign of leaving the city the Grand Vizier had Selim assassinated. The next day, 28 July, Bayraktar placed on the throne one of Selim's nephews who had escaped the murderers. This was Mahmud II who ruled from 1808 to 1839.

Bayraktar who became Grand Vizier, and his "friends of Rutshuk," did not remain in power long. The problem of reforming the Janissaries and replacing them with a new force was still uppermost and the Ayans had to be brought round to the idea. In mid-September all the Ayans of Rumelia and Anatolia were brought together to a lavish assembly at the Sultan's summerhouse in the "Soft Waters of Europe," and agreed on the organization of a new corps—Seymen—parallel to the more traditional forces. This was the Nizam i Cedid under a new name. The Janissaries were not to be duped. Jealous of the Seymen whose pay was to be much higher, they found allies within the conservative Ulemas and gained the support of Mustafa's mother. In November 1808, in the middle of Ramadan, the capital's Janissaries rose up once again and took over the city. Abandoned by everyone, Bayraktar's last stand was in a tower near the Porte and he was blown up together with the tower on the 15 November.

Mahmud II did not try to save his Grand Vizier but gauging the opposition to the reform process postponed it for a while. By the end of 1808 the unreformed Ottoman Empire was clearly the "sick man" of Europe.

The Complexities of Ottoman and Balkan Culture

The failure of the State to reform itself would not put into question what was the most crucial event in the Ottoman 18th century (even though it might not have seemed so at the time) namely opening relations with the west. The Tulips of Ahmed III had quickly faded but they had left their seeds. First the military advisers who continued to arrive: French, English, German, Dutch and Italian who unlike the first renegades were no longer required to convert to Islam. Dressed in a European manner they could move freely within Istanbul, often had their families with them and would mix with Muslims. They might even have organized balls and receptions to which Muslim friends would be invited. It was said that Selim himself had some Italian actors brought to the Palace to give performances, liked Mozart's music and bought paintings depicting human figures. After the Revolution the French colony split into supporters and opponents, the partisans of the Convention eager to spread pamphlets in the bazaars about the rights of man and the constitution. In the same way the royalists, with the help of the English, Austrian and Russian embassies, circulated anti-revolutionary pamphlets. This ideological struggle came up against a basic barrier, that of translation. It was well known, with a few exceptions, that the Ottomans paid little attention to learning foreign languages and translators complained of the difficulty of finding a Turkish equivalent of the trilogy: "Liberte, egalite, fraternite." Furthermore the embassy Dragomans—translators—formed a closed community, with strict family ties: for example the Fontons who were originally French were in the service of Louis XVI but later in that of Russia, yet a nephew remained in the French embassy and a niece married the Austrian internuncio Baron Sturmer. Later there was fierce competition in the form of the Frankini brothers, a new Dragoman dynasty in the service of General Sebastiani. News of the great European confrontation came filtered through these intermediaries, yet their prime worry would not have been objectivity. Notwithstanding, a small military, political and administrative elite had sufficient access to information on the Revolution to reject its message, by a large majority, as it was held to be a threat to Ottoman ideas. As for the reports sent to Istanbul by the Sultan's ambassadors in Europe, they suffered from the same lack of knowledge of foreign languages and culture so that the events which they described were largely incomprehensible. Besides like all diplomatic messages they would have been read by a very small number of officials.

This major political and ideological struggle in the end had very little impact on Ottoman life. Less noticeable but having wider implications was contact with European sciences. First of all through Toth's military academy and those that followed. It was under Selim that was laid the basis for a cultural revolution, for young men, often from influential families would for the first time learn about mathematics, geography, astronomy and medicine, and would understand that the world is round and orbited the sun, and that plague epidemics were an illness that could be fought against by isolating it and not the punishment of Allah.

Yet resistance to these ideas was very powerful in the form of the Ulemas who represented "religious science"—theology and law—and had the monopoly of education through the Medresses and the various types of teaching posts. They therefore had a hold on large sections of the population and could defend traditional values, and their own privileges, by mobilizing thousands of students on the streets. In Istanbul they constituted a threat almost as large as the Janissaries. Furthermore they had enormous financial power through the Vakifs, controlling at least half the wealth of the Empire. Even so, since the 17th century they had lost some of their cohesion, due in part to nepotism and corruption in recruiting and promotion. The differences in levels of education and moral training had increased tension within and in the same way as in the army and the administration, had led to the creation of factions and tendencies, resulting in a decline in their power. Yet very few supported reform ideas even traditional ones. This driving force during the conquest had by the end of the 18th century become a break to progress, of conservatism based on an obsolete vision of the world. However it still retained its prestige in the eyes of the illiterate masses (more than 90% of the population) who willingly believed in their superiority and practised, sometimes fanatically, their religion. It was these masses who rallied to the Janissaries and allowed them to depose Ahmed III, Selim III and Mustafa IV in the belief that they were defending the Prophet's inheritance.

Ottoman literature exemplifies the complexities of Ottoman culture and the traditional forms continued to flourish. S. Shaw even writes that: "the 18th century was the most Turkish literary period of Ottoman rule, for by and large the influence of the east had been rejected and the domination of western culture, which was to characterize the period of modernization in the 19th and 20th centuries, had not yet really begun." Poetry had pride of place with the affected style known as the "literature of the divan" which since the 17th century was counterbalanced by a lively popular literature. Sultan Selim himself wrote poetry of the most traditional type. Historical writing continued to be limited to chronicles without any attempt at analysis; in any case the job of "Court Chronicler" was ended under Ahmed III and from then on this work was done by a low-ranking scribe. Yet unconnected with this office Asim Efendi (1755–1809) emerges as the first modern Turkish historian, researching sources and able to speak French. This short summary makes us conclude that even though there were many Europeans in Istanbul, their native literature had little impact on the writers of the Empire which shows the limited scope of the opening of Ottoman culture to the west in the 18th century.

The culture of the Christian Balkan peoples on the other hand, began to experience a profound change under the double influence of capitalism and Aufklarung. A form of capitalism had of course always existed and under the Sultans, as already during the Byzantine emperors, there had been rich Greek, Jewish or Armenian merchants who would have undertaken financial dealings rather than ordinary commercial transactions. But in the 18th century these transactions, which until then would have been uncommon and mostly concentrated in Istanbul, flourished all over the Empire and even outside, and formed veritable conduits for the circulation of capital. In the Balkans they made use of the long period of peace following the Peace of Belgrade in 1739, which made Vienna one of the foremost trading partners of the Ottoman Empire and on which Wallachian, Serbian and especially Greek merchants were to converge. In the Mediterranean, the reduced threat to shipping led to English and Dutch companies to join the French and Italians in plying the wealthy "Levant ladder": Istanbul, Smyrna, Salonika, Aleppo, Beirut, Cyprus, Alexandria and the Islands of the Archipelago. As previously mentioned there was a permanent imbalance to the detriment of the Empire and to such an extent that from the end of the 18th century, it can be seen as semi-colonial. Even though this increase in trade was of little benefit to the Sultan, it did benefit some of his subjects, and in the area of finances the fundamental inequality of the system could be overcome since the Muslims did not really have control. Wealth did have it place in the scale of values which the Prophet handed down, especially gold, yet Ottoman thinking had remained very traditional on this question; wealth was a gift from Allah and would increase in his service, mainly through war or administrative office in Dar el Islam. The idea that money begets money through lending or exchange was totally alien, whereas this idea is at the very basis of capitalist thinking. Hence it was in Christian circles that there emerged and developed a type of capitalism in the modern sense of the word. The prime movers were the Greeks: from the diaspora, from Vienna and their district of Griechengasse behind the cathedral of Saint Stephan, from Leipzig which still has its Griechenhaus, and also Cologne, Budapest, Lemberg and Kiev, and the new trading posts of Southern Russia. Also within the Greek territories of the Ottoman Empire: Thessalonika strategically placed on the end of a land route from Central Europe, Thrace and Macedonia to the Mediterranean, whereas the Hydra, Spetsa and Psara Islands equipped ships bound for Italy, France or the North African Barbary states. In Bulgarian areas craft skills such as tanning, furrier, carpet making, wool textile making and soap manufacture were being concentrated in the hands of merchants who would sell the finished products in Istanbul, Alexandria, Odessa, Vienna and Marseilles. In the Danubian Principalities the commercial restraints due to the mandatory delivery of food to Istanbul was counterbalanced by a huge trade in contraband. So much so that in certain towns there was formed a veritable capitalist merchant class, such as Constantin Cincu of Bucharest who specialized in currency speculation in liaison with his cousin who lived on the other side of the border in Hermannstadt (Sibiu). He was the head of the Greek company and his brother-in-law Hagi Nicu, who came from Janina in Epirus, operated in Cracow and Brasov. They had contacts, relatives and associates in Constantinople, Saint Petersburg and Vienna, where several obtained titles of nobility like Baron Belu and Nilta and other loyal Habsburg supporters. These deep changes were to have two consequences: fracture the old feudal-military structures of the Empire and the vassal states, rendering them virtually obsolete and would introduce new hierarchies into the Rum Millet, based on wealth. The appearance of capitalism was to lay the foundations of revolutionary change.

The Aufklarung or the Enlightenment, the central European or French term, was the second shock to come. Vienna under Joseph II was for the Balkan merchants a showcase for reform: abolition of serfdom and corvee work, religious equality and setting up registries to guarantee ownership; measures which widened the gap between the Ottoman system and what was to be the new model "police state." Under Maria-Theresa there had already been moves by Abbot Felbinger to organize education with primary and high schools. Their compatriots in Leipzig, Munich, Amsterdam and Marseilles also witnessed similar changes. So in all these commercial towns there took place a slow alchemy which transformed these avid merchants intent on making money into a middle class thirsting for social status, like Monsieur Jourdain their forerunner in the time of Louis XIV, wishing to educate themselves. More down to earth they hoped to give the benefits to the next generation and subsidized the opening and running of schools in their adopted towns, and later in the villages from which they had originally come, above all in the Greek islands but also in Bulgaria. On top of this basic schooling the Phanariot Princes and some of the wealthier bourgeois began to send their protégés or offspring to the high schools and universities of central and western Europe and in this way not only were the ideas of Paris and Vienna absorbed but also the customs and fashions. It was again in Vienna that the Sultans's subjects first encountered the press and understood its importance. A Greek paper was started in 1790 and was followed in 1791 by the first Serbian paper published with the help of merchants from southern Hungary. During the same period the university press at Buda supplanted that of Venice, printing texts in Cyrillic type and helping to spread new ideas.

Added to these factors was the impact of the French Revolution and Empire. If this did reach the general masses it varied greatly depending on geographical location, social structure and the cultural development of the constituent groups, so its impact was delayed but would sound the revolutionary message during the whole of the 19th century and be linked to the Serbian, Greek, Romanian, Bulgarian and Albanian nationalist movements.

Notes

1. Corfu, Ithicca, Lefkas, Cephalonia, Zakynthos, Paxos and Cerigo (Cythera).
2. In Romania 60 miles to the east of Bucharest.
3. The work of the Soviet A. F. Miller: Mustafa Pasha Bayraktar—translated into French and published by the A.I.E.S.E.E. in Bucharest in 1975—466 p. Written during the war it is based on Russian sources which were unpublished yet its interpretation of the role of Bayraktar and his "circle of Rutshuk friends" does not always command support.

10

The Serbian and Greek Revolts

By the end of the 18th century the Balkans were undergoing such deep changes that an explosion could be expected and it appeared that the Greeks would be the first to experience it. Yet it was the Serbs who were first. The difference between the two cases is illustrated by the differing terms their historians use. The Serbs use the word Ustanak which means revolt and uprising and also distinguish between two successive movements, that of Karageorge and of Milos Obrenovic, whose combined action resulted in the creation of a modern Serbian state. The Greeks however use the term Epanastasis which means Revolution, Great Revolution or War of Independence, which above all places the accent on the remarkable and irreversible nature of the insurrection. In fact both events reflect complex relations with different social structures, cultural development and international interference. But both led real revolutions: the creation of Christian countries out of the Empire of Islam.

The Serbians at the Dawn of the 19th Century

Since the end of the last Serbian state—that of the Brankovics in 1459—this ethno-cultural group had undergone a north-westward migration. After the Ottoman conquest many had fled the combat zones and taken refuge north of the Danube, to the Hungarian plains, followed two centuries later by the Velika Seoba of 1690. So there grew up between the river Sava and Drava, and the Danube and the Tisza (now Voevodina) a "Serbian Hungary" whose heart was Karlowitz (Sremski Karlovci) the Metropolitan See and Neusatz (Novi Sad) the commercial and cultural centre. Emperor Leopold I had guaranteed his new subjects, with the 1690 and 1691 decrees, religious freedom and a self-administration of their

Church and Barbara Jelavich[1] emphasizes how this presents many similarities with the Ottoman Millet system. Despite these decrees the way in which the 18th century evolved was not very beneficial for the peasant classes who were to experience the oppression of the large landowners, the Magyar nobility. However the organization of a defensive border—Militargrenze—did have its advantages for a number of peasants for it guaranteed their individual freedom, their right to farm the land and their own autonomous government within Zadrugas. At the same time there emerged a small officer class who, together with the merchants and the small town intelligensia were to form the embryo of a Serbian petit-bourgeoisie. They were to establish in 1790 a Serbian Lycee in Karlowitz and another in Neusatz in 1810, and in 1791 the first Serbian language newspaper appeared in Vienna.

Separated from the land of their fathers these Serbs, known as the "Serbs from the German territories," were able to retain their own culture by staying faithfull to their own Church. The attempts by the Hungarian Catholic hierarchy to attract them to Uniatism only served to reinforce their ties with the Orthodox Church and to turn their hopes of protection towards Russia. In 1726 in response to a letter sent to Peter the Great a Moscovite opened in Karlowitz a school that taught Russian Slavonic[2] and in 1733 the Kiev Academy sent six teachers, around whom was built a lycee and for whose use some elementary school books were published. In the opposite direction, certain clerics went to study in Russia, for instance the future historian Jovan Rajic (1726–1801) who was a student at the Ecclesiastical Academy of Kiev. Not forgetting the monks from the monastery of Fruska Gora who went on pilgrimage to Zagorsk or to Petcherskaya Laura and came back from the Tsar's country with the idea of having seen the Promised Land, to the extent that in 1727 refugees from Belgrade and Slavonia established around the Dnepr an ephemerial "New Serbia" which was to provide some good officer material for Catherine II's armies. The Aufklarung and Maria-Theresa's and Joseph's reforms had quite a profound effect on this ecclesiastical rural culture: the peasants benefitted from the legislation passed during Joseph's reign, the Orthodox clegy from the Edict of Tolerance and no longer feared the pressure of the Uniates. All were filled with hope when the Emperor joined Russia in its war against the Ottoman Empire in 1788. In this new climate of telerance several scholars tried to discover in their past a sense of pride which their fellow German and Hungarian citizens denied them: Pavlo Julinac published in 1765 a "Short Introduction to the Historical Development of the Sloveno-Serbian People." Yet its very title shows clearly how difficult it was to be certain of the truth. Emile Haumant wrote that: "Even though it was a mediocre work it shows at least an effort to rediscover and define what was difficult at the time to define ie. Serbia. The people could understand the territories of Morava, Posavina and Sumadja but these were recent names, or else they would use the Turkish names of the Pashaliks and Kazas (districts). More than this, a muddle, Bosnia, Serbia, Bulgaria and even Albania. Yet Julinac, more erudite, starts with the idea of Illyricum, and Serbia as part of the diocese of the Patriarchy of Pec. In his opinion the nation was still a question of religion[3]." The secularization of this idea was the work of Dositej Obradovic (1742–1811). Born in Cakovo in the Banat region of a craftman family, he became a monk at the Monastery of Hopovo. In 1760 he left for Zagreb and then Mount Athos. Disillusioned he went to study in Halle and Leipzig and them settled in Vienna from 1789 to 1802. From here he encouraged his compatriots to revolt and joined them in 1806 as the teacher of Karageorge's children to become the first minister of Public Education in liberated Serbia. He died in Belgrade in March 1811. His major work was his autobiography—Zivot i prikljucenija—(Life and Destiny) which was published in Belgrade and Vienna. Influenced by the Aufklarung Obradovic wanted reason to triumph over religious differences. "Even though he was a Catholic he was a good man" he writes of a Croat officer who was a follower of Karageorge. Therefore it would be possible to unite all the Southern Slavs which he observed were in Dalmatia, Bosnia, Serbia and Slavonia part of the same "Family." Yet, at least in terms of education in Serbia he advocated the use of dialect rather than Church Slavonic and in this was, together with Vuk Karadzic, a driving force for modern literature. His life was an attempt to bridge the gap between Aufklarung and the Serbian revolt.

However the greater part of this ethno-linguistic group had remained south of the Danube and the Sava within the Ottoman Empire. As the Sultan's rule did not respect the borders of language and culture the Serbs were to be found in the Sandjaks of Vidin, Krusevac and Novi Pazar yet their centre was Smederevo which in the 18th century was to become the Pashalik of Belgrade following the Austrian occupation. As in the rest of the Empire this Sandjak was further divided into Kaza, Nahije and Knezin. The rule of Vienna from 1718 to 1739 had organized these into a hierarchy of Serbian Knezes—the village chiefs, the Knezina chiefs and the Nahije chiefs which were to survive in some form after the return of the Ottomans. The Knezina was the basic unit made up of several villages from out of which the main Zadrugas (extended families) elected a council of elders who chose from out of its participants a Knez who was responsible for the contacts with the Ottoman authorities, for collecting taxes, for general law and order and for meting out justice on the basis of local customary law. In theory therefore completely self-governing on this level and the Ottoman administrator—the Subasi for the army and the police, the Kadi for justice and the Multezim for finance—would live in the towns and only had contact with the Knez. The Nahija however had at its head a Musselim who was appointed by the Pasha. On the eve of the uprising the Pashalik of Belgrade was divided into twelve Nahijes, each one grouping together three or four Knezins and so the Nahija of Sabac incorporated those of Macva, Porcerina and Tamnava which were three natural regions which still figure on modern maps.

The population of the Pashalik is calculated by historians at about 400,000 inhabitants with about 20,000 Ottomans as well as troops. Almost all the Muslims lived in the towns, were refered to as Turks—Turci—they were mostly of Bosnian extraction or in other words Islamized Slavs. The Serbians, 90% peasants were alone in most of the villages but in the mountains in the east lived in close proximity with transhumant Wallachian shepherds—Vlasci—who numbers are unknown. Also worth mentioning that the Serbs themselves had not necessarily been settled there for all that long. The Austro-Turkish wars of the 18th century had often taken place in the Pashalik and it is obvious that the movement of armies, be they friend or foe, was always mirrored by the flight of peasants. The Protopope Matija Nenadovic[4] tells of how his grandmother remembered arriving in the Valjevo region which was completely deserted, and as for Sumadja in the 18th century it was not inhabited and the oak forests were used for rearing pigs.

The status of the Reaya was the same as in the rest of the Empire. The peasants were individually free, were allowed to pass on the Cift as inheritance and even sell it to anyone who would fulfill their obligations. Most of the land belonged to the Timars whose income supported about 900 Spahis, while the Sultans possessions were rather sparce with two areas of privilege administered in any case by the Serbian Knez and a few Mukatas under the obligation of paying tithe which amounted to roughly that of the Spahi's. Vuk Karadzic[5] who cannot be accused of being indulgent to the Ottomans paints a quite idyllic picture of life in the village of his youth and mentions that most of the peasants had come to an arrangement with the Spahi of the village to pay the tithe—Disetina on wheat and the Glavnica which was a secondary tithe on other produce—in one go with payment in cash of ten Piasters[6] per year. In contrast to what had happened in other regions of the Balkans the Pashalik had not been yet transformed from Timar to Ciftlik—the Serbs called it Cifluk—and its occurrence at the end of the 18th century was one of the reasons for the peasant revolt. The Spahis lived in the towns and only came to the village in the autumn to collect taxes. Belgrade—Beograd the White City—stretched out over the plateau, a small conurbation of a few thousand inhabitants to the east of the fortress of Kalemegdan which the Austrians had rebuilt during their occupation. Uzice, well known for its mosques and the tradition of its Koranic schools, had 5,000 houses, some 20,000 inhabitants who were in the main muslims. Karanovac which is now called Valjevo had 12–15,000 inhabitants. The conurbations were not for the Serbs.

It was through its church that the group defined its identity. This Church went back to Saint Sava—the brother of the first king Stephan Nemanja—which in 1219 had received from the Byzantine Patriarch, who was taking refuge in Nicea at the time, his consecration as the autocephalic Metropolitan of serbia with its see first at the Monastery of Zica near to Kraljevo, and then at Ipek (Pec). In spite of the opposition of the "Great Church" in Constantinople, Emperor Dusan had given it the title of Patriarch in 1346 which was the solemn declaration of the independence of the Serbian Church. The Ottoman conquest made it disappear and in 1459 following the fall of Smederevo Gennadios the Oecumenical Patriarch dissolved the autocephaly of Ipek and placed the see under the Metropolitan of Ohrid who in turn was subordinate to Constantinople. Henceforth the title holder of Ipek was for a hundred and fifty years a Greek or a Hellenic. But in 1537 under Soliman the Magnificent the Grand Vizier Sokollu restored the patrirachal rank to the venerable see of Saint Sava. Born a the Serbian village in the Novi Pazar sandjak, Sokolovic who because of Devsirme had become Ahmed Sokollu, had a brother at the head of the monastery of Milesevo and he was installed by the Grand Vizier as the Patriarch of Ipek. For the faithful who had kept alive the memory of the Empire of Dusan the calculation was plain, the Patriarchate of Ipek signified the Patriarchate of Serbia. On top of which it took advantage of the Ottoman expansion to extend its jurisdiction to Central Hungary where there was already quite a large Serbian population and it was because of them that the new Patriarchate appointed from 1557 the Bishops of Buda, Pecs, Szegedin, Arad, Temesvar and Vrsac. Hence almost all the serbs were brought into a single church whose liturgy was in Serbian Slavonic which was quite difficult for the ordinary people to inderstand but still quite close to the spoken language. The Millet system in turn defined an administrative Serbian community by entrusting the election of the Patriarchate to an assembly—Narodno-crkveni sabor[7]—made up of the Bishops, the igoumens from the large monasteries and secular nobility. In the minds of the faithful it in some ways replaced the lost authority of the Christian sovereign. So the historian Ch. Jelavich spoke of the Patriarchate of Ipek as an Ersatz State for the Serbs during the 16th and 17th centuries. Its abolition in 1756 was therefore a very harsh blow. The flight of the post-holder Arsenje III Cernojevic in 1690 gave it the fatal blow for while he continued to use the title in Karlowitz the Phanar saw him as deposed and appointed to Ipek a Greek called Kallinakos I. But the Porte remained wary for the region was very insecure following Albanian incursions and the Patriarch had difficulty maintaining its standards and accumulated some large debts. In 1756 a deal was struck. The Greater Church took on the liabilities of the See but abolished the rank of Patriarch. Ipek was to become merely a Metropolitan whose title-holder was more often than not, a Phanariot rich enough to buy it as was common practice for the bishoprics and the monasteries. This Hellenization of the hierarchy was followed by a growing Greek influence in the Liturgy. The old Church Slavonic was replaced by ecclesiastical Greek. However the heart of the Serbian Church was beating at Karlowitz with the Metropolitan on of the Viennese Emperor's subjects. As seen above it was in the German lands that a learned Serbian culture was being formed. The villages of the Kolubara or the Sumadja remained close to their culture based on traditional customs and which was best known through the oral literature of songs—Pesmes accompanied by the Guzla[8]. Going back a very long way, specialists discern a pre-Christian cycle, the most popular Pesmes were those that recalled the glory of the medieval kingdom, the fight against the Ottomans—above all the cycle dealing with Kosovo and the exploits of Marko Kraljevic—the struggle of the Hajduks who had become well-meaning Robin Hoods. The stories of the Pesmes and the frescoes in the churches recreated for the illiterate peasant a mythical world were Serbia was always portrayed in a good light and which made up for the oppression of the 18th century.

The First Serbian Uprising:
Karageorge, 1804–1813

Disorder and corruption resulting from the crisis of the Ottoman system were very much in evidence in the Pashalik of Belgrade. Its geographical position made the battle-ground between the Austrians and the Ottomans in the space of one century, which meant that its inhabitants were extremely used to weapons and their use in a way which it was difficult to match elsewhere. During its occupation the Austrians had recuited soldiers and administrators from among the population and Serbian became officers and N.C.O.s in the Imperial army. When hostilities once more broke out in 1788 the Austrian General Staff formed a free corps—Freikorps—where several of the future leaders of the uprising were formed for instance Karageorge, while at the same time, encouraged by the various agents that Vienna sent into Serbian territory, a merchant called Koca Andjelkovic gathered an army and occupied for some time Pozarevac and Belgrade, remaining in the eyes of the people the hero of Kocina Krajina "Koca's War." The Serbian suprise was therefore even greater when Emperor Leopold II signed the separate Peace of Sistova in August 1791. On the Ottoman side war was to bring to the region many Janissaries who were as brutal and indisciplined as everywhere else and many of whom stayed on at the end of hostilities. It was in these circumstances that the phenomenom of change from Timar into Ciftlik took place which up until then had not happened on the frontier zone. The scene is easy to imagine and is told by the

Serbian memoirs writers; the Janissary surrounded by his henchmen arrives in a village and under threat forces the peasants to recognize him as their Aga promising protection against bandits and even help in paying their taxes to the Ottoman authorities in return for the delivery of a quarter or even half of their harvest and an arbitrary number of corvee work-days. In the same way as the Beys in Bosnia, from where they often had come, the Janissaries would therefore become Ciftlik Sahibija, the lord of the land over which the Spahi would continue to enforce his own rights. Hence an increase in the peasant burden who might then prefer to run away into the forests and the increase in the numbers of Hajduks in the Sumadja and southern mountainous regions was in part caused by these developments.

The Spahis and the whole Ottoman system had problems with this and the insubordination of the Janissaries were to transform the Pashalik into an anarchic area which was even more serious as this was on the frontier of Dar el Islam. In the framework of his reform of the Empire Sultan Selim III promulgated in 1793, 1794 and 1796 three Firmans which forbade the Janissaries the settle in the Sandjak, gave greater powers to the Serbian Knez, gave real autonomy to the Nahijes and finally allowing the population, including the Christians, the right to have arms and form their own militias to keep order. As for the Ciftliks these were declared illegal. To institute this policy the Porte appaointed as Governor of Belgrade Hadji Mustafa Pasha, who was of Greek extraction. He encountered desperate resitance on the part of the Janissaries who appealed to Pasvanoglu the rebel Pasha of Vidin, for help. To face him Hadji Mustafa apparently armed up to 15,000 Serbs who repulsed the rebel and forced him to shut himself away in his fortress on the Danube. The cooperation between the Ottoman authorities and its Christian Reaya was shown to work. But in 1798 Bonaparte landed in Egypt and Istanbul recalled its soldiers from the Balkans. Selim bowed to the pressure of the rebels. Pasavanoglu was officially appointed Pasha of Vidin and the Janissaries were allowed to enter the Pashalik of Belgrade as long as they obeyed the orders of the governor. In fact they were quick to put to death the governor who is known as the "mother of the Serbs. A time of anarchy followed and the Janissaries imposed a reign of terror on the Christians as well as the faithful Ottomans such as the Spahis. In 1802 they were to be found shoulder to shoulder in revolt around Pozarevac which was drowned in blood. In the same year four Janissary leaders were to emerge and concentrated complete power into their own hands. These were the Dahis[9] whose infamy is recorded in a famous Pesma. The terrorized Serbian sought shelter in the forests of the Sumadja and forming a resistance movement which by the spring of 1804 had reached some 30,000 men.

Everything was primed for an armed revolt. The Dahis were aware of this and hoping to stifle it before its birth began to systematically kill the leaders, the Knezes. In the Memoirs of Protopope Matija Nenadovic is an account of the murder of his father Alexa, the Knez of the Valjevo region who had been found guilty of corresponding with the Austrian commander in Semlin (Zemun) and from whom he requested weapons and instructors. In two months 72 heads of Serbian notables were hung on the walls of the Belgrade citadel. The remainder had no time to lose. On the 2 February 1804 three hundred gathered at Orasac near Topola vowed to fight to the death and chose as their leader Karageorge. The first Serbian uprising was about to begin.

Little is known about the childhood of this character who we call Karageorge or in other word George the Black but in reality was called Djordje Petrovic. He is traditionallymeant to have been born in the Sumadja at Visevac near to Raca where they maintain is the baptismal font where he was baptized between 1762 and 1769. From a poor family he worked the land of others and had no education, remaining illiterate right through his life. In 1787 for unknown reasons, perhaps to escape from the exactions of the Janissaries, his family left the Pashalik and settled in Voevodina where they came under the control of the monastery of Krusedol. When Austria declared war on the Ottoman Empire Karageorge who was something like twenty years old joined the Serbian Freikorps and fought in western Serbia. He learned the art of war in the best army that existed in Europe at the time and became an N.C.O. Following the peace of Sistova he went back to his homeland and settled at Topola as a pig trader. His knowledge of the "German lands" and no doubt former military friends gave him the opportunity to make some very profitable transactions. He consequently became a local worthy. When Hadji Mustafa organized his Serbian militia Karageorge became a regional Baljukbasa—leader of a hundred soldiers—and under the Pashas command became conscious of Ottoman tactics. When the Janissaries came back he felt it was more prudent to withdraw into the forests while at the same time getting ready to use his experience of warfare. In terms of the forces that were at his disposal they were very light: his own personal troops which all Knezes surrounded themselves with (called Momci[10]) who were part soldiers and part servants who were paid by the Knez and the equivalent belonging to other notables, some Hajduks who tended to be very good at hand-to-hand fighting but very poorly disciplined such as Stanoje Glavas and also some mercenaries, known as Becari, generally Wallachians, Albanians and Bulgarians who went from Pasvanoglu's service to that of any warlord able to pay for their services. Above all were the peasants who took their time to become mobilized and Karageorge was often forced to use violence to make their minds up for them, for example hanging a Janissary at the entrance to the village which would result in the withdrawal of all able-bodied men into the forest for fear of reprisals. Furthermore their numbers were limited due to the low number of population. At the height of the revolt in 1807–08 Karageorge only had at his disposal at most 60,000 men. As for weapons these were primitive. Rifles from the old militias or imported from Austria but above all seized from dead Janissaries, cutlasses, sythes and even forks. They did not have artillery apart from a small iron canon which was sent to Matija Nenadovic by the Bishop of Temesvar. Another problem soon came to light, that of overall command. At Orasac Karageorge had been made leader—Voevoda—by the Sumadja notables. But other regions had their own Knezes who were proud of their antecedents and jealously maintained their control. The Nenadovics in the Valjevo region while the Stijkovic and Dobrnjac Zadrugas dominated the Morava sector. It was only with the first victories in the spring of 1804 that they were won over by the military ability of this poor peasant's son who lacked their own prestige. At a second reunion of notables, this time from all the regions of the Pashalik, held at Ostruznica[11] at the end of may 1804, Karageorge was given the title—Vrhovi Vod—"Supreme Commander." Yet right up to the end a simmering and sometimes violent rivalry divided the leaders of the uprising especially as Karageorge turned out to be quite often brutal and authoritarian. At least under the iron grip of Karageorge the Serbs were not to experience the disappointment of their Greek neighbours.

Despite this lack of means the uprising quickly spread. The

Turks, Ciftlik Sahibije Janissaries first of all but also greedy Spahis were put to death and the large villages were liberated from all Ottoman control. As for the towns, Pozarevac was captured at the end of March 1804, the garison of Smederevo were trapped in the fortress while Karageorge's army was fighting in the outskirts of Belgrade where there was stiff resistance from the Dahis.

It was above all against them that the Serbs had taken up arms. In 1802 several Knezes had entered into negotiations with the Porte's representatives and an agreement was reached which foresaw the elimination of the Dahis followed by a total amnesty for all and then the granting of autonomy within the Empire based on religious and commercial freedom, deciding on a fixed tribute, the nomination of a "Supreme Serbian Knez" who would be empowered to deal with matters of government, fiscal and justice and finally the restriction of the right of Muslims. This was what Protopope M. Nenadovic negotiated at Semlin (Zemun) with the Ottoman representatives on the 10 May 1804. This was to remain the basis and the Serbian demands were sent to Istanbul together with declarations of loyalty to the sovereign. In the context of general reform it was only a question of correcting some abuse of power and a return to the good methods of the past. Austria, on whose territory these negotiations had taken place, advised they ask for more and its agents did not refrain from talking of total separation from the Empire in the form of the ephemeral Serbian Kingdom of 1718 to 1739. Aware of this danger Selim III entrusted the popular Vizier of Bosnia Abu Bekir Pasha with helping the Serbs to oust the Dahis. In July 1804 the Pasha at the head of an strong force appeared in front of Belgrade and met Karageorge who had assembled 2,000 horsemen to make an impression on the Porte's envoy. In fact it was the Dahis who were scared and fled towards Vidin to seek support from Pasvanoglu but were caught in the process and their heads were sent to Karageorge who gave them as a present to Abu Bekir who had the idea that the the revolt was over.

In fact it was to change form. Everything was conditional on the word of the Vizier of Bosnia whose position turned out to be quite delicate since he was imprisoned by the new leader of the Belgrade garison and freed only after payment of a ransom from the Serbian insurgents. This episode confirmed the latter in their resolve, which had already been expressed at Semlin, to obtain a guarantee of the agreement withthe presence of an official Austrian witness. Abu Bekir had of course refused but neither was Austria very keen on giving. Dissappointed with the Austrian position the Knez turned to Russia. Taking advantage of the end of operations over the winter period they sent a delegation headed by the Protopope Matija Nenadovic. Via Bucharest and Kiev they reached Saint Petersburg on the 7 October 1804 but had to wait for more than a month before they were given audience with the Minister of Foriegn Affairs the Polish prince Czartoryski from whom they requested weapons, officers and money to obtain an autonomous government from the Porte and a Russian consul as mediator. Czartoryski realized the benefits which this could bring but Tsar Alexander was rather preoccupied by the actions of Napoleon. The delegation was given 5,000 golden ducats and the promise of diplomatic support in Istanbul. In this was the Serbians became a part of Tsarist policy from the Treaty of Kutcuk-Kajnardji. The rebels of the Pashalik had became part of international politics and following on from the revolt against the Dahis there appeared a revolt against the Sultan.

The Porte understood this for the Serbs spent the winter making contact with the troublesome tribes of Herzegovina, the Klephtes gangs of Thessaly and Epirus but also the Phanariot Hospodars of Wallachia and Moldavia. Of course the path to take was not quite clear but the idea of an uprising of all the Christians of the Balkans was in many people's thoughts and was encouraged by the emissaries of Vienna and Saint Petersburg. It was the Sultan who made the first move. After much hesitation Selim appointed Hafiz Pasha of Nis as governor of Belgrade and sent him to take up his post at the head of an army. In August 1805 Karageorge's soldiers came into contact with, for the first time, a regular army at Ivankovo[12] and forced it to retreat. This unexpected victory resulted in the last resistance coming to an end. The town of Smederevo was taken in November and became the first capital of a ressurected Serbia. 1806 was spent trying to get support from the Austrian and Russian emperors but to avail as they were both mesmerized by Napoleon's actions and stopping a double Ottoman offensive coming from Bosnia and Misar towards Sabac (13 August) and the other from Nis which brushed against the Serbian fortified positions at Deligrad[13]. With 50,000 men and 40 cannons Karageorge's army marched on Belgrade. The city was captured after a full-scale

The Serbian and Greek Revolts

attack on the 30 November 1806 on the night of Saint Andrew which is still a special day in its history. The fortress of Kalemegdan surrendered a month later. The Turks fled from the city and many of them were massacred. Belgrade in turn was made the capital and as Sabac had been conquered the previous day all the Pashalik territory was liberated save for the two Ottoman garrisons of Uzice and Sokol.

While the country of Serbia was starting to develop with all its territory and a capital the international situation was changing with the reversal of the Porte's alliances. Bonaparte's expedition into Egypt had led to a rapprochemnet with England and Russia. However following his victory over the Third Coalition Napoleon sent General Sebastiani to Istanbul to renew the old ties. In November 1806 war broke out once more between the Ottoman Empire and the Russian Empire. From then on the fate of the Serbs would depend on the vicissitudes of the new conflict. At first it seemed to go in favour of the rebels. Anxious to destroy this bed of unrest on the very borders of the Empire the Porte agreed to negotiate. Petar Icko, a merchant from Semlin was sent to Istanbul and reached an agreement based on the autonomy of Serbia under the Sultan's tutelage and to whom a tribute would be paid. Yet the ratification of this agreement with the sovereign's Firman was delayed and when hostilities between the Ottoman and the Russians began the Serbs, egged on by Russian agents, answered a call to arms by the Porte in the following terms: "Serbia considers itself an independent country and refuses to pay tribute as well as refuses to take up arms against its brothers in religion." The rejection of the "Peace of Icko" would mean war till absolute victory.

During the following summer Russia was as good as her word. Saint Petersburg sent Colonel F. O. Paulucci to Serbia on a mission to study the situation. On the 10 July he signed a "Convention" with Karageorge which was very different from the proclamation of independence in their reply to Istanbul. The Supreme Commander agreed on nothing less than a Russian protectorate in all matters. First of all on the military level the Serbs were allotted a specific task in the operations of the Tsar's army, then Russia sent administrators to the territory, set up garrisons in the main cities and promised economic aid. In Serbia Saint Petersburg was able to apply what it wanted to do in the Danubian Principalities. Once peace was restored was there any hope of real independence? Some historians believe this to be the case and attribute Karageorge from this time on, of a firm intention for independence. Events were going to preclude this. On the 17 June contact was made between the Russian and Serbian troops close to Vidin and Constantine Rodofinikin who was of Greek extraction and the permanent representative of the Tsar came to the Karageorge's headquarters. Prior to this there had been two significant events. In Istanbul Sultan Selim III had been overthrown on the 29 May which resulted in a crisis which lasted for one year and was to paralize the Ottoman army. In Tilsit on the 7 July Napoleon and Alexander had made peace and made an alliance. As a result the Tsar would withdraw his troops from the Balkans and sign an armistice at Slobozia on the 24 August with the Porte. None of these documents made mention of the Serbs who in terms of international recognition still remained the Sultan's subjects.

Isolated in this way the Serbian position was very serious. The simmering rivalry between Karageorge and the chief Knez reached such a stage that from 1807 or 1808 it is possible to speak of the existence of an proper "opposition" within the leadership. Since 1805 under Russian pressure, a "Council of Governments" had been organized which acted as a counter-balance to the Supreme Commander. The arrival in August 1807 of Rodofinikin heightened the tensions. The Tsar's representative anxious to increase his own influence played one side off against the other and Belgrade became a smaller version of the Seraglio. Karageorge reacted by proclaiming himself "Supreme hereditary Commander" in 1808. Behind the personal rivalries there was also the opposition between Russia and Austria. Whereas the "opposition" manipulated by Rodofinikin looked to Saint Petersburg, Karageorge played the Austrian card. In discussions held in the spring of 1808 with Marshall von Simbschen the commander of the border zone he did not hesitate to accept that Serbia would become a Habsburg protectorate under the authority of Vienna rather than the kingdom of Hungary whilst Belgrade would become an Austrian stronghold. Once more external events were to decide otherwise. In the spring of 1809 hostilities started up once more between the Russians and the Ottomans. Karageorge rejected a peace proposal from the Porte but .agreed to coordinate his actions with those of the Russian army. Therefore he launched two offensives, one in the direction of the Sandjak of Novi Pazar which succeeded in linking up with the Montenegrins who were also in rebellion. The other in the direction of Nis was to fail. During this offensive Stevan Sindjeldic was surrounded at Kamenica blew himself up with his men and the Ottomans to take revenge made the Cele Kula "Tower of Skulls" with the heads of the Serbs, described by Lamartine[14]. The road was clear for the Ottoman army to go down the Morava valley and capture Pozarevac and threaten Belgrade. There was panic in the capital; thousands of Serbians crossed over the Danube and amongst them Rodofinikin. Not knowing who to turn to Karageorge appealed to the one person who seemed to control the whole of Europe's destiny at the time. In October 1809 he sent Captain Vucinic with a message to Napoleon who was in Vienna at that moment, placing Serbia under the protection of the French Emperor and offering him the Sabac stronghold to put pressure on Hungary. The letter arrived too late for Napoleon had already left for Paris. A second message was taken to Paris by Vucinic from Laibach[15] but there the messanger was only managed to meet a head of division of the Ministry of Foreign Affaires. Napoleon was never to read Karageorge's famous letter. The Serbs were only a small piece on the European chessboard. In the meantime Karageorge mobilized all the men from 12 to 70 years old and halted the Ottoman advance into the Sumadja. Soon after an offensive by Prince Bagration in Moldavia forced Istanbul to divert its forces away.

The Serbian revolt was for a time saved but the territory under its control had been reduced and dissention was weakening the movement's leadership. Luckily in June 1810 Russian forces reached the Danube at Orsova and military collaboration with the Great Protector made the future seem better. Russian garrisons were put into place in Belgrade, Sabac and Deligrad. But these hopes were to be shorth-lived. Alexander I feeling that Napoleon was about to break his agreement was hoping to free his commitments on the Ottoman front. Negotiations were started secretly which led to the Treaty of Belgrade of May 1812. Article VIII dealt with the Serbians. They would have to destroy the fortifications built during the revolt and agree to the replacement of Ottoman garrisons to their 1804 positions in return for a general amnesty and internal autonomy limited only by a fixed tribute to the Porte. Yet the subject of this article had not been informed and only found out about the signing of the treaty through their enemy.

Kurchid Pasha the Vizier appointed to Belgrade demanded the towns and fortresses covered by Article VIII.

In front of what they saw as Russia's abandoning them the Serbs were shocked, especially when the Tsar's envoy advised the leaders who had gathered at the monastery of Vracevsnica to treat with Istanbul. In August 1812 the Russian garrisons left Serbia. There was no other alternative save to negotiate with Kurchid Pasha. His proposals were considered to amount to nothing less than surrender and an assembly formed in January 1813 at Kragujevac rejected them and demanded a greater autonomy under the suzerainty of the Sultan marked by the payment of tribute. The Porte replied by once more starting up military operations. The defeat of Napoleon in Russia spurred Istanbul to settle matters before the Tsar was completely free to react. The Beylerbey of Rumelia was placed at the head of three armies that converged on Belgrade whilst against this force Karageorge gathered 41,000 men. However sick and discouraged he had since April made arrangements for his exile to Russia. Despite the heroism of the Hajduk Velijko, the Ottoman army in the east captured Negotin, the army from Bosnia overcame the resistance at Cuprija in August 1813 and the road to the capital lay wide open. The Supreme Commander sent appeals for help to Russia who agreed to take in refugees, to Austria who advised on discussions with Kurchid Pasha. The request to the latter for an armistice remained unanswered. When the Ottomans started to advance the whole country was seized by panic. Accompanied by the Russian envoy and the Metropolitan, Karageorge and his family crossed the Sava river at Semlin (Zenum)on the 3 October 1813. The Ottomans entered the burning and half empty city on the 7 October and began to commit brutal acts of repraisals. The first Serbian Revolt had ended with bloody failure.

The Second Uprising and the Struggle for Autonomy: Milos, 1815–1834

The consequences of this failure were still quite important. Firstly for what became known in the collective memory as the "Epic of Karageorge" which became a fundamental reference point for the building of a nationalist ideology during the 19th century for the Serbia of 1804 to 1813 was felt to be the first independent Serbian national state, the natural legacy of the medieval kingdom which after three and a half centuries of Ottoman "Yoke" it again was linked. In terms of Europe, the rebels had made a point, that the Great powers had heeded especially public opinion and for Panslavist Russia, of the possibility of an independent Serbia. More tangibly and although it only was to last a short while, the organization of a state was to put in place structures which survived its failure. So for the peasants the complete liberation from the Ottoman system transformed them into free small-holders whose land was under market pressures and the richest amassed the best. The most adventurous or the poorest villagers flocked to the towns and as always war and its demands enriched some and ruined others. Hence patriarchal agrarian communities experienced the first shocks of the penetration of capitalism. On the political front the opposition between the Supreme Commander and the Knez foreshadowed the two tendencies of centralism of a military monarchy and decentralized government of the nobles. It was Karageorge's opponents who first came up with the term "Constitution"—Ustav—and the struggle in the "Council of Government" presaged the political conflicts of the 19th century. On a more positive note were the innovations in the realms of culture. The needs of war, of government and trade brought to the new Serbia their compatriots from Hungary who were shown to have had a higher cultural development. They became teachers especially after 1806 and the most famous is Dositej Obradovic who organized the setting up of primary education which was completed in 1808 by the Velika Skola—University—which was intended to turn out the highest-ranking state officials. It was also in Belgrade that this writer from the Aufklarung realized the importance of vernacular as a foundation of the culture of whole population.

This was not evident however in 1813–14. Following custom the conquerors were given several days to do as they liked with the booty. On one day, the 17 October, 1,800 women and children were taken in Belgrade to be sold as slaves. After two weeks Kurchid Pasha arrived and restored Ottoman rule. The Pashalik regained its previous borders, its garrisons and the peasants their Spahis. At the same time he gave a wide amnesty and many took advantage of it. Among them some of the leaders of the revolt for instance Milos Obrenovic who was appointed Knez for the Rudnik[16] region. Towards the middle of November 1813 most of the fugitives had returned home however resentment was high between the Serbs and the Ottomans. The Muslims demanded that reparations be made for the damage suffered during the uprising while the Serbs in the meantime buried their weapons. Those that stayed in Hungary tried to maintain contact and a secret society Opstina—Community—spread news and plans for an uprising. The Russian victory over Napoleon raised hopes and in 1814 Protopope M. Nenadovic who had stayed at Neusatz was given the task of sounding out the Tsar's intentions at the Congress of Vienna, yet to no avail. At the end of the year a former leader Hadji Prodan led an uprising in the Cacak region. The neighbouring Knez Milos Obrenovic proposed to the Pasha that he appease the rebellion with a promise of amnesty. The governor pretended to do this and then massacred the leaders. In the same way as the Knez of 1804, Milos felt threatened and decided to lead a revolt. In mid-April the Muslims were attacked in the Valjevo, Gruza and Rudnik regions. Pressured by their peasants the leaders assembled at Tarkovo on the 11 April 1815 and renewed the events of Orasac; war was declared against the "Turks" and an oath of obedience was sworn to Milos Obrenovic. The second Serbian uprising was on the point of beginning.

The new military leader was born in 1780 on the edge of the Sumadja region near Cacak[17] into a family who were by no means rich. As a young boy he guarded the herd and accompanied the pork merchants as far as Voevodina or the coastal area. These were his only contact with the outside world. In 1804 his half-brother Milan answered Karageorge's call and became the Oberknez of the Rudnik, Pozega and Uzice regions while he himself obtained the title of Voevode but was soon in opposition to the Supreme Commander. However he continued to fight until 1813 but refused to follow Karageorge into exile. No doubt it was part of his make-up but also from his analysis of the failure of the first uprising for he was to stress the dipolmatic side over the military.

The second uprising was limited to a short period. The call to arms of Takovo was taken up, the peasants dug up their weapons and went for the Ottomans, encouraged by the rumour of Russian help or of the return of Karageorge at the head of 15,000 Cossacks. Milos stopped near Cacak the troops sent by the Pasha of Belgrade against him, while the victory at Palez enabled them to smuggle arms from Austria much more easily. The insurgents gained control of the towns, hunting down the Ottoman authorities and soldiers. Kragujevac, Karanovac[18] and Pozarevac were thus liberated and by July all the Pashalik was in the hands of the Serbs while the Vizier of Belgrade remained shut up in his fortress. Istanbul was making preparations for a counter-offensive bringing up the army of Rumelia under the command of Ali Marachli Pasha from Nis and that of Bosnia under Kurchid Pasha who was newly appointed to this province. The unequal size of the forces was manifest. Milos asked for help from Austria but Matternich refused to help revolutionaries. As for Russia the memory of its betrayal in 1812 was still fresh. He therefore concentrated on the Ottomans. First by showing on the field of battle various humanitarian gestures, to the wounded and the prisoners, and by negotiating separately with the two Pashas who were jealous of each other. On the 21 August Kurchid Pasha summoned him to his camp but they failed to reach agreement since the Bosnian demanded that they lay down their arms. A few days later Milos met Marachli Ali at Cuprija and proclaimed his loyalty to the Sultan requesting a return to the "peace of Icko" which had been rejected, according to him, on the bad advise of Russia. The request was carried to Istanbul which appointed Marachli Ali Vizier of Belgrade and entrusted him with the task of sorting out the problem. Milos stood his ground while at the same time distributing many presants and Baksheesh At the beginning of November 1815 they reached agreement. Milos Obrenovic was recognized as the head of the Serbs with the title of Supreme Knez—Vrhovni Kniaz[19]. He was to have responsibility over justice together with the Kadis and the Nahijes and to raise taxes which were due to the Sultan. Beside him there was to be a Chancellery of the People—Narodna Kancelarija—which was to act as a sort of Supreme Court. This purely verbal agreement was ratified in 1816 by 7 firmans dealing with taxes, customs duties, trade, the power of the regional Knez and amnesty for the insurgents. In none of these texts was there mention of a Supreme Knez and the Porte did not see Serbia as an independent country. As in other regions of the Empire, the Sultan was granting his Serbian subjects certain privileges. Even so it was on these shaky foundations that Milos" talent managed to build an autonomous Serbia.

His effort was to stretch over a period of seventeen years, from 1816 to 1834. The first difficulty was a problem that was widespread in the Balkans: the many movements, including those who wanted to reform the Ottoman system and those who wanted complete emancipation of its subject peoples. One of these organizations—Hetairia—which was to play a leading role in the Greek revolt, aimed at a general uprising of Christians and its centre in Odessa of course established links with Karageorge and his fellows who had emigrated to Bessarabia. The former Supreme Commander joined and swore allegiance to the leaders of the movement and committed himself to leading an uprising in Serbia, while the Romanians of the Principalities and the Balkan Greeks would simultaneously revolt. In June 1817 Karageorge crossed the Danube at night near Smederevo and asked for protection from his old friend Knez Vujica Vulicevic. From there he sent a message to Milos requesting a meeting to organize an uprising with the support of the Tsar. The Kniaz' reply was swift. On the 13 June 1817 on Milos' orders, Vulicevic killed the hero of the first uprising[20] and sent his head to the Kniaz, who in turn sent it on to Istanbul. This was the origin of a vendetta which throughout the 19th century was to bathe the Serbian throne in blood. Apart from personal rivarly this action can be explained by Milos' analysis of the political situation: Hetairia in 1817 was far less powerfull than it pretended and the desertion of the Serbians by the Russians in 1812 meant that he was no longer willing to risk a further adventure. What above all counted for the Kniaz were the Serbs, and they were still exhausted by ten years of fighting. Their fate would be improved by getting concessions from the Porte. He did in fact enter into contact with the Hetairists in 1819 and exchanged letters with their leader Prince Ypsilanti, but during Tudor Vladimirescu's revolt in Wallachia and the uprising in the Peloponnese in 1812, Milos was so cautious that Hetairia partisans tried to overthrow him and replace him with Alexander, the young son of Karageorge. To strenghthen his power he gathered an Assembly—Skupstina—of people loyal to him in November 1817 who proclaimed him hereditary Kniaz. The ratification of this title was from them on the first objective of his negotiations with the Porte.

The accession of Nicholas I in December 1825 hardened Russian policy towards the Ottoman Empire. During the Greek revolt, Mahmud II was forced to sign the Akkerman Convention (Belgorod Dnestrovski) in October 1816 in which he promised to apply article VII of the Treaty of Bucharest relating to Serbia and recognizing the right of Russia to oversee its implementation. The Serbian question had once more resurfaced on an international level which gave support to Milos' policy but it also gave him cause for concern as it limited his freedom of movement. Above all the Convention made no mention of the hereditary nature of his title. When the Russo-Turkish war broke out in April 1828 following the battle of Navarino, Milos was extremely cautious. He was not forgotten however in the Treaty of Andrinople in September 1829: together with the Greeks and the Danubian Principalities, the Serbs had the promises of Bucharest and Akkerman duly and solemnly recognized. The Porte once again did not hold to the agreement and Milos once again conducted a policy of Baksheesh: he gave the Sultan half a million piasters[21] as well as the Grand Vizier and various intermediaries so that a right of inheritance be added to the other clauses. The Hatti Sheriff was ready by October 1830 and was solemnly read out in Belgrade on the 12 December of the same year. Milos Obrenovic was recognized as hereditary Prince of Serbia[22] and was aided by a council made up of members appointed for life. The Pasha of Belgrade was not allowed to intervene in matters of internal government nor interfere in sentencing in Serbian courts of justice. Ottomans were not allowed to live in Serbia apart from those in the garrisons and those that had lived there were forced to sell their property. The Kniaz was also to have a permanent representative in Istanbul. Finally there was a promise to return to the frontiers set by Karageorge. The Hatti Sheriff was to mark a decisive step and henceforth Serbia was a hereditary autonomous principality within the Ottoman Empire.

There still remained two problems: the borders and the level of tribute. Between 1806 and 1813 Karageorge had had control of six Nahijes, the Sandjaks of Novi Pazar, Krusevac and Vidin as well as the Pashalik of 1804. Yet the Pashas involved were unwilling to agree to this decrease in their own territory and revenues. Taking advantage of a revolt in Bosnia, Milos encouraged similar movements in the six Nahijes, sending as many as 6,500 soldiers. The Porte gave in and in May 1833 issued a Hatti Sheriff recognizing the new frontiers: Serbia grew from 24,000 to 37,000 km^2, which was to stay the same till 1878. At the same time, before the agreed deadline, Milos forceably expelled the Ottoman population from the country areas. The Spahis no longer existed. As for the size of the tribute, a sign of vassal status, this was settled using the diplomacy of Baksheesh. A Hatti Sheriff in December 1833 fixed it at two million piasters payable in Austrian gold ducats.

As well as settling the international status of the new Serbian state, Milos also had to set up its internal structures. The 1815 agreement with Marachli Ali had established the Kniaz as a simple adjunct to the Pasha. For 15 years Milos was to try to change this situation and to reduce the role of the Pasha, in the face of a governing prince, to merely a passive representative of the Sultan. Hence he concentrated all the powers into his own hands having progressively wrested from the Ottoman authorities, while at the same time retaining in the exercise of power many of the characteristics of the old system. The confusion between the state coffers and his own purse worked to his advantage and he received taxes, as well as customs duty and a monopoly on salt. In the same way, Timar land and land which had been confiscated from the Ottomans in 1815 became his own personal property and a proportion were farmed with corvee peasant labour. These practices explain why in 1837 this poor peasant's son enjoyed a revenue estimated at 1,600,000 piasters—17% of the principality's income. It is easy to understand the discontent that was to explode following the declaration of autonomy but together with these negative aspects one must also bear in mind the rapid growth of a real Serbian identity, and although still patriarchal this was enriched by the contributions of the Svabos (Serbians from the Banat who were the butt of jokes by their compatriots) who had flocked to the new country bringing with them the ideas, customs and fashions of Central Europe and above all Vienna.

The real founder of modern Serbia, this illiterate swine-herd, is still known in his country as Milos the Great—Milos Veliki.

The Greeks at the Dawn of the 19th Century

If the Serbian uprisings were shadowed by the Napoleonic epic, the Greek revolt was to be one of the major events of Europe following the restoration, for other countries as well as for the ethnic groups involved.

The first reason was due to the greater complexity of the Hellenic world which had become deeply interwoven into the fabric of Europe. Of course the great majority of this ethno-linguistic group which were termed "Greek" were down in the south of the Balkan peninsula. The population in the area prior to the uprising and based on what was to become a kingdom in 1830 are estimated at around 900,000 of which 7% were Turks. The highest concentration was in the Peloponnese where half a million Greeks lived with 45,000 Muslims. Yet the areas lived in by Hellenic peoples stretched well above the Arta-Volos line into Thessaly, Epirus, Macedonia, Thrace, the coast of Asia Minor and also Istanbul. This leads to a figure of two to three million. The different levels of sophistication were enormous between the Peloponnese or Epiriote farmer, the fishermen of the islands and the Phanariot diaspora already mentioned as having spread all over in the 18th century.

There were many types of Greek peasants, determined primarily by the type of land they cultivated and the climate. Some areas were better suited to animal husbandry than growing crops. The ever present mountains suited wandering flocks and short term field farming methods, while the rarer but very rich plains of Thessaly, the central Peloponnese (formerly Arcadia) and Arta were used for growing wheat. But on top of the natural problems, man had added his own. The Ottoman Ciftliks had multiplied in Thessaly and in the Peloponnese while rich Greeks had grabbed the fertile lands surrounding the towns. Thus a quasi-serf class had emerged which was burdened by dues and bound to the master, hence to the soil, by crippling debt. In other places the free peasants lived on the Timars or the Vakifs but the shortage of good land kept them in a state of desperate misery. They were at least were protected from Ottoman misrule by belonging to traditional self-governing communities based on customs going back to Byzantine law. Their leaders the Archons were equivalent to the Serbian Knezes. In certain regions where travel was difficult, for instance Suli in Epirus, Agrapha in Pindus and Mani in the southern Peloponnese, a strict tribal organization had survived. There were also Wallachian peoples, Arumans in Epirus and Macedonia and Tsintsars in Pindus, who were nomadic stockbreeders, whose language and customs were of different origin but who over the centuries had been to varying degrees assimilated with the hellenic population.

Much more than their Serbian neighbours, the Greeks had been allowed to retain their own forms of self government. In the north and the south, the Ottomans had often gathered villages into Armatoliki, an area of responsibility of armed Christian troops under a Kapitanios who were in principle supposed to police the area and above all fight against the Klephtes, the Greek hajduks. In fact the families of these hereditary captains had become the notables and they dominated and exploited the peasant communities. The Peloponnese, following the expulsion of the Venetians in 1715, had preserved a large degree of autonomy. The village communities had been systematically organized and empowered to send representatives from their "council of wise men" to the "Divans"—consultation—of the Vilayet; these in turn sent delegates to a Peloponnesian Senate which had jurisdiction over administrative and fiscal problems and from which two Christian members would meet with two Muslim members of the Divan of the Vizier of Tripolis. The islands were the Sultan's prerogative in the form of a Has but were controlled by a Kapudan Pasha who was represented *in situ* by a navy Drogman who in the 18th century would have been a Phanariot. In return for supplying sailors for the Ottoman squadrons the islands enjoyed some very large fiscal privileges, were self-governing and possessed their own military bodies. Shipowners and merchants made up a very wealthy class which dominated the local assemblies and were used to collaborating with the Porte's representatives. As for the Phanariots, whose origins and spectacular scope have already been mentioned, as well as in Istanbul and the Danubian Principalities they were present in all the ports. In Thessalonika, a town of 70–80,000 inhabitants, mostly Jews and Ottomans, the Greeks controlled maritime trade and had made the town the largest port in the Balkans next to Istanbul. There were 8 consuls and 18 trading companies, from the main European countries. The islands of Hydra, Spetsia and Psara near Naupli, were examples of commercial activity aiming at trade with the western Mediterranean while retaining their monopoly on Egyptian wheat. Also the Greek merchants in Smyrna and in the capital had a prominant role to play so a bourgeois class in the modern sense of the word sprang up and according to Apostolos Vacalopoulos[23], the first examples of millionaires and capitalist. Among the Balkan peoples it was the Greeks who were the most receptive to the ideas of capitalism.

They also benefitted the most from the influence and prestige of the Church. Since 1453 the Oecumenical Patriarch had been Greek, as well as all the higher hierarchy after the abolition of the Serbian Patriarchate of Pec in 1756 and the usurpation of the power of the Bulgarian Metropolitan of Ohrid. This Hellenization of the Church, already outlines in the case of the Serbs, explains why most travellers refer to the Balkan Christians as "Greek Orthodox" thus creating an ambiguity which even today troubles Balkan relations.

In reality in this Church, termed Phanariot, only the hierarchy were Greek and the low clergy varied depending on the regions they served, however it did give primacy to the Greek liturgy. Added to this is the role of the numerous elementary schools set up by rich members of the diaspora. From this there emerged a layer of the population who though Hellenized did not have a firm ethnic identity, for example the Arumans and the mixed populations of Macedonia and Thrace.

In the face of the desire for change which was to shake the Christian Reaya, this church appeared profoundly conservative in its origins, its structures which went back to the time of the apostles, its theology which rested on the first seven oecumenical councils[24] and which after the first centuries of heated discussions had been submerged in silence for the whole of the Ottoman period. It was to remain untouched and untroubled by such things as the Humanism and the Reformation. Its traditional anti-Latin attitude made it anti-western in general and hostile to both the missionary counter-Reformation in the Balkans and the Austrian Aufklarung. These were for secular as well as religious reasons, for in the Ottoman system the Patriarch, as the Basi of the Rum Millet, had the rank of Pasha with three "Tugs" and the church had vast possessions as part of its Vakifs. This explains why in 1798, Patriarch Gregory was to give "fatherly advice" to the faithful stating that "the Sultan, after God, was their Christian sovereign, guardian of their property and lives and that those who advocated dreams of freedom were going against the Holy Scriptures and were inspired by the Devil."

As was seen above the Greeks through their diaspora had come into contact with new European ideas. Two writers were to put themselves forward as the apostles of the French revolutionary message; Rhigas Velestinlis (1757–1798) and Adamantios Korais (1748–1833). Rhigas was born in Thessaly yet was brought up in the Phanariot milieu of the Principalities where he became the secretary of the Hospodar of Wallachia and was to read the works of Voltaire, Rousseau and Montesquieu. He became a passionate supporter of the French Revolution and wrote poems about it. The most famous "Thurios"—warrior anthem—was to inspire the Marseillaise. From 1796 he was based in Vienna and shared the dream of various Hellenic groups, of a uprising of the Balkan Christian peoples yet introducing principles of Human Rights and the French Constitution which he had translated. He rallied students and merchants to his idea of a Balkan Federation and went to Trieste and his homeland. Watched by the Austrian police he was arrested and as one of the Sultan's subjects was handed over to the Pasha of Belgrade who had him executed in Kalemegdan on the 23 June 1798. The memory of his death was to remain fresh in people's memories and his poems stirred the hearts of the 1821 fighters, especially since they were written in the popular tongue—Demotic—which was within the reach of everyone. The "Thurios" became a sort of national anthem.

Adamantios Korais was the great representative of the Enlightenment in its French form. From Smyrna he went to study medicine in Montpelier, prior to settling in Paris in 1786/7 where he stayed until his death in 1833. An eye-witness of the Revolution he hoped to wrest his compatriots from their servile role. In 1798, placing his hopes on Bonaparte who was embarking on his Egyptian expedition, he published a pamphlet dated "Year 1 of Freedom" and which called on the Greeks to revolt. At the same time he was convinced that the Enlightenment had prepared the ground for the Revolution and embarked on the publication of a "Collection of Greek Works" republishing the great authors of antiquity; as this was supposed to make his compatriots aware of their glorious past. As a scholar, he elaborated a language some way between ancient Greek and the popular tongue, to be called Katharevusa and to become the language of modern literature. It was in this way above all that he influenced neo-Hellenism although his correspondence did help to spread the message of the French Revolution in the Greek world.

These well-known figures were also aided by ordinary sailors who came into contact with the new ideas in the French Republic's ports and upon their return home would spread them among ordinary people. Nor should Napoleon's fame be ignored, for whatever one might think about him, undoubtedly his imperial policy was a powerful motor for a particular aspect of the revolution which was symbolized by the French tricolour. The Klepht Kolokotronis, the heroes of the future war of independence saw the Emperor as the "God of War" who brought freedom to the ordinary people. For the Greeks, news of the Italian revolutions, the abolition of the Doge's Republic and the invasion of the Adriatic coastal territories raised their expectations. The occupation of the Ionian Islands by French troops from 1807 to 1814 brought an alternative civilisation within range of the Ottoman coast; its architecture is still visible in the famous esplanade of Corfu with its neo-Classical arcades. Following Bonaparte's first occupation in 1798, a Corfu printing-press printed the Thurios anthem by Rhigas in Greek.

The Greek Revolt, 1821–1825

Yet it was not from the ashes the Enlightenment that the Greek revolt was to emerge but more directly from a pan-Hellenic dream inspired by the Russians and based on traditional peasant movements.

After the tempests of the Napoleonic period, Tsar Alexander took advantage at the Congress of Vienna to reaffirm Russia's role as "Natural Protector of Greek Orthodox Christians under Ottoman rule, in the same way that Austria and France were the protectors of the Catholics." Russian agents once again became active all over the Balkans and the political and religious mysticism which was rampant in Saint Petersburg at the time, also influenced the Greek, Serb and Bulgar exile circles in southern Russia. In September 1814 three merchants: Xanthous from the island of Patmos and two Epiriotes; Scuphas of Arta and Tsakalov from Janina, formed a "Friendly Society"—Philiki Hetairia—in Odessa, a secret society which was modelled on the masonic model with oaths, rituals and a strict hierarchy. Its aims were similar to traditional Russian policy, fomenting a widespread Greek Orthodox uprising throughout the Balkans which would lead to Russian armed intervention. Of course this implied an uprising not only of the Greek people, as nationalist historians have taken it to be, but of all Greek Orthodox Christians. Propagandists would intimate that above their leaders, the Hetairia had a mysterious "Arch" who quite possibly was Tsar Alexander. In 1818 the society established its centre in Istanbul and organized itself in the Balkans. Regions were entrusted to twelve "apostles" who formed a select network and acted together with the Russian consuls who were generally of Greek origin. So Hetairia recruited the best known figures of the day; Karageorge in Odessa, T. Kolokotronis the Klepht leader in the Peloponnese, the Metropolitan bishop of Patras Germanos, Mavromichalis the leader of the Mani and in the Danubian Principalities the son of the Hospodar of Wallachia Alexander Ypsilanti and many boyars. Above all, merchants—more than half the membership were merchants—their businesses helping to spread the message. The basic plan consisted of an uprising in Serbia which was still reverberating from the failure of the first uprising and also in Greek areas. The refusal of Milos Obrenovic and the assassination of Karageorge in June 1817 forced them to find another starting point in the north of the peninsula. The Danubian Principalities were thought to fit the bill as the Phanariot Hospodars willingly looked to Saint Petersburg for help and the Boyars hoped that Russia would force the Porte to accept reform. Lastly the Hetairists were quite strong there. The revolutionary movements in Spain and Italy in 1820 set an example. They needed a leader. They sounded John Capo d'Istria, a Greek from Corfu, who was at the time Minister of Foreign Affairs to the Tsar. Consequently he was unable to accept and refused the offer graciously. They had better luck with Alexander Ypsilanti (1792–1828), who was from a Phanariot family from Istanbul and whose grandfather and father had been Hospodars in Wallachia and Moldavia. Alexander had fought in the Russian guards division against Napoleon, had lost an arm at the battle of Dresden and was a personal friend of the Tsar. Of course he concentrated on developments in the Principalities but was forced to ally himself with the leader of Oltenia, Tudor Vladimirescu who led an army of peasants in an uprising against "bad" Boyars. This divergence of interest and failure to coordinate led to a bloody end: Tudor Vladimirescu was assassinated by the Hetairists in June 1821, while the rebel army was crushed by Ottoman troops at Dragasani. Alexander Ypsilanti fled to Austria where Matternich had him imprisoned at Theresienstadt[25] until 1827. The following year he died in Vienna without having been able to join in the war of independence.

In Greek areas there were two regions which appeared especially ripe for revolt: Epirus and Morea. It is to be remembered that two of the founders of the Hetairia were from Epirus. The region was ruled at the time by Ali who was Pasha of Janina and in open revolt against the Sultan since 1819. Ali was quite favourable to the suggestions of Hetairia and so was able to rally the support of the Greeks, Albanians and Wallachians in his Pashalik. But in January 1820 Mahmud issued a Firman stripping him of all his titles and the Sheik el Islam summoned him to Istanbul to make amends. The Pasha responded with a general levy which was supposed to give him an army of 40,000 men, however his appointed successor Bey Ishmail Pasha came at the head of a huge army and the resultant encounter ended with the route of Ali's soldiers. Even his family deserted him. At the end of August Ottoman forces began the siege of Janina where the old Pasha had shut himself up in his island fortress in the center of the lake. Henceforth he was neutralized. The siege lasted for 17 months and ended in betrayal. The "Lion of Janina" of Albanian legend was killed on the 22 February 1822 and his head was sent to Istanbul.

Morea had enjoyed some degree of autonomy, yet there was much social unrest because of the many Ciftliks which had been set up in the central plains. In Tripolis however, commerce was controlled by Muslims together with a few rich Greeks. Aware of Hetairia's intentions, the Vizier assembled in March 1821 a conference of bishops and leading figures from the Peloponnese, although many were absent because they were worried and suspicious of such proceedings, for instance the Hetairia bishop of Patras Germanos and the Mani leaders. The time was right for action yet they had difficulty in coordinating the initial stages. From the 2 April 1821 Kalamata rose up, soon followed by the whole of the Mani, while small gangs under local leaders attacked the "Turks." Traditionally Germanos is given credit for a spectacular act of bravery, worthy of Karageorge, when on the 6 April in the monastery of Aghia Lavra, above Kalavryta, the bishop waved the cross of insurrection. In fact the first acts were directed against unarmed Ottoman Ciftlik owners, Timar holders, Ulema officials and merchants. Massacres took place such as in Tripolis after the capture of the town in October. D. Dakin the historian estimates that 40,000 Muslims were killed in the Peloponnese. Nor were the "Turks" to remain idle. At Easter 1821 a group of Janissaries hung Patriarch Gregory V at the door of the Phanar church, even though he had condemned the rebels. Several bishops and numerous Greeks in Istanbul and other towns were put to death in the same way. In 1822 there were several thousand victims of massacres in Chios which are depicted in "L'Enfant grec" by Victor Hugo and the famous painting of Delacroix. The Greek revolt was fast becoming an European problem.

On the ground it was running out of momentum. The liberation of Morea had been rapid and the capture of Tripolis had limited the Ottoman presence to a few fortresses along the coast. The islands of Spetsia, Psara and Hydra revolted in April 1821 and their ships were to wage a piratical corsair war against ships flying the Sultan's flag anywhere in the Aegean. North of the Isthmus of Corinth the Ottoman garrisons withdrew or were trapped in their fortresses. Missolonghi, Thebes and Athens were besieged. However in Epirus, Thessaly and Macedonia the Armatolikia were unable to resist the regular troops that the Porte had sent against Ali of Janina and carried out limited guerilla operations. On the military front the situation did not change much until 1825.

In the meantime the organization of a Greek state was proving a big problem. The Hetairia called on Demetrios Ypsilanti (1793–1832), brother of Alexander Ypsilanti who had been eliminated by his defeat in Wallachia in June 1821. He immediately proposed a general assembly to set up a centralized but constitutional state. After agreement with the Klepht leader, Th. Kolokotronis, a constituent assembly was brought together at Epidaurus in December 1821. Dominated by the local worthies, it was not willing to entrust power to any single person and at the instigation of Alexander Mavrocordatos drew up a constitution inspired by the French 1795 model, giving executive power to five members each representing a region. This first Greek government was set up in Missolonghi and presided over by Mavrocordatos, who on the 13 January 1822 proclaimed Greek independence. But in the Peloponnese, where Koloktronis' guerilla forces were in control and felt they represented the nobility and the island people, it was not recognized. At the end of the year following the capture of Nauplia, Koloktronis called together another assembly at Astros[26] where a fight broke out between his supporters and those of Mavrocordatos whom he had arrested. Finally a new government was set up at Kranidi[27] headed by a reputedly very rich man, G. Kountouriotes, whose first action was to relieve Koloktronis of all military power. From then on there were two rival forces within the rebel ranks: the old Klepht supported by gangs of peasants who controlled the important town of Nauplia and the civil government, supported by the population of the islands but also by an Epiriote, John Kolettes, who had close links with the Armatolikia of Rumelia. There from 1824 virtual civil war between the two sides, punctuated by momentary reconciliations, lasted for four years. Often portrayed as a struggle between "politicians" and "generals" it was also that of the people of the Peloponnese against those of continental Greece and the islands.

The Ottomans were fortunate that this occurred, for they were bogged down by operations conducted against Pasha Ali and also had to confront a guerilla force which stretched their resources and continually reappeared. By 1825 the military situation was deadlocked. Mahmud decided to ask his vassal, Mehmed Ali (1769–1849), Pasha of Egypt for help. In fact he had previously intervened in Crete which had been in revolt since July 1821. In May 1822 he made an initial landing which freed Canea and pushed the Spakiots back into the mountains. Mehmet asked that Crete be included in his Pashalik in return for his intervention and that his son Ibrahim be appointed governor of Morea. The Egyptian intervention transformed the situation. In February 1825 Ibrahim landed in the Peloponnese. The Greek forces were no match for this modern army which had been trained by French instructors. At the same time the Sultan's army went into attack in the north. In April 1825 Missolonghi fell and in June the Acropolis in Athens. The Greek revolt appeared to be over.

Greek Independence:
A European Problem, 1826–1833

It was to be saved by the Great European powers whose intervention gave birth to a new Christian state: Greece.

From the very beginning public opinion had been attracted to the Greek revolt by its "Romantic" side, the Christian ideology of the Holy Alliance and by the Liberal ideas of opposition to tyranny. There grew up a pro-Greek movement which managed to combine these contradictory elements and on a Periclean backdrop brought together such different characters as Goethe, Byron, Chateaubriand, Beranger and kings such as Louis I of Bavaria and Charles X of France. It encouraged the departure of various volunteers to the area who became the first officers of the rebel army. Their disillusionment at the actual experience of a country which did not match up to their idea of classical antiquity was to be great.

The Great Powers took their time to react, Russia was the most directly concerned and Hetairia appeared to be one of its creations, yet the Tsar refused to get involved and Saint Petersburg condemned the uprising in the Danubian provinces. Even though the Holy Alliance encouraged him, Alexander refused to support subject people in a rebellion against their rightful sovereign.

However the protector of the Orthodox Church could not remain unmoved by the massacre of Christians, and the hanging of the Ecumenical Patriarch sent a crusading shockwave right through Russia. In the summer of 1821 Saint Petersburg sent a letter to the Porte which mentioned respect for the Church and its Christian subjects but in no way threatened war. England saw its own advantage in the Russian hesitation. In August 1822 George Canning became Prime Minister and although faithful to the traditional policy of maintaining the Ottoman Empire as an obstacle to Russian expansion in the south seas, was more flexible than his predecessor Castlereagh, especially since the needs of the rebels in arms and munitions were of direct commercial benefit to the Ionian Islands which since 1815 were British protectorates. He felt that these initial bases near the Greek coast could be enlarged and above all the possibility of an independent Greece under Russian protection should be avoided. In 1823, on a tide of pro-Greek public support the English government recognized the Greek rebels as belligerents and agreed to loan the Kountouriotes government 2.4 million pounds. In December 1825, Alexander I suddenly died and his brother Nicholas I, renowned for his martial and messianic ideas, came to the throne. Canning preempted him, taking advantage of the coronation of the new Tsar in Saint Petersburg in April 1826, he sent a "Protocol" through his envoy in which he suggested that both countries offer to mediate between the Ottomans and the Greeks over the creation of an autonomous Greek state on the model of the Danubian Principalities. Nicholas however wanted to consolidate his influence over the Principalities, so in March 1826 he sent the Porte an ultimatum demanding that they keep to the terms of Article VII of the Treaty of Bucharest in relation to Moldavia, Wallachia and also Serbia. Mahmud bowed to this pressure in October and the Convention of Akkerman placed the three regions under the protection of the Tsar. This alarmed Canning who persuaded Charles X, also pro-Hellenist, to become involved in the Greek question as well as the two other European powers. So Russia, France and England signed the Treaty of London in July 1827 once more confirming the Saint Petersburg protocol as a basis for action: from mediation to the creation of an autonomous Greek state within the framework of the Ottoman Empire. Furthermore as they wanted the departure of Egyptian troops, the three European powers decided to blockade the Greek coast and send a French expeditionary corps to the

Peloponnese. In October an unexpected event occurred: the battle of Navarino[28] (20 October 1827). The Anglo-Russo-French fleet came to the harbour where the Turkish\Egyptian fleet of Pasha Ibrahim was riding at anchor. A warning manoeuvre to make it leave the coastal area led to out-and-out confrontation. This "deplorable misunderstanding" as George IV was to call it, cost the Ottoman Empire a fleet of 4,000 men, many of them of Greek origin. Istanbul replied by proclaiming Holy War while the new English government under Wellington condemned the policy which had led to Navarino and adopted a very firm attitude towards Russia. Encouraged by this, the Sultan reneged on the Convention of Akkerman and in April 1828 Tsar Nicholas declared war on the Ottoman Empire. His troops crossed the Danube but were halted by the Ottoman fortresses of Sumen, Silistra and Varna. The English and French took advantage of this to sign an agreement with Mehmet Ali for the evacuation of his Egyptian troops from the Peloponnese which would take place during the winter of 1828–29 under the supervision of the French expeditionary corps commanded by general Maison. In March 1829 the Three Great Powers met once more in London to sign a Protocol which anticipated the creation of an autonomous Greece, dependent on the Ottoman Empire but governed by a prince of their own choice. In July the Russian armies broke the deadlock and advanced rapidly on Istanbul. Adrianopolis fell without a shot being fired in August and Russian cannon could be heard from the capital. Panic seized the palace and Mahmud called on France and England to mediate. Peace was signed at Adrianopolis on the 14 September 1829. The terms were moderate for Saint Petersburg understood that the Sultan was under threat from Mehmet Ali who might prove more dangerous. Russia increased its influence in the Danubian Principalities, annexed part of the Caucasus and on the Greek question forced the Porte to accept the London protocol. International sanction was given for the Treaty of London and on the 3 February 1830, a Greek state was created, still a vassal paying tribute to the Sultan, governed by a king chosen by the three European countries and with a territory extending to the north to the Arta-Volos line which was to become the frontier between Greece and the Ottoman Empire.

All that remained was to decide who should be king, a task for the European powers, and to apply the terms which would be a Greek affair. To end the civil war a new national assembly was convened, the third, in the spring of 1827 at Trezin—formerly Trezen near Epidaurus—in order to draw up a new constitution. This was relatively liberal and allowed for a president (Kubernetis) who would be elected for seven years and share power with a house of representatives. The assembly called on John Capo d'Istria who had been living in Switzerland since leaving the service of the Tsar. The new president arrived in Nauplia, the temporary capital, in January 1828 and was greeted with great emotion by the population. He could count on the support of the Peloponnesian nobility and also on Kolokotronis. A good administrator he was well able to judge the problems that lay before him: to set up a state in an economically devastated and politically divided country. He tried first of all to restore order, incorporating the armed groups into an army under the command of an English general, Richard Church. He also set a budget and formed a national bank. He was confronted with the problem of the distribution of Ottoman land. The peasants felt it belonged to them and often had occupied it without any legal titles. In terms of foreign affairs Capo d'Istria was distrusted by France and England who felt he was Saint Petersburg's man. There was unrest among the nobility who disliked his authoritarian methods, for example his dissolving the national assembly and its replacement with a simply consultative council. Local leaders were also jealous of him and there was a vendetta against him by a powerful Mani family: the Mavromichalis. After several attempts at coups d'état some members of this clan managed on the 27 September 1831, to assassinate the founder of the modern Greek state.

His death was followed by a renewed period of anarchy and civil war almost broke out once more between the leaders of the clans who were organized into political parties known as English, French and Russian. It was in these extremely fraught times that the king chosen by the European powers was to arrive. The crown had been offered first to Leopold of Saxa-Cobourg who refused, since he felt the Arta-Volos line would not be agreed by the Greeks and the financial assistance promised by the European powers was not sufficient. Following the assassination of Capo d'Istria the three nations turned to the Hellenophile King Louis I of Bavaria who accepted the crown for his second son Otto who was only 17 and therefore a minor. The agreement was ratified in London in May 1832 and the border was moved slightly to the north. Prince Otto became king on the 1 June 1835 but until then was advised by a council of regents. In July of the same year the Sultan agreed to the independence of Greece in return for an indemnity of 13 million gold francs. In February 1833, Otto—in Greek Othon—reached his new kingdom. A new Christian country, independent Greece, had come into existence in the Balkans.

Notes

1. History of the Balkans. Vol. 1 p.148/9.
2. Cf. Unbegaum (B): Les debuts de la langue litteraire chez les Serbes. Paris 1935 pp. 35–.
3. Haumont (Emile): La formation de la Yougoslavie. Paris 1930 pp.165/66.
4. Memoari. Belgrade 1893 p.6.
5. In Sprski Rjecnik. dealing with the term Spahija. Vienna 1852.
6. The Piaster was calculated in 1800 to be worth approximately 2 Germinal Francs.
7. Translated as the "Popular ecclesastical assembly" rather than the "national Church assembly" which is an anachronism. The German term Volkskirchen Versammlung is exactly the same.
8. The Guzla is a simple form of violin made from a block of maple tree, hollowed out and covered with sheep-skin. It only had on string and was played with a bow.
9. A rank in the Ottoman army carried by the leader of a Yamak unit which was made up of Janissary auxiliaries recruited from among craftsmen.
10. In the singular: Momak—boy.
11. On the river Sava 10 kilometres upriver from Belgrade.
12. Ivankovo, beside the monastery of Ravanica, near Cuprija.
13. Above Aleksinac on the Morava.
14. Stll distinguishable 2 kilometres from Nis on the Dimitrovgrad to Sofia road.
15. The Staff HQ of the Illyrian provinces.
16. In the Sumadja near Topola.
17. In the village of Srednja Dobrinja which controls the valley which goes to Pozega.
18. Now Kraljevo.
19. Term used instead of Knez.
20. In 1818 the murderer, helped apparently by Ljubica who was Milos' wife, built a church of Pokajnica—Repentance—near the place where the assassination occured at Staro Selo 6 miles from Velika Plana. It is still standing.
21. A large coin called by foreigners "piaster" was in principle worth two francs.

22. Milos was henceforth known as Kniaz Srpski.
23. Histoire de la Grece moderne. Horvath. Roanne 1975. 330 p. (History of modern Greece see p. 98 for quotation).
24. From Nicea in 325 to that of Constantinople in 680.
25. Terezin in northern Bohemia.
26. Twenty miles south of Nauplia.
27. Kranidion opposite the island of Spetsia.
28. Pylos on the very edge of the eastern Peloponnese coast.

11

The Eastern Question: Crises, 1832–1859

The birth of two Christian nations within Dar el Islam, the second delivered by the forceps of the European powers, made the Ottoman Empire the "sick man of Europe," at whose bedside governments of diametrically different political complexions would keep watch. Henceforth every internal problem that might possibly destabilize the Porte was to become transformed into a European crisis, at the time alluded to as the "Eastern Question." There were four crises before the end of the Empire: that of the 1830–40s, provoked by the ambitions of Pasha Mehmet Ali of Egypt, the Crimean war from 1853 to 1856 which marked the end of Russian hopes of hegemony in the Balkans, of 1875–78 which ended in a new map of the Balkans being drawn in Berlin, and finally 1912 to 1918 which was to join the Balkan wars with the First World War and lead to the end of the Ottoman Empire. Yet this descent into oblivion was not viewed with resignation by all the descendants of Soliman the Magnificent: the problem of reforming the system, legacy of the 18th century, was to remain right to the end, punctuated however by periods of frenetic activity that eventually was to transform the inheritance of Osman into a modern state, and periods of inertia which highlighted the inability of the Sultan to shoulder the responsibility of the Empire's continued survival.

The Tanzimat

The term "Reform" which is sometimes associated with the year 1839 in fact covers the period from 1826 to February 1856, from when the Janissaries were disbanded up to the Treaty of Paris which imposed a further "Edict of Reforms"—Hatti Humayun[1].

The death of Selim III was perpetrated by all those opposed to reform, and in particular the Janissaries who felt that their existence was threatened by the creation of the Nizam i Cedid—the model army. The Russo-Turkish War of 1807 once again underlined the Sultan's military weakness. Nor could the Janissary troops overcome Ali of Tepelin's troops or subjugate the Greek rebels. Their inability was so patent that Mahmud was forced in 1825 to ask the Pasha of Egypt, who had an army trained by French officers, for help. The Sultan could no longer delay. In May 1826 he promulgated a new military law that even though it did not disband the Janissaries integrated them into new structures. Once again they overturned their cauldrons as a sign of revolt. On the 14 June they gathered on the At Meydani—the former hippodrome—and demanded the Grand Vizier's head and went and looted his palace. The Sultan sought advice from the Ulemas who distanced themselves from the rebels while in the meantime the Grand Vizier mustered loyal troops, the artillery for instance who already had been reorganized, and ordered them to open fire on the rebels. The barracks where the Janissaries had taken refuge were systematically shelled and the ensuing man-hunt ended with many of the survivors being killed. According to the report of the English ambassador 6,000 were killed and 18,000 deported to Asia and their names outlawed. So one of the pillars of the Empire ended its existence in blood after half a millennium of history. The corps of Spahi cavalry were also disbanded together with the Janissaries and also the Bektasi religious orders who had maintained close links with them. From now on Mahmud could form a modern army trained by European officers. Yet he had to hurry for there was the Convention of Akkerman (October 1826), the war against Russia after the battle of Navarino (October 1827), the Treaty of Adrianopolis (September 1829), the independence of Greece and autonomy for Serbia, not forgetting the conquest of Algeria by the French in 1830. All were to sap the military energy of the Ottomans. The daring of Mehmet Ali was based on this assumption. During the period 1832 to 1840 when the first Eastern crisis had occurred the race was on between the effectiveness of the Porte's reforms and the adventures of its opponents: Egypt, Russia, and at one time France. In 1835 Helmut von Moltke—the future victor of Sedan—arrived with a group of Prussian officers to instruct the new army, the British were asked to improve the navy and young Turks were sent to the main military schools of Europe.

On a political level Mahmud, who had been humiliated by the condescension of European statesmen and diplomats, wished to adopt the same organization for his own government; in May 1836 a Ministry of the Interior and a Ministry of Foreign Affairs were created and in 1838 a Ministry of Trade and Public Works. Yet the most incredible event was the Sultan wearing western style clothes and above all the Fez which became a sign of support for reform. The capital's papers mention that at his investiture[2] on the 11 July 1839, his successor Abdul Medjid wore a Fez.

In 1831 Mahmud ordered a census for administrative purposes yet the primary objective of this operation was for tax purposes. It only covered the male population in various religious and arbitrary age groups. The results were not published but the registers remained open for regional government administrators. In the field of communications it is worth mentioning the publication of the first Turkish language newspaper in 1832 and in 1834 the organisation of a postal service, not only for the Sultan but for everybody. Mahmud then turned to two major problems. He wanted civil servants to be directly controlled by the central government and paid a salary direct by the treasury and not from local income tax. Yet for this to be possible (apart from the question of finance) there was also the need to recruit educated young people that underlined the need to create a secondary education system. Teachers and money were sorely lacking. The second problem were its relations with foreign governments. The traditional humiliating practice of ambassadors being received at the Palace ended in 1796 when the French Directoire's envoy, Aubert-Dubayet, refused to submit to it. But although the European powers had had permanent representatives to the Porte for some time, the opposite was not true, such was the disdain of the Ottomans for foreign sovereigns. It was only in 1834 that the Sultan agreed to send permanent ambassadors to capital cities, to Paris, London, Saint Petersburg and Vienna, thus introducing to international life and modern civilization such men as Rashid Pasha (1802–1858) who were to play a crucial role in the Tanzimat. Contact with the outside world posed the problem of language: this had been resolved with the Drogman system but these had been above all Greeks. After their independence they were replaced by an Office of Translations which chose French as the diplomatic language and sent students to study in the kingdom of Louis-Phillipe. As a young man Abdul Medjid had learned French in the Kafes of the palace and once Sultan was able to converse with Napoleon III on their journey to the Crimea.

Abdul Medjid (1839–1861) gave the reform movement its fundamental impetus with his Hatti Sheriff of Gul-Hane on the 3 November 1839. He brought together all the high-ranking officials of state at his "House of Roses"—Gul Hane[3]—the leaders of the religious confessions and foreign ambassadors and Rashid Pasha, the Minister of Foreign Affairs, read out the Hatti Sheriff which was intended to reform the old Empire, product of Jihad (Holy War), without however fundamentally altering its religious tenets: the Koran and Sharia. According to the introduction of the charter, it was a question of setting up new institutions to bring back good government. In fact, without overtly expressing it, the document placed all his subjects on an equal footing which in itself was in contradiction to Islamic law. Everybody was guaranteed "security of life, honour and possession" covering, and this was emphasized, "those of any religion or sect." Everybody was consequently under the equal before the law and accountable to the law; in terms of taxation everybody would have to pay a tax in proportion to their wealth—the end of Djizya for Christians; in terms of defence every area had to provide troops in proportion to the number of inhabitants so Christians would be expected to take up arms. On these new foundations an government was set up which owed much to the European model. Rashid Pasha who as Grand Vizier was in charge, had been posted to London and Paris and the French influence was very clear with the Civil Code, published in 1840 and owing much to the "Code Napoleon." The Sultan remained the highest authority in law and the ultimate master of its enforcement. He was aided by the Grand Vizier and the Sheik ul Islam who had the same rank in the hierarchy; the former in charge of all public affairs, had the sovereigns seal and presided over the Divan (council) while the latter kept the right to examine the Fetwas, prior to their being promulgated by the Sultan, to make sure the new laws respected Koranic law. The Divan, seen as a kind of privy council, was enlarged in the ensuing years. As well as the heads of the traditional departments such as the army, navy, treasury and foreign affairs, now referred to as ministers, there was a president of the Council of State created in 1840 and in 1846 a minister of police. The Empire was divided up into 36 Elayets (formerly the Beylerbeyliks) 15 in Europe including Wallachia, Moldavia and Serbia still sub-divided into Sandjaks, Cazas and

Nahijes. The non-Muslim population which is estimated to have totalled some 12 million souls, were divided up into five Millets: the Greek community (Rum Millet), the Armenian community which was divided since 1838 into Armenians and united Armenians (in other words Catholics attached to Rome), the Jewish community and the Latin or Catholic community. Each had at its head a Millet Basi: the Patriarch, the Grand Rabbi of Istanbul or the bishop. In 1840 Rashid Pasha tried to set up a system of local government with a Majlis (council of notables) together with the governor of the Elayet, chosen by him, and on which Christians could sit.

All these attempts at reform encountered such strong resistance that in May 1841 Rashid Pasha preferred to give up his post of Grand Vizier and go to London as the ambassador where he remained until 1845 when he once again returned to the Sultan's side. In the meantime most of these innovations remained unimplemented. Passive resistance by those whom the reformers were to call "Old Turks," paralysed central government and to a even greater extent regional government. Yet there was change in certain areas. The army system, set up by Grand Vizier Riza Bey in 1843 with the Law of Recruitment was based on equality: drawing lots, five years active service and seven years of reserve service with training a month every year. This was supposed to provide 300,000 men on active service, divided up into five army corps which, at least on paper, placed the Ottoman army on an even footing with the Prussian army. In 1845 a blueprint for reform of education was elaborated by Rashid Pasha who by then had returned to the job; with the French example as a model he foresaw primary schools—Mektebs—compulsory and non-fee paying, secondary school with six lycees which would open in 1850 and higher education encompassing traditional high Medresses and modern high schools for medicine, the army, the navy and agriculture. Yet despite the fact that education was aimed solely at Muslims and relied almost exclusively on the income of the Vakifs, results were slow due to lack of resources. The lycee at Galata Saray opened in 1868 with the help of the French ambassador and had a statute very similar to a Parisian type lycee. The provinces were rather slow in following, while the Christians continued to send their children to the few schools which were run by the clergy of their denomination. In 1847 a reorganization of the legal system transferred some areas of jurisdiction from the religious courts to the civil and administrative courts: this was the start of a secularization which opened up for the Sultan's Christian subjects equal access to the process of the law.

Even so it was only with the intervention of the European powers in 1856 and the Treaty of Paris together with a new Hatti Humayun that the basic reforms of Gul Hane were brought to fruition.

The First Balkan Crisis: Mehmed Ali, 1832–1841

Mehmed Ali, whom the French called Mehemet Ali, was from an Albanian family. Born at Kavala in Greek Macedonia in 1769, he became a soldier and was sent to Egypt to fight against Bonaparte's expedition. At the head of Albanian Janissaries he intervened in the disputes between the Mameluk governor of the province and the representatives of Istanbul. In 1804 he forced the Mameluks out of Cairo and the following year had himself appointed by the Porte, Pasha of all Egypt. Mameluk unrest still continued so he summoned their leaders and had 480 of them massacred on the 1 March 1811 and so became ruler of the country. A reformer, he set up a modern army with the help of a French captain called Selve who became Soliman Pasha. Due to this his son, Ibrahim, was in a position to defeat, for the Sultan, the Wahabites of Hedjaz [4] so when in 1825 Mahmud II was unable to put down the Greek revolt with his Janissaries, he made use of this formidable force. In return for intervening in Greece Mehmed had obtained for his son the governorship of Morea, yet the creation of a Greek state in 1830 scuppered this idea. Instead he demanded Syria. The Sultan refused and proposed Crete where Ibrahim had already intervened in 1821. A Firman in early 1832 joined the island to the Pashalik of Egypt. Yet Mehmed was not to be placated and following a further conflict over Saint John of Acra he simply broke off relations. Ibrahim's army crossed Palestine, captured Saint John of Acra in May 1832 and advanced through Damascus, Aleppo and Antioch to Konya where it encountered the Sultans' forces which it thoroughly defeated. In December 1832 the road to Istanbul was open.

The Turkish-Egyptian crisis therefore became a European problem: each Great Power was reluctant to allow another to benefit from the diminishing or dissolution of the legacy of Osman. French public opinion was fired by Mehmed Ali who was seen as a disciple of Bonaparte. In the government of Marshall Soult the Minister of the Interior, A. Thiers, with links with the port of Marseilles, militated for a policy in support of Egypt. Yet England was against, faithful to its policy of support for the "sick man." Taking advantage of this difference of opinion between the two western nations, Russia intervened vigorously. Their ambassador to Istanbul persuaded the panic-stricken palace to ask for the protection of the Tsar: a Russian fleet went to the Bosphorous and Russian troops landed near the capital. Immediately the other Great Powers forgot their differences, England, France and Austria agreed to put pressure on both Mahmud and Mehmed to force them to settle which led to the Treaty of Kutahya in May 1833 which ceded Syria and the Elayet of Adana in return for the retreat of Ibrahim's troops. There still remained however the withdrawal of Russian forces: in the face of the three Great Powers Nicholas I was unable to do anything else yet he managed to capitalize on their withdrawal. With the Treaty signed on the 8 July 1833 at Unkiar-Iskelesi on the eastern shore of the Bosphorous, he became guarantor of the independence and territorial integrity of the Ottoman Empire, committing himself to sending troops in its defence and also obtaining the closure of the Dardanelles to foreign warships. In London and Paris there was alarm at the idea of a Russian protectorate of the Empire and pressed Mahmud to break the agreement, that in any case he had been forced to sign. Palmerston, who had just arrived at the Foreign Office, also was worried about the Pasha of Egypt's ambitions in the Red Sea area, so in 1838 he had Aden occupied in order to protect the route to India. He was unable however to convince Thiers to adopt a joint policy towards Egypt.

Conscious of disagreement among the Great Powers and placing too much hope in his army which had barely begun to be modernized, Mahmud dreamed of erasing what he considered to be the shame of Kutahya. In April 1839 he made his troops advance into Syria and once more they were halted by Ibrahim Pasha who on the 24 June 1839 crushed the Ottomans at Aintab[5]. The defeat became a catastrophe when Mahmud suddenly died on the 30 June. Istanbul was open to the victor and the Pasha of Kupidan surrendered his fleet to the Egyptians at Alexandria. Not much apart from his age—16 years old—was known of the new Sultan Abdul Medjid and Europe foresaw the destruction of the Empire. The Great Powers reacted swiftly. On the 27 July a joint letter, signed by England, France, Austria and Prussia requested the Sultan "not to undertake any negotiations with Mehmed Ali without their agreement." This was the death knell for the Pasha's ambitions. All he could hope was for favourable mediation by France where Thiers, once again in power, was supporting Egypt's interests. Palmerston manoeuvred however in such a way that he gained the support of Russia and in July 1840 a "Convention for the Pacification of the Levant" was signed in London by England, Russia, Austria and Prussia in the presence of the Sultan's envoy. It enjoined Mehmed Ali, under threat of the use of force, to accept Egypt as a hereditary pashalik and the lease of southern Syria but to hand back the Sultan's fleet and the territories which he had occupied: northern Syria, Mecca and Medina and lastly Crete. Mehmed was given ten days to agree. Encouraged by Thiers, the Pasha refused these terms and Palmerston sent a fleet which landed Austrian and English troops in Syria. In quick succession the fortresses of Beirut, Sidon and Acra fell to British cannon, and Ibrahim faced with popular unrest was forced to withdraw from Syria. French public opinion was seized by war fever which Louis Phillipe stopped by forcing Thiers to resign in October: Guizot, the king's man, took over control of foreign affairs and tried to end France's diplomatic isolation. Mehmed Ali, now alone, negotiated with the British: he agreed to relinquish Syria and to hand back the Ottoman fleet yet he would retain his hereditary title over Egypt. The Porte prevaricated but on the 1 June 1841 it recognized Mehmed Ali as the governor of Egypt and his hereditary right of succession. As for the Great Powers they were reconciled with France by the signature of the "Convention of the Straits" which closed the Dardanelles off to all warship in time of peace. This was the end of Russian hegemony dictated at Ukiar-Iskelesi and the sanctioning of a new balance of power in the Middle East with Russia up to the Black Sea and Britain in the eastern Mediterranean. As for the "sick man" he was to emerge further weakened from this crisis since one of its richest provinces, Egypt, was separating itself from the Empire.

The Danubian Principalities Under Russian Protectorate, 1812–1847

The natural openness of the Phanariot world had favoured the spread of "new ideas" from Europe into the Danubian provinces, while the power struggles at the end of the 18th century had placed them in the orbit of the European Great Powers. This double influence would result in the creation of a nationalist movement and within half a century, the problem of a united Romanian state.

It was while living in the Phanariot Hospodar Alexander Moruzi's entourage that Rhigas the Greek first heard of the French Philosophes and became an ardent admirer of the French Revolution. It was fashionable for the young nobles of Bucharest to see themselves as disciples of Voltaire, Rousseau and Mirabeau even though many had never in fact read any of them. Of more impact was the role of the "Courrier de Moldavie," a bulletin published in French after 1790 by the Russian Army of occupation that mostly mirrored the views and positions of the more moderate French revolutionaries; in fact Russian liberalism was to be experienced in the Principalities right up to the 1840's. It was in this atmosphere that John Cantacuzino set out his plan for a Aristocratic Democratic Republic at Jassy which owed much to French ideas and English political practice. In 1796 the Directoire sent a consul to Bucharest to counterbalance the Russian and Austrian representatives, but also to spread the great principles of 1789. Napoleon was in turn interested in the Principalities due to their strategic position and sent Captain Aubert on a mission of information and who was to come back having written the "Notions statistiques sur la Moldavie et la Valachie." In response to this show of interest by the French Emperor, in October 1807 the Moldavian Boyars sent him a petition asking for his support in ending the Phanariot regime and the creation of an independent republic. Even though similar memoranda were sent to the Austrian and Russian Emperors this action was a further step on the path of national consciousness; the idea of the "Grand Nation" was to be even more attractive for the next generation.

In the near future the influence of Russia was dominant. Since the peace of Kutchuk-Kainardji in 1774 the Boyars had used the "right of grievance" which the Tsar had acquired against the Porte. In 1791 the boyars of Wallachia had asked for the appointment of local princes, the abolition of Ottoman monopoly over cattle trading and the return of the Turkish Raias—the military areas of Braila, Giurgiu and Turnu in Wallachia and Akkerman and Binder in Moldavia. In 1802 the hospodar of Wallachia Constantin Ypsilanti, who had a vision of a "Kingdom of Dacia" combining the two principalities, tried to organize an army, which was an idea of Catherine II and the Porte quickly tried to change this excessively Russophile hospodar. This was the pretext for a renewal of hostilities between Saint Petersburg and Istanbul in 1806. Constantin Ypsilanti once more on the throne of Wallachia, supported by the Tsar's armies, in turn became the supporter of the Karageorge Serbians and the pre-Hetairist Greeks but encountered the opposition of conservative Romanian Boyars. Even so he left the task of leading the Greek revolt to his two sons Alexander and Dimitrios.

Circumstances were so propitious in the Principalities that Philiki Hetairia contemplated launching a widespread uprising of Christian in the Balkans from these territories. Also because of its geographical position it was possible for the Tsar's armies to intervene immediately. All that was needed were some allies. The Principalities were at the time experiencing peasant discontent. Of course in Wallachia and Moldavia individual serfdom had been abolished since the edicts of Constantin Mavrocordat in 1746 and 1749, however even though they were free most peasants still remained dependent on the landowners: the boyars and the monasteries. To use their family plots they still had to pay corvee—claca—usually fixed at 12 days together with a tithe on all the produce from cultivated land as well as the monopolies of the master and above all alcohol. Corvee was usually paid in money for, in contrast to Poland or Russia, the lords reserve was quite small; the boyars gained most of their income from the tithe and could sell quite a lot. In the Ottoman Empire's trading system, the Principalities were to provide the palace and capital with livestock which gave the Boyars profits on wheat, but as of 1783 following the loss to Russia of the Khanate of the Crimea, the granary of the Empire, the Sultan was forced to turn to the Romanian areas. The demand for wheat grew so landowners tried raising the tithe on enclosed land and extending this to pastures and woodland that the peasant communities had traditionally used, yet they did not increase size of the reserve as certain historians have suggested for this was not really very profitable. The extension of this capitalist sector based on production and destined for export, lead to a heightening of tension in the countryside, in particular in Oltenia where the shared border had exposed it for decades to the exploits of Pasha Pasvanoglu of Vidin the rebel, and following his death, to the Ottoman Kirdzhali who often cross the Danube to embark on pillaging raids. Furthermore the area had experienced Austrian occupation between 1719 and 1739, in other words a European order whose negative aspects had over the years been forgotten and which contrasted sharply with the continuing decline of the Sultan's system of government.

There emerged someone able to be a catalyst for unrest in the region: Tudor Vladimirescu (1780–1821). Born about 1780 in the village of Vladimir in the Gorj district, the son of a minor Boyar or of rich free peasant, he had a certain degree of education. Around 1800 he joined the Panduri who were free peasants made up into militias and organized by the villages to defend them from Pasvanoglu's gangs. He also took part in the Turkish Russian War of 1806 on the Russian side and had contact with the Serbian leaders amongst Karageorge's entourage. By 1812, ennobled with the honorific title of "Sluger"[6], he was at the head of a district of Oltenia. He also was involved in cattletrading and his business activities took him to Transylvania, Budapest and Vienna. During the Congress of 1814–15 he stayed in the Austrian capital and made contact with the Tsar's Phanariot entourage and became acquainted with the Hetairia movement. When Alexander Ypsilanti made plans to stage an uprising of the Principality he approached Tudor who, even though he was not a member of Hetairia, agreed to cooperate. While Ypsilanti's Odessa army invaded Moldavia, Vladimirescu was supposed to come from Oltenia and capture Bucharest where the two allies would meet. In January 1821 the Wallachian Hospodar Alexander Sutu died and was replaced by a "Governing Committee" made up of Boyars, supporters of traditional reform ie. local princes, abolition of Ottoman trading monopolies etc. Tudor who was part of this "coup d'état," was rewarded with Oltenia where he found serious unrest in the countryside. On the 23 January at Pades in the Oltenian mountains, he delivered a "Proclamation" in which he denounced "Tyrannical Boyars," however promising any of the nobility who joined the rebels immunity. He entrusted power to the "People's Assembly" made up of Pandurs and peasants assembled around Tudor, which was supposed to represent the people of Wallachia. On the basis of these vague promises thousands upon thousands of peasants rallied to him and their often limited demands made Vladimirescu right the injustice, relieving local authorities of power and threatening landowners and monasteries. Many boyars fled from these gangs who would burn their

Kule[7] and threatened them with death. From out of this rabble the Sluger assembled a Pandur army of 8,000 men with which he marched on Bucharest yet assuring the Russian Consul General and the Porte's envoy that the movement was only directed against "bad" Boyars. On the 21 March Tudor entered the Wallachian capital from which the majority of its inhabitants had fled, even though a proclamation had been made which was meant to reassure them.

At the same time Alexander Ypsilanti, the official leader of the Philiki Hetairia, arrived in Moldavia on the 22 February accompanied by George Cantacuzenos—Colonel in the Russian army—and about twenty other Hetairists. With the agreement of Michael Sutu, who had rallied to Hetairia's cause, Ypsilanti issued a proclamation to all Christian subjects of the Ottoman Empire, to rise up in revolt. It also suggested that if the Turks reacted then a "Great Power" would confront them, obviously referring to Russia. There was no reaction from the Romanians of Moldavia who hated the Greeks. The Hetairists were forced to form an army from the region's Greeks, Bulgarians and Serbians. Lightly armed, these indisciplined troops massacred the Ottomans of Jassy and Galati and also a few hundred merchants, as well as some Jews. There was panic among the Moldavian boyars who together with their families evacuated the capital. In Istanbul the memory of these massacres was to be remembered for a long time. The army advanced into Wallachia at Focsani at the same time as Hetairia received some bad news: George Cantacuzenos, dispatched to Laybach where the sovereigns of the Holy Alliance were having a meeting was not even given audience by the Tsar who dismissed the venture out of hand. This was the end of any hope of Russian intervention and the end of their supposed alliance: the departure of the Russian consul general from Bucharest plainly showed this and was to create confusion among the various allies. Ypsilanti's army then arrived at the gates of the capital however the Oltenians dissuaded them from entering the city. The two leaders met on the 8 April—it was a stormy meeting. Vladimirescu reproached the Hetairists for having promised the support of the Russian army and so exposing the Principalities' inhabitants to harsh reprisals. Ypsilanti in turn tried to place this action within context of a wide Hetairia plan and urgently requested that they give support to the uprising which had just started in the Peloponnese. There was no possible agreement between such widely differing objectives and fearing conflict between the two armies they split Wallachia into two zones: to the north Ypsilanti's with his headquarters at Tirgoviste and in the south Vladimirescu's with its centre on the edge of the capital at Cotroceni.

To avoid Ottoman intervention Vladimirescu made contact with the Danubian ashas but to no avail. On the 1 May the Sultan's troops crossed the river. Two weeks later the Sluger, together with the People's Assembly and his army, evacuated Bucharest and withdrew to Oltenia. Ypsilanti, afraid, accused Vladimirescu of treason because of his negotiations with the Ottomans, had him arrested and tried in Tirgoviste by a Hetairia court. In the end he was tortured and put to death by two Greek officers during the night of 27 May 1821: his body was thrown into a well and was never found. His army melted away after a few small skirmishes with the Ottomans; as for the Hetairia they were beaten by the Sultan's troops at Dragasani and Ypsilanti fled to Austria. By July 1821 Mahmud's army had finally crushed the movement and reoccupied the two principalities. The main reason for the failure of this uprising was the ambiguity of its objectives since Hetairia had seen it as a regional events within a general uprising of the Ottoman Empire's Christians, while Vladimirescu had attempted to reform the system of the principality and had been forced by a peasant uprising to stage a rebellion whose objective had been unclear. From his own speeches and attitude, it is feasible that influenced by the example of Karageorge with whom he had had links, Tudor Vladimirescu might have wanted to become the prince—Domnul—of a Romanian or Wallachian Principality, or in other words joining both vasal states together. With this in mind terms 1821 was to be a setback for the Romanian people.

Yet the movement did have some important consequences: it marked the end of the Phanariot period and historians see this as the start of modern Romanian history. The boyars negotiated with Istanbul. For 16 months the continued to occupy the two principalities but due to pressure from the Tsar they obtained the exclusion of Greeks from ecclesiastical and secular posts and the restoration of local princes. This was the first victory of nationalist policy. The supporters of reform in Moldavia demanded more: the lifelong election of the prince, the creation of an army and the exclusive use of Romanian in legislation. The Russians taking advantage of Ottoman problems in Greece, and of the crisis which resulted from the abolition of the Janissaries, demanded the immediate evacuation of the Principalities by the Sultan's troops and complete compliance with the 1812 Treaty of Bucharest which was reiterated in the Convention of Akkerman in 1826. This provided for the boyars meeting as a Divan and electing a Prince for 7 years (except if both the Tsar and the Sultan were to disagree with their choice), the elaboration of a statute governing the boyars, the regulation of their administrative powers, the end of Istanbul's commercial monopolies and finally the deferment of payment of the tribute for two years in compensation for the occupation. The Convention in effect established a Russo-Ottoman condominion over the two principalities which were beginning to develop modern constitutional systems. The condominion only lasted for a short while: the battle of Navarino in October 1827 renewed hostilities between Russia and the Ottoman Empire. Once again Moldavia and Wallachia were used as a battleground and were completely occupied by the Tsar's army; in December 1828 Nicholas I set up a Russian military government. Hostilities ended with the Treaty of Adrianopolis in September 1829 which dealt with the Principalities specifically. The Porte gave back the three Raias on the left bank of the Danube (the territories of Braila, Turnu and Giurgiu) to Wallachia, so restoring the border along the river; administrative autonomy over what was left of the Empire's Elayets was agreed with the election of princes for life, freedom of trade for all goods, freedom of navigation on the Danube, limitations of the right of the Porte to intervene and continuation of the Russian occupation until reparations for war damage had been paid. Wallachia and Moldavia passed from a Russo-Ottoman condominion to a Russian protectorate. The occupation by Nicholas' army lasted till March 1834 and marked an important stage for Moldavia and Wallachia. Even though he was an autocrat, the Tsar wanted to modernize his Empire and hoped to have trial runs in the Principalities. He gave General Count P. Kisseleff, the head of the military government, carte blanche, and the general not only managed to repair the damage caused by the war but overcame a cholera epidemic, reorganized government, the political organization and even social life within the Principalities. This was the result of two ad hoc councils—Divans—with four boyars on each, under the presidency of the Consul General of Russia worked out the "Organic Regulations" which were completed in March 1830.

These were almost constitutions, an expression much in favour during the 1830s and which Nicholas had wanted to avoid due to its liberal associations. They were approved first by the sovereigns of Saint Petersburg and Istanbul and then by the Extraordinary General Assemblies of Wallachia and Moldavia, and were to come into effect in July 1831 and January 1832 respectively. The regulations organized the Principalities into two states with identical institutions and introduced the modern principle of "separation of power." The prince was to be appointed for life by the extraordinary general assembly (formed with boyars, members of the high church and a few merchants) and would govern with a six ministry council (Interior, Finance, Justice, Religious matters, War and Secretary of State). Legislative power was the province of the General Assembly, with 42 members in Wallachia and 35 in Moldavia, presided over by the Metropolitan; it would pass the budget but was not allowed to depose the Prince. In terms of administrative machinery the two countries were divided up into departments with a prefect at the head.

In terms of society in general the "master of the land" was now referred to as the owner, for the first time in a Romanian legal document, and was allowed to divide up the land: he had exclusive right over a third while the other two thirds were reserved for peasant tenants in return for 12 corvee days per year. As before, corvee days could be converted into money. The regulations can be seen as the introduction of a capitalist economy into the countryside with the immediate consequence of large scale land clearance and the extension of wheat production considered more profitable since it was geared for export. Yet in the end it resulted in the seizure of the best and richest land by the most affluent sections of society and above all by the boyars who began to build up estates with extensive land-stock thus changing into large landowners with all the social tensions that this entailed. As with the July monarchy in France, these documents confirmed the supremacy of the wealthy over the Prince, but also over the majority of the people. Finally on a national level both Principalities were linked together by being given similar regimes thus advancing the idea of a possible union.

In January 1834 the Porte recognized the "Organic Regulations" and agreed to choose together with the Russians the first two "ruling Princes"—their new title. They were A. D. Ghica (1834–1842) in Wallachia and Mihail Sturdza (1834–1849) in Moldavia who both tried to modernize their countries by programmes of road building, opening schools and setting up postal services.

They were in fact kept under strict scrutiny by the Russian Consul General in Bucharest and Jassy but were supported by boyar clans who were Russophiles and only opposed by those who looked to France or England for support.

The Romanian Nationalist Movement and the Crimean War: United Romania, 1847–1859

The modernization of society and state, together with the fact of being a foreign protectorate (Russian), resulted in a rapid development of nationalist consciousness with an aim to a united Romania. This developed among minor boyars, victims of the capitalizing of the countryside and among the small layer of bourgeois which had been built up with the establishment of free trade. Both groups had had the habit of sending their sons to study in the west, especially in France. Therefore between 1835 and 1846 C. A. Rosetti, Nicolae Kretzulescu, Alexandru Ioan Cuza the future prince, Nicolae Balcescu were sent to Paris and together with the great boyar Ion Ghica, formed a "Revolutionary Romanian Circle," often called the "Circle of the College of France," around Lamartine, Michelet and Edgar Quinet. They dreamed of a unified country of Moldavia and Wallachia, independent of Russia as well as the Ottoman Empire, with a constitutional government similar to that of France and the July Monarchy. Their political romanticism went hand in hand with an absolute ignorance of the Romanian people, especially those in the countryside. Their ideas however were echoed by urban groupings and around 1838 several secret societies were founded in Moldavia and Wallachia such as "Fratia" (Fraternity) in Bucharest which formulated the basic ideology of 1848. At the same time there was a cultural revival. On top of the first newspapers published in 1829 under the watchful eyes of the Russians in 1837 the Bucharest daily "Romania" was started, its very name showing its position, and in 1840 the "Literary Dacia" was published by Kogalniceanu in Jassy which, as well as being strongly involved in patriotic theatre, was to make the Moldavian capital a second centre for Romanian nationalism.

The Paris revolution of February 1848 sent shock-waves as far as the Principalities, above all since several members of the Romanian circle who took part in it: Balcescu even tore a strip of velvet from Louis Philippe's throne. There was unrest in Moldavia when on the 27 March A.I. Cuza, M. Kogalniceanu and a few other old "Parisians" had a petition to Prince M. Sturdza read out and approved by several thousand people in Jassy. It demanded individual freedom, a government answerable to the Assembly, the organization of a militia, the setting up of a national bank and the end of censorship, all measures copied from the French model. However nothing was said about the fate of the peasants nor of union with Wallachia. All that was asked for was a reform of the Organic Regulations which were mentioned so as not to disturb the Russian and Ottoman protectors. The Prince however reacted vigorously: many of the protestors were arrested and 13 of the leaders, among them I. A. Cuza who was sent to exile in Turkey. However 6 escaped and made their way to Austria. The unrest lasted 3 days.

In Wallachia it was more like a revolution. This was because of Balcescu, Bratianu and Rosetti who had just returned from Paris and were joined by some liberal boyars. They formed in Bucharest a "Revolutionary Committee" which adopted a programme similar to that of the Moldavians but also demanding the abolition of peasant corvee work and the redistribution of land to those in need. The start of the revolution was fixed for the 9 June and on that day an assembly was called at Islaz[8] on the Danube. In front of a large crowd a programme was read out. Known as the "Proclamation of Islaz" which on top of the previous demands, called for the abolition of the foreign protectorate, the election of the Prince by an assembly representing the whole of the population and the emancipation of Jews and Gipsies. Immediately a provisional government was formed and the next day unrest reached the capital. Prince G. Bibescu agreed to the terms of the Proclamation, accepted the creation of a government to include some of the leaders of the movement: Balcescu, Rosetti and Golescu, and then abdicated and left for Austria. On the 14 June the two governments at Islaz and Bucharest fused together under the presidency of the Metropolitan of Neofit. There was continued unrest in the capital. A large square was renamed the Field of Liberty and people were allowed to meet and applaud the measures taken by the government: adoption of the three coloured blue-yellow-red flag, the abolition of noble titles, creation of a national guard and the abolition of the death penalty. The French example was clear, yet soon there emerged conservatives and liberals who were opposed to the emancipation of the peasants and the ownership of land. Some argued for union of the two

Principalities and issued a proclamation "to our Moldavian brothers." During this time the Russians and Ottomans were getting ready to intervene. The Sultan's army was ready to cross the Danube on the 13 July and in a speech on the 19 July the Tsar condemned the revolutionary disturbances and reaffirmed his opposition to union. In the face of this threat the leaders began to argue among themselves. Finally a commission of three members was selected to negotiate with the Porte, yet Fuad Effendi's army had been advancing quickly and entered the capital on the 13 September after only slight resistance. Two days later Nicholas' troops crossed the border of Wallachia. The revolutionaries took the road to exile.

The occupying powers were keen to restore a constitutional order and this was the aim of the Convention of Balta Liman near Istanbul. This altered in a reductive manner, the "Organic Regulations." The nomination of the princes for a period of seven years was to be the prerogative of the two powers, the General Assemblies were to be replaced by "ad hoc divans" whose members would be nominated by the Princes. The Sultan and the Tsar agreed on Barbu Dimitrie Stirbei in Wallachia and Grigore Alexandru Ghica in Moldavia. These were the last Hospodars. Under the watchful eye of their protectors they embarked on a policy of social reaction and among other things the Agrarian Laws of 1851 which made relations between landowner and peasant much more difficult.

The failure of the revolutions of 1848 was due to the cooperation of Russia and the Ottoman Empire and an end this cooperation could only improve chances for the Romanian patriots. Those exiles in Paris clearly understood this and tried to make Napoleon III, who called himself the champion of the small nations, interested in their cause.

The second eastern crisis, the Crimean War from 1853 to 1856, was for the revolutionaries a dream come true although the Romanian question was never to be a central question. Despite Nicholas I's every effort the Anglo-Russian positions on the "sick man" remained irreconcilable. Free Trade Britain had greatly increased its trade with the Ottoman Empire which in 25 years had quadrupled and was more keen than ever on its continued existence. Russia on the other hand had tried to capitalized on the discontent of the Sultan's Christian subjects over the almost total absence of reform since 1845. Also Nicholas I felt that Abdul

Medjid had undermined his position by receiving Polish refugees in 1831 and Hungarian refugees in 1849. A further point of contention arose over the Holy Places in Palestine, further complicated by French intervention. Emperor Napoleon II had needed the support of the Pope and therefore put himself forward as the champion of Catholicism in this area of the Ottoman Empire where there had always existed a tension between the Latin and Greek Orthodox clergy. Tough negotiations were held in Istanbul in January 1853 where the Russian envoy Menshikov showed himself to be intractable. London sent the navy to the Dardanelles where it later met up with French warships. In June 1853 once again the Tsar ordered his troops to invade Moldavia. The Porte protested and the people of Istanbul showed their desire for war while over the following three months the Great Powers—England, France. Austria and Prussia—tried to find a compromise. On the 4 October 1853 in the face of the Russian refusal to evacuate Moldavia, the Sultan declared war on the Tsar and skirmishes took place along the Danube. More disturbing was the destruction on the 30 November 1853 of the Ottoman fleet by a Russian squadron in front of the port of Sinope. After the failure of further attempts by the European Powers meeting in Vienna, at mediation, France, England and Turkey signed an alliance demanding the evacuation of the Principalities before a certain date. If not then they would be at war with Russia. Austria however only promised cooperation. In April 1854 the Tsar's troops began to withdraw to their borders and the Austrians replaced them in Romanian territory. However, since March, France and England were at war with Russia. Franco-English troops based at Gallipoli were preparing to land north of the Danube, but the Russian withdrawal forced them to aim further north. In September 1854 military operations began in the Crimea and, following the battle of Alma, the bloody seige of Sebastopol began which was to last a year.

In the meantime princes Ghica and Stirbei, who at the arrival of Russian troops had fled to Austria, returned to their capitals after the intervention of Francis-Joseph's troops in September 1854. They were now more open to Romanian nationalist demands. The Patriots produced a unionist paper at Jassy called the "Star of the Danube" under the management of M. Kogalniceanu. He was later sent to Belgium to mobilize western public opinion. At the same time as military operations were under way, difficult negotiations were also under way which resulted in the Treaty of Paris on the

30 March 1856. This reaffirmed Ottoman territorial integrity guaranteed by the European Powers, made the Black Sea neutral and opened it up to all commercial shipping, made the Danube and its delta an international waterway and forced the Sultan to institute reforms promised since 1839. As far as the Principalities were concerned the treaty ended the Russian protectorate although it maintained Ottoman suzerainty with guarantee of the European Powers: it returned to Moldavia the southern part of Bessarabia which had been annexed in 1812 (Bolgrad, Cahul and Ismail) and, as far as internal affairs were concerned, entrusted the reform of the "Organic Regulations" to a number of ad hoc Divans.

The Eastern crisis was about to end with a measure of success for the Romanian patriots: Moldavia and Wallachia continued to be separate despite the support for "union" of the French Minister of Foreign Affairs, Count Walewski. In July 1856 the Princes resigned and were replaced by regents—Caimacans—appointed by the Porte to prepare for the election of the ad hoc Divans. These took place in July 1857 in Moldavia although the results were contested. France together with Russia, Prussia and Sardinia protested to the Porte, who had the support of London. A meeting between Queen Victoria and Napoleon at Osborn was held in August 1857 to avoid a further international crisis. Istanbul gave in and new elections were held. The result in Moldavia was a large majority in favour of union. In September Wallachia in turn voted and the unionists won.

The two "ad hoc divans" worked from September till December 1857. In Moldavia Kogalniceanu straightaway drew up a outline for the uniting of the two Principalities into a single country called Romania. A prince from a European royal family would be placed on the throne; the new state, a constitutional monarchy based on a representative system and guaranteed by the seven signatories of the Treaty of Paris. The project was agreed by six votes to two. In Bucharest Constantine Kretzulescu put forward an identical project which was unanimously approved. These were moves contrary to the terms of the treaty and the Porte could have obstructed them. Napoleon III took charge and called a conference in Paris of the representatives of the Seven Powers in May 1858. The discussions were difficult but ended with a Convention on the 7 August 1858 which gave the Principalities a new status. From then onwards they would be known as the "United Principalities of Moldavia and Wallachia," each having a local Prince, a government and elected assembly, yet with the same court of justice. The Porte remained suzerain and would have to agree on the appointment of the Prince. Once again disappointed the patriots multiplied their efforts only sending to the two assemblies supporters of union. On the 5 January 1859 the Moldavian Assembly unanimously elected Colonel Alexander Ion Cuza to the throne, and on the 24 January the Wallachian Assembly unanimously asked the same A. I. Cuza to be their prince. A de facto union had been achieved.

All that remained was for it be agreed by the Great Powers. Napoleon III once more offered to mediate and a further conference, held in Paris in April 1859, gained the approval of France, England, Prussia and Sardinia; Austria also agreed in June following its defeat in Italy, yet it was only in September 1859 that the Porte finally gave its approval.

The second crisis in the Orient therefore was over. The result the birth of a new Christian state in the Balkans, a consequence of the union of two of the Sultan's vasal Principalities into "Romania."

Notes

1. Hatti-Humayun: Noble Writ.
2. The investiture of the sword Taklidi Seyf involved girding the sword of Osman in the Eyeub mosque. The ceremony was normally held five days after the accession of the Sultan.
3. Outside the Topkapi Palace in what is now the garden of the Museum of Antiquities.
4. A strict reformist movement which was founded by Abdel Wahab in the 18th century and adopted by the Saud dynasty of Arabia.
5. Now Gaziantep on the Turkish Syrian border.
6. First mentioned in Wallachia in 1480 the Sluger was in charge of the supply of meat to the Prince's court.
7. In Turkish Kula: tower. The Romanians called the large Boyar houses "cule." In Albania the kula is still used to denote a traditional house which is set high up in the mountains.
8. Next to Turgu Magurele.

12

The New Christian States and the Third Eastern Crisis, 1833–1878

Devising the new legal structures of the two new Christian countries was by 1833 completed: on the 25 January[1] young King Otto of Bavaria arrived in Greece and on the 4 December Milos Obrenovic received the Hatti Sheriff confirming the size of Serbia's tribute and recognizing its borders. The two princes were confronted with a similar task: to transform two former provinces of the Ottoman Empire into states; independent in the case of Greece, autonomous for Serbia but as the Serbs said at the time "Baptized and regulated" or in other words under Christian laws. This was the beginning of a new order in the Balkans.

Greece Under King Othon, 1833–1862

Hemmed in to the north by a frontier which went from the gulf of Arta to the gulf of Velos, independent Greece was made up of the Peloponnese, Livadia including all the territories north of the Gulf of Corinth and the Eubean and Cyclade isles: in all 35,000 square miles—a tenth of the size of France. Its population had gone down a lot during the war. The "Turks" had been massacred or had fled so there were no longer any Muslims in the kingdom. On the Greek side there had also been many killed, in the order of 200,000 leaving a total of about 800,000, an average of 22 to the square mile which was less than Serbia. This population was not the sum total of all Greeks for it is estimated that there was at least twice as many Greeks living in the Ottoman provinces of the Balkans, in Asia Minor or in the English Ionian Islands. Istanbul still remained the largest Greek city with more than 100,000 but was closely followed by Adrianopolis.

Greece in 1833 has been described as a "Rump State" unable to act as the pole of attraction that nationalists had hoped for. For the Phanariots of the diaspora this small impoverished state was not exactly seductive, nor for merchants used to western life and culture; as for the Greeks of Istanbul they felt it was to blame for the loss of certain economic and social roles (such as dragomans) and for ordinary everyday discrimination, a lasting phenomenon following the anti-Greek riots of 1821\22. On a more basic level peasants had for many years emigrated to neighbouring regions such as Thessaly and Macedonia which were still under Ottoman rule but had been spared the fighting. Even in 1850, A. Ubicini, a traveller, writes that the Greek villages in Turkey looked more prosperous than those in Greece. Disappointment and reversal gave rise to the "Grand Idea"—Megale Idea—mixing memories of Classical antiquity and dreams of the Byzantine Empire, which became for almost a hundred years the sole programme for political expansion and development.

The sovereign who landed at Nauplia was eighteen years old. Back at home in the Wittelsbach House he had known the romantic atmosphere of the Grecophiles of Bavaria but was totally ignorant of the reality of Greece. His father had selected a council of regents for him presided over by Count Joseph von Armansperg (1787–1853), a lawyer who had been Minister of the Interior of Bavaria and then of Foreign Affairs and had a reputation for being a liberal. As well as the three regents there were Bavarian administrators destined to be heads of government and 3,500 German and Swiss mercenaries. Adapting this alien framework to the Greek people was to prove very difficult especially since certain things had become accepted practice during the war and were not appropriate in peacetime. Since the assassination of Capo d'Istria in September 1831 there had been three National Assemblies in quick succession which had resulted in outbreaks of violence between rival armed groups. The countryside was crawling with "Bandits," often the term used for representatives of the new regime. Dragumis, the former secretary of the assassinated president, was to end his dramatic description of the situation in 1832 with the following words: "there was once more arbitrary rule and abominable anarchy taking over the new Greece." Everything was to be rebuilt or built: the constitutional order, the administration, the army, the Church and the economy. The Bavarians reacted as politicians used to European criteria: in order to govern properly money and order were necessary. These two priorities dominated the first thirty months of the council of regents' administration.

The coffers were empty and the soldiers' and administrators' salaries remained unpaid. They turned to the European Powers for support. This however made them arbiters of the political structures. The traditional client groups of noble families began to develop into political parties and were known as the Russian, French or English parties. To their own personal aims and ambitions the leaders would add a foreign policy dimension to attract support: each tutelary Great Power would be put forward as the best able to accomplish the Megale Idea. The Russian party claimed to follow in the steps of Capo d'Istria and had as its leader Theodor Kolokotronis, the strong man of the Peloponnese; he emphasized the religious fraternity of the Russian Empire and would stress that the Tsar's policy up to the Treaty of Adrianopolis had been fundamentally hostile to the Ottoman Empire. The French party had its support in Livadia where its leader John Kolettis, former doctor to Ali of Janina, had his power base; he would hark back to the French Revolution and expressed great admiration for Napoleon. He was a real demagogue and proved to be particularly mercenary. The English party was the last to be formed for Great Britain had always stood by the territorial integrity of the Ottoman Empire; nevertheless Canning managed to attract Alexander Mavrocordatos from a powerful Phanariot family from Istanbul; an educated and ambitious man he envisaged the introduction of the English model of government to make Greece into a modern state. Through these parties the three Great Powers intervened unashamedly in the internal affairs of the country and their respective ambassadors made and unmade governments from the 1840s onwards. Thus right from the start the political system was being constructed on rather shaky foundations.

To restore order to the country and fight against bandits the authorities needed an army and a police force. Edmond About in his "Roi des Montagnes" caricatures these brigand gangs which were generally made up of old soldiers from the independence struggle or peasants ruined by war. The regency first decreed a blanket amnesty going back to 1821 which was followed up by a very harsh criminal justice act for further criminal acts. The old regular and irregular military units (about 6,000 men) were disbanded and replaced by ten battalions of Evzones, which absorbed some of the old soldiers, and together with the 3,500 Bavarians of Othon's guard constituted the new army. In 1835 there were 7,000 men altogether, including the police, with about half well paid mercenaries and alone absorbing half of the young state's budget. As for those who were forced to leave they most likely joined gangs of bandits which have left such a lasting impression on foreign travellers.

However the most urgent task was the restructuring of the administration. During the war of independence there had been attempts at setting up a hierarchy of provinces, cities and villages. Capo d'Istria had divided up the Peloponnese and the islands into Eparchies yet he made the mistake of giving these positions to Phanariots, or else Greeks from the islands, who had not been popular with those they governed. The Regency set up ten provinces—Nomos—subdivided into Eparchies and Demes with those in charge appointed by central government. The Minister of the Interior, which had been created by Capo d'Istria still continued to operate and was even expanded; a "Population Bureau" was formed which was very active and was headed by two Frenchmen: Alexander Roujoux and Gustave Eichtal, the latter being a former disciple of Saint-Simon. Yet the administration that was built up was out of touch with the ordinary Greek people, who during the whole of the Ottoman period had been used to living under their own nobility—the Tsakias—who also had almost always been hereditary holders of local office. Therefore the King's officials remained as remote from the ordinary citizen as the Beys in the past. Greek society itself remained organized around the family clan, with traditional codes of honour and vendettas. The clan would act as their political representative vis-a-vis the authorities. Right from the start the ability of the Greek state to influence society was limited and its shortcomings clearly apparent.

The regents also needed to tackle the problem of the Church which was complicated by their being of a different religion than their subjects'; the young King and von Armansperg being Catholics and the regent von Maurer Protestant. There had been since 1818 in Bavaria a concordat separating the Church from the State. The Greek Church had in fact been independent of the Patriarch of Constantinople since 1821, when the Porte had forced him to excommunicate the whole of the Greek hierarchy; yet during the war years the Church organization had been in chaos. L. von Maurer, son of a minister and a lawyer himself, drew up new regulations and submitted them to an assembly of bishops. The Greek Church was declared autocephalic and would be administered by a synod whose members were appointed by the king, notwithstanding the fact that he was a Catholic. Monasteries of less than six people were dissolved and their property confiscated by the state to help pay for the clergy and for educational purposes. Only 82 male and 3 female convents continued to operate. Further reforms encountered resistance from within the Greek Orthodox Church and the Ecumenical Patriarch refused to recognize Greek autocephalism; negotiations were held under the auspices of the Russian ambassador to Istanbul and resulted in 1850 in a Tomos of communion. This was entrenched in Greek law in 1852. Supreme authority was entrusted to the synod, presided over by the Archbishop of Athens, and not the king. The recovery of its own power against secular authority was to have important repercussions on social and political life in modern Greece.

In 1835 Othon was declared of age and transferred his capital to Athens. The following year he married Amelia of Oldenburg a Protestant who was well liked by the people but who failed to provide him with any children. The king's government, still advised by Bavarians who were referred to as Camarilla, was to retain its authoritarian character and fail to deliver the promised Constitution. The European Powers were above all eager to see the return of peace to a country which was also in the throws of a very severe economic crisis. Agriculture on which four-fifths of the population relied had been ruined by years of war: in some areas olive trees and vines had been systematically destroyed and elsewhere abandoned. As for trade it remained in the hands of the Greeks of the diaspora and was largely closed to those of the kingdom. Financial needs were however so urgent that in the countryside the Ottoman tithe paid in kind continued to be collected in the same way as before through "farmers," who were now Greek, but with the same scope for corruption which for centuries had been decried.

The situation became worse in 1840 because of the crisis in Europe. In 1842 despite the efforts of the Frenchman de Regny, appointed head of the exchequer, the royal government let it be known that it would not be able to continue paying the national debt. The Great Powers demanded savings, above all on the army, which reacted by staging the first of many coups d'état. On the 3 September 1843 the Athens military marched to the palace and forced the king to give power to Andrew Metaxas the leader of the Russian party and promise to form an assembly to draw up a Constitution. This assembly met from September 1843 to March 1844 and was made up of representatives not only from the kingdom but also from the "subjugated territories" of Thessaly, Epirus and Macedonia, hence the title "National Assembly" that Greek historians have given it. The ideas of Guizot and Robert Peel were to have an influence since J. Kolettis, ambassador to Paris, and A. Mavrocordatos, leader of the English party and appointed to Istanbul, were to be very influential in the Assembly. The two Powers were agreed that the king should retain a large amount of power, the right of veto and the right to appoint ministers. Guizot also wanted a Senate appointed by the sovereign yet appointed for life while parallel to this a House of Representatives elected by a large male franchise. The Constitution was proclaimed on the 18 March 1844 and inaugurated the constitutional period of Othon's reign, marked by violent disputes and ministerial instability, which was to become characteristic of Greek politics: there were fourteen Prime Ministers in eighteen years, the party leaders returning to power as if on a merry-go-round following elections marked by violence and scandals. The Greek historian A. Vacalopoulos paints the following portrait of John Kolettis, leader of the government from 1844 to 1847: he maintains he was rarely present at parliamentary debates but was always willing to meet the electorate who would queue up outside his home, near Hadrian's Gate, to consult him on personal matters or Rusfeti as it is called in plain language. He maintains that this terrible state of affairs was not unconnected with the neo-Greek tradition of Turkish domination—the Kodjabassides, Greek notables, who petitioned the Turkish authorities on behalf of ordinary Greeks; this was to continue well after the end of their rule and was a characteristic of national politics. Finally he points out that Kolettis was the first politician to acquire a fortune of 630,000 drachmas while in office.[2]

To distract public attention from this abuse of power Kolettis would raise the programme of Megale Idea and outline the territories that they should conquer: Thessaly, Epirus, Thrace, Macedonia, the Ionian Islands, Crete, the western coast of Anatolia, the islands off the coast and even Rumelia right up to the Balkan mountain range. So not only ethnic Greek areas but all the areas where Greek civilisation had once held sway in the past. This expansionist dream was the mainstay of Greek nationalism until 1922. This policy was the opposite of the traditional English position and in 1850 Palmerston did not hesitate to send a fleet to blockade Piraeus to protect the interests of a British citizen David Pacifico (who was also a racketeer). During the Crimean War Greek public opinion, stirred up by the King, was on the side of the Russians and armed gangs tried to provoke uprisings in Thessaly and Epirus. A Franco-British military landing at Piraeus was staged to force Othon in May 1854 to hand over the government to A. Mavrocordatos who once more calmed things down.

On the home front ever since independence, the most urgent problem had been that of "National Land" involving up to half of the population of Greece. This was Ottoman land—Ciftliks, Timars, Has and Vakifs—which had been abandoned by their owners who had either fled or been massacred. This amounted to almost a third of all the arable land of independent Greece and from the very beginning of the war had been the object of much argument: much had been occupied illegally by the peasants or seized by military leaders. Capo d'Istria had proclaimed it "National Land" but had encountered the resistance of the nobles. The Regency promulgated a law, known as the "Law of Endowment of Poor Families," which allowed former soldiers to settle the land. Yet its implementation was very slow and smacked of influence. In 1862 the State still owned 35% of the arable land and out of about 200,000 agricultural families barely 16% owned the land they cultivated. As well as the tithe which everybody had to pay, these tenant farmers were obliged to hand over 30% of their harvest to the owner. This was a rural society made up of very small holdings, some dependent on the state, others on absentee landlords and all subject to taxation. Extreme peasant poverty was to become a permanent feature of modern Greece.

In the area of education Othon opened a university in Athens in 1837 whose neo-classical architecture links it with that of the 5th century B.C. Yet many of the teachers were German, at least at first. This return to the ideal of Classical Greece sparked off a further dispute over the use of language. The Katharevusa of Korais was an inflexible in their use of the learned tongue that was very different from Demotic which was spoken by ordinary people and had made the poetry of Rhigas so popular.

Despite Othon's many efforts, thirty years on the throne did not made the people like him as a king and his pro-Austrian attitude during the War of Italian Unity further alienated him from his people. He also lacked an heir: the 1843 Constitution stipulated that his successor must be Orthodox yet all the king's brothers were Catholic. In October 1862, taking advantage of the royal couple's absence on a tour of the provinces, the garrisons of Nauplia and Athens staged an uprising, egged on by a triumvirate of politicians: Constantine Canaris, Demetrios Vulgaris and Venizelos Rufos, who forced the king and queen to leave Greece under threat of bloodshed. Othon returned to Bavaria but refused to abdicate[3] The three conspirators formed a council of regents and called a new National Assembly, while the European Powers who had approved and perhaps encouraged Othon's departure, tried to find another King. After three decades of independence the Greek state still seemed very weak, torn by political feuds and plagued by financial problems; a poor small country, only important in terms of its strategic position in the Mediterranean which was the prime concern of the European nations.

The Autonomous Principality of Serbia: Obrenovic and Karageorgevic, 1834–1868

After seventeen years of persistent warfare, backed up by some lavish Baksheesh, Serbia had become under Milos' leadership an autonomous political entity: the content was Serbian but the packaging was Turkish. The Kniaz resided at Kragujevac, dressed and lived like a Pasha, was surrounded by his family and heads of government treating them like servants, even on occasion having them flogged. Any thought of constitutional government was alien to him and the Assembly—Skupstina—which he called at various times to announce important decisions was nothing more than a meeting of the heads of the Nahijes and those in charge of the villages, who in any case were his appointees. Until 1833 Milos' Serbia had every characteristic of being the Kniaz' very own extended domain, patriarchally administered using traditional peasant hierarchies and without any codified laws.

In Vormarz Europe this was an anomaly and the 1830 Hatti Sheriff had made provisions for the prince to govern with a Council and an assembly. Milos did not take any notice of this therefore anyone unhappy with his rule: jealous nobles, administrators in disgrace, merchants ruined by the Prince's monopolies and of course the Karageorgevic family, would support the idea of a constitution—Ustav. A revolt in December 1834 made the Kniaz decide to act. His secretary Dimitrije Davidovic, a Hungarian Serb and an enlightened man, was entrusted with the task of drawing up a document based on the revised French Charter of 1830 and the Belgian Constitution of 1831. The outcome was ratified by a grand Skupstina of more than 4,000 people. The conservative governments of Saint Petersburg and Vienna however were preoccupied by the republican ideology which they saw was behind the project, while Istanbul was violently opposed to the foreign policy implications of having a Ministry of Foreign Affairs, which was also being put forward. Milos made use of this opposition and repealed the text three months after it was published and it became known as the Constitution of the Visitation—Sretenjski Ustav[4]. There was once more a period of authoritarian government by the Kniaz yet his rule was henceforth the object of European intrigue through their consuls who were to arrive in Belgrade between 1837 and 1839[5]. The Prince, more absolutist than ever, looked to Colonel Hodges, the representative of the English Liberal Lord Palmerston, for support, and those disaffected with his reign (foremost among them the Kniaz" own wife Princess Ljubica who was angry at her husband and his younger brother Jevrem's escapades) collected around Matternich's envoy . This was the embryo of the first Serbian political party: the Constitutionalists—Ustavobranitelji—whose leader was Thomas Vucic-Perisic. To neutralize them Milos published three reform texts which guaranteed individual freedom, freedom of trade, the end of the peasant corvee duty and a review of the tax system. In November 1837 a commission was appointed to draw up a Constitution yet it did not make much headway. Finally several proposals were unveiled and the Great Powers—Austria, Russia and Great Britain—decided to have them examined by their representatives in Istanbul. Advised by Hodges, Milos agreed to this and a final draft was discussed by the ambassador of Russia and the Porte's, newly created, Minister of Foreign Affairs: the Kniaz would share power with a seventeen member council—Savet— appointed for life, which would appoint and dismiss ministers; the Skupstina would be abolished despite the opposition of Milos who had hoped to be able to use the ordinary people's representatives against the nobles on the council. The people called this the

"Turkish Constitution" of December 1838[6] yet in fact it was a text which corresponded to Russian requirements similar to those expressed in the "Organic Regulations" of the Danubian Principalities: the balance of power between the Prince and an oligarchy, against the people. The constitution of the Council prompted a bitter struggle with the Kniaz and in vain he tried to make "his" peasants rise up in revolt. Isolated and disheartened Milos abdicated in favour of his son Milan on the 13 June 1839.

The years spent trying to get an Ustav were not wasted years for Serbia. The Kniaz succeeded in organizing an administrative machine with the help of former Hungarian Serbs. In 1839 there were 672 of these working in Serbia with 201 in the police force. Their model of course was the Habsburg bureaucracy. On the religious side he had laid the foundations of an independent Serbian Church using the 1830 Hatti Sheriff. A convention was signed with the Phanar authorities in January 1832 which gave the Kniaz and the people the right to choose a Metropolitan and the bishops, also making the Bishop of Belgrade the Metropolitan of all Serbia. This reduced the role of the ecumenical Patriarch to simply confirming the appointment. The Serbian Church therefore became a national church answerable to the Kniaz who elected his own secretary Pavle Jovanovic as the first Metropolitan. In 1833 he became Metropolitan Petar (1833–1859). One of the most difficult problems that the prince had to deal with was, as in Greece, what was he to do with the abandoned Turkish land. The main difference however was that in Serbia the unoccupied areas and forests were on a vast scale. Following the second uprising the peasants had seized the property of the Beys and the Spahis and felt they had full right over it, yet mostly properties without title deeds. The Hatti Sheriff of 1830 changed this situation from de facto ownership to legal ownership by abolishing the Spahiliks in return for compensation which was to be included in the tribute. In fact the tribute was set in 1833 and included the "income of the Timars, Ziamets and Mukatas." To pay it Milos retained the old tithe system which from then on was paid to the Prince's administration. This method, above all when it involved payment in kind, perpetuated traditional abuses of power and provoked much resentment. This was especially so when the 1817 Skupstina confirmed the Kniaz" hereditary title and hence the Kniaz as heir to the Sultan's privileges and consequently under Sharia law, owner of vacant land and forests. To increase the size of the population, and so the resources of the Principality, he implemented a policy of colonization which paid little attention to what traditionally had been considered to be communally owned land. He himself personally seized Ottoman land on which in 1832 he was to raise 150,000 pigs. He also retained the Ottoman system of corvee work to maintain the roads and bridges and even added work on the Sultan's land, which now of course was his own. From 1830 onwards Milos felt growing opposition from the nobility who wanted to become Boyars ie. large landowners similar to those in the Danubian Principalities, therefore so as to preempt their attempt he decided to win the support of the peasant masses who made up about 95% of the population. The agricultural laws of 1835 and 1836 confirmed the ownership of forests and pastures by village communities, thus guaranteeing the peasant a minimum level of agricultural production which was inalienable even if he was in debt. This measure stabilized the condition of the Serbian peasant and made them into a community of small-holders. The 1838 Ustav added a legal dimension to this situation recognizing full ownership of the land by the peasants. They thought this to be the work of Milos and right to the end remained his strongest supporters.

The illiterate Kniaz was wary of educated people, while at the same time recognizing their usefulness to the state organization. There was therefore an improvement in the education system but this was a very slow process. In 1815 there were only three private schools in the whole of the Pashalik. In 1839 when Milos abdicated there were 72 primary schools, three lycees with two levels, one with five levels at Kragujevac, also the Velika Skola in Belgrade which had become a "Licej" and the Metropolitan seminary. In all 3,000 students for a population of 800,000. Most of these were established in the 1830s and it was in 1832 that Milos appointed a Minister of Public Education. The Kniaz used the press for propaganda purposes. In the tradition of the princes he turned to a well known German historian Leopold Ranke to produce a booklet together with Vuk Karadzic on the "Serbian Revolution"[7]. But Milos also realized the usefulness of a periodical. A Serbian paper had since 1813 been published in Vienna called Srpske Novine which he transferred in 1834 to Belgrade into a newly installed printing press where an ordinary single page daily was produced which gave the Prince's point of view and a bit of foreign news. It is worth mentioning that in the same year the first theatre in Serbia was set up in Kragujevac.

All this did not amount to much and on a cultural level the centre of attraction for Serbs was still north of the Danube in Vienna or in Pest with the Matica Srpska in 1827 or in Neusatz (Novi Sad) with its Serbian Lycee. It is with "Hungarian Serbia" that Vuk Karadzic (1787–1864) is linked. Born on the border of the Pashalik, on the river Drina, Karadzic studied at the Velika Skola in Belgrade and was the Senate secretary to Karageorge. In 1813 he fled to Vienna where he married a Catholic German woman and was to remain most of his life, publish most of his works and where he died. He only made short journeys to Milos' Serbia and a long trip in 1830 to draw up a legal code which was never implemented. In 1832 he fell out with the Prince sending him a letter which denounced the arbitrary nature of his rule to which the Kniaz replied by not only denying him access to the Principality but also banning his works. Vuk's cultural and linguistic revolution was to take place outside the frontiers of Serbia.

The abdication of the Kniaz was followed by the protracted death (a month) of his eldest son Milan who had contracted tuberculosis. A regency was formed which ruled the country until the Porte recognized the youngest son Mihailo (Michael) (1829–1868) who was only 17 years old at the time. The Constitutionalists were on the ascendant with Toma Vucic-Perisic, Milos' most fervent opponent, together with young Ilija Garasanin, while the supporters of the Obrenovics rallied round the Kniaz" family. Here were two rival embryo political parties and their struggle was to last for most of the reign of the Prince who was totally out of his depth. A bid for power by Vucic-Perisic forced Mihailo to flee to Austria during the night of 25–26 August 1842. The hastily assembled Skupstina unanimously voted in Karageorge's son, who had been in exile since 1813 and was to become Prince Alexander Karadjordevic (1806–1885).

The change of dynasty only served to reinforce the power of the Council oligarchy whose rule was to characterize the history of Serbia until 1858. It was based on a centralized administrative machine which created a city bourgeoisie which generally came from Austria and whose ideas were coloured by the Habsburg system. The first need was therefore to give Serbia a codified legal system which had not existed under Milos. What emerged was the

1834 Civil Code which owed much to the Austrian Code and laid down the rules of ownership, providing a firm basis for capitalism to build on. Furthermore the reorganization of the criminal justice system in 1858 heralded the end of patriarchal laws. The second worry was to create a military force. The 1830 and 1838 Hatti Sheriffs proscribed this, but in 1845 a regular army of two battalions and six cannons was set up but solely for internal use. Progress in the field of education had been primarily motivated by the needs of the administrative machine. The number of schools quadrupled in 20 years and an embryo university developed around the Licej of Belgrade, while the first "Serbian Scientific Society," formed in 1849, was the precursor of the Academy of Sciences. The National Museum and the National Library were created in 1847. When one thinks that a public postal service was organized in 1843 and that a telegraph was transmitting from 1855 onwards, one must acknowledge that the Council oligarchy did go quite some way in trying to modernize Serbia. Yet between the Savet and the Prince there developed a struggle for power which was aggravated by the intrigues of Milos, exiled in Vienna and his supporters who were still active within Serbia. Furthermore after 1848, following the revolutions in Hungary and Austria, liberal pressure mounted for the restoration of a governing Skupstina. The slightly paradoxical alliance of supporters of the old Kniaz and liberal intellectuals that formed in Paris, forced the government to call a National Assembly, known as the Saint Andrew's Day Skupstina and ended with the flight of Alexander and the return of Milos.

Aged 78 it was said that he never forgot anything: his old opponent Vucic-Perisic was arrested and died in hospital in suspicious circumstances. He abolished the 1838 Constitution and dismantled the administrative hierarchy; with the support of the peasant masses his second reign was one of reaction against the bureaucratic system which had emerged. Twenty months later however, in September 1860 he died, having obtained from the Porte recognition of the hereditary title of Prince on behalf of his son.

Mihailo returned to power enriched by years of exile and travel and Serbian historians readily acknowledge him to have been the country's best prince up to 1914. His reign (1860–1868), coincided with the large nationalist movements of Europe: Italian unity, German unity and the Austro-Hungarian compromise, and was important especially in terms of Balkan history because of his foreign minister Ilija Garasanin (1812–1872) who was in office from 1862 to the end of 1865. On the home front there occurred an experiment in authoritarian monarchy which, as with Alexander, was to rely on a central administrative organization and the army, however without the restraining influence of the Council who following a law passed in 1861 had been transformed into a mere advisory body. The prince appointed his ministers who were directly responsible to him, and after 1862 they were organized into seven ministries in the modern sense of the word. A conscript army (1862 Law) was headed by a Minister of War and was in the hands of a Frenchman Lieutenant Colonel Hippolyte Mondain. In 1866 it had sixteen brigades and 14 artillery batteries: some 90,000 men for a population of 1,300,000 inhabitants which made it the largest army in the Balkans. It allowed Mihailo to achieve one of the dreams of his father: the evacuation of the "Turks" from Serbian territory. Since 1830 the Ottomans had retained garrisons in seven fortresses: the main ones being Belgrade, Sabac, Smederevo and Ulice and when he came back to power Milos once again demanded their departure. In June 1862 a young Serbian was killed near the fountain of Cukur in the Serbo-Ottoman quarter of Doreol in Belgrade by a soldier from the fortress. The population of the capital were outraged and Serbia and the Empire came within an inch of declaring war. The Great Powers intervened and following long negotiations the fortresses were evacuated in April 1867. The authoritarian rule of the prince was cloaked in a constitutional robe since the Skupstina met regularly however he encountered opposition from groups claiming to model themselves on western liberalism. There were two political parties: "conservatives" with Ilija Garasanin as their leader and who supported Mihailo, and the "liberals" who were often exiled and had at their disposal newspapers abroad. Furthermore there were of course conspiracies by the Karageorge family. One of these did in fact succeed and on the 29 May 1868 Prince Mihailo was hit by pistol shots in the Kosutnjak park near Belgrade.

Montenegro: From the Vladika to a Secular Prince, 1830–1860

Hidden in the mountains, Montenegro was a social and political curiosity in 19th century Europe. Since 1696 the Bishop—Vladika— of Cetinje had been chosen from among the Petrovic family from the village of Njegos and so the office was transmitted from uncle to nephew right up to 1918. Another family, the Radonjics had the less prestigious office of civil governor—Governador—however real power rested in the hands of the thirty or so leaders of the various tribes aided by their councils of wise men. It was they who would call men to arms, raise taxes and mete out justice based on ancient values and the rules of vendetta. Separated by "debts of blood" the tribes would only join forces to fight against their Bosnian and Albanian neighbours and especially against the Ottomans who maintained that the Montenegrin region was an integral part of the Sultan's Empire and would every so often send a military expedition to collect Harac. The borders of the country were not secure and raids on the territories of the Pashalik in the plains brought much needed resources to a land where starvation was endemic, notwithstanding the high level of emigration. Since 1702 there were no more Muslims in the highlands for on Christmas day all Turks, Albanian and renegade Serbians had been massacred during what was known as the "Montenegrin Vespers." At the start of the 19th century Montenegro had a population of 120,000 divided into 36 tribes and living in 240 villages. They had no outlet to the Adriatic for with the Treaty of Vienna, Austria had reoccupied the mouth of the Cattaro (Kotor) which had been fought over by the French and the Montenegrins during the Napoleonic period. Since Peter the Great the Vladika was a Russian protectorate and Russian subsidies made up more or less for the lack of a fixed income through taxation.

In 1782 Vladika Petar I, canonized after his death, began a 50 year reign which was to profoundly change the country. A meeting of the heads of the tribes in 1798 reached agreement on the coordination of administrative and defence matters through a body which was both the Vladika's council and a court of law, using a legal code—Zakonik—which was the first such law the country had known. Yet this success was not to last and throughout his reign he would have to fight to receive taxes and to keep down the number of bloody vendettas. It was only at the end of his life in 1830 that he was able to do away with the Radonjic family and abolish the office of Governador. From then onwards the Vladika was to become the sole ruler of Montenegro. In alliance with Russia and Austria in its struggle against the Ottoman Empire it did not get anything from the peace of Sistova in 1791 nor Jassy in 1792. In 1799 however in a further outbreak of fighting with the Sultan they managed to obtain a declaration in which it was confirmed that the Montenegrins had never been the Sublime Porte's subjects; this statement was later contested by Istanbul but was never forgotten by Cetinje. At the same time Petar almost doubled the territory of the Principality, incorporating the wooded slopes of Brda[8]. As the Tsar's ally they fought against the French in the Illyrian Provinces and were to occupy Cattaro. They were made to evacuate it in 1815 after Russia promised to give Montenegro an outlet to the sea, yet this only happened about 70 years later.

His nephew Petar II (1830–1851) was interested in poetry and was not at all interested in religion, yet he was swiftly made into a monk, consecrated bishop and became "Bishop-lord" of Montenegro for a period of 20 years. He was widely known by the name Njegos, author of the epic "The Garland of the Mountains" (1845) he was considered one of the greatest Serbian poets. He continued his uncle's efforts to transform the Principality into a unified state and on the advice of the Russians in 1831 organized a Senate with 12 members, who he managed to keep in their place unlike the Prince of Belgrade, although several times he did have to travel to Saint Petersburg to assert his authority over advisers whom the Tsar had sent and who became overbearing. He set up a printing-press in Cetinje, opened the first primary school in 1833, had a permanent guard, tried to establish a tax system and refrained from calling the Popular Assembly the "Zbor" which was supposed to make decisions on matters such as war and peace. Being denied access to the sea by Austrian territory he went in the direction of Scutari (Skoder) and in 1832 captured Zabijak on the lake. The last years of the poet warrior's reign were disturbed by revolts in the Brda region and by food riots. Petar II Njegos died of tuberculosis in 1851; he was the last Vladika Gospodar.

His nephew Danilo had been brought up in Saint Petersburg but, wanting to marry, did not wish to become a bishop. With the approval of Russia and Austria he separated the two positions into civil and religious, appointed the Vladika of Cetinje and proclaimed himself the Gospodar-Prince. He was Danilo II (1852–1860) The Porte complained at this constitutional change and Omer Pasha the governing Pasha of Bosnia was entrusted with restoring the old order. But the Gospodar appealed to Vienna which based its case on the 1799 Ottoman statement and this was the end of the crisis. Danilo quickly attempted to build up a military organization: soldiers were registered and equipped by the Prince even though the tribe still remained the basic unit. In 1855 he introduced a civil code of law which had as a basic tenet equality in law and the protection of private property; both principles operated against the tribal set-up and were to encounter some stiff resistance. During the Crimean War he was urged by Vienna to refrain from supporting Russia. At the Treaty of Paris in 1856 the Porte tried to have Montenegro recognized as an integral part of the Ottoman Empire and Danilo turned to Napoleon III to reaffirm the independence of the Principality, to request the exact delimitation of the borders and demand the annexation of the port of Bar. None of these issues had been settled by the time Danilo was assassinated by a Montenegrin outlaw at Cattaro in August 1860.

The Prodomes of the Third Balkan Crisis, 1840–1868

With the steady development of Christian countries in the Balkans there was a growing need at the same time to define their aspirations. At a time of nascent and assertive nationalism this could not fail to be other than national, aiming at the political, economic and cultural development of this such defined group. Two models were predominant: the Jacobin model which married State and Nation into one sole organization and needed a homogenous group within common borders, and the romantic German model which emphasised language and culture over frontiers and territory. Yet the great obstacle to the Christian countries was still the Ottoman "yoke" which continued to be felt in many parts of the Balkans and was a powerful stimulus to the wish for freedom. Also in some Balkan regions there was still remained alive the 18th century hope of emancipation under the protection of Russia, which in the meantime had changed from the idea of a Holy Alliance to the concept of Pan-Slavism. Western models and traditional Balkan views combined together in mobilizing the peninsula's nationalist movements.

The Megale Idea drew from the German theory of Volksgeist but tried to base it in reality on historical proof from Classical antiquity and the Byzantine period. The Serbs on the other hand combined with the dream of unification the French nation state and the ideal of Slav solidarity, brought together to form the grand "design'-Nacertanje [9]. Strangely enough this idea was brought to

Ilija Garasanin's attention by some Polish nationalists. The leader of the Constitutionalists exiled by Prince Mihailo in 1840 met agents of Prince Czartoryski in Istanbul. The latter while in exile in Paris had built up a huge network of support all over Europe against Russia which had suppressed the Polish revolt of 1830–31. In the Ottoman capital he had strong support and his envoys were spread out all over the Balkans trying to mobilize opposition groups to destabilize the European powers and spark off a European war. The ultimate objective was a reassessment, or so the Prince believed, of the division of Poland. The Poles were not very optimistic about the future of the Ottoman Empire and to avoid the whole of the Balkans falling into the hands of the Tsar they encouraged the Christian nationalities. The little Serbian Principality was at the time a Russian protectorate however its suzerain, the Porte, was wary of it and Austria was suspicious as it had its own nationality problems which included Serbs in Hungary. Generally Francophiles Czartoryski's men directed the Serbs towards Louis Phillipe in whose name they sometimes pretended to speak.

Upon his return to Belgrade and in his function as head of government to Prince Alexander, in 1844 he drew up a "project" governing foreign affairs. He toned down the Polish idea to put forward the Yugoslav idea which had been agreed by the Illyrian Movement but which encountered the absolute opposition of their suspicious and powerful neighbour Austria. However he emphasized Serbian unity with Montenegrin Serbs and those in the Ottoman territories of Bosnia and Herzegovina which would have meant that the Principality would have an outlet to the sea. To achieve this expansionist dream they summoned up the memory of Dusan and his 14th century kingdom. So historical romanticism combined with Jacobinism was to provide Serbia with a foreign policy until 1914.

In the 1840's nationalist movements in Austria were very active in the Balkans. Clubs and Societies were founded in Greek and Serbian areas. The latter were generally for educational purposes; A "Society of Friends of Learning" founded in Athens in 1836 dealt with setting up and maintaining schools for Greeks in Thessaly, Epirus or Macedonia using contributions from rich merchants of the diaspora. Other patriots went further and taking advantage of the problems that the Ottomans were experiencing, gathered gangs of bandits—Klephtes—on the frontiers and would make incursions into Ottoman territory, sometimes even with the blessing of the Athens government, as in 1843-44 when Kolettis was in power or at other times against his wish, as during the Crimean War. The Serbs had to be careful due to their position vis-a-vis Austria. The "People's Spring" in the Empire was preceded by a close collaboration between Belgrade and the Illyrian Movement, its leader Ljudevit Gaj making three journeys to the Principality during 1874-6. Together with the territories referred to in Nacertanje, "Yugoslav" patriots would quite happily add Srem, Backa and the Banat taken away from the Habsburgs by a union of Serbia with Croat areas and with Montenegro. Yet the 1848-9 Revolution showed the limits of these aspirations. The Hungarian Serbs demand for more rights within an autonomous Voevodina under a restored Patriarch was to make Budapest react violently. Patriots from the Principality, about 8,000 in all, rushed to help their brothers north of the Danube and the Belgrade government took part in the popular Assembly at Karlowitz in May 1848. Yet Vienna's ambiguous attitude, only supporting the movement against the Hungarian revolution, and above all Russian intervention which crushed the revolution in August 1849, showed how specious it was for a small country like Serbia to want to trouble the Habsburg Empire. Garasanin understood this and began once more to think of Nacertanje directed against the Ottomans. From 1849 he developed in concert with some Bulgarians, a plan of political propaganda which aimed to make all "oppressed peoples rise up" but which was really targeted at the Slav regions: Bosnia, Herzegovina, northern Macedonia and western Bulgaria. An organization was set up with Garasanin as its leader which included propagandists but also sharp-shooters—Cetniks—for whom the printing-press of Prince Alexander produced a "War Regulations for the Cetnik," a translation of Czartoryski's instructions to the Poles.

The Crimean War reminded Serbia of its subordinate position vis the Great Powers. Russia demanded the dismissal of Garasanin in 1853 while Austria threatened to occupy Belgrade if Prince Alexander did not remain neutral. At the Congress of Paris it was quite plain that the balance of power in the Balkans was dependent on Europe's attitude. During the 1860's which were dominated by the problem of Italian and German Unity the peninsula was influenced by Russian Panslavism. In these circumstances Garasanin, back in power in 1862, was to adapt Nacertanje and give it renewed scope. He began by once more setting up a "Serbian Committee" to coordinate propaganda with the aim of an uprising which would involve the Greeks, Bulgarians and mixed populations of Bosnia and Herzegovina. The Bulgarian patriot G. St. Rakovski organized in Belgrade a "Bulgarian Legion" of 600 men, while detachments were trained and armed in Bosnia and Herzegovina as well as Greeks in Thessaly and Epirus. In a memorandum sent to Napoleon III the head of the Serbian government predicted the imminent dismembering of the Ottoman Empire. At the same time he renewed links with the Yugoslav movement which was at the time headed by Bishop Strossmayer and his Croatian Nationalist Party. In 1866 there was agreement on a Yugoslav state which would neither be part of Austria nor of Turkey and preparations went ahead for an uprising in Bosnia and Herzegovina. Contact was also made with northern Albanians who promised to join the uprising. These plans, which were more or less secret, greatly inspired young Serbs who were having problems with liberalism and nationalism. Garibaldi and Mazzini became the idols of a generation which changed from a vague Panslavism in 1848–50 to a form of Serbian nationalism: from the Slav Empire to the Empire of Dusan. In 1867 an association called "United Young Serbians" would meet joining students and writers from both sides of the Danube but was soon suppressed since Prince Mihailo felt it was too liberal.

Taking his cue from this vibrant nationalism, Garasanin tried to give it an international hearing. An initial alliance was signed with Montenegro. The great writer Vuk Karadzic went on a mission to Cetinje in 1860 and Belgrade gave financial aid to Prince Nicholas who came to power that same year. In 1866 after Austria's defeat at Sadova, a treaty was signed at Cetinje which made provision for a joint uprising of the Serbs against the Ottomans and the union of both Principalities into a Greater Serbian state. With the Greeks the initial discussions were more difficult for Megale Idea overlapped in areas covered by Nacertanje. In 1860 Garasanin started discussions with the Greek representative in Istanbul but they broke down because of Greek insistence on including the whole of Thrace up to the Balkan range while Serbia wanted to incorporate the Bulgars into the projected Yugoslav state. The Serbo-Ottoman crisis over the fortresses in 1862 went some way in bridging the gap between Serb and Greek positions, but negotiations were held up by the change of king in Athens and the insurrection in Crete which in fact set off a nationalist backlash in Greece itself. In the end the alliance was signed in August 1867 near Vienna with the encouragement of Russia. The two Balkan states committed themselves to fighting shoulder to shoulder against the Ottoman Empire. Greece would get Thessaly and Epirus while Serbia would take Bosnia and Herzegovina. As for the territories of Macedonia, Bulgaria and Albania their fate would depend on the wish of the people themselves. Garasanin also sounded out Bucharest who had made approaches to Greece but his fall from power in November 1867 halted further discussions.

His departure from the political stage followed by the assassination of Prince Mihailo while Greece was to become fully occupied by the revolt in Crete ended this first attempt at a Balkan alliance. For historians it might have seemed premature since these Christian states had neither the political strength nor the military power to stand up against the Ottoman Empire. Yet the premises of 1866–68 were to bear fruit fifty years later during the Balkan Wars.

The Making of a Romanian State, 1859–1875

The 1859 union of Wallachia and Moldavia was only in fact a question of sharing an elected prince, Alexander Cuza. The two principalities were to retain separate governments and armies, until the Sultan's Firman of the 20 November 1861 recognized the "United Principalities" yet limited to the duration of Cuza's reign.

Alexandru Ioan Cuza (1820–1873) came from an old Moldavian Boyar family. He had studied in Paris where he associated with the "revolutionary" circle of the College de France around Michelet and took part in the 1848 in Jassy. After a short exile he returned to Moldavia and served in the Hospodar's army and in 1858 became commander-in-chief, with the rank of colonel. With no real political leanings, he was thought to be a liberal and even a Freemason. A rather unassuming character he managed during his brief reign (7 years) to lay the foundations, in every field, of modern Romania. Political life revolved around two tendencies: the Conservatives, representing the large landowners who because of the limited franchise dominated the elected assembly; and the Liberals who came from the small urban bourgeoisie—civil servants and professionals—who wanted the implementation of the 1848 revolutionary programme, as well as land reform to improve the peasant condition. Yet political life, whatever similarities it might have had to that of western countries, suffered from the narrow franchise and the backwardness of the illiterate peasant masses. Often it was nothing more than clan struggles coloured with the traditional Balkan phenomenon of "client groups." After having used Conservative support to make his initial moves: forming a unionist government, reunion of a joint Parliament and proclamation of Bucharest as the capital (February 1862), Cuza asked the liberal Mihail Kogalniceanu, the revolutionary leader of Moldavia in 1848, to form a government. This government which lasted 14 months managed to implement several essential reforms.

The first and most remarkable reform was the "Secularization of Church land," in other words land that had been bequeathed over the centuries to large monastic orders abroad (the Holy Places, Mount Athos, Sinai, etc.) which in fact made up about a quarter of the total territory. Despite the resistance of the monasteries and the protests of the Ecumenical Patriarch and of Russia, Kogalniceanu decided to nationalize the estates in December 1863. The assembly agreed to this and both boyars and peasants, who coveted the land, strongly supported this decision. The government organized the army, set up an Audit Office, a Council of State based on the French model and then tackled the problem of agrarian reform. This was to deal with the final abolition of tithes and the redistribution of land to the peasants. The Assembly however tried to oppose these latter measures, was dissolved by the Coup d'Etat of the 2 May 1863 and finally was brought to heel by a referendum changing the Constitution set out by the Congress of Paris. Ultimately the reform was promulgated by decree in August 1864. About 500,000 peasant families were able to take over more than 2 million hectares. This was a very important step for the social development of the country which from then on was relatively open to a capitalist (as opposed to feudal) organisation and therefore create new tensions for the boyars were becoming more and more large exporters of wheat while the peasants increasingly subject to "land hunger."

The uproar did not stop the Prince and Kogalinceanu from passing civil and criminal legal codes based on the Napoleonic Code, organizing the first education system which was "compulsory and free," creating two universities at Jassy and Bucharest and declaring the independence of the Romanian Church in spite of the opposition of the Patriarch of Constantinople who only finally accepted it in 1885. This extensive reform programme of course antagonized many people while the Prince's private life opened him to criticism. Nor did he have a successor. On the night of the 11 (23) February 1866 a group of conspirators forced the Prince to abdicate[10]. Napoleon III had been forewarned by a coalition of large landowners and liberals.

The Putsch underlined the problem of the union as the 1861 Firman had only endorsed it for the duration of Cuza's reign. However the French Emperor had promised his support and helped the provisional government to find a successor. Having been turned down by the son of Leopold II of Belgium it asked Prince Charles Hollenzollern-Sigmaringen a relative of the Prussian King, and through his mother, of Napoleon III. His candidacy was approved by a overwhelming plebiscite of 680,000 votes to 224. On the 10 (22) May 1868 the Assembly declared the twenty-seven year old their Prince, Carol I. A constitution was drawn up based on the Belgian model. The Prince would be head of government and the army, whereas the legislature belonged to the Senate and the House of Representatives still elected on a restricted franchise. The United Principalities became the Principality of Romania whose flag was the blue-yellow-red tricolor. The Porte agreed to this and issued a Firman on the 11 (23) October recognizing the permanent union of the two Principalities. A constitution promulgated on the 1 (13) July 1866 created a western style state organization, which together with a desire to emulate the French cultural model hid the Balkan nature of the new state. However this was to be seen right from the start. Political life was still dominated by the former boyars and the disgruntled peasants began to cause disturbances. In the towns the Francophile middle classes were opposed to the German Prince during the 1870 Franco-Prussian war. Carol was saved by the dynamic Lascar Catargiu who stayed in power for five years and was to stabilize the situation at home. The first Romanian railway lines were joined up to the Austrian and Russian railway networks, trade agreements were signed with the European powers despite the protests of Istanbul. Yet the question of independence, similarly with Serbia, had not been settled. Legally Romania was subject to the Porte. The Prince felt humiliated—a Hollenzollern considered to be the Sultan's vasal. The Third Balkan Crisis of 1875–78 was to provide the opportunity for the third Christian state in the Balkans to declare its independence.

The Bulgarian Problem, 1840–1876

After the final bits of their kingdom had been conquered in 1396 by Bayezid, the Bulgarians were incorporated into the Ottoman Empire, the territory annexed to the Elayet of Rumelia and divided into the Sandjaks of Nikopol, Vidin, Silistra, Kjustendil, Filib (Plovdiv) and Ormenon (Cirmen). They were mainly used to produce wheat for Istanbul yet in the extensive towns they became organized into specialized corporations for leather and wool production. Being Orthodox they were included in the Rum Millet together with the Greek, Serbian and Wallachian Christians, yet their Church retained the Old Slavonic liturgy at least in the Ohrid metropolitan area. The ecumenical Patriarch under Sultan Mustapha III, in 1767 managed to have this autocephalic church abolished and the see of Saint Clement subject to his direct authority. From this time onwards almost all the archbishops of Ochrid were Greek and tried to impose the Greek liturgy on their diocese. Thus the Church was for the Bulgarians a powerful forum through which they expressed their particular difference.

During the four and a half centuries of Ottoman occupation this ethno-linguistic group remained largely ignored for their geographical location kept them isolated from the powerful Christian countries fighting against the infidel. At the end of the 16th century European diplomacy did finally become interested when, inspired by the exploits of Michael the Brave the population of Tirnovo revolted against the Sultan and subsequently had to seek refuge in Wallachia. In the next century Habsburg and Vatican policy coincided and resulted in the creation of a Catholic Bishopric in the mining town of Ciprovci. A Bulgarian Internuncio was appointed to the Viennese court to supervise the freedom of worship which had been granted by the Sultan to his Catholic subjects. These events brought the Bulgarians to the limelight but Bulgarian historians also recall the numerous uprisings which they identify as specifically Bulgarian. In reality however they were part of the long list of religious or social uprisings which the Balkan Christians were to stage irrespective of their ethnic origins.

It was not until the second half of the 18th century that the first signs of Bulgarian nationalism were to be seen. As mentioned previously all over the Empire there was an extensive trade network using maritime as well as land routes and although the

Greeks were the main group involved and who benefitted most, the Bulgarians were also involved. There were very famous trade fairs at Kjustendil, Tatar Pazardzik and other places, and crafts were to develop in the lowland areas where there was plenty of water power for example at Kotel, Kalofer, Klisura and Panaguriste. Leather saddles and saddle-bags were produced for the Ottoman army also braid, woollen blankets and soap. From Istanbul the Bulgarians products were sent all over the Middle East while thread from Macedonia was to be seen in the markets of Vienna and Pest. In the same way as in the Greek expatriate community, there emerged a rich class of merchants, often moneylenders or bankers, capitalists who were also to create textile factories after a textile factory at Sliven was set up in 1834 by the Ottoman authorities for the manufacture of military uniforms.

This middle class, imbued by the ideas and ways of Europe were not the first to form an awareness of their national identity for they had been forestalled by several individuals who were ecclesiastics. The most famous without a doubt was Paisij of Hilendar (1722–1789) who was commonly held to be the father of the "Bulgarian Renaissance." Born in the commercial town of Bansko in eastern Macedonia he became a monk in the Hilendar monastery on Mount Athos and studied there in the "Greek Academy" where the scholar Eugene Bulgaris taught. Bulgaris was a scholar who was familiar with European philosophy including contemporary French encyclopedists. It was in this enlightened neo-Hellenic atmosphere that Paisij became aware of his Bulgarian identity. In his search for documentary material he visited the Serbian monasteries of Fruska Gora in the "German lands" where he came across, among other things, the work of M. Orbini the "Reign of the Slavs" (1601)[11]. Upon his return to Zographou Athos he wrote a "Slavo-Bulgar History"—Istorija Slavobolgarskaja— which was published in 1762. Basing himself on the legendary traditions of the ancient kingdoms he made a plea to his compatriots in favour of their language in the dual fields of education and ecclesiastical liturgy. Yet it was not the "Ottoman Yoke" that he decried but the Greek domination of the Church which at the time was undergoing an onslaught from the Phanariots which was to lead five years later to the occupation of the Metropolitan See of Ohrid. However this appeal to Bulgarian pride was taken up: numerous copies of the manuscript were made and Paisij himself gave readings at various monasteries[12]. His work was continued by the that of bishop Safroni of Vraca—Vracanski—(1739-1813) to whom he passed on his educational ideas and whose "Sunday Sermons"—Nedelnik—were the first book to be printed in neo-Bulgarian at Rimnic in Wallachia. He also advocated the defence of the old Slavonic liturgy and education in the Bulgarian tongue.

It was round these two aims that the nationalists first concentrated. Spurred on by the growth of Greek schools set up by the Greek diaspora in the villages, the rich Bulgarian merchants also wanted to compete by creating secular schools for the clergy were either too Hellenized or else too uneducated. Yet the first establishments which were opened in 1815 and in the following years: in Svistov, Kjustendil, Kotel and Sliven by their forerunners: I. Vlaskidovic and R. Popovic were to use Russian, Greek and even French school books. It was Petar Beron (1795-1871), a medical student in Munich and then a merchant in Paris, who published in 1824 his famous ABC "Riben Bukvar"[13]. Based on the mutual learning method of Bell-Lancaster it combined the alphabet, grammar, moral teaching, natural history and arithmetic. Beron financed several schools in the Stara Planina area and his Bukvar henceforth served as the basis for all secular establishments. In 1834\35 a group of rich merchants from Gabrovo, on the advice of one of their numbers Vasil Aprilov, who had been a student in Vienna and had settled in Odessa, founded the first Bulgarian secondary school where Physics, Chemistry, History and French were studied, becoming a nursery ground for the future leaders of the independence struggle. In 1845 there was already 54 schools and thirty years later an American journalist travelling through Bulgarian territory was to remark on the high number and good standard of these establishments, all supported by Bulgarians, and with no help from the Ottoman authorities. The development of education was mirrored by the birth of a Bulgarian press. The first publication in Bulgarian appeared in Smyrna in 1844 and others followed in Vienna, Istanbul and Moscow while a paper was published in Leipzig from 1846 onwards. However it was in Novi Sad and Belgrade that, with the help of the Serbian government, a political press came into being in the 1860s producing the newspapers of the leaders of the revolutionary movement.

The second major problem was the struggle for the Slavonic liturgy that resulted in the Bulgarian Church becoming autonomous. The suppression of the autocephalic see of Ohrid in 1767 sparked off avaricious competition for the bishoprics and parishes under its authority. The main method used was Baksheesh yet threats and other ways of exerting pressure were used by the Phanariot prelates and Jirecek[14] describes how it was not at all uncommon for a priest to be beaten in public in front of his altar by the bishop. In 1833 the inhabitants of Samokov sent the Ecumenical Patriarch a petition asking for a Bulgarian Bishop instead of the Greek tile-holder and more was to follow. The greatest resistance came from the numerous and rich Bulgarian colony in Istanbul. This was supported by Ilarion Makariopolski (1812–1875) who was born in Elena to the north of the Balkans but who was a product of the Greek Gymnasium of Athens. Their petitions, accompanied by Baksheesh resulted in 1849 with the celebration of mass in the Slavonic liturgy in their church in Istanbul. The Tsar's representatives to the Porte were attracted by these moves and promised them support, while in the Bulgarian regions the appointment of bishops, in Tarnovo and Makariopolski as well as other places, who did not reside there and ecclesiastical conflicts which ensued, led to outbreaks of popular unrest. Bishop Ilarion decided to act decisively. During the sacred Easter office on the 3 April 1860 he omitted to mention the name of the Ecumenical Patriarch: this was tantamount to ending the communion with the larger Church, rejecting of the Patriarch's authority and to embark on the road to schism. The Phanariot excommunicated Ilarion who was exiled to Asia Minor but the popular movement gained strength and in many villages there was open support for Greek and Bulgar popes. The outcome was decided by the European powers. The Treaty of Paris had imposed reforms and the Sultan, by the Hatti Humayun of February 1856, renewed his promise of equality for Muslims and Christians. The Bulgarian petitions increased in number to such an extent that the inhabitants of Kukus[15] turned to Pope Pius IX promising to change to Catholicism if they were guaranteed Bulgarian priests.

The Russian ambassador, Count Ignatiev, actively supported these demands and in March 1870, Sultan Abdul Aziz promulgated a Firman which created the "Bulgarian Exarchate," or in other words an autocephalic Bulgarian Church whose leader the Exarch would have his residence in Istanbul until independence, with jurisdiction over all the Bulgarians within the confines of the

Empire as well as outside, for instance the Bulgarians of southern Russia. This was an important stage in the Bulgarian renaissance.

All that remained was to translate this into political terms. Opposition to the Ottoman Empire had for many centuries been epitomized by the Hadjuks yet this had not been a specifically Bulgarian expression, even though in the 19th century the popular songs were to "nationalize" these characters. Similarly the participation of Bulgarians in the Serbian and Greek uprisings in 1804 and 1821 and the numerous volunteers who had joined in, had done so with the idea of a generalized revolt of all the Balkan Christians and whether their participation was an influence on the national Bulgarian movement it was only in terms of example that this could have been felt. But the nature of events were to change from the 1870s onwards under the influence of ideological, religious and economic stimuli as well as the European phenomena of the People's Spring of 1848 which produced a national reawakening. Certain nationalists began to openly advocate an independent Bulgarian state. Foremost was Georgi Rakovski (1821–1867) who had been a student in Athens and Paris and began his revolutionary activities in Braila in Wallachia where in 1841\42 Bulgarian emigres were planning a futile uprising of all the lands south of the Danube. A poet and a merchant in Istanbul and then in Odessa, he was familiar with the works of Russian admirers of the west and settled in Belgrade with the patronage of Garasanin. There he started to publish a Bulgarian newspaper—Dunavski Lebed—the Danube Swan, in Bulgarian and in French to publicize his people's cause. In 1861 he drew up his "Plan for the liberation of Bulgaria" which foresaw an armed struggle. In this context he formed in 1862 the "Bulgarian Legion." In fact these took part in fighting in Belgrade against the garrison of the Ottoman fortress but were disbanded the following year by the Serbian government. Withdrawing to Bucharest, Rakovski became a supporter of the idea of a Balkan federation there was argument among emigres over the question of borders for the future Bulgarian state which often conflicted with Serbian and Greek aspirations. Vasil Levski (1837–1873) was next to follow, he served in the Bulgarian Legion in 1862 in Belgrade and then emigrated to Romania where he joined in operations against Ottoman territory. In the face of the lack of impact that this type of operation had he spent two years, from 1868 to 1869, organizing clandestine revolutionary committees to lead the uprising in the event of outside intervention. He was aided by Ljuben Karavelov (1837–1897) who had been moulded in Moscow by Slavophiles and who in 1867 had come to Belgrade. He came into contact with the "Young Serbian Movement" prior to going to Bucharest to collaborate with Levski. Their joint efforts led to the creation of a "Revolutionary Central Committee" whose programme was to form a democratic republic of Bulgaria. Arrested in Ottoman territory, Levski was hung in Sofia in February 1873. Although the revolutionary movement gained a great martyr, the central committee was to become dormant as Karavelov concentrated his energies on journalism and literature.

It was from the Central Committee however that Hristo Botev (1849–1876) was to emerge. A teacher's son and disciple of the enlightenment, he studied in Odessa where he was attracted to Russian revolutionary socialism. On his return to Bulgaria in 1866 he came into conflict with the Greek Orthodox clergy and was forced to emigrate to Bucharest where he engaged in journalistic activities in support of a Balkan Federation. At the same time he published some poems which were to make him one of the greatest Bulgarian poet. In 1875 he persuaded the Central Committee to support the Bosnian revolt which ended in failure in April 1876.

The Bulgarian nationalist renaissance produced a revolutionary anti-Ottoman movement which was too weak to act alone against the Sultan's Empire, yet even so it had managed to be noticed by the European powers.

The Third Balkan Crisis: The 1875/76 Uprising and the Russo-Turkish War

Following the Serbs and the Greeks, the emergence of another country once again threatened to disturb the balance of power within the peninsula, especially as at the same moment the Bosnia-Herzegovina area was in a state of turmoil. The ambient climate in which these two disturbances were to occur made the European powers worried and was to become known as the Third Balkan Crisis.

The former kingdom of Bosnia and the duchy of Herzegovina had been made, since the Ottoman conquest of 1463, into an Elayet with the status of a Pashalik. Its governor, a Vizier with three Tugs, resided since 1851 at Sarajevo[16]. The medieval structures had remained until the 19th century: the Bogomils or Catholics who had converted to Islam had formed a martial nobility dominated by the Kapetan, the head of one of the 39 sub-districts of the Elayet. These nobles, of Slav origin, gave themselves the titles of Begs and considered that they were the owners of their land: they worked the land through the Reaya (either Christian or Muslim) and enforced dues in kind, corvee work and taxes as in the Ciftlik system. Next to these Beyliks there existed what was called Agaliks where the peasants had a similar status to those on the Spahiliks but were generally worse off. Travellers tended to corroborate each others findings that the Bosnian peasant was one of the most oppressed and poorest in the region. Furthermore the history of the Pashalik over the centuries had been one of brutal disturbances followed by pitiless repression. After 1683 its frontier location had meant that it was invaded by the Habsburg armies which was followed by the flight of large portions of the population who had collaborated with the occupiers: in the ten years that preceded the Peace of Karlowitz (1699) some 40,000 Christians crossed over to the north bank of the Danube. In the absence of any official statistics the estimates of population vary wildly depending on the observer. In 1807/8 Chaumette des Fosses[17] estimated 1,200,000 for the whole population with half Muslims, 40% Orthodox and 10% Catholic; these figures clearly must be taken together with those of the Austrian census of 1910[18]. Whatever the true number might be the Muslims were generally more numerous in the towns, the Orthodox in the east and the Catholics in the west.

This Slav population lived in a climate of latent strife which was made worse in the 19th century by the Porte's attempts at reform. The Bosnian Beys, who were said to be "more Turk than the Turks" showed a religious fanaticism and a conservatism which brought them into conflict with the Istanbul authorities. In 1821 they took up arms against revolting Greek and Albanian "Giaurs." In 1828 during the Russo-Turkish war they revolted against the "weakness" of the Grand Vizier. In 1831 Mahmud's reforms unleashed such opposition that the Sultan was declared a traitor to Islam and a local leader Hussein Aga declared war against the central authorities. This resulted in the abolition of the Kapitanate in 1837, and its replacement by Sandjaks as in the rest of the Empire, and again there was rebellion. When two years later the Hatti Sheriff of Gul Hane declared equality of rights between

Muslims and Christians the whole of the Pashalik rose up in arms and for ten years Bosnia experienced a state of latent war outside the Porte's control. In 1850 Istanbul decided to reaffirm its authority and entrusted this to Omer Pasha who transferred his seat of power from Travnik to Sarajevo which was far from the main concentration of the Beys' estates and he systematically imposed his authority on them.

The peasants' condition had scarcely changed at all. In 1858 the land was registered and the legal rights of Agalik tenants were defined. Nothing changed however in terms of the power of the Beys who continued to take up to 40% of the harvest and above all demanded much corvee work. A bad harvest in 1874 was all that was required to rekindle unrest: the reaya (Christians and also Muslims) rose up against the Beys in a Jacquerie which was far removed from a nationalist uprising. Yet the revolting masses of Herzegovina and Drina were Orthodox Christians and were seen as Serbs by their Montenegrin and Serbian neighbours. Furthermore the Nacertanje provided for the annexation of Bosnia and Herzegovina and Serbian committees had been formed in Bosnian towns. These in turn rose up but this time against Istanbul thus adding to the peasant insurrection a political angle. Montenegro as well was supplying arms and ammunition to the Herzegovina tribes near its border. Volunteers came forward from the two Principalities and the Christian states were on the brink of war with the Empire. The European powers intervened and it became a European crisis.

In fact Prince Milan, in power in Belgrade since 1868, was slightly wary but elections had taken place in August 1875 amid an atmosphere of nationalist fever and this had put strong pressure on the government to act. In Cetinje however Prince Nicholas was ready for conflict. Panslavism was the dominant ideology in Russia at the time and both the Tsar and his ambassador to Istanbul, Count Ignatiev, were partisan of this idea. But Austria-Hungary was closely following the situation and put forward its own particular interest in BosniaHerzegovina. The governments of the "Alliance of the Three Emperors"[19] proposed a programme of reforms to solve the Bosnian conflict in December 1875 but to no avail.

In the spring of 1876 there was a crisis in Istanbul. The Bulgarians taking advantage of this tried to stage an uprising which is known as the April Uprising. Launched by the revolutionary committee in Bucharest it was meant to involve first of all the regions of the Stara Planina—Oboriste and Koprivstica—but after a bad start there only took place a few disconnected encounters with Ottoman troops and their auxiliaries: Albanian or Circassian Basi Buzuks. The poet Hristo Botev died at the head of his Romanian troops who had crossed the Danube. In less than a month everything was over but the subjugation had been accomplished with such brutality that the world press was outraged. Gladstone in a pamphlet and Victor Hugo made a famous apostrophe in the Senate: the "Bulgarian atrocities" were a European problem. Sultan Abdul Aziz was overthrown and replaced by his nephew who in turn was forced from the throne after three months in favour of Abdul Hamid (1876–1909). This power vacuum in Istanbul encouraged the Christian states. The Russian Panslavists sent General M.G.Chernayev, hero of the central Asian wars, to Belgrade to take command of the army and reacting to the war fever which had taken a grip of his subjects, Prince Milan was forced to bring back Jovan Ristic to power, who had been a partisan during war. He was to set out the objectives: the annexation of Bosnia and the Novi Pazar Sandjak by Serbia and the division of Herzegovina with Montenegro. In July 1876 Belgrade and Cetinje invaded Ottoman territory. Yet contrary to what had been hoped by the other Christian peoples of the Balkans, especially the Bulgarians who had been subject to repression following the April uprising, they failed to make much headway even though the Montenegrins obtained a measure of success. Chernayev proved to be an abysmal strategist an was continuously in dispute with his allies. The European powers intervened once again and forced an armistice, then broken by the Serbs for the Ottomans had managed a spectacular recovery laying Belgrade wide open to attack. Panic seized the inhabitants of the capital and Saint Petersburg sent an ultimatum to Istanbul: the armistice signed on the 3 November 1876 froze the positions of both armies but left unresolved the revolt of Bosnia-Herzegovina.

Russia and Austria, who already in July 1876 had outlined a plan for the division of the Ottoman Empire, proposed that a European conference be held in Istanbul, which started on the 2 December. Ostensibly it was a matter of obtaining a commitment by the Porte for reforms for otherwise further revolts would patently result in the disintegration of the Empire. But while Alexander III of Russia was the mouthpiece of Panslavism and demanded the liberation of all the Balkan Slavs, Disraeli remained true to the hope of the survival of the Empire. The Sultan took advantage of this divergence of views and on the 23 December drew up a Constitution, announced by the firing of guns which was to terrify the European diplomats. This put into place a constitutional monarchy while at the same time maintained the indivisibility of the Empire. According to the Porte, under these circumstances the European conference no longer had any further purpose. This was a failure for Saint Petersburg and Russian public opinion, worked up by events, clamoured for war. This the Tsar declared on the 24 April 1877 having in the meantime obtained Austrian neutrality in exchange for the promise of Bosnia-Herzegovina.

Disraeli was convinced that the Russian armies occupy Istanbul within nine weeks and therefore the Balkans in turn would be occupied. Yet their advance was halted with the siege of the Pleven fortress which Osman Pasha defended from July to December. The Balkan allies: the Romanians, Serbs and Greeks, who until then had been ignored by the Russians, suddenly became important. Prince Carol wanted to use the war to gain legal independence from the Porte. He agreed the movement of Russian troops through his territory and this led to war with Istanbul. Ten days later a declaration of independence by the Chamber of Deputies (9/21 May 1877) was made. But on an international front this vote did not have any significance unless it were followed by diplomatic recognition. The Prince, against the advice of his entourage, came out strongly for armed intervention. The Tsar recalled this and asked for the participation of the Romanian army in the seige of Pleven. Carol himself took command of his forces and the Romanian army received its baptism of fire at the siege. In return for this blood letting, Romania requested: international recognition of its independence, a war indemnity and the Ottoman territories of the Danube delta and Dobrudja. Serbia was more reticent. In March 1877 they had signed with the Porte a return to the status quo ante the unfortunate episode with Cherbayev, and were aware of the Russian promise to Austria for the secession of Bosnia-Herzegovina. Above all they were worried that the creation of Bulgaria would mean it would have a preferential status in the Balkans in relation to Saint Petersburg. To the request for military aid they responded so slowly that it was only on the 10 December that they entered the war, three days before the surrender of

Pleven. As for Greece, in spite of the grand designs of Megale Idea, it was under intense pressure from Great Britain to stay out of the fray. Furthermore they were worried about Serbian and Bulgarian ambitions in Macedonia and Thrace. Public opinion was in favour of intervention but discussions with Russia were so drawn out that Greece was still getting on a war footing when the fighting ended.

The surrender of Pleven on the 10 December 1877 opened up the road to Istanbul to the Russian army. While Queen Victoria was sending letters to Disraeli, verging on the hysterical, Russian troops reached Adrianopolis where an armistice was signed on the 31 January 1878. Peace negotiations began at San Stefano[20], a small seaside resort about thirty miles from the English fleet which had been sent in haste by the British government.

The two opponents signed the Treaty of San Stefano on the 3 March 1878. Under its terms Bulgaria was created from the plateau north of the Balkan mountains up to the Danube, Thrace up to Adrianopolis, Macedonia together with Uskub (Skopje), Ohrid, Debar, Korca in the Albanian area, Kostor (Kastoria) in Greek lands and a large outlet onto the Aegean Sea from Maritza to Salonika but which would still remain Ottoman. Montenegro doubled its territory towards the north-west but was separated from Serbia by the Sandjak of Novi Pazar which was entrusted to Austrian occupation. Serbia only received the Nis region (about 375 sq.km.). Romania, although it was Russia's ally, was forced to cede once again the south of Bessarabia—the Kilia region and Ismail—lost in 1856 with the Treaty of Paris—but in compensation was given the Danube delta and the Dobrudja up to Silistra which had been Ottoman territory. Finally the former Ottoman protectorates of Serbia, Montenegro and Romania were proclaimed independent. As soon as the terms of the treaty were disclosed they raised a storm of protest. The occupation of greater Bulgaria and the need for Russia to maintain this for two years to organize the internal government, would mean that Saint Petersburg would dominate the Balkans; London threatened to use its fleet, Vienna demanded it be given Bosnia-Herzegovina which had been promised in 1876 and which although at the origin of the crisis was not even mentioned in its settlement. As for the Christian states they were all unhappy: Romania because it was being forced to cede territory, Serbia because they were only being given very little and Montenegro because it did not have an outlet to the sea.

Bismarck concerned for European stability put himself forward as an "honest broker" and the European powers, including France, brought together in European consultation, met in Berlin for a Congress in June 1878. The Balkan states and people were not represented but were allowed to send emissaries to plead their cause in front of this "Areopagus" which conducted itself like an international tribunal. The European powers had however already settled their differences: in May London and Saint Petersburg came to an agreement to split Bulgaria into two states while Austria had received assurances that its request for Bosnia-Herzegovina would be taken into consideration. Romania sent ministers Bratianu and Kogalniceanu who protested in vain against the annexation of southern Bessarabia but obtained the limitation of Russian troop movements over its territory during the two year period of occupation of Bulgaria. Serbia made it plain that it was not happy and the Russian representative sent a protest to Austria-Hungary. Prince Milan quickly took this up and in July 1878 Vienna and Belgrade signed an economic agreement and an agreement on communications which marked the start of a greater Austrian orientation for the Principality which from now on would be independent. Greece who had stayed out of the fighting tried to make its voice heard: its minister Deliyannis demanded Thessaly, Thrace and Crete, which had been in revolt since 1875. With only the support of France they had to make do with a promise of reform in Crete. In the name of the Albanian people the nationalist organization the "League of Prizen," which had been formed specifically for this purpose, put forward the question of their future, but received Bismarck's reply that "there was no Albanian nation."

In the end the European powers redrew the map of the Balkans. Russia occupied southern Bessarabia and set its border on the Prut and the Kilia branch of the Danube delta. Austria-Hungary occupied militarily Bosnia-Herzegovina and the Sandjak of Novi Pazar. The Bulgarian entity produced by the Treaty of San Stefano was divided into two states: to the north of the Balkan mountains the "Principality of Bulgaria" with its capital at Sofia, autonomous but subject to the Sultan, and to the south "Eastern Rumelia" which would be semi-autonomous with a Christian governor chosen by the Porte. The remaining areas, Thrace and Macedonia were to remain Ottoman territory. Serbia received Nis, Pirot and Vranje (about 300sq.m.) which was slightly more than agreed at San Stefano. Montenegro on the other hand got less but acquired

Niksic in the north and above all Pogorica and Antivari[21] which gave it an outlet to the sea. Romania retained what had been agreed at San Stefano: the Danube delta and the Dobrudja area. Greece was promised that future discussions would be held with the Porte over its borders. Finally on the diplomatic front the three Christian states were recognized as independent.

Further to these changes in the peninsula, Russia's total occupation of the Caucasus and of the Ottoman region of Kars, together with Britain's occupation of Cyprus, the Treaty of Berlin was an significant moment in the decline of the Ottoman Empire. In the Balkans the Empire only retained a fifth of its territory: Thrace, Macedonia, Epirus and the Albanian regions. Yet even this shred of Dar el Islam was coveted by the Christian states: Greece, Serbia, Romania and now Bulgaria, each with competing expansionist dreams. To attain their objectives each state turned for support to one or other of the European powers who were only too pleased to extend their influence in the region. Ethnic tensions and imperialist competition would turn this into the "powder keg of Europe."

Notes

1. 6 February in the western calendar. This is the date mentioned by several historians.
2. Histoire de la Grece moderne. cf. 157. (The history of Modern Greece) One drachma was worth one gold franc.
3. He died at Bamberg in July 1867.
4. The Visitation of the Virgin—Sretenije—which is on the 2 February. Roman Catholics call it the presentation at the Temple.
5. The French consul came to Kragujevac on the 16 March 1839. Cf. G. Castellan: "Aux origines de l'etablissement des relations diplomatiques entre la France et la Serbia." (The origins of diplomatic relations between France and Serbia.) Conference in Belgrade on its 150th anniversary. Delivered in December 1988.
6. It was promulgated in Belgrade on the 25 February 1839, therefore there are two dates 1838 and 1839 in history books.
7. Die Serbische Revolution, Hamburg 1829—based on interviews of Vuk Karadzic in Vienna. He in turn was to publish in Budapest in 1828 a work later translated into German by P. D. A. F. N. Possart: Das Leben des Fursten Milosch und seine Kriege. Stuttgart 1838.
8. The region east of Durmitor (2529 m).
9. From Nacrt which means plan or project.
10. He was to die at Heidelberg in 1873.
11. Mavro Orbini (died in 1614) a Ragusan monk was seen as the

"Father of Panslavism." His "Il regno degli Slavi" is a compilation of historical legends.

12. The work was only printed at the start of the 19th century.

13. The "ABC of Fish" on account of the engraving on the front cover.

14. Constantine Jirecek (1854–1918). A Czech historian and Minister of Education in Bulgaria from 1881–82. In 1878 he published in prague a "History of Bulgaria" which is still used as a reference.

15. Kuklis near Strumica in Yugoslav Macedonia.

16. In medieval times known as Vrhbosna it became Bosna Serai—the Palace of Bosnia. It was the capital until it was burnt down by Prince Eugene in 1697. The Vizier was to reside until 1851 at Travnik.

17. Chaumette des Fosses (1782–1841) who was in charge of the French Chancellery in Travnik from December 1807 to July 1808. His "Travels in Bosnia in 1807 and 1809" was published in Paris in 1816.

18. Total: 1,900,000. Orthodox 44%, Muslims 33% and Catholics 23%.

19. Formed under the auspices of Bismarck in September 1872 between the tree Emperors of Austria, Germany and Russia.

20. Now Yesilkoy—Istanbul airport.

21. Now Titograd and Bar.

13
Rivalries Between the Various Christian States, 1878–1912

At the Berlin meeting the World Powers sought to build a balance between the Balkan states while giving precedence to its Christian peoples. In fact the territories which remained under the Sultan amounted to one fifth of the whole of the area and consisted of Thrace, Macedonia, Epirus and the Albanian regions. However, these remnants of Dar el Islam were coveted by neighbouring countries: Greeks opposed the Bulgarians in Macedonia, Albanians in Epirus and Serbs clashed with Austro-Hungarians and Italians in the Albanian region. To reach these "national" aims and objectives the Balkan states approached one or the other of the World Powers which were quite willing to promise their protection in order to further their own interests in the area. Thus the conjunction of ethnic struggles with imperialist rivalry was soon to turn the Peninsula into a "European powder keg."

The New Bulgarian State: Princes Alexander and Ferdinand

Nationalists were by and large disappointed by the outcome of the Treaty of Berlin for their historians saw the San Stefano settlement as the only equitable answer to the Bulgarian question. The numerous street names in the capital and provincial cities called San Stefano bear witness to this.

Soon the autonomous principality became the cradle of dreams of unity. The World Powers had asked Russia to preside over its birth: the policies which had been applied half a century earlier in the Danube provinces were put into practice again. In the nine months of military occupation that he was given, the Tsar's representative, Prince Dondukov, made Sofia, a town of 20,000 inhabitants, into a capital, laid the foundations for the administration and judiciary, and also prepared an outline of the "organic regulations." This was sent to an assembly of worthies for approval, of which a third were elected and two thirds appointed, which met at Tirnovo, the old capital, in February 1879. The assembly was split into two tendencies, the "conservatives" who favoured a strong executive and a narrow electoral franchise, in opposition to the "liberals" who had often been through Russian universities where they had been influenced by Nihilism and demanded wide legislative powers. The latter won the day: the Russian outline "Organic Regulations" became a "Constitution," known as the Tirnovo Constitution, which was remarkably liberal for the time, for it established universal suffrage and gave full legislative power to an assembly chosen by the electors. Later the assembly unanimously elected as Prince, Alexander von Battenberg (1857–1893), the candidate put forward by the St. Petersburg authorities, a nephew of the Russian Empress and Bismarck's protege. On July 13, 1879, Alexander entered Sofia in pomp and ceremony, the Principality of Bulgaria became a reality and the Russians withdrew even though they left behind many military and civilian advisers. Henceforth they would be remembered as benevolent guardians as well as instruments of liberation.

South of the Stara Planina the possibility of the return of Ottoman soldiers greatly worried the population and an intervention by the Tsar's representative in Istanbul was needed before Abdul Hamid gave up his plan for military intervention. The organic statutes of the Rumelia Province were drawn up by the representatives of the Great Powers, but while England and Austria-Hungary wanted to make the Elayet administratively autonomous, Russia was in favour of setting up a separate state, with Bulgarian used in the administration, the army, etc. In the end it was decided that a Christian governor would be appointed by the Sultan, after the World Powers had given their assent. The governor would then select a directory made up of ten members, to be backed up by an assembly of which two thirds of the members would be elected. As a sign of its vassal status Rumelia was to pay a yearly tribute of 245,000 pounds to Istanbul. Obviously the ethnic complexity of the Province was a problem which made Bulgarian historians emphasize the importance of the first elections taking place in October 1879: out of 36 mandates the

Bulgarians received 31, the Greeks 3 and the Turks 2; although these results were challenged by the Greeks. Notwithstanding from the start the principle of Rumelia being part of the Principality was to have a strong influence on political life.

Prince Alexander made use of this notion also to buttress his position. As a Prussian officer he was uncomfortably aware of two areas lying outside his power: the Constitution was excessively liberal to his mind, the tsar's protectorate was still visible in the person of Russian ministers at the head of both army and police. Hence several coups which made the beginning of political life rather chaotic. Though the Assembly had a Liberal majority, the Prince asked the Conservatives to form a government, before he quarrelled with them on the subject of the War Minister, a Russian general. In 1881 he withheld the Constitution and put another Russian general in charge of government, only to dismiss him after two years. This caused a break between him and his touchy protector, Alexander III. As the Prince felt isolated in the face of the large group of Liberals who were in favour of Union, he decided to use it to assert his authority. In Rumelia itself the movement for Union was taking shape and in 1885 a "Secret Revolutionary Committee" was set up at Philippopolis (Plovdiv) with Zacharias Stojanov at its head. The latter was a writer and editor of a unionist newspaper; after the Prince agreed to it he got in touch with officers of the Bulgarian Army who won over their colleagues in the Rumelian gendarmerie. On September 18, 1885, members of the conspiracy had the Governor under arrest and returned him to the Ottoman border. A Provisional government was formed and a telegram sent to Prince Alexander: "Today a declaration of Union was approved in the name of your Highness. Your faithful subjects." The Prince was soon in Plovdiv to receive a tremendous welcome, which put a seal to the state of Union.

One obstacle remained, to have it endorsed by the Great Powers, though this was a considerable infringement of the provisions of the Berlin Treaty. Russia was in favour, but did not approve of Alexander von Battenberg who had fallen out with the tsar; this is why an official communique issued in Petersburg denounced the Prince's initiative in Rumelia, while the Russian ambassador in Istanbul gave warning to the Porte that any military intervention on the part of the Turks to return to the status quo ante would be opposed by Russia. The Ottoman protest went no further than diplomatic representations especially as Austria-

Hungary, feeling uneasy at the significant changes brought about in the balance of power established in the Balkan area, encouraged the Serbian King, Milan, to take action. While a conference of the Great Powers' ambassadors was taking its time discussing the solution to give to the new problem, Serbia declared war on the fledgling Bulgarian state in November 1885. The latter found itself on the brink of disaster: the Prince had dismissed the Russian generals from the army which was now led by captains and majors, its artillery equipment was inferior to that of the Serbian army, the main worry being that all Bulgarian troops were deployed in the south along the Ottoman border, which left the capital exposed to an invasion from the west. Milan attacked from Pirot going towards Sofia and Vidin. However, the Bulgarian foot soldiers, all of them of peasant extraction, resisted fiercely in the region of Slivnitza, which gave enough time to the southern units to arrive in forced marches. On November 19, Bulgarian troops counter-attacked and the Serbs withdrew in complete disorder leaving the way clear for a march on Nis and Belgrade. To save Milan, its protege, Vienna warned that if the Bulgarians advanced beyond Pirot they would be repulsed by the Austro-Hungarian army. An armistice to be confirmed three months later by the Peace Treaty of Bucharest (February 1886) restored the status quo ante between Serbia and Bulgaria. Meanwhile the Istanbul conference recognized the "union" of Bulgaria and Rumelia, in exchange for small corrections to the Bulgarian-Turkish border to be ratified by the Agreement of Tophane signed on April 5, 1886. Bulgaria was to keep its frontiers unchanged until 1912 and was becoming the largest of the Balkan countries with 96,000 square kilometres and over three million inhabitants.

Yet the tsar bore a grudge against Alexander who had to face a conspiracy of Russophile officers and fled in August 1886. Later another coup led by Stefan Stambolov, the President of the Assembly, enabled him to return with the agreement of Austria-Hungary and England. However, Alexander III was inflexible and Battenberg had to abdicate, which he did on September 7, handing over power to a Regency Council under Stambolov.

He was the son of a Tirnovo innkeeper and had taken part in the 1878 uprising, after which he became one of the Liberal leaders and emerged as President of the Chamber. He was hostile to Russia and was supported by the bourgeoisie which had common interests with Austria and England. In spite of strong opposition from the officer corps he had Ferdinand, a Saxa-Coburg, (1861–1948) elected as Prince, in July 1887, by a wide Assembly. In reality Stambolov was to rule for seven years as a dictator, imposing his regime and disrupting the Russophile party so that he could steer Bulgaria towards cooperation with Austria-Hungary and Germany. The clergy refused at first to recognize Ferdinand but was soon brought into submission. It came to an agreement with Istanbul and the Exarchate was allowed to appoint bishops to the sees of Ohrid and Kuprulu (Veles) thereby increasing the influence of Bulgaria in Ottoman Macedonia. However, the Prince became weary of his Prime Minister and wished for a reconciliation with Russia: in May 1894 he accepted the resignation that Stambolov had rashly offered him. In his rage the latter started campaigning violently against Ferdinand. The Court gave an officer the task to do away with the "ex-tyrant." In July 1895 in the centre of the capital he was attacked and dealt several blows from a sabre and died three days later.

The advent to the throne of Nicholas II one year earlier made reconciliation between Sofia and Petersburg possible: Ferdinand, though he was a Catholic, consented to have Boris, his son, baptized under the Orthodox Rite, with the tsar as a Godfather. This immediately led to his being recognized by Russia as Prince of Bulgaria. He went on to assume personal power, becoming increasingly authoritarian and relying on corruption. As elsewhere in Serbia or in Greece political life was no more than clashes between factions: over seventeen years thirteen governments came and went and the old Conservative and Liberal parties broke up into National-Liberal, Progressive-Liberal, People's parties and so on as a result of rivalries between personalities. Yet two new political tendencies made their appearance under the effect of economic pressures; socialism and the agrarian movement. The first one, in the shape of the Bulgarian Social-Democratic Party started as an underground movement in Stambolov's days in July 1891 under the impulse of Dimitur Blagoev (1856–1924). He had lived in St Petersburg as a student, discovered Marxism and introduced it into his country. Similarly to the Russian Social Democrat movement, the party underwent fierce internal struggles, until it split in 1903 into two, the "narrow"—tesni—close to the Bolsheviks, and "wide"—shiroki—related to the Mensheviks. Though they were few in numbers, the Bulgarian socialists made an impact on the Internationale because of Blagoev's striking personality. The

Peasant movement which arose from the Agrarian Union was much more significant. The Union was created in 1899, mainly to protect the rural masses against usurers and to achieve a more equitable distribution of taxes which had so far been disproportionately heavy in the countryside. Its leader, Alexander Stamboliski (1879–1923) a talented orator of advanced views, turned it into a proper political party.

In foreign affairs, since he now had Russian support, Ferdinand entertained hopes of reuniting all Bulgarian territories to return to the San Stefano borders. Hence he played an active part in the political life of Thrace and especially Macedonia. He thought he could repeat in these provinces the Rumelia experience, and to that end tried to enhance the Bulgarian state's prestige. In June 1908, taking advantage of the Young Turks rebellion and with the approval of Russian and Austrian authorities, he declared the abolition of the last remaining feudal links with the Porte, which had been symbolically represented by a tribute, and at Tirnovo, on September 22, 1908, proclaimed Bulgaria's independence; it was henceforth a Kingdom under a tsar: Ferdinand I.

Serbia: Dynastic Upheavals and Radical Domination

In assassinating Prince Mihailo, who did not have an heir, the conspirators meant to put the Karageorgevics back in power, but they were outdistanced by the army. While the government convened a broad National Assembly—like the St. Andrew Assembly of 1858—in order to elect a successor, the War Minister had the Belgrade garrison acclaim Prince Milan, a nephew of Milos, who was fourteen year old and attending at the time classes at Louis I Grand Lycee in Paris[1]. A Regency Council was appointed under the chairmanship of Jovan Ristic, the Liberal leader. The Great Assembly voted a new constitution in—known as the 1869 Constitution—which adopted the guiding principles of European Liberalism and gave Parliament—Skupstina—the responsibility of initiating laws, while the Prince, belonging to the Obrenovic dynasty, was able to dissolve it. This theoretical balance of power was preserved over thirty years of unrest: while the parties were trying to settle to a western type political life, the Prince seized every opportunity to come out on top by using their dissensions and leaning on the army for support.

The establishment of national states in Germany and Italy caused Serbian nationalists to give up their dream of "Dusan's Empire" and settle for more realistic aims compatible with a balance of power in the Balkans. The old Conservative and Liberal parties lost splinter groups of their younger elements, such as "Progressive," who were Neoconservatives with western sympathies rather than looking to Russia like their elders. On the other hand the Russian opposition with its mass appeal and Marxist and anarchist doctrines provided ideological guidelines for political action among the rural classes which had to face the disruption caused by nascent capitalism. These conditions gave rise to the Radicals who advocated local government in preference to central power, universal suffrage and the sovereignty of the Skupstina. They benefited from a strong organization and a talented leader, Nikola Pasic (1845-1926) who was trained as an engineer and was to hold a crucial position on the Serbian political scene for forty years.

To start with the Principality was faced with the insurrection of Bosnia-Herzegovina in 1875, a primary target for Nacertanje. While public opinion gave its approval to entering the war against Turkey, the Prince remained undecided and even contemplated abdicating, but in the end he chose to go to war—the Serbian-Turkish war of 1876—only to end in a disaster: more than 5,000 were killed and the Timok Valley was laid waste. The Bulgarian insurrection of 1876 in which Serbian volunteers took part, led to the third Eastern crisis and another war between Serbia and Turkey (1877) on Russia's behalf. Milan's army won several encounters and the Serbs asked for their reward: the Sandjak of Novi Pazar, the Kosovo, part of Macedonia and the port of Vidin on the Danube. However, the Petersburg authorities favoured Bulgaria and the Treaty of San Stefano was signed which ruined Serbia's chances as she was wedged between Greater Bulgaria in possession of the Vardar Valley and Austria-Hungary who had been promised Bosnia-Herzegovina by Russia. At the Berlin Congress Count Andrassy, Foreign Minister of the Dual Monarchy, suggested that J.Ristic, who attended the proceedings as a mere observer, sign a commercial agreement and an undertaking for building a railway line to Salonika, and in return he promised to champion the interests of the Principality. As a matter of fact the Great Powers proclaimed Serbia to be independent internationally and she was given the regions of Nis, Vranje, Pirot and Toplica.

Yet since the administration of Bosnia-Herzegovina devolved to the Viennese authorities much of the Nacertanje became inoperative as Serbia had to look to Macedonia and the plain of Kosovo because she had no access to the Adriatic.

It remained to be seen whether Austria-Hungary represented an ally or could still be a threat. Ristic was aware of the need to turn to Vienna since Russia now favoured Bulgaria. In April 1880 an Austro-Serbian agreement made provision for the building of a railway from Belgrade to Nis and Vranje on the border with the Ottoman Empire. However the agreement became commercially impossible to implement as Austrian industrialists wanted to sell their goods to Serbia but Hungarian producers of wheat refused to let cereals from Serbia enter the country. Prince Milan dismissed Ristic and replaced him with a Progressive leader who signed the commercial agreement, but he took care to supplement it with a secret arrangement signed in July 1881. Without letting the government nor the Skupstina know about it, he promised not to participate in any enterprise that would benefit Serbian populations living on Habsburg territories, including Bosnia-Herzegovina, not to sign any treaty with a foreign power without informing Austria beforehand: in return the Prince could rest assured that his dynasty would be protected and the state would become a Kingdom, moreover Austria would encourage the Serbs to expand to the South-East, that is to say Macedonia. In reality the convention created an Austrian protectorate in all but name, and when it came to light in 1893 it raised a storm of protest. Meanwhile, in February 1882, after Austria had given her consent and persuaded the other Great Powers to agree, Serbia became a Kingdom with Milan I at its head.

The country at the time was divided between the Progressives favouring Austria and the Radicals leaning towards Russia. In June 1882 the bankruptcy of the Bontoux General Union of Paris, which was to finance the building of the railways, meant a net loss of some 35 million francs for Serbia, more than the national budget. Ministers and even the Prince were involved in the scandal which was without precedent in a stable patriarchal society. The same year a fiscal dispute with Mihailo, the Metropolitan, caused the government to revoke him, but his successor was not recognized by some of the clergy, so that a "new" and "old" hierarchy coexisted, in extremely strained circumstances. Though the new King was popular, this was not enough to restore peace in the population; after the Assembly was dissolved and an attempt had been made on Milan's life, the Radicals resorted to force. The Timok Rebellion took place—Timocka Buna—in 1883; peasants in the area refused to surrender the arms that had always been kept in their homes and a bloody encounter followed with the regular army crushing them in a matter of days. A court martial passed some death sentences, in particular against Pasic who had fled the country, and twenty insurrectionists were executed. The army was becoming the main support of the monarchy, but it was still shaky. Since the creation of the Principality of Bulgaria border clashes had taken place, and in 1885 the union with Rumelia led to a war that Milan had provoked but of which Pasic from his place of exile and the Radical majority did not approve. When defeat came it greatly humiliated the young King who considered abdicating, but instead he decided to try a rapprochement with the Radicals. Whereupon his troubled relations with his wife, Queen Natalia, came into the open: personal quarrels were compounded by political disagreement; the Queen being temperamentally pro-Russian while Milan looked to Austria. He was afraid lest the Petersburg authorities, with his wife's support, force him to abdicate, as had happened in 1886 with Prince Alexander of Bulgaria. The Queen left the country together with her son, Alexander the heir apparent, upon which two government crises took place. The King asked for a divorce, which the Metropolitan pronounced in October 1888. Public opinion was indignant and the political parties took advantage of this to impose a new constitution on the King. Elections for a Constituent Assembly won a victory for the Radicals who obtained four fifths of the seats. The Constitution of 1888 introduced real parliamentary institutions: this was an open challenge to the King. Milan drew the right conclusions and abdicated in February 1889 in favour of his son, not without securing a generous pension for himself; he was only thirty five.

Alexander was thirteen and Ristic was again appointed as Regent, but as he was known to be pro-Russian he had to consent to Austrian wishes to have the "secret convention" of 1881 prolonged until 1895. Pasic was allowed to return and reorganized the Radical Party which won 80% of votes at the general elections. Thanks to the new Constitution the party was able to control all the administrative services of the state and, in foreign affairs, it steered Serbia towards Russia as was shown by the visit paid by the young King accompanied by Pasic and Ristic. Vienna riposted with curbs on imports from Serbia into Austria-Hungary, but kept silent on the subject of the convention which was known only to the regents but not to ministers. Once again quarrels between members of the Royal Family stole the limelight. In spite of the government's ban ex-Queen Natalia returned to Belgrade, soon to be followed by the ex-King: the press and parties split between supporters of Milan's and those of Natalia's. Pasic after negotiations obtained the departure of the ex-King: for three million francs, two million of which came from the tsar's purse, he gave up all his rights even his Serbian nationality. Taking advantage of his parents' unpopularity and of the Liberals new won majority, the young King carried out a coup d'état in April 1893: he declared himself to be of age, he dismissed the regents and the Liberal cabinet before asking his tutor who was close to the moderate Radicals to form a government. Yet again the King drew support from the army, while the electorate continued to back the Radicals. Nine months later ex-King Milan was coming back and for three years Serbia had to all intents and purposes two sovereigns: the 1888 Constitution was abolished and the 1869 was restored because Milan saw it as more favourable to a King's rule. Since the administration had been discredited by its subjection to political parties, the Army represented the core of a ruling apparatus increasingly isolated from the masses as seventeen cabinets in succession had presided over the destinies of the country in fourteen years.

Farce soon turned into melodrama. King Alexander had chosen for his mistress a person of dubious reputation who had been lady-in-waiting of his mother, Draga Masin. She was twelve years older than he was and in spite of the opposition of his mother and father, who for once were in agreement, he decided to marry her. The engagement was announced in July 1900, quickly followed by Milan's and Natalia's expulsion, as well as a purge from the army and administration of all their followers. The tsar acceded to a request to witness the wedding ceremony in the person of his representative in Belgrade. However, the new Queen was unpopular and the King found it difficult to form a stable government. He changed the Constitution repeatedly, without being able to stem the electoral progression of the Radicals. The latter frequently denounced in the European press "the dictatorship of the King's whims."

Then a fresh scandal broke out: only one month after they were married the King announced that the Queen was going to give him an heir. Yet Queen Natalia knew that the ex maid-in-waiting was barren and not long before the expected birth she sent a doctor from the Russian court to Belgrade. The trick was brought to the open, there was no pregnancy. This was too much; the officer class, humiliated by the international outcry, decided to take action. Lieutenant Dimitrijevic-Apis led a conspiracy of fellow officers, among them a general, who approached Petar Karageorgevic, the pretender to the throne. All hundred and twenty conspirators made their coup on the night of May 28/29, 1903; the King and Queen were struck by gunshot and their bodies thrown out of the palace's windows. The European Powers voiced their horror, but Serbia put up no resistance to the disappearance of the last Obrenovic.

The Karageorgevic option was the obvious choice. Petar was the grandson of Karageorge, son of Prince Alexander, who had been sent into exile in 1858, forty five years back. He had been educated in Hungary and later in France where he attended the military College of St Cyr before taking part in the 1870 war. Five years later, under another name, he joined the rebels in Herzegovina to fight the Turks. In 1883 he married the elder daughter of Prince Nikola of Montenegro who gave him three children. After his wife died and he had fallen out with his father-in-law, he settled in Geneva to lead the life of a scholar. This is where the conspirators of the 28 of May approached him indirectly. The Skupstina which had a Radical majority offered him power two days later after a short debate, and on June 15, 1903, he became King under the name of Peter I of Serbia (1903–1921) aged fifty nine. Though he was easily recognized by the authorities of St Petersburg and Vienna, England was afraid to have its representative in Belgrade forced to meet regicides and waited until 1906 to give her consent. The 1888 Constitution was brought back, and the Radicals had the upper hand in politics except during the 1908/9 crisis; Pasic was Prime Minister five times in ten years. The political line was definitely pro-Russian, in spite of the troubles encountered by the tsar who was faced with the Russo-Japanese war and the 1905 revolution. On the other hand bad relations with Austria led to a customs war—known as "war of pigs" (1906–1911) during which under pretext of veterinary safety all import of pork from Serbia was banned. In this context France came to the rescue by having the animals go via Salonika where the meat was exported to the West.

The French-Serbian rapprochement was also marked by the choice of artillery equipment; in 1907 the Schneider-Creusot 75 cannon won an order in preference to the 77 cannon of Skoda of Austria. Seeing the worsening of tensions in the Balkans, Peter I forced the pace of reform of the army which had started under Milan. Through a national service of two years the Narodna Vojska could muster 350,000 men, and the officer corps started to attract well educated young men to its ranks. The mood of the nation was in any case running along patriotic lines and more or less secret societies such as "National Defence" and "Union or Death" nurtured a climate of exaltation in Croatia-Slavonia, Bosnia-Herzegovina, as well as Macedonia and encouraged the creation of Greater Serbia which would embrace all Serbs under a popular King and an officially ultra liberal Constitution.

Greece Under George I, 1863–1913

After Otto's departure, the Great Powers, especially England, set to map out, one again, the Greeks' future. The search for a monarch was made difficult by the impossibility to select a candidate who was connected in any way with one or the other of the main European capitals; the process of elimination led to Prince William, younger son of Christian IX King of Denmark. He was seventeen years old, a Lutheran, knew nothing about Greece and was bringing the gift of the Ionian Islands which had been under English occupation since 1815. The National Assembly which had been convened by the Provisional Government and suitably prepared by Sir Henry Elliot, the English envoy, chose him as King under the name of George I (1863–1913). The Great Powers—England, France, Russia—gave over the Ionian Islands to the Kingdom, with their 2,000 square meters and 200,000 inhabitants. A new Constitution—called by the year 1864—was drawn up to change the Constitutional Monarchy into a "Parliamentary Monarchy": the King of Greece became King of the Greeks, meaning that the sovereign was no longer on the throne "by God's grace" but "by the will of the nation," as represented by the Assembly. Universal suffrage was introduced, civil liberties were confirmed, judges were proclaimed irrevocable. The young King swore obedience to the document which he was to uphold for half a century, he undertook to have his heir baptized in the Orthodox religion and gave a free hand to various political parties.

In reality political parties continued to be less bound by political programs than lobbies following a leader. Yet the new generation—coming after the 1843 "revolution"—ready to assume power, was a reflection of the young middle class, responsive to progressive ideas but eager to reap immediate benefits: what was at stake in an election was the allocation of jobs in local and central government according to a "system of benefit" which discouraged any possibility of long-term political action. Fifty eight governments came and went in quick succession between 1864 and 1910, often under the same men: Alexander Kumunduros nine times, Charilios Trikupis seven times, or families such as Delighiannis, two brothers and a nephew, who presided over twelve. However, in contrast to the previous period, there was an effort at organizing the parties and the long winded rivalry between Charilios Trikupis and Theodorus Delighiannis is somewhat similar to that of Disraeli and Gladstone, as the British model was ever present. Some of these politicians rose to the level of other European leaders, for example Charilios Trikupis (1832–1896) who was Prime Minister over two long periods (1882/85 and 1887/90) and left a lasting imprint in the country's modernization by building railways and reforming the army through the help of French officers.

Though the various parties were at odds on internal policy, such as matters of taxes, public works, etc. they all agreed on the Megale Idea. Yet of all the lost territories they claimed only a few were recovered in fifty years: the Ionian Islands, Thessaly and Southern Epirus, in spite of repeated attempts in Crete and Macedonia. This is to be explained by the wide gap between the resources of the Kingdom and the potential destabilization that this ambition represented for South Eastern Europe and of which the Great Powers, though not always in agreement, were keenly aware. The gift made by England of the seven isles caused much rejoicing among the inhabitants of Corfu and Athens, and young King George was received in triumph in the summer of 1864. Yet economically they changed very little the position of the country since they were similar to all other parts of Greece. Besides the government headed by Kanaris made two serious mistakes: it abolished the Ionian Academy, an Institute of higher education which had been the guardian of Hellenic studies since 1824. Worse still it subjected the Islands' Church to the autocephalic Metropolitan in Athens while previously it had been under the authority of the ecumenical Patriarchy in Constantinople. Protests were voiced but to no avail, and the religious quarrel which had smouldered up to 1850 flared up again.

The third Eastern crisis and the Congress of Berlin enabled the Greeks to express their grievances to the European concert mainly because of French sympathies, but they had to be content with a promise of straightening their borders with the Turkish Empire in Thessaly and in Epirus; it was suggested that the frontier should henceforth follow the valleys of the Salambria, which is today called Pinios, and of the Kalamas River. No mention was made of Crete, Macedonia, Thrace, the Aegean islands which were still under the Turks. To conform to the promise made at Berlin tense negotiations took place in Istanbul under the auspices of France and England. In Thessaly the Pinios Valley gave the Ottomans the use of the town of Trikala which the Greeks meant to turn into the capital of their new province since Larissa was mostly Muslim. In Epirus they clashed with Albanians who were sounded over the possibility of setting up a Kingdom of Greeks and Albanians which would have as its monarch King George or his son, yet the move came to nothing. Finally in May 1881 the Great Powers forced the Sultan to cede the whole of Thessaly and part of Epirus—the Arta region: some 13,400 square kilometres and nearly 300,000 inhabitants as compared to a total of 1,680,000 inhabitants in the census of 1879. The plain of Thessaly was a wheat granary and therefore the object of much desire on the part of Greek peasants but their hopes were frustrated. Since the 18th century the region had been an area of Ciftlik, which after the Tanzimat and above all the Ottoman agrarian law of 1858 became large agricultural concerns of capitalistic character. Early in the 1870's when Greek claims became more pressing, many big Turkish landowners preferred to sell rather than being turned out: the French traveller, L. Heurey observed how the land in Thessaly was "taken over by the Greeks from the Turks"; they also mentioned a person called C. Zographos, Foreign Minister to be, who acquired for a small amount of money a large estate on which some four hundred peasant families lived. It was not until the beginning of the 19th century and the reform of Venizelos before share croppers in Greek Thessaly—the Collighi—who kept a third of their produce, could become, at least in part, independent farmers.

In Berlin the assembly of statesmen remained deaf to the pleas coming from Crete. Let us remember that the island had been given to the pasha of Egypt by the Sultan as a reward for his assistance against the Greek uprising. In 1840 at the time of the second Eastern crisis the Porte regained possession of it. The situation on the island was similar to that of Bosnia: about half of the Cretans had gone over to Islam, but the efficient administration of Mehemet Ali made it attractive for many to return from their exile and by the middle of the century it is estimated that the population had reached some 160,000 inhabitants, a good third of which were Muslims who owned the numerous Ciftliks in the plains. The return of the Sultan's functionaries upset the inhabitants and riots had flared up in 1841, 1858 and 1866/67. The last one was felt keenly by young George who married in that year Grand Duchess Olga, herself attuned to the Panslavist ideas current in St Petersburg. Greek public opinion was in favour of the island being united to the mainland—Enosis—and counted on Russian support: the Queen had just given birth to an heir who was called Constantine like her ancestor Catherine the Great. Yet nothing could be done without the consent of the other Great Powers and France remained undecided, while England refused to give up her support of the "sick man." In August 1866 Enosis won the vote in the Cretan Assembly, fighting broke out and volunteers rushed in from Greece. The story of the Hegumen of the Arcadi Monastery who blew himself up together with Greek assailants caused a stir throughout the world. Friendship societies in support of the Greeks sprung up in Europe and the United States. The government in Athens tried to persuade the Serbs to join them into attacking the Turks, but the agreement signed in Austria, the first of a series of Greek-Serbian treaties, failed to bear fruit. General Omar Pasha methodically put out all centres of resistance by blocking supplies in weapons and men. In 1868 the Greek government under Vulgaris decided to calm down the situation and the Porte granted the Cretans an "organic status" providing for Christian functionaries to administer the island, the adoption of the Greek language as the official one, and the creation of mixed tribunals. Crete went through a period of tranquillity lasting a few years until the third Balkan crisis. Then once again patriots took up their arms but they could not get a hearing: the Turks had made promises in 1868 and the Great Powers were waiting for her to put the Organic Law into practice. As elsewhere reforms were slow to come and in 1890 the island's governor was still a Muslim, while the mixed Assembly had failed to materialize. Agitation started again but the Greek government under Trikupis pleaded for time as the country was financially exhausted and politically isolated.

The repeated failures experienced in Crete together with uneasiness about the situation of the Greeks in Macedonia, especially after the birth of the Bulgarian state, caused a revival of interest for patriotic ideals. In September 1895 some junior officers in Athens started a "National Society"—Ethnike Hetaira—which lost no time in sending arms and volunteers to Crete. With this encouragement Cretan patriots proclaimed once again Enosis. Under the pressure of public opinion the Greek government under Delighiannis sent 1,500 men to the island under the command of one of the King's aides-de-camp. The Porte took offense, and after making sure the other Balkan countries would not intervene, declared war against Greece early in April 1897. The Greek army under the heir apparent, Constantine, cut a poor figure opposite Abdul Hamid's troops which had been efficiently trained by German officers. Several encounters on the Northern border, in Macedonia and Epirus, ended badly for the Prince. The Great Powers felt disquieted and Russia with Austria-Hungary pressed for peace. After a month the war was over. The peace treaty signed in December 1897 was not too harsh on the Greeks; the Porte obtained slight alterations to its benefit on the Epirus-Macedonia frontier and, this being more of a blow, war reparations amounting to four million Turkish pounds and international financial control. Yet at that time the massacre of English soldiers on Cretan soil made the Great Powers demand a withdrawal of Ottoman troops from the island and propose that the King's younger son—Prince George—be appointed High Commissioner in Crete. This was a major step towards Enosis.

This martial episode had dealt a blow to the King's prestige and to that of his son, not to mention a worsening of the financial crisis; the fact that public finances were subjected to the scrutiny of an International Commission was deeply wounding to national pride. It was evident to a large number of citizens that serious reforms were needed. Political life was still intrinsically unstable as was proved by the assassination of Delighiannis in June 1905 and the disarray of his party. At the same time the situation in Macedonia was becoming explosive and the "Macedonian question" was now on the international agenda. Greek public opinion was clearly in need of a man who could understand its frustrations.

Cretan society was then under the sway of a new star: Eleftherios Venizelos (1864–1936). Born on the island he had read Law in Athens and gone back to work as a barrister. He took part in the rebellion against the Ottomans and was elected to the Cretan Autonomous Assembly; in 1898 he was put in charge of Justice but soon clashed with the High Commissioner whom he saw as ineffectual. In March 1905, Venizelos called for Enosis once again and convened a Provisional National Assembly. Prince George resigned and the ex Prime Minister Zaimis took his place. He was a friend of Venizelos and appointed the latter as Prime Minister of a government formed to prepare the way for Union. Following on the annexation of Bosnia-Herzegovina by Austria-Hungary and the European crisis caused by it, the Assembly in Crete declared Enosis (October 1908) and an executive Committee of five members took charge of the island's government in the name of King George I. However, in view of the loud protests of the Young Turks and the resentment of the Great Powers which had not been consulted, the government in Athens remained undecided and cabinets came and went in quick succession. A "military league" was set up among members of the Officer Corps, with Colonel Zorbas as leader, and on August 15, 1909, he carried out a coup d'état. In spite of support from the population of Athens and Piraeus, the officers soon found out that political problems were beyond them and called on the Cretan Prime Minister for help. Venizelos assumed power in Athens in October 1910. This was the beginning of a new period in modern Greece.

Romania Under Carol I, 1878–1914

Carol I had been on the throne since 1866 and trying to usher in Western type political institutions though he was hampered in his task by the Principality's legal vassal status. The third Eastern crisis provided the opportunity for Romania to break free.

The rebellion of Bosnia-Herzegovina in 1875 instantly provoked demonstrations in support of it among the population and in the following years elections took place in an atmosphere of heated nationalism. Liberals came to power and under the firm guidance of I.G.Bratianu (1821–1891) remained in office for twelve years. The Ministry of Foreign Affairs was at first in the hands of Kogalniceanu, the spokesman for revolution in Moldavia in 1848 and the man who carried out Prince Cuza's sweeping reforms. By June 1876 he sent a memorandum to Turkey and to the Great Powers, in which he requested the "individuality of the Romanian state" and the name of Romania to be recognized. However he took care to remain neutral in the war between Serbia and the Ottoman Empire, but in the course of an interview at Livadia in the Crimea he accepted the principle of the Russian Army crossing Romanian territory on condition that national integrity was guaranteed. When the Ottoman Constitution of 1876 was promulgated by Abdul Hamid there was much indignation in Bucharest: Romania figured in it the "most favoured province of the Empire." This enabled Bratianu to protest in Parliament "Never have Bajazet and Mohammed been able to wield their Yatagan in the heart of the Romanian mountains where now Midhat Pasha dares to tread with his Constitution." With the Prince's encouragement in April 1877 the government and Russian envoys signed an agreement to let the tsar's armies cross national territory. In answer to the entry of Russian soldiers in Moldavia, Turkish artillery fired on Braila and other Romanian towns along the Danube. On 29 April /11 May, the Chamber declared war against the Ottoman Empire with 58 votes for to 29 against. Ten days later, speaking at an extraordinary session of Parliament, M. Kogalniceanu solemnly declared: "We are a free and independent nation."

To encourage the Great Powers to endorse these words, the Prince urged a military intervention alongside Russia. He took command of the army, crossed the Danube and threw his soldiers into the fray round Pleven (August-December 1877). They sustained heavy losses but Romanian soldiers showed great valour, especially in the action to seize the redoubt at Grivitsa. Yet neither at San Stefano nor at the Congress of Berlin the Romanian government was granted all its requests. The return of the regions of Bolgrad, Cahul and Ismail to Russia in exchange for the annexation of Turkish territories in Northern Dobrudja and in the Danube delta made the question of Bessarabia an object of dispute between Romania and Russia for a long time. Nonetheless the Principality achieved its ambition to be recognized by the European concert of nations as independent on the juridical and diplomatic levels.

However, there remained a proviso which was to poison relations with France and England for many years to come. Article 44 of the Treaty of Berlin made an obligation for the new state not to discriminate between subjects of different religions. Yet the 1866 Romanian Constitution made it impossible for non-Christians to be naturalized: this seemed to apply to the Moslems living in the Dobrudja mainly, but it also extended to the Jews who were at the time emigrating in large numbers from the Russian Empire. As they were not allowed to buy land, they congregated in the towns where, by the end of the century, they made up 19% of the population, while in the countryside they were inn-keepers, moneylenders and, especially in Moldavia stewards, which often made them unpopular with the local population. Economic antisemitism reinforced the old Christian traditional antagonism. The "World Jewish Alliance" which had his headquarters in Paris and whose President in office was Adolphe Crémieux, invoked the Treaty of Berlin to demand that France and England delay their recognition of Romanian independence until Article 7 of the Constitution had been abrogated. Russia at the time did not respect the principle of equality as regarded her own Jews and was adopting a policy of antisemitism which reached a peak with the pogroms occurring early in the century. There ensued a bitter quarrel between Bucharest, Paris and London, since the Romanians rejected such interference as an attack on their national sovereignty. Late in October 1879, nevertheless, the Bratianu government agreed to amend the article in question: Jews could become Romanian citizens on strict conditions, but only Romanians, whether by birth or naturalized, could own the land, which made it impossible for a large majority of Jews. France, England and Germany agreed to the new law and in February 1880 recognized Romania as independent "de jure." The Jewish problem still remained, especially since immigration from Russia went on at an accelerating pace until the Fist World War. Antisemitism became part and parcel of political life in Romania.

On the strength of this international victory Prince Carol whose only daughter had died young, tried to buttress his dynastic line by adopting as his heir a nephew, Ferdinand von Hohenzollern-Sigmaringen, who was fifteen at the time. He then had himself crowned on 10 /22 May 1881. Romania had become a full fledged Kingdom.

Politics took on an ever increasing Western look. The political parties, Conservative and Liberal, now officially recognized, expressed the aspirations of different social classes: large landowners supported by the Church for the former and big business and civil servants for the latter. However, they retained their "Balkan" characteristics: political figures had their private clientele; thus for three generations the Bratianus led the Liberal Party up to World War II. There sprang up a number of splinter parties, such as on the Conservative side the Junimists, looking to the Central Powers for inspiration, and on the Liberal side, the National Democratic Party under Nicolae Iorga, an historian. The electoral system still depended on a census and at the 1911 elections, 0,2% of the population held 41% of the seats. This purely formal democracy in reality kept the rural masses and the workers away from politics. Moreover fraudulent electoral practices and the system of patronage for candidates distorted political life permanently.

The Liberals adopted a policy which benefitted trade and industry. In 1885 Bratianu took protectionist measures which started a customs war with Austria-Hungary (1886–1893) rather similar to the "war of pigs" between Vienna and Belgrade. Above all he tried to encourage foreign investments in industrial concerns, mainly in oil fields round Cimpina-Ploiesti. However, there was a very small industrial workforce; in 1901: 37,000 men worked in 600 enterprises of more than 25 employees. Working in the harshest conditions they were organized in the 1880's into workers' circles from which in 1893 there emerged the Romanian Social-Democratic Party. An intellectual called C. Dobrogeanu-Gherea represented Marxism in this party; he was in close touch with Engels. After an interruption the party came back on the political scene in 1910 thanks to trade union support; it took an active part in the proceedings of the Second International. At home strikes were organized which helped to gain some social benefits such as the 1912 law on labour insurance; yet Social Democrats had little impact on political life.

In fact the main social and political question in politics up to 1914 was that of the peasantry. In spite of Cuza's reforms, in 1864, Romania was a country of large landowners; in 1895, 6,500 owned half of the agricultural land, with as many as a million peasant families farming it. These landowners lived in Bucharest, or even Paris, and let most of the land to farmers who themselves sublet to peasants. Insecurity of tenure meant minimal technical progress. Landowners and farmers were concentrating on the international wheat market, in which Romania was a big exporter. However, this trade meant there was little to consume at home: peasants fed themselves almost exclusively on maize, in the shape of mamaliga, with the result that the population suffered from dietary imbalance and consequently from disease such as pellagra. At the bottom of the social scale 300,000 landless peasants, that is 20% of the population including their families, made up a reserve of labour for the estates, but also a group of people hungry for land and desperate.

This led to an explosion called the "great peasant revolt of 1907." It started in February in Moldavia where it took on an antisemitic colouring, then spread to Oltenia and the Danubian plain; everywhere streams of agricultural workers headed for the cities. Bucharest was seized with panic and D. Sturdza, a Liberal, asked General A. Averescu to take repressive action. He used the greatest brutality and sent canons to fire at villages; 10 to 12,000 were killed but by the end of April the last peasant rebellion in Romanian history was over. Parliament was forced to vote some reforms which were soon to be wiped out by demographic pressure. "Land Hunger" remained one of the features of Romanian society until 1921, while the state administration remained aloof, if not downright opposed to the rural population.

Foreign policy was largely the preserve of the King. His long reign allowed to maintain continuity but in any case the balance of power in Europe did not leave much room for manoeuvre. The large resources of the Russian and Austrian Empires made all dreams of uniting Southern Bessarabia and Transylvania to Romania completely impossible. The only area for action was claims on southern Dobrudja which now belonged to Bulgaria and the Vlach population in Macedonia with cultural affinities with Romanians, which is why the country had its share in destabilizing the Balkans. As he knew that Sofia had Russian support, Carol appealed to Vienna in spite of the Romanian populations living under Austro-Hungarian power. In August 1883 I.C.Bratianu called on Bismarck and in October the King signed a secret treaty between Romania and Austria to form a defensive alliance in the event of Russia attacking either. Germany joined it straightaway and Italy likewise in 1888. The treaty was renewed regularly up to 1914, but was never submitted for approval by the National Assembly and the ministers involved were kept in the dark. The German monarch chose to draw Romania into the orbit of the Triple Alliance, though it was culturally nearer to France, and promised to guarantee its borders.

Capitalist Advance and the Discovery of National Identity

L.S. Stavrianos summed up the years 1878–1914 in the Balkans as "the age of imperialism and capitalism." It would probably be more apt to reverse the order and to trace the penetration of capitalism to the end of the Crimean War (1856) and of increasing imperialism on the part of the Great Powers after the Treaty of Berlin (1878) to culminate from the early 1880's and become, like Africa but in a different way, the theatre of political and economic confrontations.

The Treaty of Paris by making the Black Sea neutral and accessible to all civilian shipping as well as turning the Danube into an international waterway opened to the industrialized countries—Great Britain, France, Austria—the whole of the Balkans as a potential market. At the same time in each of the new Christian states a class of entrepreneurs was emerging which was also entrenched in the administration and the army and combined the prestige of their education—Bildungsburgertum—with the privileges and attributes of power. They modeled themselves on London, Paris and Vienna in politics as well as way of living. They bought books, clothes, pieces of furniture, household goods from the best manufacturers and while in Serbia under Kniaz Milos only the sovereign's nieces were dressed in the Viennese fashion, twenty five years later all civil servants under Prince Mihailo wore a frock coat and top hat. These new consumers needed another class of tradesmen: whether large or small all Balkan towns now belonged to the network of European capitalism.

Through osmosis, since the new townsfolk often had their parents in the countryside, changes occurred everywhere to a certain extent. Also there was the need to export in order to buy European goods. Capitalism entered the remote areas by way of pigs in Serbia, wheat in Romania, currants and sultanas in Greece and tobacco in Bulgaria. Agriculture had to evolve from producing products for the home market to those internationally in demand. The change over was slow and partly thwarted by a major phenomenon of the 19th century: the population explosion which led to tension in the countryside and "Land Hunger" evinced in Romania, with absentee landlords, as well as in Serbia and Bulgaria where there were more small landowners. Between 1880 and 1910, without any alteration of the borders, the Romanian population grew from 4.6 to 7 million, the Bulgarian one from 2.8 to 4.3, and in Serbia from 1.7 to 2.9 million. This happy development reflecting progress in security and hygiene was a source of problems which had to be solved by either emigrating to the cities or to far away countries. The number of Greeks lured to America and its riches went up from 1,100 in 1890 to 40,000 in 1910; all in all, in the twelve years between 1899 to 1911, Greece lost 200,000 of its people. As a counterpart they sent to their families an influx of dollars which made its way to the most remote villages where these "Americans" retired after building spacious villas, such as those that are still to be seen in the Pelion near Volos, or on the Albanian Riviera and the Rhodope in Bulgaria.

The rush to the towns meant, like everywhere else in Europe, a source of cheap labour and a strong incentive to industrialization. Early in the 1860s the Greek ports—Piraeus, Patras, Naupli and Syros—saw a surge of small factories, producing wine, paper, or processing cotton. In 1872 at Ermopolis on the island of Syros, hand machines were replaced by steam engines and a gas factory was opened together with another one at Piraeus. In the following years many factories were set up to such an extent that a "Bank of Industrial Credit" was founded, proof that industrialization was taking off in Greece. In Serbia the exodus from the countryside was a phenomenon occurring in the 1870s. Only in 1874 did the urban population reach 10% of the whole. Industrialization there was delayed by the country's geographical position right at the door of Austria-Hungary, whose manufactured goods flooded the market, but also by the government's timidity as it waited until 1868 to mint its own currency; up to that year forty different kinds of Austrian and Turkish coins were circulating in Serbia, and the dinar was chosen as the monetary unit in 1873. In the same year the government promulgated a law aimed at helping industrial enterprises. The result was mediocre and it was only in 1890 that Serbian industry can properly be said to have come into existence, in two centres, Belgrade and Kragujevac. In Bulgaria the first developments went back to the 1840s while it was still within the Ottoman Empire, but long after independence there was still no industrial framework. As in Serbia Austro-Hungarian competition stifled any attempt at self-sufficiency in this area; only under the policy introduced by Stambolov (1887–1894) did the country see a flowering of small textile, wine, tobacco and sugar factories. In 1911, 800 industrial enterprises produced only 14% of the national income.

Romania experienced a similar development and did not start real industrialization until the law of 1887. However, it was different in one respect because of the enormous share of foreign investment in its enterprises—82% in 1911—and the international aspect of its oil interests. Oil production began in 1957 in a modern fashion, to rise from 50,000 tons in 1890 to 1,885,000 tons in 1913, which put Romania in the fourth rank in the world. Most of its production was refined on the spot by firms owned partly by German capital (27%), later Dutch, English, French and Belgian (8%). This financial penetration of the Great Powers occurred in Bulgaria through the agency of banks since heavy industry remained undeveloped because of scarcity of raw material. The 29 banks in existence early in the century doubled in numbers in a decade and had investments in 170 public companies with an admittedly modest capital of some 136 million gold levas. In Serbia, mines which had been exploited since the Middle Ages, attracted French and French capital. A "Serbian Industrial Company" established in Belgium in 1887 started exploiting the Timok coal basin and later lead at Crveni Breg, copper at Majdanpek and coal at Alexinac, while the French invested in antimony at Zajaca and copper at Rebelj. In Greece mines also attracted foreign capital: in 1874 the Laurion mines were taken over by a French-Italian company controlled by Marseilles' Freyssinets, while the English were interested in the Kymi lignite, since the country was terribly short of coal. However, British ventures went to the area of shipping: shipbuilding, fitting and insurance.

Only states went into what can be called imperialism. In the beginning Christian nations appealed for capital to set up administrative services, build roads and organize their armies since they had none. The wool stockings of French peasants which had made it possible for the July Monarchy to take off economically, had no counterpart in the agricultural societies of the Balkans because they had been freed so recently, and the financial resources of Greek traders had no chance of being sunk into ventures in such kingdoms as Otto's or George's. The Christian states therefore turned to the Great Powers whose banks controlled important reserves of gold. Ludwig, King of Bavaria, Otto's father, made sure his son could draw on a European loan to mop up the debts incurred during the war and the period of anarchy that followed, so that the National Bank of Greece was founded in 1841 thanks to a Swiss banker with Greek sympathies. Heavily overdrawn from the start Greek finances suffered a haemorrhage which meant that in 1890 the national debt amounted to 700 million francs; three years later the authorities had to claim bankruptcy at 30% and their creditors, on the insistence of Germany which had lost heavily in the exercise, had the capital placed in 1898 under international control. Serbia managed her affairs more prudently up to 1873, but then her fledgling banking system was shaken by the Austrian monetary crisis. Belgrade appealed at that time to Russia to meet the expenses of the 1875 war, then she borrowed heavily from the French at first, later from Germany and Austria-Hungary. In 1900 the national debt reached 422 million francs and the creditors sent representatives to the Directors of Serbian Financial Monopoly to ask for reassurance. The Bulgarian government made similar decisions in the late 1880s and servicing of the debt went up from 4,3% in 1887 to 19,7% in 1911, which put the yearly budget permanently in the red. Sofia had foreign visitors also to control public finances. Romania was lucky to avoid this mark of financial imperialism particularly wounding to national pride, but only because foreign involvement in the main sectors of her industrial riches ensured a high degree of indirect control. Nevertheless the Romanian debt rose in 1914 to 1.7 billion francs representing the heaviest one in all the Balkan countries.

Besides administration and the army the third financial burden at the time was the building of railways. It was a necessary infrastructure for modernizing national economies, as it created an organic link with the European market, thereby causing economic changes in the areas concerned, but also social and cultural improvements. The earliest railways in the Balkans go back to the 1860s. In Romania a law passed in October 1868 granted two companies, one Anglo-Austrian, the other based in Prussia, the exclusive right to build the first four lines round Bucharest and Jassy, and in 1872 the Bucharest station of Filaret was opened. In Bulgaria up to 1878, there was only one line running between Varna, a port on the Black Sea, and Rustchuk on the Danube, which belonged to an English company. In 1885 the government in Sofia nationalized the railways and making use of foreign capital, mainly from Austria, started laying a proper railway network: in 1911 Bulgarian Railways had nearly 2,000 kilometres of railway lines. The Serbian territory was included in a vast plan of Baron Hirsch who, in 1869, was granted by the Sultan a concession to establish a link between Vienna and Constantinople. In reality only in 1884–1885 was the line across Serbia completed and the first train ran between the capitals of Austria and the Ottoman Empire on 12 August 1888. The building of these railways always went beyond the financial means of the countries concerned; they had to borrow on the European markets and these transactions were often an opportunity for banking malpractice and corruption on the part of politicians.

Capitalism burst suddenly and sometimes disruptively upon societies which consisted mostly of the rural classes. In 1911 the proportion of people employed in agriculture was 80% in Bulgaria and Serbia, 75% in Romania and 60% in Greece. In respect to standard of living the changes were beneficial to villagers but what had always been the scourge of depressed areas in the countryside, usury, was replaced by a system of debt repayments more sophisticated but just as heavy. Rural exodus to the towns or emigration often came to be the last resort for smallholders reduced to the condition of proletarians by their debt burden. The impact the rise of capitalism had on the population was painfully brutal leading to a deep cleavage. Between town and country a climate of hostility developed, made up of a mixture of envy and resentment, which reflected in the ideologies used by political parties: Serbian Radicals, Bulgarian and Romanian Agrarians. There were many theorists and politicians like Stamboliski who attacked Sofia, however small a capital, as the modern "Sodom and Gomorrah."

Paradoxically the inroads made by the values and way of living of industrial Europe went hand in hand with rediscovery of national cultures. The fact that independent states functioned with their vernacular used in the administration and schools, meant that ethnic and linguistic societies were provided with a unified means of expression. Thus the problem of the literary language found a solution, apart from Greece where Katharevusa and Demotic went on competing. The educated class now able to avail itself of the new publishing and press technical advances evolved rapidly and culture spread everywhere. However, it fed on books and newspapers from abroad, which made for complicated responses among readers unable to choose between acceptance and rejection. All the new countries experienced confrontations, "Westerners" versus "Nationalists." Technical progress benefited the former, but the latter were served by political tensions within the state which gave cohesion to various factions. These exhibited a common feature of importing their ideological tenets based on patriotism from abroad, since it was in the air at the time. This phenomenon of action and counteraction produced a number of literary achievements at par with any found in more advanced countries, such as Mihail Eminescu (1850–1889) considered as the greatest Romanian poet and his fellow countryman Ion Caragiale (1852–1912) a playwright, the Bulgarian poet and prose writer Ivan Vazov (1850–1921), and the satirist Aleko Konstantinov (1863–1897), the Serbian poet Djura Jaksic (1832–1878) and the village novelist Milovan Glisic (1847–1908), Dionysos Salomos (1798–1857) and Kostis Palamas (1859–1943) from Greece whose poems encompassed a century of national history.

Yet these cultural manifestations were bookish, with an appeal limited to the educated minority in cities and a few village worthies. The rate of illiterates at the beginning of the 20th century was still enormous: 40% in Romania, 45% in Greece, 55% in Serbia, and the proportions were even higher among women. In spite of education laws, peasant masses remained outside the scope of these learned national cultures, as they clung to the cultural tradition of their particular ethno-linguistic group. The process of becoming an integrated a modern nation, with an awareness of its identity was still incomplete and the decade of upheavals lasting from 1912 to 1922 was to put an end this process.

Notes

1. He had Albert Malet as a tutor, and thanks to his texbooks several generations of French schoolchildren came to be familiar with names such as Obrenovic and Karageorgevic.

14

The Balkans "Under the Yoke," 1878–1912

The Powers meeting in Berlin not only left Balkan peoples under Ottoman rule but also transfered others—from Bosnia and Herzegovina—to Austria-Hungary so making the Habsburg Monarchy an important element within the Peninsula.

Bosnia-Herzegovina Under Austrian Occupation, 1878–1903

It would have been unthinkable that the Bosnian Pashalik should have been left as it was prior to the rebellion of July 1875 which had been the signal for a Third Eastern Crisis and Vienna from the start was to keep a close watch on the situation. In March 1876 while in Bohemia, at Reichstadt Castle, Franz-Joseph offered Alexander, the tsar, an arrangement: Russia would regain Southern Bessarabia which had been lost after the Crimean war and Bulgaria would remain a vassal territory while Austria-Hungary would get Bosnia-Herzegovina, the hinterland of Dalmatia which had come under Habsburg rule in 1815. However, the plan was a subject of argument even among the Emperor's subjects: German-speaking Liberals, above all the Hungarians objected to such an increase in Panslavist links which would raise the proportion of the Slavonic population of the Dual Monarchy. As for the representatives of the Porte, while in Berlin for consultations, strongly opposed further loss of Dar el Islam territory. Serbia also felt unhappy about this wiping away an integral part of Nacertanje. With Bismarck's support Vienna secured an advantageous compromise: Austria-Hungary would receive Bosnia-Herzegovina, but only in the guise of military occupation to restore order, while the Pashalik would remain under Turkish sovereignty. As a bonus she also got the Sandjak of Novi Pazar which was useful to the Austrian military staff for strategic reasons. As a matter of fact it was to threaten Serbia on its southern border and isolate it from Montenegrin Serbs. Hence the garrison towns of Priboj, Prijepolje and Pljelja, situated at a distance of over a thousand kilometres from Vienna, which were manned by forlorn Austrian troops and their officers.

Unexpectedly the occupation proved more difficult than a mere military show of force. The 13th Croatian Corps under General Filipovic met with spirited opposition on the part of the Muslim population and fierce fighting took place to the North around the towns of Doboj, Jajce and Maglaj. However, in October 1878, all the troops were well entrenched in their quarters. The political problem was more serious. The Croats who were encouraged by the advance of their 13th Corps and provided most of the civil servants in the occupied areas, asked for the incorporation of the Pashalik to their Kingdom; it would considerably strengthen the Yugoslav Movement. The authorities in Budapest objected strongly for precisely this reason, but neither were they keen on too much Austrian influence. A compromise was reached, leaving the Commander-in-Chief in charge of the territories as a substitute for the Emperor, and putting the Finance Minister of the Dual Monarchy at the head of the administration, with a governor endowed with dictatorial powers residing in Sarajevo. Below him the administrative tiers of the Ottoman Empire were kept in place—Sandjaks and Nahije—henceforth to be called Kreise and Bezirke, and the economic and social organization was left untouched. Between June 1882 until he died, twenty one years later, the Finance Minister in charge of the administration—Landesregierung—was Benjamin von Kallay, (1839–1903) a Hungarian, who knew the Balkans well, had been Consul in Belgrade and had written a "History of the Serbs." He was convinced that he was working for a good cause in raising the Bosnians to a European level of civilization and organizning a large bureaucracy. He replaced the 120 Ottoman Muslim Kadis by civil servants in government departments: Finance, Justice and Public Works, who numbered 9,500 by 1908. Only a quarter of them were local people, the rest was half Croats, and from all over Slavonic regions of the Empire: Bohemia, Galicia and Slovenia. The Catholic element—18% of the population—naturally benefited greatly from coming under Imperial rule; the Church hierarchy which was established—an archbishopric, three bishoprics and 150 parishes—were able to start building many churches such as the Neo-Gothic Cathedral at Sarajevo to be completed in 1889, and open religious schools. Austrian historians often emphasize the modernizing effect of their occupation. It is true that the first railways, mostly narrow gauge, go back to this era, as well as a proper road network, hospitals and museums such as the National Museum at Sarajevo which opened in 1889. Austrian architects gave the capital the look which was seen during the Winter Olympic Games of 1976. This positive balance-sheet must be viewed in the contrast to that given by Serbian nationalists, with five-fold tax increases under the Kallay government which was more strictly enforced than under Ottoman rule and was spent on the army—barracks and strategic roads—or monuments such as cathedrals and museums. Whether these achievements improved the lot of local people is a matter of debate shared by all colonies. The lack of independence of the economy was obvious since by 1881 the occupied territory was included in the Austro-Hungarian customs union: manufactured products were imported from Cisleithania and wheat from Hungary in exchange for exports of iron ore, bauxite, chromium, manganese and lead, which they had in plenty.

Another grievance voiced by the people under the occupation was the conditions under which the peasants lived. The rebellion of 1875 originated in an uprising of the Kmets against the oppressing Beys. In reality the Imperial administration adopted Ottoman laws, especially the arrangement of 1859 doing away with old feudal ties but turning the Beys into large landowners and the Kmets into sharecroppers. By 1880 the official figures were of 6 to 7,000 Agas or Beys exploiting 85,000 Kmet families, three quarters of whom were Orthodox, one quarter Catholic and only a few thousands Muslim. Thirty years later, the policy of encouraging the Kmets to buy land applied by the Austrian authorities was made null and void by the demographic explosion: the number of Kmet families had risen and these were still for the most part Orthodox. Their exiguous smallholdings did not allow for more than subsistance farming and land hunger went hand in hand with hunger itself.

The most flagrant failure of the Kallay administration was in the area of nationalities. In writing his History of Serbia he had to admit that Bosniac Serbs, of whatever religion, belonged to the Serbian ethnic grouping. Croats could not recognize this principle; this is why when he was appointed Governor, he had to ban his own book in the occupied territories. The favoritism towards Catholics was not only confined to religion; in the 80's he applied a policy of systematic colonizing of the plain of the River Sava, encouraging the settlement of Croats, and also of Germans, Poles and Czechs. Yet the attempt to achieve a better balance between religious groups only increased national tension: the Croats saw it as a first step towards the establishment of "Greater Croatia," especially when in 1882 Dr. Josip Stadler who had been made Archbishop of Sarajevo started to champion this theme. At the same time, Belgrade became the capital of the Kingdom (1882) so the Orthodox in Bosnia naturally looked to it for support. To avoid the danger of separatism, Kallay tried to promote awareness of the Bosnian identity; in so doing he thought the Muslims could be rallied to the cause, yet their attachment to the Koran wiped out all manifestations of their historical origins. It soon became apparent that every effort in this direction was futile. As clashes between nationalities increased in the Habsburg Empire and the Balkans, the dual equation gained credibility. Catholic meant Croat, Orthodox meant Serb, while the Muslims remained apart, not really belonging to any national grouping. Vienna and the whole of the Dual Monarchy adopted the policy of divide and rule in the region, only to make a conflict of large proportions more probable.

The Macedonian Imbroglio, 1850–1908

The name Macedonia, came back into use in the 19th century but dated from the days of Philip and his historical kingdom. It had become a purely geographical entity, an area of the Byzantine Empire, inhabited by Slavonic tribes since the 6th century, completely annexed in Simeon's Bulgarian Empire (893–927) and partly in Tsar Dusan's Serbian Empire (1331–1355). The Ottomans conquered it in the latter years of the 14th century and divided it into Vilayets and Sandjaks whose borders were often altered. In the middle of the 19th century European geographers applied the term Macedonia to the region lying between the Stara Planina to the North, the Olympus and Pindus to the South, the Rhodopes to the East and Lake Ohrid to the West, with 62,000 square kilometers it was twice as large as Belgium, and its population amounted to some two million inhabitants. It was divided into two Vilayets, Thessalonika and Monastir (Bitola), part of the Kosovo Vilayet created in 1877 and the autonomous Sandjak of Selfice (Servia).

Economically the region was poor, as it was mountainous and difficult to reach or plains on the banks of rivers and lakes such as Ohrid, Prespa, Kastoria, Vegorritis, together with the coastal plains of Thessalonika, Kavala and Xanthi. These were the only fertile areas and this is why the Ottomans had set up Ciftliks there; since the 1858 law these had been in theory changed into latifundia where cotton could be grown, as well as tobacco and rice. It should be observed that many Ciftliks, still called by their old name, were now owned by Greek or Jewish Thessalonikan merchants. Elsewhere a pattern of smallholdings of one or two hectares was common, which made for subsistence farming, with often heavily mortgaged land, whose excess population provided an army of season workers employed in cotton and rice cultures on the large estates.

The neighboring countries were attracted to Macedonia not by its riches but by its strategic position as it commanded the traditional highways leading from the Danube to the Aegean Sea through the Vardar Valley, the Sofia Basin and to the sea through the Struma Valley (Srymon to the Greeks) not to mention the main through road of the old Via Egnatia going via Ohrid, Bitola and Florina which joined the Adriatic and the Aegean Sea. As for Thessalonika where all these roads ended it had the advantages of a large harbor, 140,000 inhabitants and was the second largest European city in the Ottoman Empire and the third largest Balkan city south of the Danube. Hence Greece, Bulgaria and Serbia all coveted it.

In a century when nationalities were impressed by the French model of the nation state as exemplified by developments in Italy and Germany, the three neighbors fought over the inheritance of the "sick man" with reasons drawn from history and also making use of the ethnic complexities of the area. Statistics were kept according to the old Millet system of the Ottoman Empire and only took into account differences between Moslems, Jews and under the name of Rum Millet—the populations under the Patriarch of Constantinople and those which depended from 1870 onwards on the Exarchate. To translate the religious figures into ethnic groupings was a difficult task because the language factor was obviously lacking in precision. In an area where competition between various schools became fierce, the number of pupils registered in Greek, Bulgarian, Serbian, and even Wallachian establishments depended on their geographical position, the scholarships available and the pressures that were exerted locally. Observers were amused by the fact that Greek fathers could have a "Bulgarian" son because he attended the exarchist school where he was taught the Bulgarian language, history and culture, while a Bulgarian father could have his son turned into a Greek by the patriarchist school or a Serb if he was taught by masters sent from Belgrade.

On these bases the Porte drew the following census:

Muslims: 1,145,000
Orthodox Greeks subject to the Patriarch: 623,000
Orthodox Bulgars of the Exarchate: 626,000

The Muslims called "Turks" in fact included peasants of Anatolian extraction, descendants of the Yuruks, a nomadic tribe and the Konariots, shepherds established as settlers in the Konya region by the 14th century, as well as Ottomans working in the administration, converts of Slavonic stock, or Greek, Jewish (the Donmes), Moslem Albanians living in the North-West, Bulgarian Pomaks in the Rhodope, Circassians who had taken refuge in the Ottoman Empire in 1860 after fighting the Russians in the Caucasus and finally Gypsies.

Orthodox Greeks mentioned in the census represent all the Christians under the Patriarch's juridiction. It was also the term used in the field and recorded by travelers: a Greek was a person who attended the Greek church. Yet the meaning evolved slightly after the 1821 Revolt: a number of inhabitants in Macedonia had taken part and discovered that it was possible to be a Greek without depending of the Patriarch who had excommunicated the rebels. The birth of an independent kingdom provided these precursors with an aim for their nationalist ideals and state propaganda for the Megale Idea. Henceforth each crisis which shook the "sick man" had its share of attempted insurrections in the border areas with more or less direct support from Athens, while secret patriot associations organized various conspiracies and assassinations against the Ottoman authorities which were accurately listed by Constantine Vakalopoulos. If one adds the numerous Greek schools that were opened in towns and the countryside, it is clear that up to 1870 the Macedonian Greeks were the most culturally significant of the Christian population in Macedonia. Several future leaders of the Bulgarian or Macedonian movement began as fervent believers in Hellenism; for example Dimitar Miladinov (1810–1862) a Greek primary school teacher, that is a pupil of the Greek school, was converted to Slavism around 1850 after coming under the sway of a professor at the Kazan University. This uncertainty as to national identity explains the ambiguous answers made by Slavonic speaking inhabitants at Ohrid in 1851 to von Hahn. They admitted to being Greek but did not go so far as saying they were Slavonic speaking Greeks, as nationalist historians in Greece proper have claimed.

The situation was altered when a Bulgarian Exarchate was created, and by 1868 demonstrations in support took place in the Kastoria region. The March 1870 Firman made provisions in article 10, besides the seventeen dioceses already taken to be Bulgarian, that other Eparchies could come under the jurisdiction of the Exarch if a majority of their inhabitants were in favour. It is easy to imagine what pressures and counterpressures could be exerted on illiterate peasant populations. Russian funds also came in aid of the Slavonic Church and from 1872 there was a sharp increase in petitions in favor of the appointment of Exarchist bishops and priests, sometimes accompanied by fierce clashes, as at Monastir (Bitola), Resen (Bosilegrad) and Ohrid. After 1878 the Bulgarian government enthusiastically endorsed this cause and for the authorities in Sofia, Exarchism, meaning Bulgarian, became the foundation of their Macedonian policy. Primary schoolteachers, who had played a major part in the Bulgarian national revival, were encouraged to renewed efforts. In 1896 in the whole of Macedonia there were 843 Bulgarian schools with 1,300 teachers and 32,000 pupils. This Bulgarian offensive met with a spirited counter-offensive on the part of the Greeks. In 1867 Greeks from Ohrid and Monastir set up another Philiki Hetairia to organize an uprising against the Turks since there was already a rebellion in Crete; it was the driving force behind the 1878 uprising in Western Macedonia and in the Olympus region but it met with opposition from Macedonian Bulgarians, so that a modern Greek historian tells of 12,000 volunteering in 1869 to fight the Cretan rebels alongside the Ottoman troops. In reality the Kingdom of Greece, fully engaged in the annexation of Thessaly (1881) and the endless Cretan business was forced to remain comparatively passive in Macedonia while the Bulgarian government took an active part: the cause of Hellenism suffered a set-back examplified by the fact that eight dioceses were lost to the Exarchate in the area. While local conflicts became more frequent between Christians divided by nationalist activists, a war of propaganda was going on in Europe which drew arguments from "neutral" experts such as the Austrian geographer, Heinrich Kiepert who supported the Bulgars while Stanford, an Englishman, was on the side of the Greeks.

A third party later joined the fray, Serbia. The 1844 Nacertanje mentioned the Empire of Dusan which had encompassed all the Western part of Macedonia up to the Struma but, until 1875, Serbian public opinion had been mainly concerned with Bosnia-Herzegovina. The government in Belgrade, however, was in favor of opening Serbian schools, at least in the Northern part up to Uskub (Skopje); J.Ristic, the Prime Minister boasted of opening over sixty between 1867 and 1878. Anyway, though Serbia was able to advance historical and linguistic arguments she could not avail herself in Macedonia of a powerful organization such as the Patriarchate and the Exarchate. Nevertheless from the 1880's an effort was made in the shape of the railway joining Belgrade to Thessalonika. In 1885 the Saint Sava Society decided to set up schools to counter the Bulgarian Society of Cyril and Methodius which had been founded the previous year. In 1892 there were 110 Serbian schools, in 1907 226, together with three colleges at Uskub, Monastir and Thessalonika, even three high schools for girls. Thus some 10,000 young Macedonians were taught the literary Serbian language, which differed appreciably from their own dialects, as well as the history of Serbia through which they learnt that they were descended from Tsar Dusan's subjects. As regards churches any improvement had to be fought for; there were long negotiations with the Porte and the Patriarchate, accompanied by payment of baksheesh, before they were allowed to use the Slavonic liturgy in the Patriarchate's churches and before Serbian bishops were appointed. Only in 1897 did Firmillan Drazic receive confirmation of his appointment at Uskub, but as a mere diocesan administrator. On arrival he was the butt of stone throwing on the part of Exarchists and Patriarchist Tsintsars and was forced to stay for several days in the railway coach he had traveled in; only in 1902 did he really become a bishop.

About the same time as the Serbs another competitor made its appearance on the Macedonian chessboard: the Romanian government. Because Bucharest was so far from the region there was no question of territorial conquest but Romania was interested in the legacy of the Ottoman Empire and therefore in her brothers living there. Ottoman statistics include them in the figures for Patriarchists and the Greeks did not mind annexing them, especially the Tsintsars in the Pindus. Bulgars and Serbs alike put them at 70/80,000 towards the end of the century. Bucharest paid for Romanian schools and sent teachers. This of course helped to keep their cultural identity alive, but had little impact on the Macedonian question: it only served as a pretext for Romania to intervene in Balkan affairs.

The outcome of half a century of religious and educational rivalries as well as propaganda which made use of arguments drawn from history, linguistics and ethnography, showed in contradictory statistics given by the various protagonists by more or less impartial experts. The report of the International Commission of the Carnegie Foundation dealing with the Balkan wars emphasized this ambiguity:

	Statistics Bulgarian (1900)	Statistics Greek (1904)	Statistics Serbian (1889)
Turks	449,200	634,000	231,000
Bulgarians	1,181,000	332,000	57,000
Greeks	228,700	652,700	201,100
Serbs	700	—	2,048,000
Wallachians	80,700	25,100	69,600
Albanians	128,700	—	165,000
Jews	67,800	53,100	64,600
Gypsies	54,500	8,900	28,700
Others	16,500	18,600	3,500
Total	2,258,000	1,724,000	2,870,000

The commission published as an annex to the report two ethnographical maps, one drawn by V. Kancov, a Bulgarian geographer, the other by his Serbian colleague, J. Cvijic, which were almost identical as regards the distribution of Turks, Greeks and Wallachians, but the former made no mention of the Serbs, while the latter simply replaced Bulgarians by Serbs and Macedonian Slavs, and called the Arnauts "Albanian speaking Serbs."

Christian solidarity which had been much in evidence in the days of Ottoman power simply vanished in the 1850s and the religious conflict between Patriarchate and Exarchate showed few signs of brotherly love. The fact that country-states intervened in the 1870s somewhat took the religious aspect out of the matter exacerbating nationalisms and resulting in terrorism and war. A significant step in radicalizing the issue was the appearance in 1893 of the Macedonian Revolutionary Organization of the Interior (IMRO). It was created at Risen, a village lying near Lake Prespa and originally was a group of intellectuals who wished to prepare an uprising against the Ottomans. In the general situation of all imperial territories striving to achieve Tanzimat the aim was to insure that Christian populations should enjoy "personal security and guarantees of law and order as well as justice in the administration." The long term objective was to make Macedonia autonomous under the slogan "Macedonia to the Macedonians." The noise of Greek, Bulgarian and Serbian propaganda drowned the voices of the local population which had something to say to careful observer: in 1902, J.Cvijic called "Macedonian Slavs," as distinct from Serbs and Bulgars, the Slavonic speaking population living south of the line Ohrid—Prilep—Veles—Kratovo, and in 1905 the German geographer K. Oestreich ignored Serbs and Bulgars and called them Macedo-Slavs and evaluated their number at two million. Thus Macedonians did exist! A movement by the name of "Macedonian Renaissance," according to Skopje historians, started around the 1850s. From then on Dimitar Miladinov and Constantine his brother (1830–1862) made every effort to encourage teaching in the vernacular; their outlook was anti-Greek to begin with and drew inspiration from Russian Pan-Slavism. There gathered round them a group of young teachers who published the first text-books written in dialect, such as the "Primer for Children" signed by Parteni Zografski, which appeared in 1858 in Istanbul-Galata. It should be observed that this pioneering work had the support of the University of Zagreb where several of the group had attended and also of J.Strosmajer, a bishop and spokesman for the Southern Slavs, who had a Collection of Macedonian Songs compiled by the Miladinov brothers and published in Zagreb. For the 1893 generation cultural agitation was not enough for it had the example of the Bulgars fighting for political freedom. The IMRO Congress at Thessalonika in 1894 organized an underground military network which divided the territory into districts under the authority of a captain who had a cheta—a formation of comitadji, volunteers recruited among craftsmen and local lower middle class; the Organization had at its disposal a financial service which levied taxes and an "executive police" which kept control of the activists and punished spies and traitors. At the head of IMRO was Goce Delcev (1872–1903) son of a Kukus (Kilkis) craftsman living in a predominantly Greek area. He had attended the Thessalonika high school and later the Military Academy of Sofia, before becoming a primary schoolteacher at Stip. He followed the "autonomy" doctrine, and dreamt of an independent Macedonia inside a Balkan Federation. In spite of his military training in Bulgaria political leaders in Sofia backed his rivals: they supported the "Supreme Macedonian Committee" or Macedonian Organization Abroad, known as Vrhovists or Supremists, which started in Sofia in 1895 and whose aim, originally kept secret, was to join Macedonia to the Bulgarian Kingdom. Operations against the Ottomans started immediately and harsh reprisals followed: between 1898 and 1902 the Organization could boast of 132 armed encounters or assassination attempts which claimed 4,373 "Turk" lives. IMRO was at the time provided with weapons and financial assistance by Bulgaria and if necessary the comitadjis could rapidly seek refuge behind the frontier; there was no doubt that the Bulgars were gaining the upper hand in Macedonia. The Greeks were worried by these developments and in 1894 reorganized the Philiki Hetairia which acquired a military organization. Groups of Andartes (rebels) made similar operations, attacked Ottoman public services, levied taxes among the peasants, closed Exarchist churches and if necessary fled to Greece. Macedonia became a combat area for terrorist activity which went beyond the domestic scene since the French railway going from Thessalonika to Gevgelia was sabotaged twenty times in one month, English tourists suffered exactions on their travels and the French Ottoman Bank of Thessalonika was blown up.

On July 20 (August 2) 1903, the feast of Elias—Ilinden—IMRO and its Bulgarian supporters tried to strike a major blow at the enemy: they wanted to free the Monastir (Bitola) Vilayet from Ottoman occupation and then become masters of the whole of Macedonia. The rebels had some initial success and the creation of the "Republic of Krusevo" was declared, later the fundamental idea of separatists. They claimed to have used 27,000 men to fight against 350,000 Ottoman troops. One thing is sure, that by mid-September the last rebels were crossing into Bulgaria and the IMRO leadership was decimated, among those killed Goce Delcev.

Reprisals were brutal: it was reported that 200 villages were destroyed, 4,700 inhabitants were massacred, 3,000 women were raped and 12,000 houses burnt down. Europe was waking up again to the "Bulgarian massacres" deplored by Gladstone in 1876.

In reality, for a while Macedonia had been uppermost in the minds of European leaders. The massacre of the French and German Consuls in Thessalonika in 1876 was still fresh in people's memories and in 1897, during the Cretan crisis, Austria-Hungary and Russia talked of a partition of the region which would have allowed for an Albanian state. In the meantime the Istanbul authorities were requested to bring in "reforms": yet again the Porte made promises, but nothing came of them. In October, 1903, Franz-Joseph and Nicholas II met at the Murzsteg Castle near Semmering and decided on a reform program, known as "Program of Murzsteg," which the Sultan accepted. Hilmi Pasha, the Ottoman Inspector General would be assisted by two "civilian agents," one Austrian, the other Russian; the territory was still divided into five police areas but an international police force would be answerable to the Five Great Powers (England, France, Italy, Austria and Russia); also in 1905, London asked for a Finance Control Commission to be created. This was only to be a provisional arrangement to restore a minimum of order, but Article IV of this program, laid the ground for the division of Macedonia into "National" Zones, Bulgarian, Greek and Serbian. Hence each of the protagonists was intent in pushing the others out of their zones—which meant physical expulsion. Terrorism went on unabated, especially as IMRO was torn by internal conflicts. The Verhovists with pro-Bulgaria sympathies felt the autonomy tendency, also known as "centralists," were responsible for the Ilinden failure and the congresses at Thessalonika and Rila in 1905 gave rise to heated exchanges which were mirrored on the ground with firearms. On this occasion the principle of setting up a separate Macedonian nation-state was advocated as a solution. However, the coup d'état in Belgrade in June 1903 and the difficulties encountered by Peter I at the start of his reign tempered Serbian enthusiasm, while the Greeks, who had to deal with the Cretan situation, could scarcely do more than operate in the southern area of the region. In 1906–7 the Bulgars seemed poised to win in Macedonia, when once again the Great Powers made demands on the Porte in favor of the Christian populations. In July 1908, however, the nationalist movement of the Young Turks took over power in Thessalonika, the nerve centre of Macedonia.

The Albanian Renaissance:
Rilindja, 1850–1908

Statistics for Macedonia all mentioned the Albanians whose numbers were said to be between 120 and 160,000. This represented only a fraction of the ethnic group speaking the same language, which according to a map drawn up by Ami Boue in 1847, stretched along the Adriatic coast from Antivari (Bar) to the north down to the Gulf of Corinth and went inland as far as a line going from Prizren, Lake Ohrid, Kastoria, Trikala and Lapanto. In 1875 Elisee Reclus made an estimate of 1,400,000, with north of the Shkumbin River 600,000 Gegs, made up of two thirds Muslims and one third Roman Catholics and to the south of the river 800,000 Tosks, with two thirds Muslims and the others Orthodox; the largest city was Prizren said to have over 40,000 inhabitants, while Tirana had less than 10,000. The geographer remarked on the Albanians extending up to the plain of Kosovo and the banks of Lake Ohrid, while in the south, in Epirus they were rubbing shoulders with Greeks: Arta, Janina and Prevasa had become Hellenic and "only a few Moslem families are still using the Albanian language." They called themselves Shqiptars, the Sons of the Eagle.

In terms of administrative organization the Albanians were distributed in four Vilayets, Janina (Ionnina), Monastir (Bitola), Kosovo and Scutari (Shkodra) mixed with Greeks, Serbs, Wallachians and Macedonian Slavs. These areas were as poor as Macedonia, but apart from the port of Durazzo (Durres) start of the Via Egnatia, did not have the same strategic importance. The Ciftliks were concentrated on the coastal plains while in the mountainous parts the population lived in autarchy. The latter retained their tribal social organization—the Fis—such as the Catholic Mirdites with their Kapedan, who ran their own administration under the distant tutelage of the Shkodra Governor. Since the conquest in the 15th century, the Ottomans had found it difficult to administer these regions without roads, in which the inhabitants, well armed because of the vendetta tradition, and always ready to greet the Sultan's representatives with gunshot. In 1826 the abolition of the Janissary system in which many Arnauts had served, had repercussions on Albanian society due to the end of Timars. Later the Tanzimat met with fierce opposition. The families of Beys such as the Toptani, Vrioni and Verlaci, turned into large landowners with estates ranging from 5 to 12,000 hectares whose relations with peasants were feudal and who resisted any attempt at centralization on the part of the Porte. Craftsmen and tradesmen in the cities complained of the burden of taxation getting heavier, and the mountain tribes insisted on keeping their traditional liberties. They all joined in opposing the ruling of compulsory military service—the Nizam—in 1843 and uprisings broke out, primarily a refusal of modernization by a conservative society. Nevertheless they were the first stirrings of national awareness.

Yet the Albanians, unlike Greeks, Bulgars or Serbs, were hampered by fierce conflicts between various religious groups. There was an estimated 70% Muslim population in the area between the Kruja-Lake Ohrid line to the north, and Vlora-Permeti to the south; there were 20% Orthodox Christians who were dominant in the south; Roman Catholics were confined to the northern mountains. It should be observed that Muslim Sunnites were balanced by Bektashis who, following the abolition of the Janissary system, took refuge in Albania until the end of World War II, and by crypto-Christians (crypto-Orthodox and crypto-Catholics) who had two first names, one Christian in their villages and one Muslim for the Ottoman administration. This kind of tolerance or compromise did not mean that rivalries and religious opposition disappeared, especially since these were often fueled by clergymen who benefited from the generosity of their patron-states: Greece for Orthodox, Austria and Italy for Catholics.

Whatever the reason, economic and social changes in the 19th century meant there was a large emigration to Istanbul, capital of the Empire, which by 1850 had become the largest Albanian city, with a colony of 60,000, and to Greece, Egypt, the Romanian Principalities, Southern Russia, and later America, and even Australia. As they came into contact with other national minorities, the Albanian colonies played a great part, in conjunction with older settlements such as the Arbrechians in Southern Italy, in rforming a national identity. The Ottoman reform plan in the field of education, adopted in 1845, made provision for compulsory school attendance had remained a dead letter, but opened the way for religious schools. The Albanian regions had many new schools,

Turkish-Muslim, Greek for the Orthodox and Italian for Catholics. A few Albanians realized the risk of fragmentation and insisted on language and school being the only possible foundation for their identity. Thus Naum Vegilharxhi (1797–1854), who was born at Korca, and emigrated to Romania where he took part in the rebellion of T. Vladimirescu (1821) took the first initiative in defence of the vernacular and national culture by publishing text-books in Albanian and in 1850 forming an "Albanian Cultural Association." At Istanbul, K. Kristoforidhi (1830–1895) who went to England as a student, did the same and tried to simplify the alphabet, which got him into trouble with the Sheik ul Islam and the Patriarch who would not tolerate any changes in the transcription of religious texts. At this point the Arbrechians made an important contribution; they had preserved their Orthodox liturgy in the Albanian language and in 1794 a high school was opened at San Demetrio Corone in Calabria where all classes were in Albanian. In the days of the Risorgimento some of their intelligentsia became aware of their national identity and found inspiration in it for their own work. One such was Girolamo de Rada (1814–1903) whose epic poem Skanderbeg (1866) was translated into several languages and found admirers in Lamartine and Mistral, or Demetrio Camarda (1821–1882) who in 1864 published an essay on the Albanian language tracing its history back to antiquity.

In the country itself the movement incited hardly any interest. The Porte ran Turkish public schools through the education offices of each Vilayet, while the Phanar Patriarchate in 1872 formed a "Cultural Association" in order to spread the use of the Greek language in Epirus, a region with a mixed population. Faced with this two-pronged offensive the teaching of Albanian was slow to develop: in 1878 in the three most advanced Sandjaks Avlonya (Vlora), Belgrad (Berat) and Ghirokastra (Gjirokastra) there were 80 Turkish schools, 163 Greek schools and not a single Albanian one. The language was taught as a subject only in two Catholic schools at Shkodra, but it was of minor importance and classes were in Italian. However, at this time there was a concerted effort to record the oral folk traditions; in 1871 Zef Jubani, secretary of the French Consul at Shkodra, published a "Collection of Popular Songs and Albanian Rhapsodies" in Trieste, while in 1878 Thimi Mitko at Korca produced Collected Songs and Proverbs of South Albania under the title of "The Albanian Bee," which refered to the romantic movement of the Slavonic Matice. Such were the beginnings of what is known in Albanian history as Rilindja, the Renaissance.

Events in Europe gave a political aspect to the movement. The Eastern Crisis of 1875-77 and the Treaty of Berlin (1878) put the Albanians in a difficult position. The London Protocol signed by the Great Powers in March 1877 made no mention of them: the regions of Debar (Dibra), Kalkandelan (Tetovo) and Gorice (Korca) were joined together to form a western Bulgarian Vilayet. Hence the Albanian "patriots" were in a quandary: should they fight the Ottoman Empire alongside the Christians who had no inkling of an Albanian nationality, or should they join the Sultan's forces to receive, as a reward, recognition of their separate identity. Thus the Albanian movement suffered from a certain ambiguity from the start, which hostile neighbors were not slow to exploit and they invoked the existence of a Muslim majority to denounce the Albanians as the natural allies of the Turks. In the face of the decisions taken in London, an assembly met at Janina in April 1877 at the invitation of Abdul Frasheri (1839-1892) scion of a family of southern Beys and a deputy for Janina at the first Ottoman Parliament. In a memorandum sent to the Porte they requested the Albanian regions become an autonomous Vilayet, under the administrative authority of local civil servants, and whose official language in public services and education would be Albanian. Though it remained unanswered this memorandum was the first political initiative taken by the Rilindja. The Serbo-Ottoman war in 1878 caused Serbian troops to move into areas with an Albanian majority which gave rise to contradictory accusations of atrocities: feelings of hatred developed between the two communities. The Treaty of San Stefano (March 1878) made arrangements for the Shqiptar territories to be completely dismembered, and to prevent this happening a large gathering took place at Prizren on June 10, 1878 at the request of Abdul Frasheri, during the Berlin discussions between the Great Powers. 80 delegates from the Kosovo, Shkodra, Monastir and Janina Vilayets attended, representing all three religions, and decided to form a league, by the name of League of Prizren, just as Skanderbeg had done before them. Among the Balkan neighbors and the Great Powers this body roused suspicions of being a device for the Porte to prevent its empire falling apart. It is true that Muslim conservatives could be found in it, but there were also nationalists who wanted an autonomous Shqiperia. The Great Powers gathered in Berlin remained unmoved and Bismarck declared: "There is no Albanian nationality." Local League committees took up arms therefore to protest against the decisions taken by the European Powers: Montenegro had to fight for two years and thanks to the support of an international squadron managed to take Dulcigno (Ulqin), as for Greece she was forced to give up the occupation of Janina when Thessaly was annexed in 1881. Most of the Albanian territory remained within the Empire as the League had wanted. Another of its aims was to achieve autonomy, but this met with a blank refusal from the Porte and, in December 1881, when a "Provisional Albanian Government" was formed, Istanbul sent an army which occupied Prizren and dispersed the patriots, 4,000 of whom were tried, among them Abdul Frasheri and sentenced to death. He was later pardoned but had to remain in jail until 1885. The Prizren League ended in failure but was a precedent for future patriots as well as bringing the Albanian cause into sharp focus.

Culturally the movement went ahead. Sami Frasheri (1850–1905) a brother of Abdul set up a "Albanian Learned Society" in Istanbul through which text-books were published and he developed a new alphabet, while the third brother, Naim Frasheri (1846–1900) took over from his brother who was still in prison and wrote an epic poem "The History of Skanderbeg" (1889) which won him the reputation of being the Albanian national poet. The Society opened a private school at Korca in March 1887; it was the first "national" school for Orthodox as well as Muslim children, which is why the Patriarchate excommunicated it. Abroad Arbrechian communities were encouraged by the chairman of the Italian government, Francesco Crespi, a Sicilian of Italo-Albanian parentage, and above all in 1908 the large Boston colony broke from the Greek Church to create an Albanian Orthodox Church. This was brought about by Fan Noli (1882–1965) a young patriot who had a long and uneven career. He was born near Adrianopolis, attended school at Athens and later studied in Egypt where his fellow Albanians talked him into going to the United States to look after their brothers. He was ordained into the priesthood and organized a missionary Church under the authority of the Russian Patriarchate.

Politically the struggle for autonomy continued and the question of Albania remained on the European agenda together with the Macedonian imbroglio. In 1905 a "Committee for Albania's liberation" was constituted at Monastir (Bitola) by B. Topulli and a few young intellectuals. Following the example of their neighbors they set up underground local committees and guerrilla units—Cete—which became active in the south in 1906 with attacks against Turkish gendarmes and Greek Andartes. Thus the Albanians could be counted among potential inheritors of the Ottoman Empire.

The Rebellion of the Young Turks and the Fourth Eastern Crisis, 1908–1912

The Porte had experienced a crisis in 1876 with the fall of Abdul Aziz, the short reign of Murad V, his nephew, and the accession to the throne of his brother Abdul Hamid II (1876–1909). The prime mover of these changes was Midhat Pasha (1822–1883) one of the Tanzimat dignitaries, who had been sent to Vienna, Paris and London, before becoming Grand Vizier for a short while, before the conservatives forced him to step down. Immediately after the Treaty of Paris (1856) there had been a Turkish "revival," similar to that of the Bulgars and Macedonians: together with the wish for modernization by preceding reformers, there was the desire to assert the Turkish identity, in the face of Western power and of the Christian subjects in the Empire. In 1865 some of these innovators, Namik Kemal, Ibrahim Sinasi, Abdul Ziya got together under the banner of a journal "Musbir" which became involved in countering the Persian influence in literature and in the spoken language, and upholding the concept of a Turkish national identity within the Empire. It was banned by the Porte in 1867 and its editors emigrated to Paris and London where they adopted the name of "Young Turks" which was that of a short lived Committee formed in 1868. Meanwhile Abdul Aziz, faced with the opening of the Suez Canal (1869), took a few measures towards modernization. He opened a Medical Institute (1867), the Imperial Lycée at Galatasaray, with assistance from the French (1868), the University of Istanbul (1869), and a Law Institute (1870) while the press was allowed to develop. In 1872 there were three dailies and several weeklies, but their sales remained lower than the six French newspapers published at Istanbul, Smyrna and Alexandria. The Sultan was also keen on railways and in 1869 he granted a Bavarian banker, Baron Hirsch, the right to build the Vienna-Istanbul line. All these undertakings were costly and in 1872, when Abdul Aziz decided to take charge of government in person his impulsive temperament got him into financial trouble. Following the Crimean War the Porte was burdened with a debt which to service constantly needed fresh loans. In 1875 fourteen loans had to be made amounting to 200 million pounds sterling—which pushed the yearly interest up to half the income of the Empire. European lenders expressed unease and when the rebellion broke out in Bosnia, spreading later to the whole of the Balkans, the reforming party in the administration took action. In conjunction with the war minister and with a Fetwa granted by the Sheik ul Islam, Midhat Pasha forced Abdul Aziz to abdicate in favor of his nephew Murad (May 30, 1876). The latter did not stay in power more than three months: as Midhat found him unstable, he replaced him with his brother, Abdul Hamid II, whose reign was to last from August 1876 to April 1909. In order to pacify European public opinion after the Bulgarian atrocities, the new Sultan tried to project the idea that he was a reformer. He appointed Midhat Pasha Grand Vizier and promulgated a Constitution. This came as a surprise and the Empire's enemies saw this move as an "oriental farce." On December 23, the Russian, English, Austrian and French ambassadors met to examine the reforms to protect the Christian peoples feeling that the Porte was under pressure to accept them. However they had to suspend proceedings because of artillery fire. The envoys of the Great Powers learnt that the Sultan had granted a Constitution to his peoples, which made all their efforts pointless! The consequences of this theatrical coup were far reaching in terms of foreign affairs and also internally for the Ottoman Empire had a Constitution, known as Abdul Hamid Constitution (December 1876). It upheld the principle invoked in the Gulhane Hatti Sheriff of 1839: all subjects of the Sultan were equal whatever their confession or nationality, although Islam was still the state religion; the constitution allowed for political institutions such as an elected parliament, an independent judiciary and decentralized the Empire with representatives influencing the governors' decisions. However, the Sultan retained considerable powers: he appointed ministers, called Parliament into session, dismissed it and retained authority to send individuals seen as dangerous into exile. In short it was an "authoritarian Empire" in which Abdul Hamid stood for Napoleon III before he became the "Bloody Sultan" remembered for the 1895–96 Armenian massacres. In February 1877 he dismissed Midhat Pasha who went to live in exile in Europe and governed with a camarilla of courtesans from his Yildiz Palace.

The Parliament which had been elected through indirect suffrage met in March 1877 and this first session of a Legislative Assembly in the history of the Empire was the scene of picturesque exchanges. In April the Sultan took advantage of Russia's declaration of war to adjourn Parliament; the Constitution was never applied: every year the document was printed in the government's agenda but the Assembly was not convened until the Revolution of 1908.

During this lengthy suspension of constitutional government Abdul Hamid came to rely increasingly on the Muslim religious hierarchy to oppose the Great Powers and their economic ascendancy and played on his role as Caliph of 300,000 million of the Prophet's faithful. To this end he encouraged pilgrimages to Mecca and in 1900 built the Hedjaz railway starting at Damascus. The ideology of return to the roots of Ottoman greatness went hand in hand with press censorship, close police watch on individuals through an army of spies, and curtailing higher education as well as travel abroad. This served to increase the number of Turkish opponents living in Paris who were known as "Young Turks" but who were in fact from many tendencies as was clear from the 1902 Congress in which Turks, Arabs, Armenians, Kurds and Albanians took part. It ended in deadlock naturally since the plans made by all these exiles were mutually antagonistic: the various "national" programs of the Albanians, Kurds or Armenians were opposed to the dreams of the "Ottomanists" who saw the Empire's future as a symbiosis of different peoples, or the "Panturanians" who wished for the reunification of all the Turkish peoples of the Ottoman and Russian Empires.

A solution was found by a small group of officers who suddenly made their voices heard. The military class was dissatisfied with the reversals suffered by the Empire in quick succession in the Balkans and the European Powers meddling in the area. It was especially incensed by the international gendarmerie which kept law and order in Macedonia: the most vociferous were officers of the 3rd Army Corps in Thessalonika. Among them was Captain Mustafa Kemal (1881–1934) founder of modern Turkey. He was born in the town and was a graduate of the Military Academy set up by the Germans; he was an officer of outstanding ability who in 1905 chose to enter the underground movement for national revival advocated by the "Committee for Union and Progress" formed in Paris in 1890 under Ahmed Riza (1859–1930), whose aim was to return to the 1876 Constitution. Yet the Committee seemed too heterogenous to the military and they formed a secret society called "Society for Freedom," which was organized, like the Macedonian revolutionaries, into small independent cells and sworn to absolute secrecy. One of these officers was a cavalry captain by the name of Enver Pasha (1881–1922) who was in favor of the Panturanian doctrine and was in touch with the Young Turks in Paris. This is why the revolt that followed bore his name.

In July 1908 the Sultan's police managed to infiltrate the organization and the Great Powers made preparations for another intervention in Macedonia: the conspirators thought the time had come for action. On July 23, a telegram from the general staff of the 3rd Corps was sent to the Sultan: the Constitution had to be put back into force within 24 hours or the 3rd Macedonian Army would make for Istanbul. Abdul Hamid, who was under pressure from European governments and in severe financial difficulties was forced to accept the conditions. In the town of Thessalonika Christians and Muslims fell into one another's arms, Comitadjis and Andartes came down from the mountains to fraternize and Enver Pasha exclaimed: "Henceforth there are no Bulgars, Greeks, Wallachians, Jews or Muslims. We are all brothers, equal and proud to call ourselves Ottomans." This was the Young Turk Revolution of July 24, 1908. It was in fact a military coup which is why there were limits to the changes that followed.

In the next days the Constitution was restored and Abdul Hamid swore to uphold it, the Yildiz camarilla was dismissed. However, the Committee for Union and Progress did not come to the fore and the Empire lacked a strong executive. Another Eastern Crisis broke out. Since 1878 the Austrian military hierarchy dreamt of becoming masters of the Adriatic by annexing Bosnia-Herzegovina which was under the administration of Vienna. Yet the Serbs were as touchy about it as the French about Alsace-Lorraine, and it was difficult to deprive Milan or Alexander of this region since they were political allies of Austria. After Peter I's accession to the throne the kingdom started looking to Russia, the arch rival of Austria-Hungary in the Balkans: the seizure of Bosnia-Herzegovina could be seen as compensation and a step towards restoring the balance of power. Count Aehrenthal, who became Foreign Minister in 1906, was convinced of this and prepared for a redistribution of Ottoman territory. His counterpart in St Petersburg, A. Isvolsky was of a similar mind and wished to make up for the humiliation of the Japanese war by giving Russian ships access to the Straits of the Black Sea. Early in July 1908 he sent a confidential diplomatic note to suggest an arrangement: Russia would not object to the Austrians' seizing Bosnia-Herzegovina, if in return the latter helped the Tsar gain access to the Straits from which his warships had been banned since 1841, like all foreign ships. The Young Turk Revolution occurring a few days later and seemed to provide the pretext for this. The ministers met in Moravia at the Castle of Buchlau in September and agreed on the principle of a deal, but did not fix a date and there was no official report of their conversation. Soon afterwards Prince Ferdinand of Bulgaria arrived in Vienna to inform the authorities there of his wish to break his vassal ties with the Sultan; Aehrenthal saw this as a chance to strengthen Austrian influence in the region and advised him to take the title of tsar which was in use in the Middle Ages in Bulgaria. On 5 October 1908, Ferdinand declared Bulgaria independent and became Ferdinand I, Tsar of the Bulgars. The next day Aehrenthal announced to the chancelleries of Europe the annexation of Bosnia-Herzegovina by Austria-Hungary.

This raised a storm of protest and led to the 4th Eastern Crisis in the 19th century, taking Europe to the brink of war. Serbia was indignant and turned to Russia for redress, which in turn meant involving France. The Russian authorities were faced with public demonstrations of anger from Panslavists. The Foreign Minister who had kept his government colleagues in the dark cut a mean figure, his denials contradicting Aehrenthal's assertions. As there were no minutes of the Buchlau conversation the Russian was accused of lying and could not explain himself; the ensuing dispute went on for several months and gave rise to fierce debates in diplomatic circles. Wilhelm II came down in favor of Austria and on March 21, 1909, addressed what seemed to be an ultimatum to Isvolsky: the Russian Minister had to accept full annexation or he would have to face combined action from Germany and Austria-Hungary. Isolated, Isvolsky bowed to the inevitable and promised to make the Belgrade government calm down. A note dated March 31, addressed by Serbia to Austria-Hungary and the other European Powers, stated that her interests had not been affected by the "fait accompli" in Bosnia-Herzegovina. In April an agreement was reached between Istanbul, Vienna and Sofia: in return for financial compensation and Austria returning the Sandjak of Novi Pazar to the Ottoman Empire, the Sultan consented to the loss of Bosnia-Herzegovina and Bulgaria.

The crisis on the diplomatic level was over, but not without serious consequences. In Serbia nationalism was asserting itself, in the Ottoman Empire the Young Turks suffered a blow to their reputation and were accused of losing more territory than Abdul Hamid after thirty years of absolutist rule. The legislative elections, held in accordance to the Ottoman Constitution, took place right in the middle of the crisis, in November-December 1908. They took place under the system of two-tiered indirect suffrage, the right to vote applying only to men over 25 years of age. A movement of opposition to the central Union and Progress Party rallied round Prince Sabaheddin, a nephew by marriage of Abdul Hamid, who advocated decentralization and enjoyed support from the various nationalities in the Empire. Yet this liberal Ottoman Party came into play too late and only candidates who represented "Union and Progress" were elected to Parliament. A conflict immediately erupted between the Chamber and the Grand Vizier which ended with the latter's resignation, while the masses in Istanbul demonstrated against the Young Turks who had been denounced by the Ulemas as miscreants, free masons and heirs of the French Revolution. As for the representatives of the nationalities they accused the Young Turk committees of being authoritarian. Tension increased in April 1909 under the impact of the painful conclusion to the European crisis and in the night of April 12 to 13, a mutiny by soldiers stationed in the capital, with the participation of religious leaders, led to a march on Parliament. There were violent scenes involving Young Turk officers and Armenians while Greeks and Albanians clapped their hands. As disorder spread the Macedonian Army under Shevket Pasha marched on Istanbul on 24 April 1909, to place it under martial law. Three days later, Parliament on the strength of a Fetwa signed by the Sheik ul Islam dethroned Abdul Hamid who had to go into exile to Thessalonika and was replaced by his brother Mehmed Reshad who took the name Mehmed V (1909–1918).

The new sultan was not a danger for the Unionists who could now rule unimpeded through men such as David Bey the Finance Minister, Talat Pasha Minister of the Interior and above all the army under Shevket Pasha. Yet the Central Committee itself remained in the wings and underwent a reorganization to set up a secret hierarchy which shadowed the official authorities. In the countryside it was assisted by large landowners, while in towns it attracted the middle class officials, barristers, doctors and teachers. It was described as a "complex organization which is something like a masonic lodge, a revolutionary cell, as well as a komitadji group and a modern political party."

After achieving their first objective—turning the Empire into a Constitutional Monarchy—the founding members had to deal with its second aim—Union—and spell out its policy vis-à-vis the various peoples of the Empire. The Young Turks did not approve of the Millet system, which to their mind was anachronistic and divisive. As they were influenced by Jacobin ideas put about by the French Revolution, they wanted Greeks, Albanians, Jews, Armenians, Arabs and Turks all to be integrated as Ottoman citizens equal in rights and obligations. Yet the Balkan peoples had their own ideas ranging from autonomy to independence. In Macedonia they made their point with guns but were now also able to voice their claims in Parliament, which included at this time 147 Turks, 60 Arabs, 27 Albanians, 26 Greeks, 14 Armenians, 10 Slavs and 4 Jews. All over the world there reigned a climate of nationalism. In the winter of 1908–9 Bulgarian comitadjis and Greek andartes once more took up arms, while the Albanian countryside once again rose up. What fueled discontent was the discriminative laws passed by the Young Turks, after the April 1909 coup, concerning associations, the press, education. Non-Turkish populations protested at the cultural hegemony under cover of Ottomanization. They were also subjected to pressures on the part of the European Powers, now divided into Triple Entente and Triple Alliance, and fiercely competing for imperial influence in the field of railways, such as the Bagdad line, or oil round Mosul. France unwilling to jeopardize the loans made to the Sultan remained on the sidelines, and rejected a request from the Young Turks for a loan, though they had always looked to her for support. In September 1911 Italy went on the attack in the Tripoli region.

At the time the Albanian provinces were up in arms. In 1908 a Berat notable, Ismail Kemal (1844–1919), went to Parliament at the head of the Albanian group. Disappointment soon followed. The Young Turks tried to impose their language and spelling in schools, and above all they ordered the people to give up their arms, which was contrary to their tradition. The Kosovo region rose up in March 1910, soon followed by the populations of the northern mountains, under Ded Gjo Luli who adopted the Skanderbeg flag. In the spring of 1912 answering the call of two deputies, H.Prishtina and Ismail Kemal, the whole Albanian country rose up and the Ottoman administration was paralyzed.

The Balkan powder keg was about to explode.

15

The Balkans as a Source of Conflicts in Europe, 1912–1918

If you visit a cemetery in any Serbian village, or those in Greece, Bulgaria or Albania, you will discover graves of soldiers dead "in the field of honour" which European historiography list separately as the Balkan Wars (1912–1913) and World War I (1914–1918)— 1922 for Greece. It is clear that for the unfortunate people there was no break in these terrible conflicts, which signified developmental crises and accession to maturity of contemporary Balkan states.

Balkan Wars, 1912–1913

They were local conflicts in the sense that only local people were involved in the fighting and the objectives remained limited, they should not be seen only as clashes between European imperialistic powers. Yet the Balkan Wars were encouraged by rivalries between the great European countries, especially those opposing the Triple Alliance to the Triple Entente. The crisis following on the annexation of Bosnia-Herzegovina ended a tacit agreement of non-aggression that, since 1886/7, had ruled relations betwen Russia and Austria-Hungary in the Peninsula. Isvolsky and his successor, Sazanov, felt the insult deeply, especially as it came after the humiliation of the Japanese defeat and the disruption caused by the 1905 Revolution. The Balkan dispute offered the tsarist Empire an opportunity to recover its pride without a head on clash with the Triple Alliance powers. The Balkan states sought the protection of the Saint Petersburg authorities before making attempts at entering alliances in view of sharing out the Ottoman heritage in Europe.

The Young Turk Revolution as it led to intolerance, exacerbated latent nationalist movements, which feared the renewal of the old Empire under the guidance of "Union and Progress." Could the sick man recover? It became urgent to act and in December 1908 Isvolsky spoke to the Duma of the creation of a "Balkan bloc." Serbs and Bulgarians carried out reciprocal opinion polls and in April 1911 Venizelos made soundings in Sofia. The war between Italy and Turkey raised hopes among all potential heirs and in the spring of 1912 plans for concrete action began to take shape. Talks between representatives of Belgrade and Sofia were long and difficult. In March 1912 their outcome was a defensive alliance against attack by a third party, either Austria-Hungary or Turkey, but a secret protocol defined the conditions of sharing out Macedonia and adjacent regions. Old Serbia, that is to say Kosovo and the Novi Pazar sandjak, would return to Serbia up to the Sar Planina line; territories east of Rhodopus and the Struma Valley would be allocated to Bulgaria; as for the central part between the Sar Planina and Lake Ohrid it would become an autonomous province as Bulgaria wished or it would be divided between the two states which would refer to the tsar for arbitration. In the event of a war with the Ottoman Empire, Bulgaria would provide 200,000 men and Serbia 150,000. Two months later, Athens and Sofia entered into a similar agreement, clearly hostile to Istanbul but with no mention of territorial clauses since they both wanted Thessalonika. In October, Montenegro in turn signed with Serbia and Bulgaria agreements on intervention in possible hostilities against the Ottoman Empire. This series of diplomatic undertakings was called the "Second Balkan League" (this refered to the League of 1865/1868 which was aborted when Prince Mihailo was assassinated in Belgrade.)

Istanbul, like the European capitals, was well aware of these dicussions, but the Porte was unable to react due to the turmoil in which its internal policy found itself and the disarray of the army which was under pressure from the Italians in Libya and Albanian rebels. As for the Great Powers they were hopelessly divided: they were of course apprehensive of an explosion in the Balkans, but Russia urged the Slavic states to go ahead before she tried to calm them down, and Austria-Hungary followed the latter course all along as she herself was involved in difficulties with nationalities, while England stood on the sidelines ready to intervene with her diplomacy.

In reality the Balkan peoples decided to act entirely on their own. On September 30, 1912, they issued mobilization orders, and an ultimatum demanding far-reaching reforms in the administration of Macedonia. Istanbul sent troops to the strategic places and remained silent until, on October 8, Montenegro sent an army to "restore order" in Northern Albania. A week later, the Porte requested the Serbian and Bulgarian ambassadors to leave the capital: war was declared on October 18 and Greece, invoking the cause of Cretan Enosis, joined her allies. The General Staffs of the European Powers deep in preparations for the major conflict they could see was approaching, sent their experts to the area to observe the manoeuvers "in real life." Newspapers and specialized reviews did the same and the European press was full of reports of fine military manoeuvers as well as the horrors of war. All the specialists expected a quick victory of the Sultan's troops which were trained by stars like Von Moltke and Von der Goltz, and were equipped with Mauser guns and Krupp cannons. In fact the Balkan armies added together were larger than those of the Ottomans in Europe, because the Empire had to protect its eastern borders against Russia and to keep order among its Arab populations. Moreover the Christian soldiers fighting for "national" aims proved more efficient, mobile and determined than their enemies.

The Bulgarians' campaign was the most successful. The main Ottoman forces being massed in Thrace, Ferdinand I launched his armies there. They held Edirne in a pincer movement and won victories at Luleburgaz and Buna Hissar only to stop in front of the Cataldja fortified lines, 50 kilometers from Istanbul. Another offensive towards the Aegean Sea brought them to the Struma River (Strymon) and one of their battallions entered Thessalonika, though this was twenty four hours after the Greek troops. In the end the Bulgarian detachment was allowed to remain in the town but did not share in the Provisional military command. George I's army came from the South to occupy Prevesa on the Gulf of Arta, then advanced towards Janina and, on November 8, seized Thessalonika. On the sea the Greek Navy tried to prevent Ottoman reinforcements arriving from Asia and occupied many islands in the Aegean Sea. Meanwhile the Serbs were descending on Macedonia where they won a victory at Kumanovo, occupied the sandjak of Novi Pazar before advancing south towards Prilep, Monastir (Bitola), and Ohrid while another army of Peter I crossed the Albanian region to occupy Durazzo (Durrès) and besiege Scutari

(Shkodra). Within a few weeks the Ottoman Empire had lost most of its Balkan territories. The new Grand Vizier, Kamil Pasha, who was an Anglophile, asked the London authorities to mediate: he was offered an armistice with Bulgaria on the basis of the Cataldja line and a conference in London of all the participants in the war to be held in December. However the Christian states' demands were such that no agreement seemed possible. Turkish patriots rose in anger and on January 23, 1913, some officers led by Enver Pasha, gun in hand, drove the government out and asked Shevket Pasha, the Commander-in-Chief, to assume power. Negotiations in London were broken and military operations resumed early in February. The Ottomans proved better organized then and fighting was more intense, but the Balkan armies were still superior and the Ottoman forts fell one after the other. On March 6, the Greeks were entering Janina, on March 28, after a bloody battle at Bulay, the Bulgars under General Ivanov took Edirne which had been under siege for five months, and the Montenegrins entered Scutari late in April. Shevket Pasha had to submit. The London Conference (May 30, 1913) forced the Ottoman Empire to give up all Balkan territories west of a line Midya on the Black Sea to Eniz on the Aegean Sea, as well as losing Crete which was given to Greece, while the European Powers were left to decide on the fate of the Albanian regions and the islands of the Aegean Sea. Shevket Pasha, the old patriot of "Union and Progress" paid with his life for having signed the infamous document. On June 11 he was assassinated in the street, while another coup was in the making. The Unionists took strong measures and all opposition parties were forbidden: Istanbul was settling to another dictatorial régime.

Now the Balkan Allies had to share out the spoils of war. Previous agreements which were only sketchy in the first place seemed grossly unsatisfactory to the Bulgarians who, since they had proved to be the decisive military element, claimed for themselves the whole of the unattributed zone, the central part of Macedonia from the Sar Planina to Lake Ohrid. As for the Serbs they had hoped to lay their hands on the Albanian regions and felt frustrated that an independent Albanian Principality was created. In compensation they insisted on being given territories in Macedonia. Thessalonika was a bone of contention between Greece and Bulgaria and Romania, joining the fray, wanted compensation for "giving up" her Walachians in Macedonia: she asked from Bulgaria the town of Silistra on the Danube and Southern Dobrudja up to the resort of Balcik. These disputes took place against a background of discord among the Great Powers; St Petersburg wished to preserve the Balkan League while Vienna wanted to put an end to it.

In the field tensions increased and there were many clashes between "allied" troops when they came into contact. Early in June Serbia and Greece agreed not to enter into separate arrangements with the Bulgarians and to have the River Vardar as their frontier (the Axios for the Greeks); in the event of a refusal from Sofia the two countries might resort to a combined military operation. The Russians when they heard of these negotiations felt they had to intervene: a telegram sent to Athens and Belgrade demanded that the tsar be consulted. However, the Bulgarian Command was afraid to be overtaken by events and public opinion was fired to enthusiasm for Macedonia. In the night of June 29/30, 1913, Ferdinand I ordered his troops to move back the Serbian and Greek lines. Belgrade and Athens immediately responded with declaring war: this was the start of the second Balkan War (June-July 1913).

The decision taken by Ferdinand I, besides indignation in the two capitals concerned and criticism on the part of many Bulgarian historians, gave rise to contradictory judgments: was it a full out attack or a mere show of force to react to the Serbo-Greek agreement? Was the government consulted and did it give its assent? A judicial enquiry later left the questions unanswered. What is certain is that Bulgaria found herself isolated facing her erswhile allies, while the Istanbul government under pressure from public opinion ordered the army to march. On July 22, Enver Pasha was back in possession of Edirne—a symbol since it was the first Ottoman capital in Europe. Everywhere Bulgarian troops were forced to yield and were unable to prevent the Romanian army to occupy the Dobrudja, without a declaration of war, and advance on Sofia. On July 31, Bulgaria asked for an armistice. The negotiations took place in Bucharest this time and a peace treaty was signed on August 10. The conditions were harsh for Bulgaria who had only a little piece of Macedonia in her share: the Struma Valley between Gorna Dzumaja (Blagoevgrad) and Petric with the Strumica enclave. Greece received all Macedonia south of Lake Ohrid and the coast with Thessalonika and Kavala. Serbia was given Northern Macedonia and the center up to Ohrid, Monastir (Bitola) and the Vardar. Romania moved into South Dobrudja. As for the Ottoman Empire it signed a treaty with Bulgaria late in

September dealing with the territories in dispute in Thrace: because of Enver Pasha's victories part of it was recovered with Edirne and Kirklareli, to be called eastern Thrace henceforth, while the Bulgarians obtained western Trace between the Maritsa and the gulf of Kavala which gave Sofia an opening on the Aegean Sea.

In fact these Balkan Wars were a disaster for all the countries in the Peninsula as they became divided by tales of atrocities and hatreds still burning fiercely at the time of World War II and beyond. In politics they were the preliminaries of the Great War: on the one hand Bulgaria and her dreams of revenge against Serbia in Macedonia, against Greece with Thessalonika and the whole of Thrace, against Romania with South Dobrudja, while all these countries which had not much in common clubbed together to defend the new status quo.

The Creation of an Albanian State, 1912–1914

While national armies were at war the Albanian regions rose up again. In April 1912 mountain tribes from around Djakova (Djakovica) in Kosovo took up arms in answer to a call from M.Prishtina, a member of parliament in Istanbul, while his colleague Ismail Qemal, the deputy for Berat, put forward the Albanian cause to the European Powers and supplied the partisans with weapons. The uprising spread rapidly and in July 1912 the whole of the Albanian regions had joined in. The military operations of the first Balkan War made the situation more confused as the offensives against the Ottomans took place in part on Albanian territories. The Serbs advanced through Kosovo up to Prizren and Uskub (Skopje) which had fallen to the Shqiptar rebels; through the sandjak of Novi Pazar they joined forces with the Montenegrins on the lake of Scutari and let them take the town, then they occupied Kruja, capital of Skanderbeg, Tirana, Durazzo (Durrès) and Elbasan, that is the northern zone of the Albanian parts up to the River Shkumbi. The Greeks coming from the south took hold of Epirus and occupied the capital Janina (Ioannina), before reaching Argyro Kastro (Djirokastra) and arriving at the gates of Avlona (Vlora).

In October 1912, some leaders meeting at Uskub had decided not to join in the war between the Balkan allies and the Ottomans, but there were clashes, especially with the Serbs. Ismail Qemal who was in Istanbul at the time realized that something had to be done. He went to Vienna where he met the Foreign Minister, Count Berchtold, and the English and Italian ambassadors, then went on to Trieste, with a small party of patriots, landed at Durazzo where they were joined by some Central Albanian notables before reaching the port of Avlona. There while Greek soldiers were encamped in front of houses, on November 28, 1912, an Assembly of 83 delegates chosen from the three religions was held. It took the name of "National Assembly" and after a speech by Ismail Qemal Albania was proclaimed independent. The same leader was asked to form a provisional government made up of seven Christian and Muslim ministers, and to inform Istanbul and the European Powers of the birth of a new state. In reality the chancelleries made no response and the Avlona decisions had no impact on the rest of the world. The situation was no better on the home front since most of the territory was occupied by foreign armies. The authority of the "Vlora government" as it was called by Albanian historians, was confined to a triangle going from Avlona to Berat and Lushnja. Everywhere else begs and leaders of fis scorned these important men dressed in European clothes who had taken it into their heads to meet in a small harbour of the Myzeqe.

Yet the Great Powers assembled in London since December 1912 to arbitrate on the first Balkan War could not ignore the Albanian problem, since the area was right in the middle of the Ottoman territories to be shared out. Ismail Qemal joined the international gathering chaired by E. Grey, secretary of the Foreign Office. The Ambassadors' Conference was divided between Austria-Hungary and Italy on the one hand, in favor of an independent Albania under their protection, while Russia and France, who encouraged Serbian expansion, thought that Albanian nationalism was an artificial creation of Vienna. Experts drafted various schemes, according to the fluctuations of military operations, and in May 1913 when the Treaty of London forced the Ottomans to give up all their territories west of a line running from Midye to Eniz, the diplomats had to pronounce on the fate of those regions lying outside Macedonia. On July 29, 1913 they declared that a "Neutral Sovereign Principality under a Hereditary Monarch and guaranteed by the Great Powers" was constituted. After the uneasy beginning at Vlora came the official recognition on the international scene.

There remained to give the new state an organization. A seven member commission—representatives of the six Great Powers plus an Albanian—was given the task; first of all "existing authorities" had to be abolished, among others the Vlora government, then an organic statute had to be drafted on the pattern of the Romanian and Bulgarian ones, and finally following the Macedonian example an international peace keeping force had to be set up. As was the custom in the 19th century, the head of state was to be Prince selected by the European Powers. As for the territorial borders two commissions were to draw them on the basis of decisions listed in the Treaty of London. Serbia had been given, apart from Central Macedonia, the Kosovo and the land of the Black Drin from Ohrid to Dibra (Debar). Montenegro had received the regions of Ipek (Pec) and Gjakova (Djakovicz), while Greece had Janina and the whole of Epirus. There remained for the Principality 28,000 square kilometers from Lake Scutari and the Prokletije in the North to Butrint and Konitza (Korça) in the South, with about 800,000 inhabitants out of one and a half million Albanians living at the time in the Ottoman Balkans. Even then only the threat of naval intervention at the hands of the Great Powers was enough to make Montenegro leave Scutari (Shkodra), while the Greeks went on exerting pressure on Konitza and Argyro Kastro. In reality the question of frontiers dragged on until 1925 and the lingering effect of it inspired Albanian claims ever since.

In June 1913 the last Ottoman troops left the country, but the Vlora government had failed to get any recognition and Paul Cambon saw it as an "Austrian enterprise." Power had passed into the hands of the large landowners, real feudal lords, such as the Toptani in the Durazzo region: this is what Albanian historians called "xenocracy." However, in December, not without difficulty, the Great Powers had agreed on the choice of a Prince, Wilhelm von Wied (1876–1945) scion of an old Rhenan family, ruined by Napoleon. He was a captain in the Prussian Army and nephew of the Queen of Romania, but received no encouragement from the Kaiser to become the Mbret of the Shqiptars. He nevertheless arrived at Durres—short-lived capital—on March 7, 1914, on an Austro-Hungarian ship, with an escort of Italian, English and French units. His reign was to last six months.

Completely in the dark as to the country's real situation, he appointed to assist him ex civil servants from the days of the Ottoman Empire or wealthy feudal lords like Esad Toptani, ex-deputy for Durres who became Home and War Minister, flanked by some German, Austrian, Italian and even English experts. The new government immediately became a nest of intrigues. The main problem was that of frontiers which were to be drawn up by an international commission and ended with the Protocol of Florence of December 1913. Yet the final arrangement was not to the Greeks' liking; the Prime Minister, E. Venizelos, put his weight behind a movement for secession. There appeared at Gjirokastra a "Provisional Government for North Epirus" under an ex-Minister in the Athens government, J. Zographos. He was defeated at Korca and bloody reprisals followed on both sides. The Mbret agreed to enter negotiations with this government and the Protocol of Corfu (May 1914) gave a measure of autonomy to the region where the Greek language became the official language together with Albanian. This was an insult for the Patriots. In June-July peasants in the central part who did not feel happy about the power given to landowners advising the Prince on his interior policy, and also were antagonized by the exclusively Christian flavor of the "Court," started to rise in the Tirana and Elbasan regions. To the south Greek andartes were roving the countryside terrorizing the inhabitants and causing whole villages to leave. On the eve of the Great War the Wied government only controled the towns of Durres and Vlora. When war broke out in Europe the Mbret declared Albania neutral: international experts departed and Austria-Hungary suspended her payment of subsidies to the tune of 75 million francs that had gone to the national budget so far. As he had no financial means left, Wilhelm von Wied had no choice and boarded another ship on September 3, 1914, to return where he came from.

Once again the poor people was left to anarchy and foreign interventions.

The "Yugoslav" Question and the Sarajevo Assassination, 1878–1914

The gun fired by Gavrilo Princip, a Serbian student, on June 28, 1914, at Sarajevo, marked the growth of a movement so far largely ignored by the Western Powers which were still impressed by the majesty of the Dual Monarchy, the Yugoslav movement.

History had driven a wedge between the Southern Slavic peoples—Bulgars, Serbs, Croats, Slovenes—to start with by making them develop after their conversion to Christianity, under two different Churches, the first two rallied to Byzantium while the other two came under the authority of Rome. To this was added the fact that if Bulgars and Serbs constituted independent kingdoms or empires in the Middle Ages, able to resist the Byzantine Empire, the Slovenes never had their own government and from the days of Charlemagne were the subjects of successive Germanic Empires, under the Carolingians, the Ottonians and the Habsburgs, while the Croats after two centuries of having their own kingdom, from 1102 came under the crown of St Stephen and for eight centuries shared the fate of the Hungarians. The outcome was that Bulgars and Serbs came to be under Ottoman rule for four to five centuries, while Croats and Slovenes lived in the shadow of Vienna and Budapest. Hence their cultures and religions were radically different. The only thing left was the language, though the dialects had also evolved, to such an extent that Slovene became a specific language, while Serbs and Croats in the 19th century came to an arrangement on a common literary language with two distinct scripts, Cyrillic and Latin. At the end of the 18th century, when in Central Europe there was a revival of national consciousness under the influence of Aufklarung, the French Revolution, then Herder and German romanticism, the common language gave rise to the idea of a Slavic community and from there the notion of Yugoslavia emerged. Ljudevit Gaj, a Croat, (1809–1872) became the apostle of Illyrism, advocating the union of all southern Slavs of the Habsburg Empire. The 1848 Revolution was the signal for an alliance between Croats and Vojvodina Serbs to counter the Hungarians under Kossuth, but it was crushed by the oppressive measures taken by Bach (1849–1859). From then on together with a Croatian nationalism looking back to the early Middle Ages to differentiate itself from the Magyars, there grew a Yugoslav movement under Bishop Josip Strosmajer (1815–1905) spokesman of the Illyric cause in all the Balkans, who tried to establish close relations with Belgrade; yet he was unsuccessful since Serbia in the days of Garasanin was dreaming Nacertanje. The Austro-Hungarian Compromise reached in 1867 was a disappointment for all the Slavic populations of the Dual Monarchy and was followed by nationalist disorders which ten years later came to the boil with the occupation of Bosnia-Herzegovina. For a quarter of a century strong antagonism opposed Croats and Serbs, but the Yugoslav trend had not vanished completely. Until his death in 1905 Strosmajer now bishop of Dakovo in the Serbian

Strem remained the champion of the cause, and in 1903 the accession to the throne of Peter I of Serbia fueled a revival of Pan-Slavism which was expressed in feelings of solidarity between Southern Slavs. In 1904 an association, Slovenski Jug, created in Belgrade by intellectuals and students preached union between Serbs, Croats, Slovenes and Bulgarians. At the same time in Croatia, under the influence of ex pupils of Thomas Masaryk in Prague, there appeared a generation of people ready to cooperate with the Serbs living in the Habsburg Empire; the "Fiume (Rijeka) Resolutions" (October 1905) envisaged turning the Dual Monarchy into a Triple Kingdom of whom Serbs and Croats would be the third wing. On these premices a "Croat-Serbian coalition" was organized, a political body whose aim was to bring about a federation of all Southern Slavs within the Empire, yet with privileged relations with Belgrade: it was the most influential formation in the Zagreb Parliament (Sabor) in the years 1906/09 and its leaders, Frano Supilo, Ante Trumbic and Svetozar Pribicevic were behind the creation of Yugoslavia after World War I.

The annexation of Bosnia-Herzegovina (October 1908) was a major blow to the patriots in each community and an association for "National Defense"—Narodna Odbrana—came into being in Belgrade which recruited Serbs as well as Croats to fight Austrian troops. Simultaneously there was an intensification of Croatian nationalism, together with the Yugoslav cause gaining ground among the Croats. As for Serbia there was increasing opposition there to the idea; it is true that Peter I was now a focus for union among Southern Slavs, but the Radicals in power were not in favor of this, and the army strongly opposed the idea as it dreamt of Greater Serbia with Bosnia-Herzegovina part of it, among others. At the core of this movement was a secret society called "Union or Death," also known as "the Black Hand" whose leader was Colonel Dragutin Dimitrijevic, nicknamed Apis (1876–1917) who had been one of the conspirators in the assassination of King Alexander; now head of Intelligence at the General Staff he had a network of agents in all the lands under Ottoman and Austrian authority. He was especially active in Bosnia-Herzegovina where Gavrilo Princip was working for him.

On June 28, 1914, on the feast of St Guy—Vidov Dan—the anniversary of the Kosovo disaster in 1389, the Crown Prince of Austria-Hungary, Archduke Franz-Ferdinand (1863–1914) after a tour of inspection of military manoeuvers, was visiting Sarajevo with his wife, the Duchess of Hohenberg. They were both shot by a young Serb and the phrase "these gunshots caused over eight million deaths" is apt, because the assassination proved to be the start of World War I.

The story is well known. On a Sunday morning about 10 a.m. in a city manned by insufficient security forces on the occasion of a state visit, eight young Serbs, split into two groups, were waiting for the Archduke to pass on his way to the Town Hall. The procession—two open cars and two others tailing them—drove along the Quay Miljacka where the first group was standing. Cabrinovic threw a bomb on Franz-Ferdinand's car, but he missed and an Austrian officer in the second vehicle was seriously wounded. The procession rushed ahead to the Town Hall where Franz Ferdinand made a scene and shouted to the Mayor "What kind of welcome is this?" After the reception the Prince decided to visit the injured man and the convoy had to be re-routed: the Archduke's car was second in line, his wife sitting next to him on the back seat, with the Governor of Bosnia facing them. However, on the same part of the way, as they reached the Latin Bridge, a driving error forced the vehicle to go into reverse. Gavrilo Princip was waiting there and fired a first shot on Franz-Ferdinand who was hit in the neck, another shot caused the Duchess who had stood up to fall. When the convoy arrived at the Governor's Konak the Duchess had already died, and the Archduke expired a few minutes later. Meanwhile the police were taking into custody Cabrinovic, Princip and five other associates without any trouble, only one of the eight escaped to Montenegro. Though the sequence of events is clear beyond question, the search for responsibility is still controversial. The Viennese authorities immediately cast the blame on the Serbian government and therefore decided on war. Belgrade and its protectors in Russia and France accused Austria of deviousness: "Everything points at the Austrian governments' s fault" Emile Haumant still wrote in 1930. Contemporary historians tend to peg responsibility at a lower level. The basic fact is the heated atmosphere of nationalism which was vented in acts of terrorism all over Bosnia-Herzegovina and Macedonia at the time. Vl. Dedijer provided a long list of assassination attempts, made by Serbian or Croatian students against representatives of the Austrian masters. These young people, raised on stories of Russian revolutionaries, saw in assassination an heroic deed which gave meaning to their lives. "I am a Serbian hero!" cried one of the conspirators when he was arrested. Who provided their weapons? Undoubtedly the secret societies such as Narodna Odbrana, Crna Ruka, Mlada Bosnia. One can assume that it was The Black Hand under Dimitrijevic-Apis which sent the weapons taken from army magazines, and found a way to take the bomb carrying conspirators across the Serbo-Bosnian frontier. Did the mysterious Colonel directly order the assassination? Both friends and enemies claimed that he did to glorify or denigrate him: the execution mast to which he was tied in Salonika on June 26, 1917, for his participation in a plot against Alexander, the Prince Regent, may have heard his confession. What is sure is that the Serbian government had received a warning that a plot was being hatched, but there were so many! and that the Viennese authorities , though forwarned, did not take elementary precautions in a city like Sarajevo which was torn by religious and nationalist hatreds.

After the deed was done forces came into play competing to derive most benefit from it, for the time being the Austro-Hungarian military establishment and the Ballhausplatz. Since 1906 General K. von Hotzendorf had been in favor of a preemptive strike against Serbia which represented a hotbed of Slavic subversion on the periphery of the Empire. Count Berchtold, who had replaced Aehrenthal in February 1912, was also for a strong arm policy against this thorn in the flesh of the Dual Monarchy which to his mind was the vanguard of the Russian advance in the Balkans. In Vienna itself they met with the reluctance of the old Emperor—84 years—and in Budapest that of the Prime Minister, Stephen Tisza, who did not wish to increase the proportion of Slavs in the Empire. The balancing act that ensued went on for over a month. Yet as William II had promised his support, the government of Austria-Hungary chose to wage war though with limited aims and of short duration if all went well: a "punitive expedition" against a nest of terrorists. On On July 22, at 6 p.m. the Austrian chargé handed the Serbian Finance Minister, who was standing for N. Pasic in his absence, an ultimatum demanding that publications showing hostility to the Habsburg be banned, and that officers together with teachers who shared this attitude be revoked; it was also required that Austrian experts be admitted into Serbia for carrying out an enquiry into the Sarajevo assassination. Belgrade was allowed 48 hours to accept the conditions, otherwise diplomatic relations would be broken. The Serbs appealed to the other European Powers for their mediation but made preparations for general mobilization and half an hour before the ultimatum expired the order was issued. They accepted the conditions except for the last which was seen as an infringement on the Kingdom's sovereignty. Vienna took it that the ultimatum had been rejected and the Austrian chargé departed from Belgrade. On the next day Berchtold is said to have informed the Emperor of a "fight" on the Serbo-Hungarian border, which step was later denied as the incident remained unconfirmed. Yet on July 28, Austria-Hungary declared war on Serbia. Through the system of alliances Russia mobilized on July 30, Austria-Hungary on the 31st, Germany and France on August 1, and between August 1 and 4 declarations of war were issued.

The Sarajevo "incident" resulted in an European later to become a world war.

The Calvary of Serbia, 1914–1916

Though Western historians presented it mostly as a military contest between France and Germany, regarding the "Eastern Front" as of minor importance, such cannot be the view of the Balkan peoples whose territories were partly or wholly ravaged by the war and accompanying destruction and violence not to mention atrocities.

First to suffer were the Serbs who started the tragedy. On July 28, the Austrian artillery started to bomb Belgrade from the banks of the Sava and the Danube. The Viennese authorities, as well as those of other European capitals, were convinced that the Dual Monarchy with 51 million inhabitants and armed forces estimated at 1,800,000 men, would walk over Little Serbia with 4.4 million inhabitants and at the most 520,000 soldiers. However, the threat from Russia on Galicia forced the Austrian General Staff to alter its mobilization plans. The 250,000 troops under General Pocorec attacked on the Drina but had to make two separate assaults to occupy temporarily the Serbian capital. Then a counter-offensive launched by general Putnik drove them out twelve days later. For eleven long months the tiny kingdom was exposed to bombardment from the Austrians and its population was decimated by a terrible typhus epidemic which claimed over 150,000 victims.

The situation was made more complicated through the intervention of the Ottoman Empire. The nationalist leaders of the

Union and Progress Committee could not tolerate remaining passive in a widespread European crisis. By August 2, at the instigation of the War Minister, Enver Pasha, and of the Minister of the Interior, Talat Pasha, a treaty was signed with Germany, ostensibly a defensive one aimed at Russia. Yet as they were eager to seize the opportunity to wipe out the humiliation of the Balkan Wars, the Young Turks did not mind entering the operations. After a few weeks of a semblance of neutrality, the opportunity was offered by the "Breslau and Goeben incident." The two German cruisers were caught in the Mediterranean at the start of hostilities with both exits closed at Gibraltar and Suez; they took refuge in Istanbul to the intense frustration of the Allies who denounced the violation of the Statute of the Straits. The Young Turks answered with a certain amount of cheek that the ships had been purchased by the Ottomans and French newspapers grew indignant at the masquarade of Turkish sailors with fair hair and blue eyes! The Grand Vizier canceled the proposed surrender and closed the Straits to commercial shipping. However, the Russian victories in Galicia and those of the French on the Marne kept the Palace undecided until crates of gold arrived from the Kaiser. On October 22, Enver Pasha ordered the Black Sea fleet to put itself at the disposal of the German Admiral Souchon, commanding the two cruisers, and attack the Russian harbors at Odessa, Sebastopol and Novorosisk. On November 2, 1914, Russia declared war, on the 5th France and England joined her. Sultan Mehmed V called for the Djihad and William II sent his ally a gaggle of generals—von Sanders, von Seeckt, von der Goltz and von Falkenhayn—to take the Ottoman army in hands.

An immediate consequence was closure of the Straits to Allied fleets, which increased the difficulty of liaising with the Russians as it left only the North Sea and the Pacific Ocean. As for Serbia it was accessible only through the mountains of Montenegro or through Greece which was still neutral. The British Admiralty under the First Lord, Winston Churchill, decided to respond to this new situation with force: the unfortunate Dardanelles expedition was launched in March-April 1915. An attempt of an English-French squadron to force its way resulted in heavy losses (5 out of 18 ships) and a landing of five divisions on the Gallipoli Peninsula followed; they managed to hold out for eight months in harsh conditions without achieving anything. This failure was a heavy blow for the British flag and Winston Churchill as well as putting into light differences between the Allies. Petrograd was afraid of England taking control of Istanbul and the Straits, and on March 4, the Foreign Minister, S.Sazonov, in a memorandum spelt out Russian aims: after a victory he would claim Constantinople, the two banks of the Bosphorus, Eastern Thrace, as well as various places in Asia. Moreover when Venizelos, the Greek Prime Minister, offered the English and French to join sea and land forces in an attack against Constantinople, Russia opposed the idea which would represent the realization of the Megale dream. In the spring of 1915 Constantinople was still a priority for the tsarist Empire.

In the meantime the Central Powers had control of access to the Balkans. Due to her geographical situation Bulgaria had a key role in bringing supplies to Istanbul as well as Serbia which was completely isolated; this is why the two sides in the war vied with each other for an alliance with her. The Austro-Hungarian invasion of Serbia in July 1914 had been greeted by most Bulgarians as a reversal of the Treaty of Bucharest. Yet public opinion was divided on this. The coalition in power in Sofia, just as the Court round the Saxa-Coburg king were pro-German, while the opposition rallying round the intelligentsia rather looked to the Allies. When Turkey declared war, the Entente immediately offered the Bulgarians Thrace and Macedonia, that is to say a part of Serbia which had been the reason for her going to war in the first place! Vienna generously promised a sizeable part of the Karageorgevic kingdom. However, the military situation was still unclear and Ferdinand I wanted more time. The failure of the Dardanelles operation and German victories in Poland and France helped him make up his mind. As he now believed in the superiority of the Central Powers, he accepted their offer: Turkey would immediately give up part of Eastern Thrace to widen Bulgaria's access to the Aegean Sea, after the war there was to be a return to the 1912 frontiers and Romania would cede the Dobrudja if she sided with the Entente, and finally a loan of 200 million marks would be forthcoming to modernize the army. These were the main lines of the secret treaty of alliance signed on September 6, 1915, between Vienna and Sofia in which Bulgaria promised to open hostilities against Serbia within thirty days. Opponents to the war among Stamboliski's Agrarians and Blagoev's Socialists were brutally silenced and the leaders thrown into jail.

By September 22, the Austro-German front on the Sava and Danube showed signs of increased activity while Bulgaria ordered general mobilization. Belgrade found itself threatened in the rear and appealed to Greece who was still bound by the May 1913 Pact. However, King Constantine whose wife was the Kaiser's sister, insisted on remaining neutral against the Prime Minister, Venizelos' advice. The latter suggested that the Western Allies land troops—150,000 men—at Thessalonika to support the Serbs. In effect on October 3, 1915, the first Allied soldiers landed in the port, but the King objected and forced Venizelos to resign. On the following day Feld-Marschall Mackensen threw sixteen Austrian and German divisions against the Serbian Western Front; after three days of fierce fighting Belgrade fell on October 9, five days later the Bulgarian army launched an attack, barred the Morava-Vardar road at Vranje and proceeded to occupy the whole of Macedonia. General Sarrail, commanding the Allied forces in Salonika, tried to go to the rescue of the trapped Serbians, but he could only muster a few thousand men with insufficient equipment. Late in October the Bulgarians effected junction with Mackensen's troops in the Kosovo region, ill-fated as ever. The Serbs with their backs to the Sar mountain, had only one exit: the higher Ibar Valley and the Northern Albania road down to Scutari (Shkodra) and the Adriatic. There followed, between November 25, 1915 and January 20, 1916, the terrible retreat which remained as a durable imprint in the Serbs' collective memory: old King Peter, a sick man lying in a waggon drawn by oxen, the members of government, the General Staff, ordinary troops and many civilians with women and children, monks and priests carrying the coffin of King Stephen I, the remains of a proud people making its way through rocky mountains; in the depths of winter, armed only with guns, with no food supplies, in the midst of the Albanian population still smarting from the exactions of the previous year. An estimated 20,000 died on the way, the survivers reaching the ports of Antivari (Bar) and Dulcigno (Ulcin) after unaccountable delay were picked up by French, English and Italian ships. The government and the general staff were taken to Corfu, without consulting the King of Greece, while the troops were sent to Bizerta to end up in camps and hospitals set up on Tunisian territory, and many civilians made their way to France via Italy. By late January 1916, the whole of Serbia was occupied by the Austrians and Bulgarians, but on the other side of the Mediterranean a Serbian army was taking shape with French equipment and instructors, which was to reach 125,000 men in July.

The Transylvania Dream and the Romanian Disasters, 1914–April 1918

Like all other European leaders the Romanian ones were taken by surprise when war broke out. The Liberals had regained power in January 1914 under I. C. Bratianu, and were preparing two reforms, the agrarian one and the electoral reform. In foreign affairs since 1883 a secret alliance bound Romania to the Central Powers and, in the crisis of 1914, King Carol who was a Hohenzollern sided with his "relatives" the Austrian and German emperors. Public opinion, especially among intellectuals, looked to France but resented imperialistic Russia after Southern Bessarabia had been annexed in 1878.

There was also the lure of Transylvania. It was then only in the minds of a few patriots: the annexation of Transylvania was not included in the program of any Romanian political party, as the very existence of the Dual Monarchy, the trend towards the Triple Alliance and the personality of the German King precluded any such notion. On the other side of the Carpathian Mountains the Romanians subjected to the Habsburgs were acutely aware of their nationality and fought for a separate status which would put them a par with the other peoples in the Empire, while remaining in the Dual-Monarchy. After the 1848 revolutions during which they fought against Kossuth's Hungarians with the Emperor's armies, the Romanians were disappointed at Vienna's lack of gratitude as they were treated harshly under the "Bach system" (1849–1859). The decree issued in October 1860 in which Franz-Joseph laid out a new legislation for his Empire, made them more hopeful: Transylvania was made autonomous again in relation to Pest and could have a Diet at Klausenburg (Cluj) once more. Yet the Hungarians raised objections to the new arrangement and in January 1861 the Romanian leaders meeting at Hermanstadt (Sibiu) decided to uphold the two claims which formed the basis of their political action up to 1914: recognition of their "national" identity similar to that enjoyed by Transylvanian Hungarians, Germans and Szeklers, especially in respect to the language. The 1863 Diet gave them a relative majority and they succeeded in the Romanian language passing into official use like German and Hungarian. However, the February 1867 Compromise let them down in favor of the Magyar nobility. Then the Romanian subjects of the Austrian Empire depended of two distinct administrative systems, the Hungarian kingdom and Bukovina which was one of the lander of Cisleithania. From then on the history of the Romanians living in the Hungarian kingdom was one of protracted struggle by the "patriots" against Budapest and its policies. The "Nationality Law" of December 1868—known as Law 14—passed by the Hungarian Parliament made for equal rights and the use of the language but at the same time stated that there was only "one Hungarian nation." The Prime Minister Koloman Tisza, in power from 1875 to 1890, applied it in a restrictive manner and the Romanian leaders protested his Magyarization practices. In 1881 they responded by creating a National Romanian Party which remained faithful to the Emperor, but demanded autonomy for Transylvania and equal rights. In January 1892 the party sent Franz-Joseph a "Memorandum" signed by several hundred patriots who denounced the oppressive government in Budapest. The Hungarian authorities' reaction was to put the agitators in jail and take them to Court which rallied Liberals all over Europe to the Romanian cause. As it was made illegal because of the judicial proceedings the National Romanian Party resumed its action only in 1905 and obtained some seats in Parliament; the 1906 elections gave it 16 Romanian deputies in the Budapest Chamber among them two statesmen to be who would represent Romania at Versailles, Alexander Vaida-Voevod (1872-1950) and Julius Maniu (1873-1951). Some of them thought it opportune to turn to the Crown Prince who was known to be against the Hungarians: in 1909 his visit to the King of Romania, Carol I, caused a furore among Magyars. However, the movement for universal suffrage in Hungary was opposed by Stephen Tisza's government (1913-1917) and on the eve of the war the "Romanian question" was frozen. Yet the 1910 census revealed that in the twelve circumscriptions of what used to be Transylvania, where they lived next to Hungarians, Szeklers and Saxons, the Romanians made up 55% of the population, one and a half million, compared to 34% of Hungarians and Szeklers and 9% of Germans. Moreover they had spread outside the borders of the old Principality: in the land of Marmaros (Maramures), Szatmar (Satu Mare) and Bihar (Bihor) there were over 600,000 of them making up 37% of the population; to the south in the Banat there were 835,000 Romanians, 42% of the population. All in all, for the Kingdom of Hungary, there were nearly 3 million Romanians, that is 20% of Budapest's subjects. In Bukovina there were 275,000 making up 35% of the population, coming after the Ruthenians (38%) but before the Germans. Whatever weight these masses, mostly rural, represented, it was clear that nothing less than an European war was needed for the Patriots' dream of union to become reality.

In the meantime the Crown Council meeting at Sinaia on August 3, 1914, was the occasion for heated debate between those who wished to intervene on the side of the Central Powers, the King and the Conservative Leader, P. P. Carp and those who advocated neutrality, Bratianu and the Liberals together with a number of Conservatives. The latter carried the day. This made Romania, like Italy and Bulgaria, a subject for attention on the part of both parties in the war. Russia raised hopes for union with Transylvania, while Germany magnanimously promised Bukovina which belonged to her Austrian ally and a separate status for the Romanians living under the crown of St Stephen. This was a point which Tisza refused categorically, especially as mobilization in Hungary had proceeded smoothly because of the population's fear of a Russian invasion.

On October 10, 1914, Carol I died after being on the throne for forty-eight years. His successor as expected was his nephew, 49 years-old Ferdinand, a Hohenzollern whose wife was Princess Mary of Edinburg, a grand-daughter both of Queen Victoria and Tsar Alexander II. Ferdinand I lacked his predecessor's prestige and political flair, as for the Queen her natural sympathy for the Entente made the situation more complicated for the Court. The new King confirmed his country's neutrality, but as the war was dragging on, public opinion became increasingly hostile to Austria-Hungary. In December 1914, the ancient moderate "League for Cultural Union of All Romanians" based in Bucharest, turned into the "League for Political Union of All Romanians," under the chairmanship of a Transylvanian Vasile Lucaciu, a Uniate priest and hero of the Memorandum lawsuit, who was assisted by Nicolae Iorga, a Bucharest University professor, Take Ionescu an anti-German Conservative, A. Marghiloman, Octavian Goga a Transylvanian poet who had chosen to live in voluntary exile in the Kingdom. It requested immediate intervention on the side of the Entente, which alone could help Romania to realize the

"Unitary state." Yet in 1915, Austro-German successes in Poland and above all Bulgaria declaring war on Serbia, made the Romanian government think again. In June 1916, another Russian offensive in Galicia seemed to tilt the scales towards the Allies and I. C. Bratianu entered into secret negotiations with them. The outcome was a treaty of alliance signed on August 17, 1916, between Romania on the one hand and Russia, France, Great Britain and Italy on the other. In return for military intervention by Romania within ten days, the Entente gave the new ally "carte blanche" to annex Bukovina, Banat, Muramures and the whole of Transylvania up to a line Debreczen-Szeged which meant including purely Hungarian territories. The treaty was followed by a military agreement which contained plans for a Russian offensive in Bukovina while the French Army of the East was committed to attack Bulgaria from Salonika and the other countries of the Entente were to supply arms and equipment. On August 27, 1916, another Crown Council decided, with the King, the Liberals and Conservatives in agreement, except for P. P. Carp, to declare war on Austria-Hungary; which was done the very same day. The King had asked that Germany should not be mentioned, but Berlin declared war on Romania on August 30, soon to be followed by Bulgaria and Turkey.

On August 28, the army under General Averescu entered Transylvania and seized Kronstadt (Brasov); it was greeted with joyful demonstrations by the Romanian speaking population, while the Hungarian population took to their heels, sign of ethnic tensions which gave rise to accusations of "atrocities" on both sides. On September 1st, the day they declared war, the Bulgarians attacked the Romanian bridgehead of Turtucaia (Tutrakan) in Dobrudja on the right bank of the Danube ; after six days of fierce fighting the 3rd Romanian Army had to capitulate and leave behind several thousand corpses and 25,000 prisoners. For all the assurances given General Sarrail's Eastern Army was unable to launch its offensive and the country's morale was seriously affected by this disaster. Beyond the Carpathian Mountains in a campaign which lasted for a month Averescu moved up to the outskirts of Hermannstadt (Sibiu), Segesvar (Sighisoara) and Tolgyes (Toplita) but under threat of an Austro-German counter-offensive from Petrosani was forced to order a retreat. On October 3, the Romanians were crossing the border on their way back. General Falkenhayn was following close behind and he advanced through the

Carpathians to sweep over Wallachia along the Jiu and Olt valleys, while the German-Bulgarian troops of Marshal von Mackenzen went to the attack in Dobrudja and seized the port of Constanta. On November 25, the Court and government had to evacuate Bucharest which was occupied by the Austro-Germans and took refuge at Jassy. With Russian support the front was stabilized in January 1917 on a line south of the Siret and the Danube.

Thus Romania was split into two. The armies of the Central Powers were occupying Oltenia, Wallachia and Dobrudja, that is two thirds of the Kingdom's territory and they ran a military government in the capital whose main task was requisition of agricultural produce (wheat, cattle and wine) as well as oil to send all those to Vienna and Berlin. In the remaining third of the country—Moldavia north of the front line, the government and Parliament now at Jassy tried to carry on as best they could. The death of Emperor Franz-Joseph (November 1916) and Charles I's accession to power allowed a breathing space of six months which the French Military Mission under General Berthelot put to good use in re-organizing the Romanian army. Large quantities of military equipment, rifles, cannons and about hundred aeroplanes were received. Nevertheless the situation was precarious in Moldavia where thousands of refugees put pressure on food supplies. As the neighboring areas of Russia were engulfed in chaos after the Revolution of March 1917, the spread of subversion was also probable. To avert the danger Ferdinand I issued a proclamation on April 5, 1917, promising to distribute the land to peasants and more say in political life. In June a "Constituent Assembly" representing the non-occupied area of Moldavia was convened by I. C. Bratianu and passed a wide-ranging land reform as well as electoral universal suffrage. Yet these were only promises for the future. In July in response to the wish of the Entente Powers and in conjunction with the last Russian offensive in Galicia the Romanian army under General Averescu attacked on the Siret. In spite of fierce fighting and the presence of Russian troops alongside the Romanians, the Austro-German front not only held fast but became dangerous. Following on the October Bolshevik Revolution and the cease-fire agreement between Lenin's government and the Central Powers, the Romanians were compelled to seek an armistice which was signed at Focsani on December 9. Peace talks started in January 1918 and proceeded simultaneously with the Brest-Litovsk ones, though they were held at Buftea near Bucharest, I. C. Bratianu refusing to have any dealings with the Bolsheviks whom he cordially detested. Nevertheless he could not keep the country from contamination from revolutionary ideas: some sailors of the Romanian fleet in the Black Sea rebeled and troops had to be brought in from the front to arrest and expel Bolsheviks who were in control of the Headquarters of the Russian army near Jassy.

Romanian leaders were divided on the price to pay for peace. Bratianu resigned in January 1918 to let General Averescu, the war hero, discuss conditions with the victors. The Treaty of Brest-Litovsk (March 3) made tergiversations impossible: on March 18 the preliminary treaty of Buftea seemed so harsh that the King thought to improve it by calling A. Marghiloman, a known Germanophile, to power. This was not sufficient to make the German General Staff unbend though. The treaty that was signed in Bucharest on March 7, 1918 between Romania on the one hand and Austria-Hungary, Germany, Bulgaria and Turkey on the other forced the losing party to give up Southern Dobrudja in favor of Bulgaria, to accept alterations to the border in the Carpathian Mountains to the advantage of Austria-Hungary, giving her some 150,000 inhabitants, economic clauses allocating part of the production of wheat, meat and oil to the Central Powers together with a monopoly of navigation on the Danube; last Wallachia remained under occupation until war was ended on all fronts. Romania was condemned to remain passive militarily and diplomatically under German protectorate.

Paradoxically Romania succeeded in making Moldavia return to its pre-1812 frontiers and be given Bessarabia back. Since the tsar's fall from power, this province the population of which was mixed but with a Romanian majority was in turmoil. The Russians were divided into revolutionaries and those who were against changes, Nationalist Ukrainians wanted to have the province annexed by Kiev, and the Romanians started a "National Democratic Moldavian Party." Then with the encouragement of French representatives at Jassy they they declared the existence of a "Democratic Moldavian Republic" on December 2, 1917 at Kishinev (Chisinau) under Ion Inculet, a nationalist Romanian. As he was afraid of Bolshevik reprisals the latter called in Romanian troops and the whole of Moldavia was occupied. An Assembly—Sfat—elected in doubtful circumstances, first of all declared Moldavia independent of Russia, then on April 9, 1918, voted in favor of union with Romania. Lenin's government refused to recognize the Sfat's legitimacy and its freedom of choice in the presence of Romanian troops. The Bolsheviks saw in this the first intervention by the Entente against them, so they refused an annexation which is still nowadays a bone of contention between the two countries.

The Rape of Greece and Allied Victory in the East, 1910–1918

In October 1910 when Eleftherios Venizelos came to power in Athens he embodied the hopes of the patriots who wanted to modernize the country after centuries of stagnation. With the support of the Liberal Party the "semi-dictator," in the words of the Austrian ambassador, who had chosen able personalities to assist him in the task, launched a series of reforms while retaining the main lines of the 1864 Constitution. A body of independent civil servants made its appearance as well as a Council of Judges. The army was re-organized under the guidance of the French General Eydoux, while an English Admiral took the navy in hand; the financial administration was overhauled and the budget balanced. In the sensitive area of agriculture Venizelos carried out an agrarian reform in Thessaly, where could still be found the traditional ciftliks: 150,000 hectares were shared out between 4,000 peasant families. Everywhere in the country modern methods of agriculture were encouraged through the appointment of agronomists and the opening of technical schools; these measures all came under the authority of a new Ministry of Agriculture. He made primary education compulsory and promulgated the first code regulating employment of labor, though the country had no industry to speak of as yet. Thus slow changes were beginning to appear in Greece when the Balkan Wars broke out. The army and the navy made a credible show and by November 1912 Thessalonika was in Grrek hands. This roused Bulgaria to anger as her spokesman in London had said earlier "Thessalonika or it is war"; George I responded by symbolically moving into the city after its conquest but he was assassinated there in February 1913, by a madman according to the Greeks and a patriot according to the Bulgarians. Another delicate question was that of Northern Epirus which was given to the new Albanian state by the Florence Conference (December 1913). The Greeks claimed that the area had 120,000 of their fellow countrymen, with three bishoprics and 376 parishes as well as 360 schools numbering 22,000 pupils. The European Powers had to put pressure on Greece for the region to be evacuated, after a "government" had been established in the self-proclaimed independent North Epirus (March 1914). One way or the other after the Balkan Wars the territories under the Greek state had nearly doubled in size, to reach 108,000 square kilometers while the population went up from 2.6 million to 4.4 million inhabitants.

The Sarajevo assassination and the European war caught Greek public opinion in a acute nationalistic mood: Constantine, the new king (1868–1923) son of George I, took the name of Constantine XII, as the successor of the last Byzantine Emperor, Constantine XI who had died fighting Mahomet II in 1453! In the name of the Megale Idea Venizelos offered the Entente Powers to add his forces to theirs for an attack against Turkey, but the Allies balanced as long as Bulgaria remained neutral, because the Russian government cast a greedy eye on Constantinople and was not keen on Greek intervention. The Anglo-French expedition in the Dardanelles in January 1915 turned the port of Thessalonika into an Allied base with the island of Lemnos also under military occupation. Wilhelm II made representations to Constantine, his brother-in-law, who had at his court a group of solid Germanophiles, including Queen Sophia (1871–1932), the Kaiser's sister, G.Streit her secretary and various officers who had been trained at the Berlin Academy such as Ionnis Metaxas (1871–1941) who was Chief-of-Staff at the time. The latter was opposed to Greece joining the expedition and on March 5, Venizelos had to resign. Like Bulgaria Greece saw the two sides vie with each other for her favors; yet the situation was still unclear. In June 1915, the general elections brought the Liberals to power with an absolute majority; Venizelos was back as Prime Minister in August. From then on Greece remained divided between the King and his Court who believed in victory for the Central Powers, and the government who played with the Entente. The press was equally split and the diplomatic personnel of both coalitions turned Athens into a hotbed of rumors and intrigues. In September the fact that Bulgaria declared war on Serbia brought the difference into the open. As Venizelos wanted the Allies to land troops in Thessalonika to rescue the Serbs who were exposed on two fronts, he met with strong opposition from the King and the pro-German party; he was forced to resign on October 5, just as the first Allied soldiers were setting foot on Greek soil. The "Rape of Greece" denounced by the press of the Central Powers, plunged the country into the turmoil of war conditions. The Anglo-French occupation of Thessalonika did not go without its share of unpleasantness, General Sarrail acquired a reputation for " bad temper and suspiciousness" and late in December German aeroplanes bombed Allied positions in the town. In the following spring the General Staff of Mackenzen informed the authorities in Athens that the General was going to advance into Eastern Macedonia and occupy the fort of Rupel on the Bulgarian frontier in the Struma Valley; Sarrail responded by declaring Thessalonika under siege and occupying the Island of Thasos. The Anglo-French Conference which took place in London on June 8/9, 1916, made plans for the Greek blockade and a naval show of force, it also drafted a note requesting the government's resignation, fresh elections, demobilization for the army and exile for high civil servants in the administration and military personnel who were hostile to the Entente. As for the German-Bulgarian troops they occupied the port of Kavala sending the 8,000 strong garrison to POW camps in Germany. This was the last drop, especially as six governments in quick succession—over two years—showed clearly that the people in power were hopelessly divided.

On August 29, 1916, a Greek Committee for National Defense, was created in Thessalonika, with Sarrail's blessing, to support intervention on the Entente's side. Venizelos went to Crete where he was born and announced that he was forming a Provisional Government based in Thessalonika where he landed on October 9. Greece was then under two governments. The Allies recognized the Thessalonika one "de facto" and increased their pressure on the King: French and English officers took control of the railways, arsenals and fortified positions in Athens, while sailors under Admiral Dartigue du Fournet patroled the streets. Early in September the troops of National Defense seized the town of Katerini on the Thessalian border on the highway Larissa-Athens: fifteen people were killed and it looked like the beginning of civil war. In Athens tensions increased between Royalists and Venizelists: the city was full of rumors of impending massacres. On December 1st, Dartigue landed 2.500 men to take control of the capital. Regular street fighting took place round the Zappeion in the National Park and on the Philopappos Hill; the French-English squadron opened fire and sixty four cannon shots were aimed at the city: there were on both sides about sixty killed and 150 wounded, Allied casualties being slightly heavier than the Greek ones. On the two following days there was a witch hunt among

Venizelists. There were reports of lynchings, there were acts of violence, pilfering and the press of the Entente countries denounced the "Athenian Vespers." The King seemed to bear some responsibility for the troubles so the Allies decided on a complete blockade of sea access to Greece.

Meanwhile in November 1916, the Thessalonika government had declared war on Bulgaria, and dispatched the first battallions to the front where after six months there were 40,000 men; the reward for this was official recognition by the Entente in December. The government in Athens was confronted with increasing pressure from the Allies who had established a "buffer zone" between the King's troops and that of the Venizelists and now demanded that all those responsible for the December disorders be sacked and even arrested and handed over to the Allies. In April 1917, the United States' declaration of war made the position of the neutral powers precarious, and the changes occurring in the French government with the arrival of war leaders more determined—the Nivelle offensive started on April 7—made the Allies decide to liquidate the "Greek affair" and force the King to abdicate. The operation was to take place under Charles Jonnart (1857–1927) ex-Governor General in Algeria and Foreign Minister in the Briand Cabinet in 1913 ; he received the title of "High Commissioner of the Greek Protectorate," representing France, England, Russia and Italy. As for Venizelos, who had been publicly excommunicated by the Archbishop in Athens in December, he chose to institute a Republican régime in Greece with the support of a group of émigrés meeting in Paris. On the English side after many hesitations Jonnart was permitted to go ahead. By June 6, his ship was at anchor in the Piraeus harbor, and he took command of the situation. To avoid provoking another bloodshed he got in touch with the government under Zaimis and at the same time with Venizelos and Sarrail in Thessalonika. On June 11 he handed the Greek Prime Minister an ultimatum demanding the King's abdication within 24 hours and the Crown Prince to be excluded from the succession. Constantine bowed to the inevitable and went into exile in Switzerland, to be replaced by his younger son, Alexander I (1893–1920); the capital demonstrated for the fallen king, but the rest of the country remained quiet and the way was open for the reunification of Greece.

On June 27, Venizelos became the head of the government in Athens, where he remained in power until November 1920. He immediately declared war on the Central Powers while the Allied troops evacuated the capital, as well as Thessaly and various other centers of occupation apart from Thessalonika. There was a complete purge of the administration to eliminate the pro-Germans; but the main effort went naturally into the military machine. The Greek army soon counted fifteen divisions, ten of which, though under strength, were sent to the Salonika front to fight alongside eight French divisions, six Serbian, four English and one Italian.

The Allied victory started precisely on this front. While the offensives launched by Foch on the Marne and the North were sucking in all the German reserves, the Central Powers had to rely on Bulgarian troops for the most part in the South-East of Europe. Their numbers were about the same as that of the Entente and they had showed great fighting spirit so far. Yet the Bulgarians were beginning to feel weary while news of the Bolshevik Revolution and a crisis in supplies did nothing for the troops' morale. In May 1918 an Allied offensive in the region of Skra-Gevgelija on the Vardar River put into relief the shortcomings of Ferdinand's army. By September the fruit seemed ripe; General Franchet d'Esperey, the commander of the Eastern Army, on September 15, launched his 280 battaillons against the 260 Bulgarian ones. After three days of violent fighting the front was pierced in the Dobropolis east of Bitola and Franco-Serbian troops soon occupied Prilep, Veles and Skopje. The 100,000 Bulgarians escaped being encircled by means of a quick retreat, but when they returned home they found an uneasy situation which led to the short lived Radomir Republic (September 26–30) based on Bolshevik ideas. The Bulgarian High Command had to accept an armistice which was signed on September 29, 1918, at Thessalonika. The capitulation of Bulgaria opened the way to Belgrade to the Allies and Prince Alexander's troops entered the city on November 1st, which meant that Serbia was now free. On September 30, the Ottomans signed the armistice at Mudros thereby opening the Straits and Constantinople to Allied shipping. This was the first chapter of the Central Powers' defeat.

Romania was quick in seizing her opportunity. The Marghiloman government still quartered at Jassy took a long time before ratifying the Treaty of Bucharest signed in May 1918, while Bratianu, the opposition leader, let it be known that he was ready to declare war again if the Allies guaranteed the clauses of the alliance treaty of 1916. On November 6, 1918, King Ferdinand asked a general to assume power while the first French and Serbian echelons of the Eastern army were crossing the Danube; on the 9th, the Romanian government sent an ultimatum to Feld-Marschall Mackenzen commanding the occupation forces ordering him to leave the territory. On November 10, he announced that Romania considered herself at war with the Central Powers, but on the following day while hostilities ceased on the other fronts, the German troops withdrew to Transylvania followed by the Romanian army coming from Moldavia. On November 13, the Belgrade armistice signed by General Franchet d'Esperey and the Budapest government established the demarcation line which ended the Romanian advance into Hungary.

King Ferdinand and the government led by Bratianu who had been recalled to power returned to Bucharest where they feasted the French troops under Franchet d'Esperey's command. Together they toasted the Union; this was decided on November 15 by a Romanian Committee for Bukovina, to be followed on December 1st at Alba Julia for Transylvania and Banat, and last on January 8, 1919, by the Saxons at a meeting in Medias. On December 12, during an extraordinary Parliamentary sitting at Bucharest, I. C. Bratianu had these declarations of Union endorsed: Greater Romania had become a reality.

The victorious Entente Powers could draw the map of the Balkans anew.

16

The Triumph and Failure of the National States, 1919–1939

The peoples of the Balkans emerged from the "seven year war" badly bruised. From the Dnestr to the Gulf of Corinth each had direct experience of fighting, invasion and occupation (be it by friend or foe): thousands had fallen on the field of battle and above all untold levels of exaction had been experienced by all the civilian populations. The Greeks speak of 45,000 dead and 40,000 deported from Macedonia by the Bulgarians. Their economies were in ruins and there was famine in Sofia and Athens. The ethnic conflicts of the past had become transformed into hatred and the assertion of national identity was synonymous with aggressivity and xenophobia. As everywhere else in Europe it was a time of nationalism and in these particular countries it was a far cry from the Wilsonian discourse of self-determination of peoples and Anglo-Saxon style democracy. The French model of "Nation State" was the highest point of reference but papered over inter-ethnic strife heightened by social and religious tensions. This made the "Nation" state a fragile construction which occillated between dictatorship and dissolution.

The Versailles Order: Victors and Vanquished

It would be wrong to think that the four countries at Versailles divided and united territories in the same way as the sovereigns of the past. Expert advice was sought whose reports, now in archives, form a priceless source of historical research. A few countries, their representatives, or rather those who put themselves forward as such, were listened to. But only some; the "good" with the basic manicheanism of victor and vanquished, with on the one side those in the allied camp: the Serbs, Romanians and Greeks; on the other the cobelligerents, Germany, Austria-Hungary, Bulgaria and Turkey; further confused by the victor's friends arguing over the same territories, for example the Serbs and the Romanians over the Banat of Temesvar. The Versailles order in the Balkans was a compromise between the national interests of the victors and the political and economic interests of the victorious Great Powers, in the 19th century tradition.

The southern Slavs did not wait for the Allied victory for setting out their goals. While N.Pasic's "heroic Serbia" maintained its visibility at the side of the French and English, the Yugoslavs of Austria-Hungary were organizing themselves to face a new situation: the final demise of the dual-Monarchy. Their task was complicated by the Allied commitment to Italy. In April 1915, eager to have Italy on their side the Allies had signed a secret treaty in London in which the government of Rome was promised, as well as Trent and the Austrian south Tyrol, the mainly Slav areas of Trieste, Gorz, Gradisca, Istria apart from Fiumi, some of the Dalmatian Islands, the coast from Zara (Zadar) to Sebenico (Sibenik) as well as the Albanian port of Valona and the Greek Dodecanese Islands. As soon as the terms were known Pasic complained. Ante Trumbic (1864–1938) and Frano Supilo the Croat leaders, won over by the idea of a Yugoslavia in May formed a "Yugoslav Committee" which was transfered to London and with the support of activists such as R.W. Seton-Watson and H.W.Steed was to become until the end of the war the mouthpiece for union of Croats, Slovenes and Serbs. It soon obtained the support of powerful emigre groups in America but even then the secret treaty was to spoil relations with Yugoslav and Serb representatives both diplomatically and in the field. As for Bulgaria, Allied promises of compensation in Macedonia were rendered void in October 1915 by her intervention on the side of the Central Powers: However it had unsettled Pasic and sowed the seeds of distrust further aggravated by the secret treaty of Bucharest in August 1916 in which the Allies promised Romania, among other things, the Banat region which was also coveted by the Serbs. Therefore there were a few points of contention. In France in the meantime the Yugoslav Committee of London rode a wave of sympathy which Serbian suffering generated and attracted to their cause Slavists such as Ernest Denis, Emile Haumant and Louis Leger. Paris was the meeting place for Alexander of Serbia and Ante Trumbic and after complicated and difficult negotiations, an agreement was finally reached in Corfu on the 20 July 1917, on a declaration expressing the wish to form, following victory, a "Serbian, Croat and Slovene Kingdom" under the Karageorgevic dynasty. An independent and democratic country, respecting freedom of belief and the equality of the peoples. This programme was immediately accepted by the National Montenegrin committee in France where King Nicholas had found refuge in 1916 after the occupation of his country by the Austrians. Although Trumbic proclaimed that the Corfu agreement marked the end of the ideology of a greater Serbia and anticipated the creation of a Yugoslav federation, Pasic continued to advocate a form of centralism which closely resembled the previous defunct ideology. Neither were the Allies in a hurry to decide: the Americans waited until June 1918 to accept the declaration without however recognizing the Yugoslav committee, while the first official French mention of a "Yugoslav state" was on the 29 June 1918 and Balfour the English minister only lent his support on the 25 July; meanwhile Italy continued to insist on the Treaty of London.

The collapse of Austria-Hungary forced all the protagonists to put all these projects and promises into practise with policies which were to prove incoherent. On the 29 October 1918 a National Council—Narodno Vijece—was formed in Zagreb bringing together Ante Pavelic (1889-1959)[1] a Croat, a Slovene priest Anton Korosec (1872–1940) who was head of the church party and Sv. Pribicevic a Serb from the Serbo-Croat coalition. Supported by Emperor Charles, this council decided to form a "national government" which was empowered to carry through the union of Serbia and Montenegro. The provincial assemblies of Bosnia-Herzegovina and Vojvodina also joined and so, from the border of Serbia to Italy, was formed de facto a Yugoslav state, whose leaders negotiated with the London Committee and with the government of Belgrade. After prolonged discussions in Geneva with N. Pasic a short-lived coalition government was formed, but it was ultimately in Belgrade that a delegation led by Ante Pavelic and Svetozar Pribicevic reached an agreement for union under the Karageorgevic dynasty with a central government based in Belgrade. Four day before the Skupstina of Montenegro had assembled at Podgorica and with King Nicholas still in France, had decided on uniting the small kingdom with Serbia and the other Yugoslav countries. On the 1 December 1918, in the royal palace of

Belgrade, the heir to the throne, Prince Alexander, solemnly proclaimed the "Union of the Kingdom of Serbia and the independent states of Serbia, Croatia and Slovenia into a united Kingdom of Serbia, Croatia and Slovenia." A few days later a coalition government was formed, presided over by Stojan Protic a Serb, Ante Trumbic a Croat, Anton Korosec a Slovene, a Serb from Croatia Sv. Pribicevic while Nicholas Pasic, who had fallen out with everone, was sent to Paris to represent the new kingdom at the Peace conference.

However, even before this was officially recognized by the victors, a serious crisis developed with Italy. The armistice which Italy signed at Vila Giusti with Austria-Hungary on the 3 November 1918 was followed by the occupation of Trieste, Pula, the isles of Istria, Zara and Sibenik and an advance in the direction of Laibach (Ljubljana) by the troops of General Diaz. All these places had been promised to Italy by the secret treaty of 1915. The Nardno Vijece of Zagreb was immediately mobilized and appealed to Foch. Serbia informed Italy that it was ready to engage its own armed forces. Diaz retreated but stayed in Trieste. Franchet d'Esperey, who since the armistice of the 13 November with the Hungarians was able to intervene, hoped to occupy the port to make it into a staging post for his army in Hungary. Foch resolved the matter by leaving Serbian and Yugoslav troops in Ljubljana and the Italians in Trieste. The Rome government wanted to take part in the peace conference basing its case on the terms of the secret treaty of London, so they continued to blockade the Yugoslav coast and launched a campaign of agitation and a violent press campaign. But on the 18 January 1919 the peace conference began at Versailles. It was to give form to a Yugoslav state.

After a month and a half of existence the kingdom of Yugoslavia remained a state without frontiers. Pasic put forward territorial demands which were not very different from those of the Yugoslav Committee of May 1915 in London: Serbia, Montenegro, Southern Styria, Carinthia, Istria including Fiume, the area of Trieste-Goriza, Dalmatia and the islands. In all 250,000 sq.km. with a polpulation of 12 to 13 million of which 1 million were not Slavs. Yet this project placed the new kingdom in competition with every one of its neighbours apart from Greece: Hungary for Vojvodina (Backa and Baranya), Austria with Styria, Carinthia and Medjumurje (the area between the Drava and the Mur), Bulgaria over the strategic area along its frontier between Vidin and Petric, Romania over the Banat, Italy over Trieste, Istria, Fiume, Dalmatia and the islands and finally Albania over the land north and west of the Drim. The Paris discussions were therefore heated and prolonged and the Yugoslav delegation with 93 members representing all the political parties needed all its expertise: the geographer Jovan Cvijic and the historian Sl. Jovanovic to justify the statistics of Baranya and Prekumurje. In the meanwhile the Italians acted as if the territories they were occupying belonged to them even though President Wilson on the 14 April laid out a compromise. Orlando, the Italian Prime Minister left the conference furious leaving the problem of the Italian-Yugoslav border wide open. Following a plebiscite the Treaty of Saint-Germain on the 10 September 1919 established the separation of the Austrian Klagenfurt basin, with its small Slovene minority in the southern zone, as part of Austria; the Treaty of Neuilly with Bulgaria on the 27 November 1919 settled the border in the Struma valley giving Serbia the districts of Vranje, Tsaribrod and Negotin, about 2,800 sq. km. and a population of 100,000 of whom the great majority were Bulgarians; the Treaty of Trianon with Hungary on the 4 June 1920 divided the Banat region between Romania and Serbia and gave Backa and Baranya to the Yugoslavs. With Italy there had to be a special treaty, concluded on the 12 November 1920 which drew the new frontier north of the line promised in London, with an Italian enclave at Zara and neighbouring islands and Fiume becoming a free town. As for the frontier with Albania this was only to be resolved at the Conference of Ambassadors in 1924. The Yugoslav union had succeeded.

Romania also had problems getting the victors to agree to a united Greater Romania, declared on the 24 January 1919. Their compatriots in Transylvania had taken things into their own hands as soon as the dual Monarchy of the Habsburgs had collapsed. On the 12 October 1918 at Nagyvarad (Oradea) the Romanian National Party of V. Goldis declared the right of self-determination, six days before Emperor Charles' manifesto transforming the Empire into a federal state. A "National Romanian Council" was then formed at Arad, similar to those of the Hungarians and Czechs which had negotiated with the revolutionary government of Count M. Karolyi and the Minister for Nationalities, O. Jaszi. Yet the Armistice between Franchet d'Esperey and Karolyi, signed on the 13 November at Belgrade, was to set the line of demarcation roughly on the edge of the old Transylvanian Principality, slightly less than that agreed in the August 1916 alliance treaty and giving the Banat to the Serbians. Rather worried, the National Council therefore decided to hold at Gyulafervar (Alba Julia) a Grand Assembly of Romanians from Transylvania and Hungary on the 1 December 1918. It was to consist of delegates elected by universal suffrage together with representatives of Romanian organizations such as the church, teachers and cultural societies in Transylvania, Maramures, Crisana[2] and Banat regions. The elections gave a large majority in favour of union with Romania. In an atmosphere which recalled the reunion of Blasendorf (Blaj) in 1848, the 1228 deputies, including 5 bishops, teachers, national guardsmen and 61 delegated from womens' groups, accepted the borders drawn up by the Conference of Paris. A provisional government was appointed and on the 14 December Bishop Miron Cristea—the future Patriarch—came to Bucharest to announce the decision of the Grand Assembly to the King. On the 14 December Ferdinand I issued two decrees: one sanctioning the union and the other organizing a provisional government for these regions represented in the Bucharest government by three ministers without portfolios. Budapest protested in vain in the same way as Russia had, refused to accept the union of Bessarabia, which it denounced as blatant annexation of its own territory.

In Paris, London and Rome since 1916 the ground was being prepared for the Romanian side and in the French capital there had been formed in early 1918, alongside a Czech and Polish lobby, a Romanian lobby, active among university professors with the support of such men as Seignobos the historian, the geographer de Martonne and politicians such as Albert Thomas the Minister for Armaments. Its newspaper "Romania" advocated union with Transylvania and Bukovina. In April 1918 some Romanians from Transylvania participated in the "Congress for the oppressed nations of Austria-Hungary" in Rome and set out their demands with the already foreseeable perspective of the division of the Empire. In early September, General Berthelot, the head of the French military mission in Jassy, advised the Conservative leader Take Ionescu that in view of the speed with which events had been taking place, he should go to Paris to form a "Romanian National Council" to represent all the regions of Romania. This actually happened on the 3 October and he became the recognized spokesman for the Allies. It was also Take Ionescu who persuaded the government in power in Bucharest to once more start hostilities against the Central Powers. The consequences on the battlefield and its end on the 24 January 1919 have already been mentioned.

Guilty in their opinion of having signed a separate peace agreement in May 1918 with the Central Powers, together with the fact that the United States did not recognize the secret August 1916 treaty, meant that the victor nations refused Romania the status of "ally" and only allowed 2 delegates which was less than Serbia. Bucharest complained and I. C. Bratianu himself came accompanied by a large delegation that included Al. Vaida-Voevod who represented the new provinces. On the 31 January 1919 Bratianu explained the Romanian position to the Council of Four Powers as well as its claim to the Banat region and the conflict of interest with Serbia which was already militarily in situ. It was sent on to the Territorial Commission which following long and detailed examination of the advice of experts, simply agreed to the transfer of Austrian Bukovina and Bessarabia, formerly Bolshevik territory; it however rejected the Romanian idea of river Tisza as the western border and limited Transylvania to east of the Arad, Oradea and Szatmar (Satu Mare) axis; furthermore it divided the Banat into two and only the north up to Vrsac was Romanian, the rest was Serbian. Bratianu was to protest but to no avail and furious he left Paris on the 15 June.

The Romanian question was further complicated by the outcome of events in Hungary. The revolutionary government of Bela Kun, called the "Republic of Councils," in power since March 1919, was clearly inspired by the Bolsheviks and consequently was having problems with the west. Marshall Foch foresaw the need for military intervention in the same way as in Russia, but Lloyd George and President Wilson were more inclined to negotiate. Encouraged by General Franchet d'Esperey who also wanted Serbia involved in the question, the government of Bucharest sent its troops right up to the Tisza, thus acquiring what it had been promised in 1916. London threatend retaliation if it went any further, but a bungled counter-offensive by the Hungarian Red Army took the Romanians up to Budapest which they entered on the 3 August, two days after the fall of Bela Kun; they were to stay there until November and the arrival of the counter-revolutionary army of Admiral Horthy. Accused by the Hungarians of numerous exactions, their presence in the Magyar capital led to a virtual end to relations between the four Great Powers and Bucharest and when the Treaty of Saint-Germain was signed with Austria on the 10 September 1919, although the question of Bukovina concerned Romania it was not consulted. Bratianu resigned. The four western powers then sent what amounted to an ultimatum, demanding that Romania accept a treaty guaranteeing minority rights, the division of the Banat with Serbia and the evacuation of Hungary up to the line established at Versailles. Bucharest had to comply. General elections brought Al. Vaida-Voevod a Transylvanian to power, who immediately resumed discussions with the allies: on the 10 December he signed the treaties of Saint-Germain and Neuilly and Bukovina and southern Dobrudja became officially part of Romania. The dispute with Hungary was resolved by the Trianon texts of the 4 june 1920: Transylvania, Maramures, Crisana and northern Banat were in turn recognized as an integral part of the Romanian state. In Paris that same year, on the 28 October, France, Great Britain, Italy and Japan recognized Romanian posession of Bessarabia; Bolshevik Russia protested and the United States refused to condone the "carving up of Russia without its consent." Thus the question of Besarabia was to continue to remain wide open.

The defeated Bulgarians could do nothing more than accept the conditions set out by the victors. As in Germany and Austria-Hungary, military defeat was to lead to revolution, largely inspired by the Russian October revolution. This was even more so since the two countries had very strong links and the two armies had been in contact with each other in Moldavia. Numerous acts of fraternization had taken place on the Siret front helped by the fact that the soldiers could understand each other. When they were forced to retreat following the defeat at Dobropole, some rearguard units in Macedonia rose up in mutiny. The revolt reached Radomir[3] which was an important railway junction and where the Bulgarian H.Q. was positioned. It was surrounded and the officers were arrested on the 24 September 1918, on the same day that the Sofia government requested an armistice. There were attempts at negotiations but the peasant leader, A. Stamboliski, declared the "Radomir republic" which was to last four days. After having tried to make the mutineers march on Sofia he was arrested by loyalist troops. The armistice imposed by General Franchet d'Esperey and signed on the 29 September, ordered the retreat of all Bulgarian troops to behind the 1913 borders and the occupation by the allies of certain strategic points; also King Ferdinand, considered too sympathetic to Germany, was forced to abdicate on the 3 October 1918, in favour of his son, who became Boris III (1894-1943). Elections were held in the midst of economic and social crisis and brought the Stamboliski government to power.

As in Germany it was to be the role of the centre left parties to settle the state of war. Without the participation of the Bulgarians the victors decided the fate of the country and envoys from Sofia in vain were to ask for plebicites in contested areas. The treaty signed at Neuilly on the 27 November 1919 was far worse than that of Bucharest in 1913: Romania was to occupy southern Dobrudja, Greece would get the whole of Aegean Thrace thus depriving Bulgaria access to the Aegean and Serbia would be given the Strumica valley, Caribrod (Dimitrovgrad) and Bosilvegrad (Bosilegrad). On top of this Bulgaria would have to pay its neighbours, its former enemies, large reparations: 2,250 million francs and deliver cattle and coal. Finally the army would be reduced to 33,000 men. Human loss was estimated at 150,000 dead and 258,000 wounded, the economy was in ruins and there was famine in Sofia. Some 250,000 refugees from Macedonia and Thrace were to bring with them to this tired and humiliated country the seeds of an aggressive expansionist dream, while the centre left parties were left tainted by their acceptance of the victor's terms. Bulgaria was in the camp of the unhappy with Versailles.

The Greeks experienced the pride of being victorious: their armies joined in autumn 1918 in the eastern army's offensive and contributed to the Bulgarian armistice of 29 September. This opened the way to Istanbul just as much as that of Vardar and forced the panicked Porte to sign an armistice on the 30 October on a British ship anchored at the harbour of Mudros[4], felt by Turkish nationalist to have been a total surrender of the Ottoman Empire and in terms of the Balkans, allowed the Allies to station troops in the area of the Straits and to use them freely. On the 13 November the Anglo-French force which had landed at Istanbul took control of the city and on the 8 February 1919 General Franchet d'Esperey made a triumphal entry. In the meantime the Greek army, whose losses had up till then been slight (about 5,000 killed or wounded), was getting ready to occupy Thrace as far as the walls of Istanbul. Once more the dream of the Megale Idea stirred Greek hearts and Venizelos, who had come to Paris for the Peace Conference, defended brilliantly the Greek position. Yet he came across Italian opposition who claimed northern Epirus for Italy and a vassal Albania and also the Dodecanese islands and the Smyrna (Izmir) region which had been promised to them in the April 1917 Saint-Jean de Maurienne agreement. Prime Minister Orlando, having left the Conference, allowed the Greeks to occupy Smyrna and the surrounding region to assure the protection of the Greek population under threat from the Turks: there had been talk of 900,000 Greeks either killed or deported from Asia Minor during the war[5]. King Alexander's troops disembarked on the 15 May 1919 amid great popular support. The Treaty of Seves which the Ottomans signed on the 10 August 1920 was to confirm these positions giving Greece eastern Thrace up to Istanbul and the Smyrna region if after five years a plebiscite showed it was the wish of the population. For Venizelos and his supporters this was the start of the restoration of the Byzantine Empire.

Yet in the meantime there took place an act which was to prove to be a national disaster for Greece for in Athens, participation in the victory had not erradicated the divisions that had resulted as a consequence of the abdication of Constantine and Venizelists and Royalists continued to oppose each other. Following the signature of the Treaty of Sevres two navy officers tried to kill Venizelos at the Gare de Lyon in Paris and these differences once more came to the foreground. On top of this a short while after an unfortunate accident occurred. King Alexander was bitten by a monkey and died on the 25 October 1920 in the midst of an election. Attention was turned to the problem of the succession since Prince Paul, the third son of Constantine, refused to mount a throne that neither his father nor his elder brother had volutarily renounced; in his opinion the pro-German king who had been forced to abdicate should lawfully return to his throne. The outcome of the November 1920 elections was a suprise for Venizelos since he was not reelected and his supporters became a minority in the House. Three days later he left for exile. The Allies, worried by these developments, intimated to the government in Athens that a return of King Constantine would free them from any prior agreements with Greece. Notwithstanding, a plebiscite recalled him and on the 19 December 1920 the monarch made a solemn entry into Athens, to the acclaim of the population.

In contrast to these political intrigues the Ottomans were experiencing a remarkable national renewal, personified by Mustafa Kemal. He had become a general during the fighting in the Caucasus and was appointed inspector of the 3rd Army to restore order in Anatolia; on the 19 May 1919 (four days after the Greek landing at Smyrna) he landed at Samsun, the largest Turkish port on the Black Sea and began what is known as the "Kemal Revolution." In Istanbul a weak Sultan, Mehmed VI, who had succeeded his deceased brother Mehmed V, allowed elections to be organized at the end of December 1919 that resulted in a strong majority for the nationalists. The Ottoman parliament voted on the 28 January 1920 a "National Pact," similar to the text which Mustafa Kemal had passed in Anatolia: it requested acknowledgement of the abolition of the capitulation treaty decreed by Enver Pasha in 1914, freedom of movement in the Straits, guarantees of security for Istanbul and the recognition by the Great Powers of the sovereignty and absolute independence of the Turkish nation. The eruption of English sailors into the assembly rooms to arrest supposedly pro-German representatives, led to the dissolution of parliament and most of its members joining the Grand Kemalist Assembly in Ankara in April 1920. Henceforth the centre of Turkey was in Anatolia while Istanbul was occupied by the Allies.

In contrast to the provisional government of Mustafa Kemal, the Sultan and the Porte as an institution appeared to be on its last legs, yet it was with them that the victors were to sign the Treaty of Sevres, immediately denounced by the Kemalists as a betrayal. The Allies themselves were well aware of its weakness. The Italians, angry at being excluded from negotiations had designs on establishing a foothold in the Smyrna region to the detriment of the Greeks and the French had had problems with the English over Syria and the eastern Mediterranean. Hence in March and October 1921 agreement was reached with the Ankara authorities that was to lead to the withdrawal of French and Italian troops from Anatolia[6]. Greek historians still decry this relinquishing territory above all since the arms that these troops left behind were to fall into the hands of the Kemalists and were to be used against Greek troops. In June 1920 the latter had in fact extended their own zone of occupation and intended advancing on Ankara; they were halted the following spring by a defeat at Inonu by Ismet Pasha (hence the name Ismet Inonu 1884–1973). In March 1921 they once again advanced and reached the Sankarya river (called Sangarios in Greek) so stretching their lines of communications over more than 250 miles of arid land. On the 26 August 1922 Kemal counter-attacked and the Greek lines were cut in two. There followed a terrible retreat that was executed in the utmost confusion towards Smyrna, the army becoming entangled with a flood of refugees fleeing possible repraisals. On the 9 September 1922 Mustafa Kemal entered triumphantly into Smyrna, evacuated by Constantine's troops who had gone to the islands. Shocked by this disaster some officers in Chios formed a Revolutionary Committee around Colonel N. Plastiras, and a telegram was sent to Athens demanding the abdication of the king. For the second time Constantine yielded and on the 27 september 1922 he left for exile[7], leaving the throne to his eldest son George II.

The international implications of this dramatic misadventure still had to be resolved. The Turks insisted on the evacuation of Greek troops from eastern Thrace, occupied following fighting in July 1920. This was settled in October 1922 with the armistice of Mudanya that settled the Greek-Turkish border on the the river Evros (Meric). The Kemalists however were moving towards the Straits and the Allies were forced to negotiate with them. Discussions opened at Lausanne and were dominated by disagreement between Lord Curzon the head of the Foreign Office and General Ismet Inonu. This was to last till July 1923. In the meantime, on the 2 November 1922, the Grand Assembly of Ankara abolished the position of Sultan and Mehmed VI fled aboard an English warship[8]. The Ottoman Empire was finnished. The document which was signed in Lausanne on the 24 July 1923 "erased the humiliation of the Treaty of Sevres"[9]. As far as the Balkans were concerned it restored to Turkey eastern Thrace together with Edirne and the islands of Imbros and Tenedos while the islands of the Aegean Sea went to Greece (apart from the Dodecanese which went to Italy and Cyprus to England). The Capitulations were abolished. As for the recurrent problem of the Straits this was settled with the free passage of merchant shipping at all times, the passage of warships yet not in squadron formation in peacetime and the demilitarization of the Dardanelles and the Bosphorous. The Turkish Republic, proclaimed on the 29 October 1923, no longer had a major stake in the Balkans: eastern Thrace with some 15,000 sq.miles and 500,000 inhabitants of whom 95% were Turkish, together with the cosmopolitan city of Istanbul with 600,000 inhabitants competing and envious of the new centre of the Kemal state: Ankara.

One futher calamity was to befall Greece: the movement of whole sections of the population. Massacres had taken place in

Asia Minor, some involving tens of thousands. An act signed in Lausanne on the 30 January 1930 foresaw a forced transfer of gigantic numbers of the population: 1,300,000 Greeks from Asia and 400,000 Turks from Europe. This was the end of the Megale Idea. A. Vacalopoulos the historian called it: "the worst disaster to befall the Greeks since the fall of Constantinople in 1453."

Yugoslavia Under King Alexander

"The Kingdom of the Serbs, Croats and Slovenes" proclaimed in Belgrade on the 1 December 1919 was a project rather than a fact. First because on top of the three peoples already mentioned there were Germans, Hungarians in the Vojvodina, Albanians in Kosovo and in Macedonia, Romanians in the Banat, Turks from Bosnia-Herzegovina and Macedonia, some Czechs, Slovaks, Ruthenians, Italians, White Russian refugees and 70,000 "other" nationalities. In all more than 2 million from ethnic minorities or 17% of the total population. Furthermore they defined Serbo-Croats through language, which was supposed to give a complete picture, yet in fact it was possible to break them down further in terms of religion: 5,400,000 Serbs and 3,700,000 Croats bearing in mind that the Macedonian Slavs were identified as southern Serbs and so included in this total. Of the 1,300,000 Muslims nobody could tell how many were Serbs and how many Croats.[10] Several of these minorities—the Magyars, Germans, Albanians, Romanians and Italians—still had links with their homelands and so there were many types of irredentist tendencies. As for the three founding peoples who had wanted union they had not agreed on a organization for union. In opposition to the vision of a "Greater Serbia," in other word the Kingdom of Serbia expanded to the borders of the new state, the federal concept shared by the Croats and the Slovenes who had been part of the Dual-Monarchy that declined precisely because it had been unable to transform itself into a Federation of Peoples.

The Yugoslav State was therefore still at its inception and its architect was to be the Serbian heir apparent, Prince Alexander Karageorgevic (1888–1934), the great-grandson of the legendary George the Black. Ruling since 1914, instead of his father Peter I who was afflicted by illness, he had shown great energy during the war although at times this had smacked of brutality. A Serbian patriot, he had more confidence in his army rather than Parliament, to build up a strong structure. Having got rid of the "Black Hand" opposition in June 1917 following the Salonika trials[11], he allowed a "White Hand" to be organized, made up of officers who were exceptionally loyal to the prince. On the death of Peter I in August 1921 he became Alexander I (1921–1934) and was known by his supporters as the "Knight king and the unifier." In June 1922 he married Princess Maria of Romania, daughter of King Ferdinand, who in 1923 gave him an heir Peter.

At first political action augured well for the new state: the first elections in November 1920 were above board and a dozen political parties shared the 419 seats in the Constituent Assembly; the largest was Pasic's Radical Party, the Democratic Party which was a coalition of former radical politicians and Serbs from the former Austrian territories, the Peasant Party and the Communist Party. The latter above all had made significant gains with 58 seats (more than the Croats). Stemming from the old Social Democrat Party that had existed before the war on each side of the Drava and the Danube, which as everwhere else had split into two following the victory of the Bolsheviks. In June 1920 its left wing had formed a Communist Party with the aim of creating a Yugoslav Soviet Republic, part of a Danubian-Balkan Federation which would be part of an international Federation of Soviet Republics. Its appeal had more to do with widespread war-weariness and peasant disaffection (still largely illiterate and not yet benefitting from the agrarian reforms of the previous year) more than belief in idealistic theories. Added to this there was much agitation from Serbs and Croats from the Austro-Hungarian army who had been made prisoner in Russia and been set free by the October Revolution; among these was a certain Josip Broz, known as Tito (1892–1980). The Prince Regent, who had been brought up in the Nicholas II's Russia and had a visceral hatred of the Bolsheviks, was shocked by their success but soon found a way of dealing with them. An attempt on his life and the assassination of the Minister of the Interior by a young Bosnian communist was the perfect pretext for passing a law of "State Security" which outlawed the Communist Party: the 58 representatives were banned from attending the Skupstina and its newspaper and agitation prohibited. Right up to the Second World War the Yugoslav Communist Party was forced to operate underground.

The Croat Peasant Party on the other hand was to have a

The Triumph and Failure of the National States 421

prominent role to play. Set up in 1904 in Zagreb by the Radic brothers: Ante Radic (1868–1919) and Stjepan Radic (1871–1928), they were similar to the Serbian Radical party in that their supporters tended to be small proprty owners, relatively progressive and very chauvinistic. Its manifesto which advocated autonomy for Croatia within a Yugoslav federation had appeal within the new kingdom and was to generate political conflict for the next twenty years. Its leader S. Radic was opposed to the constitutional blueprint which N. Pasic, who had been returned to power for the tenth time, drew up. Despite the opposition of Croat representatives it was passed on the 28 June 1921 (hence the name Constitution of Vidovdan) by Serbian Radicals, the Democrats, Bosnian Muslims and those representatives whose vote were bought for various forms of privilege. Even so this was less than half the possible votes. This constitution was based the pre-War Serbian constitution and gave strong central control the King who was head of the army and chose the prime minister. It had a single House of Representatives—the Skupstina and an administration totally under the control of the government. As well accusing the government of corruption, Croats could not avoid observing that for the first ten years of the Kingdom the position of Prime Minister had been held by a Serb for 117 months out of a total of 121 months, while the Ministries of War and the Navy were consecutively held by Serbs.

Only on the surface were these ten years politically "democratic." The Croat Peasant representatives boycotted the Skupstina until 1924. Radic was increasingly drawn to the idea of a "Green International" advocated by the Bulgarian Prime Minister Stamboliski and went on a journey to Moscow which landed him in prison for several months accused of high treason. N. Pasic, president for the 17th time, got him out and made him Minister of Education in a coalition which ended following the death of the former. His death further aggravated the situation and there emerged a grouping called the Precani—those on the other side of the river or the former Austro-Hungarian provinces—opposed to the Serbian Carsija—the "Market" or business world. Their conflict was to lead to disaster. On the 20 June 1928, during a session of the Skupstina, a Montenegrin Radical representative opened fire on the Croat representatives and Stjepan Radic and two of his colleagues were killed. All Croatia denounced the "Bloody Skupstina" and the kingdom was split in two. The King gathered the leaders of the various parties together, above all the sucessor of S. Radic, Dr Vl. Macek (1879-1964), and confronted them with the division of the kingdom into two countries. The Precani turned this down fearful of the expansionist dreams of Hungary and Italy. On the 9 January 1929 Alexander I dissolved parliament and abolished the Vidovdan Constitution. There began what is known in Yugoslav history as the "Royal Dictatorship."

In contrast to other European dictatorships this was meant to be a temporary measure and was not supported by any specific organization. The king was to be in charge of the government of his people who in turn, at least at first, saw this as solving the existing problems. The government was entrusted to a general who was responsible only to the sovereign. Decrees were issued which cracked down on terrorism but also on Communist agitation. Political parties and associations were dissolved and the press strictly controlled. In October a decree reorganized the administrative machinery of government, regrouping the 33 administrative departments into 9 Banovinas, provinces headed by a Ban, thus repacing the old territories and the kingdom adopted the official name of Jugoslavija. Yet the Precani soon realized that Serbian hegemony would continue since the Prime Minister, Minister of War, Minister of the Navy and Interior Minister were still from the old kingdom. Some Croat leaders emigrated; the moderates in Switzerland called for autonomy for Croatia, others, more radical, such as Ante Pavelic went to Bulgaria and then to Hungary and were helped and finaced by Italian and Hungarian fascists. They were at the origin of the terrorist organization Ustasa—Rebel— which was formed in Italy in 1930 and whose aim was for an independent Croatia, by every means possible. Inside the country itself Dr Macek was put on trial but was acquitted. Meanwhile the numbers of Croat nationalists and communists in the prisons mounted up. There they were ill-treated and tortured. Even so, in January 1931 the King and Queen visited Zagreb and Alexander talked with his suprised subjects in the street. In September he promulgated a new Constitution that pleased neither side. He also created a "Democratic Yugoslav Peasant Party" that almost became the official King's party. The worsening economic crisis was mirrored politically by an increase in tension in Croatia and Slovenia and even an armed uprising in Lika[12] aided by Mussolini's Italy. The Croats openly demanded autonomy in the "Zagreb Manifesto" that again earned Dr Macek three years in prison. The system of policing became more repressive while the number of political murders increased. It was in this atmosphere of mounting fear that the Marseilles incident took place. Alexander landed there for an official state visit to France and was killed together with the French Foreign Minister, L. Barthou, by an Ustasa Croat.

The whole country was to experience a short lived feeling of unity around the royal coffin but the heir to the throne Peter II was only eleven years old and the regency was placed in the hands of a triumvirate controlled by Prince Paul (1893–1976), a cousin of the dead king. He attempted to institute a policy of liberalization yet the 1935 elections were so rigged that the Croats once more boycotted the Skupstina. The regent reached an agreement with Dr Macek who was out of prison and brought into government an economist Dr Milan Stojadinovic. The attention of Europe was at the time fixed on the Third Reich and historians have mainly concentrated on the Yugoslav government's attraction into the orbit of the emerging great power. Internally the Croat problem was to dominate everything. The Vidovdan Constitution had abolished the previous constitutional clause whereby the Orthodox religion had been the state religion of Serbia and instead an Orthodox Yugoslav Church, bringing together the followers of both regions, had been created. At the same time the Muslim community was also reorganized. There was the problem of the Catholics mainly in Croatia and Slovenia. Prior to his death King Alexander had started negotiations with the Vatican to reach a Concord and this was finally signed in July 1935. The Skupstina took its time ratifying this but agreement had been reached when the Patriarch of the Orthodox Church torpedoed discussions by excommunicating all representatives who had voted to ratify it. This was followed by violent demonstrations and Stojadinovic was forced to withdraw the proposal. The rift between the Serbs and the Croats grew wider. The regent then took direct control of the situation and direct talks were held between Prince Paul and Dr Macek. The urgency of the task was underlined by the entry of German troops into Czechoslovakia in May 1939. They reached agreement on the 26 August 1939, ten days before the start of World War II. The agreement—Sporazum—set up the Great Banovina of Croatia which brought together inner Croatia and Dalmatia with a polulation of 4,400,000: 860,000 Serbs and 160,000 Muslims. The Banovina was centered on Zagreb, restored to its past preeminence with a Diet—Sabor—with competence over internal affairs. Yet this development was still too little for the Croat extremists who continued to look for support to Hitler and Mussolini.

This chaotic political drama was being played in an essentially rural country. In 1918, 78% of the population lived off the land. One of the earliest measures taken by the new state was agrarian reform, started in February 1919. In Serbia it was essentially a case of purging the system of the after-effects of war, in Macedonia and Bosnia-Herzegovina of erradicating the last traces of Ottoman feudalism and destroying the large Muslim landowners who were often considered Turks; in Croatia, Vojvodina and Slovenia it was a question of, at the same time destroying the power of the mostly Austrian or Hungarian landowners—latifundiaries—and giving land to the demobilized soldiers who were open to revolutionary ideas. The contrast between the regions, the large estates of the Habsburg nobility and the small democratic Serbian rural peasant communities needed to disappear to make the initial foundations of a new unity. For although many of the Habsburg supporters had left their land and castles after the end of the war, thus simplifying the task of the Division Commission, the Muslim Beys of Bosnia had managed to maneouver politically, lending support to Pasic in return for guarantees for their property. In the end, on the eve of the Second World War, not all the problems had been ironed out yet it has been calculated that about 2 million hectares of land had been redistributed, about a quarter of all the arable land, and that half a million peasant families (a quarter of all peasants) had benefitted from this redistribution. Although quite extensive this reform was largely rendered ineffective by the growth in population which for the country as a whole was to rise from 12 million in 1919 to 16 million in 1940. This increase of 1.4% per year meant that the number of people living off one square kilometre of arable land rose to 100 which meant a rural overpopulation of 62%[13]. Yet emigration abroad, to the United States, South America or Australia was not as easy as prior to the war for these countries were implementing stricted immigration controls. As for industrial growth this was very low. In 1938 the proportion of the population who lived in the countryside had only gone down by 3% to 75% while the number of industrial workers had not even reached 400,000 even though successive governments had concentrated on industry and had implemented policies to encourage investment from abroad. In 1937 it is estimated that a third of all industrial capital was in foreign ownership, for example the copper mines at

Bor belonged to a French company. The shortage of national capital was one of the biggest weaknesses of Yugoslavia between the wars and Marxist historians have been able to speak, as elsewhere in the Balkans at the time, of a semi-colonial economy. Its institutions did experience a few years of relative prosperity following the post-war recovery but the Great Depression of 1929 was to hit hard an economic system based on agricultural production: prices were to fall between 1929 and 1933 by 44% for wheat and 26% for maize, so reducing the purchasing power of three quarters of the population. It was therefore easy for Germany, in the very midst of its rearmament effort, to appear as a saviour.

Twenty years after uniting, Yugoslavia had not achieved the cohabitation of the southern Slavs: its nationalist peasantry, up to 40% illiterate and 70% in Macedonia, were a great burden for the small layer of urban bourgeois torn between the Anglo-French democratic model and the attraction of German-Italian fascism.

Romania Under Carol

Great Romania which was recognized at Versailles covered almost 200,000 sq. miles and in 1920 had a population of 15.5 million with 70% Romanians. Unlike the 8% who had lived in the "Old Kingdom" before the war—the Regat—these 30% aliens[14] came from the new territories and in general contested the way in which they had been incorporated into the kingdom. The Magyars together with the Szeklers made up, according to the 1925 Romanian census, a quarter of the population of Crisana, Maramures, Transylvania and the Banat. The Germans included the Transylvanian Saxons (270,000), the Swabians from the Banat and the German speaking people of Bessarabia, Bukovina and the Dobrudja. There were Ukrainians and Ruthenians in Bessarabia and Bukovina, and Bulgarians, Turks and Tatars in the Dobrudja region. Their geographical position laid them open to the irredentist influence of neighbouring countries. Their legal status was defined by the Treaty for Minorities which was forced on Romania in December 1919 when they agreed to the Treaties of Saint Germain and Neuilly. This guaranteed full equality under in law. These considerations were also enshrined in the Constitution of 1923, the Hungarians however complained over their practical application. In terms of the agrarian reform of 1920 they brought the issue to the League of Nations which discussed it for seven years. Internally the minority groups defended their rights with the aid of political parties such as the Magyar Peasants Party, the Magyar Union of Workers (MADOSZ), the German Party which became the party for Germans with Nazi sympathies and the Bulgarian Party which had seats in the Parliament and gave their support to the Romanian parties in return for concessions over eductation and the press. In reality the minorities problem was a handicap for Greater Romania. In Transylvania, Hungarian nationalism, based on a feeling of cultural superiority to the Balkan peoples of the Old Kingdom was keenly nurtured by Budapest irredentism. In the Dobrudja area the Bulgarian peasants complained of a policy of colonization of the best lands. In Bessarabia, which had the reputation of being the "worst administered province of all of Europe," unrest was virtually permanent and came from two sources: antisemitism and Bolshevism. As for the Germans, from 1934 onwards they were taken over by the propaganda organs of the Third Reich.

Romanian political life was dramatically changed by the introduction of universal suffrage which had been agreed at Jassy in 1917 and was in effect introduced through a decree issued in June 1919. The old Conservative Party, discredited because of its pro-German tendency and deprived of its social base due to the agrarian reforms, broke up and virtually disappeared from the political scene. The Liberals, reorganized into the National Liberal Party were to dominate the 1922–1928 period under the firm leadership of the Bratianu family: Ion (1884–1927), his brothers Constantin and Vintila and his son Gheorghe (1898–1954). Firm supporters of union and centralism they represented the bourgeoisie of the Old Kingdom, called for the development of industry and banking, fought vigorously against the labour movement and opposed all separatist tendencies. They had voted the Constitution of 28 March 1923 which declared in its opening article: "the Kingdom of Romania is a United and Indivisible National State." Against these traditional organizations there emerged a new movement: the Peasant Party, which had been founded in Bucharest in 1919 by a group of medium sized farmers, Church popes and school teachers led by a Wallachian teacher called Ion Mihalache (1882–1965). Its manifesto laid out plans for the expropriation of large estates, the organization of peasant cooperatives and a system of rural banks. Brought into the 1919 coalition as Agriculture Minister, I. Mihalache elaborated an agrarian reform which was seen as so radical that the king forced his resignation. The Peasant Party went through several years of decline before merging in 1925 with the former National Romanian Party of Transylvania and forming the National Peasant Party whose new leader Iuliu Maniu oriented it to a policy of openness to foreign capital while at the same time denouncing the "corruption and nepotism of the Liberal Moldo-Wallachian bureaucracy." Another movement, the People's Party was also for a time very successful, under General Averescu who was remembered for his victory in 1916. Using the slogan "Work, honour and legality" he advocated national solidarity. Brought to power in May 1920 with 43% of the votes, Averescu implemented agrarian reform (July 1921), was brought back to power in 1926 but his party, weakened by internal divisions, was to disappear a year later while its leader was made Marshall.

These various political parties were to dominate the political scene until 1938 but whatever the Peasant Party or the Peoples Party might have wished and proclaimed, political life retained many of the characteristics of the Old Kingdom: corruption, election rigging and nepotism. Therefore elections sometimes led to suprises, for instance the Liberal Party gaining 103 seats in November 1919, only 9 in May 1920 yet 227 and an absolute majority in the House in March 1922. The People's Party's results varied from 7 to 224 and then 12 seats. Hence there occurred short-lived coalitions based on alliances between individual politicians and also many politicians leaving their parties due to personal antipathies. On top of all this there was the dynastic problem for King Ferdinand was getting old and wished to settle the question of his succession. Although his marriage with Mary of Edinburgh had been stormy this had resulted in 1893 in the birth of a son—Carol—who was the heir apparent. He had married Helen of Greece, daughter of King Constantine who gave birth to a son Mihai in October 1921. But Carol's marriage was to be no happier than his father's and the heir apparent engaged in a public liaison with a divorcee, Elena Lupescu—born Magda Wolf—of a Jewish family from Jassy. This was doubly shocking for a court that was traditionally antisemitic. In 1925 the king made his son choose between the throne and his mistress and Carol abdicated in favour of his son Mihai and went abroad with Elena Lupescu on the understanding that he would not return for ten years. Ferdinand died two years later and Mihai aged six became Mihai I with a council of regents presided over by Patriarch Miron Cristea. Yet three years later, at the height of an economic and political crisis, a group of officers and businessmen brought the self-exile back in secret and two days later, on the 8 June 1930, Parliament restored Carol II to the throne while Mihai became "Grand Voevod." Despite his promise to I. Maniu, the leader of the government, to break with his mistress, Carol who had divorced Helen of Greece in 1928, brought Elena Lupescu back and had her living in the palace so sparking off the departure of the Queen mother. The new king was 37 years old, was intelligent but lacked education, had few scruples and was brutal as his personal life had demonstrated. He was an admirer of Mussolini, despised politicians and parliamentary life and dreamed of becoming the regenerator of his country. At first he acted cleverly, giving power over a seven year period to all the main leaders of the parties who through their own failure eliminated themselves. So by 1938 the way was open for him to impose his own power. This was the start of the royal dictatorship.

On the 18 January 1938 he dissolved the newly elected House and entrusted government to Patriarch Miron Cristea who promptly declared a state of emergency. A new constitution was drawn up on the 20 February giving greater powers to the king, abolishing political parties and repacing them with the "Front of National Rebirth." Mussolini's model was imposed on everyday life and corporations of workers and employees were set up. In reality the regime was based on a camarilla made up of Elena Lupescu, some industrialists such as Nicolae Malaxa who was of Greek origin, and bankers so giving the regime an appearance of racketeering alien to the nationalist ideology that was supposed to be developed in the country. Ultimately Carol ruled with the support of the army and the police over a people disillusioned and politically apathetic.

In economic and social terms Greater Romania like the Old Kingdom was a agricultural country with 78% of the population peasants. The most serious problem was therefore that of land. As has been previously mentioned the king in Jassy had in 1917 promised land reform and in December 1918 the method of redistribution was fixed by decree. A very radical plan, drawn up by Mihalache the leader of the peasants, was not implemented but finally in July 1921 a law was passed. It foresaw the transfer of Crown land, limited ownership to 100 hectares, but with exceptions and following compensation the distribution of the surplus into plots of 5 to 7 hectares. For the country as a whole, almost 6

The Triumph and Failure of the National States 429

million hectares were expropriated and 4 million distributed to 1,400,000 peasants. The remaining 2 million hectares were retained by the villages for pasture or forests or for services such as schools or roads. The result was controvertial. In Transylvania the Hungarians, who generally had large estates, complained that they were the only group to suffer. In Bessarabia the peasants taking cue from the Russian Revolution had already divided up the land and refused any further change. Everywhere there were accusations of corruption. Whatever the truth might be, land reform was to assure that serious outbreaks of violence, such as those that occurred in Romania in 1907 did not happen again and was called by Mihalache: the "safety valve against the Bolshevik threat." Nevertheless in 1930, 24% of the land was controlled by 6,700 large landowners as opposed to 28% owned by 2,500,000 poor peasants. The average holding had clearly increased yet the demographic rise of 1.2% per year meant that this continued to be divided up and rural overpopulation continued even though it was slightly lower than other Balkan countries. The Romanian peasant however remained very poor due to the low productivity: wheat production was 8 to 9 quintals per hectare as against 16 in France and for maize 10 to 11 as against 15 to 16. Cereal production dominated but wheat was for export and maize remained the basic foodstuff used in a dish called Mamaliga. Lastly the 1929-33 economic crisis brought increased hardship to rural areas with the collapse of agricultural prices.

Industry was to undergo a remarkable expansion. The Old Kingdom had previously produced petrol and wood but Transylvania added a wealth of mining resources in the Jiu Valley and non-ferrous metals, coal and salt. Under the guidance of the Liberals, post-war reconstruction was rapid and growth was high. From 1923 to 1938 industrial production doubled yet still remained proportionately less in terms of GNP to agriculture: 30% as against 38%. Oil production was the most important industry, rising from 1.1 million tons in 1921 to 8.4 million in 1934 but then declining showing the first signs that it was being exhausted. Following the nationalization of prewar German companies, the Romanian government became the largest partner with 60% of all capital, ahead of about 100 French, English and American companies. The petrochemical industry refined about 90% of its crude oil around Ploesti and 4 million tons were exported in 1930 and 6.6 million in 1935 due to increased demand from the Third Reich. There was large public investment in metallurgy—the king himself investing in the Malaxa plant—and in 1930 about 70% of total production was for the state, especially arms production, hence a slightly particular form of protective tarifs which operated within this industry.

In conclusion in 1938 the standard of living of most Romanians remained low and among the lowest in Europe with a per capita GNP of 94 dollars. In Greece it was 76 dollars, in Bulgaria 81 dollars and in Yugoslavia 106 dollars while in France it was 246 dollars.

The economic and political situation naturally gave rise to opposition movements, both Marxist and Fascist. The former's fleeting popularity was due to Romania's geographical proximity to Bolshevik Russia rather than because of the workers movement which in any case was very small. Since 1917 Moldavia had been a place of refuge from the Russian Revolution and had experienced its effects. In December 1918 workers took to the streets of Bucharest in despair at their condition. The Romanian Socialist Party which had spread to the new provinces was split by the question of affiliation to the Third International and in May 1921 a Congress held in questionable circumstances decided to set up the Romanian Communist Party. Exposed to Bratianu's police it enjoyed three years of open political activity and obtained 75,000 votes (0.25% of the electorate) in 1922. Two years later it was made illegal, its organization dissolved and its newspapers banned. This period of illegality was to last from April 1924 to August 1944 and was extremely dangerous. Outlawed, the Comintern made its problems worse. Its congresses were held in Vienna, Kharkov and Moscow and the Secretaries General were in turn a Hungarian, a Ukrainian and a Pole, all imposed by Moscow. In 1924 the International declared the new Versailles States "Imperialist" and called for the right of recession for the Transylvanian Hungarians and the Ukrainians of Bessarabia and Bukovina. This however was impossible for the Romanian Communists to advocate since it laid them open to attack from the Bucharest government for high treason. There were internecine struggles within the Party between left and right wing fractions. The Party did achieve a measure of success in organizing strikes in 1933 in the railways and in the petrochemical industry. During these strikes a few of the leaders of the future distinguished themselves, for example: Gheorghiu-Dej, Vasile Luca and Lucretiu Patrascanu. In 1935 it joined the "Anti-Fascist Front" but its leaders were arrested and were given harsh prison sentences. On the eve of the Second World War the Romanian Communist Party, still outlawed, only had a few thousand members.

The main force for anti-government activity was fascism. It was to develop over several distinct periods. During the immediate post-war period, as in Germany and Italy, when people became disillusioned with the peacetime order, mainly intellectuals or from the army who formed small groups and during the Great Depression of 1929-33 when it attracted large sections of society who had rejected Marxist policies and analysis. In 1923 in Bucharest a Fascia was formed along the Italian lines by university students. In the same year Professor Alexander Cuza (1857-1947), from the University of Jassy, set up the "National Christian Defence League" whose nationalist and antisemitic ideology combined with a "peasantism"—taranismul—which also influenced I. Mihalache and his associates. During the 1926 elections it got 10 seats. It then went into allience with the Transylvanian poet Octavian Goga which resulted in the latter occupying for a short time the post of Prime Minister in 1937 and putting into practise a brutal and economically disastrous policy of antisemitism.

Its roots grew from the same humus as the "Iron Guard"— Garda de Fier. Corneliu Codreanu's movement(1899-1938) was more clearly fascist in its organization. Codreanu was from a middle class Jassy family, had been a student of Professor A. Cuza and organized an anti-Bolshevik force of irregulars on the Moldavian border. His violence to Jews and Communists brought him into conflict with the police, prison and exile to Grenoble where he was to study law. In 1927 he organized the movement around the Nazi model with "Green Shirts" with himself Capitanul. They began to agitate against the Jews in Bessarabia where Codreanu was elected representative in 1932. The participation of Iron Guardists in the 1933 strike made the government abolish the movement. It took its revenge by assassinating the Prime Minister on the platform of Sinaia station. Codreanu reappears in 1935 with an alliance called "All for the Nation" with whom the leader of the peasants I. Maniu signed a "non-aggression pact." In December 1937 Codreanu's supporters got 19% of the vote so becoming the third largest force in the country. His alliances with other parties was to end in January 1938 but the King had not forgotten the provocation of the murder of I. G. Duca as he left the royal palace. Arrested in April 1938, Codreanu was sentenced to ten years hard labour. On the 29

November he was transfered with thirteen fellow prisoners to another prison and shot "while attempting to escape." In fact the fourteen men had been cold-bloodedly executed in the forest. The "Capitanul" was dead but the Iron Guard was still to be reckoned with. Codreanu's form of fascism of course borrowed elements from the German and Italian models: the cult of leader, the uniforms and the Roman salute, but its fundamental ideas: anticommunist, antidemocratic and antisemitic were deeply entrenched in the country itself. It also glorified Orthodox Christian values, peasant culture and folklore and had a slightly morbid cult of death. This amounted to a vague and sentimental philosophy of violence and rejection of the modern world. It was therefore attractive to unemployed intellectuals, the rejects of peasant society and also the working class. The Malaxa works was one of its bastions and after the depression the movement benefitted from the tacit support of several goverments. From 1937 onwards it enjoyed the help—including financial—of the Third Reich. It would however be an exaggeration, at least before 1941, to portray the Iron Guard as German 5th columnists. Fascism was a relatively developed element on the political scene of crisis ridden Greater Romania.

On the eve of the Second World War Romania gave the impression of being culturally part of post Versailles Europe, with its cafe culture, writers and artists who had studied in France and lawyers and businessmen living in Bucharest in a cosmopolitan way. Yet behind this lively facade there was the shocking backwardness of the peasantry who were 40% illiterate (in Bessarabia 60%), badly nourished, as in the 19th century afflicted by pellagra, with the highest child mortality in Europe and second only to Yugoslavia for tuberculosis.

Divided Greece

On the side of the victors in 1913 and again in 1918, Greece suffered greatly from the trauma of defeat in Asia Minor in 1922. In fact it was the army and the king who had been defeated and they were immediately to pay the price; the king by abdicating and going into exile and the army with the execution of its commander-in-chief General G. Hatzianestis, executed together with the leader of the government and four other ministers following their trial in November 1922. More importantly however, was the end of the idea of Panhellenism which had been present for 2,000 years on the shores of the Aegean and around the Black Sea, from Bulgaria to the foothills of the Caucasus; it was the end of the Megale Idea. All the Greek expatriates were forced to return to the mother country; 1,300,000 refugees to a country with 4,500,000 inhabitants[15]. Most of them had fled from Kemal's Turkey but 170,000 also came from Bulgaria and Macedonia, now part of Serbia. Only a small ethnic Greek population of a few thousand at most would remain in Istanbul. With the help of the League of Nations these refugees settled in Thrace and Macedonia, the new territories of the kingdom, about half as farmers and half in the towns, above all in Thessalonika and Athens. Although there were severe economic and social problems caused by this resettlement it should be mentioned that the northern regions rapidly became Greek, to the point that the Slav speaking population protested that by denying them their native language the Greeks were implementing a systematic policy of integration. Henceforth, ethnically, Greece was Greek.

However it was still deeply divided. Out of these dramatic events there emerged, in opposition to the royalists, a Republican movement. Constantine's eldest son George II (September 1922–December 1923) could rely on support from elements within the army such as General I. Metaxas and a small political party, the People's Party, headed by P. Tsaldaris (1868–1936). The Republicans had officers such as N. Plastiras, Th. Pangalos and the Democratic Union of A. Papanastassiou. They could also count on the support of the Communist Party, formed in November 1918, which only gained seats in the Athens Parliament in 1926. In between these was the Liberal Party of Venizelos under the leadship, in the absense of its founder, of Th. Sophoulis (1860–1949). Venizelos had fallen out with Constantine but was in favour of a moderate monarchy and in 1923 argued for the preservation of George II on the throne. However many of his supporters were to fluctuate in their support for the monarchy depending on the political mood of the moment and the result was the proclamation of the Republic following a plebicite in April 1924. The Venizelist period from 1928 to 1933 came to an end with a military coup d'état organized by General N. Plastiras, the return of King George II to Athens in November 1935 and on the king's initiative the dictatorship of General Metaxas from April 1935 to his death in January 1941. The political imbroglio was further complicated by the intervention of the army which took power four times: in 1922, 1926, 1933 and in 1935. It was also true that politicians had virtually become a professional class and generally came from the legal professions, torn by clan rivalry and indulging in nepotism and corruption in the worst Balkan tradition. More and more remote from the preoccupations of those they were supposed to represent, they showed themselves to be out of touch with the country's real problems[16]. Venizelos himself was to escape an assassination attempt organized by the Chief of Police of the royalist government and two years later was condemned to death for his involvement in the Plastiras coup d'état. He sought refuge with the Dodecanese Italians prior to going to Paris where he died.

Greece, glorified for the invention of Democracy, was to succumb to the scourge of Europe at that time experiencing dictatorship from 1935 omwards.In November 1935 a plebiscite was held to recall George II which gave a 97% vote. According to A. Vacalopoulos this was an "electoral parody" in a country which was subject to martial law and press censorship. The elections which took place after did not give a straight majority to any of the parties and the Communist party came fourth with 6% of the vote and 15 seats. This was reason enough for the king, without any consultation, to appoint General Metaxas head of the government. A general strike, claimed to be communist inspired brought about a dictatorship. On the 4 August the king signed decrees dissolving Parliament without setting a date for forthcomming elections and revoking those articles of the constitution dealing with individual freedom. A wave of arrests sent many political leaders to the islands and 400 union and communist activists were imprisoned or sent to camps. The system put in place was called the "4 August Regime" with its leader the "Archigos" who unlike the Fuhrer or the Duce was unable to attract the support of the masses. Its ideology was based on a simplified view of Greek history: three period of glory all characterized by authoritarian systems: Pericles who had been a dictator hiding behind a veneer of democracy, Byzantium with an imperial autocracy and the third Metaxas'. Teachers were forced to pass on these new realities to the youth who were indoctrinated in a "National Organization" E.O.N. based on the Italian and German model with uniforms, Roman salute etc. The regime was supported by the Church who had control of education and was favourably rewarded by the state, but it also relied on a very energetic police force. On a more positive note it elaborated social laws such as the eight hour working day, settlement of land debt to improve the plight of the peasants and encouraged the use of the Demotic language in education. It implemented at the same time a defence policy which was to become more urgent in view of the deteriorating international situation: the Metaxas Line (a replica of the Maginot line) on the country's northern border at least repelled the Italian army even though it fell to the Wermacht in 1941. This was the paradox of the dictatorship for although it immitated the German and Italian models and had a policy of closer ties with Rome and Berlin, Metaxas was forced to face up to the Italian ultimatum in October 1940 and, before he died in January 1941, had the pleasure of seeing his small army inflict a series of defeats on Mussolini's armies.

In terms of its economy and the social development of its population Greece, during the 1920's, was less a "peasant society" than its neighbours: 60% of its population lived off agriculture and there was also a need for a redistribution of land. The settlement of refugees made the need for agricultural reform more acute. The two processes were combined in a transfer of property without precedent since independence in 1821. Thanks to the League of Nations a loan of 12.3 million pounds sterling was granted to Greece under the auspices of the "Committee for the Settlement of Refugees"; 1.1 million hectares of land was given to 143,000 farming families. Ten pre cent of this land was state property but the rest was Church land, land from the 2,500 Ciftliks of Macedonia, Epirus and Thessali and above all land belonging to the 600,000 "Turks" who had been expelled. In all this amounted to 38% of all the cultivated land. Yet in the same way as in Romania and Yugoslavia this attempt at a redistribution of land was to be thwarted by population growth which, with a birthrate of 30% and a rate of mortality of 17%, was the highest in the region. Unable to emigrate to the United States as had been common prior to the war the Greeks were to experience severe overpopulation with 87 people per square kilometre of arable land giving rise to the usual consequences of excessive division of land, lack of tools and equipment and low yields. The industrial base was more developed than in neighbouring countries with 19% of GNP and they were quick to point out that in the decade following the war it had grown by more than during the whole of the previous century. The refugees from Asia Minor brought with them the carpet industry which was concentrated on Athens and Piraeus but the most important industries were farm produce, followed by cotton textiles and chemical fertilizers. About 90% of this industrial production was the output of small concerns employing less than five workers. There was however a real shortage of power generation especially with coal and hydroelectricity.

As in the past there was the problem of the national debt. The balance of trade was in the red. Exports were mainly traditional products such as tabacco, raisins and wine but imports were of manufactured products such as machinery, raw materials and a third of the annual wheat requirements. On top of this deficit there were increasingly large State loans, the European powers as always maintaining their control of the Greek economy, as they had done since the 19th century.

So Greece in 1940 was a very poor country. The diet of its population was among the worst in Europe, just above the Portugese and the Albanian: 2,400 calories per head of population per day or a third of the meat consumption of North Americans. In educational terms, proud as they were of their glittering past, illiteracy was among the highest in Europe: 41% in 1928 with 58% for women but falling to 27% in 1940 following concerted efforts at improving this during the Metaxas dictatorship.

Unrest in Bulgaria

Coups and violence were to be a characteristic of the interwar years. Although Bulgaria was a more egalitarian country than its neighbours such as Greece or Romania, two factors were to make it rather more fragile: the weakness of the authorities and irredentist philosophies. King Boris III (1894–1943) had succeeded his father amidst the crisis of defeat in October 1918, and like his father before him, lacked the active support of the populace, his powerbase being the military and bureaucratic oligarchy. This was joined by a technocratic middle-class which was often the product of German schools. Bulgarian irredentism was essentially a refusal to accept the Treaty of Neuilly and harking back to the victories of 1912 as well as the Treaty of San Stefano in 1878. Yet to the outside world this was expressed through the violence of IMRO, isolating Bulgaria while at the same time punctuating internal politics by bloody incidents.

Victor of the first post-war elections, A. Stamboliski the leader of the peasants formed a government in October 1919. His party the Agrarian Union, had gained a third of the seats but the Communist Party B.K.P. had a fifth, thus becoming the largest Communist party in the Balkans, even though they had only emerged in the previous spring from the Tesna—strict—fraction of D. Blagoev's Social Democrat Party. But through the efforts of its Secretary General, Vasil Kolarov (1877–1950) who towed the line of the nascent Third International, the B.K.P. took part in the largescale strike movement of autumn 1919. The government did not hesitate to use force against the protesting railway workers leading to a rupture with the Communists. Having quelled the social unrest and signed the Treaty of Neuilly, Stamboliski hoped to set up an "Agrarian" regime based contrary to the Marxist class theory on the peasant taken as a whole. The March 1920 elections confirmed the strenghth of his party with 40% of the votes and almost half the number of seats. He was therefore able to form a homogeneous agrarian government. In 1922 land reform limited agricultural ownership to 30 hectares of land which affected few farmers but did distribute some of the state and village land. Already normal practise, small holdings were encouraged; in 1926 only 3% of Bulgarian farmers were landless farm labourers and 80% landowners. The government developed agricultural education, spread ideas of hygiene in the countryside and instituted a "Service of Obligatory Labour" which was intended to bring together young town and rural inhabitants by employing them in building roads, railway lines and irrigation channels. Still clinging to his pre-war pacifism Stamboliski dreamed of a "Green International" bringing together peasants in Central Europe into international cooperation, in opposition to the "White International" of the capitalists and the "Red International" of the communists. This was his message in 1921 when he travelled to Prague, Warsaw and Bucharest.

This agrarian government clashed with numerous sections of society and its leader's methods made him violently hated by some. The King and his court detested these "peasants" and following Serbia's lead a "League of Officers" was formed in 1913 which brought together journalists, lawyers and university teachers. There guiding light was Professor Alexander Tzankov (1879-1959) who was a former socialist and had been an administrator for Mussolini. They formed the "National Alliance"—Nroden Sgovor—to fight against Stamboliski. But the April 1923 elections were a triumph for the agrarians who won 212 seats out of 245.

The opposition decided to use violence while the Communists, the second largest group in Parliament with 16 seats, declared themselves "neutral." A coup d'état took place on the 9 June 1923. Taking advantage of the absence of Stamboliski, at the time in his native village, some officers of the league took over control of the capital and arrested all the ministers. The King who had not been forewarned and was at Varna agreed on the composition of a new government headed by Professor A. Tzankov. Stamboliski tried to organize a peasant resistance but was captured by an IMRO hit-squad, mutilated, forced to dig his own grave and killed on the 14 June. The experiment in agrarian democracy had ended in a bloodbath.

The Tzankov government began to supress both agrarian and communist sympathizers, even though the latter had not intervened. The Third International became worried, blamed the B.K.P. leadership and issued a directive for joint action with the peasants. An attempted armed uprising in September 1923 ended in disaster: the Communist leadership went into exile and only returned in 1944, while a "White Terror," exposed in A.Barbusse's pamphlet "The Executioners," lasted for two years and is said to have caused 20,000 deaths. Professor Tzankov ended his political career in September 1944 a genuine "Fascist," to use the term used by Bulgarian historians, leader of the government in exile in the German Reich. Their use of "fascist" is not intended to cover a regime having a democratic facade ie. multi-party Parliament with regular elections but with no real involvement of the people, rather the "conservative reaction" pursued by Tzankov until 1931 and by his more moderate successor A. Liaptchev. One of the first measures was the banning of the Communist party which was the start of 21 years of illegal activity, marked by sharp internal conflict. Left-wing deviationists carried out an assassination attempt against the King in 1925 in the Church of Sveta Nedelja in Sofia which resulted in 128 dead and 300 wounded. The white terror increased in intensity. Another problem faced the government was IMRO. (Liaptchev was in fact Macedonian). Supported by the Minister of War the organization infiltrated the army and completely controlled the Petric region where it supplanted the normal authorities and raised taxes and meted out justice. Since the Macedonian question had been legally settled and was enshrined in international law IMRO could only operate as a terrorist organization without any specific aims. Its leader since 1925, Ivan Mihailov, was in the service of the highest bidder and the organization began to splinter into tendencies which asserted themselves through violence and bombs. Komitadji violence became an international problem from 1927 to 1930 for while Mussolini was financing IMRO activities, Britain and France were asking for its dissolution. King Boris who had his uses for it procrastinated until the Komitadji blew up the Orient Express near Tsaribrod. Liaptchev decided to take action and arrested I. Mihailov who then managed to escape. The visit to Sofia of Ante Pavelic the head of the Ustasa demonstrated that the two terrorist organizations collaborated with each other and this was borne out by the assassination of King Alexander in Marseilles.

The 1929 economic crisis resulted in a political crisis by strengthening the democratic opposition forces. To resolve the problem a group of soldiers and intellectuals formed a group called Zveno—Ring—on an authoritarian but republican platform and advocated a federation with their Yugoslav neighbours. On the 19 May 1934 they staged a coup d'état and the king taken by surprise was forced to agreed. The assembly was dissolved and all political parties banned. These republican officers stayed in power for only a short time, for in January 1935 the King forced them out and appointed one of his own supporters, G. Kioseivanov to lead a government which was to last till 1940. This "Royal Dictatorship" ressembled that of Carol in Romania and allowed the King to send the army back to barracks and rule using state employees and the police.

As with all the neighbouring Balkan countries Bulgaria between the wars was mainly a peasant country: 80% of the population were engaged in agriculture in 1938 which provided 73% of the GNP. This was subsistence farming with the land very often divided into small units. Peasants would also produce soap as well as ersatz coffee and used oil lamps for lighting. The methods of farming remained primitive and tractors were almost unheard of. The most serious problem was that of indebtedness notwithstanding serious efforts at promoting a cooperative movement. Bulgaria did export some products but to the detriment of the standard of living of the rural population: primarily tabacco but increasingly fruit, wine and wheat were sent to Germany.

Next to Albania, Bulgaria with only 7–8% of the GNP was the

least industrially developed country in the Balkans. The only largescale mining concern was the Pernik coal mine, close to Sofia while the rest was predominantly light industry such as agricultural produce and textiles. On the eve of the Second World War the country did not produce one single ton of steel and only 400 concerns employed more than 50 workers. A few areas were flourishing such as textiles and sugar production where the state was involved and there had been large investment from abroad: in 1936 this amounted to 42% and was mainly from Germany. In 1937 68% of Bulgarian exports went to Germany and 66% of the imports came from there. Bulgaria under Boris III was economically as well as politically in the Third Reich's sphere of influence.

Unrest in Albania

Following the departure of the Prince of Wied in September 1914 the state of Albania no longer existed, its territory becoming the battlefield over which neighbouring countries were to fight and a bargaining chip for the European powers. The Allies used it as bait to draw Greece and then Italy into its camp. The former were allowed to occupy the Koritza (Korca) and Argyrocastron (Gjirokastra) regions; the latter took the port of Valona (Vlora) and the island of Saseno (Sazan)[17]. In the meantime Serbians and Montenegrins advanced up to Elbasan, Tirana and Scutari. In fact there took place the destruction of the Principality with the permission of the European Powers who had created it in 1913. The defeat of the Serbians in 1915 meant that they were replaced by the Austro-Hungarians who extended their rule to Scutari and Durazzo (Durres) facing the Italians at Valona. The English and French, in conflict with King Constantine of Greece, allowed Italian troops also to occupy the Gjirocastra area even Janina which had been given to Greece in 1913. To link up with these allied troops, elements of General Sarrail's eastern army advanced on Korca which was reached by French troops in October 1916. By the end of the year all of Albania was occupied and was to remain so up to the peace treaty.

This tragic situation mobilized Albanian patriots, including emigres in the United States. Their organization Vatra (the Home) under the presidency of Bishop Fan Noli, managed to interest President Wilson in their cause. In December 1918 a congress of 48 delegates met at Durazzo which was occupied by the Italians and formed a "Provisional Government" entrusted with the task of pleading the Albanian case at the Paris negotiations. It was strengthened in the French capital by representatives of the Albanian communities in the United States and Istanbul. The peace conference kept on stalling over the opposing desires of Italy, Yugoslavia and Greece over the nothern and southern areas of the countries, whereas President Wilson felt that secret treaties made during the war were unacceptable. By spring 1920 there was agreement of a return to the 1913 Albanian borders. In the meantime however the situation on the ground had developed. Worried by the Versailles machinations a group of patriots had called a congress like the one held at Valona (Vlora) in 1912, at Lushnja outside the Italian occupation zone. This met on the 20 January 1920 and entrusted government authority to four regents, to replace the absent King[18] They were to be supported by a legislative assembly and a new government was formed headed by Sulejman Bey Delvina, a former companion of Ismail Qemal. The organs of power moved to Tirana which from being a small town of 1,500 inhabitants thus became the capital of Albania. They now had to liberate the territory from occupation forces. The French evacuated Korca transferring authority to the Albanians despite an attempted raid by the Greeks. In Vlora however the Italians only gave in after a full scale battle in June 1920 in which volunteers from all over the region participated. An Italian-Albanian peace protocol was signed at Tirana under which all Italian troops were to withdraw from the whole of Albanian territory apart from the island of Saseno (Sazan). Albania from now on had a government with effective authority over most of the territory established at the London Conference of 1913. This was the necessary condition for its recognition in international law and Fan Noli went to plead their cause in Geneva. The League of Nations admitted Albania into its midst in December 1920 against the wishes of France who upheld the Serbian and Greek positions. The two neighbouring countries in fact continued to put forward their respective claims. The Conference of Ambassadors in 1921 agreed on a return to the borders of the 1913 London Treaty but the two countries continued to refuse and following some incidents and a hearing of the League of Nations and the International Court of the Hague, agreement was reached in August 1925. Albania gave up the monastery of Saint

Naum on lake Ohrid to Yugoslavia and Greece withdrew from the 14 disputed villages around Korca. Even so a section of Greek opinion was to continue to demand the return of the "Empire of the North" together with Korca, Gjirokastra and Himara.

On the home front the Albanians had to learn the ways of a modern country. The obstacles were enormous: economic underdevelopment combined with a tragic cultural underdevelopment with 90% of the population illiterate and an intelligentsia formed in the north by the Austrians, the Italians on the coast and the Greeks in the south. The political tradition was of multi-secular opposition to Ottoman rule with tribal solidarity in the mountainous north and feudal ties in the central plains area: only in the south was there an embryonic middle-class with merchants and seamen yet it had little real power. The only possible political leaders were the former Beys of the Ottoman administration in alliance with the large Muslim landowners. More than anywhere else in the Balkans, parliamentary rule was nothing more than a pastiche, hiding client group rivalries under the leadership of heads of wealthy families of differing religious traditions.

This would mean that Fan Noli's attempts to modernise and create a democracy in 1924 were doomed to failure. The first government which the 1921 elections produced was dominated by Ahmet bey Zogolli, known as Zogu (1895–1961). Son of a tribal chief in the Muslim area of Mati, he studied in the high-school, then the Military Academy in Istanbul and fought the Serbs and the Montenegrins during the Balkan War. Having participated in the Lushnja Congress he became the Interior Minister in the Delvina government, organized the police force under his control, repulsed a Yugoslav incursion from the Kosovo region and in 1922 declared himself Prime Minister. His authoritarian methods created strong tensions and the opposition, grouped round Fan Noli, forced him from power with an armed uprising in the spring of 1924. This is what Albanian historians call the "Democratic Revolution of 1924" which put Fan Noli into power. He was to remain for six months. His programme aimed at establishing a humanist, pacifist and Wilsonian democracy. This was more than the feudal lords in the hinterland could bear or the Italians or the Yugoslavs. A trip by the "Red" bishop to the U.S.S.R. was reason enough for them to refuse to recognize his government. Zogu who had taken refuge in Belgrade was getting ready for armed intervention with the help of the Yugoslav army and veterans of Wrangel's White

Russian army. He crossed the border on the 10 December 1924 and four days later entered Tirana from which Fan Noli appealed in vain to the League of Nations.

Zogu had a total monopoly of power: a severely limited Parliament proclaimed the republic in January 1925 and elected him president for seven years. He put in place a tailor-made constitution, appointed himself the commander-in-chief of the army and gave military rank to the mountain tribal chiefs—the Bayraktars. Wishing to modernize the country but lacking in capital he turned to Mussolini who had been one of the first to recognize the Republic of Albania. In September 1925 a national bank was set up with Italian capital making it into a virtual subsidiary of the Bank of Italy. At last Albania was given a national currency called the Lek instead of the fifteen types of coins which had been used until then. Mussolini's hold continued to grow in this way and also through the "Society for the Economic Development of Albania" (S.V.E.A.). Mussolini then went from economic to political questions: Rome asked Zogu to recognize its exclusive right to ensure the defence of Albania and in November 1926 was forced to sign a "friendship and security pact" called the "Tirana Pact" which led to heightened tension with Yugoslavia. Assured of the support of Mussolini the President summoned a Constituent Assembly which unanimously decided on the 1 September 1928 to transform Albania into a "Democratic, Parliamentary and Hereditary Kingdom" with Zogu as the Albanian King, Zog I (1928–1939). The constitutional texts were changed but not the form of government. The royal family and the court were proving expensive consequently Zog turned more and more frequently to Italy to obtain loans together with hefty Baksheesh for himself. On occasion he tried to resist. In 1932 he sent General Pariani's military mission away but the arrival of 22 warships put an end to this impulsive resistance. For ten years Zog was to rule under the protection of Mussolini, to the growing anger of the nationalists, youth and the army.

Yet this was not enough for Count Ciano, Zog's witness at his marriage with Countess Geraldine Apponyi from whom the King hoped to have an heir. The Duce's Minister for Foreign Affairs decided on a radical solution and his father-in-law let himself be convinced, which was all the more easy since he was jealous of Hitler's successes in Vienna and Prague. On the 25 March an ultimatum was sent to Tirana demanding that Italian troops take over all the strategic points, Italians be allowed to colonize the best land

and that the two countries join in a customs union. Zog resisted completely isolated. On the 7 April—Good Friday—at dawn 30,000 soldiers, preceded by a violent naval bombardment, landed at Shengjin, Durres, Vlora and Saranda and encountered isolated resistance which was quickly quelled. The following day the Duce's army entered Tirana from which Zog had fled across the snow covered mountains to Greece accompanied by his wife and Prince Skender his heir, born three days earlier, but also with part of the state treasury. Democratic Europe showed indignation but did nothing. Independent Albania was dead.

This period had undeniably been one of progress for the Albanian people yet on the eve of the Second World War Albania remained the most backward nation of Europe. The per capita average value of its industrial production was of the order of 8 dollars, as against 20 in Romania and 140 for France. The country remained fundamentally agricultural with 85% of its population and 90% of its production from the countryside. However only 9% of its land was under cultivation, pitting the large hereditary ciftlik estates in the plains against the small holders from the peasant villages—Fis—in the mountains. Everwhere the farming methods remained primitive. Maize production was predominant in the north and in the centre with tabacco, olives and wine in the south; but generally sheep rearing was more important than crop production which in the mountains was left to the women. Industry only accounted for 10% of the GNP. The quantity of electricity per capita was 9Kw per hour in contrast to 38 in Greece and 75 in Yugoslavia, nor were there many villages with electricity. It had quite large natural ressources yet the coutry did not have the necessary capital for its exploitation and its geographical position meant that only Italian investment was coming in from abroad. It was the Italians who were responsible for the oil field in the Vlora, Berat and Fieri triangle, which rose from 11,000 barrels in 1933 to 934,000 in 1939 to supply the Italian military campaign in Ethiopia. Having no railway network and only 2,000 km of roads reputedly suitable for motor vehicles, Albania was only really accessible via its ports yet none of the ships which docked in its ports were Albanian. The standard of living of its inhabitants was commesurate with these economic factors: the peasants suffered from severe malnutrition which led to tuberculosis as well as the scourge of the fertile coastal plains: malaria.

From the Light of Democracy to the Shadow of Dictatorship

For the peoples of the Balkans the 1919/20 peace settlement was to have a fundamental flaw. On the one hand the great majority had been able to realize their dreams of unity and copying the French "State-Nation" model had managed to bring together most of the same national community within the frontiers of a state. This was the case for the Romanians, Yugoslavs, Greeks and up to a point the Albanians. These peoples felt that this was the result of their nationalist struggles and revolutionary processes such as that of the union of Alba Iulia or that of Belgrade. In fact these so-called revolutions had only succeeded due to agreement by the four Great Powers and only in respect to those who had ended the war on their side. The lines drawn at Versailles was an unegotiated compromise between the wishes of the Balkan peoples and the self interest of the victorious Great Powers.

In effect the 19th century situation was being perpetuated yet the principal actors had changed: the large Empires who had dominated since the 18th century—Russia and Austria had disappeared to be replaced by the French and the English, joined by a new-commer Italy. But as in the past these Great Powers were rivals and were playing their own cards: France saw herself as the protector of Yugoslavia which she considered an elarged Serbia and of Romania which was Latin, England was more interested in Greece as a strategic base in the eastern Mediterranean and virtual guardian of the Straits and Italy, who felt that she had been cheated by the outcome of Versailles, was in confrontation with Yugoslavia and Greece over control of the Adriatic; Mussolini's brand of fascism succeeded in making Croatia, Albania and Bulgaria its accomplices in redrawing the borders. When economic crisis resulted in the weakening of these democracies there emerged a fourth player, Germany, now the Third Reich, which was about to end a relatively peaceful parenthesis of 17 years and plunge the Balkans once again into the tragedy of a World War.

Wreathed in the aura of victor and present on the ground until 1920 with its Eastern Army France appeared to be the guarantor of the new Balkan order. She strongly supported Greece against Albania and Yugoslavia against Italy and Bulgaria in their territorial claims. Sticking strictly to the terms of the Treaty of Neuilly the French oversaw the effective disarming of Bulgaria whose army was reduced to 93,000 men, but agreed that the Ambassadors Conference authorise an increase of 10,000 to fight against the communists after the bomb attack at the Sveta Nedelia Church against King Boris in 1925. Yet was to support Belgrade in its protests over the exactions and terrorist activities of IMRO in Macedonia. It was only in 1934 when the Zveno military took power in Sofia (Paris was suspected by some of having encouraged the coup d'état) that the French bias was translated into a rapprochement with Yugoslavia. With the same aim of continuing the status quo in Central Europe, especially in the face of Hungarian aspirations, E. Benes had from 1921 onwards nurtured what is called the "Little Entente" which brought Czechoslovakia, Yugoslavia and Romania together in alliance. France was to be the advisor and reinforced it by signing a military alliance with Romania in 1926 and with Yugoslavia in 1927. During this period Belgrade and Bucharest were to be the dual pillars of French policy in the Balkans.

France had since 1923 increasingly come up against Italy. Having been forced to concede over Yugoslavia, Greece and Albania, in the post war years due to internal problems, Italy under the Duce had willingly embarked on an aggressive foreign policy. In August 1923 some Italian members of the frontier commission on the Greek-Albanian border were killed in Greek territory; Mussolini sent an ultimatum to Athens, shelled and occupied Corfu but was forced to withdraw on the orders of the League of Nations. His ambition was to have control of the Adriatic and for this to happen it was necessary for him to destroy the state of Yugoslavia. Mussolini therefore encouraged Hungarian and Bulgarian expansionist aspirations and tried to destabilize the Kingdom by supporting the Croat Ustasa terrorists as well as Bulgarian IMRO. In 1926 Ante Pavelic found refuge in Italy. At the same time the Duce tried to isolate Belgrade by signing friendship and arbitration treaties with Romania in September 1926 and Greece in September 1928. He also tried to counter-balance French influence in the region by building an axis between Turkey, Greece and Italy. Yet having settled their differences in October 1930 with a friendship treaty of neutrality and arbitration, Turkey and Greece became supporters of the status quo in the Aegean Sea and the presence of Italian troops in the Dodecanese went against the interests of both of these neighbouring countries.

The economic crisis of 1929/30 which was to hit agricultural countries so badly, made the Balkan capitals try to mend fences. The initiative came from the Greek agrarian A. Papanastassiou who revived the idea of a Balkan Federation. An initial conference took place in Athens in October 1930 followed by further ones in Istanbul, Bucharest and Salonika, with the support of the League of Nations. A series of commissions were set up to cover economic, cultural and healthcare issues but were to fail due to political considerations. Bulgaria continued to demand the return of Bulgarian people in Macedonia and an outlet into the Aegean Sea. Egged on by Mussolini, Sofia proved intransigent and once more the idea of a Balkan Federation came to nought.

The other countries then concentrated on a pact involving four countries: Greece, Yugoslavia, Romania and Turkey which finally was signed in Athens in February 1934. The participants mutually guaranteed each others borders and promised consultation in case of conflict; the pact remained open to other countries which was meant as an invitation to Bulgaria to treat. The Treaty of Athens was drawn up in October in Ankara by the editorial statutes board of the Balkan Alliance presaging a permanent Council of Ministers of Foreign Affairs, a Balkan bank and coordination in legislative matters. Once more this wonderful plan came unstuck because of international opposition. France had wanted to take it under its wing yet things had changed for Hitler since January 1933 had been building the Third Reich. The first blow to the alliance was the murder of King Alexander in Marseilles in 1934. Behind the Ustasa, the hand of Italy was discernible to Belgrade but Paris, worried lest it force the Ducé into the Fuhrer's arms, went for appeasement. This was perceived by Balkan minds as a climbdown by the French. The Ethiopian escapade and the failure of the League of Nations sanctions was a further blow since it showed that small countries could not rely on international solidarity for their security. Yet the most serious blow was the reoccupation of the Rhineland in 1936 clearly showing French military weakness and consequently her inability to help its allies in Central Europe as well as in the Balkans. The conference held by the alliance in Belgrade in 1936, clearly showed this change in thinking, for from then on Balkan cooperation was to be limited to political issues and not to questions of defence. Four months later Turkey raised the problem of the defence of the Straits which had been forbidden by the Treaty of Lausanne in 1923. The convention of Montreux in July 1936 gave complete control of the Straits over to Turkey. Free passage to merchant shipping but the militarization of points of passage and its closure in time of war were to be allowed. The international commission of observers was dissolved. The influence of democracy was declining in the Balkans. That of Hitler was starting to be felt. One of the first signs was the dismissal in August 1936, by Carol II, of his Minister of Foriegn Affairs, Nicolae Titulescu (1883–1941) a keen supporter of the French alliance and a foremost figure in the League of Nations. With him went the idea of "collective security" or put in another way the belief in alliances such as the Pittle Entente or the Balkan Alliance. From then on the Balkan countries played a free for all in the face of the "Brown Peril." Romania and Yugoslavia refused to make any sort of alliance with the U.S.S.R. and abandoned Czechslovakia (linked by the May 1935 pact) to its fate. M. Stojadinovic's Yugoslavia settled its differences with Bulgaria with an agreement in July 1938, signed a treaty with Italy in March 1937 and began to look economically to Germany, soon doubling its trade. The Munich agreement in September 1938 was the finnishing blow for France and England for they were alone, the last Great European democracies. Romania, the favourite of Versailles, as well as Bulgaria, the least popular, were both gravitating into the orbit of the Third Reich.

Notes

1. The future Croat head of State during the Second World War belonged at the time to the "Party of Law" and was the heir of A. Starcevic, but was quite open to collaboration with the Serbs.

2. The Oradea region (Nagyvarad).

3. Near Pernik, 27 miles south-west of Sofia.

4. On the island of Lemnos.

5. Vacalopulos in "Histoire de la Grece moderne" p. 228 mentions 900,000 dead and 450,000 expelled.

6. The agreement at Saint-Jean de Maurienne in April 1917 had envisaged the division of Anatolia into French, English and Italian zones, as well as Greek and Armenian zones, which was implemented after the Treaty of Sevres.

7. He died at Palermo in January 1923.

8. He was to die at San Remo in May 1926. A son of Abdul Hamid, Abdul Mesid, succeeded him as Calif (1922–1924) and died in Paris in 1944. His descendants still live in the French capital.

9. P. Dumont in Mantran ; Histoire de l'Empire Ottoman. op. cit. p. 646.

10. The first census undertaken in the new state on the 31 January 1921 outlined:

Languages		Religion	
Serbo-Croat	8,911,509	Greek Orthodox	5,93,057
Slovenes	1,019,997		
Germans	505,790	Roman Catholic	4,708,657
Magyars	467,658		
Albanians	439,657	Greek Catholic	
Romanians	231,068	(Uniates)	40,338
Turks	150,532	Muslims	1,345,271
Ruthenes	25,615	Protestants	229,517
Russians	20,568	Jews	64,746
Poles	14,764	Other	1,944
Italians	12,553		
Other	69,878		

11. The "Salonika Affair" in which officers of the "Black Hand" were accused of contact with the enemy and attempted assassination of the Prince Regent. Three officers including Dimitrijevic-Apis were condemned to death and executed while about 200 others were put in prison or interned in military camps in Tunisia.

12. A region of Croatia which is cut off from the coast by the Velebit River behind Zadar and has a minority Serb population.

13. For France during the same period the incrase in the population was 0.44% which gives 28.8 persons per sq.km.

14. Romanian Census of 1930: Total Population 18 million.

Romanians	12,985,000	71.9%	Bulgarians	361,000	2.0%
Magyars	1,426,000	7.9%	Gypsies	270,000	1.5%
Germans	740,000	4.1%	Turks/Tatars	180,000	0.8%
Jews	722,000	4.0%	Poles	54,000	0.3%
Russians	415,000	2.3%	Serbo-Croats	52,000	0.3%

15. Under the exchange of populations it was anticipated that "Muslim Citizens" ie.Turcs but also Abanians would leave. By 1926, 606,000 inhabitants had left Greece in this way.

16. Cf. the very critical passages from A. Vacalopoulos. Histoire de la Grece Moderne op. cit. pp. 240/1 and 252/3.

17. At the entrance of the Valona Bay.

18. Wilheim von Wied had not legally abdicated.

17

The Balkans in World War II, 1939–1945

The watchword of 1919—national independence and democracy—had led the region to failure on two counts. On the one hand to nationalism of a violent or mild nature in Transylvania, Macedonia, Thrace, Epirus, Dobrudja, Bessarabia, Bukovina, Dalmatia, Istria, Vojvodina, Kosovo, in the Dodecanese Islands and Cyprus, not to mention antagonism between Serbs and Croats or Serbs and Slovenes, racial tension among the Transylvanian "Germans" or those of Banat and Bessarabia, with Turks in Bulgaria, Macedonia, Bosnia, or latent unrest among the Romanians of Macedonia and Greece, Lipovans in the Danubian Delta, Gagauzians in Bessarabia and many others. As for democracy, instead of spreading it had given way to dictatorship in Yugoslavia under King Alexander, Carol in Romania, Boris in Bulgaria, Zog in Albania and General Metaxas in Greece. On the international stage Italy and its fascist regime had the upper hand in Albania, was very influential in Greece and Yugoslavia, while Hitler's Reich was exerting political pressures on Romania and Yugoslavia through its Saxon and Swabian "Volksdeutsche" and above all it had extended its economic imperialism over Romanian oil, Yugoslav and Bulgarian wheat and mineral resources, 60 per cent of which were exported to Germany. On the eve of another world war the Balkans looked more fragile than ever.

The Axis Powers Impose their Rule over the Balkans, 1939–1941

Unlike Hitler who managed to occupy Austria, the Sudetenland and Bohemia and Moravia without firing a single shot, Mussolini, his ally, began military operations in World War II by invading the smallest of the Balkan states, Albania, on Good Friday 1939. On 11 April Count Ciano set up a "new order" represented by an Assembly of large landowners which called itself Constituent and appointed Serget Verlaci as Prime Minister who had been involved in a family feud against King Zog. Soon a vote of union with Italy was made and Victor Emmanuel who was already Emperor of Ethiopia was offered the crown. In reality the "little king" was represented by his deputy, Francesco Jacomoni who had been the Italian Minister in Tirana and had been instrumental in the invasion of Albania. The Verlaci government soon showed itself to be a puppet in the hands of the Roman power which instituted a campaign of Italianization by means of imported civil servants, agricultural settlers, compulsory teaching of Italian, and above all domination of the economy setting up over 350 Italian enterprises over a two year period which resulted in the destruction of traditional crafts.

Britain and France refused to recognize this coup de force and after pledging support to Poland in opposing German claims on Danzig, acted likewise with two other countries who seemed under threat, Greece and Romania. Therefore the Balkans were sucked into the stormy atmosphere of a world war. On May 22 the Fuhrer and the Duce signed the "Iron Pact," a military alliance to be applied automatically, and on 23 August 1939, the Third Reich concluded a pact of non-aggression with Stalinist Russia strengthened by a secret agreement on spheres of influence. The Baltic countries and Poland had been neatly divided and another item dealt with the Balkans "As for South-eastern Europe the Soviet side stated its interest in Bessarabia. The German side replied that it has no political designs at all in the area." (art.3). The Bessarabian question was thus settled before the start of the conflict, but the whole of the Peninsula remained open to future rivalries. Grigore Gafencu, the Romanian minister, tried by diplomatic means to set up a "neutral bloc" round the existing Balkan Entente and on 6 September Bucarest proclaimed itself neutral, just as it had done at the beginning of the First World War. It strictly respected this undertaking, in spite of the collapse of Poland its neighbour and ally and the fact that the Warsaw government sought sanctuary on Romanian territory with some 100,000 nationals and the gold reserves of the State Bank. After being imprisoned for the sake of appearances most of the able-bodied Poles and half of the gold made their way to France and England, much to Berlin's fury. The Prime Minister, A. Calinescu, was shot by the Iron Guard right in the center of Bucharest, in retribution. His successor was Gh. Tatarescu who kept to the same neutral policy and in March 1940 King Carol launched his theme of "national reconciliation" which was accompanied by the release of Iron Guardists from prison.

After 10 May 1940, the Wehrmacht offensive in the West depleted the Reich's oil reserves, and as early as 27 May, Berlin insisted on Romania signing a "Petrol Pact" by which three million tons of crude oil would be supplied at a third of the world market price. As compensation Romania expected to receive arms and if need be support to enable her to stand up to the USSR. Stalin was indeed made uneasy by the enormous gains of his Nazi ally and was desperately trying to reap the benefits of his agreement with Hitler. On 25 June, on the day of the armistice signed by Petain, the head of the Soviet government, V.Molotov, informed Berlin of his plan to annex Bessarabia in keeping with the terms of the secret agreement, but also the old Bukovina which had never been Russian, although its northern part had a population with a majority of Ukrainians. The next day an ultimatum was sent to Bucharest ordering that all territories shown on an accompanying map be ceded to the USSR. Carol appealed to Berlin and Rome but in vain. On 28 June 1940, the Red Army occupied Bessarabia and Northern Bukovina, an area some 50,000 square kms with almost three million inhabitants. Stalin had made up handsomely the losses incurred by the Tsarist Empire in 1917.

As he felt isolated Carol tried to fully use his German connexion. The head of the Iron Guard, Horia Sima, a Transylvanian primary school teacher, joined the government under Ion Gigurtu, admired the Axis and as a gesture, withdrew from the League of Nations where Titulescu the Romanian representative had played a prominent part. On the home front a "National Party" was set up, the sole political party permitted which was a replica of other fascist parties. At the same time Hungary and Bulgaria put forward their claims in Berlin, one on Transylvania, the other on Dobrudja. I.Gigurtu and his foreign minister rushed from Salzburg to Rome only to be told by the Fuhrer and the Duce to deal straight with Budapest. The talks taking place at Turnu Severin failed and Ribbentrop and Ciano sent for the two contenders to come to Vienna and hear the brokers' verdict. On August 29 1940, the Romanians were shown a map of Hungary's new territories which led to Manolescu fainting on the spot. On the following day the crown council agreed to this decision by 19 votes in favor to 10 against and one abstention which was from the king. That evening, in Vienna a text was signed giving Admiral Horthy's Hungary the northern part of Transylvania, up to the line Oradea-Cluj-Tirgu Mures-Brasov, Cluj reverting to the Hungarian name of Koloszvar, while Brasov remained part of Romania: 43,000 square kms and 2,667,000 inhabitants with a Romanian majority. In exchange Germany and Italy promised to protect the new borders of Romania. As a matter of fact Bulgaria had also put down her own demands: the return of southern Dobrudja lozenge which had been lost during the second Balkan war in 1913. Bucharest had to swallow its pride once again and accept the border agreement of Craiova (September 7). Patriotic feelings ran high and for a whole week all over the country public demonstrations took place drawing on members of all political bodies including the communist party which reflected the USSR concern at feeling excluded from the new territorial arrangements. Using the communist move as a pretext the Iron Guard tried to take over power. Then the king turned to General Ion Antonescu (1882-1946) who had been Defense Minister in 1938, greatly admired the Third Reich and was reputedly well disposed towards the Guard. On 6 September, the next day, with the support of the German Legation in Bucharest, Antonescu forced Carol II, who by then was totally discredited, to abdicate in favor of his son Michael who became once again Michael I (1940-1947). Romania was turned into a "Legionary state" under Conducator Antonescu, ruling on the same lines as the Fuhrer or the Duce, but the regime soon fell into disrepute because of a series of bloody episodes: for example the assassination of Nicolae Iorga, a historian, who had stood against the Guardists in his capacity as Prime Minister. In foreign affairs Romania joined the Tripartite Pact—Germany, Italy, Japan—and in October allowed a "German military mission" to move in, soon reached 20,000 men complete with armored and mobile units. These forces ostensibly were supposed to protect supplies of wheat and oil to the Reich, but in fact served to dissuade the USSR from taking any action in the Balkans.

Meanwhile the Duce made a move in the area which led to the setting up of another front. The part Italy had played in the French campaign had been singularly modest and Hitler had not even taken the trouble to inform his ally of his moves with Romania. Mussolini vented his frustation in Greece. In spite of his ideological ties with fascism, and though England and France had promised to protect his country, Mataxas declared himself neutral. If he took hold of Albania the Duce would become the leader of Shqiptar nationalists who were agitating against "persecution" suffered by their fellows in Epirus. Feeling worried by the campaign being waged by the Italian press and after various incidents at sea and in the air during the summer of 1940, the government in Athens appealed much to their surprise to the authorities in Berlin. Not until they met in Florence on 28 October did Mussolini inform Hitler that his troops had launched an attack on Greece. On that same day at 3 p.m. the Italian Ambassador had delivered an ultimatum to Metaxas giving him three hours to agree to the Italian occupation of several bases in Greek territory: the answer was the famous "no" uttered by the Greek. The Duce sent his armies across the Albanian border. Some 80,000 well armed soldiers advanced along the coastal highways up to the River Thyamis, and another column marched across the Pindus, while the airforce was dropping bombs on cities that had been declared open with devastating results. Contrary to the Duce's expectations, Greek resistance was fierce and General Papagos skilfully conducted operations soon launching a counter-attack. From the Pindus the Italians were driven back to the Albanian border, then pushed back until the towns of Korca, Saranda, Delvina and Gjirokaster which were occupied by Greek units. They succeeded in establishing a continuous front and wintered there.

The other Balkan states remained passive while this was going on. Bulgaria was tempted to intervene to take Macedonia and Thrace but Turkey warned her that in this case she would also take action. Sofia understood these words and stayed quiet. It was another matter for Britain, isolated after the French defeat but could not afford to let the Axis powers hold sway in the Eastern Mediterranean, especially as Greece had been garanteed the integrity of her borders in the spring of 1939. Churchill offered to help therefore, but Metaxas did not want British intervention which might force German troops stationed in Romania into action. Thus he only asked for naval and air support and did not want an expeditionary corps to be involved. On 11 November combined British air and naval forces bombed the port of Tarento sinking three battle cruisers thus putting the Italian fleet out of action for a long time. On the other hand the Greek dictator refused to have any dealings with King Zog of Albania who was in London at the time. He refused to come to an understanding on the subject of Greece returning the occupied zones off Epirus. However, Metaxas died on 29 January 1941. King George II seized this opportunity to restore a semblance of parliamentary respectability to the regime. The head of the State Bank, A.Korysis, was asked to form a government. He showed himself more willing to listen to suggestions from the British who were occupied since early December 1940 on a major counter-attack in North Africa. He agreed to British troops landing in Greece, but out of the 100,000 men expected only half arrived and they were badly equipped. This "British army" in the Balkans all the same was considered as a major threat by the German General Staff, the OKW.

Meanwhile relations between the Reich and the USSR had deteriorated. The Kremlin authorities had been alarmed at the changes made without their consent to the Romanian border, and expressed their displeasure when Molotov visited Berlin in November 1940. He complained at the Tripartite Pact that was signed without his knowledge and made clear his views on the Balkans: the USSR demanded free access for her battleships to the Straits and military bases in the area; moreover she wished to give Bulgaria the same guarantees as the Germans. Stalin thus made it clear that nothing could be done in the Peninsula without his agreement. Hitler then took two decisions: On 13 December the OKW issued Directive No 20 on intervention in Greece (Operation Marita) and on December 18 Directive No. 21 for an attack against the USSR (Operation Barbarossa). The latter had been planned by the Fuhrer as early as the summer of 1940 and anticipated "a speedy military campaign even before the end of the war with England": it was meant to be only the preliminary step before a final assault against Britain in which the seizure of Greece was the first move.

However an intervention in the southern Balkans made it imperative to hold the northern parts. This had been achieved in Romania after she joined the Tripartite Pact in November 1940, together with Hungary and Slovakia. There remained Bulgaria, Yugoslavia and possibly Turkey to be persuaded. In Bulgaria the Italian misadventures in action strengthened the wish for neutrality in the population, which still felt grateful to its Russian "liberator" represented by the statue of Alexander II on the main square of Sofia, though Germany's influence was strong in political and academic circles. In February 1940 King Boris appointed Bogdan Filov as prime Minister; he was professor of Art History and strong admirer of Germany. He listened favorably to the propositions that Ribbentrop made in the autumn of 1940 on Bulgaria joining the Tripartite Pact. At the time the USSR was also offering him a treaty of friendship and non-aggression which had the support of the Communist Party expressed in a petition signed by thousands of people. Stalin promised the Bulgarians an outlet on the Aegean in Thrace. Boris tried to play for time, but the Germans became insistent and from December 1940 he had to agree to the presence of many odd German "tourists" who were dressed as civilians but in reality were military experts preparing an intervention in Greece. The USSR pointed out that Bulgaria and the Straits were part of its "security zone," but to no avail. On March 1941, Boris in Vienna signed a treaty in which he entered the Tripartite Pact, which meant that the Reich's tourists could don their uniforms and military missions could openly prepare Operation Marita.

However, the operation was delayed by an event outside the borders: Yugoslavia split apart. Since the Serbo-Croatian-Sporazum signed on 26 August 1939, Yugoslavia had a coalition government headed by D. Cvetkovic, a Serb, whose deputy was D. Macek, the Croatian leader. Following the example of the other Balkan republics Yugoslavia declared itself neutral in September 1939, while trying to improve relations with Bulgaria and establish diplomatic ties with the USSR, which up to then had been nonexistent. The defeat of France in May 1940 forced the Yugoslav authorities to consider their geopolitical situation between Italy and Germany. The fact that German troops were stationed in Romania and Bulgaria, and Italian armies had entered Albania thus threatening Greece, left no room for manoeuver. Early in 1941 the Germans pressed their case harder: if Yugoslavia entered the Pact she would be awarded the port of Thessalonika, a natural outlet for the Vardar region which had been coveted by the Serbs since Emperor Dusan first claimed it. Prince Paul was in no hurry to commit himself and after visiting Hitler in Berchtsesgaden on March 3 was deluded into thinking that if he signed the Pact his country would not be drawn into any military arrangement. After long and heated discussions on March 21 the government decided to join the Pact with 16 votes for and 3 against. Four days later the document was signed in Vienna and announced officially in Belgrade. Though there was an addendum to the effect that Yugoslavia would take no part in the Axis military operations and would be given Thessalonika, it remained a hidden agenda and gave rise to the most disturbing rumors. Public opinion went wild and overnight on 25–26 March a military putsch took place in the 19th century Serbian tradition. General Dusan Simovic and a party of officers took over power: the regents and government leaders were arrested while King Peter was declared of age a few months before reaching the legal limit. Simovic assumed premiership, and kept Macek on, while M. Nincic, a supporter of the Germans, was made foreign minister. Meanwhile popular demonstrations showed clearly that the country was against the Pact to such an extent that Churchill, the British press and Pravda were unanimous in praising the people of Yugoslavia for rising in defence of its independence and freedom. Feeling deeply offended, Hitler ordered Goebbels to run his propaganda machine at top speed and the civil servants in Wilhelmstrasse promised Hungary and Romania the division of Vojvodina, as well as assuring Bulgaria that her ambitions in Macedonia would be realized. At the same time the OKW was expanding Operation Marita to the whole of Yugoslav territory. Himmler's services were also busy undermining the stability of the state, which was an easy task as, Macek having refused to create an independent Croatia, they could turn to the separatist Ustasa movement who promised to declare independence as soon as the German troops entered Zagreb.

Military operations started on April 6, 1941. The Wehrmacht launched its main thrust from Bulgaria in the direction of Nis, Skopje and the Vardar region, while another armoured column seized Thessalonika and linked up with the Italians who had come from Albania at Lake Ohrid. Hence the German Panzers drove up towards Kragujevac and Belgrade where they were joined by an Army Corps arriving from the Romanian Banat. Other units from Austria entered Zagreb, while Italian soldiers pushed to Ljubljana and occupyied the Dalmatian coast. Hungarians made their way into the Vojvodina up to Osijek and Novisad and Bulgarian troops took over from the Germans in occupying Macedonia. After heavy bombing resulting in thousands of casualties, Belgrade was taken on the 11th: the king and the government first withdrew to Montenegro later to fly to Greece under British escort. On 17 April the

Yugoslav high command was forced to surrender: it had taken 11 days for Yugoslavia to fall.

Greece fell just as easily. Early on 6 April just as the German army was attacking Yugoslavia, the Reich's Ambassador in Athens handed Premier A. Koryzis a declaration of war and the German divisions stationed in Bulgaria started the pincer movement which took them to Belgrade. The Greek Maginot line, known as Metaxas line was by-passed and the soldiers manning it had to surrender after three days. The units of the Albania front withdrew to the south where, after joining the British Expeditionary Corps, a number sailed to Crete. On 18 April the Prime Minister took his own life, while the King and other political leaders went away to Canea. On 20 April the generals of the Army of Epirus, without prior discussions with civilian leaders signed a surrender treaty and one of them, G. Tsolakogiu, became head of government under German protection. It took fourteen days to wipe independent Greece off the world map.

Meanwhile Yugoslavia was falling apart. On 10 April 1941, the Wehrmacht entered Zagreb and Ante Pavelic's Ustasa declared Croatia independent. In Slovenia, a "Slovene National Council," representative of all political parties apart from the Communists, on April 11, proclaimed itself to be the only authority for the nation. However, the next day Italian troops entered Ljubljana. On April 20/22, in order to coordinate his operation with those of the Hungarians and Bulgarians, Hitler met the Duce in Vienna and the dictators shared out the Yugoslav territories into nine separate districts: the northern part of Slovenia was to be occupied by German military forces, as well as Serbia confined to its pre-1878 borders, and the whole of the Banat; Italy, not content with occupying Montenegro, annexed southern Slovenia, the coastal plain of Dalmatia as far as Dubrovnik, together with the Kotor delta (Cattaro) adding also to her Albanian kingdom, Kosovo and part of Macedonia; Hungary annexed western Vojvodina (backa); Bulgaria was given most of Macedonia and the Pirot region; finally Greater Croatia including Bosnia-Herzegovina was created which was independent in theory but not in practice.

Late in April 1941, the whole of the Balkans from the Prut and the Danube Delta to the end of the Peloponnese was subject to Axis rule. Symbolically Crete partly occupied by British troops was outside their power. The European dictators could not tolerate this: on 20 May a daring attack by German paratroopers, coupled with heavy bombing from the air, soon put Greek and English forces out of action. King George II and his government fled to Egypt where they remained under British protection. For the warlords the Balkan episode was over, they henceforth could concentrate on Operation Barbarossa, but contrary to their expectations the latter would not last just a few weeks but over three years and during this time the strategic importance of the Peninsula would turn it once again into one of the main areas that the two world coalitions would try to secure for themselves.

Romania and Bulgaria Under German Occupation, May 1941–Spring 1944

Romania was on the front row in the contest opposing Stalin and Hitler that started on 22 June 1941. The "Legionary state" created in September 1940 was not to last for long: excesses committed by the Iron Guard made not only the Conducator uneasy but also the OKW as its main concern was to ensure the safety of the rear of the future eastern front. On 21 January 1941, the Guard took control of Bucharest and cruelly massacred 350 people including many Jews. The following day Antonescu sent Romanian officers and soldiers, supported by Panzers fielded by the Wehrmacht, after the Legionaires who were eventually executed. Only Horia Sima and a few survivers succeeded in fleeing to Germany where they were kept by Himmler as a means to exert pressure on the Romanian dictator: the Iron Guard was eliminated for ever from the political scene in Romania. The country found itself under an authoritarian regime based on "active nationalism" and on close cooperation with the Reich.

On meeting the Fuhrer in November 1940—the first of fourteen such meetings—Antonescu promised to take part in the campaign against the USSR that was being prepared. In fact after refusing to intervene against Yugoslavia, unlike Hungary and Bulgaria, the Romanian leader declared war against the Soviet Union as early as June 1941 and the Conducator himself was to be Commander in Chief of Romanian forces. From then on the war in the East was to be the dominant factor of Romanian national life. The general—later to become marshall—put in charge of the government his namesake, Mihai Antonescu (1904–1946) a professor of law. Public opinion was split between anti-Russian feelings which was traditional, heightened by the prospect of regaining Bessarabia and

Bukovina, and pro-British leanings in spite of England having allied itself to the USSR; the Romanian Communist Party alone, still illegal, lost no time in denouncing this attack against the "Motherland of Socialism," but it was too small to make itself heard for a long while. The old politicians, I.C. Bratianu, and I. Maniu convinced King Michael that he should end hostilities after 11 July when the lost territories, lost in June 1940, had been regained. This was to no effect: Antonescu refused to listen and sent fifteen divisions to the front where they helped capture Odessa (October 16). This was a bloody operation with 70,000 casualties among Romanian troops. The country as a whole became aware of the horrors of modern warfare just when a message from London asked Romania to recall her troops or risk finding herself at war with Britain. The Conducator took no notice of this and on 7 December 1941, war with Romania was declared in London and five days later, according to the terms of the Tripartite Pact, Bucharest issued a declaration of war on the United States following the Japanese aggression against Pearl Harbor. Thus Romania was in tow behind Hitler's war machine for better or for worse.

For the 1942 campaign Hitler needed his Hungarian and Romanian allies, but they could not agree on the question of Transylvania. As compensation for the losses incurred by Romania, Antonescu asked for Northern Transylvania to be returned, but Ribbentrop calmed the Hungarians down with promises that the "Vienna arbitration" would stay in place. The German population of the area—Saxons and Swabians—made relations between leaders in Bucharest and Berlin highly complicated. As the only legal political organization, the "Romanian-German Party"—Deutsche Volksgruppe in Rumanien—represented all 750,000 German-speaking inhabitants. Since they were of Romanian nationality they could be called up to join Antonescu's army, but Himmler insisted on their being eligible for S.S. units or the Wehrmacht; some 75,000 dazzled by the prestige of these formations—better equipped and better paid than the Romanian army—opted for the German uniform, which raised many eyebrows among Romanian recruiting officers. To pacify the Romanian authorities Hitler gave Romania the right to administer, not to annex, Ukrainian territories lying beyond the Dnestr (Nistru in Romanian) up to the River Bug including Odessa: these regions went by the name of Transnistria. It became an area for economic pillaging and concentration camps to hold the Jews and the inhabitants of Bessarabia and Bukovina who were not of Romanian stock. Under pressure from the Nazis, Antonescu introduced antisemitic laws: Jews were forbidden to practise as doctors, barristers, journalists, they could not own a wireless set, a motor car, were not allowed to enter cinemas etc.; however, Romanian Jews were not made to live in ghettos, nor sent en masse to the death camps of the Reich. The country was also systematically exploited: oil, wheat, the labor force all served the German war machine. The black market flourished and prices rose sharply: by 1944 they were seventeen times higher than in 1940. General poverty led to a fall in morale, reflected in memos addressed to the Marshall by ex-political leaders who had been banned from any form of action apart from informing him.

The battle of Stalingrad (September 1942–February 1943) was the turning point of the Romanian military operations. Antonescu had fielded thirty divisions in the summer offensive of 1943 and they has suffered heavy casualties. When the Red Army counterattacked in November, the Romanians vainly begged the OKW for air cover and armoured vehicles. A Romanian division was in the army of General Paulus who was forced to surrender and others had to retreat precipitously in disastrous circumstances. 300,000 men had been killed, wounded or taken prisoners during the ill-fated campaign and Romanian units no longer able to control the Transnitria had to be relieved by the Wehrmacht. This disaster made all the forces who had advocated staying out of the war from the beginning: the Liberal and Peasant Parties traditionally close to France and England whose representatives could not accept waging war against Britain and the United States; the Communist Party drawing support in favor of peace from the masses suffering from economic restrictions; military cadres resentful of overbearing German ways, and also as the war was dragging on the majority of the soldiers who were increasingly uncooperative: between June 1941 and June 1944 86,000 of them were sentenced as deserters. Against this widespread discontent, those in favor of "collaboration" were disunited. At the highest level, while the Marshall remained loyal to Hitler right till the end, the head of the government, Mihail Antonescu, felt closer to the Italian form of fascism and from January 1943, in concert with Mussolini attempted to withdraw from the war. The two Romanian leaders embroiled by their womenfolk (Mme Antonescu, Mme Goga etc.) in a web of intrigues at times were no longer on speaking terms. Even more serious were tensions with the German authorities over the Volksdeutsche and with the Hungarian "allies" over Transylvania: Horthy in 1942 in order to protect his border with Romania had no qualms in holding on to German equipment that was supposed to go to the Russian front, much to Hitler's fury.

Taking this into account opposition to the war began in ernest in the spring of 1943. In foreign affairs several steps were taken with tacit approval from the government to make contact with the Anglo-Saxons. A number of personalities concentrating on Romanian embassies in the capitals of neutral countries such as Lisbon, Stockholm, Bern, Ankara and Madrid, tried to persuade politicians in London and Washington of the need to defend Romania against Stalin's ambitions. The Allies remained unresponsive and on 1 August 1943, the British-American airforce made its first massive attack against the Ploesti refineries. As for the Soviet Union they agreed to hold talks in Stockholm during which they insisted on Romania breaking relations with the Reich and fighting alongside the USSR till the end, and in exchange Transylvania would be returned to her. At home, all political parties had been banned by Carol II in 1938 but the Communist Party was experienced in surviving underground as it had done since 1924. Though it had few members and several of its leaders were in jail such as Gheorghiu-Dej, others had found sanctuary in the Soviet Union: Ana Pauker, Vasile Luca, Emil Bodnaras and in November 1943 they set up a division, called "Tudor Vladimitescu," after recruiting Romanian POWs. As early as June 1941 Communists in Romania were responsible for strikes and "anti-war" sabotage: the Tirgoviste arsenal was set on fire, the Buzau ammunition depot was destroyed, as well as other acts, which made them into the favorite target of the dictatorial regime. Party historians claimed 313 "martyrs"—either shot or killed in action—between 1941 and 1944. On Stalin's advice Communists also adopted the policy of cooperation with all the forces opposed to fascism. In November 1942 they helped to promote the "Union of Patriots" which published an underground paper "Free Romania"—Romania libera. In the summer of 1943 another step was taken with the "Anti-Hitler Patriotic Front" formed after an alliance between the Communist Party, the "Ploughmen Front" headed by Petru Groza, Madosz (Union of Hungarian Workers in Romania) and local sections of the Social Democratic Party. The Peasant Party let by Maniu refused to join since it wanted to include in its program the return of Bessarabia and Bukovina to Romania. Very soon the Front appeared to be controled by the RCP which was its most dynamic component and whose leaders, L. Patrascanu and E. Bodnaras, having secretely returned from Moscow, kept in touch with Gheorghiu-Dej in prison, through his lawyer, Ion Maurer.

Bulgarians were not affected by the war to such an extent and Barbara Jelavich wrote: "of all the Axis allies they enjoyed the best conditions." Up to King Boris's death, in August 1943, the way of life of ordinary citizens was not significantly altered. As it now belonged to the Tripartite Pact the country had to put up with the presence of Wehrmacht units which were to be used in Greece, but also played a major part in the campaign against Yugoslavia. The fact that the latter fell apart enabled Bulgaria to realize its dreams of domination over neighbouring areas. The Bulgarian army did not have to intervene: the OKW informed it that it need not bother, but Hitler entrusted his ally with the occupation and administration of three quarters of Yugoslav Macedonia, Greek Macedonia as well as Thrace. Boris won the name of "Unifier" and his image as champion of the national cause increased his prestige among the population. By June 1941 the Bulgarian government had annexed the part of Yugoslav Macedonia under occupation; the German authorities did not show any concern. The official policy was to win the population over, since according to the government Macedonians were Bulgarians. The campaign of appeasement included a National Theater for Skopje, as well as a Bulgarian Library, a Museum and a "King Boris University," while in the rest of the province 800 Bulgarian schools were opened with imported teachers and popes. This was in sharp contrast with the heavy-handed Serbian administration, but soon there could be heard similar criticisms of the new masters who were accused of acting as victors: corruption and nepotism flourished in the accustomed style of the Balkans. Whether the new policy was successful remains to be proved. One fact is certain, the Resistance in Macedonia developed early in 1943 in the shadow of Tito's Yugoslav Partisans, and because Bulgarian troops were involved in the fight against guerillas alongside the Germans, the rebellion spread rapidly. In the old Greek territories of Thrace and Macedonia, Bulgarian officials were much less easy going. The Greek authorities intent on increasing the Greek population in these parts, in 1923 settled the Greeks who had been expelled from Turkey in the early days of Kemal in the area, at the expense of the Slav population which was forced to leave. Thus the latter had become a small minority when the Bulgarian government enforced the same policy but in reverse: Greeks were pushed out to the benefit of Bulgarian settlers. However this was done in such a merciless way that Greek researchers claim that thousands of people were executed. There is no doubt that public opinion in Greece violently turned against Bulgaria following these events.

It is probable that Germany imposed on Bulgaria economic agreements that were favorable to the former, though it is hard to believe some Bulgarian historians when they claim that the country was "occupied" and "economically plundered." King Boris's government was entirely responsible for the incredibly harsh measures taken against the Resistance in the early days and the countryside grew rich during the war years as could be seen from villagers suddenly buying furniture and radio sets. The campaign against the USSR in June 1941 did not involve Bulgaria in any operations since public opinion leant heavily on the side of the Russians and the political leaders were not sure of their position. However, on 13 December 1941, as a symbolic gesture, B.Filov declared war on the United States and Great Britain. The USSR Legation in Sofia and Soviet consulates in Varna and Burgas remained open and had a number of military experts under their roofs. The German authorities expressed their displeasure and in April 1942 Hitler in an interview with Boris insisted on his breaking relations with the Soviet Union, but the King only closed the consulate at Varna. The German defeat at Stalingrad effectively put an end to the faintest possibility of Bulgarian intervention on the Eastern Front: the reservists who had been called up openly declared their opposition. Instead the political leaders put out feelers to America through diplomats in Bern. Meanwhile on 28 August 1943, King Boris died suddenly at the age of forty nine; he had just returned from visiting the Fuhrer in Eastern Prussia and rumors were rife in Sofia of his being poisoned by Himmler's henchmen. A child aged six ascended the throne under the name Simeon II (1943–46). According to the constitution the National Assembly was to elect a Regency Council but Hitler sent a telegram to point out that B. Filov was "best qualified to lead the country." The Prime Minister selected Prince Cyril, brother of the dead monarch, and a general to form with him a Regency Council and entrust D. Bojilov, Minister of Finance, with the task of pursuing the same authoritarian pro-German policy.

In internal affairs B. Filov had often modeled himself on the Nazi example: a Movement for young people was created, a system of civilian mobilization which prevented workers to move from factories and there were even antisemitic laws in spite of the small number of Jews, 50,000, living in Bulgaria. A law for "the National Salvation" (December 1940) was passed making it compulsory for Jews to wear a star of David, and the possibility of expelling them from the capital. However, when Hitler asked to have them deported to the Reich the Filov government unwilling to provoke public opinion chose to arrest Jews only in occupied territories in Yugoslavia and Greece (some 10,000); as for those living in the kingdom the Assembly protected them: 43 MPs among them the Vice-President of the Chamber protested and the government backed down. Thus Bulgarian Jews were the only ones in Nazi Europe to avoid being deported to the death camps.

This move was one expression of a larger pattern of "Resistance" which due to the characteristics of the Bulgarian situation was different from that of other countries. There were similar difficulties to overcome: repression on the part of the authorities, being forced to go underground, but there were also specific obstacles. First of all the country was not waging war against the USSR and war against the Anglo-Saxon countries remained entirely theoretical. As it happened this official policy of "neutralism," which amounted to "soft collaboration" with the Reich, had been to great advantage; besides what was termed "the completion of territorial unity" brought about by annexation and occupation of neighboring regions, there had been a steep rise in the price of agricultural produce from which the peasants benefitted while the numerous workers working in Germany were able to send large pay packets home. These factors were very important for keeping the population quiet since it was politically unsophisticated. Resistance arose out of the ranks of the Bulgarian Communist Party, banned since 1923, but which was, on the eve of the war, the strongest in the Balkans and the most obedient to the 3rd International, whose secretary was G. Dimitrov. By June 1941 he came down in defence of the "Motherland of Socialism," and tried to prevent Bulgaria from being a rear base for the Wehrmacht. He decided straighaway to take up arms "against the German occupier and their Bulgarian servants." Up to July 1942 he concentrated on acts of sabotage against military establishments, fuel dumps or railways and roads. He must have found a sympathetic hearing in

The Balkans in World War II 467

the army for in June 1942 General Wl. Zaïmov was sentenced to death and executed as a "Bolshevik agent." In the USSR G.Dimitrov had arranged for a radio station "Hristo Botev" to broadcast news and directives which listened to by many people. To tap a larger section of the population, in July 1942, the Bulgarian CP appealed for a joint effort from all progressive forces and launched the "Patriotic Front"—Otetchestven Front—which attracted, not other political parties, but prominent individuals such as Nikola Petkov of the Agrarian Union, G.Cheshmedjev of the Social-Democrat Party. The Front's program included breaking the alliance with the Reich, toppling the Filov government and replacing it with a broad National Democratic Union. By the end of the year about a hundred committees were circulating large numbers of underground newssheets. The day after the German defeat at Stalingrad the Front set up the first guerrilla camps in the Rhodopes, Rila and Pirin with active participation of the Communists. They established links with Tito's Partisans and with the Greek ELAS who sent them arms and equipment. In August 1943 the movement was strong enough to need a "National Committee" to head the Front which included representatives of the five political tendencies. It also was in contact with London through British officers who had joined Tito after being parachuted in. Early in 1944 it is estimated that about 10,000 men were involved in guerrilla warfare.

Peoples at War: Yugoslavs, Albanians and Greeks, Spring 1941–Spring 1944

In Yugoslavia the surrender of the Army's High Command on 17 April had not gone done well with all the fighting units. In Northern Bosnia a small party of Serbian officers gathered round Draza Mihailovic (1893–1946), a Staff Colonel, and set up a Resistance center in the Ravna Gora run on the lines of the Chetniks—irregulars—of the 19th century. As for the outlawed Yugoslav PC, which had taken part already in demonstrations against the Tripartite Pact it reacted enthusiastically to Stalin's appeal for help after Hitler's aggression of 22 June 1941. Its Secretary General was Josip Broz, nicknamed Tito, (1892–1980) who had been elected in 1938. He was a metal worker, born in Croatia at Kumrovec to the north of Zagreb from a family of poor peasants. He had served in the First World War in the Austro-Hungarian Army and had been taken as a POW to Russia where during the Bolshevik Revolution he became a Communist. He returned home in 1920 and became an active member of the Yugoslav PC; he was sent to the USSR several times for training and worked in the Comintern before being made Secretary General of the YCP. His close assistants included Alexander Rankovic, a Serbian, Eduard Kardelj, a Slovene, Milovan Djilas from Montenegro and many others some of whom were experienced in military matters after having been involved in the Spanish civil war.

The two centers of Resistance were not only dissimilar but also hostile; besides the fight against German or Italian occupation forces and their puppet governments, they also waged a civil war. The Chetniks were "Great Serbians," royalists and devoutly Orthodox, they were also against Croatians and radically anti-communists. The YCP dreamt of a Yugoslavia that would be changed into a Soviet Republic but for the time being Tito applied Stalin's orders of wide "union of popular forces": the Partisan movement took in members outside the narrow party base and and aimed at uniting the various peoples in a large brotherhood to fight fascism. From the start Tito appealed to all Yugoslavs, while Mihailovic's scope was traditionalist Serbians. They also differed on tactics: Mihailovic thought that attacking Axis forces while these powers were on the ascendent, was both illusory in terms of military tactics but also harsh on the civilian population who would be exposed to brutal reprisals. It was therefore imperative to wait for an Allied landing—British in the main—which would make it possible for the Chetniks to join in the military operation and help restore the Monarchy. Tito was convinced that these very reprisals would force people to choose sides and besides the hardships endured under the occupation regime would arouse such resentment in the population that could later be exploited: this is why he advocated taking up arms straighaway to lead to the victory of the people. For several weeks they cooperated while the leaders met on two occasions. However, members of the two movements started fighting each other by November 1941. German troops took advantage of this to harass the Partisans who withdrew from Serbia and settled in the Sandjak of Novi Pazar. Massacres in reprisal for assistance to the Partisans by the population amounted to 7,000 inhabitants at Kragujevac including about hundred children who were shot with their masters—whole classes at a time. As for the Chetniks they partly joined the Belgrade government forces in collaborating while Mihailovic was left undisturbed with his party of followers in the Ravna Gora.

At the same time the German occupation authorities had established in Belgrade a government headed by General Milan Nedic, ex-War Minister and a convinced Germanophile. However, this "Cabinet of National Salvation" was an administrative façade and was constantly the butt of interference by Wehrmacht representatives. It soon lost what little credibility it had with the population, after first appearing as a saviour à la Pétain. In any case Serbian citizens had to put up with harsh restrictions due to German requisitionining.

In Croatia the independent state had to let the Italians take the whole of Dalmatia, but it had received Bosnia-Herzegovina in exchange making the nationalists' wishes come true and they rejoiced over the birth of "Greater Croatia." The latter then boasted 6.5 millions inhabitants, but only half of them were Croats; there were also nearly two million Orthodox who were called Serbs, and 700,000 Moslems who refused any specific nationality but who were regarded by the Ustasa as "the most unaldulterated Croats." Thus religion became a criterion for identity, which meant allowing the most fanatical acts imaginable: Ustasa had their weapons blessed before massacring Serbs, Moslems returned to the call for Jihad and Orthodox believers forced to choose between death and having their children forcibly baptized set Croatian villages on fire as well as mosques. The wave of enthusiasm which had carried the country in April 1941 was of short duration: Macek, leader of the Peasants, retired to his farm before being interned and Archbishop Stepinac who had first issued a call for supporting the Pavelic government was frightened by the excesses of its armed forces. In any case the "independent" state did not remain so for long: as early as May 1941 Prince Aimeri of Savoy, Duke of Spoleto and a relative of Victor-Emmanuel, became King of Croatia under the name of Tomislav II, but the situation was so chaotic that he never set foot in his kingdom. The civil war made it impossible for the administration to function and German military rule was enforced in Zagreb: all lines of communications were under its control, mineral ores were requisitioned and labour sent to work in Germany. On the other hand only the Croatian armed force was available to the occupying power since the Ustasa were terrorists and not soldiers.

In Montenegro, Mussolini tried to recreate an independent

kingdom as the Italian Queen was a daughter of Nicholas the last monarch. However, there was little support for a royal regime were and the attitudes of these mountain people to foreign occupation was so antagonistic that by July 1941 the country was in open rebellion. In spite of Italian troops who were occupying Albania making several attempts to regain control, Montenegro throughout the war served as a base for the Resistance. The Partisans under the command of Arso Jovanovic, soon to be Tito's Chief of Staff, got the upper hand in the region, while Milovan Djilas, a political commissar, followed a rigidly communist line of action in opposition to the Secretary General's orders.

When he was forced to evacuate Serbia, Tito concentrated his men in Eastern Bosnia and, making good use of the climate of violence created by Ustasa raids against the Serbian population, decided to strike right at the center of Pavelic's regime. In the summer of 1942, he conquered the whole of Central and Western Bosnia, and, making Bihac his headquarters, organized the "National Liberation Army" as well as a "Council Against Fascism" (AVNOJ) (November 26, 1942), empowered to administer the regions recovered by force of arms. Dr Ivan Ribar, who had been President of the Constituent Assembly in 1920, headed the new Council, which in time was to pronounce on the future of Yugoslavia and chose a federation with wide autonomy for individual republics. In Macedonia, under occupation by King Boris' army, this policy led to a clash with the underground Bulgarian Communist Party and an appeal was made to the Kremlin for arbitration. The decision came down in favor of the Yugoslavs and the Partisans set up an organization in Macedonia under Vukmanovic-Tempo, an envoy of Tito. The same happened in Slovenia: in spite of an Italian offensive in the summer of 1942 and the presence of paramilitary units supported by the religious authorities who opposed the communists,the Partisans gained a strong hold over the region.

For the European continent, completely dominated by the Axis Powers, the appearance of an oasis of freedom on Yugoslav soil presented a new problem. Since its fall in April 1941, the Belgrade royal government, in exile in London, was the only body recognized by the Allies. Tito's emergence changed the outlook altogether. As a communist he was out of bounds for the emigres who appointed a "Great Serbian," Professor Slobodan Jovanovic as head of the government and as a symbolic gesture included Draza

Mihailovic—with the rank of general—who became War Minister. The BBC presented a picture of the Chetniks and their leaders as Resistance heroes, while it was the Partisans who on the ground were victorious and Churchill sent liaison officers to Mihailovic. On the other hand Tito should have enjoyed support from Stalin, but in fact he received no assistance other than verbal encouragement on the radio, and the Yugoslav royal legation in Moscow was raised to an embassy. The Kremlin leaders wanted the situation to be clearer before committing themselves. As for Hitler he saw the Bihac meeting as naked provocation: he demanded that the Duce and his protege Pavelic launch a joint operation to wipe out the Partisans. Surrounded on all sides Tito and his men retreated through the Bosnian mountains in hazardous conditions, routed the Chetniks who were blocking their way over the Neretva and withdrew to Montenegro and Eastern Bosnia. The Partisans called these operations the 4th and 5th enemy offensives: they were to last from January till June 1943, and the Chetniks fought alongside the Wehrmacht during this time. Tito himself was wounded, but he now had two British officers dispatched by the British Prime Minister to contact him.

Italy's surrender in September 1943 completely altered the strategic map by doing away with the Duce's occupation zones—Slovenia, Croatia, Montenegro—where Italian soldiers were replaced by Germans. In those areas there followed desperate efforts on both sides to seize arms and military equipment left behind by the Italians. Tito's troops took the greater part of the booty which amounted to ten full divisions: their strength increased significantly. Tito then called another meeting of AVNOJ in Jajce in Bosnia in November 1943. The Council became a real Parliamentary Assembly of sixty seven members representing the various peoples of Yugoslavia and was empowered to legislate and administer the country. The Council appointed a "National Liberation Committee" as a kind of provisional government, with Tito, now a Marshall, as its leader. The Assembly decided to rebuild the country as a federation, to annex a few districts at the expense of Italy and to ban the return of King Peter to Yugoslavia while waiting for elections. In the face of this new power which enjoyed wide popular support, and was backed by a 300,000 strong army, the King's government was helpless. It sat in Cairo and relied on the Chetniks for support, but the latter because they had collaborated with the enemy had few friends outside of Serbia. Churchill had sent a military mission to Tito under Brigadier Fitzroy Maclean and was informed that it would be wise to switch his support to the Partisans. Churchill mentioned this fact to Stalin and Roosevelt at the Teheran Conference in December 1943 and in the following months withdrew British officers from Mihailovic who saw many in his entourage leave to join General Nedic instead. Meanwhile the Germans had invaded most of the areas previously under Italian control and an operation which was launched to take Tito prisoner almost succeeded: he had to fly to Italy and set up his headquarters on the Island of Vis which was under British control (May 1944).

The Albanians, having been subjected to forced Italianization, were soon to show their discontent. On the occasion of the National Holiday, on November 28, 1939, demonstrations took place in Tirana and most major cities, mostly young people taking part. The Italians, giving nationalists hope of annexing Greek and Yugoslav territory, tried to enrol Albanian units to assist them in the Greek campaign of October 1940: a few battalions marched off shouting "Freedom for Cameria." When a Greek counter-offensive took Metaxas' soldiers to Gjirokaster and Korca, they were initially well received by the population which resented the Italian occupation, but the policy of forced Hellenization followed by the Athens government alienated patriots. On the other hand they went wild with joy on hearing about Yugoslavia's disintegration. Hostility to Serbia was well entrenched and in 1912 when the region of Kosovo Metohija, which was called "Old Serbia" in Belgrade, was taken over, there had been indignation. Thus Albanian national pride was well served by the return of Kosovo to the crown, as well as annexing the Macedonian zone running from Tetovo to Lake Prespa and the part of Montenegro round Ulcinj and Bar, together with administrative rule over the Cameria, which amounted in all to 7–800,000 new subjects, mostly Albanians. Italy was able to claim that thanks to the Axis "Greater Albania" had recovered its racial borders. Rome put in charge of the country a representative of the nationalist bourgeoisie, called Mustafa Kruja, who was allowed a measure of autonomy.

This, however, was not sufficient to stop the organization of a Resistance movement. From the beginning of the Italian invasion in April 1939, King Zog, from his exile in London had tried to regroup his followers into a fighting force. There were many other exiles in Belgrade and late in 1940 some of them gathered round

Abaz Kupi, a local chieftain opposed to King Zog at the time, to carry out raids across the border with the help of the British. Yet most of the country's nationalist leaders adopted an attitude of wait and see. The impetus for armed struggle came from the recently constituted and very small Albanian Communist Party (ACP). This was the youngest of European communist parties dating back to November 1941 when it started in Tirana. It was the union of three small Marxist groups created by intellectuals at Korca, Shkodra and Tirana, but the former proving the more dynamic because of its leader, Enver Hoxha (1908–1985). He came from a Moslem family belonging to the trading middle class of Gjirokastra. He attended the Lycee Français at Korca and later the Montpellier University, became a Marxist in France under the influence of members of the FCP, then taught French at the Tirana and Korca lycees until 1939, when he had to go underground. The Founding Congress from 8 to 14 November 1941, was a modest affair; it was a gathering of 15 activists from the three existing groupings who appointed a Central Committee of 7 members headed by Enver Hoxha to draft a program of strict adherence to Marxism-Leninism and endorsing the Comintern policy of antifascist union. Two Yugoslav CP members took part in the proceedings and later an argument was to arise with Vl.Dedijer, who described the creation of the ACP as a Yugoslav initiative, and Enver Hoxha who claimed to have acted on his own. Anyhow the ACP like Tito's Partisans chose to take up arms for "the national independence of the Albanian people and a democratic people's government." On this basis, late in 1941, Enver Hoxa's comrades prepared for action. In towns they organized "guerrilla units" to attack the Italian occupation forces, while in the mountains they revived the old tradition of cheta, small parties of irregulars who attacked lines of communications and transport vehicles. At the same time the ACP carried out a propaganda campaign by distributing tracts and its underground newspaper "Zeri i Popullit" (The People's Voice). To start with they received advisors, equipment and arms from Yugoslavia. In the same way as Tito's Partisans, but three months earlier, the ACP issued a call for a Conference to be held at Peza, near Tirana, in September 1942, to bring together communists, followers of King Zog and leaders of the Catholic North; it was decided to set up a "National Liberation Front" (L.NC.) under an eight-member Council including Enver Hoxha and Abaz Kupi. This being settled the armed struggle developed fast. Late in 1942, there were 22 cheta amounting to some 2,000 men who had liberated several areas of the Central and South mountains. Their success was carried outside the national frontiers and in December 1942, Anthony Eden, Cordell Hull and V.Molotov in turn paid homage to Albanian Partisans and came down in favor of a restoration of Albanian independence.

Another focus of resistance developed round nationalist leaders who soon became strongly anti-communist. It is true that from the start they had been opposed to the occupier, but only after the Partisans had won a few successes and the Allies had reacted favorably, did they overcome their old political and clan rivalries. In December 1942 they formed a "National Front"—Balli Kombetar (BK) an underground organization calling itself "nationalist and opposed to King Zog." This movement was ill disposed towards Yugoslavia because it claimed the Kosovo territories and looked to the Anglo-Saxon Allies for assistance as it was opposed to communism. They were able to infiltrate administrative services and recruited the Minister of Justice to their cause, but also set up guerrilla camps which competed with the Partisans. Some members of the YCP, such as Vukmanovic-Tempo who had been sent to help the Albanians, stongly advised their comrades to turn immediately against the B.K. As for the Italians feeling unsure of themselves after the defeat at Stalingrad, they approached the nationalists and gave the Albanians back their flag, their own currency and a measure of freedom. The new head of government, Malik bey Bushati had dealings with the Balli. In the circumstances the ACP called its first National Congress at Labinot near Elbasan, in March 1943, at which Enver Hoxha attacked the Yugoslav policy of fighting the BK. However, it was not long before they fell out and Mussolini's fall in July 1943, marked a meeting between by two movements which ended by an admission of failure. The Partisans organized an "Army of National Liberation" which at the time of the Italian surrender seized the equipment and armament of five divisions. However, the Germans did not remain idle: 70,000 soldiers came from Greece to occupy all the towns. They declared Albania an independent state in the capital, setting up an Assembly, a Regency Council and a government. The Balli Kombetar had many connections with the new authorities and issued an order not to attack Wehrmacht soldiers. The Catholic leader in the North and Zog's followers made their arrangements but their attitude remained ambiguous since the Germans had no wish to return the Kosovo to Yugoslavia and made capital out of this; they allowed "another Prizren line" to develop in the area and harassed the Serbs.

As they felt politically isolated, the Partisans whose army numbered about 20,000 men, launched an all out struggle against all so-called "collaborators"; like Yugoslavia and Greece, Albania was drifting into civil war. Seeing that the nationalists were incapable of restoring order, the Germans took the situation into their own hands and with the help of some Albanian elements in November 1943, launched a major offensive against the Partisan camps. Enver Hoxha experienced the same problems as Tito and had a narrow escape. He was lucky that a counter-offensive by Mehmet Shehu's brigade, in January 1944, succeeded in rescuing his military staff from encirclement. A strong base was then established in the Dumre east of Lushnja. By the end of March 1944, the Red Army had reached the Romanian border and the Wehrmacht had to deal with more pressing matters, so the crisis in Albania ended.

On 20 April 1941, following their surrender, the Greeks were subjected to occupation by three foreign powers. The Germans only stayed in Athens and a few neighbouring islands, at Thessalonika and its region to control access to the Vardar; Western Thrace, the islands of Thasos and Samothrace were entrusted to Bulgaria, while everything else was given over to Italy. The three successive heads of the Athens government—of whom only the last, John Rallis, was an experienced politician—all claimed to be there to make foreign occupation more bearable, but they had to obey the victors' orders. Germans were interested in agricultural production, mineral ores and ensuring the safety of lines of communications. Italians aimed at a close ideological and cultural rapport, but corruption put paid to these hopes, as well as the growth of black marketeering which they themselves fueled. The Bulgarians, as was shown earlier, applied a policy of moving of populations which led to many excesses: Greek historians pass the harshest judgement on the latter form of occupation. There is no doubt that that the Greek people suffered great hardship in the exceptionally severe winter of 1941–1942: cold and hunger caused havoc among the population, subjected as it was to an inefficient system of rationing. A figure of 3,000 deaths from starvation is given for Athens alone, in spite of efforts on the part of the Greek Church to limit suffering. To this must be added, after July 1942, antisemitic measures taken by the Nazis: the 45,000 Sephardic Jews of Thessalonika who were deported to the death camps of Birkenau and Bergen-Belsen.

These various factors help us understand the rapid growth of a strong resistance movement, which was helped by the difficult terrain and historical traditions of the Klephtes. However, just as in neighboring Yugoslavia and Albania the movement split up into rival and later enemy factions so that in the end the wretched country was engulfed in civil war. Even emigre Greeks were divided: the King's government in exile in London, later in Cairo, was of doubtful legitimacy because it came from Metaxas' dictatorship. King George, who enjoyed Churchill's patronage, was the embodiment of legitimacy for the Allies, but the Republicans disagreed. From the start, the question of the "King's return" was at the heart of political quarrels both among emigres and within the country. In the meantime the main objective was fighting the occupying forces.

The first to open hostilities were the KKE communists. As they were driven underground by the dictatorial regime, they answered Stalin's plea and worked among workers and trade unions to create a central organization which called itself, on 22 September, 1941, the "National Liberation Front"—E.A.M.—which was joined by socialists and various left-wingers. Its program was broad: after the country's liberation, a government of national union would be set up, which would ask the people to decide on whether the King should return to power. Though there was no mention of socialism or communism in the document, it was drafted by Glinos, a Communist, and members of the K.K.E. held all the key positions in the organization. The Front then turned its attention to preparation for a spring offensive and armed units were trained to become the "People's National Liberation Army," E.L.A.S. The first Resistance groups became operative in May 1942 in the Pindhos region under orders from an energetic guerrilla leader called Velukhotis. The Andartes (Partisans) then spread out to the whole country. In the same way as Draza Mihailovic in Yugoslvia, a number of army officers rejected the surrender and answered an appeal from General Plastiras, who had ruled as Republican dictator in 1933 and was at the time in exile in France. In October 1941 they decided to form the "Greek Democratic National Army," E.D.E.S. to operate in the same mountain area between the Gulf of Corinth and the Albanian frontier. In July 1942, Colonel, later General Napoleon Zervas was in charge of a Resistance group, being supplies by

Britain, which in the beginning willingly cooperated with E.L.A.S.. Together they blew up the Gorgopotamos viaduct, breaking railway communications to the North and to the German garrison in Athens for six months. Another party of officers who had gained support from the British General Headquarters in Cairo, founded the "National and Social Liberation Movement"—E.K.K.A.—who included Republicans and Royalists and took orders from Colonel Sparos who operated in the Parnassus region from March 1943. There existed other smaller organizations and in Athens the old political parties began operating underground.

Conflicts soon began to appear between the various Resistance groups: the E.L.A.S. and the E.D.E.S. quarrelled over control of the "liberated zones" in Central Greece and half way through 1943, some sections of the E.D.E.S. defected to join the security forces of the pro-German government in Athens. As for E.K.K.A. it aimed at maintaining a balance between its two bigger rivals but had to contend with E.L.A.S. whose men brutally disarmed its units in the Parnassus. These clashes were very disturbing for the Allies who had sent by parachute officers to liase with the various resistance groups and arms and equipment. However, Winston Churchill was a staunch friend of George II and was intent on restoring the monarchy, which put British policy at odds with the major Resistance groups. British advisers, such as Colonel Woodhouse, realized that the Communists were the most dynamic element and tried to divert supplies to E.D.E.S. and E.K.K.A. to restore a certain balance. This infuriated the men of E.L.A.S., but nevertheless by the autumn of 1943, while there were 120,000 Andartes, E.D.E.S. counted only 1,300 men in the field and E.K.K.A. a few hundreds.

The British used these freedom fighters in planning the Sicily landing (July 1943) with a joint operation in Greece. It was called "Animals" and included the three factions in a wave of acts of sabotage in Thessaly and Epirus, where railways, bridges and telephone lines were systematically destroyed. Pleased with these successes which immobilized many German units in the country, the British then tried to establish political agreement between the various movements. In August their military mission in Greece sent six Resistance leaders to Cairo in order to meet representatives of the government in exile of E.Tuderos, a banker. This Cairo Conference was a failure: the three factions agreed on forming a government of National Union after the liberation, but disputed their respective share of seats, they also wanted to postpone the King's return until the referendum, while George II insisted on landing before that time. These quarrels upset Churchill who sent the resistance leaders back home and in fact broke relations with E.L.A.S. However, the question of the King's fate was also dividing the Greek Army in Egypt, two divisions of which had valiantly taken part in the battle of El Alamein. Metaxists-Royalists and Republicans opposed one another, officers and soldiers alike. Verbal clashes were followed by acts of violence degenerating into open rebellion in February 1943. Another mutiny in the army and the navy, in March 1944, was firmly handled by British forces: 10,000 officers and men found themselves locked up in a camp in Lybia. The new Greek Army was entirely Royalist.

On 8 September 1943, the Italian surrender completely changed the balance of forces. Most Italian units had—not always of their own accord—surrendered their arms to E.L.A.S. which from then on was not discriminated against for a share of British air drops. E.D.E.S. and E.K.K.A. became extremely worried, especially as the Allied Conference at Teheran (November-December 1943) decided against a landing in the Balkans. Churchill therefore planned British intervention to restore the King to his throne after the liberation. Meanwhile E.L.A.S. taking advantage of superior numbers attempted to wipe out Colonel Napoleon Zerbas' movement. In October bloody clashes occurred between the two bodies. However, as the Germans regained control of the parts occupied until then by the Italian troops, they launched on 16 October an offensive against all resistance forces. There followed uninterrupted assaults by the Wehrmacht until its departure in September 1944, resulting in losses on the Greek side estimated at 20,000 deaths, slightly more taken prisoners and around 5,000 executions as reprisal. In spite of this enemy action, clashes between members of E.L.A.S. and E.D.E.S. went on until February 1944, and in April an operation mounted against Colonel Psaros' group, E.K.K.A., ended in tragedy: its leader and 150 of his men after being taken prisoners were executed. E.A.M. then believed that it was strong enough to set up a real "Mountain State"—Kedros, Cedar—complete with schools, tribunals, newspapers, civilian services, roads, factories and even theaters. Each liberated village was administered by a "People's Council," elected as in areas held by Partisans in Yugoslavia. E.A.M. was loud in proclaiming its aim of achieving national union and boasted six bishops and 1,500 officers of the old army in the ranks of E.L.A.S., but it was an organization controled by the 15–20% communist members in its midst. On 10 March 1944, without any consultation, the Front set up a "Political Committee of National Liberation," P.E.E.A., a kind of provisional government which held secret elections with an alleged one million Greeks participating. The Committee chaired by Svolos, a lawyer, was thus assisted by an elected National Council with its seat at Karikades in the Pindus.

The government in exile in April seized the initiative and appointed George Papandreou (1888–1968) as Prime Minister. He was previously personal secretary to Venizelos and was opposed to Metaxas who managed to escape from Athens and reach Cairo. The new program was: "One Motherland, one Government, one Army" and its aim was to reconcile antagonisms in every sector. To this end the head of government called a conference of representatives of all political parties and all resistance movements which took place at Dar-el-Saouer in Lebanon in May 1944. A "Lebanese Charter" was adopted after heated discussions, which created a "Government of National Union" to be recognized by all resistance forces , but in which four ministries were allocated to E.A.M.; after the liberation a referendum would settle the question of the régime and whether to have the King return or not. This was the political basis for the Greek people to embark on the last stage of the war and shake off the chains of German occupation.

Arrival of the Red Army, April–December 1944

The whole of the Balkans saw the day of liberation ushered in by the arrival of the Red Army: once again men of the Great Northern Power crossed the Danube and ventured as far as the River Morava. This time though Russia had become the Soviet Union and was under Stalin's control and together with its troops a political and social "revolution" occurred, winning the day in Romania, Bulgaria, Yugoslavia and Albania, but failing in Greece at the cost of civil war and much bloodshed, due to the British divisions sent by Churchill.

It started on 26 March 1944, when Generals Malinovski's and Tolbukin's troops reached the River Prut. At the same time the Romanian government under Mihai Antonescu was still negotiating to pull out of the war and in Cairo, Prince Stirbei, once a minister, met with the British, American and Soviet ambassadors. The Allies demanded an immediate end to operations against the USSR and a declaration of war against Germany, Allied troops to be allowed free passage through Romanian territory and reparations, in exchange for the return of Northern Transylvania. Molotov, the Prime Minister, in a public declaration added that his country intended to keep Bessarabia and Bukovina. Marshall Antonescu refused these conditions. On 4 April the British-American airforce carried out heavy bombing of Bucharest to show solidarity with their ally. At home the Resistance had organized a "Patriotic Front" since the previous summer, under the control of Communist leaders, and set up its first guerrilla groups in the capital, in the Prahova Valley, in the Banat region, while intellectuals went into action with a "Memoir" addressed to the Conducator, and got in touch with King Michael's aides. Early in August, Marshall Antonescu met the Fuhrer for the last time in East Prussia and was promised air support. However, on August 20, battle raged all along the front from Jassy to Kishinev; within three days the Romanian front had crumbled and Russian soldiers were in control of the Moldavian capital. On August 22, Antonescu returned from his HQs to Bucharest and with the agreement of his Council of Ministers, made the decision to offer an armistice to the Soviet authorities. He arranged an audience with the King for the following day at 4 p.m.

Upon hearing the news, on 23 August in the morning, I.Maniu, leader of the Peasant Party, urged Michael to take action: the Russians were advancing and the Germans would turn the country into a battlefield in halting their advance. Since June an action committee, including three representatives of the palace, three delegates from the army and three envoys from the Front, had been formed in order to prepare for the overthrow of the Marshall, but the date was left open. Officers and communist leaders agreed that the time had come for action. On 23 August when both Antonescu, the Marshall and the head of government, presented themselves to the King, the latter announced to them that they had to resign, he had them arrested by officers of the Palace Guard and locked up in the strong room built by Carol for his stamp collection. The monarch asked one of the conspirators, General C.Sanatescu to form a government made up of army people and technicians including one representative from each of the main parties: Maniu for the Peasants, C.I.Bratianu for the Liberals,

C.Petrescu for the Social-Democrats and L.Patrascanu for the Communists who emerged from twenty years of illegality. Meanwhile units of "Patriotic Guards" trained by the RCP were at gun point taking control of the strategic points of Bucharest and Bodnaras, their leader, took charge of the Antonescus and locked them up in the secret Party headquarters, which gave him another winning card. In the evening, at 10 p.m. the King issued a radio declaration to announce the fall of the dictatorship, the formation of a government of National Union and the end of the war against the Allies. He then withdrew to a remote village called Dobrita near Tirgu Jiu. On the following day, 24, the 3rd Romanian Army withdrew from the Moldavian front opening the way to Bucharest to the Red Army while German troops went on fighting. In the capital the garrison of 8,000 German soldiers put up a strong resistance and fought the Romanians for three days, while the Luftwaffe razed the city center to the ground. As a reprisal King Michael, on 25 August declared war on Germany and Hungary, much to Hitler's anger. The latter formed a "national" Romanian government round Horia Sima, ex-leader of the Iron Guard. On 30 August the Red Army entered Bucharest where it enjoyed a mixed reception, due to Romania being traditionally wary of Russia. An armistice was signed in Moscow on 12 September in the presence of British and American representatives. According to its terms, Romania was now taking part in the war against Germany, it gave the Red Army free access to any part of its territory, promised to pay 300 million dollars in kind as reparations, recognized the cancelation of the "Vienna Arbitration Pact" and therefore North Transylvania was returned to Romania, while Bessarabia and North Bukovina remained part of the Soviet Union.

Thus the government of National Union under General Sanatescu (23 August 1944–March 6, 1945) endeavored to put the nation back into some kind of order and to continue the war effort intending to first liberate all national territory, then when this was achieved on 26 October taking part in further military operations which took the Romanian Army as far as Slovakia by the time of the cease-fire in May 1945. Bucharest estimated that her entering the war on the Allied side had cost 170,000 men and one billion dollars. In the autumn of 1944, Romania had regained most of her territory, her king and a government representative of all the various political parties. However, at the same time Churchill in Moscow offered Stalin 90% influence over the country, leaving only 10% for the "other powers." This meant the Soviet Union could please herself.

Bulgaria naturally came next in being overcome by the Red Army. The ambient climate here was very different from its northern neighbour, since the traditional Russophile feelings of the local population had been boosted by the Soviet victories at Stalingrad and in the Ukraine, an enthusiasm which the Soviet envoy in Sofia had taken care to nurture. On 18 May 1944, the Moscow government asked for its consulates at Varna and Burgas to be reopened immediately, under threat of breaking diplomatic relations. There followed a crisis in the government. The new Cabinet which had been sworn in on 1 June attempted to negotiate with the Anglo-Americans in Ankara to avoid the Red Army entering the country. However, the about turn in Romanian policy of the 23 August laid the way to Sofia open to Tolbukin's troops. Parliament was convened to declare Bulgaria "neutral" and ordered Bulgarian troops to evacuate Yugoslav Macedonia. On 2 September the Regents chose K. Muraviev, member of the Agrarian Party, as Prime Minister. He issued a declaration to the effect that Bulgaria was no longer at war with the United States and Britain, but it was too late. The Communist Party had for some time been preparing a coup against the government and the National Committee of the Pariotic Front (O.F.) which was a coalition of all left-wing parties in an "illegal opposition" announced the new policy on 1 September. Meanwhile Soviet authorities had taken Muraviev's declaration to end the war with the Anglo-Americans as a manoeuver to keep the USSR from interfering in Bulgarian affairs; on 5 September they reacted by declaring war on Bulgaria. Muraviev asked immediately for an armistice, issuing orders not to resist Soviet troops if they entered the country and broke off relations with Germany. On September 8 the Red Army crossed the border into Bulgaria while the O.F. called for a general strike and performed many acts of sabotage. Overnight irregulars took over Sofia and arrested the Regents together with members of the government ; on 9 September at 6.15 a.m. a radio announcement informed the population that a new Council of three Regents had been formed, one of them being Todor Pavlov, a Communist, and a new government was in power—the First Government of the Patriotic Front—headed by Colonel Kimon Georgiev, one of the participants in the coup d'etat of 1934.

In the meantime Soviet troops had seized all strategic positions without encountering any opposition. A provisional armistice was signed with Marshall Tolbukin on the 9 September and the population in Sofia gave a hearty welcome to his troops, handing flowers to them. The government evacuated the occupied territories of Macedonia and Thrace and ordered a general mobilization. In fact, without waiting for the armistice treaty to be signed in Moscow on 28 October the Bulgarian Army was sent to the 3rd Ukrainian Front and moved on from Nis and Skopje towards Vienna; there were 30,000 casualties.

By the end of October Bulgaria had returned to her 1939 frontiers, she retained young King Simeon, aged seven, under a Patriotic Front government controled by the powerful Communist Party basking in the prestige of its real leader, George Dimitrov, ex-secretary general of the International in Moscow. There were few obstacles in their way since Churchill had granted the Soviet Union 75% influence over Bulgaria, with 25% for the "others powers." Stalin was thus given a free hand and in fact even more so than in Romania.

In Yugoslavia the situation was more complicated. Since the Jajce meeting the Partisans had set up a proper government under Tito to counter the one in Cairo under King Peter II. Yet in May 1944 Tito, under pressure from the German army, had been forced to take refuge on the island of Vis which was under British occupation. The British authorities naturally tried to bring the two rivals to some kind of agreement. Peter put Dr Ivan Subasic, a Croat who had previously been outlawed, in charge of forming a government. General Mihailovic had been removed from the list of ministers in the reorganizing of the preceding Cabinet and his Chetniks found themselves in two different camps: some joined the Partisans while others collaborated with the Germans. The British had finally made up their mind: they were putting their bets on Tito. As a gesture the Marshall met Churchill in Naples early in August. The British Premier had to assent to most of his visitor's demands. He then had to talk Peter II into putting his weight behind the enterprise. In a radio broadcast on 26 August 1944, the sovereign appealed to his subjects asking them to join the Army of Liberation and recognized Tito as the leader of all freedom fighters in Yugoslavia. The surrender of the Bulgarian army left Macedonia open and the Partisans took a strong hold on the region. They set up "Liberation Committees" in the liberated area as everywhere else, making sure members of the YCP had the lion's share of seats. In

September Tito flew to Moscow to coordinate the Red Army's advance with Partisan operations; the Marshall complied with Stalin's wish to have Soviet units enter Yugoslav terrritory, but only in the Danube valley on their way to Hungary. On the other hand he insisted that his men would be first to enter Belgrade. This is what happened: on 20 September, the Yugoslav capital was liberated by joint forces. General Nedic, head of the pro-German government, had tried to prevent this Partisan advance by making an alliance with Mihailovic, but the Chetniks, who by then numbered only 10,000 men, were soon disarmed by the Red Army and handed over to the Partisans who massacred them almost all of them. Their leader fled once again into the Ravna Gora and wandered in the mountains until he was captured in March 1945.

Dr. Subasic had entered into an agreement with Tito early in September under a proviso that two representatives of the Partisan Movement would join the King's government but that the sovereign himself would not return to Yugoslavia until a referendum was held. In September the agreement was competed by setting up a Regents' Council which did not operate until a dispute over its composition had been settled. It was not until the three Great Powers met at the Yalta Conference (February 1945) that the three Regents were appointed, one Serb, one Croat and one Slovene, all approved to Tito but non-Communists. Subasic then retired and on 5 March 1945 handed over the reins of government to Tito who, under various titles, was to govern the country until his death in 1980.

Meanwhile fighting was going on. Using Belgrade and Serbia as a base, the Partisans conquered the whole of the Western region. The Wehrmacht, on its way north from Greece and Albania from which it departed in November and December 1944, put up strong resistance in Western Bosnia and in Croatia where it was assisted by the Croatian Army and the Ustasa. Only in May 1945 did the Germans lay down their arms. Pavelic and his partisans could only hope to save their necks by fleeing: the Poglavnik and its dignitaries managed to cross into Austria among a stream of refugees and disappeared into thin air. Another group of about a hundred thousand people together with women and children was intercepted by the British at Bleiburg in Austria and were handed over to the Partisans in accordance with Allied agreements; they were for the most part summarily executed. This last act of mass murder of the Yugoslav civil war was to leave deep scars on the collective memory. In Slovenia the Partisan movement did not have such an impressive rise to power and on 1 May the Yugoslav army entered Trieste twenty four hours before a New Zealand division, laying the foundations for one of the most thorny problems of the post-war period.

In Moscow Churchill had offered 50% Soviet influence and 50% for "others." He probably had in mind Italy which was firmly controled at the time by Marshall Alexander. Yet the Partisans were all powerful in Yugoslavia and proclaimed themselves faithful supporters of Stalin. The latter left few soldiers in the country besides a number of "experts," so Tito felt entitled to treat Stalin as an equal and informed him of the fact when in Moscow in September 1944. In the end the Red Army had to strike a bargain with the extremely popular Croat communist who had become Marshall and head of the Belgrade government.

The Red Army never set foot in Albania and later Enver Hoxha's followers were to boast that their country had freed itself entirely by its own resources. In reality Tito's support was significant and the Albanian and Yugoslav Partisans coordinated their operations with the objective of Albania becoming the seventh or eighth Socialist Republic in a Federation of Southern Slavs. Before this could happen the British and the Americans sent military missions to the various resistance movements, in view of the fact that from the spring of 1944 the question of liberation was seen in terms of political power. In May the Communist Party held a "First Anti-Fascist Congress of National Liberation," at Permet, to appoint a Council of 121 members and a 13 members Committee to serve as a Provisional Government under Enver Hoxha, the ACP secretary general. The latter was also appointed as Commander-in-Chief of the armed forces with the grade of Army General and an impressive number of stripes! Albania followed the Yugoslav model to the letter. The assembly adopted a program of reconstruction of the country on a new basis, excluding King Zog and his followers. The British attempted to bring together the other resistance groups but Churchill would not hear of the Cairo government in exile being included because the sovereign had lost his support. As for the Balli Kombetar it concentrated its recruitment campaign on the circles close to the collaborationist government with the slogan "Let us save our homeland from the Communist danger."

The outcome was to be settled in the field. Enver's Partisans were in control of the South where they counld rely on the Epirus Andartes for support and mustered some 35,000 men; Central Albania was in the hands of Zog sympathizers and the northern parts were held by the old chieftains more or less affiliated to B.K. Late in May 1944, the Germans, flanked by Albanian units, launched an offensive which forced the Partisans to move north which brought them into conflict with Zog's men. The occupation authorities established a new government of collaboration which formed an "anti-communist front" round Abaz Kupi, leader of the Northern tribes who had joined forces with Zog. A full scale civil war followed ending with a victory for the Partisans: one after another Berat, Gjirokastra and the other towns fell. By the end of September 1944 three quarters of the country was liberated. Enver Hoxha sent a mission to the Allied HQs at Bari and succeeded in persuading the British to stop helping the other resistance groups after they had attempted to land a commando which had to be evacuated together with their military mission and Abaz Kupi their associate.

On 22 October the Anti-Fascist Committee meeting at Berat became the "Albanian Democratic Government" under Enver Hoxha its President and Minister of Defence, assisted by nine Communist ministers. In November the Wehrmacht, after evacuating Greece, withdrew from Albania, though there was fierce fighting to the end. Tirana fell to the Partisans on 28 November 1944, the anniversary of the 1912 Independence. On the following day Shkodra also fell and the whole country had been liberated.

The Albanian Communists found victory heady after they drove out their adversaries away and started a series of bloody purges. Yet the victory was also partly due to Tito's actions and his buttressing the ACP. Stalin was well aware of this and had promised to allow him to annex Albania, but he was unaware of the particular circumstances of the country which in any case remained out of the Red Army's reach.

Greece was the theater of occupation from another direction: Churchill sent his troops. After a year of quarreling, which often ended in fighting, the various resistance movements signed in May 1944 the Lebanon Charter which should have immediately created a "National Union" against the German occupiers. In reality ELAS did not endorse the decisions of its delegates to Lebanon and the four ministries allocated to EAM in the Cairo government remained unfilled. In July the arrival in Greece of a Soviet envoy from Yugoslavia led to a change of attitude. Stalin who could rely on the Red Army to enforce his influence on the rest of the Balkans, was willing to leave Britain in charge of its Greek preserve. Three months later he raised no objection against the proportions offered by Churchill for the area: 90% British influence, 10% left to others. The EAM leaders became more accomodating and in September occupied the ministerial offices which Papandreou had kept vacant for them. Soon afterwards the Greek government moved from Cairo to Naples and an agreement was signed in Caserta by which all resistance forces were placed under the authority of the English General R. Scorbie, who was due to land British troops as soon as prossible and occupy Athens. This put an abrupt end to the ambitions of EAM. In September the presence of the Red Army in Bulgaria and its march towards Belgrade threatened to cut off the Wehrmacht's supply lines and its means of retreat; the OKW ordered withdrawal early in October and it was effected under difficult circumstances with its troops being harrassed by ELAS. There followed reprisals against villagers while the population of industrial suburbs were getting out of control. The Germans evacuated Athens on 12 October 1944. On the 18th the Greek vessel "Averof" brought G.Papandreou and his government to the port of Piraeus, as well as General Scorbie leading 4,000 British soldiers. They made their way together to the Acropolis to unfurl the Greek flag, but following Churchill's instructions General Scorbie acted as if the city was under occupation.

The Papandreou government ordered all the Resistance fractions to lay down their arms by 10 December. The 70,000 ELAS men refused to comply, their ministers resigned and, on 3 December a large demonstration of their supporters in the center of Athens ended in a bloodbath: at least fifteen demonstrators fell under police fire. This marked the start of the first civil war which lasted six weeks and forced the British to bring two divisions over from Italy their numbers reaching 50,000 men together with air support. Everywhere in the country White terror replaced Red atrocities: people were put in jail, or shot dead on the basis of their political opinions, neither always bearing much relation to the truth. Churchill who from the beginning had ordered the use force, arrived in Athens with Anthony Eden on 25 December and acted as arbiter: the King was not to return until a referendum had been held and a Regent, Archbishop Damaskinos, would rule in the interval; the government was changed and Papandreou replaced by General Plastiras, the official leader of EDES, who was republican and anti-communist. Stalin who was concentrating on the Yalta Conference did not react and sent an ambassador to Athens. EAM and ELAS troops had to accept the situation. On 15 January 1945, an armistice was signed and on February 12 the Varzika agreement laid the foundations for peace in the country: all military organizations were to lay down their arms, in exchange for an amnesty and guaranteed equal political rights. Peace had cost 11,000 lives and was to prevail for twenty months before another civil war erupted, to last for three terrible years.

In this volatile part of the Southern Balkans, the British forces helped counter-balance Stalin's hold on all the rest of the Balkans.

Conclusion

1945 figures in the History of the Balkans as the start of a period of forty five years which is quite unlike any other.

Not only did it raise the "Iron Curtain" on a line going from Epirus to Thrace which isolated Greece from its natural hinterland, but above all the Peninsula lost its balance as its southernmost tip turned into an advanced position of an Atlantic military alliance whose command center was in Washington, while all the neighboring countries, except for a while the Yugoslav enclave, represented the southern flank of an Empire ruled from the Kremlin. From a political point of view the Balkans no longer existed and any attempt at a regional agreement met with an ukase from one or the other Big Power: Moscow objected to the American bases in Greece, while Washington was wary of proposals for denuclearization of the Peninsula.

This awkward situation had an effect not only on countries but also on their peoples, as it offered the ones the Soviet and the others the American model. It may be that Greece, though a member of NATO, was less developed than most of her allies and its intermitent democratic régime, interrupted by the authoritarian rule of Marshal A.Papagos (1952/55) and by the Colonels' dictatorship (1967/74), was still influenced by Mediterranean traditions. To such an extent that Marc Marceau, correspondent of "Le Monde" in Athens, wrote in 1967 "the deputy is bound to his electors from the day he is born until he dies. This makes for a strange relationship between slave and master, but not for sound and coherent political life."

Communism also had acquired specific characteristics in the Balkan Peninsula, as the Russian model had to fit different historical and cultural traditions. Speaking of "Balkan communism" would be complete nonsense and whoever traveled frequently to these parts could only be aware of the difference between the Romanian nomenklatura, heir to boyarism, and the Bulgarian apparatchik, mere village people who had made good while the Albanian ones were traditional chieftains. Naturally these régimes were similar in some respects because of the common factors of their development in time. In the beginning they all enforced Marxism-Leninism in multinational or plurinational countries and predominantly rural societies, two characteristics they had in common with bolshevik Russia in the 20s. This advantage was compounded by the prestige of the Red Army which arrived in Romania and Bulgaria in the blaze of its victory over Hitler's armies, though in Yugoslavia and Albania only military and other advisors intervened. Not to mention that many communist party leaders had been trained in Moscow, such as Dimitrov, the Bulgarian, Romanian Ana Pauker and Tito. All these factors go to explain the staunch Stalinist régimes that were installed to start with, though Tito's dissidence in June 1948 broke the monolithic pattern of the Soviet Empire, not that Yugoslavia in practice became any freer under its "self-governing" guise. As Stalin's successors wove their webs of intrigues as of old under the tsars, their emulators in the Balkan Peoples' Democracies had to learn to decypher them to play the trump card when the time was ripe. The various capitals had in turn their Krushchev and their Brezhnev men as rulers, sometimes they were the same, as Gheorghiu-Dej who turned from being an arch Stalinist into a partisan of "national communism" which N.Ceausescu inherited before ending up as a caricature of Stalinist power.

However, although the main actors on the world stage wore the same masks, at the grass roots life was more complex as ancestral village traditions had to adapt to suburban conditions, an abrupt change which willy-nilly one third or even half of the population had to undergo, sometimes at a high social cost like everywhere else. Official Marxist practices had to put up with christenings in the countryside "to placate the wife," the diplomatic bag bringing television sets and hi-fi equipment for the happy few, or various incursions into the world of capitalism with Peace Conferences or other international gatherings. There was a long list of privileges, large and small, available to Party members through solidarity networks which had less to do with ideology than family ties, in the manner of Ceausescu's Romania, or clan relations on the Mediterranean pattern, as in Albania under Enver Hoxha. Nepotism and corruption, the two Balkan illnesses, survived happily under Marx's moralizing shadow.

A more important flaw lay in the fact that the sense of nationhood did not develop. A Slovene in Ljubljana felt just as much under the yoke of the Serbs, not to mention the Albanians in Kosovo, the Turks in Bulgaria, the Hungarians in Romania. Under fine internationalist phrases there remained cultural differences, language rivalries, even religious disputes flaring up between Orthodox and Uniates in Transylvania. The Party made much propaganda over Cuba, Vietnam, Angola, Ethiopia or other global problems but paid little attention to the many daily irritants that meant little chance of the Fatherland, for all its communist ideology, being anything other than the majority racial grouping.

A common language had little impact deep down on attitudes within the family circle. It is true that one of the first measures taken by the new regimes had been the ban women from wearing a veil and this was been achieved in spite of strong opposition. As for equality between men and women, proclaimed in labor legislation, it was achieved more because of urbanization and women being employed in factories than under pressure from the Party. In remote parts of Macedonia, Albania, even in Bulgaria, foreign tourists can take "picturesque snaps" of women carrying heavy burdens walking behind their husbands who sit on a mule or a donkey. The mad escape of fourteen year old Albanians to Brindisi and its bright lights shows both shortcomings in family relations and the utter failure to indoctrinate the grandsons of Enver Hoxha.

The revolutions that started in the Balkans in 1989 were an attempt to break with half a century of applied communism but they also are in line with a particular tradition which is visible at every turn of the new road. In the Peninsula just as in Central Europe the signal came from Gorbachev's Perestroika. Whatever may have been at the root of the reform it acted as a catalyst for the Socialist Republics of Bulgaria, Romania, Albania, and not forgetting the Socialist Federation of Yugoslavia which was already independent.

It had a direct effect on Bulgaria and Romania since they were traditionally bound to follow the same course as "Big Brother" and pay homage to the new power in the Kremlin. This was no easy matter, much harder than in the days of Krushchev's campaign of destalinization, since only a man and his practices had been at stake then, while Gorbachev was dealing with dogma and behaving like an ally of "American imperialism." Hence a deep reluctance to follow the new direction which for four years created tensions between the various leaders and bad relations between the Parties. Meanwhile the Western media reported the thaw taking place in Moscow to the Balkan inhabitants in sharp contrast to the freeze imposed by their ancient leaders, Todor Zhivkov who had been in power for thirty three years and Nicolae Ceausescu for twenty four years. Of course these internal conflicts were of little concern to the man in the street whose cares were mainly directed to the difficulties of daily life. However, Perestroika had a bearing on this as Bulgaria like Romania did most of their trade with the USSR and were dependent on her for balancing their budgets. First the changes in policies, later disruption of the Soviet economy made all commercial contracts void, interrupting supplies of raw materials and domestic shortages in all countries. The COMECON crisis, as it affected the economies, already badly hit by the world recession of the early 80s, or reeling under the impact of Ceausescu's megalomania, had a devastating effect. Romania and Bulgaria were again the scene of endless food queues as in the aftermath of the war, thus giving rise to the most alarming rumors. Popular discontent was likely to lead to social upheaval which would do away not only with the people in power but also with the nomenklatura and their privileges. They had to act decisively: both in Sofia and Bucharest the "Revolution" came from inside the Party, as some leaders made the old leaders into a scapegoat and took over with promises of "reforms." Yet in towns the population demanded more than that and started an open ended train of events whose outcome it was impossible to predict.

In Yugoslavia and Albania the situation was different. Tito had broken with the Soviet model in 1948 and Enver Hoxha in 1960. Though Belgrade resumed official relations and commercial dealings with Moscow, while Tirana remained outside COMECON, the economic crisis raging in the USSR was not an important factor in the populations' demand for changes. In reality since Tito's death in 1980 the Yugoslav federation was in a state of permanent crisis and the worsening economic situation reflected the administrative confusion and economic competition between the various republics. The collapse of communism in neighbouring Central European states was to shake the Party—the Communist League—which was completely discredited and broke into republican splinters. The Yugoslav peoples, understandably anxious in the face of mounting economic difficulties, were drawn towards the bright lights of a market economy well known to millions of temporary workers in Germany, and to the nationalist dreams which they have inherited from their warring ancestors. In fact one cannot speak of a "Yugoslav Revolution" but several revolutions, Slovene, Croatian, Macedonian, Bosnian, Serbian and Montenegrin, putting into question both the nature of the régime within each republic, either communist or democratic, and the future of the federation itself. As for Albania, locked inside its 28,000 square kilometers of infertile territory, by the will of its original head of state, it was sinking further into economic, social and cultural backwardness, thrown into sharper relief by the technological revolution of the last decades of the 20th century. Thus in March 1991 E.Nano, the Prime Minister, evoked the need to bring Albania into the "world of civilization." Townspeople, especially the myriads of youths who were immune to the heroic memories of the war, became increasingly aware of this sorry state of affairs, due to the influence of Italian television networks and their dazzling publicity. Hence the primitive reaction of fleeing to Italy. University students were more sophisticated in their demands for democratic freedoms and the Party leader, Ramiz Alia, was forced to make concessions. Yet the elections which took place on 31 March 1991, were unclear as they have been in Bulgaria and Romania.

What next? The last two years gave the Balkan populations the power to choose for themselves. Western media, in their utter ignorance of these peoples' particular characteristics, have not been slow in advising them how to choose: pluralist democracy, market economy, putting regional, even European interests above national claims. Churchill was fond of saying that democracy was the least dangerous political system there was, but in its parliamentary guise, it took two centuries to evolve in France and Britain. The Balkan peoples need time to get organized in their own way; the only demand that can be made by the world community is for human rights to be respected.

Culturally, except for Greece, they find themselves in the same situation as in 1945, or even 1918 or 1912. They must first of all return to this distant past, re-examine the problems that were swept under the carpet by half a century of artificial institutions. They must get reconciled to their particular history, do away with rigid Marxist attitudes going back to the 19th century, take into account the glory and the squalor, the successes and disasters of past centuries which helped to turn them into Romanians, Bulgarians or Albanians as well as creating the Yugoslav alternative. In short they have to delve into the recesses of their specific national consciousness, but in so doing remember the new conditions in which they live as the 20th century is drawing to an end and technological advances make disputes over boundaries and aggressive nationalism pale into insignificance. Even the Greeks who often succumb to the grand visions of Athens in the age of Pericles or Byzantium as it was in the days of the Macedonian emperors, must learn to establish a dialogue with their neighbours, not only with more distant European countries, in order to assert their own characteristics as well as modernize their country.

After surveying five centuries of shared adventure which the Balkan peoples have experienced, one is aware of their rich variety in human terms. They are answerable for these riches to the whole of mankind, but above all to the rest of Europe because without the Albanians, the Bulgarians, the Greeks, the Romanians, the Turks and the Yugoslavs, it would be truncated and therefore that much poorer. In the shared structure which is to be built, whether a confederation or a federation, let them fulfill their part, completely, bringing their own specific contribution to the old dream of the Olympian Paradise.